From Journey's End to
The Dam Busters

To Joan, of course, and at last.

From Journey's End to The Dam Busters

The Life of R.C. Sherriff, Playwright of the Trenches

Roland Wales

Pen & Sword
MILITARY

First published in Great Britain in 2016 by
Pen & Sword Military
an imprint of
Pen & Sword Books Ltd
47 Church Street
Barnsley
South Yorkshire
S70 2AS

ISBN 978 1 47386 069 8

A CIP catalogue record for this book is available from the British Library.

Typeset in Ehrhardt by
Mac Style Ltd, Bridlington, East Yorkshire
Printed and bound in the UK by CPI Group (UK) Ltd,
Croydon, CRO 4YY.

Pen & Sword Books Ltd incorporates the imprints of Pen & Sword
Archaeology, Atlas, Aviation, Battleground, Discovery, Family History,
History, Maritime, Military, Naval, Politics, Railways, Select, Transport,
True Crime, Fiction, Frontline Books, Leo Cooper, Praetorian Press,
Seaforth Publishing and Wharncliffe.

For a complete list of Pen & Sword titles please contact
PEN & SWORD BOOKS LIMITED
47 Church Street, Barnsley, South Yorkshire, S70 2AS, England
E-mail: enquiries@pen-and-sword.co.uk
Website: www.pen-and-sword.co.uk

Contents

Acknowledgements

This book began with the Sherriff Nights at Kingston Grammar School, and so my thanks must begin with Jackie Steinitz, who signed up to the entire idea from the start, and was my partner in crime throughout: without her (and especially her outstanding musical talents), none of the Nights would have taken place, and this book would not have been written. Rowing master Phil Simmons was also a great supporter of the Sherriff Nights, as was Richard Smalman-Smith, who also doubled as an uncanny Sherriff lookalike. Above all, I have to express my gratitude to the many KGS rowers and parents who participated in the events so wholeheartedly over the years, and who made the Sherriff Club the best parent support organisation on our stretch of the Thames.

I must also express my thanks to so many staff at the school who tolerated the (slightly raucous) Sherriff Nights, indulged my slightly obsessive interest in Sherriff, and then ensured that the school would partner with the Surrey History Centre in the Heritage Lottery Fund project, which resulted in Sherriff's papers being catalogued, collated and archived. Most important, as far as the HLF project was concerned, were Head, Sarah Fletcher; School Archivist, Marianne Bradnock and Bursar, Edward Lang. Since they moved on, I have been extremely fortunate to have had the complete co-operation and assistance of Heads Mark Wallace and Stephen Lehec, archivist Joanne Halford, and the new bursar, Jane Smith. I should also like to thank Nick Bond, who has been a firm supporter of the project throughout, as well as contributing greatly to the writing of my play about Sherriff, and directing it, or extracts from it, on several occasions.

A great deal of the information in this biography comes from Sherriff's papers at the Surrey History Centre, where I have been lucky enough to receive a great deal of support and friendship. Above all, I would like to express my sincerest appreciation to Mike Page and Di Stiff, who have encouraged me with Sherriff since the very earliest days, and who steered the HLF project through its many phases: they have made me feel incredibly welcome at the Surrey History Centre, and have afforded me assistance and co-operation well in excess of what I had any right to expect. I feel that they treat me like a colleague instead of a customer, for which I am immensely grateful. I should also like to thank Janet Nixon, who was an invaluable source of help and support in the early days, and Zoe Karens, who was the archivist recruited to organise the Sherriff papers, and who gave me the benefits of her extensive knowledge. Zoe was assisted in her endeavours, particularly in the organisation of Sherriff's press cuttings, by a number of volunteers, but especially Linda and Barry Oliver, without whom this book would have been much the poorer. More generally I want to thank all of the staff at the SHC, who are unfailingly helpful and polite, even in the face of my persistent and unreasonable demands. Here I have particularly in mind the Document Assistants – Teresa Gray, Guz Gonzalez, Martin Starnes and Joanna Murtagh – who are charged with locating vast tracts of Sherriff papers whenever I visit, and who do so with great efficiency, and even greater tolerance and good humour.

While researching the book I have had the good fortune to have enjoyed support and assistance from many archives, both in the UK and the US. I was greatly aided by the staff at the Margaret Herrick Library in Beverly Hills (and especially by Kristine Krueger, to whom I am very grateful); by Brett Service in the Warner Brothers Archives at the USC School of Cinematic Arts; and by the staff in the Special Collections Section of the Library at UCLA. I would also like to thank the staff at the Special Collections Library of the University of Michigan, and especially Juli McLoone and Kate Hutchens, for the photos and correspondence they so generously provided from the Maurice Browne archives.

In the UK, I would first like to thank KGS, The Scouts and Curtis Brown for permission to quote from Sherriff's published and unpublished works. I would also like to acknowledge, with gratitude, the support and assistance of Gillian Butler at the Kingston Borough Archive, Simon Donaghue at the Havering Local Studies Centre, Jennifer Thorp at New College, Oxford, and archivists from many other organisations, including the Imperial War Museum, the Lambeth Palace Library, the Devon Records Office, the Modern Records Centre at the University of Warwick, the V&A Theatre and Performance Archive, the Senate House Library at the University of London, the Bodleian Library at the University of Oxford, the British Library, the John Rylands Library at the University of Manchester, and the Reuben Library of the British Film Institute.

I am grateful to these organisations and others, including Studio Canal Films Ltd, the David Lewis Estate and the New York Public Library for permission to publish various pictures. I am also grateful to the Society of Authors for permission to publish extracts from the letters of G.B. Stern and George Bernard Shaw, to the beneficiaries of the literary estate of James Hilton and Curtis Brown for permission to quote from his letters, and to the Cazalet, Dearmer and Booth families. Every effort has been made to contact other copyright holders where relevant, and I would be grateful for the names of additional copyright holders who may have been inadvertently omitted, that we may correct the record.

In preparing the draft of the book I took advantage of the good nature of many friends and colleagues who read through early (and much longer) drafts of various chapters of the book. As well as those mentioned above, I benefited greatly from the comments of Loretta Howells and David Cottis, and, especially, Howard Seabrook and Michael Lucas. The standard disclaimer is hardly necessary, but I am happy to acknowledge that remaining errors are definitely all mine. I would also like to thank Loretta's colleagues, Sam Thompson and Pete Allen, at the R.C. Sherriff Trust, who have shared their knowledge and contacts with me in the very friendliest fashion. I am also very happy to record my appreciation to Olive Pettit, Chris Manning-Press, Michael Dixon and Anne Hutton for taking the time to share their memories of Sherriff, and their papers, with me, and for providing an insight that cannot be gleaned from dusty papers. I was fortunate, as well, to benefit from the recollection of a number of Old Kingstonians who had been lucky enough to meet Sherriff, or be coached by him, over the years, and in that regard I would particularly like to thank Robin Blooie and Fred Dickenson. I am also grateful to Marilyn Smith for sharing her knowledge of Selsey, and for her generously offered skills as a tour guide.

Finally, I wish to thank the members of my family who have been such a help throughout the endeavour. My sons, Peter and Lewis, have had to put up with the exquisite embarrassment of a parent who organises musical and dramatic events at their school in honour of some unknown, out-of-date writer, while simultaneously having to endure an apparently endless sequence of black-and-white movies. Not only that, but they have accompanied me on several archive trips, located sources, taken notes, read drafts of the manuscript and generally been a great help in bringing the project to fruition. The same goes double for my wife Joan, who has not only shared in all of these tasks, but has additionally supported me in every conceivable way, not only in the preparation of this book, but throughout our forty or so years together. I literally cannot thank her enough.

Introduction

Turn thy thoughts now to the consideration of thy life, thy life as a child, as a youth, thy manhood, thy old age, for in these also every change was a death. Is this anything to fear?

Marcus Aurelius, *The Meditations*, Book IX.

Since 1980, the parent support organisation for rowing at Kingston Grammar School has been named the Sherriff Club, because he was a generous benefactor to the school while he lived, and still is, because half of all his royalties go to the school (the other half to the The Scouts).

My sons attended the school, and both were keen rowers, so in 2008 I became Chair of the Sherriff Club, still only dimly aware of the achievements of the man for whom the club had been named. I knew, of course, about *Journey's End* – who could not? It had been a staple of school halls and local theatres for many years, and even ventured into the West End from time to time. But, having grown up at the time when the First World War was crudely summarised as 'Lions Led by Donkeys', or by the scathing satire of Joan Littlewood's *Oh, What a Lovely War* (a film that had a tremendous impact on my 10-year-old self when I saw it in Glasgow on its release), *Journey's End* seemed utterly out of touch – featuring characters one could never believe had existed, speaking words that surely no one could ever have uttered. But it was I who was out of touch, for it was the play's claim to authenticity that had made it such a phenomenal success when it was first performed: it was based, after all, on the author's own experiences as a soldier on the Western Front, and was instantly hailed as a classic and truthful account.

Feeling duty bound to find out more about Sherriff, I quickly discovered that he was not a one-play wonder: he had written many plays in his life, although none displayed the resilience of *Journey's End*: in fact, very few have been revived in the commercial theatre since 1960. Much the same was true for his books: he had written several novels, but none were (at that time) in print. But his films were a completely different matter. Even a cursory investigation turned up films that had been among my favourites as a boy: *Goodbye, Mr Chips*; *The Four Feathers*; *Quartet*; *The Invisible Man*; and, of course – on every schoolboy's list of great movies, then and now – *The Dam Busters*. I was beginning to warm to Mr Sherriff.

Like all school parent organisations, the primary goal of the Sherriff Club is to raise money to support the rowers' endeavours. One way to do so was to organise a theatrical night in which the rowers would perform, thus ensuring the attendance of their parents in the paying audience. The more rowers, the more parents, we reasoned, so rather than have one play featuring a handful of students, we would have extracts from many plays, featuring many students. And where better to find source material than in Sherriff's own works. So, in November 2008, the first Kingston Grammar School Sherriff Night was born, featuring extracts from his plays: *Journey's End* (of course), *The White Carnation*, *St Helena*, and *The Long Sunset*; and also from his films: *Goodbye, Mr Chips*; *The Four Feathers*; and *Lady Hamilton*.

The evening was a huge success, so a repeat the following year seemed only sensible: in fact, the Sherriff Nights would continue for seven years, during which time the rowers of Kingston Grammar School performed extracts from almost every published Sherriff play. Some of his unpublished writing was performed as well: his first ever play, *A Hitch in the Proceedings* (ironically written for a fundraising venture not unlike our own) was seen on stage for the first time in ninety years; and his *Sequel to Journey's End* was performed for the first time ever. Nor were his movies forgotten: extracts from the most popular were performed, including, on one notable occasion, an all-girl version of *The Dam Busters*. One wonders what Sherriff would have made of that, and also of the fact that his boys' grammar school had become co-educational.

As the Sherriff Nights proceeded, the need to discover more about Sherriff himself became more pressing. Unfortunately, no biography of Sherriff had ever been written. This seemed at the very least surprising, because, in his day, Sherriff had been a famous and well-regarded literary figure. He had enjoyed huge worldwide success with *Journey's End* in 1929–30 (the closest analogy today would be the *Harry Potter* series), and although he was never ranked among the literary titans, he wrote about ordinary people and their everyday lives with great empathy and compassion. His dramas may have lacked the breadth and psychological depth of some, but they were seen as perceptive and truthful (and never over-written); his three 1930s novels won sweeping praise for their honest examination of the lives of the English middle class; and his name on a film script was seen as an absolute guarantee of quality.

One account of his life did exist, however – no longer in print, but still obtainable: his autobiography, *No Leading Lady*.[1] It is a wonderfully written book, an admirable showcase for Sherriff's storytelling abilities. But it is, at best, a partial account, omitting almost all of his wartime experiences (which is curious, to say the least, because his army years are those of most interest, given the avowedly autobiographical nature of *Journey's End*), and skirting over most of the post-1945 years. But there is an even bigger problem with *No Leading Lady*, which is its unreliability.

When Sherriff bequeathed his royalties, in part, to Kingston Grammar School, he also bequeathed his papers, over a hundred boxes of letters, scripts, diaries and ephemera, reaching back to the second half of the nineteenth century. In their wisdom, the school governors deposited the papers at the Surrey History Centre, conscious that their archivists were in a much better position to look after Sherriff's vast collection of writings. With the aid of a grant from the Heritage Lottery Fund, the papers were completely re-examined and catalogued, revealing much about Sherriff that was unknown, or had been forgotten, and laying bare the inconsistencies in Sherriff's memoir. For although there is a thread of truth that runs through the narrative of his memoir, in many of its details it is misleading, or just plain wrong. Quite why he should have had such disregard for the truth is not clear, but throughout his life Sherriff was a very private individual (becoming more so as time went on), and it may have suited him to construct a particular persona, to keep people at arm's length from the real Sherriff. He was also a natural storyteller, so must have been sorely tempted to embellish more mundane accounts, if only to please his audience. Even in the early years of his fame he left a trail of false impressions, and the embellishments grew with the writing of his autobiography.

His collected papers give a much more complete picture of the real Sherriff, especially when supplemented by the autobiographical details that suffuse his writing. A fictional account of a young soldier, Jimmy Lawton, bears such a resemblance to Sherriff that we can better understand his thoughts and moods through his fictional alter ego. The family in his first novel, *The Fortnight in September*, mimics Sherriff's own family in so many ways that we learn more about his early years from its pages than we do from *No Leading Lady*. Most famously, *Journey's End* reveals the boredom and anxieties that afflicted the young Sherriff in the trenches, as we can see from both his letters home and his subsequently written 'Diary' of some of those terrifying months.

The first Sherriff Night came shortly after the hugely successful David Grindley revival of *Journey's End* in the West End and Broadway, and over the past few years *The White Carnation* has been revived as well, while Persephone Press have successfully reprinted three of his books, so the time seems to be ripe for a reappraisal of his life and career. There have been books published recently that skilfully examine aspects of Sherriff's life – focusing on his East Surrey battalion[2] during the war, for example, or on his 'classic war play'[3] – but no comprehensive account yet exists. That is what the following pages are intended to provide.

Roland Wales
August 2016

Chapter 1

Into Uniform, Beginning – 1916

Men seek retreats for themselves, houses in the country, sea–shores, and mountains; and thou too art wont to desire such things very much. But this is altogether a mark of the most common sort of men, for it is in thy power whenever thou shalt choose to retire into thyself.

Marcus Aurelius, *The Meditations*, Book IV.

Throughout the whole of a bleak November day a queue of men slowly worked around the big gymnasium. Standing in the gallery above, one could almost tell the time by the position of any man you cared to watch – they moved so slowly and surely. Take, for instance, a certain very young boy – he doesn't look more than seventeen – he started at the door of the gymnasium at two o'clock, had reached the first corner at two-thirty, the next at three-thirty and now as the light in the great room grew dim at the close of a dull, wintry day he was just disappearing by inches up a flight of steps leading to the recruiting room.[1]

Robert Cedric (Bob) Sherriff joined the Army on 20 November 1915, applying at the Duke's Road depot of the 28th Battalion, The London Regiment (Artists Rifles). We can't be sure exactly how the day went, but there's quite a good chance it followed the pattern described in Sherriff's story of young Jimmy Lawton, from which the above extract is taken. It was the first extended story he ever wrote – more than 20,000 words long – and it reveals a pattern that would be exhibited throughout Sherriff's writing career – one in which his personal experiences were recycled in his fiction (while his autobiographical accounts, ironically, often contained fictional experiences).

There is no record of how army life went for Sherriff in the first few weeks after he joined up – nothing, in fact, until he takes his place at the Gidea Park Camp in Essex around New Year 1916, and begins to send letters home to his mother and father. But it seems reasonable to presume that his first few weeks were a fair reflection of young Jimmy's, in which case he began his training being handed his uniform in a storeroom in his local depot, and struggling to get the knack of putting on his puttees. In a group of thirty or so, he likely spent the next few hours being taught how to 'dress properly – how to clean buttons, boots etc.', and how to do some basic drill, before being dismissed, and enjoined to take home his civilian clothes and remember to salute any army officers he might meet on the way home.

For a month he trained in London: in the morning he would travel up by train to parade in Regent's Park,[2] followed by route marches into the suburbs, squad drill, physical training; in the afternoon, lectures 'on musketry – on blisters – on discipline'.[3] Sherriff 'loved the route marches along the country lanes, singing the marching songs with the band ahead of us. I loved the manoeuvres across the downs and guard duty at night, watching the dawn come up behind the trees.'[4]

After five weeks it was time to move into camp, so, shortly after Christmas, Sherriff struggled to pack his kitbag with everything he might need – his clothes, his mess tin, his plate, knife, fork, his toilet outfit, boots and socks – and after a fitful night's sleep, would have awoken, like Jimmy:

> with rather a pang of regret that he was leaving home for the first time in his life without the company of his parents. ... When he said goodbye to his mother that morning she gave him a little leather-bound book of the meditations of Marcus Aurelius and told him he would find comfort in it if he were lonely. His father gave him five pounds and told him to keep cheerful and develop his sense of humour – then he had taken a final look round the house and said goodbye. Ten minutes later he was saying another goodbye out of the carriage window to the old Grammar school in the trees.[5]

That extract from young Jimmy's story reveals a great deal about Sherriff's frame of mind as he left for camp: the excitement of leaving on what he saw as a life of adventure, but at the same time the nervousness of a rather unconfident boy; the longing for home (which would be a regular theme in his letters from both training and the trenches); the volume of Marcus Aurelius, with its attendant stoicism, speaking of his mother's desire that he do himself – and her – proud; the stiff upper lip bonhomie of his father; and finally, the attachment to his old school, which seemed to deepen the longer he had left it behind.

By the end of that day, Sherriff and his comrades were in camp – in huts of thirty men, in a camp designed to hold 2,000, with 'huts in a great square and duck boards running between them ... across the camp road were the medical hut and the YMCA reading room and other places of amusement and in the centre ... stood the cookhouses and the quartermaster's stores and the many other departments necessary for a large camp.'[6] He would have suffered great pangs of homesickness as he dwelt on what his family would be doing that evening: 'It was seven o'clock – his sister was probably doing her foreign stamps – possibly a little lonely about not having anyone to exchange duplicates with – he could imagine his mother sitting by the fire reading and his father at the table working on his diary or his accounts – and whilst pondering on all this he realised what a very fine home he had.' Sherriff, like Jimmy, would have spent his first night in camp learning 'the comfort of a good home by losing it'.[7]

Joining Up

Jimmy is Sherriff's alter ego in some things, but not all. For unlike Jimmy, Sherriff had volunteered once already, before he was accepted into the Artists Rifles. In fact, he had tried just a few days after Britain had declared war on Germany, on 4 August 1914, shortly after he returned from the river camping trip he was enjoying with his former school friend, Dick Webb.

Sherriff had left school in 1913 and had immediately gone to work at the Sun Insurance Office, where his father had already worked for more than twenty-five years. He hated it. His autobiography is very clear on that point:

When the First War came I'd just left school and started work in a London office. I'd been a big shot at school: captain of rowing and cricket, and record holder of the long jump in the sports. From that I had become a junior clerk on a high stool, sticking stamps on envelopes, writing 'paid' against names in ledgers, filing away old letters and running errands. After that last triumphant term at school it was a demoralising comedown. I hated wearing a high stiff collar and a bowler hat; I hated the journeys in a crowded train; above all I hated the miserable, hopeless monotony of it all.[8]

In an article he published in 1968, Sherriff gave an account of his first attempt to volunteer. He headed down to the headquarters of his county regiment, and was interviewed, along with several other boys, by the adjutant. The two boys ahead of him, he wrote, were admitted on account of having been educated at renowned public schools. He was turned down because, although Kingston Grammar School was founded by Queen Elizabeth in 1561, it was not on the list of recognised public schools. 'And that was that,' wrote Sherriff. 'I was told to go to another room where a sergeant major was enlisting recruits for the ranks, and it was a long, hard pull before I was at last accepted as an officer.'[9]

Like many of Sherriff's stories, however, a certain amount of embellishment masks the truth. Sherriff's army record is available at the National Archive,[10] and it confirms that he did, indeed, attempt to sign up shortly after the war had begun. His application is dated 13 August, 1914, and it was countersigned by W.P. Etches,[11] the second master at Kingston Grammar School (attesting to his 'good standard of education'), and by Major H.P. Treeby, commander of the East Surrey Regiment Depot in Kingston upon Thames on 15 August, who attested that 'I have seen Mr Robert Cedric Sherriff and can recommend him as a suitable candidate for appointment to a temporary commission in the Regular Army for the period of the war.' The Royal Army Medical Corps doctor passed him medically fit on the same day. But Sherriff's form then disappeared into the bowels of the Army system and emerged with a stamp showing 'Not Accepted' on 25 March 1915.

Major Treeby's assent is clearly at odds with Sherriff's version of the story. But, if he was not rejected (on account of his school) on the day he applied, why was he turned down? Probably for one of two reasons. First, he was not old enough. The Army was recruiting 19-year-old junior officers, and at the time of his application, young Sherriff was only two months past his eighteenth birthday. The second may indeed have had something to do with Kingston Grammar: officer candidates were being accepted from the 'renowned public schools', if they had a history of serving in their school cadet forces, but the cadet force in Kingston Grammar School was not formed until 1915. Sherriff was effectively applying for an officer position, despite being too young and having no previous experience whatsoever: it is not surprising that he was turned down.

While awaiting the results of his army application, he continued to work at the Sun Insurance Fire office in Oxford Street, but he chafed at the life, feeling that he had been taken from school too soon. The evidence comes in part from the *Jimmy Lawton Story*,[12] and a subsequent play fragment,[13] both of which contain scenes in which a headmaster consoles a pupil forced to leave school before he was ready. There are also a couple of letters from Mr Clayton, an ex–schoolmaster of his, written in early 1914, replying to a letter from Sherriff expressing a desire to become a schoolmaster himself.[14] At some point, however, Sherriff probably began to realise that, without a university degree, his dream of becoming a schoolteacher was likely to remain unfulfilled, and perhaps that added fuel to his resentment at being torn from school earlier than he would have wished.[15]

Possibly to relieve the monotony of his daily grind, Sherriff and his friends seem to have decided to organise an event in support of the soon-to-be-formed KGS cadet force. The files of the Kingston Rowing Club[16] contain a programme advertising a *Magical Entertainment* on 25 and 26 September 1914. The evening consisted of a series of individual acts (in the music hall style), including comedians, singers and two magicians – Akron and Karlroy – who were to be assisted by, among others, Ali 'Breedoonbootah', 'Jeenjah Biskit' and 'Disis de Waiout' (say them out loud for maximum effect). The picture of Akron in the file bears a strong resemblance to Sherriff (see Plate 4), and the groan–worthy puns are symptomatic of the sort of music hall humour that would characterise his early plays.

The Reproach of Impertinent People

While still awaiting a reply from the Army, Sherriff wrote to his employers asking for permission to join the Army, and for his salary to continue to be paid, or at the very least, for his post to be kept open until he returned. But they turned him down, on account of his age ('he is not included in Lord Kitchener's invitation to enlist as he has not yet reached the age of nineteen years'), and because of the number of people who had already left the office to enlist.[17] Sherriff appears to have let the matter rest at that point, and seems to have started to work longer hours (with accordingly higher pay) and to be given more responsibility than would be normal for someone of his age and experience – a direct result of the thinning of the office ranks. He felt no guilt about not being in the Army; he had tried to apply directly, and also to secure the support of the firm, but with no success, which was hardly his fault. And having heard of the hardships of training undergone by those who had already left,[18] and being aware of the casualties on the Western Front, it would be surprising if, like Jimmy, Sherriff did not console himself with the thought that at least he was safe.

His birthday came on 6 June, and with it another letter to his manager at the Oxford Street branch. Again his employers tried to discourage him, and again he decided to bide his time.[19] He received a letter from Sun Insurance's General Manager (George Mead), appreciating 'the correctness of the decision at which you have arrived in connection with recruitment', commending his patriotic instincts, and stressing how damaging it would be for the office if he left, especially since the Oxford Street Fire office had now taken on the additional business of managing government anti–aircraft insurance (a 'colossal' addition to the burden of work).

There is an additional paragraph of interest in the letter that hints at some of Sherriff's concerns about remaining out of uniform. Mead writes that:

> I am well aware of the reproach implied by the glances and remarks of irresponsible and impertinent people, who would constitute themselves judges in other people's matters; but such interference is now open to the reply that you are engaged upon work for the government.

It must have been difficult for a young man of military age to remain out of uniform, and Mead's response suggests that Sherriff might already have fallen foul of remarks, or perhaps only glances and gestures.[20] But he was a young man who was keen to be seen to do the right thing – in fact, that would be an important motivation throughout his entire life, likely due to the expectations placed upon him by his mother, who exerted considerable influence upon him, and to whom he was devoted.

Sherriff continued working at Sun Insurance until the end of October, when he again requested permission to join up, and he was turned down, but with a warning that:

> the Directors do not feel in a position to pay your salary whilst away from the Office. You will be regarded as having resigned your position but I shall hope at the close of the war to be in a position to offer you reappointment, in the event of your so desiring it.[21]

That seems to have been the company's best and final offer, but it was clearly not enough to prompt him to remain on his stool in Oxford Street. Three weeks later, he was standing in the midst of a long line of men in that draughty gymnasium in Duke's Road.

What prompted him to swap the safety and security of his well-paid office job for a life of drill, discomfort and danger? The *Jimmy Lawton Story* suggests that the catalyst may have been the death at Loos of one of his former colleagues. In the latest version of the story,[22] several pages are devoted to Jimmy's anguished wrangling over whether he should stay in the office ('he, a boy of eighteen, lording it over men of fifty or sixty'), or whether he should join up. But when news arrives that Mason has been killed at Loos – Mason, whose work he is covering at that very moment, and whose signature lies on some of the papers before him – he feels he has to go. The manager, protesting his decision, points out that he is doing Mason's work, and Jimmy replies: 'That's the very reason I must go, sir, I'm doing Mason's work. I feel I must go on doing it now, sir.'[23]

The Battle of Loos, which was the British Army's contribution to the wider offensive in Artois and Flanders in the autumn of 1915, began on 25 September and lasted, in the first instance, for three days: casualties were very heavy. The timing is such that it is entirely possible that one of Sherriff's former colleagues was killed, and that the news of the death came through to the office by the end of October. Unfortunately, there is no confirmation from Sherriff's letters, nor from his father's diaries, but the overlap between Jimmy and Sherriff's experiences is so great that it is hard not to conclude that the death of a colleague was at least partly responsible (probably coupled with public disapproval of a young, healthy man not in khaki) for Sherriff's change of heart.

The Artists Rifles

A couple of months after the Loos offensive ground to a halt, and six weeks after he first paraded at Duke's Road, Sherriff found himself wrenched away from home, on his own for the first time in his life. The camp to which he was sent was the Hare Hall Camp, in Gidea Park, near Romford in Essex, which had been the Artists Rifles' training centre in the UK for only a few months.[24]

The Artists had originally been formed in 1859, and had been conceived as a regiment for artists, actors, painters, musicians and other artistic types. Establishing its headquarters at Duke's Road in 1880, it fought as part of the Rifle Brigade until the government's formation of the Territorial Force in 1908, when it joined with twenty-five other volunteer battalions to form the 28th (County of London) Battalion of the London Regiment. It became a popular battalion for middle–class volunteers (from public schools, universities etc.), and was inundated with volunteers when war broke out in 1914.

Initially, the Artists were allocated to protection duties in London, but by the end of October they embarked for France, establishing, at the War Office's behest, a second training battalion at Duke's Road. Recruiting for the Second Battalion began on 31 August, and within a week more than 5,000 had volunteered. What kind of men? According to the account in the Regimental Roll of Honour: 'Varsity blues, rowing men and athletes of every description, mostly without any previous military training'.[25] Gregory reports that:

> During that week there was such a crowd assembled outside the front door in Duke's Road that several NCOs changed into civilian clothes and mingled with the crowd. The men they liked the look of were presented with a card requesting their presence at an interview the following day, the remainder being ignored and left to draw their own conclusions. Four thousand of them had perforce to be refused.[26]

The first battalion went to France at the end of October 1914, and a few days after grave losses among the officers of the 7th Division at Ypres, 'some fifty "other ranks", public school and university men who had taken Lord Roberts' warning and trained in peacetime, were rapidly given some practical tips, promoted to second lieutenant and the next day went straight into action (still wearing their Territorial private's uniform and Artists' badge with the addition of a "pip").'[27] The promoted officers were held to have performed 'splendidly', and more were demanded from the Artists, and duly supplied (this time, at least, after a few days' training).

So the battalion in France became established as a training corps for officers in the field, and at the same time, a 3rd battalion began to be formed on New Year's Day 1915. Training was initially done at Duke's Road, and at Kenwood (on Hampstead Heath, where the work involved construction of trenches and dugouts 'on the most up–to–date Continental models')[28] and then at camp in Richmond Park, where, with the amalgamation of the first two battalions, it was designated as a revamped 2nd Battalion. In May 1915, a new 'School of Instruction for newly gazetted Officers of other Territorial Regiments' was established within the battalion. It ran along similar lines to the school in France, and within a few months more than 1,500 of them passed through the school course and examination. In the meantime, in July, the battalion moved to High Beech in Epping Forest, before settling at Gidea Park. In November 1915, the Artists Rifles Regiment was officially recognised by Army Order[29] as an Officers' Training Corps, and the Home Battalion became the 2nd Artists Rifles OTC, which is the official designation given to the regiment that young Sherriff joined on that bleak November day at Duke's Road.

Early Days in Essex

Sherriff arrived at Hare Hall camp in the last week of December 1915. From that moment on he wrote regularly to his mother and father – more than 160 letters covering his time in the Artists, and his brief time with the 3rd East Surreys in England, before he was posted to France in late September 1916 – which gave a very comprehensive account of the Artists' training. Like Jimmy, Sherriff was at first miserably homesick, getting up in the dark and washing in a cold hut along with twenty-nine other men – one of them a 'drunkard'. The first letter we have is to his mother, dated New Year's Day 1916, by which time he had spent 'nearly a week' at the camp, 'and am still alive'.[30] A couple of days later,[31] he reports that he's very lonely, but tries to reassure his mother that it's not that he's not popular, it's just that if he goes out with others he'll be too miserable to be good company. He finds the other men rowdy, and cannot understand how they can enjoy themselves: 'I don't suppose they have such a nice home as I have, or I am sure they could not enjoy themselves so much here.'

Although he quite liked the men in his hut, he would rather have been with two of his friends who were in the Engineers, and he was trying to join them there. By 5 January, his request was granted and he wrote to his mother from a new address, no longer in the camp, but now billeted in a house at 24 Manor Road, Romford, along with Trimm,[32] a friend from Kingston who had joined the Artists at the same time. Throughout his time in the Army, Sherriff would struggle to adapt to new situations, or unexpected turns of events, but on this occasion, despite the short notice, he was thrilled: 'We've got one of the most comfortable billets that could exist, and I have got in with my friend from Kingston, Trimm,' he wrote.[33] Unfortunately there was something that he saw as a 'drawback' – namely Trimm's 'extreme fondness for girls'. He explained that 'There is a lady (Mrs Harvey) and three girls here, and all are very kind and considerate,' but added, in a PS, 'I do hope I won't be made to go out with the girls, as you know I dislike them. I shall let Trimm do so, but I shall not.'

This postscript and the comments in the *Jimmy Lawton Story* are the first pointers to an apparent antipathy to girls on Sherriff's part. A certain discomfort around women can be identified at various points in his life (described, for example, by Olive Pettit, a secretary who worked for him, and by his godson, Lieutenant Colonel Christopher Manning–Press).[34] To counter this, he had very close and productive working relationships with a number of very capable and impressive women throughout his working life,[35] and their correspondence with him is generally warm and enthusiastic. Without giving too much of the later story away, it may have been less that he was antipathetic to girls, and more that he was averse to a romantic attachment to them – perhaps because of an overprotective mother, or because he was happier in the company of young men.

Sherriff soon accustomed himself to the rhythms of the Artists' training, and seemed happy with his lot. He wrote to his father that 'Things are going quite well at present,' although, exhibiting his usual anxiety about the prospect of change, he could not resist adding, 'although one never knows when we may be moved.'[36] A couple of days later, they were jolted from their usual routine by what he called a 'Great Field Day'.[37] He was part of an enemy force (1,500 men of the Artists) advancing on London via Romford and Brentwood, and being opposed by about 700 men of the Officers' School. As one of the Engineers he was to be engaged in building a bridge to allow the attackers to advance, but 'as only about five of fifty knew anything about bridge building, we all sat on the bank and looked on' while others did the work. Owing to the delay, some of the troops had crossed further up the river, and the commander was sufficiently upset that 'everyone was made to walk over in single file and back again.' He and his colleagues seem to have had a most enjoyable day, with additional diversion provided by the rearing of the commanding officer's horse, nearly knocking his staff down.[38]

The account in the letter is one of the first occasions in which Sherriff gives an extended description of an event, and it makes for very entertaining reading, especially owing to his ability to highlight passing absurdities. Although a man of fairly conventional views – very much a product of his middle–class home counties background – he seemed to embody the spirit of the slightly cynical external observer, reserving his gentle tones of mockery for many of the things that he held in quite high esteem. In this case, he felt himself very much a part of the Army – and wanted to do well – and yet seemed unable to resist a smile when things failed to go according to plan. A much more detailed account of the event also crops up in the *Jimmy Lawton Story*.[39]

The other part of the routine with which he was familiarising himself was leave. Every second Saturday, he had the chance to go home – usually around Saturday lunchtime (although not if there were special drills planned, or extra duty etc. – which, if it happened with short notice, would knock him into something of a tailspin). He spent the two weeks between leaves waiting desperately for the next one. In fact, even when he only had a one–day pass, he would travel all the way to Kingston, just for the pleasure of four hours at home.[40] In the intervening weeks he did something rather odd: where other recruits might be out socialising with each other, he would devote every other Sunday to seeing his mother, who would travel out to meet him in Romford. His letters to his mother are suffused with references to recent leaves, impending leaves, or contemplation of her visits (recent or prospective). For several weeks he attempted to rent a room in Romford, mainly for the purposes of giving him and his mother somewhere quiet and private to meet on a Sunday. That must have been hard to explain to his fellow recruits.

The next few weeks show Sherriff relaxed and happy – bar the occasional bout of toothache – and gazing with amusement at the activities of the Army. Training seemed focused on drill, marches and trench digging, although with the odd creative touch: on the day of a particularly heavy snowfall, for example, they were taken into a large field, and while some of the men dug miniature trenches, the others practised 'bombing' with snowballs – to see how many they could throw into the trenches at 50 yards.[41] For trench digging they would go out into the Essex countryside (usually to Mountnessing, which was a 9-mile train journey and 2-mile march away), but getting home was not always straightforward. On one occasion, 'our march [back] was considerably longer than coming because the officer took a short cut.'[42] Earlier that month, on returning from trench digging, they were delayed when their train back from Brentwood was cancelled due to a Zeppelin raid, and they were forced to sit in a train in the dark for two and a half hours.[43]

As well as writing to his parents, he also kept in touch with old office and school friends. A couple of letters from Cyril Manning–Press arrived during January, sharing some gossip about former school friends and his colleagues – noting in particular that 'our newest member of staff (a lady) is a BA of Cambridge, but she is quite a "sport".'[44] Sherriff's friends at Sun Insurance were also disposed to gossip about new women recruits. G.B. Doland writes that 'Watson has not been gazing forth into the world so much lately. I think the novelty of the lady staff interests him a little.'[45] Doland seems to have been close to the mark – a letter from Watson just a few days later remarks: 'The girls – oh! The girls. There is one here that would just suit you. Eighteen years of age and lives at Barnes.'[46] Perhaps he hadn't told his colleagues about his antipathy to girls – or maybe he only expressed the antipathy to his mother (possibly because he felt it was something she wanted to hear).

With all that he was happy with his lot at the time, he was at a loss about what to do in the future. In the course of a few short weeks he applied for a number of branches of the service. First, of course, he had moved to the Engineers to be with Trimm, among others. Next he talks of wanting to be a 'Fire Surveyor'[47] (although acknowledging that he is having difficulty in the Surveyor's Section, since he has trouble with trigonometry, angles and theodolites). By 16 February,[48] he has applied for a commission in the Royal Field Artillery, because he thinks he won't make it in the Engineers, and because it is better than the Infantry (perhaps, too, he was swayed by Trimm, who did eventually end up in the Artillery). A week later, he was interviewed by the captain about his application,[49] and yet just one week after that he had applied for a commission (as an Engineer) in the Royal Leicester Regiment (noting that he did not expect to get it, since there were sixty applicants for just four positions, and in the end they went to three experienced Engineers and a Surveyor).[50]

At first blush it may seem difficult to understand just why Sherriff chose to apply for so many different positions, but given that he sensed that he was out of his depth in the Engineers, it may be that he was simply trying to find a graceful way out. He obviously knew he was not ready for France (had barely shot a rifle), but he may have felt that leaving the Engineers would at least give him a chance of succeeding, whereas if he stayed in he might lack the necessary technical skills to be offered a commission, leaving him in the ranks instead. In all of this, one thing is clear: Sherriff wanted to be an officer – he felt it was appropriate to his talents and to his education, so in all probability he was likely to clutch at any commission opportunity that might come his way. But the issue soon became moot – at the beginning of March the Army broke up the Engineering School and Sherriff was quickly beset by anxiety once more.

Family Beginnings

Sherriff was never good with change. Throughout his time in the Army he exhibited a willingness to do his duty, to do what was expected of him, and this he seemed to do in resigned fashion, notwithstanding the natural tendency to fear death or injury. But time and again his letters highlight the agonies he suffered when circumstances changed suddenly, or were about to change. Even in France, he was, in some ways, less anxious in the trenches than when he was in reserve, or rest, contemplating moving up into the trenches again. Why this should be is difficult to ascertain, for he seems to have had a very comfortable and happy upbringing in a loving family, with extended family readily at hand.

He was born on 6 June 1896 to Herbert Hankin Sherriff and Annie Constance (Connie) Sherriff (née Winder). His older sister, Beryl, had been born three years earlier, and his brother 'Bundy' would follow three years later.[51] Both mother (whom in his letters he called 'Dearie', although when talking about her within the family she was known as 'Mimsie') and father (whom he wrote to as 'Pips') came from middle–class backgrounds.

Herbert was born in 1857[52] to a father who had followed his own father as governor of Aylesbury Prison. He was the eighth of eleven children, although three of them failed to live long enough to see his wedding to Connie Winder in 1892.[53] Connie was also from a large family – she was born in 1871,[54] fourth of eleven. In census records her father's occupation is initially given as 'baker', but then as 'master baker', so there was no real difference in their social status. There was, however, a big difference in their ages: Herbert was thirty-four when they married, Connie only twenty. He seems to have been excited about the prospect of his marriage – in his diary, on his wedding day, he marked in large black letters: 'My Wedding Day'; he also wrote that, in the carriage on his way to church, he had 'never felt so uncomfortably respectable in my life'.[55]

They lived in Hampton Wick, which Sherriff described as 'still a village: not quite in the country and yet not quite a part of Greater London',[56] in a house called 'Rossendale', at 2 Seymour Road. The house was large: the census in 1911 reports it had eleven rooms (including the kitchen, but excluding scullery, landing and bathrooms), and it had at least a parlour, a dining room and a library (all of which are mentioned in Herbert's diaries) plus five bedrooms for the family members and another for their servant. It also had a summerhouse. The status of the house reflected their social status:

Ours was the house with the double gates and trees in the front garden. Nobody else in Seymour Road had trees in their front gardens or double gates and we were glad of this because it put us on a slightly higher level, although not as high as the people in Lower Teddington Road, who had carriage sweeps and gardens down to the river.[57]

Herbert worked for the Sun Insurance Company nearly all his life, having started there in July 1877, aged just nineteen at a salary of £70 a year. 'I am now, I suppose, settled for life,'[58] he wrote in his diary at the end of that year. He enjoyed the work, and had the scope to do lots of overtime, which meant that he could earn a good salary. In 1905, the year Bob started at Kingston Grammar School (KGS), he recorded that 'The year ... has been a very prosperous one. I made £455 (salary and overwork etc.), the most I ever made in a year. Spent £425 – also the largest – but the children's schooling begins to tell up.'[59] As a comparison, average earnings in 1902 were just £70 a year, and the salary of a senior teacher at Kingston Grammar School at much the same time was £180.[60] In his draft memoir, Sherriff writes of his father that he:

was not a success in the ordinary meaning of the word. He was never a manager or head of a department: he never, in fact, moved from the cashier's office on the ground floor. He began there as a junior in 1878 [sic] and finished as a senior at the other end of the room in 1923.[61] The room was 20 yards long and he progressed across it at an average speed of 5 inches a year.[62]

Herbert was delighted when the boy (he called him Cedric at first; referring to him as 'Bob' came rather later) was born, writing that, at 11.45 on 6 June: 'A boy has just been born – very delighted – he is squalling away like anything – I recognised his voice before I knew of its sex.'[63] He was pleased, too, when Beryl was born (although it is hard to be completely sure about what he felt, since someone has taken the trouble to score out the entries in Herbert's diaries at points of maximum family interest), but his entries about Bob's birth speak of paternal pride – congratulations from all he met on the river, and so on – which is, perhaps, unsurprising in a Victorian father. But Herbert was not quite the stuffy patriarch that such a label would imply. He writes often in his diaries of spending time in the nursery with his children – sometimes while doing his 'overwork' (mainly reading reports etc.) – but also about playing games with them, or reading out loud to them from Twain, Dickens and others. Later, he writes of taking the boys camping, or taking Beryl and Bob cycling in the lanes near their house. Indeed, in 1906, when they had what seems to have been their first holiday in Selsey (just south of Bognor on the south coast – a destination that would be a regular holiday spot once they had purchased 'Sleepy Hollow', a holiday home there, and memories of which would inspire Sherriff's first novel, *The Fortnight in September*), he, Bob and Beryl cycled down from Hampton Wick, about 60–70 miles, over the period of a couple of days.

But still, Herbert liked to keep time free for his own pursuits: he was a keen cyclist and skiffer, he played tennis and cricket (indeed, was on the committee of both clubs), and chess. He also liked to go to the races, although the amount that he gambled seemed to decline as the responsibilities of parenthood took hold. And his diaries show him enjoying pursuits on his own, while missing out on family occasions. On Boxing Day 1895, for example, he writes: 'To Aquarium to see Ladies Cyclists race. The French riders very tasty. [Mademoiselles] Beany and Dalliarde especially so.' (And it's not hard to imagine how his pregnant wife (with a 3-year-old daughter) would have viewed that comment,[64] had she seen it.) On another occasion he records that 'Thursday was Beryl's party – forty-two were here including small ones and grown-ups – I took the evening off and went to the Coliseum in London, where there was a real good show.'[65]

Connie, of course, was the parent who looked after the children, but she enjoyed her own pursuits too. She became an avid member of the Skiff Club, with a newspaper cutting recording her 100th win in 1909,[66] and Herbert introduced her to the joys of cycling, noting in his diaries that she was difficult to teach and that 'she doesn't improve as much as she should' because 'she laughs too much and stops [the] machine.'[67] Nevertheless, before long she was joining the throng of female cyclists on the towpath around Kingston – and not just on the towpath: she and two friends were caught by a policeman when they were riding on the pavement, and were duly summonsed, being fined 2/6d each later that year. She also began to pursue her interest in performing, and by 1905 was appearing regularly with the Percy Richards Opera Company at small events in and around Kingston. The company seems to have been made up mainly of amateurs (except for the Richards themselves), but she seemed to be given more and more to do, her progress being marked by Herbert's diary entries. By 1907, she was being singled out in the prestigious pages of *Stage* magazine for her role in *Carmen* (still with Percy Richards): 'Great praise is due to Mrs Sherriff, who for the first time undertook the role of Carmen. She shows very great promise in both voice and acting.'[68]

There is nothing in Herbert's diaries to suggest any major disharmony in the family home. Both he and Connie obviously had plenty to occupy them, the children seemed happy at school (Bundy following Bob to Kingston Grammar School) and they stayed close with relatives: Herbert's brothers, Frank and Edgar, seem to have been regular visitors, while his sisters, Edith (Ede) and Kate, lived together in a house in Mortlake, to which the family cycled regularly; Connie's mother lived just behind Kingston Grammar School, in the same street as her sister Alice (and brother-in-law Syd), with whom Connie and Herbert seem to have been particularly close. The children had many activities themselves (Herbert remarks on their sudden stamp collecting mania, for example, which cost him dearly) and seem, from their correspondence while Bob was in the Army, to have been great friends.

The source of Bob's anxiety about change, therefore, is not easy to discern. But perhaps there is a clue in something else he wrote in the early draft of his autobiography:

> I had a habit of touching lampposts and trees when I went by them. If I missed one, I simply had to go back and touch it – even if the nurse shook me or slapped me I [would] wrench my hand away and run back and touch it – and then I felt calm and cool again. It worried my mother and father quite a lot because they were afraid it meant there was something serious the matter with me, but one day a man in my father's office told him that the great Dr Johnson used to do the same thing all his life.[69]

Olive Pettit, his erstwhile secretary, remarked[70] that Sherriff reminded her of an autistic boy who used to live near her, and wondered if that might explain his lack of interest in women, and his obvious preference for solitude later in life. Autism Spectrum Disorders are defined as: 'disorders … characterised, in varying degrees, by difficulties in social interaction, verbal and nonverbal communication and repetitive behaviours.'[71] Sherriff's writing and correspondence, and the depth of his later social engagement, conclusively refute any suggestion of problems with social interaction or verbal communication. He could obviously be great company, as his later correspondence shows. But while he could cope with social functions and audiences, he seemed to prefer to avoid them (often sometimes agreeing to attend events, yet cancelling at very short notice), especially later in life. But perhaps the hint about his 'repetitive behaviours' may provide a clue about his deep antipathy to change.

Back in Camp

The breaking up of the Engineering School coincided with a more general reorganisation at Gidea Park, where the School of Instruction was converted into four companies of cadets, to which recruits were passed on for training as officers after first receiving a preliminary training in the ranks. 'A new Cadet school is going to be started with very strict discipline,' writes Sherriff to his father on 2 March. 'The corps is to be reduced by 1,000 men, all those unsuitable for taking commissions are to be transferred as privates to line regiments.'[72] The next day he writes to his mother that he expects to be moved out of his comfortable billet and back in the huts at camp the very next day, and 'the fact is that the news of leaving billets and stopping leave has come so suddenly that it has brought back all my old homesickness for the time being.'[73] A few days later, however, he was in much better spirits. He had, indeed, moved into one of the huts at camp – Hut 25 – and although he was not with his friend Trimm,[74] he was with 'a lot of other friends, so I'm quite satisfied on that score.'[75] The huts were ready for their arrival with the beds made and the fires lit. 'It was a very different night to my first one. There were three other Yorkshiremen in our hut and they were so funny I was nearly ill through laughing.'

His letters to his mother and father were quite different from each other in tone. He would spell out his daily routines and training schedules in some detail to his father, and they would be peppered with a cynicism about the Army in general and specific individuals in command. If a parade was held for an important officer he would delight in telling his father the ways in which it had gone wrong, as if to highlight the foolishness of those in senior positions, perhaps echoing the kind of attitudes his father himself espoused. But with his mother, his tone was much more one of longing – of longing to be home, for his forthcoming leave, or to see her – often coupled with detailed travel plans. Yet the letters were also studded with bouts of stoicism (unsurprisingly, given her gift of Marcus Aurelius). In the *Jimmy Lawton Story*, he tells of Jimmy's travel home for weekend leave, and his walks in the park with his mother, when 'she urged him to do his best wherever he was and under all circumstances however hard, to always keep up a cheerful countenance for his friends,' while 'she saw with a great feeling of pride that her boy's spirit had not been bullied out of him and crushed as she had feared – but that it had grown finer and stronger.'[76]

As well as routine training, there were a number of special duties required of the recruits – hut orderly, for example, police duty on the local station, and quartermaster's fatigue. Sherriff was especially pleased to be detailed on fire picket in mid-March, the duties of which, he explained to his father, consisted of keeping back the crowds if fire occurred. They were to remain in camp for twenty-four hours, with full kit and rifles, in case of emergency (although, as he pointed out, nothing much was likely to happen unless there was a Zeppelin raid). But the upshot was that, for the first time, he was fully uniformed and equipped, and his pride in his appearance is evident in the photograph that was taken at the time [see Plate 5]. Of course, they had to return the equipment afterwards for the next men, but for a moment he felt like a real soldier.

As the month wore on, he and the others became more anxious about who would be picked to wash out of officer training and head straight to line regiments as enlisted men. He warned his parents not to be surprised if they heard he was being transferred out, reporting that, from a group of men who had applied for Royal Field Artillery commissions, that had been the fate of those who had not been selected. He had been told that those who had arranged commissions would be allowed to stay, and so he contacted an old KGS man, Colley, whom he had heard was a captain in the East Surreys, asking for his help. Having moved to the East Kents, Colley could not help him; instead he advised him that every man had to serve six months in the ranks before his commanding officer could recommend him for a commission: 'I assume that provided you pass all your exams and your CO considers you are fitted for a commission he will recommend you.'[77]

By this time, partly at the urging of Sergeant Smith, who crops up in his letters a few times and is obviously someone he trusted, he had decided to voluntarily 'wash out' of the Engineers (where there were few commissions anyway, and where he felt his lack of qualifications would count against him) in favour of a commission in the Infantry. Again, as before, it was the commission that mattered most to him, rather than the branch of the service to which he would be attached. Every fresh rumour about men being sent to France would produce a new burst of anxiety. On 7 April he wrote: 'I have just stopped writing my letter to hear a sensational rumour that all the Engineers are to be transferred.'[78] He did not know if it was true but would not be surprised if it were. Ten days later, it was something else: 'There is another draft being prepared for France and as I have "washed out" of the Engineers I am wondering if I will be included – but of course I think I would rather stay in Romford even if it is only for the sports and cricket.'[79] The rumour mill never stopped.

Sports

As the spring wore on, the cricket season had begun, and he was anxious to play – not for the regiment, where the side was 'nearly all county players',[80] but for the company, at least. There followed a litany of requests for his cricket gear, and endless instructions about how it should be brought over. Early in April he was reminiscing in a letter to his mother: 'This lovely weather reminds me of those glorious days I spent at school in my last term,'[81] and went on to express the hope that they would have some athletic sports soon. He soon had his wish, for it was announced that there would be a sports contest on the Wednesday after Easter (26 April), and he instantly started training. He doubted that he would do well, because there were so many other good athletes in the camp.

This is a typical example of Sherriff's modesty at work. His sporting performance at school had been exceptional – he had won prizes right from his very first sports day,[82] and his name was peppered throughout the school magazine whenever sports were mentioned. By his final year he was captain of cricket, and also of rowing, where he had been in the crew that had bested local rivals Tiffin School in their annual race (see Plate 3). But his final sporting performance was the most memorable, as *The Kingstonian*[83] magazine highlighted:

> Beautiful weather favoured the annual athletic sports in connection with the Kingston Grammar School … special mention must be made of R.C. Sherriff, the winner of the Victor Ludorum trophy, who is at once a very speedy sprinter, and a very beautiful jumper.

His successes on the day included winning the long jump, the high jump, the 100 yards and the quarter mile[84] – every event, in fact, that he had entered.[85]

Despite this impressive performance, and his natural athleticism, he was wary of how he would perform in the Artists' sports when the time came. The day before the heats he had written to his father that he was hoping to make the finals; but when, a couple of days later, he wrote that he had been successful, he nevertheless cautioned that 'I thoroughly enjoyed myself, but I fear I will have little chance in the finals, as there are so many good men in for them, but it is as much as I would hope to get into the finals at all.'[86] The finals came after a short spell of leave at Selsey, which he much enjoyed, and when they did he emerged with a second in the long jump and a win in the inter–company relay, and just missed out on the 100 yards and 220 yards finals, showing just what a good athlete he was, despite his own misgivings.

Throughout his life Sherriff would be modest about his own abilities and achievements. He commented in *No Leading Lady* that, because he was poor at Latin, his headmaster had 'written me off as a flop'.[87] But he was far from the worst student in his class (although nor was he the best). His 1908 Lent Term Report[88] shows him fifth in his form group of twenty: ironically, his best position was in Latin (third), while, not so surprisingly (given the difficulties he faced with trigonometry in his surveying), his worst was maths (tenth). His writing (fifth) and English skills (seventh) were in line with his average.

He tended not to write much about himself in his letters home – not, at any rate, in a self–appraising fashion. But it is interesting to see how he viewed himself, through the prism of the *Jimmy Lawton Story*, which offered him the chance to look back at his younger self from the perspective of a couple of years' additional experience. As far as appearance is concerned, he seems to have viewed himself as 'good looking … but not extraordinarily handsome, but he interested some of the older men as a typical English boy.'[89] Emotionally he felt himself rather unworldly ('it must be remembered that he was young – young even for his age – ignorant of many things which perhaps his father should have told him'), but that he was blessed with the greatest gift of all – that 'of common sense – a sense that told him by instinct what not to say, what not to do and how to address different kinds of people.' It is interesting that he couches his common sense as the ability to sense what not to do; being seen to do the right thing was ever an important motivation for him, as was eagerness to please: 'he cultivated a manner that he thought pleased different people best.' But he was always willing to listen and learn: 'In talking to older men than himself … he always tried by asking questions to get their views and advice. … And so he learnt many things gradually from his friends' unrestrained talk, sometimes not understanding, but always learning.'

The Final Months

By the middle of May, the camp was filling up – new men were arriving all the time, and accommodation was sufficiently stretched that they had to be put up in tents. Sherriff noted that one of the newcomers was a Tiffin schoolmaster (Mr

Thompson), but also an ex–master of his own, Mr Keetch, who had dined at Sherriff's home on several occasions.[90] Sherriff watched enviously one day as a batch of men who had been through the officers' school were 'given leave until they get their commissions, and I have been watching them clear out with their luggage, lucky men.'[91] One of them was Wilfred Owen, although there would have been no spark of recognition if they had passed each other.[92] By this time the progress to a commission came through selection to the Officer School, and as Sherriff watched the men in his hut go off one by one (to be replaced by new men, which did not sit well with his dislike of change), he found a new source of anxiety in wondering how long it would be before the call came for him – if, indeed, it ever did. Nevertheless, he was a little consoled by becoming even more of a soldier: 'We've now got full packs and rifles each, so feel quite like real soldiers now.'[93] Admittedly, there was more work involved in cleaning, but at least they could take pride in polishing up the leather. Having passed the required musketry tests he was now training with his own rifle at the more advanced Rainham Marsh firing range, and they had just been given their first lesson in 'bayonet fighting'.[94]

His birthday, on 6 June, was blighted by the news of the death of Lord Kitchener the previous day, when the ship in which he had been travelling to Russia, HMS *Hampshire*, was sunk by a German mine. 'You can well imagine the depression it has caused and no doubt the worst effect of the affair will be the loss of morale,' wrote Sherriff to his father.[95] This must have compounded the feeling he had of the war coming closer, for after a steady trickle of men departing for commissions, he reported that 'Yesterday we had an inspection by about thirty-five colonels who came down to pick officers from the school and finished up by picking all the 600 men there, which settles them all up with commissions.'[96]

Sherriff was ready to try anything that might help get him in, so turned to his Uncle Syd (husband of his maternal Aunt Alice) who wrote a nine–page letter to Major Higham of the Artists in support of his nephew, only to be told that the men to receive the coveted 'Blue Forms' had been selected but not yet informed. On 19 June he wrote to his mother noting the good news she had brought him, 'which I do hope comes off alright – although I think it sounds quite "official" I shall be glad to hear exactly what Sergeant Faith told Auntie – and shall be glad to get my Blue Form.'[97] Two short days later, he came back from a route march, smothered in dust, to find a Blue Form waiting for him. He sent it back to his mother to collect the various signatures he needed to attest to his character and education, and in the meantime found his name on a list of men named as 'probables' for the school. The regiment gave them a list of tailors where they could have their uniforms made. He chose Hazel & Co of Hanover Square, and went to be measured by them, but held off buying anything until his application to the school had been confirmed.

Meanwhile, things were taking a more serious turn in France. On 1 July, he wrote to his father that 'I have just got an evening paper announcing the start of the British offensive, so the next few days should have some interesting news in the papers.'[98] The Battle of the Somme had begun. Although the casualty figures started mounting quickly, there were to be no further references to the Somme in his letters. He and the other cadets must have been unnerved: it certainly gave Jimmy Lawton pause for thought:

> When a man is suddenly awakened from a happy dream and realises there is an unpleasant day ahead of him – he realises it with an unhappy shock and a sinking heart. Then, after thinking about it longer in bed for a while, he braces himself up – decides to do the best he can – and then dresses himself as happily and contentedly as he can. ... That night he lay awake some time in the darkness of the hut – and between the fitful gusts of wind, when the trees stopped rustling and were quite still – he heard the dull rumbling again far away across the sea.[99]

Four days after the Big Push began, the new recruits to the Officer School were removed from their huts and took their places in Gidea Hall, the large manor house that dominated the Gidea Park camp. He hoped to be placed in the same room as Trimm and his other friends – even to the extent of falling in line behind each other – but it was not to be. His new address was 'Y' Company, Cadet Unit, Room 53, Gidea Hall. Inevitably he was upset at the change ('I will tell you my troubles when I see you, I hope … as I am rather lonely at being separated from my friends and at being put in new quarters. … I am looking forward to seeing you so much as I always fall back on you more than ever when I am lonely.'[100]), but he was happy to be in a company with Sergeant Major Henham, a colleague of his father's from Sun Insurance. He wrote about his daily routine to his father[101] – hard at work on drills and lectures from reveille at 6.00 am until 8.00 in the evening, after which he had a few moments free to indulge his love of Scott (he was reading *Woodstock* at the time) or other historical novelists. As the month wore on he became accustomed to the new arrangements, and he and Trimm and some others collaborated in finding a room to rent in which they could work more easily. Trimm had by now decided to put his name down for the Artillery, but Sherriff was pleased that Sergeant Major Henham had helped steer an old KGS friend[102] towards a commission in the East Surreys alongside Sherriff. Despite the desperately hot weather, their training programme was undiminished (although they were allowed to perform some of it in shirtsleeves) – he writes of putting up wire entanglements and practising trench warfare, grenade throwing and much more.[103]

On 9 August, he was told by Sergeant Major Henham that he was to be one of the sixty men in the company to be allowed to take their exams at the end of August (the rest having to wait until the end of September). He wrote excitedly to his mother to tell her that he might have his commission by the end of August,[104] and after a short weekend's leave he got down to serious work: extra classes were put on for the lucky men, and there was little time for relaxation. His letters for the next two weeks were brief and functional; often to do with the organisation of his finances to make sure he had everything he needed for his uniform. The exam took place on 24 August, and there followed a couple of days of agonising and rumours, until on 30 August, during a 'very nice evening' with Henham and the other sergeants, he was told that he had scored 161 marks out of 220 in the exam ('which was surprisingly higher than I expected') and had passed. But 'they absolutely don't know what to do with us now and why they don't let us go on leave I don't know.'[105]

In fact, they did know what to do with them – they were given leave pending gazette (i.e. until they were attached to their regiments), and it must have started pretty soon after, since the next letter to his parents is dated 13 September, and is written from the 3rd Battalion of the East Surrey Regiment at Grand Shaft Barracks in Dover. After the punishing routine at Gidea Park (especially in the run-up to the exams), he found it difficult to fill his time. He was, of course, miserable and lonely ('I really can't say I like being here much – everything is so strange and I don't know any of the officers yet'[106]), and he worried that he would make mistakes ('The discipline here is very strict indeed – you go about in fear of having done something wrong all the time'[107]). He heard unofficially that he would be bound either for France or Salonica (and he hoped for the latter), but whatever the decision, he wanted it to come soon: 'I have got to go off some day or other and it hardly makes much difference if it is early or late – the longer you wait here I expect the less you want to go out.'[108] He was not completely starved of things to do: he met his uncle Syd, who was stationed nearby, and a friend lately from the Artists. He was also given his revolver and ammunition and given a course on how to use them (though he found it hard). The waiting must have been agony: if he was anything like Jimmy Lawton, he spent the time anxiously worrying about whether he had the makings of an officer:

> The discipline in the Rifles had taught him to worship the officers and look upon them as creatures far higher in every way to himself.... Now he was to become one of them he wondered whether he could ever make his soldiers feel as he had done towards his officers.

His last letter from Grand Shaft Barracks is dated Monday, 25 September, which is probably when he was told that he would be leaving for France on Thursday, 28 September. Jimmy's story provides a poignant glimpse into Sherriff's last couple of days at home – walking and talking with his parents, sitting with them at home, making the final preparations for his kit. And one of his mother's final speeches may have been pretty much what Connie said to her own son the night before she waved him off at Charing Cross station:

His mother told him how she envied him. 'You don't know yet how sad it is to gradually grow old – to gradually see your skin become wrinkled and your hair turn grey. And if it really happened that you had to die … I can think of nothing more splendid than passing away in the full vigour of manhood – under the open sky – to go at the climax of your life, instead of slowly fading out in a long weary old age in some sickly bedroom. Oh … it's fine to be a man today – in being able to feel that every hardship you endure – every twinge of pain you feel is for a great just cause – so absolutely just – with none of the shuddering doubts that the enemy must feel – to [go] with a clear conscience – and then you come home safely as I feel sure you will. To be able to feel in your inmost conscience that you have done your uttermost and that when your own time comes that there are [lots] of friends waiting on the other side – still laughing and young and cheerful as they died.[109]

Chapter 2

In the Trenches, 1916–19

*And thou wilt give thyself relief, if thou doest every act of thy life as if it were the
last.*

Marcus Aurelius, *The Meditations*, Book II.[1]

The morning of 28 September 1916 was fine and sunny in London, but
Sherriff and his mother made their way to Charing Cross station with heavy
hearts. They had made the most of the last twenty-four hours, roaming the
woods near their home in Hampton Wick, and taking moonlit walks through the wide
expanse of Bushy Park. But now there was time for just one last cup of coffee before
he boarded the ten o'clock train: '[The guard] waved his flag and blew his whistle, and
the train crawled away across the Thames towards the coast. As we went round the
bend we saw hundreds of little white handkerchiefs fluttering on the platform.'

When he arrived in Folkestone the train ran right up to the pier, and all that he
had to do was carry his luggage 'across about 50 yards up the gangway on to the
boat'.[2] A short, smooth crossing later, and he and several other men of the East
Surreys arrived in Boulogne. That evening he wrote home to his mother: 'I can
hardly realise I am in France, it seems just like a cinematograph picture to see the
Gendarmes in baggy trousers walking about and porters in blue overalls.'[3]

From Boulogne he and several others took the train to the base camp at Étaples
('Eat Apples', as the Tommies called it). One of them in particular, an older man
named Percy High, a former schoolmaster on his way back to the war again after
having being sent for officer training, would become an important source of advice
and counsel during the difficult times ahead. They arrived at the base camp at ten
o'clock in the evening: 'My first impression ... was that of blackness and rain:
innumerable huts with shining wet roofs and thousands of glimmering lights.' It
was still raining when they emerged from their tents next morning, and went to the
orderly room to receive books for drawing money from the field cashier, and to be
told to await further instructions. The first thing they did was to put on their macs
and stroll round the camp. He was amazed at its size:

Line upon line of huts seemed to disappear into the distance: here and there
cookhouses sent columns of black smoke into the air. Then there were hospitals,
recreation rooms, YMCA huts and numbers of open squares for drilling and
assembling. Thousands of men lived in this giant wooden city.[4]

After the walk there was nothing to do but 'loaf', although Sherriff did take the opportunity to draw out some money and buy himself a good pair of trench boots (boasting to his father about how much cheaper they were in Étaples than at home)[5]; otherwise, they just waited to see where they had been posted. That evening, Percy High told him that the two of them (along with Abrams, another man who had come with them from London) were to proceed by train the next morning to join the 9th Battalion of the East Surrey Regiment, 24th Division, 1st Army.[6]

At the station the next morning the three of them discovered that their destination was to be Bruay. Sherriff was greatly relieved:

> We could hardly believe that we were not going to the Somme; we had, in fact, practically made up our minds that we would go there – where the world's greatest battle was then raging at its very height, and where fresh troops by the thousand were required every day.'[7]

But the journey there was very tedious. It took them several hours to reach St Pol, where they had to wait another seven hours for the connecting train to Bruay. While there, with the weather having improved, the three men chose to relax in a nearby field while they were waiting, and while doing so, Sherriff wrote a quick letter to his mother, telling her that he had seen much to interest him on the journey, and that 'I should like to write a book about it one day if I can.'[8]

They continued their journey later that evening, another three hours or so in the train from St Pol to Bruay. As darkness fell they began to see:

> a faint flicker on the horizon, growing brighter now, then dying away, but always flickering up again. … That flicker in the distance was the reflection of the Very lights that rise and fall over no-man's-land so that the men could watch at night … there was a rustle of wind outside and in the quiet that followed came a distant solitary boom. 'Did you hear that?' said Abrams. 'You'll hear plenty more,' said Percy from his dark corner.[9]

The 9th East Surreys, the 'Gallants'

The final part of their journey came the next day, by truck to Estrée-Cauchy (or 'Extra Cushy', as it was known, since this was where the battalion was sent for rest), where Sherriff arrived on Sunday, 1 October 1916.

The 9th East Surreys was a service battalion, formed at the beginning of the war from recruits who were mainly drawn from London and the surrounding areas.[10] They had trained in England for the best part of a year, before being shipped to France in September 1915, where they were thrown straight into the Battle of Loos, suffering terrible casualties. The battalion was 'patched' up with new recruits to take the place of the casualties, and after a spell of rest, took its place in the line of trenches, in the Ypres Salient, and then facing Messines. In the spring, after a period of training, they were pitched into their next big battle – at Guillemont and Delville Wood on the Somme, 'where men fell like flies for no seeming gain. They came out with four officers and 150 men, where forty officers and 800 men went in.'[11]

While recovering from their efforts on the Somme, the battalion was again rebuilt, with returned wounded and sick, and with new recruits, such as the three officers who had just arrived at Estrée-Cauchy on that sunny Sunday in October. They reported to the orderly room, and met the adjutant, Lieutenant C.A. Clark (known to his fellow officers as Nobby). He had enlisted at the age of seventeen, and had served with the East Surreys in the Boer War, reaching the rank of regimental sergeant major by 1914, before being commissioned at the beginning of 1916. Sherriff would grow to like him very much: 'Nobby was a stout jovial man, an ex-colour sergeant and a splendid soldier who knew every detail of his work (and everybody else's too). He was very popular, and commanded respect, despite his dropped H's.'[12]

Nobby sent Sherriff off to 'C' Company, Abrams to 'B' Company and Percy High to 'D' Company. Sherriff was indifferent to being parted from Abrams, but regretted that he and High had been separated, since he clearly valued his advice and companionship.

Visiting his company headquarters, he met Lieutenant Schofield, who made him welcome by offering him some whisky. 'I accepted, as politeness suggested, but felt that twelve o'clock in the morning was hardly the time for whisky – I felt so because I knew nothing of the habits of active service.'[13] Later he met his company commander, Captain Charles ('Baby') Hilton, who had been with the battalion since December 1915.[14] Sherriff had mixed feelings about him:

> I never knew whether I really liked Hilton or not – he was a bluff, good-natured sort of man: a very good soldier who understood and did all in his power to lighten the burden of his men. Yet he had the most sarcastic, bullying manner towards people whom he disliked (who were junior to him) that I ever came across: he was quick to notice little peculiarities of voice or manner and would unmercifully imitate anyone whom he thought disliked it.[15]

There was nothing to do that sleepy afternoon, and Sherriff was surprised by how rural it was, 'no sound of guns, no sign of war'. While the officers of 'C' Company sprawled out on blankets in front of their tents he went looking for Percy High. Waiting for him in the garden of the house in which he was billeted, he was suddenly confronted by an officer who commenced talking to him at tremendous speed, telling him to take off his sword-frog,[16] since they were not worn in France. The officer in question turned out to be Gerald Tetley, a 29-year-old barrister for whom Sherriff would develop a great affection:

[He] was one of the most complex of the many extraordinary people I met in the Army. He was a pale, delicate looking man with a long straight nose, a blue chin and very short sight. He was also slightly knock-kneed, and most untidily dressed. When he fell down … he always came apart into four pieces – his hat, his stick, himself and his spectacles. … He was the quickest tempered man I ever met, flying into a rage in the most childish way on the slightest provocation. … In the line he was a marvel: naturally high-strung and nervous, he was always with his men should there be any danger. … He prided himself on being a High Churchman: he was an Oxford man and a barrister, and he had the vilest flow of the most unimaginably profane language that I ever heard.[17]

After an idyllic walk with High, they returned to the battalion's orderly room, to be addressed by Colonel Tew, the commanding officer. Sherriff began to harbour grave doubts about his fitness for the role of an officer:

My heart sank lower and lower as he lay bare the cold blunt truth of war; as he enumerated the qualities that a young officer should possess and the duties that he should understand, a cold fear came over me – Am I an efficient officer? Do I know enough? Will I be sent back to England as a disgraceful example of incompetence?[18]

Just as when he was with the Artists Rifles, changing circumstances, coupled with anxiety, brought on the usual bout of homesickness, but the friendliness of his fellow officers soon cheered him up. Later, at dinner with his fellow officers, he tells us in his memoir that 'For the first time I breathed in a little of the spirit of 'C' Company'[19]:

Doubtless there were other companies as good, but 'C' was mine and 'C' remained mine during all the time I served in France and Belgium. By degrees, 'C' Company became my most perfect ideal, and it would have broken my heart to have been transferred to any other company. 'C' Company is an ugly, colourless expression, but it became a term of loving memory to me. We wore a red diamond of cloth above a green cross on our sleeves and the very sight of those colours brought a glow of pride to me. We had five different company commanders and twenty different officers while I was with the company and my greatest pleasure to look back on is the fact that I remained with 'C' Company all the time I was on active service. Every day I became bound more surely to 'C' Company and every day I loved and esteemed it more.

The Reserve Line

Within a couple of days Sherriff was finally on his way up to the trenches. They began their journey at eight o'clock on 2 October, and arrived at Cabaret-Rouge, in Zouave Valley, a few hours later, after travelling, in the rain, 'for about a mile down a seemingly endless trench'.[20] Sherriff's sleeping quarters were in a tin shed, with two other second lieutenants, Puttock and L.H. ('Jimbo') Webb. Writing to his mother that night he reassured her that he was quite contented, and that: 'I shall be as careful as possible, dear.'[21] They settled down to life in the reserve trench, about a mile from the front line, and Sherriff began to get to know and like Webb (a pious man, and very brave).

After a couple of days, Hilton decided it would be good for Sherriff and Webb to have sight of the front line before they actually took their places there in just a few days, so on 3 October they walked along the valley, and up a series of trenches on to Vimy Ridge. Within a quarter of a mile they began to hear the sound of shells whistling overhead. He wrote to his mother:

> There is a constant crash! crash! bang! over ahead of us, but I feel that it is useless feeling miserable and so really feel quite happier than expected. ... It takes some time to get used to the shelling and you think every bang has sent a shell flying over towards you – but they probably burst miles off.[22]

On returning from this expedition he encountered for the first time another of the officers who would be a source of great comfort and strength to him. Lieutenant A.H. (Archibald) Douglass (known to everyone as 'Father', although he was only twenty-eight) had come to the battalion as a signals officer in June, and had been one of the few officers to survive the Somme.[23] Sherriff first saw him:

> sadly sitting in our shed drying a sock over the candle. ... Father[24] was one of the most lovable men I have ever known: to use an exceedingly ungrammatical expression, he was the best type of typical Englishman: he hated any form of affectation and he hated vulgarity. A man of few words, he would sit for an hour or more at a mess table without saying a word, smoking cigarettes that dangled from his upper lip – leaning forward and fiddling with his fingers under the table. He was also the coolest man I ever saw in the trenches, where nothing ever seemed to make the slightest impression on him.[25]

Four days later, he was sent up to the front line with three other officers, to make sure they knew how to get there, and to familiarise themselves with the layout of the trenches they would be taking over. After a long journey and a quick reconnaissance of the trench positions, they soon found themselves facing a bombardment of Minenwerfer (mortar bombs, or 'minnies', as the English called them):

Can you imagine what it is like to stand in a narrow trench and watch great things 2 feet long and about a foot round shoot up in the air looking like a little piece of pencil, the height is so great to which it goes – it then turns and drops down towards earth whilst we all run along in different directions and screw up into a corner and wait for the bang and then a shower of dirt about five seconds after.[26]

The four officers saw no reason to hang around, and retired quickly to the reserve line, but Sherriff was immediately sent back: Hilton wanted him to spend the night there to acclimatise himself before going up for the real thing. Sherriff was very unhappy: it was bad enough to have made the journey once, but to make it a second time, and then be forced to stay was almost as much as he could bear:

When I heard the banging going on in front ... it felt just like what it is to go to the dentists. I knew I had got to go up but my courage very nearly failed, although I knew I could not go back.[27]

He arrived back at the front-line trench at 'stand-to'. Stand-to took place twice a day – roughly at dawn and dusk, when every man in the battalion would take his place in the trench for an hour, in case of attack. The Germans did the same, so for two hours every day there were two lines of men, stretching from the Channel to the Alps, gazing across no-man's-land at each other.[28]

Sherriff had something to eat and slept for a while, then was summoned at ten o'clock to accompany Penrose, a captain in the 8th Battalion, The Queen's Regiment, as he toured their positions:

I got up with chattering teeth in the cold clamminess of the wet chalk dugout: In the dim light, with fumbling fingers I slung on my equipment, hung the gas satchel round my neck and put my steel helmet on ... 'I shouldn't take a walking stick, it's in the way'[29] – Penrose was pulling on a pair of thick leather gloves – 'Come on!' he said.[30]

The stretch of line that Penrose and his men were defending (and to which the 9th East Surreys would shortly be moving) was a tricky one. The bulk of the line was about 100 yards from the Germans, but at one end the line ran directly towards the German line (closing to within 40 yards), and at the other end the line pushed out to a bomb crater ('Ersatz crater') where 'the British lay on one lip and gazed ... into the eyes of the Germans on the opposite lip,' just 30 yards away.

Sherriff strained his ears listening to every noise that broke the silence – a crack from the German lines as a bullet flew towards the trench; a light fired from across no-man's-land, hissing and spluttering high in the air; a 'heavy' shell, making a sound like rippling water overhead.[31] He and Penrose toured the line, ending at Ersatz crater, chatting quietly to the men who lay in the two narrow trenches that jutted towards the crater rim, trenches so narrow that they could barely move along them. As he stood in the dark, he wondered how long the soldiers would be alive, and how long their captain would live, 'that elegant, courtly young man whom I regarded with feelings of admiration and awe – who looked so out of place on this ridge of corruption and death.'[32] That night, when Penrose and Sherriff had been relieved and were back in the dugout, the crater would be attacked by the Germans, who were looking for British prisoners for identification purposes. One German was killed, one British soldier missing. Sherriff breathed a sigh of relief when, after breakfast, he packed his kit and left. On the way back: 'I was resting against the side, and I saw on the opposite wall a little cluster of scarlet pimpernels, fresh and beautiful with beads of dew still on them. I picked one and sent it home.' It found its way into the memoir a few years later.[33]

Up in the Line

He got back to Cabaret-Rouge just in time to find the men packing their belongings. At nine o'clock the next morning, 10 October, 'C' Company headed towards the line that Sherriff had so gratefully departed the day before. He was bringing up the rear with the reserve platoon, and could see up ahead as the company toiled up towards Vimy Ridge, under mortar fire, since the Germans had spotted the relief was taking place. Sherriff was racked by indecision; should he carry on, or should he wait in place until the firing had quietened down? Sherriff set out the dilemma in his memoir: should the young commander take his troops up in the face of danger, at the risk of seeing them killed, and having their deaths on his conscience? Or should he wait in place, keeping them safer, but risking the relief of the men who were depending upon them?

> What a difficult job it was! If he had any imagination (and most educated men have), the thought of this responsibility haunted him secretly, day and night. It is a dreadful thing to be responsible for lives, and when times came that demanded a quick decision, and if that decision was wrong, and men died through it – what can be more awful than the thought that you are a wholesale murderer – you, who did your very best, who used your utmost judgment, but failed?[34]

In stop-start fashion, timing their movements to avoid barrages of minnies, Sherriff finally managed to shepherd his men into the trenches at the top of Vimy Ridge, and then braced himself for the eight days that would follow:

> After nearly a year of training I had arrived at the ultimate duty that the training had prepared me for. I had been clothed and fed and housed by the

country. I had given nothing of practical use in return. The time had come now when the bill was to be paid.[35]

As soon as they had arrived, Hilton posted up a duty roster for the next two days: Sherriff was on at 6.30 pm (just after stand-to) for three hours, then again at midday the following day, and at 10.30 in the evening. When he was not on duty he would remain in the safety of the dugout, and write letters home to his family. After he had been there four days he wrote to his mother of the loneliness and anxiety he felt, and how hard it was to remain stoical for the men:

> and yet through all the little tragedies that happen each day in men being killed and wounded you have to try and show to the men that you are taking it all calmly and you must be so careful not to show any weakness that the strain is awful at first until one gets used to it … I hate … the suspense of waiting for these shells to come and when they are up in the air the excitement of running along to judge their fall takes away fear for the minute – it is after the explosion that you feel cold and frightened all over – and then is the time you have got to smile to reassure the men.[36]

Three days after they arrived, Sherriff was made keenly aware of the dangers of the front line when one of his men – John Chapman, a 19-year-old farm labourer from Wisbech – was killed by a minnie blast. Sherriff deeply regretted that, earlier, he had reprimanded him for not shaving: 'Now he was dead – I had worried him in his last few hours.'[37] Over the next few days two more men in 'C' Company were killed, one from a sniper shot, and one from shock, after being buried up to his neck by a blast of earth from a minnie, and having to remain in that position as more fell around him. Sherriff continued to write home, assuring his parents that he was well, apart from an occasional headache due to the nervous strain, which he had been able to sleep off. The days passed painfully slowly for him though, and he hated every moment, especially on the last night of duty before they were due to move out of the line. Standing in the trench, next to Second Lieutenant Lechmere Thomas (the bombing officer, and consequently known as 'Tommy the Bomber') he saw a minnie rise up from the German trenches, and feared that this might be his last moment: 'for a few minutes I crouched against the trench, while Thomas stood up watching, vastly amused ("He is mad," I thought)', but it exploded harmlessly well away from them, and he was safe. Thomas, two years younger than Sherriff, wasn't mad, of course, just 'a daredevil boy who used to do amazing things, such as sitting on the parapet in the daytime.'[38]

At 3.00 pm on 18 October, after another agonising day, Sherriff and his comrades were finally relieved by the Middlesex Regiment. Even the long march back to Estrée Cauchy, where they arrived at 9.00 pm, could not dampen their spirits. Sherriff saw that his platoon was safely billeted in a nearby barn, and then went to the mess with the other officers of 'C' Company:

> It was a delightfully happy meal, that first supper out of the line, and while the rain came down steadily outside, beating on the windows and streaming off the sills, we sat round a most appetising supper on clean china plates, drank wine out of glasses, and listened to the crackle of the log fires. It was wonderful – a fit ending to the perfect happiness that had followed us away from Vimy Ridge. We laughed and talked like schoolboys on their way home for the holidays.[39]

The battalion moved back into reserve on 18 October, and the following day, after inspecting his platoon's kit (so they could arrange the necessary repairs and resupply), he turned to his sergeant and asked if he might be able to recommend a man who might serve as his batman (servant) – an older man, since a batman's job was a little easier than that of a rifleman. That was when Private Morris entered Sherriff's army life – a 'somewhat unclean, oldish man … about forty-five … a small man, with a rugged face, blue eyes and a drooping fair moustache'.[40] The sergeant acknowledged that he was not much to look at, but in the months ahead Sherriff would come to appreciate him greatly:

> Morris had his faults as every other man had. He was a rotten soldier: he never learnt to salute correctly and he never once put his puttees on neatly, but he was a humorist, and a humorist in France was worth a dozen howitzer guns to England.

The time in reserve was not all resupply and training: there was some work to be done as well, with the result that, one evening, Sherriff had to help take a working party up to the front line for trench digging in no-man's-land ('rather an unpleasant job', he told his father, 'which I was glad to finish').[41] When he returned he had a long sleep, and woke up to find Hilton in his tent, sympathising with him over the duty he had just been sent on, and telling him to take it easy:

> I got, for the first time, that 'human touch' that Hilton had. I know of no man, so gruff and apparently unsympathetic, who had underneath such a deep sense of duty to those under him. The men liked him because he did everything he could for them – he did it in a rough, abrupt way, but he did do it, and that's better than all the honeyed promises of a weaker man.[42]

Sherriff had been sent on the duty by his friend Pat (Second Lieutenant Patterson), and Hilton thought that Sherriff should not have been the one to go. Perhaps it was just sympathy for the new recruit, just back from his first difficult time in the line; or it may be that Hilton had already noticed Sherriff's anxiety under fire, and perhaps determined that he should be spared a return trip, however brief.

After breakfast, he walked into the nearest village, Guoy-Servins (about 4 miles away) to enjoy his first bath since arriving in France almost four weeks earlier. He lingered as long as he could, and counted himself lucky that, owing to the liberal application of Boots vermin powder, he had not suffered from lice as so many others had. He dressed and started back for camp, but on the way was overcome with a terrible bout of homesickness. And with the memories of his happy carefree days at home came other thoughts:

> A frantic desire to live: there was so much I wanted to do. So many books I wanted to read. So many places I wanted to go to. ... Then another desire came; the desire to worm out of all this danger. Why should I go and live in the front line, the most dangerous place, and do the work of an infantry officer, the most dangerous job? Why not get out of it, anyhow, by any means – go sick – transfer to some other service.

But just as suddenly as the homesickness had come, his thoughts changed:

> The thought of the men I lived with came to me – of Hilton, Pat, Webb, Percy High, Sergeant Clarke, Corporal Medlock, old Morris. They went on doing it, uncomplaining, patiently waiting for their time to come. Yes! It was worth it – worth all the dangers to live with such men as these: to try and live up to their level of courage, to talk with them, live and sleep with them – it was a proud thing to do this – then why be afraid to die with them? Thousands of men, far better than I, had died, men who would have done much greater things had they lived. They had gone, and whatever the place was like where they had gone to, it would not be lonely there.[43]

So the crisis passed, for now, and he had regained his composure by later that day, when he went to the local village to enjoy a concert arranged by the chaplain, in which a song by Tetley was one of the highlights (because it was 'so feeble'). He was bolstered that night by his reading of Marcus Aurelius ('Nothing happens to any man which he is not formed by nature to bear').[44] The next day was Sunday, and he enjoyed the church parade, and afterwards, a long walk with Percy High, when they told each other of everything they had done since they last parted (Percy had enjoyed rather a quiet time at the front, noted Sherriff in his memoir, rather ruefully).[45]

Even while the two were talking, they must have been aware that they were likely to be on the move again soon. The British Army at the time aimed to cycle its units in and out of the front lines on a regular basis, recognising the toll that would be taken on nerves from too long an exposure to the danger of enemy action. After serving in the front lines (usually for six days), units would be cycled out to support or reserve for similar spells, or, if they had been near the line long enough, back for a period of rest. So it would hardly have come as a shock to hear that the battalion had been given orders to move, the next day, to Noeux-les-Mines, where they were to relieve the Royal Lancaster Regiment in the support lines. On this occasion, however, Sherriff would not be moving with his beloved 'C' Company, for he had been detailed to a quite different duty.

The Mines of Hulluch

At seven o'clock in the morning of 24 October, Sherriff and fifteen men from the battalion set out to join the 254th Tunnelling Company at Mazingarbe. The tunnelling companies (Royal Engineers) were used in the digging of mines, to plant explosives under enemy trenches,[46] but also in the construction of tunnels and vaults to store men and equipment. There had been considerable offensive mining operations on the Loos Plain during 1915 and early 1916, but by the autumn the operations appear to have been more of a defensive nature – preventing mining attacks by the enemy, and developing a network of tunnel-based listening posts.

The new duty was a 'snip', as the outgoing officer in charge of the tunnelling parties had it, which raises the question as to why Sherriff was chosen for the duty. He was a new man – only three weeks in France, and with only one week in the line under his belt, so perhaps his services would be least missed.[47] On the other hand, he had barely had time to attach himself to his new company, and get to know his new colleagues, when he was whisked away. It might have seemed more sensible to send another officer, someone who had been out longer, and who might have benefited from a period of relatively easy duty.[48] Hilton's solicitude, following Sherriff's stint with the working party in no-man's-land, may suggest that he was worried about the younger man's response to the first eight days in the line. Sherriff's anxiety at the front would likely have been apparent – and it would have contrasted with Father's generally relaxed approach, and Lieutenant Thomas's sangfroid on the trench parapet in the daylight. Nervy officers made for nervy men, and perhaps the transfer to the tunnelling regiment was an attempt to allow him to get a little bit more experience of wartime France before he again faced the rigours of the line.

To his pleasure he was not the only officer on the journey, for a number of others had been sent on as an advance party to take over the trenches that they would shortly be occupying. The officers included Percy High ('D' Company) and Abrams ('B' Company), Douglass and Stevens from his own company, and Second Lieutenant (David) Hatten, from 'A' Company, whom Sherriff was delighted to discover was another old Kingston Grammar boy. From Mazingarbe they continued walking through the ruined village of Vermelles, then into a very long communications trench known as La Rutoire Alley:

It commenced ... by breaking through a red brick wall on the roadside and winding through a wild garden, full of overgrown weeds and fruit trees. Then it went under a light railway and out on to the Loos Plain, where it wandered aimlessly across towards the old front line. It was a splendid trench, 3,800 yards long, dug deep, in firm white chalk.[49]

They marched until they arrived at a trench called 'Tenth Avenue', by which time he had met the other officer who would share the duty with him, Lieutenant Gibson (whom he had known in the Artists Rifles), who had brought fifteen men of the North Staffordshire Regiment with him; the number of other ranks had been swollen by an additional fifteen of the Queen's Regiment, and fifteen of the West Kent Regiment. All in all, there were just two officers and sixty men, and the departing officer explained how things would work. The sixty men were to be divided into three groups of twenty, each working an eight-hour shift; they would be marched from the trench to their duties in the mine by a corporal, while the officers would take turns to go to the mine and supervise the work. When Sherriff asked how close they were to the front line he was not encouraged to hear that they were only half a mile away, but he 'sighed with relief'[50] that the minnies couldn't reach them, and that the outgoing officers had never been shelled in their present position.

Sherriff stayed in his dugout in Tenth Avenue for two months, returning to his battalion only after Christmas. They were to be his two happiest months in France, since the work was straightforward, and the living and working environment relatively free from shellfire. He and Gibson were to supervise the activities of the infantrymen they had brought with them, leaving the actual tunnellers, who were Engineers, to be supervised by their own engineering officers. Supervision involved arriving about 5.30 pm, and checking on the working party from time to time: a visit to the men about 7.00 pm, followed by one at midnight, usually sufficed, and otherwise he could rest in the safety of the officers' dugout, deep inside the mine. During the day the earth from the tunnels would be placed in sandbags, ready to be dragged to the surface at night, and disposed of in shell holes, before being covered up with earth to conceal the chalk from underground. Towards morning it would be Sherriff's job to go up, out of the mine, to ensure that the chalk was covered satisfactorily (and could not be seen by German airmen).

Sherriff and Gibson set to improving their conditions gradually in the first few weeks, laying in the equipment they might need for cooking, and making sure that the men's food and accommodation were acceptable. Of course, there were still problems from time to time. Sherriff writes, for example, of an occasion when all the food (and much else besides) in their dugout was eaten by rats, forcing them to take more precautions, such as fixing doors to their cupboards. But Morris had a better plan:

'What we do want,' remarked Morris, after he finished the first part of the anti-rat campaign, 'is that bloke who hypnertised [*sic*] all the rats, and tootled them away with a flute, and then took them all into a mountain and shut 'em in – Hamilton was 'is name, I think – I'd 'ave a try only I ain't got no flute, and there ain't no convenient mountain 'ereabouts – it 'ud be rotten to get 'em all out a followin' yer, and then not know what to do wiv 'em.'[51]

While he enjoyed the peace and quiet of the tunnelling duty, his 'C' Company comrades were in and out of the line. After spending six days in the support lines, they took their place in the front line again on 31 October, in the Hulluch sector, near Sherriff's Tenth Avenue, and enjoying the same spectacular sunset ('a glorious red sky', as Sherriff described to his father).[52] Thereafter, during November, they had three more spells in the front line (broken up by a few days in support or in reserve), but casualties were, mercifully, quite light.

Displeasure

Towards the end of November, Sherriff was beginning to wonder about his future in the Infantry: he had seen the life of an engineering officer, and was rather attracted to it (as he had been in the Artists Rifles). He accordingly went to see his new commanding officer in the East Surreys, Lieutenant Colonel T.H.S. Swanton (who had taken over from Colonel Tew, the man who had made Sherriff anxious about his own abilities, when Tew was badly injured in a horse riding accident). Swanton was not popular in the battalion, and Sherriff was not impressed either, noting that the CO had not seemed pleased with his application to join the RE, and he 'seemed to think I was trying to get a soft job.'[53] Swanton was not happy about giving him a character reference for the Engineers, since he hardly knew him, and felt that Sherriff had not had enough experience of trench warfare. To make matters worse, over the next week or two Swanton was so energetic that:

He comes around on the quiet and sees men of the East Surreys attached to my party in a dirty condition – the reason being that they have just come back from working, and also that the selection of men sent to me are all the worst. ... Of course, I am blamed for their dirtiness and have probably got in his bad books.[54]

Despite his anxiety about Swanton, Sherriff was still able to maintain his sense of humour, as can be seen from a letter to his father on 29 November: 'Two months ago today I set foot on the Gallic soil (to use a journalistic expression) and my appearance in the war area seems in no way to have altered the situation.'[55]

But the situation with Swanton got worse, leading to a reprimand for Sherriff:

The commanding officer noted with displeasure this morning that some of the men of the battalion were unshaved and very dirty; on being asked who they were they answered 'Tunnellers'. It is intended to relieve you in the near future.[56]

He was very upset, not just because he was likely going back into the front line, but because he was always someone who was eager to please, and for whom it was important to be seen to do the right thing. On this occasion he confessed to his mother how unhappy he was:

I always hate being 'told off' for anything and it makes me miserable – none of the other men except ours are ever spoken to – it is dirty work and they cannot help coming back dirty. ... I do not want to go back to the battalion as you know and much less to go back because I am not capable of looking after my men. ... I always take these 'tellings off' so much to heart – much more, I suspect, than the commanding officer thinks and it always depresses me for some time afterwards.

Despite being in a relatively quiet part of the front, his nerves were showing no signs of improvement:

I don't know why it is, but some men seem to stroll about the trenches when they are shelling just as though nothing was happening. They must be made very differently to me, for it makes me tremble and breathe hard even if I just go round to the lavatories – once, coming back, they sent a shrapnel shell whizzing over and it burst a bit behind us. I felt very much like running for shelter when I saw a man climb up on to the parapet and look over as unconcerned as possible and say 'that was a near one'. ... This morning a flight of wild ducks flew overhead and both armies began firing at them – unfortunately a lot of the bullets came down on our roof and round about which frightened me as much as anything.[57]

When writing his memoir he would try to explain his unusual sensitivity to the sounds of war with reference to his vivid imagination, and his better education:

Sometimes frequently, I went through agonies of dread – terrible spasms of fear – even when there was no need for it and no immediate danger. I don't believe the majority of the men felt such things – they only felt immediate and visible danger. Perhaps I am flattering myself – perhaps it may sound terribly snobbish, absurdly conceited, yet I told myself that the average man in the ranks, who had no education – did not have these awful nameless fears. I told myself this in defence of myself – I told myself that whatever I enjoyed by way of better comfort, I paid out again in mental dread.[58]

His gloomy mood worsened with the news he had just received about an old friend: Dick Webb, the Kingston Grammar boy with whom he had been camping when war broke out, had just died of his wounds. Sherriff received a heartbreaking letter from Webb's father:

> It gives me great pain to tell you that dear Dick succumbed to his wounds on 10 October at the Base Hospital, Étaples. My wife and I went over to him and I was there some days, but Mrs Webb stayed till the last. The doctors and nurses gave us every hope of his recovery and he seemed to be improving, but eventually passed away very suddenly.   You will understand the terrible blow it is to us. One which we shall never get over. He was in such splendid health when he went away. Many other old KGS boys have given their lives for their King and country: Basil Cruiser, K. Rentall, V.P. Knapp, F.N. Marsh and T.G.N. Gardiner (Master). How dreadful that so many promising young lives should be lost.   We are all very run down as you may imagine.[59]

Sherriff tried to be stoical about his friend's death:

> these are things that cannot but be expected and although they do not depress you it makes you feel all the more the hateful uselessness of the whole thing – there is nothing to do but to bear everything that fate brings along with the knowledge that it cannot be prevented.[60]

Christmas, at Last

By mid-December, change was in the air. As well as worrying about whether the commanding officer would send him back to the battalion, he had to brace himself for the arrival of two more officers and another sixty men. He was never one to embrace change, and he complained about the extra work he had to do in preparing for the new arrivals, and worried about the implications for his present living and working arrangements. He was pleased, though, when one of the officers turned out to be Second Lieutenant Patterson, his 'C' Company colleague.

At much the same time, Tetley, who was living in a dugout relatively close to Tenth Avenue, reached out to invite him round for dinner one evening. Sherriff, although not unhappy with the solitude afforded him by his existing arrangements, took up the invitation, and had a splendid evening with Tetley and Second Lieutenant Harry Lindsay (whom he describes as Tetley's 'favourite lieutenant',[61] and whom Sherriff himself thought to be 'one of the nicest boys in the battalion'),[62] marvelling at their war stories. Tetley had been in France since autumn 1915, and Lindsay had come out to the battalion just before Sherriff, and both had been wounded (Lindsay in the neck, in 1915, while serving in the ranks of the Rifle Brigade, which made Sherriff 'cold to think of'). The dinner party obviously made a huge impression on him, since it takes up several pages of his memoir, and it is most likely then that he began to develop a great affection for both men.

In the run up to Christmas, Sherriff and Pat went to great lengths to ensure a fine celebration – Sherriff's letters home are full of the thoughts of Christmas past, as well as the treats they intended to buy for themselves and their men. Christmas Eve dinner was an elaborate five-course affair, although the description of the dishes in the menu rather embellished the fare that Morris and James (Gibson's batman) were able to conjure up from the supplies available.[63] On Christmas Day they had another pleasant evening, when they were entertained to dinner by the RE officers in the mine. But Sherriff's mind was not entirely on his surroundings, because he had been told unofficially that he was likely to be relieved in the near future. It was no surprise, then, when he received the formal order on Boxing Day that he was to return with his men on 27 December. At three o'clock in the afternoon an officer arrived from 'D' Company, bringing fifteen men with him, and Sherriff and his little band set out for the small town of La Philosophe, where the battalion was currently held in reserve.

When the last moments came, I could have cried. All the hundreds of pleasant incidents came crowding back – the quiet free evenings – the walks to Bethune – and all that lay ahead were maddening hours of patrolling the front line – watching for minnies, dreading the darts, caged like an animal in 50 yards of winding ditch. The torture of Vimy Ridge would be drawn out now into one long agony of six days in, six days out, six days in, six days out; maddeningly regular, until something happened.[64]

Unhappy New Year

When Sherriff returned to his battalion he was detailed to 'D' Company, because they were short of officers. He would have preferred 'C', of course, but if that was not possible, then 'D' – Tetley's company, with Percy High among his colleagues – was almost as good. He may still have been holding out the tiniest hope of a transfer to the RE, but that was soon dashed by Swanton, who told him that he would not give him permission to go, because he was already too short of officers.[65] To make matters worse, the battalion was about to move again – to relieve the 8th Queen's in the left section of the Hulluch sector. By the evening of 30 December, he was back in the front line that he so dreaded.

The day after they arrived, the Germans welcomed them with some shelling, but 'nothing very bad', according to the battalion diary. But on New Year's Day, 'Fritz [wanted] to give us a New Year's greeting.' Throughout the morning and much of the afternoon the battalion's trenches were bombarded with 'whizzbangs, 4.2s and 5.9s. Front line, supports, reserve line Ninth and Tenth avenues all received attention. … As well as shelling, the enemy also heavily minnied the front and support line of the left and centre coys [*sic*], and slightly the right.'[66]

Six men were killed, and six wounded.[67] From the tone of his letters home, Sherriff seems to have borne up well under the strain. On 5 January, he moved back to Tenth Avenue again, in brigade support, and over the next couple of weeks they would rotate in and out of the line once more, before heading back up to the Hulluch front line again on 23 January, from where he wrote to his father, hopeful that they would soon go out of the line for a few weeks. In fact, he left much more quickly than that, for a day later he went on the sick list, and after being taken to a field ambulance,[68] was soon sent back to hospital.

He described his condition to his mother and told her not to worry:

I have had a return of my old complaint of neuralgia around the left eye, due I am quite sure to a tooth that requires stopping. So I am due to go to the dentist I think tomorrow and then a day or two of rest, which I shall welcome as the neuralgia has brought on a kind of nervy feeling.[69]

He was much less sanguine in writing to his father on the very same day:

It is no good dwelling on the awfulness of it all, for you know it only too well – the men who go up for a tour of duty in the trenches go up absolutely resigned; there is [*sic*] no fiery displays of hate as in England by certain people who have never been here, they go because they must – and although they are always cheerful they go with that thought that, although there is every possibility of them coming back safely, someone isn't. Any impartial onlooker – seeing our men going up to the trenches with such cheerfulness would never dream of the things they are to endure before they come out again. Everyone has a different temperament I know, and I may have got a more imaginative one than suits the necessities of trench life, but I must say that I cannot conceive of anything that has occurred in history that puts men to a greater test than this – think of anything that is acknowledged to have been dreadful – the battles with the dear old cannon ball which you can let fall 5 yards from you without harming you – then battles were all over in an hour or so and while on it went thick and fast – here it is the awful expectancy which is most trying – it is that that tells on different temperaments – some may not feel it at all, to others it is torture.[70]

Curiously enough, at the same time as he was explaining his fears to his father, the kind of sangfroid in the face of imminent danger that he so envied was being displayed by his colleagues who were still in the front line, and in particular by two of the younger men whom he so admired: Thomas and Lindsay. They, along with Second Lieutenant Davies (who commanded the raid), and fifty other ranks and six sappers from the Royal Engineers, had taken part in a daring daylight raid on the enemy trenches. The objectives were threefold: to obtain identifications; to inflict losses on the enemy; and to secure a sample of ration bread. The men were divided into six squads, each led by an officer or NCO. The first two were fighting squads, led by Thomas and Sergeant Walter Summers (an 'outstandingly brave fellow',[71] who was as keen as Thomas to tangle with the Germans); squads 3 and 4 (each accompanied by sappers) were mopping-up squads; and squads 5 and 6 were detailed as 'blocking and connecting squads'. The raid took place just after noon (since it was felt that the Germans would be more relaxed then than they would at night),[72] when the men moved through gaps in the wire that had been cut by shelling in the previous few days. The raiders succeeded in killing a number of the enemy[73] and taking three prisoners, while securing the desired ration bread sample, and a gas helmet. There were, of course, British casualties: three killed and four wounded. Lindsay commanded the withdrawal with great bravery, and was last to leave the German trenches. On the way back he attempted to aid three of the wounded men, and having been forced to leave one in no-man's-land, had to be restrained, when he returned to the trench, from going back out again in broad daylight. The final wounded man was brought back under cover of darkness. Both Thomas and Lindsay would receive MCs for their day's work, while Summers received the Military Medal.[74] Sherriff presumably heard tell of the raid when he eventually returned to the battalion, filing it away to be used when he wrote *Journey's End* some ten years later.

A Restful Time

From the hospital Sherriff was sent back to an officers' rest station (he described it as 'just like an English hotel, where your time is your own')[75] for a fortnight's rest, and his letters over the following two weeks show him grappling with his emotions, attempting to understand just why he appears to feel so much more wretched than everyone else. He writes most honestly to his mother, confessing that 'the last four months continual (or almost continual) trench life has rather told on my nerves', and that 'I feel I would be willing to do anything – resign my commission and work at any kind of work so long as I am only away from the awful crash of explosions which sometimes quite numb me.'[76] His letters to his father, by contrast, are longer, and dotted with supercilious commentary and observation – on religious services, French fashions, the skaters on the frozen lake – on almost everything, in fact, but himself. Almost. There is one exception, and it is an interesting one, when he raises the question of shell shock – to dismiss it, certainly, but the very fact that he was willing to raise it shows that it was on his mind:

It is just what I wanted – a few days' rest like this – I am not suffering exactly from shell shock but the last four months has tried my nerves rather – I feel absolutely well and cheerful when resting – it is the continual bang! bang! of the line that makes me shaky.[77]

He started back for the battalion on 12 February, but he seems to have been in two minds as to whether the rest had helped him. The dentist had done his work, 'stopping up' three teeth, and he told his mother that he felt better in some respects, although his headaches persisted. He didn't think, however, that his nerves had improved much, as he told his father: 'any noises worry me and I can't set my mind properly to anything.'[78] It took him several days to get back to the battalion, which, after a week in support, and another week in the line, had been marched back 20 miles to rest billets in Bas Rieux. They would remain there for the rest of the month, and the relief at being away from the line is evident in the battalion diary, which records inspections and resupply, training of various sorts, baths, and even the divisional cross-country run. Sherriff additionally records games, and boxing matches. On the downside, the very cold weather had broken, and 'the old programme of mud, mud, mud'[79] had started again.

Up the Line Again

From Sherriff's perspective, the time in rest finished all too soon, and by 1 March they were marching back to the front – towards the Calonne sector, just north of Vimy Ridge (about 15 miles north of Hulluch). He was back in his beloved 'C' Company, which was now commanded by Lieutenant Godfrey Warre-Dymond, who had taken over when Hilton was sent back to base to act as an instructor (perhaps one of those 'cushy' postings designed to ease the stress of men who had been at the front for a long time, as Hilton had). Warre-Dymond was twenty-seven, and had been educated at Marlborough and Cambridge. Commissioned in January 1915, he had arrived at the battalion at the beginning of September 1916, shortly before Sherriff himself. Warre-Dymond had been in command of 'B' Company for a couple of months, and became acting CO of 'C' with Hilton's departure. Sherriff developed a great respect and affection for Warre-Dymond, both as a person and as an officer, and was particularly impressed with the job he did in moulding 'C' Company:

I came to the company when it numbered fifty men, old battered men who had survived the Somme by a miracle, and a few men who had come in drafts. I saw them first on the morning we started from Estrée-Cauchy for the line – a column of shuffling, swearing men loaded with sacks. I saw them on Vimy Ridge – swearing, scratching, filthy. I saw the company slowly come up to strength with new recruits, and patched-up returned men, and I watched the platoons come up to strength. Then I saw them in the chalk trenches and craters round Hulluch, where some were killed; later, in the cellars and weird places in the villages of Calonne, and more were killed. Then, while resting in a little village behind the line, Dymond took charge of the company and his magic hand turned it into a living thing that became magnificent. In the cruel hot days at Hooge, the spirit of the company shone out in many ways – in clean rifles – in smiling, shaved faces, while other companies were unshaven and dirty.[80]

It took them a couple of days to get there, and Sherriff's letters from the journey are gently optimistic about his chances of facing up to the rigours of the front line. On 3 March, the battalion relieved the Canadian Highlanders on the right sub-sector of Calonne, a battered little village that had once been a prosperous suburb of Lens. Things were generally quiet, apart from some artillery activity back and forth. Hence casualties were light, with just four men wounded in the six days they were there. The weather was improving, and Sherriff liked their dugout, which was:

> very homely, it is a cellar and we've got tables and chairs and a big mirror, and pictures on the wall and a chiffonier in which we keep our crockery etc. – this is very unusual for a front-line dugout – and at mess in the evening with a party of six of us we are quite happy.[81]

He described just such an evening in a short story,[82] in which an unnamed narrator invites a visitor to walk with him through the ruins of Calonne, observing the battalion and the company in the front line as they wait to be relieved. The story is obviously based on his experiences,[83] and as the evening ends with the singing of the fictional company's anthem (an old music hall tune entitled *Call Round Any Old Time*, which was also the anthem of Sherriff's own 'C' Company), the depth of the comradeship shines through.[84] 'C' Company was clearly more than just another unit to him; it was almost a substitute family, and one that he desperately needed to help him through his repeated neuralgia crises. The affection with which he describes the company and the evening in the story suggests that they and that particular moment held great significance. The story was probably written at some point after he came back from France, but likely before he left the Army,[85] in which case it is reasonable to ask why the memory of that evening should have remained with him for so long, and been so warm. The most likely answer is that it embodies fully his feelings towards the embrace of his company, which may have been the only thing that helped him tolerate the stress and anxiety that were integral to his time in the trenches.

The Crisis Comes …

After its time in Calonne, the battalion went back into reserve in Bully-Grenay for a week, and then returned to the right sub-section of Calonne on the night of 14 March. Sherriff, however, was not with them, having been posted to a job training newly arrived recruits from England, 'a long way back from the line'.[86] He was hopeful he might stay there for a fortnight – 'it is a short rest from the line which each officer will get in turn – I got it first because I am now practically senior officer in the company.'[87] That may have been why he was chosen, but in fact he had spent only twenty days in the front line since the beginning of the year, while the battalion as a whole had been there for thirty-two days. More likely is that the battalion was keen to avoid stressing him too much, in case he again had to go sick.

After training the new recruits for a couple of weeks he returned to the line with the battalion, and at first he seems to have been relaxed. Three days later, already back in reserve in Bully-Grenay, he was complaining about the return of his neuralgia, which gave him that 'awful nervousness again', with the result that, whenever he was outside, 'I always feel I must listen for shells coming and every little noise puts me off what I am doing.' He talked about going to see the doctor, but does not appear to have done so, despite having been laid up in his bed for at least a day because of it. His neuralgia may partly explain the rather strained look on his face in the photograph that was taken of the battalion's officers while they were there (see Plate 7). He sent a further photo of the company's officers to his mother a few weeks later (see Plate 8), commenting that one of the men in it (Kiver) had been killed, and another (Trenchard) wounded.[88]

When the battalion went back into the line at Calonne a few days later, they again went without Sherriff, who was sent to train the new recruits once more. This time, at least, he understood why:

> I think the reason I came back to do this job was because I had another bout of neuralgia and I stayed a day in bed with it. I seem always to get this when I get near the guns again, but I am always hoping it will get better in time.[89]

But it didn't. As soon as he returned to the battalion it overwhelmed him again, and he remained behind with the transport.[90]

This was the very worst his neuralgia had ever been, and he went to see the doctor and explained to him, 'without exaggeration or making light of it', exactly how he felt: it is as vivid and comprehensive a description of a man suffering intolerable mental strain as it is possible to find:

> Let me explain how I feel. When you first get out here you realise that there is a certain strain to put up with – one gets to the line and is rather surprised by its quietness – shells are not flying over incessantly and in fact at the period when I arrived there were none to spare on our front at all – they were being used in a more serious place. You feel rather agreeably surprised – and then someone says 'look out! here's a minnie' and you see what appears to be a shell [rising] slowly upwards [which] then turns and comes down with a swish and makes a

terrific explosion – it may not have been near you and the explosion was not as loud as you anticipated.

This goes on day after day and then one day a man may be blown to pieces by a 'minnie' (for only one in a hundred lands in a trench) and every time you walk past the shattered piece of trench you have the pleasure of seeing pieces of his anatomy hanging on bits of barbed wire etc. – one day a man is sniped and you may see his blood-stained helmet carried away and then you begin to respect the powers of a 'minnie' and you don't feel so inclined to look over the top after seeing a man shot in the head – and so day after day goes by and you gradually get a habit of gazing into the air for 'minnies' and your ears become painfully sensitive to picking up the sound of a shell coming – and your heart throbs unnecessarily sometimes, your arm brushing against your chest makes a swishing sound and you stop to listen in suspense, a man starting to whistle makes you jump, hundreds of times you become painfully on the alert for a false alarm and at others for a real alarm. The more familiar you become with a sector of line the more you learn its danger spots and there are times when you pass certain places as fast as your legs will carry you.

It is when you get to this state – which may take any length of time according to your state of nerves (and with some men apparently never comes) that the suspense of long hours of duty in the line tell upon you – and it is then that even when some way behind the line, where only shells can reach, that you get a kind of instinct to pick up any sign of a recent shell burst – a small hole in the ground where a splinter landed, a little loose earth scattered about by the explosion all worry you.[91]

… and Passes

Luckily, the battalion was due to be recycled out for a spell in rest billets, and just a couple of days after writing to his father, Sherriff was marching alongside them, on the road to Coyecques, another tiny farming village about 30 miles behind the front line, 'almost out of the sound of guns'.[92] The doctor who had been treating him had given him some tablets, which he didn't feel helped much, but he had also given him a note for the battalion doctor, saying that his neuralgia should definitely be looked into, and suggesting that it might be due to the 'straining of the eye muscles'.[93] He didn't care about the cause, just that it should be cured.

After two days in rest, he was happily reporting that the neuralgia was better, and was hopeful that 'a few more weeks might hopefully cure it'.[94] Being away from the sound of the guns was likely the main factor, but again he had that feeling of belonging: 'We have a very jolly mess here – my company always seems to be very lucky in having nice men – I could not wish for better companions.' The weeks were filled with all sorts of diversions: there were inter-company football and tug-of-war matches, relay races, 'improvised singsongs every night',[95] but there was also more serious training such as the normal weapons handling, and 'exercises to attack trenches under a creeping barrage'.[96] If Sherriff had any inkling of what the latter training might signify, he gave no sign of it in his letters home, which became noticeably shorter, which was always a good sign; when he was feeling low he would pour his heart out on the page. After nearly three weeks they were marched off towards the sound of the guns once more: but not back to Hulluch or Calonne. This time they were marched off towards Ypres, the Hooge sector in particular, which was some 30 miles away. Sherriff enjoyed the marching, although 'the march back is never as pleasant as the one coming.'[97]

Hopeful Signs

The weather had turned very hot, and the march was long and tiring, but Sherriff seemed in good spirits when he reached the front line, hoping that the warm weather might improve his neuralgia, and he was writing to his father of the signs of spring on the battlefield.[98] He was rather fatalistic in his letters, as he had been for several weeks, constantly reassuring his mother that, while he had every hope of coming through the war safely, she should be prepared to bear any bad news about him with resignation.[99] If he died, he wanted her to take the money in his bank and buy a bungalow in Selsey, 'like Sleepy Hollow',[100] but he consoled himself with the thought that, in the event of his death, she would be well provided for through Bundy and her knowledge of nursing.

This spell in the front line passed off fairly quietly, and on 21 May the battalion went into brigade support for a week and a half, then to the town of Poperinge, about 10 miles back from the front, for a spell in reserve. Throughout all this, Sherriff's letters are relaxed and happy, betraying no signs of the crippling anxiety that had plagued him just six weeks before. Quite why there should have been such a change is difficult to fathom. A number of simple factors may have contributed: the weather was much improved, which lifted his spirits, as did his renewed walks with Percy High. In addition, he was very hopeful of being given leave at some time in the near future, which, for a while, was the main topic in his letters. The burgeoning spirit of the company under Warre-Dymond may also have been a positive influence.

Then again, he had not actually been in the line that much since coming back from tunnelling at Hulluch. Between 1 January and 1 June, a total of 151 days, he had been in the front line for only twenty-seven days, thirty-three days fewer than the battalion as a whole. He had been in rest (either with the battalion or on his own) for fifty-five days, and had been training new recruits, or back with the transport, for another twenty-five days. When he was well away from the trenches, and the sounds of shellfire were muted, he seemed able to recover quite quickly.

Off Again

Sherriff turned twenty-one on 6 June 1917, just as he and the battalion parted ways again. He was being sent off to a sniping and intelligence course, while his colleagues were sent off to Vormezeele, close to the Wytschaete-Messines ridge, where they arrived the following day, shortly after the ridge had been successfully taken in a British assault, which began with the detonation of eighteen mines, the work of several tunnelling companies. For most of the rest of the month, with only occasional short spells of relief, the battalion would occupy trenches in the immediate vicinity of the ridge, frequently under very heavy shelling. Casualties throughout the month were very heavy, with over fifty killed (as much as in the previous six months combined) and more than twice that number wounded, including Captain Tetley, who lost a foot, and was transferred to hospital in England.[101]

The best birthday present Sherriff could have received, although he didn't realise it, was to avoid going into the trenches around Messines. He had expected to go up with the battalion, but:

> a day before the battalion left for the line I was informed that my name had been selected for a course of sniping in place of another officer – as he had not served so long out here and had not had so long continuously in the line – he took over my platoon and I remain at the transport camp as a reserve pending my departure to my course.[102]

That may, of course, have been the reason for his departure, but it may also have been that Warre-Dymond felt that Sherriff would find the engagement very difficult. The battalion knew what was coming – they had done their 'creeping barrage' training while at Coyecques, and the build-up of men and materiel around the ridge would have confirmed their fears. Whether that was at the forefront of Warre-Dymond's thoughts, or maybe just at the back of his mind, the result was that Sherriff was able to celebrate the taking of the ridge from a place of relative safety. His observations are understandably buoyant, but perhaps deficient in self-awareness:

> I have been watching Hun prisoners stream by in hundreds – poor dejected looking men with a quick nervous look who do not seem to wish to meet the eye of anyone – streams and streams of them – some hatless, some with helmets and some little cloth caps – they are unshaved and haggard and bear a look that only men who are subject to incessant bombardment can bear – some old men bent with sheer exhaustion – some bespectacled – some typical 'Fritz's' – they all look very apologetic and beaten.[103]

Over the next two weeks he thoroughly enjoyed his course, but he was to be even happier when he got back to the battalion and found that, rather than joining them in the trenches around Messines, he had been granted two weeks' precious leave. Inevitably we lose sight of him for a couple of weeks, but we can guess his pursuits – walks with his mother and Pips in the park, or by the river, cycle rides out to Oxshott woods, taking to the river in a skiff – everything, in short, that he had longed for during the previous nine months. He returned to the battalion on 5 July, and although initially depressed at having left his home behind, a walk with Percy High seems to have bucked him up, as did the fact that the battalion was currently at rest – 'it would have been "wretched" to have gone up the line straightaway.'[104] In fact, the battalion had been at rest in Coulomby, about 12 miles to the west of St Omer (a long way back from the front line) since 30 June, but his company was elsewhere – in Inglinghem, 6 miles north-west of St Omer, where they 'were drilled by officers who were attending a training school there.'[105] Sherriff grumbled to his mother that the mess was in a tent, which was not to his liking; he would have preferred to be with the battalion. And yet, a few years later when he was committing his memories to paper, they were suffused with a rosy 'C' Company glow:

> But the finest memory of all was the time I returned from leave to the village where 'C' Company were doing duty as a model company to a Training School. I never saw them better than lined up on the white road in the morning – a straight line of men with clean brown faces and clear eyes – clean uniforms with bright green and red slashes on their arms that appeared with a vivid splash as they turned together, when they presented arms a line of glittering bayonets sent a flash of light across the fields. A line of clean, bronzed knees below the khaki shorts and a line of jet-black boots on the chalky road completed the rare sight of a perfectly trained, perfectly equipped and perfectly happy company of men.[106]

Hope and Trust

On 16 July, the battalion began to wind its way back to the trenches, marching all the way. It took them five days to travel the 30 miles or so, most of the marching being done in the small hours of the morning, to avoid the sun. By 21 July, they were back at Micmac camp, and the next day in the front line, where his fatalism had come back:

> It is now some time since I was last in the line, and there is no doubt, of course, as to it being my turn and I sincerely hope I shall be lucky enough to come through safely as well as through all future periods in the line. … We are bound to have a fairly rough time at some period during our next spell in the line – but some have got to come through safely and the most I can do is hope and trust that I shall be one of these.[107]

'C' Company took its place in the front line, alongside 'D' Company, in a trench known as Image Crescent, just north of Klein Zillebeke, while 'A' and 'B' companies took over the support trenches in Zwarteleen, which the other companies had just vacated. In brief letters from the front line he reassured his parents that he was safe and well, although the district he was in was very 'hot'. The battalion diary records consistent enemy shelling most of the day and night, with heavy casualties, including three officers killed (including Captain Pirie, the battalion medical officer, Lieutenant Picton and Second Lieutenant Bogue),[108] with Second Lieutenant Ellis wounded, and another fifteen casualties among the other ranks. The experience was difficult enough that Sherriff's letter writing was curtailed, even after he emerged from the front line on 25 July, as he was catching up on sleep.

Bedlam

On 1 August, the battalion moved forward from its camp in reserve at Dickebusch to the Old French Trench, 2 miles south-west of Ypres, preparatory to moving up to relieve one of the units that had been engaged in the Battle of Pilckem Ridge, which had begun with an intense artillery barrage prior to an assault on 31 July.[109] Sherriff described the barrage in an account many years later:

> The great preliminary bombardment had begun. We were surrounded by batteries of artillery, and for three nights it was bedlam. ... There was something grand and awe-inspiring in the tremendous cannonade of guns. If you stood out there at night, you would see the whole surrounding country lit with thousands of red stabs of flame as salvo after salvo went screaming overhead.[110]

While the guns may have raised the spirits, the weather and the conditions in camp did quite the opposite, for by the time Sherriff's battalion was called upon, it had been raining incessantly for three days and nights, and the conditions in which the men were living were merciless:

> The cookhouse was flooded, and most of the food was uneatable. There was nothing but sodden biscuits and cold stew. The cooks tried to supply bacon for breakfast, but the men complained that it 'smelled like dead men'. The latrines consisted of buckets with wet planks for the men to sit on but there weren't enough of them. Something had given the men diarrhoea. They would grope out of their shelters, flounder helplessly in the mud and relieve themselves anywhere. Some of the older men, worn out by the long marching and wretched food, were sick. They would come groping out of their shelters, lean their heads against the corrugated iron walls, and stand there retching and vomiting and groaning. Then they would go back to their huts. ... These were

the men who were to break through the German lines, advance into Belgium and win the war.

The battalion moved forward from Old French Trench at 5.00 pm on 2 August, to take over the brigade battlefront from the North Staffs (who held the northern half) and the Queen's Royal West Surreys (who held the southern half). 'C' and 'D' companies took over the front line, with 'A' Company in support and 'B' Company in reserve. The battalion diary recorded the difficulties the relieving troops faced:

> Heavy rain had been falling for three days, no communication trench could be used, for they were more than waist deep in water and liquid mud. Consequently all movement had to take place overland and the dark night and obstacles in the way made progress slow. In addition, on arrival at the support line, and, further, on the way to the front line, 'C' Company got caught in a heavy rain of shelling from the enemy, suffering something like twenty casualties in killed and wounded.[111]

Sherriff was one of the wounded, and it would bring his wartime career in France to an abrupt end.

In an article in 1968,[112] Sherriff wrote of the circumstances surrounding his wounding, suggesting that the battalion had been involved in an 'over-the-top' style of attack that had begun at dawn, and that he had been wounded in the afternoon, when attempting to make contact with a neighbouring company. But his account is quite at odds with the battalion diary, which must be seen as the far more reliable source. It will be recalled that the 1968 article is also the one that gave a misleading account of his first attempt to enlist (see page 3), and being written more than fifty years after the event, it is not surprising that some of the details would be incorrect. But there is no question of the veracity of his general account of the miserable conditions in the days leading up to his wounding, nor of the fearsome barrage that preceded his move towards the front lines, both of which are corroborated by the diary and other sources. Similarly, his account of the shell that caused his wounding seems authentic, as does his description of what happened immediately afterwards:

> It was a soldier's legend that you never heard the shell coming that was going to hit you, but I know from first-hand experience that you did. We heard the report of it being fired, and we heard the thin whistle of its approach, rising to a shriek. It landed on top of a concrete pillbox that we were passing, barely 5 yards away. A few yards farther and it would have been the end of us. The crash was deafening. My runner let out a yell of pain. I didn't yell so far as I

know because I was half-stunned. I remember putting my hand to the right side of my face and feeling nothing; to my horror I thought that the whole side of my face had been blown away. Afterward, with time to think about it in hospital, I pieced the thing together. The light shell, hitting the solid concrete top of the pillbox had sent its splinters upward, mercifully above our heads; but it had sent a ferocious spattering of pulverised concrete in all directions, and that was what we got.

Sherriff and his runner 'began the long trek back, floundering through the mud, through the stench and black smoke of the "coalboxes"[113] that were still coming over.' They made their way back to a dressing station, and then, after a brief examination by a doctor, they carried on to a field hospital. Sherriff reckoned they had walked for six hours, over 5 miles, to arrive at the hospital, where:

with the aid of probes and tweezers, a doctor took fifty-two pieces of concrete out of me, all about the size of beans or peas. ... He wrapped them in a piece of lint and gave them to me as a souvenir.[114]

The same night he was wounded he had an orderly write a letter to his mother, telling her he was:

feeling quite well, although I was wounded this morning in the right hand and the right side of the face. Nothing at all serious, dear, don't worry. I walked down all right ... rest content that I am quite well and there is a chance of getting home.[115]

He had a bash at writing a letter to Pips on his own, using his left hand (as can be seen from the shakiness of the letters). The sentiments to his father were the same – he was fit, and in no pain, and very much hoping to get to England. And that he did: he was admitted to the 14 General Hospital at Wimereux, near Boulogne, on 3 August, and sailed for Dover the following day on the hospital ship *St Denis*. From there it was on to the Royal Victoria Hospital in Nettley, Hampshire. Back in England at last, and with a wound that was none too serious – he had caught himself a very lucky 'Blighty one'.

Back in Blighty

Sherriff stayed at the hospital in Nettley for two weeks, writing to his mother and father while he was there, but also – very happily from his point of view – being visited by them as well. When he arrived he fully realised how lucky he had been 'to have got home ... considering the comparative slightness of my wounds,'[116] and just ten days later, he noted that 'my finger is the only damaged part now and that will soon be better.'[117] However, there was one new problem: his neuralgia had flared up again:

> I am told there are three main causes: namely, the eyes, the teeth or the nose. I had my eyes examined yesterday and they were found quite normal and tomorrow I am having an X-ray photo taken of my nose, as possibly there is a growth somewhere in it which may irritate neuralgia – in any case I think now is a good opportunity of having this cured once and for all.

The reoccurrence of the neuralgia may well have been psychosomatic. He knew his wounds were relatively superficial, and expected to be out of hospital quite soon. On 18 August, he wrote to Pips that:

> As my wounds are now practically better there is nothing for me to stop here for except my neuralgia, which will probably be cured by the application of some syringe to my ears. However, I shall not of course hesitate to report any trouble I have with my head, for I think ten and a half months is quite a sufficient spell out there and that I am due at least a couple of months off in England – and the kind of neuralgia I had several times in France was enough to knock me up – I have not had it as bad as I did in April this year but it is always hanging about.[118]

Even as he was clutching at that straw, however, a medical board had decided that he was fit for service again, as he reported in a rather glum postscript in the same letter: 'I have therefore been granted three weeks' leave commencing tomorrow, Sunday, and ending 9 September. I am then to report to Dover and to have three weeks' Home Service there, after which I am fit to go out again.'

A week into his leave, however, he again reported sick. This time he had boils – which had broken out on his neck when he left hospital, and then formed more widely in places where he had splinter wounds – and he was checked in to St Thomas's Hospital in London. The treatment took long enough that he had to write to the battalion notifying them that he would not be returning as planned, and requesting an extension of his sick leave. The cause of the boils is unknown, but while infection may have played a part, so might the stress of knowing that he was just a few weeks away from returning to the din of the trenches.

Letters from Abroad

While hospitalised, Sherriff received a number of letters from his old comrades, initially rather envious that he had been lucky enough to be sent home. His company commander, Godfrey Warre-Dymond, was the first to write: 'You lucky young beggar getting back home. I do hope you are getting along really well, but just not well enough to come out again this summer.'[119]

Although the letter seems to suggest that he was not wanted back at the battalion, Warre-Dymond probably meant it more kindly. After Sherriff had been wounded, the battalion had remained in the front line for another five days, during which they suffered heavy casualties, with the loss of a number of officers, including the commanding officer, Lieutenant Colonel de la Fontaine,[120] and also Second Lieutenant Sadler (killed, according to Warre-Dymond, by the same shell that wounded Sherriff); and the wounding of several more, including Patterson and Percy High. Serving in a 'hot' sector, Warre-Dymond probably wished no more than that Sherriff be spared the tough time they were having.

It seems likely that Sherriff had written to Warre-Dymond by this time, perhaps suggesting he was keen to get back into the fray, for Warre-Dymond's letter continues:

As regards what you say about yourself, all I can say is don't be a boob and we are all awfully sorry to lose you. However, the thing is to rejoin the battalion the day before peace is declared and we hope we'll all be there.

Percy High expressed similar sentiments: 'I was very sorry to hear that you had been hit and greatly relieved to know that it was nothing very serious. Of course you are lucky in getting home first now.'

Sherriff would have been relieved by the second part of High's letter, which confirmed that High's wounding was not too serious either:

Like a fool I could have managed [to get back to England], I think, as I had a bit chipped out of the fleshy part of the arm, but as you often say, I take matters rather seriously, so I did not even go down, but have been doctored by our own medics.[121]

Sherriff was not the only one back in hospital in London. Tetley had been in hospital for some time receiving treatment on his leg (after losing his foot), and even in September it was still bothering him:

thanks for the … invitation which I greatly regret it will be impossible for me to accept as my wee leg hasn't healed up completely yet. … I really am progressing these days – I toddle around a bit on crutches and spend the *apres-midi* in a wheelchair.[122]

Homewood was also back, receiving treatment in Guy's Hospital for 'water on the knee', although he was also being treated for asthma. When Sherriff wrote to Jimbo

Webb he noted that he had been out with both of them, which must have helped prevent the kind of homesickness he would usually feel after a period of upheaval.

Innocent and Fair

But there was something else besides. Ever since his first evening with Tetley and Lindsay, Sherriff seems to have been as close to them as to anyone in the battalion, and the letters we have from Tetley, while written in a florid manner, are shot through with great warmth. In September 1917, for example, he closes with: 'buck up and get antiseptic and lighten my loneliness by a sight of your innocent and fair countenance some old time,'[123] and signs off 'yours affectionately'. It is difficult to know quite what to make of the 'innocent and fair countenance' remark, and the 'affectionate' sign-off. The two phrases together point, at the very least, to a depth of affection between the two men, but just how deep is hard to gauge. Sherriff was clearly viewed as rather young and immature, 'innocent' certainly, and probably rather quiet and shy: that is presumably why, when Tetley wrote to him in February 1917, he counselled, 'Don't let Lizzie shock you,'[124] the 'Lizzie' in question being Harry Lindsay (Tetley's 'favourite lieutenant', it will be recalled from Sherriff's soiree with them while attached to the tunnellers). The dialogue recalls some lines from *Journey's End*, when Osborne meets Hardy as Stanhope's Company are taking over the trenches:

> Osborne: You don't know [Stanhope] as I do; I love that fellow; I'd go to hell with him.
>
> Hardy: Oh you sweet, sentimental, old darling.

Hugh David[125] dismisses these lines as symptomatic of nothing more than two soldiers needing to get along, but he acknowledges that there may be a hint of some sexual repression in *Journey's End*, in particular of the public-school 'pash' and hero-worship type ('in which reluctant subalterns could well have been indulging only a matter of weeks before their call-up'). Viewed in that context, and with the disparity in their ages, the affection between Tetley and Sherriff may not amount to much more than that between Stanhope and Raleigh.

But there are a couple of other letters from Lindsay that also merit examination. About a month after Sherriff was wounded, Lindsay wrote to him at home:

> Dear Sherriffa
>
> Was awfully pleased to hear from you, you have got well quickly. What a pity you couldn't have stayed in hospital a month longer. You saw dear old Tetley, didn't you? Did he tell you any stories worth repeating, if so, let's have 'em. My dear boy, we have eleven new subalterns but as to seduce them as you say

they are awful people. They have hardly an aitch between them, and are very terrible people, I can't stick 'em at any price. How nice it must be leading a rural life. That's the kind I should love instead of flaunting about in pink breeches in Leicester Square. I've heard things <u>and</u> I can <u>prove</u> it. I'll bet you enjoyed your sly little self. Got any rose leaf cigarettes?[126]

Twelve days afterwards, there was this:

Dear Sherriffa
So pleased to hear from you. I ought to be next but one for leave so I will look you up so get your gladdest eyed nurse to put an extra dab of powder on her nose in expectation of my visit. I have only today returned from that Gay city Paris. We were moved (the whole lot of us) and we aren't in a bad park. ... I consoled my batchelor evenings with a pair of chic pyjamas and a saucy dressing gown (the French maid used to peep at me through the keyhole). I blushed all over, yes all over deary. ... You'd have loved the hussies in Paris, one pinched my bottom. She did <u>really</u>.[127]

It is hard to know quite what to make of the letters, but they have strong gay overtones: the fact that Sherriff is addressed in a feminine style (as, indeed, was Lindsay, when referred to by Tetley as 'Lizzie'); the reference to 'seducing' subalterns (although the inclusion of the modifier 'as you say' might indicate that Lindsay is poking fun at a previous malapropism from Sherriff, or, as Tetley had warned, trying to 'shock' him?); the reference to 'flaunting in pink breeches in Leicester Square', and other details besides. All of that, however, makes the references to the 'hussies' in Paris look rather odd – unless, of course, the 'hussies' were not women, but men?

Homosexuality was effectively illegal at the time of the war – if not quite so baldly expressed, then implicitly, owing to the 'accumulated battery of legal provisions designed or utilised to suppress sexual, social or cultural interactions between men in the first half of the twentieth century'.[128] As in the nation as a whole, so in the Army, where, until the year 2000,[129] 'homosexuality, whether male or female, is considered incompatible with service in the armed forces.'[130] And yet, there is plenty of anecdotal evidence of romantic relationships developing (chastely) in the trenches, because great care had to be taken in overt displays. As one ranker remembered:

There was no sexual contact with anybody in the services. The simple reason is, I got promoted to sergeant from corporal. As you're getting promotions, you couldn't take no chances. I had several chances mind you, with two or three different private soldiers I knew. You can gauge 'em, but the point is, when you come and look at it, you say to yourself, well, is it mind over matter?

You know, you say to yourself, no I mustn't. You're jeopardising your chances, because if something happened you're going to get a court martial.[131]

Nevertheless, some officers were court-martialled and lost their commissions for 'gross indecency'.[132]

The war literature is replete with tales of homosexual crushes and dalliances. There is the homoerotic poetry of Sassoon, Owen and others, including J.R. Ackerley, of the 8/East Surreys, who became a well-known writer and editor. He later wrote[133] that, during the war, 'I never met a recognisable or self-confessed adult homosexual … the Army with its male relationships was simply an extension of public school.' Ackerley tells of his admiration for 'handsome farm or tradesboys' in his platoon, and of choosing his runners and servants for their looks ('this tendency in war to have the prettiest soldiers about one was observable in many other officers').[134] Robert Graves, in his play *But It Still Goes On*, has one of the characters remark of homosexuality in the war:

Thats another part of life that isn't generally known. Do you know how a platoon of men will absolutely worship a good-looking gallant young officer? If he's a bit shy of them and decent to them they get a crush on him. He's a being apart. … Of course they don't realise exactly what's happening, neither does he; but it's a very strong romantic link.[135]

It is easy to envisage the quiet, shy, naïve Sherriff playing the role of the young public schoolboy, being cherished and protected by the slightly older men.[136] It is also easy to imagine him being 'shocked' by 'Lizzie', but it is much harder to imagine him involved in any 'flaunting', in Leicester Square or anywhere else, although the West End of London 'was the heart of public queer life in the first half of the twentieth century,'[137] and an inspection of records shows a significant number of 'queer incidents in proceedings' in the metropolitan Magistrates' Courts and City of London Justice Rooms at the time, some of which are bound to have involved soldiers back from the war.

The paragraph in Lindsay's second letter, about the 'hussies', is confusing if he was more interested in men than women, but of course it is possible that the letter may have been in code to avoid any detection in the event of the letters being censored, or going astray. There is a long history of codes being used to conceal homosexual activity,[138] and in this case the word 'hussy' can be taken in different ways. On the other hand, it is also easy to read into such letters things that are not really there.

Taking the letters together with Sherriff's memoir, it seems undeniable that Sherriff had a very close relationship with Tetley and Lindsay, probably more affectionate than with any other members of the battalion (although he was also very fond of Percy High, as something of a mentor and teacher). But there is no evidence that the relationship was ever anything other than completely platonic, no matter how outrageously camp Lindsay's letters. And the picture of Sherriff wandering the West End in search of companionship – of either sex – is not one that bears any plausibility whatsoever. In fact, the contrast between Sherriff and his fellow East Surrey man Ackerley is quite marked: Ackerley was aware of his homosexuality before even leaving school, and admits to having searched out attractive male companions, often from the working classes. The young Sherriff never had the confidence to seek out (far less seduce) young companions: in fact, he was far more likely to be the one being chosen. Throughout his entire life there is no evidence of Sherriff entering into any kind of physical relationship with anyone. He would always remain most comfortable in the company of men – and frequently young men, especially through coaching them in rowing clubs – but most likely because he thought in the same way that they did, rather than that he was attracted to them (although that can never be wholly ruled out).

Dover Bound

Sherriff was still in St Thomas's Hospital on 13 October, when he wrote to 'Jimbo' Webb, congratulating him on winning the MC, and telling him:

> I'm in hospital but getting fit, and will be going to Dover in a week.... Naturally, I am in no fearful hurry to go to France again – but I often think of the good times we had together and I hope we shall have many more of them ... my great hope now is that I get back to the dear old 9th again when I return to France.[139]

It appears that he may have left hospital as expected, but then had several weeks' sick leave, before joining the 3/East Surreys on 9 November.

He never did go back to France, as a succession of medical boards ruled him unfit for overseas service throughout the rest of the war. In Dover he taught musketry to the new recruits, and attended a musketry course himself, as well as an anti-gas course, which he does not seem to have enjoyed much.[140] At some point during the year he also seems to have been involved in some kind of bombing accident, although his injuries were not sufficient to warrant any significant medical treatment.[141]

While in Dover he would undoubtedly have kept up to date with the news from France, which, for the East Surreys, had not been good. In March 1918, just as he was promoted to temporary lieutenant, they suffered their worst casualties since the Somme in the so-called *Kaiserschlacht* – the great German offensive against the British lines, which began on 21 March and ended with the battalion all but wiped out, with seventy-seven men killed, many more wounded, and a large number captured, including Nobby Clark and Godfrey Warre-Dymond.[142] Father, too, was wounded in the early part of the battle, and died in England a few weeks later. Private Eatwell, who was there for the battalion's last stand against the Germans, described Nobby Clark's heroic words towards the end:

> He said: 'We have nothing on our flanks and there are no supports behind. You will ether be killed or captured before the morning is out. Stick it out for the honour of the Regiment.' A very brave man, and loved by every man in the battalion.[143]

One wonders how Sherriff must have felt: great sadness for his comrades and his old company, certainly, but tinged with relief that he was in Dover; also, perhaps, a certain amount of guilt and regret?

There was more bad news to come later in the year when Harry Lindsay was killed on 3 September. By now a captain, and battalion adjutant, he was killed during a German attack while going round posts that the battalion had established in the German front-line trenches. The official History of the Regiment commented that he was 'standing up to overwhelming odds in a manner to increase even his reputation for courage and devotion to duty'.[144] Back in Dover, Sherriff must have grieved for his lost friend.

Our last sighting of Sherriff in the East Surreys is in February 1919, shortly after his promotion to temporary captain, when he wrote a letter to Pips from the Area Gas School in Greenock, where he appears to have been stationed for some little while.[145] He had just received his demobilisation papers from the Sun Insurance office, to which he intended to return on leaving the Army. Directly he received the letter, he at once asked permission to return to his battalion, which he was sorely missing:

> I am not very contented here – I think I have told you before that the battalion – your regiment – surrounds you like an atmosphere – you see the badge on every man's cap – every officer you meet is a personal friend and somehow it is like a big school.

He had, however, had one final interesting duty – as part of the military forces that were called to Glasgow in the wake of the riots in George Square (sometimes called the Battle of George Square) on Friday, 31 January 1919. An estimated 60,000 workers had marched in the square, with demands for a reduced working week, and lower unemployment, and they had been met by a fierce response from the Glasgow police. Sherriff's reaction to the events is illuminating, in the unsympathetic nature of his reaction to the strikers and their leaders: 'The riot of Glasgow was a ridiculous occurrence in which a lot of naturally empty headed idiots marched through the street making themselves (if such a thing were possible) look even more despicable and ridiculous.'

He followed this thought with a long description of the strikers (and their 'extraordinarily feeble minds') and their leaders (who were 'specimens which are rarely seen outside racecourse bars'), concluding:

> Thank goodness the ordinary Scotsman has plenty of common sense in his head and the general opinion I think favours a Lewis gun as the best cure: as long as no disinterested people were hurt – I don't think there would be any loss to the nation excepted a few good bullets.

Years later, he would write a sequence in a movie showing such a post-war riot, but in Germany, where someone does indeed get shot. One wonders whether the scene made him cast his mind back to George Square, and if so, whether he had cause to regret his juvenile judgments.

Chapter 3

A Writer in the Making, 1919–26

Practise thyself even in the things which thou despairest of accomplishing. For even the left hand, which is ineffectual for all other things for want of practice, holds the bridle more vigorously than the right hand; for it has been practised in this.
Marcus Aurelius, *The Meditations*, Book XII.

O n 26 February 1919, Temporary Captain R.C. Sherriff was gazetted out of the service. His job at the Sun Fire office had been kept for him, but he was unhappy at the thought of going back to work in the City. The *Jimmy Lawton Story* was clear enough on his dislike of that life, and reading between the lines in letters from his ex-comrades[1] it is plain that the war had not made the prospect seem any brighter. Nevertheless, with nearly 3 million men demobilising during the course of 1919, he probably assumed that any job was better than none – even if it was one that he felt he had outgrown. His friend Staddon reminded him how difficult it was to get any decent or well-paid job,[2] and so he returned to the office in Oxford Street.

At first he seems to have knuckled down to what was expected of him, but he was sufficiently unfulfilled to consider the Army once more, and during the summer he began to complete the application for a permanent commission. It is surprising, given how badly he had suffered from his nerves in the trenches, that he would even contemplate re-joining the Army. But his good friend Manning-Press had obtained a permanent commission and been sent off to India; there was much about the soldierly life that he enjoyed, and perhaps the two years he had spent away from the Western Front had diminished the memory of how unhappy he had been. Whatever the reasons for his application, and however he justified it to himself, it disappeared into the Army bureaucracy for two and a half years, before it came back marked 'Not Selected'.[3]

But by then he had moved on. In fact, he was moving on even as he submitted his application – with his engagement with Kingston Grammar School, with his rowing, and with his writing.

He had almost certainly been writing while in the Army. Two short stories in particular – *A Quiet Night* and *The Cellars of Cité Calonne* – bear the hallmarks of recent recollection, although it is more likely they were written in Dover than in France.[4] By May 1919, he had clearly decided to publish some account of his wartime experiences, for he wrote to John Lane, publishers of the *On Active Service* series[5] to see whether they would consider publishing his tale.[6] The question is: what did Sherriff have it in mind to send?

There are two possibilities: the *Jimmy Lawton Story*, or his *Memories of Active Service*. We can be reasonably sure that *Jimmy Lawton* was begun in the summer of 1917, when Sherriff was lying wounded in Netley Hospital, because an initial fragment ('Chapter III') can be found in a letter to his father dated 18 August.[7] The text was short, not much more than a page, and does not feature in later drafts of the *Jimmy Lawton Story*, but the style is similar. The *Jimmy Lawton* fragments are interesting as some of the earliest versions of Sherriff's work, the extended nature of the tale demonstrating how he began to approach structuring a longer story. Many of the elements show quite clearly his knack of picking out the little foibles in everyday behaviour. There is an extended sequence about Jimmy's train journeys into London that is funny, especially in the dialogue of some of the passengers. His description of training in the Rifles is very detailed, and betrays the cynicism of the 'old lag' that he must have considered himself by the time he wrote it. And while there is not, in general, much tension in the story, there are moments – incidents – where a real dramatic flair becomes visible, most notably as Jimmy is preparing to leave for France.

After receiving the encouraging note from John Lane, he probably laid *Jimmy Lawton* aside and began work on *Memories of Active Service*: indeed, the title itself rather gives the game away. According to a later interview:

> The turning point ... was scarlet fever, after the war. For some weeks I lay in bed with nothing to do. In a cupboard nearby were my old war letters, and I began to sort them into chronological order. That was the beginning of a diary I wrote – *Memories of Active Service*. There were to be several volumes, but only Volume 1 and part of the second got finished. Volume II ended rather limp and got bound in a stamp album. *Journey's End* was that diary crystallised.'[8]

Memories covered his time from the moment he arrived in France until he was posted back to the East Surreys at Christmas 1916. No date is given for when he first began to write it, but Volume 1 contains a dedication to his mother, and to the officers from his regiment who died while he was in France, and is dated January 1922. This is most likely when the whole account was completed, not just the first volume, because he had by then moved on to writing other things. The writing in *Memories* is clearly more assured than in *Jimmy Lawton*. Like the earlier story, much of it comes from letters he sent home, and they are comparable, too, in the way that they begin as continuous narratives, but then move towards a diary format towards the end. But the storytelling in *Memories* has more light and shade, and the comic interludes and asides are more deftly woven into the text. There are more, and longer, dialogue sections, which read very well – confirming Sherriff's skill with his characters' speech patterns – and there are some very fine descriptive sections, which stay in the mind long after they've been read.

He is less successful when he moves from a narrative account to a more thematic account of the life of an infantry officer. This is not altogether surprising, since at this point he was only about twenty-four years old, with precious little experience of anything other than his home life and the war. *Memories* confirms that his strength did not lie in political or philosophical analysis, but in observation, reporting the behaviour and the conversation of the men around him. *Memories* was never published fully in its final form, but several of its passages made their way into *Journey's End*, and sections were reproduced in the *Journal of the East Surrey Regiment* in the 1930s.[9]

While busy at work, and with his writing, he was nevertheless keen to return to his rowing. On 29 May 1919, he was part of a very well attended meeting at Kingston Grammar School, which agreed to revive the Old Boys' Association (which became the Old Kingstonian Association, or OKA), and to 'promote the movement for a memorial to those old boys who had fallen in the war'.[10] In addition, it was agreed to establish an Old Boys' Rowing Club and Sherriff was appointed its first honorary secretary – who better than the man who bought himself a sculling boat with his war wounds gratuity?[11] The club seems to have died a quick death, but Bob and Bundy quickly joined Kingston Rowing Club (KRC), with Sherriff becoming, by his own account, one of the first grammar school boys to be accepted.[12] Within a year, Bob had made his way into the KRC crew competing in the Henley Royal Regatta (HRR). He would represent KRC at Henley several times in the 1920s, and the event would remain, for him, an annual highlight throughout his life.[13]

He seemed to be reconciling himself to his work as well, if we are to judge by his role as a main author of the Christmas 1919 edition of the *Oxford Street Times*.[14] This was a small satirical magazine, full of jokes and office gossip, and written by several of the staff, although Sherriff was its editor.[15] The magazine is illustrated with several drawings, some of which are reminiscent of drawings in wartime letters to Bundy, and in other things he had written. In the editorial he thanks those who have made contributions, and a few of the names are familiar from correspondence he had with office staff during the war, including Laurence Woodley, the young man who had written to Sherriff enquiring about the progress of his application for a commission.[16] Sherriff seems to have contributed several pieces to the magazine – including a page offering (humorous) advice to (probably fictitious) correspondents, and a slightly longer story detailing the adventures of a young woman in the office. The story has a gently teasing tone, suggesting that Sherriff had begun to reconcile himself to the presence of women at his work, confirmed by him wishing, in his editorial, for every reader 'an increment in his (or her) salary in the New Year'.

Back to the Battlefields

In May 1921, Sherriff returned to France and Belgium, but this time in the company of his father, on a bicycle tour. His father wrote an account of the trip, illustrated with photographs and postcards of the time, showing the ruined villages pockmarking the area.[17] The account is rather dry, although there are some nice details, such as the care that had to be taken in importing one's own bicycle into France – taxes paid, and certificates issued for no obvious reasons other than those of bureaucracy. He itemises the hotels he stayed in and the meals he took, which provides an insight into the difficulties in reconstructing an area devastated by war. But there is none of the observation that distinguished his son's letters just a few years earlier.

Sherriff's photographs are bleakly interesting; shards of metal amongst tufts of wild grass; jagged, overgrown trenches; treeless roads; stockpiles of rusting ammunition; and, everywhere, buildings in ruins. His father shows him to be keen to explore his old stamping grounds, but there is no suggestion of melancholy, not even when he is photographing the graves of three former colleagues.[18] The trip was thorough, taking in all the places featured in *Memories*: Ersatz Crater and the front line at Vimy Ridge; Estrée Cauchie, where he rested afterwards; the craters of Hulluch, where he worked with the tunnelling corps; Cité Calonne, with its basement dugouts; Bully-Grenay; and finally, the place where he took part in the Third Battle of Ypres – a visit that might have been expected to be full of emotion, but which his father describes in a rather flat and unengaged fashion (perhaps unsurprisingly from a rather Victorian figure): 'It was in this battle – about the 1st or 2nd day – that my eldest son, Captain R.C. Sherriff of the 3rd East Surreys [*sic*], was wounded and sent home to England, where he remained until the end of the war.'

They left for England the following day, with Sherriff's father noting that 'the explosion of ammunition dumps were so frequent yesterday that one could almost imagine the war was still on and Ypres being bombarded.'

Before the trip, Sherriff wrote to Godfrey Warre-Dymond to tell him he was planning to make a journey to France and Flanders – 'not a kind of holiday to cheer one up perhaps,' but one that he had long had an ambition to make. The letter mentions the 'kind of diary' he is in the process of pulling together, and he obviously hopes that this trip will help in that regard, but there also seemed to be some unfinished business, as he confesses that, after his wounding at Klein Zillebeke:

I never went out again: the morning I got my blighty in [that] trench was the last morning I spent in the front line – not a very brilliant end up. ... Probably you are far too busy a man now to think of these things, but really I must say I often go over it again.[19]

There is an elegantly written piece in the December 1921 issue of *The Kingstonian* magazine, describing a trip the author had recently made to the battlefields, and listing many of the places that Sherriff and his father visited. It is unsigned, but almost certainly by his pen (making it his first ever piece of published work): the writing is very reminiscent of what appears in Sherriff's letters and his memoir – simple and unstuffy, but very immediate – and references to the Romans and to chickens are also quite typical.

If it is by him, then what does it tell us? Not too much. Like most of his writing about the war, it is not about anything in particular; there is no literary finger-jabbing going on here. Instead it is a gentle, rather elegiac piece, about what once was, and what it has now become. The overwhelming impression is of a landscape being reclaimed by nature, but also at the mercy of the forces of progress, about which he is uneasy: 'dingy wooden huts' and 'vulgar wooden houses' are growing up in the ruins of Ypres 'like fungus on an old tree … and you feel a sudden shock when you see a glaring red villa on the spot where the Chateau of Hooge once stood.' He misses 'the great semi-circle of Very lights that used to fall and rise round the city'. He never liked change anyway, but perhaps he felt that the changes that had already come to the battlefields – and that were sure to continue – were disrespectful to the memories of those who had served and died there. Many years later, he wrote a short story[20] about Trotter returning to the battlefields with his wife and two sons, and if we can learn anything from this article it is that, like Trotter, he does not view the war in a negative light. 'One day,' he writes, 'perhaps men will go and dig for relics in those old grass grown mounds. Pieces of the old front line will be preserved with religious care, as Hadrian's Wall on the moors of Northumberland is preserved.' Perhaps *Journey's End* would represent his attempt to dig for those lost relics.

A Hitch in the Proceedings[21]

Through his active membership of Kingston Rowing Club, and his involvement with the Old Kingstonian Association, Sherriff came into contact with the people who would join together with him to form the amateur dramatic group that would perform his first five plays. The group was initially called The Adventurers (but would become the Cymba Dramatic Club in 1923) and their first performance was on 18 November 1921, when they acted Sherriff's very first play – *A Hitch in the Proceedings*.

Sherriff tells the story[22] that the purpose of their first theatrical performance was to raise money for Kingston Rowing Club, but the programme for the evening tells a different story: in fact, it was in aid of the Restoration Fund for Kingston Grammar School's Lovekyn Chapel – an early mediaeval chapel that is still used by the school today.[23] Sherriff recalled the evening as a series of variety turns, followed by his short play; but, in fact, the evening consisted of two one-act plays separated by a short concert, consisting mainly of songs.[24] The first short play had only five characters, three of whom were played by the mainstays of the organisation: Sherriff himself, his old friend Cyril Manning-Press and W.R. Warner,[25] who was secretary of Kingston Grammar School, as well as its rowing master and a member of KRC. Those same three were closely involved with all subsequent Adventurers/Cymba performances.

There seems to have been considerably more purpose around the founding of The Adventurers than simply an ad hoc desire to fundraise. Sherriff had been writing since he came back from the war, and was obviously intent on being published in some way, and in Manning-Press he had found someone who enjoyed amateur dramatics as much as he did.[26] There seems little doubt that Sherriff was a prime mover in The Adventurers, and that, from the outset, the intention was for him to write plays that they would perform. He remarked himself that 'the two basic things you need for a play are a good story and a company to produce it when it's written.'[27] In 1925, after the performance of his fifth play, Sherriff was interviewed by the *Surrey Comet*:

> This much may be said with certainty, that even if [Sherriff's] ordinary vocation leads him into different paths, the theatre is his chosen route, and to that end he studies consistently, reads voraciously, thinks more than a little, and eventually produces something which is well worth acting, and in which it is the delight of his brother members of the Kingston Rowing Club to appear. Largely through Mr Sherriff's enthusiasm, and ably supported by members of Kingston RC, there was founded some three years ago the Cymba Dramatic Club. A committee came into being, made, inspired and ruled by youth, for none was over thirty, and it was decided to produce a play. So Mr Sherriff wrote one.[28]

The interview speaks eloquently both to Sherriff's enthusiasm for drama, and his willingness to work at his craft.

The seriousness of The Adventurers' purpose is also evident in the theatre where they held their performances. The Gables Theatre was a small private theatre, sitting in the garden of a grand house in Surbiton (also named The Gables) owned by the Boret family. Sherriff writes that someone in KRC 'discovered an old house with a small theatre in its grounds'[29]: it seems reasonable to presume that the 'someone' was one of the two Boret boys, who were at that time rowing with KRC![30] The house had originally been built in 1877 for Wilberforce Bryant (of match manufacturers Bryant & May), and in 1884 he constructed the theatre in his garden, which 'any useful or religious body' could use for free.[31] Ownership transferred to the Cooper family by 1891, and during the Boer War they allowed it to be used as an army hospital.[32] In 1905 it was bought by Herbert Boret, a shipbroker, who retained ownership until 1925, when it became a college for working women, known as Hillcroft College, which it has remained ever since.[33] But in 1921 it was still very much a theatre to be used by all – and one suspects that The Adventurers were granted its use for free, since they acknowledge Mrs Boret's assistance in their programmes.

A Hitch in the Proceedings has a very simple structure. Groups of people arrive at a 'charabanc', which they believe is bound for an excursion to Brighton. They ask a man whom they (mistakenly) believe is the conductor if this is the bus to Brighton and he confirms that it is. They pay him their money and get on the bus. At the last moment the 'conductor' departs, and the real driver arrives to ask why they are on the bus, which – as he had explained to a young man standing nearby (the fake conductor) – is broken down and awaiting repair. 'The curtain falls amidst the outrage of the cheated passengers.'[34]

The characters come from a wide range of social types: he has two elderly ladies (played by men in the performance); five young women who are described as 'government officials'; two 'beanfeasters' (i.e. drunks); a 'man of some position' and his fiancée; an old man and his granddaughter; a small boy and his mother; and a rather timid minister (the Reverend Teddington Locke, named for the closest lock on the river downstream from the Kingston Rowing Club) and his cousin. The government officials are not given much to do, but the interplay of the rest of the characters is very funny, mostly resulting from malapropisms, misunderstandings, the puncturing of pomposity (usually, in all innocence, by the small boy) and a sprinkling of music hall humour ('Why does Lloyd George wear red braces? Why – to keep his trousers up of course!'). Sherriff felt the play did not capture the audience until the arrival onstage of the beanfeasters, but this was not the experience of the Kingston Grammar School rowers who acted the play in 2010 (the only time that it has ever been revived), who found that the laughs came fairly steadily throughout. Even the rather corny old jokes went down well – the same kind of jokes that would be sprinkled throughout his early plays, to good effect.

The whole evening merited a brief review in the *Surrey Comet*,[35] which described The Adventurers as 'an accomplished group of artists', but said little about *Hitch*, other than that 'full justice was done to the play by the company engaged in its performance.' There was, however, a much fuller review in *The Kingstonian* in December 1921. It began by acknowledging how unusual it was to review an 'Entertainment' that was not a school function – but since it was raising money for the Lovekyn Chapel, and since so many masters were involved, 'we cannot allow it to pass unnoticed.' The reviewer scored it a 'complete success', adding that 'Mr James[36] and Mr Giffard[37] must have studied the ways of the Old Kent Road and its denizens many an evening to produce so life-like an effect.' Mr Lodge (who played one of the old ladies) and Mr Sanders[38] (stage manager) were also commended, as was young Jack Moriarty, a KGS pupil who played the small boy.[39] Manning-Press also merited a mention (as an Old Kingstonian), but not Bundy – although he was a stalwart of the KGSOB Hockey Club. It must have slipped the reviewer's mind, but at least he was able to applaud The Adventurers for having raised 'no less than £20 for the Fund through this effort'.

The Woods of Meadowside

'Rowing and writing went well together,' wrote Sherriff,[40] and for him they certainly did. Over the next four years he had four new plays performed by The Adventurers/ Cymba, and became an important figure in both the Kingston Rowing Club and the Old Kingstonian Association.

Shortly after the success of *Hitch* he embarked upon a new piece – a one-act play entitled *The Woods of Meadowside*,[41] which was performed, again at The Gables, for two nights beginning on 2 April 1922. In *No Leading Lady* Sherriff recalled that there were three plays on the programme this time, and that, for his cast, he had to take those left over from the other two plays. But his memory was again faulty. In practice, the evening's entertainment followed the previous style: two one-act plays, one of them an older established piece,[42] and the other written by Sherriff, with a short musical interlude between the two. Nor was he left with the dregs of the cast members – there was some overlap between the two casts, and many of those in his play had acted in The Adventurers' first outing.[43]

The play is about three racecourse ne'er-do-wells who attempt to escape from the law by disguising themselves in other people's clothes. While disguised they encounter a group of picnickers (a colonel and his wife, their two daughters with two friends,[44] and the local minister). The leader of the crooks is at heart a decent chap, led astray by gambling. He recognises Joy, one of the colonel's daughters, as a girl on whom he had a crush some time before. Still sweet on her, he confesses his crime, and thus reconciled, is willing to give himself up when the police come to arrest them.

There was no review in *The Kingstonian* on this occasion, but some pictures exist[45] (as evidence, perhaps, of the seriousness of their purpose as a dramatic club), and the *Surrey Comet* was on hand to note that 'those accomplished entertainers, "The Adventurers", made a welcome reappearance at The Gables Theatre,' before singling out Sherriff's play as its 'chief interest', describing it as 'an amusing one-set comedy' (which it is, owing to Sherriff's trademark music hall style banter).

Sherriff was obviously proud enough of his second play to do three things with it: first, have it properly bound; second, have it registered with the Lord Chamberlain's Department (which was a requirement if any professional management were to take it on and produce it); and third, submit it to an agent for consideration. Sherriff says he picked out Curtis Brown because they had an:

unpretentious name … they didn't promise anything, and didn't publish a list of their successes. They merely gave their name and address and said 'no reading fees'. Most of the others wanted a guinea and I hadn't got a guinea to spare.[46]

Whatever the reason for picking them, he sent them a typewritten, bound manuscript early in June, and received the slightly discouraging reply three weeks later from Mr G. Patching (Head of Drama) that they felt it would be impossible to do anything with the script because the cast was too big for a professional company to use in just a one-act play. But at least they had not simply dismissed it on grounds of its dramatic quality.[47]

Profit and Loss[48]

After Curtis Brown's dismissal of *The Woods of Meadowside*, he probably thought it was time to move on to longer plays if he wanted to see them performed beyond the amateur stage. One-act plays were not much in demand in the West End, and if he wanted to be produced he would need to write something more commercial. So The Adventurers moved on to new ground – a programme featuring a single three-act play. As Sherriff explained, this put a lot of pressure on them:

> No great harm was done if a one-act play misfired. People would tolerate being bored for half-an-hour when there were other items in the programme to rinse the taste away, but a three-act fiasco that went on the whole evening would have killed The Adventurers stone dead.[49]

The play went through several drafts, but was complete before the end of 1922, and to make sure the performance went well, the directorial duties were handed (for a six guinea fee) to Frank G. Randell, a veteran of Mrs Patrick Campbell's theatre company.[50] The performance would again be at The Gables ('by courtesy', as the programme noted, 'of Mrs Boret'). Flyers were printed advertising the performances on 10 and 11 January 1923, with tickets priced at 3s 6d (about £9 in today's money) – which was a pretty hefty price for an amateur production – 2s 6d for reserved seats and 1s 3d unreserved (which looked a much better deal).

The play follows the progress of William Jottings, who, just before the war, is promoted from foreman to manager, and is eager to make the most of his improved circumstances. He wants to trade up from his house in Paradise Street, Hackney, and for his children (Dick and Betty) to go to better schools, but his family is unconvinced. During the war he makes a great success in business, and is knighted, and he now lives in a fancy house in Curzon Street, Mayfair. But he is upset because he feels he is not welcomed into high society, except by the kindly and down-to-earth baronet Sir Peter Brunt.[51] His son and daughter are happy, however, for they have made friends with the Fothergill children, brother and sister Gerald[52] and Norah. In fact, they are friendly enough that Gerald and Dick each agree to propose to the other's sister, and while Betty feels she is not well bred enough to warrant Gerald's attentions, she acquiesces in the engagement.

When Jottings' investments suddenly turn sour, everything is called off, and he and his family return to Paradise Street. But, at the urging of Sir Peter, the Fothergill children arrive, eager to resume their friendship, and the play ends with fences mended, and engagements resumed, while Jottings is reunited with his old Hackney friends.

The *Surrey Comet*[53] gave a very flattering review to both the play and the participants. 'The author's aim has evidently been to present a play with entertaining qualities,' it wrote. 'Though the theme may be of familiar texture, Mr Sherriff has clothed his play with incident and dialogue of real merit, blending with considerable talent "the sublime and the grotesque, the pathetic and the ludicrous".' As for the acting, it noted that:

> the reception given to *Profit & Loss* was undeniably flattering as each member of the cast did well. … Mr Sherriff was modest and refined as Gerald … and Sir Peter Brunt, in the hands of Mr C.A. Manning-Press, appeared to be a kindly-disposed baronet whose wise words 'carried' to the end of the hall more distinctly than those of some members of the company.

As his first full-length effort, the play is different in scope and ambition from the previous two, which were largely humorous in tone. Although *Profit and Loss* was leavened with humour,[54] it focused on a serious topic that would occupy him in his future work – the relationship between money, breeding and class. Mr Jottings is a decent man who takes the opportunity of an improvement in his circumstances to seek to raise his station in life – and, more importantly, that of his children. Sherriff does not lampoon Jottings (as he does his Hackney friends), but he is punished for his overweening ambition by losing everything in his financial dealings – a warning, perhaps, that he would have been better to remain in his initial position, where he might well have been happier.[55] But at least his children can aspire to something better.

The person who comes out best from it all is Sir Peter Brunt – the epitome of the well-bred upper class – who is welcoming to the Jottings family, who has seen his sons die in the war, yet bears the sacrifice with stoicism, and who even cares enough to track down the Jottings to their Hackney home to see that the children are reunited with their suitors. As in almost all of Sherriff's works – and especially the earlier plays – the old-fashioned upper class are the epitome of the very best in attitude and bearing; something that would allow him to feel comfortable in their company once he had gained his success. And the distinction between old money and new money is always important: time and again, Sherriff shows us those who have been catapulted into financial success floundering with their lower-class manners among those who have been bred to their station in life. At this point, of course, Sherriff was still lower middle class and no more than comfortably off – but in later works it is ironic to observe him chastise those who have acquired wealth suddenly, without the taste or breeding to put it to good use.

Shortly after the successful performance, Sherriff sent the play off to another local amateur ensemble, and to Curtis Brown, for their consideration. A few weeks later, he had an encouraging reply from Patching, who considered that the play had 'excellent characterisation', and 'some really good dialogue'. Unfortunately, he did not deem it strong enough for the West End – the provinces perhaps, but they could not help place it there.[56] Almost immediately afterwards he received a similarly mixed response from the local drama group, whose committee had considered the play and found it 'interesting … but on rather conventional lines'. They sweetened the pill, however, by noting that they would be honoured if he 'would allow us the privilege of reading the future and better plays which must come from his pen.'[57]

Time and again in the future, Sherriff would endure criticism of his work, or would suffer very public failures when his work was rejected by the public or the critics. But he seldom seemed to take offence, as others might do. Instead he listened to the criticisms that were being made, and where he thought they were apposite, he incorporated them in his work (although he could be combative when he felt the criticisms unjust). His resilience would lead him to return to his writing desk in the wake of disappointments, only for him to score a 'bullseye' (as he would put it)[58] with his next piece of work. And so it was when he received the mixed reviews of *Profit and Loss* – he returned to work almost immediately, producing another three-act play that would be performed before the year was out. This time, though, the play would not be performed by The Adventurers, but by the newly formed Cymba Dramatic Club.

Cornlow-in-the-Downs[59]

The new club was an attempt to formalise The Adventurers' arrangements. Qualification for membership was membership of the Kingston Rowing Club (KRC) for male members, and for lady members it was that they be relatives or friends of members of the KRC. Cyril Manning-Press was the treasurer. Casting was to be done by a special sub-committee, and membership subscriptions varied according to whether members were acting or non-acting. While the individuals involved hardly changed, it is clear that Sherriff, Manning-Press, Warner and the others were becoming confident enough in their programme and abilities that they wanted to establish a more formal identity, one which would mark them out among the other dramatic clubs in the area. According to the interview Sherriff gave to the *Surrey Comet* in 1925,[60] the club's ambition even extended far enough to see themselves in their own theatre at some point in the future.

The Cymba Dramatic Club's first performance was a play extolling the virtues of tradition. It is set in the sleepy village of Cornlow-in-the-Downs, a village that has been immune to the scourge of progress for centuries, and whose most important inhabitants – the Reverend Burnley and Colonel Peterson – do their best to prevent newcomers arriving, trailing modernity in their wake. But the arrival of Mr Maraway, a successful businessman despatched to the village by his nerve doctor as part of a rest cure, threatens to tear the village's sleepy fabric. In particular he tempts the vicar's son, Leslie, with promises of business success if he will leave the village with him, and also persuades his sister Daphne – to whom Maraway has been making romantic overtures – to do likewise. To complicate matters still further, it emerges that the vicar's wife, Mary, was previously engaged to Maraway, and it was Daphne's resemblance to her mother that had first subconsciously attracted him.

Early in the second act, Maraway receives a telegram informing him that the moment is right for him to strike against two former competitors, whom he now has it in his power to ruin. Maraway exults at the prospect, clearly discomfiting Leslie. When he next encourages Daphne to leave with him, she says she would be happier if Maraway stayed in the village with her instead. He tries to persuade her by telling her how exciting the world of business can be, but, like her mother before her, she rejects his entreaties, telling him that the best way she can help him is by saying 'goodbye'. So Maraway leaves, and the village continues on its way, undisturbed.

Cornlow-in-the-Downs is Sherriff's version of Shangri-La – James Hilton's mythical place of peace and harmony, far from the perils of progress and the modern world.[61] And it is not so surprising that he should indulge such pastoral fancies: his letters home from the Army were full of references to the desirability of owning a farm, or moving to the country – and his happiest childhood moments include those spent on the beaches at Selsey. Several of his subsequent works extol bucolic virtues, either in themselves, or in contrast to the dangers of development.[62] But his defence of the undeveloped in this case is rather tongue-in-cheek, and a little condescending. Leslie reveals, for example, that the villagers mislead the vicar about their simpleness – that they are much less so when chatting to each other in the pub or visiting neighbouring villages. Furthermore, the pursuits to which the vicar (another in the line of bumbling vicars in his early plays) and the colonel devote themselves – croquet on the lawn, fishing for a giant carp in the local pond, ripening a single tomato – are spiced with slapstick, as though inviting us to find their efforts endearing, but perhaps rather simple and pointless. Leslie and Daphne, and the vicar's wife, are all much more knowing in their appreciation of the village way of life – aware of the compromises they are inevitably making to enjoy their rural isolation. Sherriff clearly sympathises with the village and its inhabitants against the likes of Maraway, and it is his dislike of the thrusting businessman that shines through most vividly.

The play was first performed on 10 December 1923, yet again at The Gables theatre, with Sherriff's friend Giff as the vicar ('once again responsible for an excellent piece of work', according to the *Surrey Comet*),[63] and Cyril Manning-Press who produced 'a very familiar stage colonel, full of muted oaths and loud laughs'. Sherriff's sister Beryl also popped up briefly as the maid. The play was 'enthusiastically received by a crowded house', the review began, noting also that 'in response to an enthusiastic call, the author appeared before the curtain at the end and thanked the audience for the warm reception they had given his work.' While he may have been gratified by the curtain call, he was surely less pleased with the review's criticisms of the play:

> The theme is an excellent one, but the play drags occasionally, although there is a great wind of refreshingly breezy humour running through the dialogue, and the second scene in the second act might, without any disadvantage to the action of the play which it only serves to retard, be altogether deleted. It is merely an interpolation of pure unadulterated slapstick farce.

Resilient as ever, he took the criticisms to heart and reworked the play. The next performance, on 26 March 1924 in the Teddington Parish Hall, featured a broadly similar cast (including Beryl), but a reworked script, which was still not entirely satisfactory. So he had another go, this time producing a script[64] that works much better dramatically: much (though by no means all) of the slapstick humour remains, but the overall tempo of the act is much improved.

There is one major change between the earlier and later versions that is worth commenting on – a scene in which Maraway confronts Mary, his former fiancée. In the first version of the play the exchange between them is quite bitter in its tone. She resents his earlier commitment to his business; he resents her decision to leave him. She begins by trying to hurt him and he fires back. The exchange is conducted in fairly general terms, focusing on his character faults, and her decision to settle for a 'futile' life in the country, rather than to live the London life she would have enjoyed, and for which she was meant. But in the redrafted version we see an exchange on what it means to be a wife. Mary's misgivings at being marooned in the country are elided, and instead she emphasises her role in support of the vicar. 'You were born to crash through life in front of everyone else,' she tells Maraway. 'It's so much easier to crash through alone. Hubert Burnley was born to drift through life. It's easier to drift with another boat alongside. ... Wives are at their best with men who fail sometimes,' she says. Urging him to go back to his business, she says, 'You can alter a business – build it up and extend it – it grows big as the man grows big – but you can't alter a wife: she's always a little well-meaning person who grows tinier and tinier as the man's success grows bigger.'

While Sherriff's lifelong devotion to his mother and absence of any romantic entanglements clearly suggest at the very least a certain wariness towards women, his attitude to marriage is less clear. Even if he had been a closet homosexual (and the jury is very much out on that), it is possible that, in the manner of, for example, Siegfried Sassoon, he might have been inclined to be married for the appreciation of the institution itself, and the benefits (outside the physical) that it might convey. His parents' marriage appears to have been solid and stable while he was young, although they enjoyed different interests, and probably had separate bedrooms.[65] Holidays appear, on occasions, to have been taken at different times, and as we have already seen, correspondence was separate, likewise visits to their son while he was in the Artists' Rifles. No photograph of the two together exists after the family portrait of about 1906 (see Plate 2). It is, of course, impossible to know whether they remained happy in their relatively separate existence, or whether there was a *froideur* between them as a result, but the few clues we have suggest they remained on good terms: from Sherriff's letters we see a picture of the family in their living room in the evenings, each engaged on their separate tasks; from *The Fortnight in September* we see them happy in their annual holiday together; and when Sherriff and his mother headed to Hollywood for the first time in 1932, we see Connie write warmly to her husband at home. But, of course, there would also have been strong societal pressures to remain together, and avoid the shame of divorce.[66]

Nearly all of Sherriff's early plays feature a young couple destined to be together. In *The Woods of Meadowside*, Percy declares his long-standing love for Joy, and even as he is carted off by the police we suspect they will marry when he is released. In *Profit and Loss*, the Jottings children are betrothed to the Fothergill children, who pursue the romance even after Mr Jottings' financial disaster has returned the family to Hackney. Once more in the village of Cornlow, Daphne rejects Maraway's advances to return to her long-time admirer, Jack Lomax, a young and responsible farmer. Other than *Journey's End*, it is almost[67] impossible to find an original work by Sherriff (outside of the cinema) in which marriage does not play a significant role – problems may assail married couples, but they are resolved within the bounds of their relationships. It is hard not to conclude that Sherriff was a fan of the institution in theory, even if he never had the opportunity to test it in practice.

After much revision, Sherriff despatched his manuscript to Curtis Brown, and Patching initially replied that 'we will read [it] with great pleasure. We certainly remember reading *Profit & Loss*.'[68] A few months later he wrote again,[69] to say that the play had interested them 'quite considerably', and that 'beautifully cast and produced … it has quite a good chance of success.' Noting that they had already offered it to one or two managements (to no avail), he suggested that perhaps it might be possible to arrange a performance by 'one of the best private producing societies. … Such Sunday night special performances very often led to production of a play for a run, that possibly otherwise would never have been produced at all.' Unfortunately, there was to be no West End performance for the play, although Sherriff's hopes were briefly raised early in 1925 when he received word from Curtis Brown that the RADA[70] players were interested in producing the play if certain changes were made. A subsequent letter from the players themselves conveyed the disappointing news that they had opted for another play, but that some of their members were still keen to perform the play if suitably amended (a list of potential alterations being helpfully appended). But in the end nothing came of it. Nevertheless, with only his second three-act play he had come close to achieving his goal of a West End production, and, suitably encouraged, he set to completing the play he had been working on during 1924, in the hopes that this might be the one that brought the success he desired.

1924

Shortly before the second outing of *Cornlow-in-the-Downs*, the Strolling Players performed *Profit and Loss* at the Little Theatre in Teddington, the first time that a Sherriff play had been performed by anyone other than The Adventurers/ Cymba. Sherriff had already been vice captain of the Kingston Rowing Club for a year, and working closely with the captain, E.A.S. (Gerry) Oldham. Perhaps in recognition of his extra responsibilities he had dialled back his involvement with the Old Kingstonians, leaving the committee, although some of his friends remained involved, and he was sufficiently well thought of to be invited to speak at their major functions. But he continued with his rowing as enthusiastically as ever – his name appeared in the Kingston crews at a number of regattas (including Henley) during the spring and summer – although without his brother alongside, since Bundy had departed for India the previous September, to take up a job as an insurance clerk.

Throughout the spring and early summer he continued to work on his new play, *The Feudal System*,[71] finishing it in August. Whether because he was especially pleased with the results, or because he was growing in confidence, he actually submitted the play to Curtis Brown before it had its first outing in a theatre. Mr Patching was very positive, reporting that they liked it, and thought it had a good chance of success, and consequently had sent it to Mr Harrison at the Haymarket theatre.[72]

So – what was in the play that Patching liked so much? *The Feudal System* is about the mutual obligations owed by master and servant, and returns to Sherriff's concern with class and breeding. A prologue shows us Peter Grenville, master of the great house of Merehayes, at his wit's end because he has run out of money. In despair, he shoots himself, leaving his son, Derek, in the care of his faithful, long-standing butler, Mr Jonson. Peter's cousin, Henry Mordaunt, is furious, feeling it is inappropriate that the boy be left in the care of a servant, but Jonson is happy to oblige, noting that the Grenvilles and the Jonsons have looked after each other for hundreds of years. Admittedly, the boy will not now go to Winchester, but Jonson believes that he can nevertheless provide more for the boy than a mere school could. The house is taken over by a ghastly nouveau riche businessman named Squdge (who is inevitably the butt of some of Sherriff's better barbs) and Derek moves to Streatham with Mr Jonson and his wife.

Seven years later, we are in the Jonsons' tidy drawing room in Streatham. Derek is taking night classes in estate management, and is sweet on Bessie, Mrs Jonson's niece, who also stays with them. But Mr Jonson disapproves of their nascent relationship, feeling that Derek should marry into his own class (the landed gentry). Derek has a chance to enter that world again when he attends the twenty-first birthday party of his cousin (Mordaunt's son), which is held at Mordaunt's stately home. Although nervous initially, he quickly fits in, and spends the evening with Laura, to whom he had been very attached when they were both in their early teens, just before his father's suicide. Laura encourages him to look beyond Streatham, to fight to return to Merehayes, where he belongs.

In the final act we discover that Jonson has quietly made a success of himself in business, owning a string of properties, all of which he has now sold, to fund the purchase of Merehayes. He gives the deeds of the estate to Derek as a twenty-first birthday present, on the condition that he can return to the house with him, and act once more as his butler. Mrs Jonson strongly disapproves, but the transaction goes ahead nonetheless, and the play's final scene, set some nine months later, shows Derek on the eve of his marriage to Laura, alongside his uncle, cousin and friends, and with even the Jonsons now reconciled.

The play is another encapsulation of Sherriff's attitude to class and breeding – people have an appropriate station in life, and they should stick to it. Perhaps Mrs Jonson best sums up Sherriff's attitude to the upper class: talking to her niece, Bessie, she remarks that 'Uncle George ... thinks there's only one class in the whole world that matters and that's people like the Grenvilles – the old English gentry. He'd die for any of those people if they wanted him to.' That Sherriff approved of the link between master and servant is confirmed by the quote on the front of the programme: 'And the English folk received protection from their Norman masters, giving in return their services when their masters were in need.'[73] Of course, the upper class are not allowed off scot-free: Grenville's cousin, Mordaunt, is an example of someone who fails to appreciate that the privileges and obligations of his class: he rebuffs Peter's request for financial help, and attempts to intercede on numerous occasions in ways that would be detrimental to his nephew, but he comes round in the end. Sherriff's most scathing barbs, of course, are reserved for the Squdges. Sherriff also has fun at the expense of Mr Jonson's friends in Streatham, but only as far as using them as his usual lower-class comic relief: they know their station, and are content within it, so they are treated gently. Mrs Jonson would be treated likewise, except that she wants to see young Derek remain in Streatham, a place to which, given his breeding, he is evidently unsuited, and so she is portrayed unsympathetically.

The play was given its first outing on 27 February 1925, and it received a very positive review in the *Surrey Comet*[74]:

Mr R.C. Sherriff's ... two previous essays in playwriting have not been wanting in originality – and ... although he had in his latest play a sermon to preach, or something very near it, the play was relieved of boredom and made interesting because he had brought to its conception a fine idea neatly worked out, interludes of his usual boisterous humour, some very admirable characterisation, and not a few most pungent lines.

The reviewer noted that the text of Sherriff's 'sermon' would not find favour with everyone (socialists, in particular would find it 'anathema'), but that 'those who have pride in traditions' would enjoy it, since 'duty and pride of race is the text.' With a cast of twenty-seven, nearly all the usual Cymba players were in evidence – Manning-Press as the unpleasant Mordaunt, Sherriff as the tragic Grenville, and even W.R. Warner stepping back on to the boards in a bit part. Only Giff was missing, having left for a post in the United States a few months earlier.[75]

A further review in the March 1925 edition of *The Kingstonian* was less effusive. Though unsigned, it was written by C.A. Howse, headmaster of Kingston Grammar School.[76] While commending Sherriff's characterisation and dialogue he clearly felt it rather too long: 'if Mr Sherriff would take to himself an alter ego, who would trim and prune, we feel convinced that a London theatre would not be too high an ambition.' In his letter to Sherriff he also added that 'it struck me that you fell between two stools – a desire for realism and a secret craving after farce,' although, on the positive side, 'there was a trace of Galsworthy's modern problems,' (an observation that must have pleased Sherriff immensely).

The pattern throughout 1925 was much the same as in the previous year – taken up largely by rowing and writing. He remained as vice captain of KRC, preparing for the step up to captain the following year, earning the gratitude of Oldham, who wrote to Sherriff that 'I could not leave [the club] in better hands, nor could I have had a better lieutenant.'[77] He also maintained his involvement with the OKA, laying a wreath on the memorial tablet on behalf of the Old Boys, and giving the occasional toast at their function. Curiously, Sherriff would often confess to a dislike for public speaking in his later years, but there was ample evidence from reviews of these early occasions that he was rather good at it.[78]

Mr Birdie's Finger[79]

Sherriff's eye was still firmly set on the stage. He began by paying heed to the suggestions offered by Joan Temple of the RADA players, for improving *Cornlow-in-the-Downs*, obviously hoping that he still had a chance of having it played in the West End.[80] But at the same time he started working on something new – a comedy about the efforts of a small village to resist the attentions of a wealthy developer.

Mr Birdie's Finger is set in the village of Tinker's Dell, and contains just seven characters (in sharp contrast to his previous play): the two most important inhabitants of the village, namely the doctor and the major; Mr Birdie (the parish clerk); the doctor's son, Dickie; the developer, Mr Winter, and his assistant (and daughter) Joan; and the maid, Mary. The tale is a simple one. The three main men of the village hear that a developer is interested in buying and developing some land nearby. They are appalled at the prospect, but nevertheless agree to a meeting with him. Joan talks to Dickie at length about her father's plans, and he explains why the village should be left unchanged, citing in support the needs of the three 'topping old Englishmen'. The next day, when Mr Winter has come to visit, he disarms them one by one by promising them that the development will include something dear to them, over which they can exercise some control: a new hospital for the doctor; a grand new sports club for the major; and a natural history museum for Mr Birdie, a passionate collector of butterflies. Winter has, of course, obtained the necessary intelligence on the three men from Joan's conversation with Dickie, who is, in turn, incensed at Winter's pitch to the men's self-interest. He argues against it, and as the men begin to have their doubts over their own newfound zeal, Dickie allows them to back out of their support by suggesting they had merely been stringing Mr Winter along the whole time. Mr Winter tells them that he has a meeting in London the following evening, at which he will give the go-ahead for the plans, whether or not they agree.

Next day, Joan tries to persuade Dickie to agree to the development, and it is obvious they are attracted to each other. A cricket match is about to take place against Tinker's Dell's great rivals, Ragholt, and the doctor and major are preparing for it when Mr Birdie – their star bowler – arrives with his arm in a sling, having been injured in a carpentry accident. Dickie, having heard from Joan about Winter's cricketing ability, realises that, by using him in the team, they can both win the match and save the village by delaying his departure for his meeting. Using the same tricks and flattery that Winter had earlier deployed on them, the three men and Dickie persuade him to appear in the cricket match. The final scene, like all the others, takes place in the doctor's study, but with a cricket match being played offstage and Mr Birdie running in and out with a running commentary. Inevitably, Winter bowls out half of the other team and scores the winning runs, but too late for him to leave for London. The play ends with the village saved and Dickie pledging his love for Joan.

The play is very funny – easily the funniest of his early works – and makes full use of Sherriff's humorous characterisations and one-liners. And the banter between Dickie and Joan is nicely judged, allowing for a greater development of the woman's role than in any of his previous plays (or, indeed, than most of his subsequent plays). Joan is a very strong and capable young woman, clever enough to devise the scheme for seducing the village's senior inhabitants, and also to discern Dickie's use of the same techniques to seduce her father. The doctor and major are affectionately drawn, although with a gentle mocking of their pretensions and self-importance (reminiscent of the treatment of the vicar and the colonel in *Cornlow*); Mr Birdie is in much the same bumbling mould as the line of earlier vicars. Structurally, the play works well in the first two acts, turning the villagers' disdain for Winters in the first act nicely into enthusiastic support in the second, before turning full circle again. But the elusive meeting on which the finale hinges is a rather weak plot point (could Mr Winters not simply reschedule the meeting for the next day?), while the device of having the cricket match offstage, relayed by constant entrances and exits, is not a successful one.

The play's inaugural performance was at the Surbiton Assembly Rooms on 25 February 1926. Unusually, it was performed by the Genesta Amateur Dramatic Club (another local drama group, organised and run by friends of Sherriff, including David Hatten and his twin brother Archibald), rather than by Cymba. Why this should have been the case is not altogether clear. The Cymba group was still in operation – in fact, they had performed *Cornlow-in-the-Downs* (produced by Sherriff himself) at The Assembly Rooms in Surbiton the previous December, and two weeks after the Genesta premiere, had yet another show at The Assembly Rooms – this time a production of John Hastings Turner's *Lilies of the Field*, with both Sherriff and his mother in the cast. Perhaps Sherriff was distracted by his elevation to the KRC captaincy, and felt he could not help organise a performance as well as write the play on this occasion. Or maybe he just enjoyed seeing his plays performed by others. Whatever the reason, the *Surrey Comet* reviewer was as unimpressed by the acting ('not up to the usual Genesta standard'[81]), as he was impressed by the play:

> we must praise Mr Sherriff, for in his fourth and latest dramatic work he has, at the least, excited to the full what the schoolboy termed 'our risible faculties'. More also, for the laughs come the readier that we know we are diverted at the frailties and failings of ourselves and of our neighbours. That we realise this argues that the author's creations are unexaggerated and that caricature has not ousted similitude.

Another reviewer wrote simply that the play 'pleased the audience, chiefly on account of its humour, which kept them in a continuous roar of laughter.'[82]

Curiously, despite the glowing reviews, there is no record that the play was sent on to Curtis Brown; perhaps Sherriff felt that a simple comedy would be less likely to meet with the favour of West End producers than would one of his more substantial plays. A further review in *The Amateur Stage* (dated April 1926, so probably discussing the same production, although perhaps a different performance) observed that 'If ever a play was endowed with a splendid idea, and a finely convinced set of characters to carry that idea into action, this new comedy enjoyed that good fortune.' But he chides Sherriff a little for 'having nothing interesting or witty [to say] on the subject of town-weary England seeking rural retreats.' But this is a little harsh. We might expect, given Sherriff's natural sympathies towards the countryside, that he would see nothing good in the developer's plans. But he does a fair job of giving Joan some strong arguments. When Dickie protests at one point that the development will bring the wrong sort of people, she replies:

> the people who take the houses we build in country villages have worked hard all their lives in dismal towns, scraping their savings together for the great day when they can retire and come and live in the country, and see what a dear place England is. I'm sorry if it offends you, but I've made up my mind to give a few more people the joy of living in Tinker's Dell.

And Sherriff allows that the development may be of high quality, and bring plenty of trade to the villagers, as well as much needed additional facilities. It is hard not to believe that Sherriff was actually a little conflicted on the issue – torn between his instincts towards conservation, and the view that others should be allowed the kind of share in the country that he sought himself. Ten years later, in *Greengates*, we would see him actually celebrate the same sort of village-based development that the residents of Tinker's Dell opposed.

After *Lilies of the Field* there are no more sightings of the Cymba Dramatic Club, although Genesta continued to flourish. There were further performances of *Profit and Loss* by The Strolling Players (several, in fact, during 1927) but otherwise no more productions of Sherriff's plays. Sherriff writes in *No Leading Lady* that the group folded after the fifth play, which is not quite correct, but he is probably more accurate when he says that it ended because after five years in succession, 'the novelty had gone'. 'One by one,' he wrote, 'the original members dropped away, and though we recruited new people they were never quite the same. The fires were burning low.'[83] But he then writes that he gave up the captaincy at the same time, and in this he is clearly mistaken. He had only just been made captain, and it was a job he took very seriously, as letters in the KRC files indicate. So while he may be correct that the Cymba Group had simply run its course, its demise did not coincide with the *end* of his captaincy, so much as with its *beginning*.

Even his own rowing began to take a back seat; after all, he was now thirty years old, and there were lots of keen young members arriving at the club. So 1926 turned out to be his last appearance at Henley Royal Regatta, but at least he went out in style. After winning their contests on 1 and 2 July, the Kingston Eight, with Sherriff in the two seat (the second lightest oarsman in the boat), beat Thames RC on the Saturday morning to book their place in the final later that day. But they had the misfortune to meet an on-form Selwyn College, Cambridge crew, and although they matched them through the early part of the race, the university crew were just strong enough to hold on for a half-length victory. The *Surrey Comet* reported[84] that the result 'was not in harmony with many predictions, but obviously a well-trained college crew possesses advantages over a club, whose members have to put the claims of business first.' It went on to note:

> The Prime Minister, Mr Stanley Baldwin, was an interested spectator of both Kingston's races on Saturday, being on board the umpire's launch which followed the semi-final in which Kingston defeated Thames, and in the judge's box when Kingston opposed Selwyn college in the final. His opinion was that both races had been very finely contested.

Sherriff must have been thrilled by his crew's efforts, and by the Prime Minister's attendance, and possibly just as much by the congratulatory letter he promptly received from his predecessor, Gerry Oldham, who assured him: 'Good luck Bob – only go on as you have started and the KRC will be beating Leander.'[85]

Sherriff continued to row, popping up in races from time to time, but not at the Henley level any longer. He became a 'popular captain of the club', according to the *Surrey Comet*,[86] and continued in the position for three years – three years during which he would balance his captaincy duties with writing the play that would thrill audiences around the world, and change his life completely.

Chapter 4

The Writing of *Journey's End*, 1927–28

In the morning when thou risest unwillingly, let this thought be present – I am rising to the work of a human being. Why then am I dissatisfied if I am going to do the things for which I exist and for which I was brought into the world?
Marcus Aurelius, *The Meditations*, Book V.

Sherriff began writing his most famous play in the summer of 1927, 'one August Bank Holiday in one of the railway carriage bungalows at Selsey Bill.'[1] He had not written anything since *Mr Birdie's Finger*, a year and a half before (a low rate of productivity by his standards during the early 1920s), perhaps because his duties as newly minted captain of Kingston Rowing Club were rather more onerous than those of vice captain, but the itch to write had not gone away, and after the Henley Regatta had drawn the rowing season to a close in July 1927, he picked up his pencil once more.[2]

Sherriff tells us in his autobiography that *Journey's End* started as a novel about hero worship, with young Raleigh in awe of Stanhope at school, but their positions gradually reversing as their lives went on. Finding a novel hard going, he began to think that the war might serve some purpose in the story, and then he began to think in terms of a play:

I had avoided the war in the novel because I couldn't see anything happening to Stanhope and Raleigh that would have any relevance to the story as a whole. But the more I thought about it in terms of a play the deeper it began to bite.

Once he had worked out the plan and the timing, he was on safe ground, 'Dialogue came easily: I merely had to write down what people said. ... The other characters walked in without invitation. I had known them all so well in the trenches that the play was an open house for them.'[3]

It is natural to be curious about why he came to write about the war once more, having left *Jimmy Lawton* and his *Memories of Active Service* long behind him – and in both cases, uncompleted. In the interview with *The Westminster Gazette* he remarked:

[The play] sprang not so much from the war as from my association with the post-war generation with whom I resumed rowing and football and who brought to me a fresh outlook. Subconsciously, perhaps, I wanted to perpetuate the memory of the men I'd known, but certainly no divine inspiration came to me.[4]

Maybe not divine inspiration, but there seems to have been something in the air in 1927 that made the war worth revisiting. Already in 1926 had come works by Ford Madox Ford, T.E. Lawrence and Herbert Read, followed in 1927 by Max Plowman's *Subaltern on the Somme*. By 1928, there was a flood of volumes, including Sherriff, of course, and Blunden, Sassoon, Remarque[5] and e.e. Cummings. In 1929, it grew further, to include Graves, Hemingway, Jünger[6] and O'Casey, among others. Of course the war had been addressed in earlier literature, too. On the stage, plays such as Harry Wall's *Havoc* (1923), and *The Prisoners of War* (1925) by J.R. Ackerley (another play by an ex-East Surrey man first performed by a private society) had been produced, but had failed to find a ready audience. But by 1927, the time seemed ripe. Some suggested it was because the authors had had time to process their experiences (or, perhaps, for those who had not served, their emotions). Herbert Read, for example, in *The Criterion* in June 1930, reviewing *All Quiet on the Western Front*, notes a sudden popularity in wartime memoirs, and suggests that:

> All who had been engaged in the war, all who had lived through the war years, have for more than a decade refused to consider their experience. The mind has a faculty for dismissing the debris of its emotional conflicts until it feels strong enough to deal with them. The war for most people was such a conflict.[7]

Hynes adds to that thought the possibility that 'the presence ... of a future war made the telling of the past war's story both possible and imperative,'[8] while Fussell adds a quotation from Jung for good measure: 'the war, which in the outer world had taken place some years before, was not yet over, but was continuing to be fought within the psyche.'[9]

So it is possible that Sherriff read some of the war literature that had begun to be produced, or was perhaps simply aware of it. But it is also likely that he had some unfinished business of his own. His attempts to grapple with his own experience had not been satisfactorily resolved, with his memoir rather fizzling out. As we have already seen, Volume II ended just before his return from the Tunnelling Company: before being shelled on New Year's Day 1917; before the bouts of neuralgia, which became increasingly debilitating; and well before his eventual wounding and return to England. So maybe there were some feelings he still needed to explore – feelings that he felt unable to explore in the format of a memoir, or a largely autobiographical novel. Vera Brittain, in a foreword[10] to *Testament of Youth*, explained the difficulties she faced in deciding how to approach her subject, dismissing both diary and novel formats in favour of a more considered memoir. Perhaps Sherriff went through the same decision-making process before deciding that a play (which, after all, was the format that had thus far yielded him most success) was the best way forward.

Whereas his earlier plays had benefited from being shared with others as he went along, *Journey's End* had been shown to no one else. Before he sent it to Curtis Brown ('I had already tried their patience with a string of other plays that hadn't come to anything,'[11] he wrote) he showed it to 'two men who seemed most likely to be interested and constructive' – one a local journalist who had 'written glowing reviews' of his earlier plays, and the other, 'an old army friend who had been with me in France and was now on the committee of the leading dramatic club in the neighbourhood'. The name of the journalist is, unfortunately, unknown: the reviews were never signed. But the identity of the army friend is very obviously David Hatten.

Perhaps as well as looking for comments, he had hoped that Genesta might produce his latest work. If so, he was to be disappointed; neither Hatten nor his journalist friend were very impressed, so Sherriff says that he put it back in a drawer for a while, before finally opting to send it to Curtis Brown in April 1928.[12] They replied, in fairly short order, that it was 'a very fine play' that they were 'enthusiastic' about, and that 'we shall do everything possible to secure its performance.'[13] Albert Curtis Brown,[14] in his memoir, recalled that Sherriff was 'fully aware of the prejudice that prevailed in 1928 against war-plays',[15] but they nevertheless sent the play to Horace Watson at the Haymarket Theatre. Watson agreed that 'it was an unusually fine play, but thought its grim tragedy would be too much for the feelings of the audiences; and, besides, there were no women in it. Others felt the same way about it.' So it was agreed that the best chance for it would be with the Incorporated Stage Society, one of the private societies that performed plays on Sunday nights and Monday matinees when theatres were dark.

The Stage Society

The Stage Society was founded in 1899 as a society that would produce 'non-commercial' drama that had 'intrinsic merit'.[16] It was to give at least six performances during the year, and membership would be by subscription, so that the organisation was classified as a members' club, and thus immune from the attentions of the censors in the Lord Chamberlain's office. It incorporated in 1904, with George Bernard Shaw and his wife as the only lifetime members. As well as avoiding the censor, the Incorporated Stage Society (and other private societies like it) offered a showcase to actors, directors and playwrights, and West End theatre managers would come along to observe the proceedings and weigh up the commercial potential of what they saw on stage.[17] During its first twenty-five years it had been responsible for promoting the works of many dramatists seen as avant-garde at the time (though now quite firmly part of the theatre canon): Bernard Shaw, Ibsen, Yeats, Chekhov, O'Neill, Pirandello, Strindberg, Turgenev, and many others – as well as novelists and literary figures such as Hardy, Conrad, Henry James, Joyce, Masefield, Bennett and more.

Nevertheless, it lived a precarious existence. In 1922 it had all but come to grief and the hat was passed round for additional funds. In 1927, the society joined with the 300 Club, another private club producing Sunday plays, this one run by Phyllis Whitworth (wife of Geoffrey Whitworth, a drama critic and Director of the British Drama League). It had only started up in 1923, but mounted its twelfth production at the beginning of 1928, in the form of *Young Woodley*, a play by John van Druten about the love of a young boy for his housemaster's wife (a play initially banned by the censor, but one that would subsequently transfer to the Savoy theatre, closing only to be replaced by *Journey's End* in 1929). One other feather in Mrs Whitworth's cap was the first production of Ackerley's *The Prisoners of War*, although only with some misgivings when she became aware, in advance of its first performance, that it was being talked about as the 'new homosexual play'.[18]

This was the society to which Sherriff's play was being sent, and its track record was so out of tune with his own preferences that it is easy to understand his misgivings:

> The Incorporated Stage Society was a highbrow affair. Most of the private societies that produced plays for members on Sunday nights did so in the hope of discovering plays that would become West End successes and augment their funds through a share of the proceeds. But the Incorporated Stage Society would have none of this. Their declared policy was to produce plays of merit that, while deserving production, had no likely appeal to the general public.[19]

Sherriff was invited along to a Stage Society production to talk to one of its committee members, Geoffrey Dearmer – a war poet (his poetry remained largely undiscovered for many years, but it is now very highly regarded).[20] Dearmer was a significant literary figure, who had written a number of plays himself, and was a firm believer that the society should seek to produce plays of merit, even if they *were* likely to have commercial appeal. Sherriff met him on 9 July at a performance of *Paul Among the Jews* by Franz Werfel. This was unfortunately exactly the kind of highbrow affair that Sherriff feared (and it was accordingly slaughtered in the press the next day – 'The Stage Society at its Worst', barked the *Evening Standard*). But he was pleasantly surprised when Dearmer expressed his admiration for *Journey's End*, and urged Sherriff to send it to Bernard Shaw for his opinion.[21]

There are conflicting views about just how much Sherriff needed Shaw's endorsement. Sherriff himself seems to have thought that the odds were stacked against the play in the committee, but from other sources it appears that the result was finely balanced. One thing that is very clear is that Dearmer was a great advocate for the play. W.S. Kennedy,[22] in writing to St John Ervine[23] to correct a newspaper article he had written, noted, 'The play was brought to the notice of the committee, of which I was then chairman, by Mr Dearmer.'[24] Ervine had written in his piece that Dearmer had threatened to resign if *Journey's End* was not performed, and with the committee evenly split, Kennedy had thus been implicitly forced to deliver the casting vote in favour.[25] Kennedy was having none of it. He told Ervine that he had no recollection of any resignation threat, and if there had been, he would anyway not have acquiesced. He said that he had supported the production 'with mixed feelings. It was only when I knew that no commercial manager would put it on that my own vote was given in its favour. I felt that it was stuff for the commercial stage rather than for the Stage Society.'[26]

But Dearmer had threatened to resign, not in an effort to influence the committee's decision, rather to protest its decision to overrule the Reading Committee, of which he was a member, and which had clearly been in favour of the play (in fact, another Reader, the well-known novelist R.H. Mottram, was happy to have his strong support expressed in the play's pre-publicity, describing it as 'a very graphic piece of realism, written with restraint and very obvious sincerity'.[27]) Dearmer's other concern was with the society's policy in general. He wrote to Kennedy:

> I remember your excitement when reading *JE*, and I venture to think you rated the play as higher than 'stuff for the commercial stage' at the time. I cannot myself subscribe to the view that the business of the SS [*sic*] has been (in my time at all events) to produce only plays that are not, and cannot be, commercial.[28]

So it seems that everyone agreed on the quality of *Journey's End*; the disagreement lay in whether the ISS should select only plays with no prospect of commercial production.

Sherriff sent the play off to Shaw, at that time holidaying in the south of France, in early September. He was dismayed when he read that Shaw had been bitten by a mosquito that had poisoned his hand, doubting that, in such a condition, he would be inclined to read the play. To his surprise, however, a reply came back on 16 September 'with Swiss stamps in place of the French ones I had stuck on',[29] and with the French stamps carefully peeled off and placed inside the envelope. More importantly, Shaw had returned the manuscript, and slipped inside its pages was the following report:

> This play is, properly speaking, a document, not a drama. The war produced several of them. They require a good descriptive reporter, with the knack of dialogue. They are accounts of catastrophes, and sketches of trench life, useful as correctives to the romantic conception of war; and they are usually good of their kind because those who cannot do them well do not do them at all.

They seem to me useless as dramatists' credentials. The best of them cannot prove that the writer could produce a comedy or tragedy with ordinary materials. Having read this *Journey's End*, and found it as interesting as any other vivid description of a horrible experience, I could give the author a testimonial as a journalist; but I am completely in the dark as before concerning his qualification for the ordinary professional work of a playwright, which does not admit of burning the house to roast the pig.

As a 'slice of life' – horribly abnormal life – I should say let it be performed by all means, even at the disadvantage of being the newspaper of the day before yesterday. But if I am asked to express an opinion as to whether the author could make his living as a playwright, I can only say that I don't know. I can neither encourage nor discourage him.

One wonders quite what Sherriff said in his covering letter to solicit such a response, since it seemed to focus more on Sherriff's capacities as a dramatist rather than the merits of the play itself. But Shaw was astute in spotting Sherriff's gift for dialogue and journalistic-style observation (something that would be noted subsequently by St John Ervine),[30] and he gave the play support, albeit of a qualified kind. So Sherriff took the results to Dearmer, exaggerating Shaw's support by the age-old West End trick of selective quotation, telling Dearmer that Shaw had said 'Let it be produced by all means.' And that, according to Sherriff, was that. In reality, however, the society had probably decided to produce the play anyway: the continuing pressure from Dearmer and the Reading Committee, and the obvious disinclination of any of the professional managers to take up the play meant that the ISS was probably its only chance to obtain a performance. The secretary of the society, Matthew Norgate, wrote some years later that the society had been desperate to find a show to fill its December slot,[31] which might also have helped tip the scales in the play's direction.

Sherriff must have been delighted when the ISS programme for the year was publicised at the beginning of November, with coverage in all of the main newspapers. The first production of the season would be *Journey's End*, by R.C. Sherriff, 'a dramatist who has not previously had a piece produced professionally', observed the *Telegraph*.[32] 'Unknown author's war play', read the *Daily Chronicle's* headline, 'Trench story with no woman part': the absence of any female cast members was noted quite widely among the papers. *Journey's End* would be followed by Benavente's *The Princess*, and Tolstoy's *Rasputin* (both in translation, of course), plus a further work by a well-known English author, which would be publicised when difficulties with the rights had been overcome. To those frustrated with the society's apparent preference for foreign (for which, read 'highbrow') over British dramas, and for those mindful of the recent success of another unknown British dramatist (John van Druten, with *Young Woodley*), the first item on the ISS menu must have looked intriguing.

The Play

Journey's End is set in a 'dugout in the British trenches', before St Quentin, and the action begins on 18 March 1918 – on the eve of the *Kaiserschlacht*. The story is straightforward: the officers of a company on the Western Front await the impending German attack. In fact, Sherriff said he had considered calling it *Suspense* ('but this didn't ring true because I couldn't honestly claim that it had any,'[33] he wrote, although he was being much too self-deprecating), or *Waiting* ('but it had the flavour of a restaurant or a railway station'). Instead he called it *Journey's End*, a title that, he wrote,[34] was derived from the closing words in a chapter of a book he was reading one night. Then again, he told American critic Gilbert Gabriel that he first saw the phrase 'scrawled in German on a piece of planking over an enemy dugout door'.[35] In a letter in 1939, however, his secretary wrote to Aircraftman E.P. Jones:

> [Mr Sherriff] wishes me to tell you that the title *Journey's End* was not drawn from any special previous reference or use of the words. I am sorry I cannot give you a more interesting reply, but when searching for a title for the play, the one selected came independently of any previous association.[36]

The main character in the play is the young Captain Stanhope, who has been in the trenches three years, having come straight from school when he was just eighteen. The strain of leading the company is ameliorated by his consumption of whisky, but despite his fondness for the bottle his men and fellow officers feel there is no one better in the line. His second in command is Lieutenant Osborne, known to the other officers as Uncle, a gentle, kindly presence, a schoolteacher and family man in his late thirties. The other officers in the company are Second Lieutenant Trotter, a stout and jovial man, risen from the ranks, lacking in imagination, perhaps, but utterly reliable. The final officer in the company at the beginning of the play is Lieutenant Hibbert, a weak man whose nerves are shot, who lives in a perpetual state of terror, and whose only desire is to escape from the trenches.

Early in the play, a young officer arrives: Second Lieutenant Raleigh is a young man from Stanhope's old school, who has hero-worshipped him for years, and whose sister Madge is as good as betrothed to him. He had sought out Stanhope's company, thinking how good it would be to fight alongside him, but Stanhope is terrified that Raleigh will write home to tell them of how far he has fallen. The officers come and go from the dugout as they take turns at their duties in the trench, and we watch them interact over their meals, served, with a dose of humour, by Mason, the servant.

There are three main plots that run through the play:

> Stanhope's insistence that he should be allowed to censor Raleigh's letters home – although when he finally forces Raleigh to hand over the letter he has

written, and Osborne reads it to him, he finds that Raleigh has been full of praise for his old school friend; Stanhope is ashamed of what he has become.

The second is Stanhope's response to Hibbert's attempts to 'worm out' of his duties and go on sick leave: Stanhope eventually threatens to shoot Hibbert if he leaves the dugout, Hibbert capitulates, and Stanhope confesses that he shares Hibbert's fears, but is bolstered in his duties by his whisky and the comradeship of his fellow officers.

The third relates to the trench raid that is ordered by the colonel, to obtain prisoners that they might interrogate regarding the forthcoming attack. Raleigh and Osborne are selected to lead the raid, and Osborne is killed in its execution.

After Osborne is killed, Raleigh struggles to accept his death, even as the other officers attempt to forget with a drunken dinner party that same evening. Following the dinner party the play comes swiftly to its climax: as dawn breaks on the morning of the German attack the officers leave the dugout one by one to take their place in the line, while the German bombardment crashes around them. Raleigh is quickly wounded in the back by shrapnel, and is brought down into the dugout, where he dies in Stanhope's arms. The play ends with Stanhope wearily mounting the steps to face the German advance.

Journey's End draws heavily on Sherriff's wartime experiences, especially his first few days in the trenches, as set out in *Memories* and letters:

Raleigh's account of his journey to the dugout mimics very closely the section where Sherriff shared a railway carriage to the front with Abrams and Percy High;

The discussion of Minnies recalls Sherriff's own morbid fears of them, expressed so frequently in his letters home;

The opening scene, of Hardy drying his sock in the candlelight, is an almost exact match for the first occasion when he met Douglass, and even Douglass's nickname (Father) has its counterpoint in the character of Uncle. Trotter's protests, at the lack of pepper, recall another Douglass incident in the first seven-day stretch in the line.

Of course, Hibbert's neuralgia is something that Sherriff could speak of with some experience, and even some of the dialogue used in the exchanges between Hibbert and Stanhope – talk of Hibbert 'worming out', for example, or Stanhope's urgings to stand with his fellow officers – is clearly drawn from Sherriff's own account.

These, and other examples in the play highlight its veracity (justifying Bernard Shaw's 'journalism' comment), which was, in part, why the managers had rejected the play: based entirely in a dugout, with no women, and a downbeat ending, it was hardly the thing to bring out crowds seeking entertainment and escapism. But what they had missed was its humour and the depth of its characterisation; these were people whom others would recognise and care about. The challenge was to demonstrate to the managers just what they had missed – that, in the correct hands, and with the correct cast, the play had the potential to be powerful and moving, as well as true. And, as it happens, that was exactly what the ISS was about to do.

James Whale

The Stage Society handed the reins of the production to James Whale,[37] who, according to Sherriff,[38] was a 'man-of-all-work in the theatre', who 'played small parts, designed and painted scenery, and occasionally got a job as a stage manager, but had never been in charge of a play in a West End theatre and had never earned beyond £5 a week.' In fact, he was much more experienced than that.

Whale was born into a poor family in Dudley in 1889,[39] making him some seven years Sherriff's senior. His initial exposure to the theatre came mainly from trips to the Dudley Opera House with a friend whose father could provide them with free tickets. He seems to have delayed enlisting until he concluded conscription was inevitable, and finally joined the 'Inns of Court' cadet corps in October 1915, being commissioned a second lieutenant in the 2/7th Worcestershire Regiment in the summer of 1916. He fought, like Sherriff, at Passchendaele, and it was there, on 25 August 1917, that he was captured while leading 'a stunt on a pillbox at midnight'.[40] He was sent to a prisoner of war camp in Holzminden in Germany, and it was there he began to develop his love of the theatre: 'I sincerely believe,' he said later, 'that training [in the camp] meant as much to me as anything I ever learned since. The stage presented really the only possible career for me then.'[41]

He returned from the war to the Birmingham Repertory, where he worked for a few years before moving to London and Oxford for work – as actor, stage designer, and, occasionally, director, as well as assisting in the general management of various theatres in which he was employed.[42] For a couple of years he worked in various roles for the well-known actor-manager Nigel Playfair at the Lyric, Hammersmith, but by May 1927, their relationship had fractured and Whale was left to find work as best he could. In the following eighteen months, 'Whale acted in eleven productions and designed scenery for fifteen, often labouring under the auspices of the Incorporated Stage Society, where he had become known for his ability to stretch a meagre budget for settings beyond all reasonable expectations.'[43] In early

November, while the ISS was finalising its plans for the winter season, Whale was involved in no fewer than three productions, all of which ended promptly, leaving him free to take a small part in an anti-war play called *High Treason*[44] at the Strand Theatre. While in his dressing room one evening, Whale received the approach that was to change his life, when Matthew Norgate offered fifteen guineas[45] to direct two performances of another war play for the ISS. Reluctant to accept at first, he eventually changed his mind, and agreed to meet the author a few days later.

The ISS Production

Sherriff went to see Whale at the theatre, where he was making himself up for that night's performance. 'He didn't seem very enthusiastic about *Journey's End*,' wrote Sherriff, and he said little about the play 'beyond the comment that certain scenes were too sentimental and would have to be brought down to earth or cut out. I gladly agreed to do anything he suggested. I would have cut the whole play and done it again if this got it any nearer to the West End.'[46]

For all that Sherriff was worried about Whale's commitment to the play, he was impressed when he heard of his army experience, and when he saw that he had already read the play thoroughly and 'knew it backwards'. Ending the conversation just before he went on stage, Whale invited Sherriff to his flat the next day, where he showed him 'a beautifully constructed model. I had envisaged little more than a squalid cavern in the ground, but Whale had turned the hand of art to it. By strutting the roof with heavy timbers he gave an impression of vast weight above. ... There may never have been a dugout like this one: but any man who had lived in the trenches would say "This is it: this is what it was like."'[47]

'Luck followed us through the casting,'[48] said Sherriff, noting that none of the leading stars of the time were inclined to take a chance with Stanhope, so Whale offered the part 'to an obscure young actor named Laurence Olivier', who at that time was just ending a West End run in a comedy called *Bird in Hand*. Olivier had been promised the role in Basil Dean's new play *Beau Geste*, due to begin in the West End in the New Year, so was not envisaging staying with it in the event of a transfer to another theatre (not that he thought that was particularly likely).[49]

Luck had followed in the casting of the other parts as well, although Sherriff was not aware of it at the time. Six of the cast had fought in the war. George Zucco (Osborne), had served as a lieutenant in the West Yorks, and had been wounded in a trench raid at St Quentin. Melville Cooper (Trotter) had served with the Highlanders, while David Horne (Hardy) had been a captain in the Grenadier Guards. Percy Walsh (the sergeant major) and Alexander Field (Mason) also served in the Army. H.G. Stoker (the colonel) was the most distinguished of the lot: he had been the first submarine commander to penetrate the Dardanelles minefield (a feat for which he was sure to win the Victoria Cross, except that his ship was captured a day or two later).[50] These older men were in their thirties and forties, and generally had quite extensive experience on stage,[51] in the West End and elsewhere. Olivier, at just twenty-one – the youngest of the principal actors – was obviously not quite as experienced, but had already chalked up several London appearances. The least experienced – Maurice Evans and Robert Speaight – had just begun to appear on the West End stage that year, but both were quick and clever, and eager to do well. Almost every one of the cast would use their *Journey's End* experiences as a springboard to further success in the theatre, with Zucco, and especially, Melville Cooper and Maurice Evans, going on to successful Hollywood careers.[52]

Given the long track record of Whale and so many of the actors, Sherriff must have been very nervous when he went along to the first read-through of the play 'in a shabby upstairs room over a shop in the Charing Cross Road. It was a cold November morning, and I found Whale sitting at a long bare table in his overcoat, with a muffler round his neck and the cast standing about around him. They were an ordinary looking lot of men: what you might see any evening on Waterloo station or a train home.' Sherriff was worried, because he saw Olivier looking 'bored and restless'. He obviously was: 'I told James Whale, the director, I didn't think all that highly of the play,' Olivier wrote in his autobiography.[53] '"There's nothing but meals in it," I complained. He replied: "That's about all there was to think about in Flanders during the war."'

Sherriff was even more put out when the actor who was originally hired to play Mason promptly threw his script on the table, as he'd been given a part in a play that was shortly to begin its run in the West End. Whale had told Sherriff beforehand to take notes if he wanted, but otherwise to sit and say nothing – it was important that their instructions came only from the director. If Sherriff had issues with how Whale was handling things, they could discuss them together later, in private. Sherriff had nothing to say – nor did he even take any notes – but from then on in the theatre he was mindful of the importance of clear communication and direction, and that writers should avoid getting between producers and their actors.[54]

Even at the first read-through, Sherriff was confident in his cast: 'as the reading went on it came over beyond a doubt that the team had been perfectly chosen. None had any need to act the parts: they were the men: they merely had to be themselves.'[55] Maurice Evans agreed: 'it became obvious at the play's first reading that an ideal cast had been assembled by sheer chance.'[56] Perhaps not quite by chance. Robert Speaight found himself 'deeply impressed by the script',[57] and maybe the others, too, felt they might be taking part in something a little out of the ordinary, however uncommercial it might have been deemed to be.

After the first reading, Sherriff went back to Whale's rooms and together they worked on the script. 'The cuts and alterations turned out to be very small,' he wrote, '[and] the play went on practically as it was first written.' Maurice Evans disagrees, however: 'It only remained for the script to be given the blue-pencil treatment – pretty ruthless cutting in which I took a hand.'[58] Given Evans's relative lack of experience – especially among such a band of grizzled war veterans – it is unlikely he had much of a say in shaping the script, but it is likely that some cuts were made, to trim the running time and quicken the pace of the play. Then it was simply a round of rehearsals, mostly 'in rooms with the dugout boundaries marked out in chalk on the floor'. Sherriff, however, was unable to attend: he was not (yet) a theatre man, just an insurance man, with duties to perform and his patch to cover.

The Sunday night societies ran their productions on a wing and a prayer. They would take place in theatres that were already running their own productions, so the actors had almost no time to act with their own scenery – usually just a few hours on the day of the first performance, which was also when the sound effects (so important for *Journey's End*) could be tried out for the first time. Funds were tight: the cost of 'building and painting the dugout came to £80', and uniforms were borrowed where possible. Some of the cast members wore their own old army uniforms (that would work for Zucco and Cooper, both of whom had been lieutenants); Field wore his old puttees; and Sherriff lent his tunic and Sam Browne belt to Olivier, noting modestly that, while his captain's tunic was appropriate for Stanhope, 'the MC ribbon had to be sewn on.'[59]

Opening Night at the Apollo

After a couple of weeks of rehearsals, *Journey's End* received its premiere at the Apollo Theatre, on Sunday, 9 December 1928. Sherriff recorded in his autobiography that 'the only clear memory of the first performance that Sunday night is of the endless stream of perspiration that had to be mopped off from around a stiff uncomfortable evening dress collar.'[60] He went along with his mother, his father proudly noting in his diary: 'Bob's play *Journey's End* performed at the Apollo Theatre London – so at last he has a play on the London stage.'[61] Sherriff recounts a feverish evening, prowling around the theatre, unable to keep still, haunted by anxiety: would the performance be up to snuff, would the audience appreciate it? In the end he wrote that he was disappointed in the play's reception, underwhelmed by the 'polite and formal' applause.[62]

But again, we should not take his memoir at face value. He does like to set up a story arc, and for every triumph there has to be an agonising journey towards it. In fact, we know that the play went down very well indeed. 'It became apparent on the first night,' wrote Albert Curtis Brown, 'that here was a great play, and one that had commercial possibilities, too.'[63] At the interval he was buttonholed by Victor Gollancz: 'Victor saw the performance, and was so impressed that he told Sherriff in the interval that he wanted to publish it.'[64] We also know that Maurice Browne first became aware of the play[65] when he was phoned at midnight on Sunday by Harold Monro[66] (and told, 'hazily'), 'that he had just returned from a wonderful, a perfectly wonderful play: it was the most wonderful play ever written; I must put it on at once.'

There was also the very famous West End manager Basil Dean. Having already lined up Olivier for *Beau Geste*, he took along his co-star in the production, Madeleine Carroll.[67] Dean was bowled over. In 1973 he wrote:

> The memory of that Sunday night performance is still vivid ... I was completely overcome by the play – its humour, its drama and its emotion all expressed in terms of the utmost sincerity. Immediately the curtain fell I ... scampered up the dressing-room stairs as though half the managers in London were at my heels. I was introduced to the author by David Horne. I said the production must be transferred, just as it was, cast, scenery, etc., without alteration of any kind.[68]

Even Sherriff's father knew the result of that evening: 'From all accounts it appeared to have been quite a success and there appears to be a very probable production at a London theatre in due time.'[69] There can be no doubt that, before he went to bed that night (while he was scrambling eggs with his mother),[70] he knew what a success he had on his hands.

The Reviews

The critics were out in force at the Apollo for the Monday matinee: George Bishop of *The Era*, W.A. (Bill) Darlington of *The Telegraph*, Charles Morgan of *The Times*, Hannen Swaffer of the *Express*: Sherriff must have been awed and terrified at the same time (hardly crediting that he would go on to be very good friends with several of them). One of the main critics of the time – James Agate, who worked for the BBC – had not been disposed to go. He had missed the first act, 'after his usual late lunch', when he bumped into Bishop on the pavement outside the Apollo. 'He asked me, "What piece of highbrow nonsense" was being played? My enthusiasm induced him to see the two remaining acts and at the end he was as excited as I was.'[71]

Agate was the first of the critics to make his views known, broadcasting on the BBC that very night. In fact, he had already prepared a script about another show that he proceeded to tear up, substituting for it a paean of praise to the play:

> Less than three hours ago the curtain fell on the Stage Society's production of a play called *Journey's End*, and I have to say that since I have had the honour to be your dramatic critic I have not been present at any performance which has stirred an audience so deeply. ... I cannot believe that there was any single member of the audience this afternoon who was not only deeply moved but also exalted and even exhilarated by this tragedy.[72]

And he had words for those who would argue that they simply wanted to be interested and amused at the theatre:

I have seen no audience more deeply interested than was the audience this afternoon. Nor have I often heard more laughter. There was a cook–batman in this play whose every appearance ... brought down the house. The piece was wonderfully well played by a company of ... fine young actors.

Sherriff's dad was listening in:

Bob's play *Journey's End* performed again at the Apollo. Mr Agate the dramatic critic on the wireless tonight gave a most flattering account of the play – in fact he could not have spoken better of it. Says it is too good for the public taste who only require revues, musical comedies or farcical comedies.[73]

The rest of the critics pronounced the next morning and they were well nigh unanimous. 'War Play better than *Havoc*', roared Hubert Griffith in the *Evening Standard*.[74] Bill Darlington in *The Telegraph* called it the most realistic play about the war that we have seen: 'Every man in the ... audiences which saw *Journey's End* ... who had ever inhabited a dugout on the Western Front must have felt almost intolerably moved as the once familiar atmosphere stung his throat.'[75] *The Manchester Guardian* called it 'the best play about the war that has been written. The power and passion and tragedy of it all make it one of the fine plays of the time.'[76] The *Daily Mail* reckoned it 'is in some ways the most cruelly realistic of the many war plays. The author ... has no direct story to tell; no heroics to appeal to cheap emotions. Nor are there scenes of gore. Instead he presents a study of temperament and an analysis of fear.'[77]

Almost all of the other dailies, and the weeklies, fell in line. The only slight exception was the great Charles Morgan in *The Times*, who refused to recognise the play as a work of art. 'Mr Sherriff's study of the front line, though it comes as near as the stage may ever come to precise representation of life in a dugout, is not a work of art with any prospect of endurance.'[78] (So much for his powers as a prognosticator!) He nevertheless argued that the play's substance was in an 'aggregate of portraits', and proceeded to spell out the main features of all the principal characters, before praising the performances of the actors to a man: H.G. Stoker's 'quiet authenticity' as the colonel; George Zucco's 'beautiful impression of character and the background of character', whose Lieutenant Osborne 'towered above the others'. He also commended Laurence Olivier's 'extremely able' Stanhope, and noted that Robert Speaight (Hibbert) and Maurice Evans (Raleigh) controlled their emotions 'admirably', while 'splashing their colour now and then'. Field (Mason), Cooper (Trotter) and Walsh (the sergeant major) discharged their 'plainer tasks' with 'judgment and humour'. Other papers chose to elevate some of the actors over others: some relished the more theatrical performances of the three younger men, while others (especially Darlington) valued the 'studied and deliberate unemotionalism' of the older actors, a divide apparently drawn up between those who had lived through it, and those who had not. Anchoring every review was praise for James Whale's set and direction – and the critics were not alone in that: Basil Dean had offered him a job as his assistant as soon as he saw him after the opening night performance.[79]

According to Basil Dean, following his enthusiastic endorsement of the play on the Sunday night, Sherriff 'stalked me down the side of the stalls during a *Pickwick* rehearsal.'[80] Sherriff followed this up by writing to him the next day, drawing the glowing reviews to his attention. 'I hope you consider the play worth trying,' he wrote, 'as I should so much like the production to be in your hands.'[81] But Dean was not yet able to commit to a production, being financially somewhat over-exposed because of involvements in both *Pickwick* and *Beau Geste*, so he replied the next day, pleading for time:

> I would like to make immediate arrangements for its production, but in the present state of public uncertainty, I feel I must hold my hand until we know what is going to happen. Royal demise is always a most unsettling factor in the theatre in this country.[82]

The issue of 'royal demise' was on everyone's mind, since the King (George V) had been seriously ill with septicaemia since November (and it was obviously one that occurred to Sherriff as well: in *No Leading Lady* he attributed the initial success of *Journey's End* at the Savoy to the announcement, some weeks later, of the King's recovery)[83]. But even leaving that aside, Dean was struggling to raise the cash. He had hoped that David Horne might be able to persuade his father to help, but that turned out to be a dead end; nor would his partners in the *Beau Geste* production prove willing to help. Unwilling to go it alone, he pulled out.

In the absence of any commercial offers, the cast were despondent:

> normally, at the end of a play's run, there is a closing-night party to which the actors hie themselves. ... Not so in our case, however. We just stood around on the stage, a forlorn cast of actors, watching the stagehands tear down our scenery ... to be hauled off to some warehouse, never, we thought, to be seen again.[84]

But they were united in their belief in the play, and Evans, having turned down Dean's offer of a part alongside Olivier in *Beau Geste*, sought to enlist the support of the other *Journey's End* actors to raise enough money for their own production. He was at that point under contract to Leon M. Lion (a well-known playwright, actor and theatre manager), who was in charge of the Wyndham's Theatre, and since the theatre was dark, Evans cheekily asked if he might rent it for a short while to judge the commercial potential of the play. Lion agreed, but even with this backing, and additional help from others, the actors came up a couple of hundred pounds short of their goal, 'at which time,' wrote Evans, 'we lost heart and gave up the whole idea.'[85]

Agate had said, in his talk, that he had spoken to three of the best-known managers in London, and they had no confidence that the play could be put on and make money, because they doubted the willingness of the public to attend.

> How can there be anything wrong with a theatre which can produce and act plays like this one this afternoon? The answer is that there is never anything wrong with the theatre. The wrong lies entirely with the public which will not support good plays and has a taste only for the bare knees of musical comedy. ... It is the public's fault if it is deprived of work of extraordinary quality and interest.[86]

Maurice Browne

All was not yet lost, however, for George Bishop had been busy. By his own account, after the Monday matinee performance he had 'scoured the West End' looking for Maurice Browne, a man with wealthy backers who, he knew, was currently in search of a production. Bishop ran him down at the Arts Theatre and 'told him I had found ... the perfect play with which he could start his London management.'[87]

Maurice Browne was forty-seven years old and had made an interesting way through life. His father had been a successful headmaster, but had killed himself when Browne was just thirteen. He had been to Winchester for a time, served in the Army in the Boer War, and studied at Cambridge with Harold Monro, who married Browne's sister. In Italy in 1910, he fell for a young woman called Ellen van Volkenburg (known to her friends as Nellie Van), and followed her to the United States, where, without much money, the two established their Chicago Little Theatre, a home for avant-garde theatre, and part of the beginnings of the American Little Theatre movement. But war and economics closed the theatre, and they divorced before Browne returned to England, alone and penniless.

In the 1920s, however, things began to look up, as Browne became production manager at Bronson Albery's newly founded Arts Theatre. He also began to write for, and act upon, the London stage, most notably acting the part of the soldier in *The Unknown Warrior* earlier in 1928, in a production directed by Nellie Van at the Wyndham's. At the request of philanthropists Dorothy and Leonard Elmhirst,[88] some special performances of the play were given at Dartington Hall in Devon in 1928. Before the play packed up, according to Leonard Elmhirst, 'we said to Browne, "if he did ever come across some play of such interest as *The Unknown Warrior*, we might be interested in it, or in helping with it."'[89] At some point after his late night phone call from Monro, Browne got in touch with the Elmhirsts to tell them that he had just found such a play.

At about this juncture the story becomes a little muddled: we know that Maurice Browne eventually acquired the rights to the play, but there are three competing accounts as to how he got them. Sherriff's, inevitably, is the most romantic (but his dates are hopelessly wrong)[90]; Browne's is the most entertaining (but the picture he paints of Sherriff and Whale is wildly implausible, although funny)[91]; Bishop's (backed up by Dean and Elmhirst) is easily the most reliable.

Bishop's account tells us that, after they had met outside the Arts Theatre, Browne asked Bishop if he knew where he could obtain a copy of the play. Bishop knew that Basil Dean had been making enquiries, and so he went to Dean's office, only to be told that 'he had taken no definite steps to acquire the play'.[92] Shortly afterwards, Curtis Brown was on the phone to Dean to ask him what he knew about Browne, who had apparently given Dean as a reference: 'Was he a reliable person to whom a contract for *Journey's End* could be safely entrusted?'[93] Dean replied in the affirmative. The next day, Bishop obtained a copy of the play from Curtis Brown's office, and gave it to Browne to take down to the Elmhirsts in Devon. We know from Elmhirst that Browne went to Dartington Hall on 15 December[94] to read the play to them. They liked it very much, and asked Browne how much it would cost to stage, and, 'if not a soul goes to the play', how much 'down the drain' they would be. The answer was £2,000 – so they agreed to fund it, leaving Browne to find a theatre and deal with the production details.

He returned promptly and went to Curtis Brown to buy the option to produce. Browne wrote that Sherriff's agents were 'as friendly as a Chicago blizzard' (unsurprising, perhaps, given the reputation that Browne appeared to have in London theatre land).[95] But he came away with an option in his pocket.[96]

Colin Clive

There was, however, one snag. Browne's option stipulated that, within ten days, he had to engage a cast and director, and secure a West End theatre where the play would have to open within four weeks. 'Those ten days included Christmas Day, Boxing Day, a Sunday, and New Year's Day.'[97] Clearly, James Whale was already on board, and all of the cast – bar Olivier – were willing to sign on. And with the offer of four theatres within thirty-six hours, the only issue left to settle was the name of the final cast member: just who would play the part of Stanhope?

Here, again, the story gets a little murky. Sherriff acknowledged that he and James Whale searched far and wide for someone suitable, but to no avail. Maurice Browne commented that they 'could "see" no one else in the part; they turned down every applicant, vetoed every suggestion.'[98] But then, the lessor of the Savoy told him about a young man, who had 'never played in the West End', but who would be perfect for the part. His name was Colin Clive.

Colin Clive-Greig was born in France in 1900, son of an English colonel, and a mother who came from the famous Clive (of India) family. He attended Stonyhurst College, and then went to Sandhurst. Although he was just old enough to have fought in the war, he was prevented from doing so by a knee injury. He became an actor in the 1920s, beginning in the provinces, but he eventually moved up to London, where he had been acting in the West End: in 1928, he featured in Kern & Hammerstein's *Show Boat* (as Steve, the husband of the *Boat's* leading lady, Julie), which was a big hit at the Theatre Royal in Drury Lane – although it's probably fair to say that this owed rather more to Paul Robeson's debut in the part of Joe (and perhaps to Cedric Hardwicke) than it did to Clive.

Maurice Evans disputes Browne's account of the 'discovery' of Clive, claiming that, when he and the other actors were thinking of financing *Journey's End*, he had been tipped off about Clive by Jeanne de Casalis, an actress friend of his, who was Clive's girlfriend.[99] So sure was Evans of Clive's ability to play the part – 'his accent, his military bearing, his whisky voice were exactly what the part required'[100] – that he made it a condition of *his* continued involvement that Clive would get the part. Not only that, but he spent a week rehearsing with Clive before he was interviewed, to make sure that he gave Whale exactly what he was looking for.

Clive came to interview on New Year's Eve, 1928. Sherriff wrote, in a newspaper article 'introducing' Clive (in November 1930, when Clive had already made his name in both London and Hollywood), that he had come to the interview more casually dressed than the other actors ('I'd only just arrived from the country when your call came,' explained Clive), and that 'he had not read as well as some of the others, but there was something beneath his reading that we had not heard before. It is not always the actor who gives the best first reading who achieves the finest performance on the first night.'[101]

The decision on that showing appears to have been a toss-up between Clive and his main rival, a young man named Colin Keith-Johnston, who had been through the war, and won an MC into the bargain – the very embodiment of Stanhope, it would seem. As to which way round the voting went, we are rather in the dark. Sherriff says that he and Whale tried to persuade Browne that they should take Clive over Keith-Johnston[102]; Browne, on the other hand, swears that it was he who favoured Clive, against the strong objections of Whale and Sherriff. ('My only contribution to *Journey's End* was Colin Clive,' he said.)[103] Whichever way the votes stacked up, on that evening Sherriff suggests that it was someone else who had the effective casting vote – namely, Maurice Evans, whose opinion was the most important, since Raleigh and Stanhope had so many scenes together. When asked which actor he thought was most suited to the part, Evans replied: '"Keith-Johnston's got it here" (pointing to his forehead) – "but Clive's got it here," (pointing to his heart).'[104] So Clive it was, and given that Evans had been rehearsing with him for a week, the decision was hardly likely to go any other way.

On to the Savoy

With Stanhope cast, Browne had delivered on the terms of his option. There was now nothing to stop the play going ahead, and on 7 January 1929, the contract between Sherriff and Browne was officially signed.[105] For a £75 advance, Browne was granted the British Empire rights (excluding Canada), and he agreed to produce the play 'in a first-class manner in a first-class theatre in the West End of London within three months' or he would forfeit his rights. Royalties were pegged at 5 per cent of gross receipts up to £1,000 per week, and at 10 per cent on receipts between £1,000 and £1,500 a week. If the play hit the jackpot and grossed over £1,500 per week, Sherriff would be paid 10 per cent of everything. There were three other important clauses:

Sherriff retained publication rights and amateur rights;

Browne had the option to acquire the US (and Canada) rights, on the same terms as in the UK, if he exercised the option within six weeks of the play's first performance;

Browne was entitled to 40 per cent of the film rights.

On the very same day, James Agate did yet another radio talk on the subject of *Journey's End*. He started by insulting the audience – again: 'I remember telling you all that none of you would have the chance of seeing this play performed because, quite frankly, experience had shown that as playgoers you weren't worth it.' But he had good news, too. The audience now had the chance to demonstrate that it did have the desire to see good plays, for Maurice Browne would be producing *Journey's End* at the Savoy Theatre on Monday, 21 January; he had also taken a five-month tenancy at the Savoy (after which the theatre would be rebuilt)[106]; and he would then take another theatre, for an even longer period, at which he intended to run a permanent company. If the audience were at all interested in watching good drama, they should go *at once*. If they did, promised Agate, they would have the extreme satisfaction of proving him wrong.

So the news was now out: *Journey's End* would have its West End debut, and soon. There would be no change in the set, or in the director, and – apart from Percy Walsh (the sergeant major) who dropped out, to be replaced by Reginald Smith (another veteran of the war) – no change in the main cast, despite Maurice Browne's interest in playing Uncle.[107] According to Sherriff, that was quite a stroke of luck, for although Browne 'was all right with Euripides', he was not the man for a 'down-to-earth play that stood or fell upon its realism'.[108]

Clive had three weeks from getting the part to playing it on a West End stage, at what would surely be one of the theatrical events of the year. It must have been especially nerve-wracking to be parachuted into a company that already knew the play so well. If we take Maurice Evans at his word (and he and Clive had already rehearsed some of their scenes), that might have eased the pressure a little, although even with that help his reading had been sketchy. Everyone needed him to take possession of the role, but after the first week of rehearsals he was still struggling badly. He apologised to Sherriff, telling him that he 'had always been slow in getting hold of a part',[109] and this was particularly so in this case, when he was straining to catch up with the others. It was at this point that Sherriff made what he modestly claimed was his 'most useful contribution to the production' – namely, encouraging Clive to take a drink or two before the afternoon rehearsal, to relieve the anxiety that was bottling up his performance. Clive duly did so, and returned a changed man. 'He took command of the rehearsal,' wrote Sherriff, 'as Stanhope had commanded the company.'[110]

Tinkering with the Script

While rehearsals were under way, there was time for some further adjustment to the script. Some of the critics at the Apollo performances had drawn attention to some lines that sounded out of place, and Sherriff and Whale themselves were perfectionist enough to have some views of their own as to how the play had worked on its first two outings. Some changes had probably already been made before the ISS production, but from the versions currently available, it is clear that there was some further tinkering before the Savoy premiere.

There are three early versions of the *Journey's End* script, which differ from the present text. The earliest version is in the Imperial War Museum, where it was deposited in 1929 by Sir Walter Lawrence, having purchased the manuscript for £1,500 at the 10th Anniversary dinner of the League of Nations Union at the Guildhall in London, on 14 November that year. This manuscript is not, unfortunately, a typed and bound one: the papers are a jumbled assortment of handwritten and typewritten pages,[111] with no numbering sequence.

The other two versions are very similar, and thankfully, both typewritten and sequential. One is in Sherriff's own papers at the Surrey History Centre (SHC),[112] and the other is in the Victoria and Albert Museum Theatre and Performance Archive[113]: to all intents and purposes, they are identical, except that the former is missing some pages towards the end.[114] We can regard these as the *original* script, and they differ in a number of ways from the version we know today. But the question is: when did the changes from the original come about?

As we have already seen, Sherriff said that very few changes were made before the Apollo Theatre performances, but Maurice Evans disagrees. Maurice Browne appears to side more with Sherriff: after the play opened at the Savoy he commended Whale, who had done 'a magnificent production, and ... some very wise cutting',[115] thus suggesting that the cutting had come *after* the ISS performances. On balance, it seems likely that there were cuts made both before and after those performances. Some of the changes seem to have been made solely on the grounds of length, and one imagines these being made early on in the process, to speed up the action. But the other changes are subtler in their impact, affecting the tone of the play, and altering the portrayal of the characters; these seem more likely to have been made in the light of experience, and following comments made after the initial production.[116]

There is one change that we know for sure came after the performance, since one line was identified, in a review of the performance at the Apollo, as almost the only false note in the play.[117] When Osborne tells Raleigh that he once played rugger for England, Raleigh replies, 'How topping – to have played for England!', to which Osborne then says (in the original), 'You're playing for England now.' Always mindful of critics' comments, Sherriff changed Osborne's response to 'Well, aren't you, now?' in time for the Gollancz first edition of the published play. But sometime later he changed it again, to its present incarnation (p.42): 'It was rather fun.' As ever, he was very willing (eager, almost) to make changes where he felt they would improve the play, or its reception.

On the whole, the changes do not make a huge difference to the play, but there is no doubt that the tone is affected by even quite innocuous alterations, especially where the character of Stanhope is concerned. The acid test, however, would be the critics. Having been at the Apollo, how would they regard the revised version of the play: would they look at it differently, or would they not even notice that the changes had been made?

The Savoy Production

The play was due to begin at the Savoy Theatre at 8.30 pm on Monday, 21 January. In fact, the curtain went up a little late, revealing David Horne on stage as Captain Hardy, drying his sock over a candle, just as Douglass had done, in real life, some twelve years earlier. Sherriff was there with his mother, sister and brother-in-law[118] (munching egg sandwiches and drinking whisky and soda), no doubt feeling a little skittish, since the dress rehearsal had not gone well. The rickety sound effects, which had worked satisfactorily at the Apollo, had to be upgraded for the much bigger Savoy, and the dress rehearsal had been punctuated with the ill-timed sounds of war. The rehearsal had gone on until midnight on Sunday, with further rehearsals for lighting and effects on Monday morning, and another run-through on Monday afternoon. Sherriff was convinced on his way to the theatre that the performance would be a disaster, and the play would go down in flames. His nerves can't have been helped by the glittering crowd – a host of well-known names from the theatre world (including the Elmhirsts themselves) and the military.

There were cheers when the first act curtain came down, and Sherriff found himself in a crowd of well-wishers, keeping his fingers crossed that the evening hadn't been jinxed, since there were several tricky passages in the play still to be navigated. But none of the disasters he feared came about, and eventually the curtain came down. There was silence in the crowd, and when the curtain rose again it did so only briefly, showing 'twelve figures clad in uniform, standing stiffly at attention and dimly seen against a darkness amid the swirl of smoke', according to Maurice Browne.[119] This, Browne felt, was his second contribution to the play (after the casting of Colin Clive): against the objections of some of the actors, he (backed up by author and director) argued that the impersonality of that final tableau reinforced their wartime theme. Then the curtain rose again – whether prompted by a solitary 'Bravo' in the crowd (Sherriff's version), or by the applause of the actors behind the curtain (Maurice Evans's version) is unimportant, for the next time the curtain rose the applause was deafening, and so it remained as the various actors took their bows. When, at last, the crowd had exhausted its expression of appreciation, Sherriff gave a speech – thanking Maurice Browne among others – and then called on Whale to say a few words as well. And then for Sherriff it was home to bed, to await the next morning's papers.

The reviews were stunning – and unanimous.[120] If anything, the critics felt the play was even better than they had thought before. 'Greatest of all War Plays' thundered the fearsome Hannan Swaffer in the *Express*; 'How Like it All Is', declared *The Times*; 'Stirring New War Play; Trench Life Truly Depicted', wrote the *Telegraph's* Bill Darlington, who was only just recovering from the jolt to his memories that he had received at the Apollo. Different newspapers deployed different adjectives, but the content was much the same: 'Impressive' (*Daily News*), 'Fine' (*Daily Mirror* and *Daily Herald*), 'Best War Play' (*Evening News*), 'Triumph' (*Evening Standard*) … there was not a single negative note.

There was consensus on the verisimilitude of the play. The *Evening Standard* review noted:

The effect of [the play's] actuality must have had, on all that part of the audience that had experience and memory, the effect of something entirely physical – relief, from the soles of their feet upwards, that what they saw was 'only a play', relief that their boots were not wet and their clothes muddy, that their heads no longer wore shrapnel helmets, and that it would not be their own turn in a few minutes to go up those steps at the back of the stage into the dawn of 21 March 1918.

In the *Daily Chronicle*, J.B. Priestley (who knew something of war himself) wrote that this was:

The war as the fighting man knew it – 'the line' as it really was – this is presented in stark, harrowing reality in *Journeys End*. … Real talk. Real emotion. Real men. Mixtures of good and bad, of bravery and cowardice, of saint and sinner, like your neighbour in the auditorium.

Hannan Swaffer in the *Express* wrote that 'There is no shirking the facts; there is no concession to fashion. The author has set down what he has seen,' while the *Daily Mirror* noted that 'it shows life at the front, with an unemotional realism which is a much better argument against war than sentimental propaganda plays.'[121] Priestley was of the view that the play 'could and should be translated into the language of every ex-ally and ex-enemy. It is the strongest plea for peace I know.' Sherriff would answer him the very next day in the *Express* by stressing that 'I have not written this play as a piece of propaganda. And certainly not as propaganda for peace,' but the tussle over the play's anti-war credentials (or lack of them) would rumble on for months (indeed, to some extent it does so still, despite Sherriff's protestations).

There was a generally accepted view that the play was not just an authentic account of a moment in the trenches, but also worked as great *drama*. It was not, however, viewed as great *art*. But Darlington did not see that as a criticism:

> This play is not a great play, for the very excellent reason that it does not aim at being a great play; but that within its limits it is, humanly speaking, perfect. ... A great play about the war must deal with the question: 'What does war mean?' ... Mr Sherriff, on the other hand, set out to answer quite a different and less fundamental question, 'What was our war like?' He has answered that question as fully as any man could within the compass of a play in three acts and a single setting.

The Times, too, agreed that the play was not high art, but seemed to feel that it ought to be:

> We do not feel that we have been admitted by art into any individual mood or quality of awe so felt by the author in the presence of his material as to convey the sense of universality through his play. The sweep and gathering force of tragedy are wanting in the faithful and unsentimental account of the conditions of war. ... Mr Sherriff has written an exciting play, but he has not made the wonder and the awe felt in the war articulate to ourselves or to others.

Interestingly, a few days later, *The Sunday Times*[122] reviewer took his stablemate to task:

> It is not obvious that all this sweeping and gathering could be present only on condition that faithfulness departed. ... Surely every work of art is to be judged according to its success or failure in achieving what it sets out to do. It seems to me that Mr Sherriff has succeeded perfectly. *Journey's End* is a realistic play, and a realistic play is to be judged by its realism.

All in all, the production was viewed as an improvement on even the high standards set at the Apollo, with some of the script changes noted approvingly, together with the enhanced sound effects. Across the board there were commendations for the acting and the characterisation. *The Evening News* noted that men in the interval were comparing the characters to men they had known in the trenches. And for the reviewers at the Savoy, much of the credit for that went to the actors: 'Excellent Acting' (*The Morning Post*), 'Very well acted' (*Daily Herald*), 'The acting is even better than before' (*The Telegraph*). Of course, one of the big questions about the acting was whether Colin Clive would prove an adequate replacement for Olivier – again the answer was unanimous. Darlington was the most complimentary of the bunch:

> Mr Colin Clive ... scores a personal triumph. [Stanhope] was played at the first performance on lines that suggested the theatre rather than life. Mr Clive corrects all this, with the result that his one big outburst, when Stanhope does at last give way to his grief over Osborne's death, gains enormously in power.

On the Monday evening, Sherriff's father wrote in his diary[123]:

> *Journey's End* (Bob's war play) produced at the Savoy Theatre. To have a play put on the London stage must be quite a notable event in our ordinary everyday family – what it may lead to is full of promise and possibilities.

Even surveying the reviews in the papers the next day, none of the family would have had any idea of how their lives would be upended by *Journey's End*'s extraordinary triumph.

Chapter 5

The Aftermath, 1929

Receive wealth or prosperity without arrogance; and be ready to let it go.
Marcus Aurelius, *The Meditations*, Book VIII.

At Christmas in 1928, Sherriff deposited his monthly salary cheque, of £26 12s 4d, in his account at Barclays Bank, Kingston.[1] At that point his bank account totalled just over £29 10s. On 7 January, he deposited a little over £50, being the larger portion of the sum that Maurice Browne had paid for the advance British rights on *Journey's End*. Sherriff must have been very satisfied – his play was to be put on at the Savoy Theatre, and he had just received over two months' salary in return. One month later, however, he was depositing his royalties from the first couple of weeks' productions at the Savoy – almost £250.[2] By 18 February, his royalty cheque, for just one week, was over £227 – or more than eight months' salary.

Gross receipts in the theatre in the first week were very strong – over £1,700. One week later they were up to £2,400, and they stayed there, or above, almost throughout the run at the Savoy. In the first few weeks it was word of mouth, novelty and fashion that drove the demand, but it was Browne's shrewd business sense that kept it high thereafter. The key to a long run was a good deal with the 'libraries', or ticket agencies. They immediately pursued Browne, and day after day they badgered him to do business. After several meetings they made their best offer, and when Browne refused even to let them have a commission on the seats they sold they walked out, to the despair of Clifford Hamilton (Browne's business manager)[3] and Sherriff, who was convinced that Browne had overplayed his hand.[4]

But the crowds were flocking to the play – including Herbert, who had attended the Thursday matinee (along with his aunts, Ede and Kate), and recorded that he was 'much impressed with it – a very powerful play which grips one throughout. Colin Clive very strong in a very trying part.'[5] The BBC chose to broadcast some sections of the play in their 'Surprise' slot that very evening, with the announcer warning nervous people that 'it would be desirable for them to shut off their sets during the transmission'. The recording was made in the studio, with Maurice Browne finally having the chance to play his beloved Osborne, alongside Ion Swinley (who would later pop up in *St Helena*) as Stanhope, Derek Williams as Raleigh (a part that he would perfect on Broadway), and Percy Walsh reprising his role from the ISS production (as the sergeant major). George Bishop in *The Era* reported that the broadcast had created 'an even greater demand to see the play'.[6]

With queues outside the box office, and the BBC on board, the play was well on the way to becoming a smash. It wasn't long before two representatives of the biggest agencies again stood before Browne, as he later recalled with great satisfaction:

> 'You've licked us,' they said. 'The smaller libraries won't come in on the deal; we shall have to carry them. What are your terms?' I told them; they gasped and signed. It was the first time that a five-figure deal had ever been made for a straight play.[7]

In fact, according to *The Era*, the libraries signed up to a deal worth £16,000 – 'and the run is therefore assured for the remaining four months of the Savoy tenancy.'[8] Sherriff's contract with Browne guaranteed him royalties of 10 per cent on *all* receipts if the gross was over £1,500. Sure enough, with the theatre taking in about £2,500 a week, he began to receive a weekly cheque of over £220. With the play certain to run until June, he could plan on receiving almost £4,000 in royalties from the Savoy alone – or rather, more than ten *years'* salary.

Nor was that all. Gollancz brought out the book of the play to take full advantage of the Savoy production. An initial printing of 1,000 copies was doubled before the end of January, and further printings came thick and fast, with a grand total of seventeen impressions (67,000 copies) by the end of the year,[9] by which time Sherriff would have earned the best part of another year's salary from Gollancz, with more to come.

The play quickly began to garner worldwide attention, and managers and publishers from other countries were soon beating a path to Curtis Brown's door. The market that was likely to be the most important was the United States. Maurice Browne had quickly exercised his option on the United States' rights, and several Broadway producers were already hovering around his door. He was almost ready to settle with one of them[10] when 'a tornado swept into the dressing-room'[11] – a tornado called Gilbert Miller.

Miller was born in New York in 1884, the son of an English theatrical producer who had made his home in the United States. His father, Henry, had built his own theatre in 1918,[12] and it had become known as a venue for serious plays.[13] Miller took over the theatre after his father died in 1926, but he also owned the St James Theatre in London, and had a track record studded with long and successful runs. He was known for his willingness to take English plays across the Atlantic, and in many respects there would seem to have been few producers better qualified to take on an American production of *Journey's End*. According to Browne, once the tornado found that the rights had not yet been sold:

a chair hurtled to the dressing room door; the tornado hurricaned into the chair and all night through flung me from wall to wall. By 1.00 am [the other producer] had long been outbidden. Hour by hour the price rose.

Eventually, Browne wrestled from him a remarkable deal: Miller agreed that he would 'take all the risks, claim no share in the film rights, give you [Browne] the final say-so and pay you 60 per cent of the net.' According to Browne, it was an offer 'without parallel in the history of the Anglo–American theatre'.[14]

Every Silver Lining …

The wild success of the play was not without its drawbacks for Sherriff, for it placed strenuous new demands upon him, while he still was trying to perform his duties as an outdoor man for Sun Insurance. In the first place there were the invitations to dinner and lunch, for everyone wanted to meet the shy and modest young man who had inadvertently written a smash hit. Two people in particular opened up their extensive networks of contacts to him. G.B. Stern, the novelist and playwright, was at the heart of literary London, and she fell in with Sherriff almost at once, introducing him to people like Somerset Maugham, H.G. Wells and John Van Druten, among many others. Another famous hostess who took an almost parental interest in him was Maud (Mollie) Cazalet, who introduced him to prime ministers such as Stanley Baldwin and Neville Chamberlain, and to literary giants such as Rudyard Kipling. Sherriff later described her as 'the quietest, most modest and unassuming person I ever met. … She soon found out that I'd never get anywhere under my own steam, and took me under her wing and brought me out like a debutante.'[15]

Mrs Cazalet was much the same age as Sherriff's mother, and with the same degree of maternal pride in her family, so it was unsurprising that the relationship between the two of them became close and affectionate, remaining so throughout her life.

Mollie's son, Victor, was an MP, and close to Churchill, who, despite being Chancellor of the Exchequer, had still found time to go to see the play at the Savoy. Churchill wrote to Sherriff on 1 February, commenting on how interesting he had found *Journey's End*,[16] and raising some questions about both the play and the production, which Sherriff duly answered.[17] Churchill was eager to meet him, and Cazalet arranged it, entertaining Sherriff to lunch at his club before taking him round to No. 11. After a thorough discussion about Sherriff's wartime experiences, the three went on to the House of Commons: it was all that Sherriff could do to get back to his Charing Cross office to file his reports.[18]

Perhaps, if the play had been less of a phenomenon, the additional burden placed on him would not have been so great. As well as the lunch and dinner invitations, there were rehearsals for new companies, discussions with agents and lawyers about worldwide royalties and investments, a hundred letters a day streaming into the theatre, and with the need to keep half an eye on the production itself. He complained to Maurice Browne that 'an insurance job demands nine hours a day – a theatre demands nine hours a day – I cannot do both.'[19]

To make matters worse, he felt that his customers now viewed him very differently. Before, he felt he had been more by way of a 'servant' to them, but now that they knew he had a big success in the West End they were much less natural with him:

> I think some despised me for wanting to go on in the same old way – others ran to fetch their friends to come and have a look at 'the gentleman who wrote the play' and I remember one man, who ran a radio shop. He'd always been rather offhand ... Then one day he evidently got wind of what had happened because I found him very nice and smiling. I'd never seen him smile before. He took me into the room behind his shop and said, 'Nice little business I got here, if only I had a little more capital. What d'you say to coming in as a half-share partner? You wouldn't have to work. Only just put a bit o' money up.'[20]

It had not been Sherriff's intention to give up his job straightaway. The receipts from *Journey's End* were initially impressive, but no one knew how long that might last, nor how the play would go down in Europe or the United States. His job, by contrast, was relatively safe – or as safe as any job could be in a downturn. Some years later he remarked, 'As my father said, I'd only got to stay on another thirty years and I'd get a pension for life'[21]: it was meant humorously, but there was probably at least a bit of truth behind it.

There was one other thing: Sherriff was an amateur in a world of professionals. He clearly felt very out of place, which was unsurprising given the experienced men around him. He must have looked at Whale and Browne and concluded that he had very little in common with either of them – the length of time they had worked in established theatre, the connections they had made across the theatrical world, the breadth of their romantic entanglements, all must have made him feel very quiet and suburban. They had travelled widely for their art – in Browne's case, all the way to America, which seemed impossibly exotic to Sherriff at the time – and both of them could cope with a wide range of theatre work, and do it well enough to have it displayed in the finest theatres in the West End. Sherriff's path had done nothing more than take him on a tour of small theatres and church halls. It would have been odd if he hadn't felt out of place.

Nevertheless, a decision had to be made; he could not continue with both lives. Luckily, the decision was made for him, when he was called in to see Sir William Goschen, at that time chairman of the Sun Insurance Group.[22] Sherriff had no idea why he was being summoned, and feared that he might be fired, but was delighted to find that Sir William just wanted to meet him and to talk to him about the play, which he had already seen a couple of times. Towards the end of their conversation Goschen asked about his plans for the future, and Sherriff told him his worries – could he bank his future on the promise of a play that had only been running for a few weeks in London? To his astonishment, Goschen entirely understood his fears, and sought to allay them by offering him a six-month leave of absence,[23] during which time he could concentrate on the play and his theatre work; if things should not work out, he could always return to his work with Sun Insurance.

Within a few days Sherriff had left the insurance world behind him, never to return. He was obviously nervous about what he had done – giving up the comfort and security of a place he knew well, for a world in which he felt a little at sea:

> I had belonged to the office in a way in which I should never belong to the theatre. The men there were my sort of men. We had the same background; we talked the same language, played the same games and did the same things. I got on well enough with the men in the theatre, with Maurice Browne and the actors and the men behind the scenes, but the only interest we had in common was *Journey's End*. From that point on we parted ways. I had either got to break through into their world and live their way or plough a lonely furrow of my own. The chances were against a breakthrough because I wasn't made to be a man of the theatre. It fascinated me, but no matter what lay ahead I should always remain a jumped-up amateur.[24]

On Broadway

Gilbert Miller had decided that the play would be premiered at the Henry Miller's Theater, with an all-English cast, English producers, and sets and props exactly as in the original. In part this was to retain the uniquely English tone of the play, but it was also 'to avoid the "prohibitive costs of production in America"'.[25]

So, auditions began in London in mid-February,[26] and the parts were soon assigned. Colin Keith-Johnston, who had so nearly won out against Clive for the Savoy production, would play Stanhope. Almost all the other parts were to be filled by experienced players, such as 53-year-old Leon Quartermaine (Osborne), and Henry Wenman (Trotter); Raleigh would be played by Derek Williams, who had already had a run out in the part in the BBC's abridged broadcast of the play on 25 January. Curiously, the youngest member of the cast might also have been one of the better-known, for the part of Hibbert was to be played by Jack Hawkins, just seventeen, but fresh from high-profile roles in *Young Woodley*, and most recently, *Beau Geste*. Hawkins wrote[27] that he was originally invited to audition for – and duly won – the part of Stanhope, but when Whale (whom he persists in calling Welch) and Miller found out his age they decided that it would be too risky to have the play resting on such youthful shoulders. As a consolation prize, he was awarded the part of Hibbert and got to keep the lucrative contract that had been assigned to him: $200 a week (about £40), and first-class return passage to New York.

Whale himself was not at all enthusiastic about coming to the United States with the company, preferring to maximise the opportunities in the West End that were now sure to come his way. While Browne was unconcerned, perhaps harbouring the thought that he might then undertake the directing on Broadway, Sherriff was sufficiently worried to offer Whale an additional incentive: 1 per cent of his gross royalties on all American productions, which, over the next year, would amount to some $5,000.[28]

Before taking the company to the United States, Miller had a replica set built for a try-out at the Arts Theatre Club, with six performances planned from Thursday, 7 – Sunday, 10 March. The timetable allowed everything to be broken down and packed away in boxes before they sailed for the US the following Wednesday. This was the first time ever in the West End that two companies would perform a play simultaneously, but the Arts Club performances were not well received. Few of the cast escaped the critics' barbs: Keith-Johnston was seen to have done an adequate job as Stanhope (better than Olivier, but not nearly so good as Clive), and Derek Williams and Jack Hawkins were commended as well.[29] But Leon Quartermaine was criticised for still being more actor than soldier, and Henry Wenman proved much too comic a Trotter. Like the critics, the audiences were not impressed, and Miller must have quaked at the thought of the money he was spending on taking them all first class to the United States.

A party of thirteen set out on the *Aquitania* – Miller, Browne, Whale, Sherriff and cast. During the crossing Miller took the chance to rehearse some of the younger actors in his cabin, 'smoothing down their ultra-English accents, rubbing out mannerisms, altering a few words here and there to make them fall more easily upon the American ear.'[30] He told Sherriff that if they were 100 per cent English they would be fine, but if they were 105 per cent, 'they'll go down the drain.' Jack Hawkins remembers the journey rather differently:

> The trip to America was one long party. In 1929 America was in the grip of prohibition, and faced with a long dry spell we regarded it as our duty to take on as much drink as we could while we had the opportunity.[31]

They docked in New York on 20 March. Sherriff stayed on board to enjoy lunch with some of the actors, but was suddenly faced with the members of the New York press pack who had come out on a tugboat, looking for a story. So Sherriff spun them the usual tale:

> The story the reporters had got hold of was not precisely true, but there wasn't any point in watering it down by telling them about the long string of earlier

plays I'd written for the boat club that had got me nowhere. ... It would have
been too long a story anyway. ... So I felt justified in brightening it up by
adding a bit of dramatic licence. It wasn't cheating, because everything I told
them actually happened. I simply cut the dull stuff and linked the interesting
episodes together just as I would if I were condensing a long rambling story
into a play for the stage.[32]

There, in a nutshell, is Sherriff's attitude to his own story – an attitude that persisted
throughout his life, and reached something of a culmination in *No Leading Lady*.
He no doubt had many motives for manipulating the truth – one of which was
undoubtedly the desire to spin a good yarn. But he was shy as well, and maybe
concealing some of the truth allowed him to shield his true personality. As Ervine
noted in his 1930 article:

Hundreds of portraits of Mr Sherriff have been published in the American,
the British and the European press. Scarcely a day passes but some reference
to him or his play is printed. ... The publicity has been extraordinary and
shows no signs of diminishing. Yet Mr Sherriff remains almost unknown to
the public.[33]

That was surely how he preferred it.

While Sherriff was talking to the press, Whale went to the Henry Miller's Theatre
to organise the temporary erection of the set, to allow for a dress rehearsal. The
actors had to be word perfect, since their first US engagement was the following
night in the Long Island suburb of Great Neck, where they would appear at the
Playhouse, which had become more of a cinema than a theatre. But on this occasion
the hoardings highlighted the unusual nature of the attraction: '*Journey's End*. A
play, not a film. Actors in the FLESH!'[34] Sherriff describes in detail the agony of
the performance, waiting in case the locals would take badly to the English accents
and drown the play in ridicule. But it passed off well, and the set was boxed up and
transported the 20 miles back to the Henry Miller's Theatre, where it would be on
display the very next evening.

At 8.30 pm on 22 March 1929 – twenty minutes earlier than usual because of the
length of the play – the curtain rose. When it fell for the last time at the end of the
night it did so on a production that was every bit as triumphant as the UK show,
and was received by the audience in much the same way – silence as the curtain
fell, then huge ovations: 'I hear that at the end the audience cheered, and cheering
in the theatre in America is, of course, very unusual. The critics are profoundly
impressed.'[35] The excitement of the play's overwhelming success is vividly captured
in Maurice Browne's breathless cable back to the London office:

Press and public excellent. Miller considers success assured. Offers buy me out. Offer refused. Brooks Atkinson in *Times* says cast, despite unfavourable tidings, acts with memorable perfection. Burns Mantle in *News* says performance inspiringly fine – as near perfect as such things can be; Arthur Ruhl in *Tribune* says all played without false note. Same three critics pay play glowing tribute.[36]

Gilbert Miller followed this up a couple of days later with a long telegram of his own, summarising the overwhelmingly positive reviews from thirteen different newspapers[37] – 'a great play', 'amazing', 'powerful and ... beautiful' – the plaudits were an echo of the London papers, with an American accent.

After the triumph, Sherriff stayed in New York for a few more days – handling publicity chores, and establishing a US-based company that would be the receptacle of his proceeds from the play's performances in America. It was obvious very quickly that the proceeds could easily outstrip those in the UK. His account[38] with the Irving Trust Bank in the United States shows royalties totalling $4,333 in the first three weeks, before rising to about $1,800 a week thereafter (with the sterling-dollar rate fixed at $4.87, that amounted to something over £350 a week – much better than even the best weeks at the Savoy). Maurice Browne, too, was 'having the fun of my life'. On March 27 he wrote excitedly to the Elmhirsts, to tell them that he and Miller had already begun planning to take at least two touring companies out with the play – one in the United States and one in Canada. He was also enjoying the attention of the 'movie magnates, trying to show dignity in falling over each other in their quite inadequately concealed eagerness to get the talkie rights.'[39]

On 29 March, tired but exhilarated, Sherriff boarded the *Beringaria* and headed back home from his Broadway adventure, leaving Maurice Browne there for another week and a half, closeted with Gilbert Miller, and savouring his success. James Whale also stayed behind, directing another play for Miller – *A Hundred Years Old*, by Joaquin Quintero. It did not receive good notices, but Whale had by that time set his sights elsewhere. He was keen to get movie experience, thinking it would give him the chance to direct the talkie version of *Journey's End* that was already very close to being agreed. Consequently, having picked up a contract as an uncredited 'dialogue director' for the Paramount Famous Lasky Corporation, he set out to begin his apprenticeship in Los Angeles on 1 May.[40]

Sherriff arrived back in England on 5 April, to congratulatory letters from his friends: Mollie Cazalet – so pleased the play had gone down well on Broadway[41]; Geoffrey Dearmer (now, with George Bishop, a reader for Maurice Browne Ltd at the princely sum of £3 a week) – keen to meet up[42]; G.B. Stern so pleased that he hadn't been caught by America, though apparently it was 'very much caught by you'.[43] There had even been a nice letter from Leonard Lodge (the KGS schoolmaster who had played one of the old ladies in *Hitch* all those years earlier), who admired the play and was very grateful that 'your schoolmaster is such an admirable and loveable fellow', who 'serves as a fine corrective' to the master in *Young Woodley*.[44] There was a tiny twinge of disappointment, however: the new car he had ordered – an Austin 16 – was not yet ready for collection (despite the fact that the car dealer had written personally to Sir Herbert Austin to hurry things along).[45] He would not make the same mistake again: in future years he would typically order his new car well in advance of his trips to the United States, to ensure that it was ready for his arrival back home.

Unhappiness Inevitable

There was another disappointment when he returned, which was on a much grander scale, and was linked to the difficult question of the sale of the movie rights to *Journey's End*, a saga that had begun on 7 February when Maurice Browne wrote to the Elmhirsts, telling them that 'with a gulp and a gurgle and a pounding heart' he was just about to 'refuse a £4,000 offer for the talkie rights in *Journey's End*'.[46] He had, furthermore, bought out Sherriff's interest in the rights for £2,250.

The contract between Browne and Sherriff had specified that movie rights would be split 60:40 in Sherriff's favour,[47] and that in the event of an offer being received that one party wished to accept but the other did not, the party unwilling to sell could buy out the other person's share. At first blush it seems surprising that – only (just over) two weeks into the Savoy lease, with record attendances and the libraries committed for months ahead – Sherriff was willing to sell out his share of the rights so cheaply. And Browne noted in his letter to the Elmhirsts that Sherriff had sold his interest despite his and Curtis Brown's strong urgings. 'Sherriff's ultimate decision,' he wrote, 'was based on the fact that it would ensure him £100 a year for the rest of his life, so that in this one case, at least, he decided – with his eyes open – to play safe.' Browne paid Sherriff a 10 per cent advance a few days later; it shows up in his cash book on 14 February as a payment of £202 10s (after the deduction of Curtis Brown's 10 per cent fee).[48]

By the end of February, the offer for the rights had risen to £4,500, but things really began to get going when the Broadway company boarded the *Aquitania*. By the account of George Hill (Browne's brother-in-law, whom he had designated in charge of the Foreign and Film Sections of Maurice Browne Ltd), a number of 'Film people'[49] were taking the same passage. In the course of a few days the bidding war intensified, such that the price had doubled by the time the ship berthed in New York. After ten days in New York, £12,000 was the highest bid. Then, after a brief lull, the rights were finally sold to Morris Gest for £15,000. And that's when the trouble began, for just at the point when the deal was about to be signed, Browne got word from the UK that Sherriff was unhappy at the price he had been paid for his share of the rights.

What had caused Sherriff's change of heart? Sherriff's version was that he had only accepted the initial offer because he had been seeking security to give up his job.[50] However, once Goschen had offered him leave of absence, he no longer felt the need to shore up his finances. Furthermore, he maintained that Browne had agreed to pay the money to him before they sailed for the United States, and that his failure to do so had rendered the agreement void. Upon his return from the US he had been met at Waterloo station by Clifford Hamilton, who had tried to press a £2,000 cheque into his hand. 'Smelling a rat', however, he declined to accept the cheque – believing that had he done so he would have implicitly acquiesced to the earlier deal. He then had Curtis Brown wire Browne to tell him the deal was off.

After receiving word that Sherriff wanted to back out of the deal, Browne cabled him on 8 April: 'Dear Bob, difficult believe author *Journey's End* would seek to go back on word as reported, but, if report true, consequent unhappiness inside yourself inevitable.'[51] At the same time, Browne was wiring his fellow directors, complaining about Sherriff's duplicity, and maintaining that 'Sherriff orally sold me the movie rights finally and fully and without time qualification and we paid price he asked.'[52] He then outlined two possible courses of action. Both began with the suggestion that they should attempt to reason with Sherriff; one path then darkened considerably with suggested recourse to various legal actions, while the other path recognised that litigation might 'imperil [the] play's message to the world', and that it was better to sacrifice 'pride, money and everything else' than the play itself. 'I therefore urge,' concluded Browne, 'settle with Sherriff soonest possible on best terms possible.'

The next day, Sherriff and Curtis Brown met with the Elmhirsts' (and thus, implicitly, Browne's) accountant, Fred Gwatkin, on 'neutral territory'[53] – a room at the Savoy Theatre. By Sherriff's account Gwatkin 'looked like Mussolini', and although jovial at first, quickly flared up, 'strutted round the room, slammed his fist on the desk and shouted, "A man's word is his bond! A verbal agreement, in law, is as firm and as irrevocable as a written one!"' But Sherriff, while admitting that he had accepted the agreement, maintained that he was no longer bound by it, because Browne had yet to pay up. Gwatkin told him that, if he did not stick to the agreement, Browne would withdraw the play from both Broadway and London; then, demanding a firm answer by later that day, he swept from the room. Curtis Brown told Sherriff that Gwatkin was bluffing – that Maurice Browne would never give up the profits he was raking in on both sides of the Atlantic – but Sherriff, by his own account, was not persuaded. He felt that Browne was quite capable of taking a quixotic approach: 'By instinct he was an actor who revelled in classic tragedy, and if he decided to cast himself as the hero of a real-life drama he would play it out to the bitter end, even if it meant ruin.' And so he gave up any further claim on the rights, and accepted the original settlement instead, banking the cheque on 10 April. Losing the additional money may have been a difficult pill to swallow, but it was 'a cheap price to pay for peace and quiet', he told Curtis Brown.

Sherriff's account of the whole affair is a characteristically lively one, but as so often, it is not quite the whole story. There is no doubt that he accepted the initial offer *before* being offered leave of absence from his firm, as he later wrote to Browne:

You know why I accepted your offer to purchase my interest: it was to place a little security behind me so that I could resign my position at my office – I acted against strong advice because I could not justly continue my office work and do my *Journey's End* work as well. Directly the £2,000 was safely behind me I intended to resign.[54]

But when, shortly afterwards, he received the offer of a leave of absence, he felt less need of the money, and 'my first instinct was to come to you and say "let's call the deal off" ' – I'd rather stand in on a gamble with you.' By that time, however, Browne had already received a higher offer, and Sherriff felt it would be awkward to go back on his deal, so he decided just to 'grin and bear' his loss.

The question then is why Sherriff changed his mind when he returned from America. In *No Leading Lady* he suggests it was because he felt that the £2,000 came with an implicit condition that it would be paid before his departure for America. But given the agreement was made before the Broadway rights had been sold to Gilbert Miller, this particular justification doesn't hold water. It also calls into question his entire story about meeting Clifford Hamilton at Waterloo. In the fragments of his letter to Browne he appears to suggest that he felt the deal was voidable because Browne had not signed off on the contract prepared by Curtis Brown. Browne, on the other hand – as can be seen from his telegram, and Gwatkin's response – felt that an oral contract was quite binding enough. Fred Gwatkin believed that Sherriff's wish to renegotiate the deal sprang from a simpler motive:

Apparently … [Sherriff] did not anticipate that the company would get such a large sum for the picture rights, and considered he had made a bad bargain. In this attitude he was no doubt influenced by the advice of Curtis Brown Ltd … and we cannot help thinking that Curtis Brown in turn were influenced by the fact that … if Mr Sherriff had dealt with the motion picture rights himself, they would have received a considerably larger fee.[55]

There was no residue of ill feeling between Sherriff and Browne – as Gwatkin himself noted: '[He] is not hostile by reason of the interview. In fact we had a very pleasant talk last night. I think he was sorry he was prevailed to take up the attitude he did.'[56] Sherriff was always a very principled and straightforward individual, never one to try to wrangle the last penny from a deal – on occasions offering others a share of his royalties where he felt they deserved it[57] – and his embarrassment at his attempt to wriggle out of the deal probably explains why he went to such lengths in his autobiography to construct a plausible explanation for his behaviour. But he quickly moved to make amends, writing to Browne and regretting the 'misunderstanding' that had occurred, and assuring him:

> I signed without reservation of any kind – and above all, Maurice, I want you to know that I do not feel the slightest bitterness. You have the credit of making a large and successful business deal and you owe me nothing in any shape or form beyond what has already been paid.[58]

Even with that, however, the saga was not quite over. Although Gest had won out in the bidding, he defaulted on the payments of his contract, and the rights went instead to a British firm for the sum of £16,000.[59] Actually, the rights went to two British firms, for Michael Balcon (of Gainsborough Pictures) and Tommy Welsh (of Welsh-Pearson) had decided that, rather than outbid each other, they would join forces and make the film a co-production venture. Nevertheless, as Balcon later noted, 'both Tommy and I had some explaining to do to our respective colleagues.'[60]

As a final coda, Maurice Browne later sent Sherriff a gift of £2,000 to compensate for his having lost out on the deal. It probably pleased Browne and Gwatkin that, as a gift, and free from any contract, there was no requirement that Curtis Brown receive any of the money.

Scott of the Antarctic

With the unpleasantness of the movie rights put to bed, Sherriff's mind started turning to what came next. His leave of absence had been confirmed, and the money was now rolling in from Broadway as well as the Savoy, so he began to think of how he might follow his unexpected triumph with *Journey's End*. Sherriff sent his agent, Walter Peacock, two plays that might form the basis of his next production – one was almost certainly *Mr Birdie's Finger* and the other most likely *The Feudal System* – and spoke to him about another play idea, one that Peacock was very much in favour of: 'I think the subject a very fine one, that might result in a play as important and successful as *Journey's End*.'[61] Sherriff also spoke to Hannan Swaffer about it:

> When you said a few weeks ago that I should never write another great play, it stimulated me to think of a really fine idea. I should be nervous about making into a play the last hours of a man who died so recently, except that I feel Captain Scott's life and death belonged to nobody but to the great world and that they are an example and inspiration to every one of our blood. For that reason I feel his family will not be offended.[62]

It soon became clear, however, that the family were very much offended, and Sherriff was forced into something of a humiliating retraction. In a statement he made to

The Observer[63] he denied intending to write a play about the Scott Expedition specifically. Rather, his new play 'may deal broadly with the theme of adventure through exploration, and may be set in polar regions.' He was very clear that he would do nothing that would cause pain to the families of Scott and his colleagues:

> No play, however great in its public interest and possible value as an historic story of courage, would be justified if pain were given to a single person who had already suffered such great personal loss. A play with an imaginary story – and imaginary characters – which dealt with a fine theme inspired by actual human endeavour would have just as much value without causing pain.

Sherriff had been scared off by Scott's widow, Kathleen,[64] who 'blocked all attempts to dramatise her dead husband's story in Britain.'[65] But in the process, and no doubt in the light of Sherriff's acquiescence, they became friends. There are regular missives between the two during the 1930s and he enlisted her help when commissioned to write a chapter on Scott for the book *The Post Victorians*.[66] The chapter is affectionately drawn, and focuses more on Scott's earlier exploits (especially in the *Discovery* Expedition), rather than on his unfortunate fate, which Sherriff characteristically handles with great delicacy:

> To quote passages from Scott's last diary is akin to hacking pieces from a perfect memorial. The diary must be read in its entirety: there is no more to say. Word by word it bares the character of a great man whose death now stands back from us by more than twenty years. They have been years that Scott would have lived with all the passionate energy of his nature. But a blizzard kept him from them – and a few miles of snow-clad wilderness.[67]

Going Global

The reception that *Journey's End* afforded in London and New York provoked a stampede from theatre managers, publishers and producers across the world. Before long, Curtis Brown was selling off the rights for countries throughout Europe and beyond: the German rights in February; the rights in Czechoslovakia, Scandinavia, Holland and Hungary in April; France in May; and the Far East in June. At the same time, Maurice Browne was arranging the sale of the touring rights in the UK. After he had returned from the United States he had been besieged by managers clamouring for the touring rights, but Clifford Hamilton urged him to tour the play himself, to retain more of the profit. Browne, however, growing weary of administration, offered to sell the rights to Hamilton, in a deal that Gwatkin characterised as overgenerous[68] (for which he blamed Browne's excessive reliance on Hamilton).

On Saturday, 4 May, *Journey's End* appeared on the European mainland for the first time – in Paris, in an English language production, performed by the English Players (under the direction of Nellie Van Volkenburg, with the co-operation of Maurice Browne Ltd). According to reports, 'hundreds of people'[69] had to be turned away from the premiere at the Theatre Albert I. The Players had been given permission to perform the English language version until 15 September (when they would have to give way to the producers of the French version of the play, *Le Grand Voyage*), but in the event they continued playing into October,[70] such was the demand for the play.

In July, at the same time as Hamilton was getting ready to set his touring parties loose on the English provinces, the Gilbert Miller organisation announced that its first touring company would hit the road in September, beginning in Indiana, and quickly moving on to Chicago, 'where it probably will stay for some time before continuing its wanderings.'[71] Two weeks later, the Canadian cast was being announced, with the intention of opening in Kingston, Ontario on the inauspicious date of Friday, 13 September, before moving on to play 'across the breadth of Canada and ... eventually in San Francisco and Los Angeles'.[72] Shortly afterwards, another British company set out on the steamer *Maldovia*, bound for Australia, New Zealand and South Africa.[73] On board were Reginald Tate (Colin Clive's understudy, later to become famous in the BBC's *Quatermass* serial) and up-and-comer Lewis Shaw (who had been a hit in *Young Woodley*).

Nor were they (and Jack Hawkins, of course) the only young actors to see the possibility in long runs of *Journey's End*. Auditions began in July for R.B. Salisbury's touring party to the Far East. Rejoicing in the name of 'The Quaints' (for reasons that have never been explained), these touring parties had been organised by Salisbury for several years. While on tour they would perform a variety of plays, including Shakespeare, and musicals. On this occasion, they would also perform *Journey's End*. A young John Mills, just twenty-one, hoped to audition for the part of Raleigh (having admired Maurice Evans's performance in the role), but when he went to the auditions he was asked to read for the part of Hibbert instead, which he did, but rather badly. Just before stepping off the stage, however, some mutterings among the watching managers were concluded with the invitation for him to try the part of Raleigh after all. This he did, with some success, thus securing his spot on the tour. The mutterings had come from Sherriff himself, who had been passing the Prince of Wales theatre, where the auditions were taking place. Entering on a whim, he watched the audition, and turning to R.B. Salisbury said: 'What's that boy reading Hibbert for? He looks like the perfect Raleigh to me. If you haven't already cast the part, get him to read it.'[74]

The Quaints set off on 3 August, on a tour that would bring *Journey's End* to India, Burma, Malaya, Singapore, Ceylon (Sri Lanka), Hong Kong and China. While in Singapore for the second time, in March 1930, they would run across

Noel Coward, taking the long way back from the United States. He adopted the party as his own, and even volunteered to play Stanhope for three nights, which he did, although without conspicuous success. The trickiest moment was the occasion when, on one evening, he altered Stanhope's final exit, making him return to bend over Raleigh's body one last time. In doing so his helmet fell off on to poor John Mills, injuring him either in the face (according to critic Alexander Woollcott),[75] or in a more tender part of his anatomy (according to Mills himself,[76] who really ought to have known).[77]

As well as the outposts of Empire, the play soon spread throughout mainland Europe. Germany was first. Sherriff had sold the rights to the publishers Drei Masken Verlag back in February.[78] They had hoped to hire Remarque to translate, but he declined the opportunity, partly because he feared that, in revisiting the subject of the war, he ran the risk of replacing Sherriff's thoughts with his own.[79] Within a few weeks, however, they had settled on the German poet and playwright Hans Reisiger. He, in turn, must have moved pretty smartly, because before the end of April, one of the great men of German letters, Thomas Mann (who would receive the Nobel Prize later that year), had written to tell him how much he liked the play:

> It gave me such pleasure as one at my age seldom experiences after reading a book. ... What a splendid work it is, strong – without the slightest brutality or exaggeration. Its modesty, sincerity and manly human feeling really touched my heart. I can say that I have seldom, after reading a play, had such a longing to see it staged.[80]

Die Andere Seite (the German version of *Journey's End*) was premiered in Berlin, at the Deutsches Kunstler Theater, on 29 August. It was witnessed, from a stage box, by Sherriff himself – by now a free agent, having resigned from Sun Insurance in early July.[81] The Nationalists did not like it,[82] but otherwise the play received much the same reception as in its other triumphant first outings in London and New York: 'For a few moments after the curtain had fallen upon the collapsing dugout ... with Stanhope going out to certain death, there was complete silence. Then, as the curtain rose and the players appeared, loud and prolonged applause broke out.'[83] The curtain had to be raised over and over again, and 'in response to the insistent demands, the young English author at last came shyly forward, flushed, excited and trembling, to bow his thanks.'[84] Next day, the critics were kind, impressed by the play's 'tolerance, its impartiality, its simplicity and the complete absence of rancour'.[85] It lasted ten weeks in Berlin, and reportedly[86] made £1,000 profit for its producer, Dr Robert Klein.

By the time of the triumph in Berlin, The Quaints were already ashore in India, rehearsing for their opening performance in Calcutta on 4 September, and Clifford Hamilton's UK touring companies were well under way. The Northern Tour began in Lowestoft in July, and played in nineteen different locations before ending in Cambridge at the end of November. The Southern Tour began in Cardiff in August, remaining in Wales throughout the month, before moving south, playing a total of seventeen different towns and cities before ending in Oxford at the end of November. At the same time, one of Miller's touring companies had just taken up residence in Chicago as planned, while the Canadian tour had also begun.

Back in Europe, the next stop in Sherriff's own personal tour was Stockholm, for the premiere of *Resans Slut* (the Swedish translation of *Journey's End*) in Sweden on 19 September 1929, with Prince William and several members of the Nobel Prize Committee in attendance. This, it was claimed, was the first performance of the play in a neutral country. The reception was again rapturous, and after the performance Prince William received Sherriff and his mother in the Royal Box.[87] After Sweden, the final stop for Sherriff was in Paris, for the premiere of *Le Grand Voyage* (the French version) on 26 September at the Theatre Edouard VII. The play was translated by Virginia Vernon (an American living in Paris) and Lucien Besnard (who had written a war play of his own), and produced by Vernon and her husband Frank, a well-known theatrical producer. For the translation, the words of Alice in Wonderland were dropped, and replaced instead by quotes from *A Midsummer Night's Dream*, which was thought likely to have more meaning to the French. The play again received an ovation on the opening night; after the final curtain, Sherriff was called upon from the stage, he rose and bowed his acknowledgement of the crowd's applause. But the next morning the critics were not kind: 'Dull', 'slow', 'inartistic' and 'monotonous' were some of the verdicts, while the *Paris Soir* found the play 'as long drawn-out as the war itself'.[88] Sherriff, by contrast, was quoted in the French press as having thought 'the entire play was wonderfully done. I am delighted',[89] and playgoers seemed to agree with him, since *Le Grand Voyage* ran very successfully for nearly five months.

Still the play kept rippling out to new locations. The English Players, now denied Paris because of *Le Grand Voyage*, took themselves to various venues in Switzerland and around Germany (including a couple of stops in Berlin, despite *Die Andere Seite*), before becoming the first English actors to perform in Prague, and then Vienna. When they finished in Monte Carlo on 22 December they had held eighty performances in thirty-six European towns. Elsewhere in Europe, productions started up, in November, in Warsaw and Oslo (with the usual audience reaction in the latter – a stunned silence followed by enthusiastic cheering),[90] and in Finland in December (in seven theatres, supposedly).[91] Two more American tours went out in October and November – to play the southern States and larger cities that had not yet seen the play, notably Boston and Philadelphia. In Britain, after the first two tours came to an end in November, it was decided that the country could now handle three instead: Red (which took the play to Scotland for the first time); White (which took in Ireland for the first time); and Blue (twenty-three smaller towns, ending in Chatham in June).

A Pansy Aspect

'In November there will be over twenty companies playing *Journey's End* in various parts of the earth,' declared *The Era* in September. 'Australia, India, America and almost every country in Europe are included, and on matinee days the play will be spoken in every hour of the twenty-four.'[92] Even accepting the latter comment as some creative spinning, the play was now a worldwide phenomenon. It clearly fitted the Zeitgeist, and the global success of Remarque's *All Quiet on the Western Front* at the same time suggests that the public were now ready, after years of avoiding written representations of the war, to embrace the experience.

The play had extensive appeal, surprising some of the critics who felt that at least part of its success lay in aspects that were uniquely British, aspects that might not translate well to foreign productions. The American critic Richard Littell, for example, argued that: '*Journey's End* could not have been written by an American ... it is English, or British, through and through.'[93] Its Britishness would be expected to have great appeal in the outposts of the Empire, and indeed the reception there seems to have at least matched the reception at home. But how could those countries where the play was presented in another language connect with its 'Englishness'? Sidney Carroll suggested[94] that it was through the universalisation of the play: while watching *Le Grand Voyage* he came to recognise that the play he was watching was a world play, about a world war. 'Here is an attempt,' he wrote, 'to universalise a theme and popularise for foreign consumption a set of characters, the charm and artistry of whose original creations were peculiarly and exclusively English.'

Not all critics were enamoured of Sherriff's creation, however. Much of the play's success had come from its apparent verisimilitude, but this was doubted by some in the United States, who looked instead to their home-grown war play as a guide to what war was really like. *What Price Glory?* was written by an ex-Marine officer (Laurence Stallings) and a playwright who had not fought (Maxwell Anderson, who would go on to a long and storied theatrical career). It had first been produced on Broadway in 1924, and had run for a year, but had never travelled beyond the American shore.[95] The story concerned two Marine officers tangling over a woman in France, so in that sense it was more a play about two men during a war than it was about the war itself. It was much more of a boisterous, brawling play, with earthy dialogue, more robust characters, and a 'grand, cynical attitude toward the whole bloody mess'.[96] *Journey's End*, by contrast, was viewed as 'too gentlemanly',or, in the words of George Jean Nathan, a major voice in the American theatre (and well known as a contrarian):

> There is a humorously falsetto note to the [play] and ... the late war, as the author sees it, apparently needed only a butler to convert it into a polite drawing room comedy. ... I can't resist the impression that Mr Sherriff's military men have a faint, pansy aspect that proves just a trifle disturbing.[97]

He was dismissed by many at the time, and Bill Darlington, an ardent supporter of the play (and of his friend Bob Sherriff) was still manning the barricades fifteen years later, dismissing 'American critics, who never saw service in the first war and find the tough guys of *What Price Glory?* more like the civilian idea of a soldier'.[98]

Another who was unimpressed with the play was Sean O'Casey, who disliked it intensely, dismissing its 'false effrontery … which made of war a pleasant thing to see and feel … all the mighty, bloodied, vulgarity of war foreshortened into a pretty, pleasing picture'.[99] But O'Casey had not served in the war either, and he was probably sore not just about the relatively poor reaction to his own war play (*The Silver Tassie*, which ran at the Apollo from October to December 1929), but also by *Journey's End*'s adoption by the British theatrical establishment, including Agate and Coward, whom he despised. But in fact, the very gentleness that O'Casey sought to skewer – the lack of overly demonstrative theatricality – was seen by many as a positive virtue. Even Robert Sisk, who disliked the play, let out a sigh of relief: 'You will not, thanks to Heaven, find profanity in *Journey's End*.'[100]

Most voices on the play's authenticity chimed more with Darlington than Nathan and O'Casey, and emphasised in turn the link between that quality, and the play's universality: 'There can be no reason for not seeing [this play]. It vibrates with the lives of millions of men, whatever their nationality may be. … They are all soldiers in a few soldiers.'[101] The scale of the conflict also meant that a drama of civilian soldiers would be likely to have greater reach. 'It is a better play than *What Price Glory?*,' wrote Littell, 'because it represents war as the majority of the men knew it who fought in it. … *Journey's End* is the war after four years, the war of obedient civilians who grit their teeth, the war of a nearly exhausted nation, not the war of adventure and cognac and Mam'selles.'[102]

Ervine declared himself always willing to read or watch anything to do with the war, but felt that nothing 'composed in artistry' would be written 'until the memory of it has passed out of the painful experience of mankind.'[103] He did concede, however, that Sherriff's play had value as a 'photographic' account. Littell, too, felt that the passage of time since the war had been essential to the play's quality: 'Coming some ten years after the Armistice it is the greater for an impartial tenderness and restrained, hopeless sympathy which would have been hard to achieve just after the smoke and corpses had been cleared away.'[104]

On Armistice Day the *New York Times* carried an editorial in praise of their veterans:

> Our veterans of the war make no parade of what they did in it. … More excitable and sentimental French and German soldiers have written expansively of the terrible things they suffered. … Most of our men will not even talk of such matters. They took them as a dire necessity that had to be gone through without unmanly whimpering.

Alexander Woollcott, the well-known critic for *The New Yorker*, reacted with outrage, shocked that he should have lived to hear the *New York Times* implicitly dismiss *All Quiet* as 'unmanly whimpering'. *Journey's End*, he noted, 'fairly aches with the intolerable strain of four years of modern warfare' and in that lies 'a suggestive measure of the difference between our experience and England's'. Woollcott then listed all the capitals in which the play would be performed that evening, before noting how glad he was that his own country would see more performances of the play than any other, because it was 'needed more in a country which might thereby learn that it, too, never knew what the war was like.'[105]

Back in Britain, just after the first Savoy performance, a similar thought had been voiced by Sir Laming Worthington-Evans, the British Secretary for War, who remarked that 'every boy ought to be taken to see it to show them the things their fathers had come through in the Great War.'[106] Maybe *Journey's End* was such a success because people were at last ready to know more.

Movie Ills

While Sherriff was on his European 'tour', word was coming in about problems with the script for the *Journey's End* movie.

Neither Balcon nor Welsh had a studio in the UK that could make a 'talkie', so, after snapping up the rights, Balcon had gone to New York and made a deal with Tiffany-Stahl (a small producer) to produce the film in Hollywood under 'very stringent conditions'[107] (imposed by Balcon). Tiffany would take a 50 per cent interest in the film, while the two British companies would share the remainder. The task of scripting the film was initially handed to V. Gareth Gundry, an ex-army officer who had been a director for Gainsborough, but problems began to appear quite quickly. On 21 September, Peacock wrote to Sherriff that he had had a three-hour interview with Balcon and Welsh, and that he had read the 'final' scenario, which Whale had told him was 'terrible'. Gundry's passage to New York had been cancelled, and Whale was to be given a freer hand in the scenario, which he was to prepare in collaboration with a Tiffany-Stahl 'expert'. Peacock was confident that, with Whale in charge, 'things should be much easier … and a really good film possible.'[108]

At much the same time, George Pearson, of Pearson-Welsh (a highly experienced director in his own right) was asked to go out to Hollywood to 'supervise the filming by Whale, as yet with little experience in film technique, and to see that no distortion of Sherriff's work was attempted by America, for such would be angrily resented in England.'[109] He sailed for New York on 21 September, and would not return until the following April.

Sherriff had no further role to play in the movie, but he had plenty to keep him busy. He had begun to start looking around for a bigger house; he was still captain of Kingston Rowing Club, and was elected for a further term on 23 October[110]; and he had started work for Gollancz on a novelised version of the play. Since Sherriff had not written a novel at that point, Gollancz teamed him up with Vernon Bartlett, a well-known journalist, two years' Sherriff's senior, who had also seen service during the war, before being invalided out in 1915. He had worked for a number of papers, and also as Head of the London Office of the League of Nations. At this point he was working for the BBC, giving a weekly broadcast that had a big following.[111] He had published a book of short stories about the war, *Mud and Khaki*, and a novel about a wounded soldier at Ypres, entitled *No Man's Land*. He had also just published a novel called *Calf Love* – a coming-of-age tale set in East Prussia in 1912, which was well received. Bartlett would do the bulk of the novelisation,[112] but they went off on research trips together, and would meet regularly to discuss the progress of the work.

Armistice Week

Sherriff also had another, more pressing, work commitment, for he was reworking the *Journey's End* script for a very special radio event: the broadcasting of the play on Armistice Night. It would be heard in the United Kingdom, but would also be heard around the world through short-wave broadcasts, as well as in the United States and Canada, where it would be carried coast-to-coast by NBC stations.[113]

The reworking of the script focused mainly on adapting it for radio (making entrances and exits clearer, for example – or, as Sherriff put it, covering 'movement and business'). But there was another issue as well – whether the salty language of the play (mild to our ears, but seen as racy at the time) ought to be ameliorated before the broadcast. A BBC official explained:

> We have to consider, within reason, the most susceptible of our millions of listeners. There is a great deal of difference in producing a play at a theatre and in broadcasting it. In our case it goes right into the homes of the people and is heard by many persons who would not go to a theatre. It goes to the country parsonage, the cottage, to homes of every kind, old and young.[114]

After a bit of back and forth, and following rehearsals on the Friday before broadcast, Sherriff was able to reassure the press that:

> the play has not been touched except to cut out a few strong soldiers' words where it was felt that other words could be substituted. Where it was felt that the elimination of a word would destroy the meaning or realism of the play it has not been cut.[115]

The key concern was the word 'bloody',[116] which was permitted, as Sherriff noted: 'In the last big scene, in which Stanhope goes for the subaltern … there is no expression that could be substituted.'[117]

The play went out as planned at 9.05 pm on 11 November, to an estimated 3 million listeners.[118] It lasted one and three-quarter hours, uninterrupted, and was, for most people, a considerable success – 'a better broadcast play has not been sent over in our opinion. A splendid cast spoke their lines perfectly.'[119] But there were others who criticised the broadcast for lack of atmosphere, or for having been badly performed. Sherriff seemed inclined to agree with some of the criticisms,[120] suggesting that, as ever, he was willing to learn from his mistakes, to make sure things were done better next time. Radio would remain a medium he was anxious to conquer.

The broadcast was just one among a number of Armistice events of significance to Sherriff that week. The day before there had been a special performance of *Journey's End* at the Prince of Wales Theatre for holders of the Victoria Cross. At that point there were 467 of them, and 320 had attended a dinner at the House of Lords on the Saturday evening.[121] Later in the week, on Thursday, 14 November, the League of Nations Union would hold a Peace Commemoration dinner in the Guildhall in London, at which one of the highlights would be the auctioning off of the manuscript of *Journey's End*.

At the last minute, an extra appointment was added to Sherriff's already crowded calendar, for the King and Queen (along with the Duke and Duchess of York – (see Plate 17) would be attending the Thursday evening performance of *Journey's End*, and would like to meet the play's author. This posed a dilemma for Sherriff, who was already supposed to be formally presenting his manuscript to the auction winner the self-same evening. After some negotiations they managed to rearrange the dinner timetable to allow him to leave earlier than otherwise planned, but nevertheless he had to rush across town at breakneck speed in time to be presented to the Royal party during the first interval.[122] By the end of the night the manuscript had been bought for £1,500 by Sir Walter Lawrence, who promptly donated it back to the Imperial War Museum, and Sherriff had enjoyed the honour of meeting the King and Queen.

There were many who expected a knighthood to follow at the end of this extraordinary year, but perhaps surprisingly, given what an ambassador for the country *Journey's End* had proved to be, it never came. Maurice Browne suggests that he, however, *was* tapped on the shoulder, but felt the honour was misplaced:

An Eminent Intermediary called on me. *Journey's End* was a national possession; Certain Persons in High Places felt that it deserved a knighthood; the cottage in which Thomas Hardy had been born was about to be sold; its gift by me to the nation would doubtless be suitably recognised. I was ungracious enough to grow angry: if anyone were knighted, it must be Sherriff. The Eminent Intermediary changed the subject.[123]

Plagiarism

At the end of a roller-coaster year,[124] there was one final twist in store, when Sherriff's triumphant November was marred by an accusation of plagiarism. An American woman, Katherine Burke Sherman, who described herself as 'a writer of dramatic composition, short war stories and novelties for children',[125] filed suit in the New York District Court against Sherriff, Gilbert Miller, Maurice Browne and Brentano's (the American publisher of the play), charging that *Journey's End* had been plagiarised from her own three-act play, *Flags and Flowers*. She had written her own play in 1926, copyrighted it in July 1927, and then sent it to various producers, including 'one director very closely associated with Mr Gilbert Miller'. She alleged that the plot and all 'the essentials of drama' were stolen from her manuscript (which had never been produced). Furthermore, 'much of the dialogue and all of the plaintive, poignant sentiments' of Sherriff's play were 'snatched from hers', while the climax of *Journey's End* was very similar to the second act of her own play. She was asking for $200,000 in damages, as well as all the profits that had accrued from the performance and publication of the play.

Sherriff was taken aback by the lawsuit, but not entirely by the allegations, since they had also been made by Miss Burke Sherman in a pamphlet she had prepared and circulated to theatregoers outside the Henry Miller's Theatre in New York a couple of months earlier; a similar pamphlet had been circulated in the West End more recently. He had dismissed the allegations at the time: 'I am sorry if she thinks I copied her play, but, of course, I have never seen it or her, much less heard about it or her.'[126] Miss Burke Sherman had neither the funds – nor, by all accounts, a sufficiently compelling case – to engage a firm of lawyers, so she drew up her complaint herself. Despite its obvious lack of merit, Sherriff was forced to take it seriously, and instructed his American lawyers accordingly. The case was ultimately heard at the New York Southern District Court in October 1931, and dismissed when Sherriff provided documentary evidence of the source material for the play (his *Memories*), an early draft of it, and affidavits from readers and managers who testified that they had seen the manuscript long before Gilbert Miller had been involved. Given that she had no money, Sherriff would have to foot his lawyer's bill himself, to the tune of about $3,000.

But that was two years in the future. At Christmas 1929, even with the plagiarism case looming over him, Sherriff must have been astonished at the year he had enjoyed. Certainly, there had been bumps along the road – the abortive Scott play and the squabble over the movie rights in particular. But he could still sit back and enjoy the fruits of a remarkable success – millions of people across the world had gone to see his play, and they were buying hundreds of thousands of copies of it, in all sorts of languages. When he totalled up, in his cash book,[127] the amount of money he had made from *Journey's End* that year, it came to the astonishing figure of £41,184 13s 8d – or 129 *years'* worth of his previous salary.

He had invested much of it – and owing to good advice, the investments had largely withstood the impact of the Wall Street Crash at the end of October. The play was still running in London and New York, and the touring companies were criss-crossing the globe even as new ones were setting out. The movie was in the works, in James Whale's capable hands, and the novel was well under way. The future looked secure. But he had given up his job to become a writer, and as such there was one thought still nagging at the back of his mind: was he a one-play-man? The time would soon come when he would have to pick up his pencil and find out.

Chapter 6

What Next? 1930–31

Speak both in the senate and to every man, whoever he may be, appropriately, not with any affection: use plain discourse.

Marcus Aurelius, *The Meditations*, Book VIII.

In November 1929,[1] Maurice Browne had allowed Colin Clive to go to Hollywood to act the part of Stanhope in the *Journey's End* talkie, on the condition that he was back by 13 January – a week before the first anniversary performance.[2] According to Sherriff, with Clive's departure the play's 'spell was broken'[3]: Clive was the person who had made the role his own – he was the one everyone wanted to see – and so the box office began to slip when he was no longer there.

Ticket sales certainly fell during Clive's absence – but they had already started to fall off a little before he left, and the fact that they did not rise after his return suggests that the play had begun to run its course. Receipts had also fallen at the Henry Miller's Theatre, and rather more steeply than in London.[4] But the numbers were bound to drop at some point. *Journey's End* had already been serialised in newspapers and broadcast on the radio, and with so many touring companies taking the play to new cities, it was no longer necessary to travel to London or New York to enjoy a performance. Nevertheless, both London and New York shows would continue for some months to come, because profits were still there for the taking.

In Hollywood, the *Journey's End* movie was making progress. Colin Clive had arrived in the United States on Thanksgiving (28 November) and gone straight to work with the rest of the company.[5] The others had been in rehearsals for a week and a half by then, and Clive had to work hard to fit in. He set to, working six days a week until his last scenes were shot on 30 December, whereupon he returned to England. There were a few further interior scenes to be shot, and five days' worth of exterior shooting, which was disrupted by bad weather, but eventually the film wrapped on 22 January, some three weeks behind schedule. After that, just the editing remained, but as Whale was a slow editor, it would be several more weeks before it was ready to be screened.[6]

Meanwhile, the collaboration with Vernon Bartlett was going well. Bartlett was still doing most of the work, but he and Sherriff met regularly, and travelled around the locations that would be featured in the book, to ensure their authenticity.[7] Bartlett came to appreciate Sherriff's qualities, describing him as a 'young man who was incredibly little affected by the sudden acquisition of a handsome fortune and world fame'. He noticed in particular the 'instinctive' empathy and understanding Sherriff had for ordinary people. The only man he had ever met, he later wrote, who 'seems to have the same instinct for understanding the little people about him to the same degree' was Adolf Hitler, although he observed wryly that the two had made very different uses of that particular talent.

A Special Matinee

On 21 January 1930, Maurice Browne held a party to mark the play's first anniversary; Herbert noted in his diary that Bob went with his mother.[8] A few days later, on 25 January, Herbert described another event in his usual matter-of-fact fashion: 'Bob to dinner of the 9th East Surreys. He stood 140 of them to *Journey's End* performance at the Prince of Wales theatre.'

This was his second reunion since the success of *Journey's End*. The previous year he had been toasted alongside Gilbert Frankau,[9] as two men who had immortalised the Battalion's activities in fiction. Now, at the beginning of 1930, the men of his old regiment were to be his guests at a special matinee performance of *Journey's End* at the Prince of Wales Theatre. The *Surrey Comet* reported on the proceedings at the theatre,[10] which 136 men had attended, noting that, afterwards:

> Mr Sherriff gathered a few of the party together and conducted them 'behind the scenes' and explained the various 'gadgets' used for producing the sound 'effects'. ... Some of the party found their way to the stage, where the dugout scene of the play became an appropriate place for a flashlight photograph of the group [see Plate 19].

Featured in the photo were: 'Jimbo' Webb; Lechmere Thomas ('Tommy the Bomber', who had won an MC – along with Harry Lindsay – in the raid upon which the *Journey's End* raid was based); Godfrey Warre-Dymond, the much-admired commander of 'C' Company; and Nobby Clark, adjutant when Sherriff first arrived at the battalion, who had fought alongside Warre-Dymond in March 1918, when both were taken prisoner.[11]

Also pictured on the stage, but standing rather shyly at the back, was Sherriff. Compared to the others, his wartime experience had been relatively brief, and he must have been acutely conscious of the nervous agonies he had suffered in France, agonies so astutely captured in the character of Hibbert. He had made much of the fact that his play was based on his real-life experiences, and its authenticity was the very thing that had helped the play become a worldwide phenomenon. So he must have anticipated that, at some point during the day, the conversation would turn to the question of the real-life soldiers on whom Sherriff's play was based. Sure enough, as the *Comet* reported: 'Many of those present tried to solve the question whether the characters in the play had their counterpart in former members of the battalion.' But Sherriff was ready for them: 'although a few had rather definite opinions, the playwright would not satisfy them and remained non-committal.'

Sherriff had rather hedged his bets on whether the characters were based on specific individuals. Before the Savoy production, there was this: '*Journey's End* is absolute realism: even my characters are composite portraits.'[12] A couple of weeks later, this line had changed – now the characters were more like broad types[13]:

> My play shows the effect of the strain on different types of men. The characters in the play are not actually drawn from life. They are an admixture of perhaps half a dozen different men of various types that one saw out there – the ex-ranker, the imaginative man, the schoolboy idealist, the second-in-command.

A year further on and he had decided that he had been more influenced by people he had met after the war: '[The play] sprang not so much from the war as from my association with the post-war generation with whom I resumed rowing and football and who brought to me a fresh outlook. Subconsciously perhaps I wanted to perpetuate the memory of the men I'd known.'[14]

This view was refined again a couple of years later: 'With one exception, the fellows I drew were those I met every day in the office and on the river, and in the street. The other fellows I did not remember clearly – except Osborne.'[15]

In fact, for all of Sherriff's hedging, there seems little doubt that the characters were composites, based firmly on people he knew. Starting with Osborne – whom, at least, he acknowledged as being based on a real person – it is quite clear that he embodies characteristics of both Douglass and Percy High. Raleigh is an easy figure to place too – and there is no need to worry about any composite. His experiences of coming to the line are those described by Sherriff in his own diaries, right down to the winding path that he takes to get to the trench. Sherriff is also, undoubtedly, the major source for Hibbert as well, which is a likely reason for why he is so coy about identifying source characters.

It is noteworthy that, in outlining the 'admixtures' of characters, he clearly identifies the characteristics of Raleigh (the schoolboy idealist); Trotter (the ranker); and Osborne (the second-in-command); but then refers only to 'the imaginative man' (referring, one presumes, to Hibbert). It was his imagination, it will be recalled, that he felt to be the cause of his anxieties: even when he was in the relative safety of the Tunnelling Company he found it easy to envisage imminent perils. This comment is certainly the closest he ever came to (inadvertently) identifying himself as Hibbert. In the play itself, the arguments that Stanhope uses to convince Hibbert to 'stand-in' with the others, are reminiscent of the arguments that Sherriff deployed on himself on the walk back from the local village nearly thirteen years earlier[16]; Sherriff also cautioned himself against 'worming out', using the same form of words that Stanhope uses to describe Hibbert, and the whining tone of Hibbert in the play is a clear echo of the complaints about neuralgia in Sherriff's letters. There seems little doubt that Sherriff's convincing portrayals of Hibbert (and Raleigh) come from him having intimately shared those emotions, which would be reason enough for him to want to avoid any close examination of the source of those 'admixtures'.

That leaves just two officers – Trotter and Stanhope. Most comments on the model for Trotter focus on the stout figure of Trenchard in the Bully Grenay photo (see Plate 8), but Trenchard and Sherriff spent only four weeks together in France (although they served together in Dover after they were invalided home). He had been a stockman, living in Australia before the war, and he had not been a ranker – so besides his physique there is little of the Trotter in him. The one ranker who did feature in Sherriff's life, and who had a pattern of speech akin to Trotter's,[17] was Nobby Clark – although, of course, he was of a higher rank than Trotter, and in better shape.[18]

As to Stanhope – in his heroism (and in Raleigh's hero-worship of him) it is hard not to see Godfrey Warre-Dymond.[19] There is no doubt that Sherriff found his company commander a heroic figure; his praise for his efforts in twice restoring the fortunes of 'C' Company (see pages 40–41) is proof of that.[20] Warre-Dymond's obituary in the *Journal* of the East Surrey Regiment also carried the line that, because Sherriff had served under him as a subaltern, he 'had some claim to have been the original Stanhope of the play.'[21] But Warre-Dymond was a little bit older than Stanhope, and had not joined from school. Furthermore, there is absolutely no suggestion that he drank in anything like the quantities that Stanhope did (although he was 'a great fellow for producing good dinners', as Nobby Clark remembered affectionately a few years later).[22] Tetley was another company commander whom Sherriff much admired, and although there is clearly no correspondence between a 29-year-old barrister and Stanhope, there may have been one or two aspects of his behaviour that worked their way into Sherriff's portrayal of a company CO (a rather abrupt manner when provoked, for example). It has also been suggested that a possible source for Stanhope's war weariness may well have been Hilton, Sherriff's first company commander, who had already been in France for eighteen months by the time Sherriff arrived, and was still serving at the Armistice.[23]

A Novel Approach

In January 1930, there was a flurry of press interest[24] in Sherriff's proposed follow-up to *Journey's End*, but he was much too busy to make any real progress. He was inundated with correspondence, and had also been working on the novel, so that the *Era* could report, 'The proofs of the novel have now been passed by R.C. Sherriff and his collaborator Vernon Bartlett, and it will be out early in March. Victor Gollancz told me when we met a short time ago that it exceeded his expectations.'[25]

The novel is in two sections, the second of which is a more-or-less faithful version of the play. The first section provides the youthful backstories of Stanhope, Raleigh and Madge. It begins with the 10-year-old Dennis arriving at Dr Raleigh's house in Alum Green one summer (when Madge is about eleven, and Jimmy about eight), and the first few chapters show their subsequent development. Midway through the first section the war begins while Dennis is at Sandhurst, and when he finally goes to France in June of 1915, Madge comes up to London from Bournemouth (where she's working as a nurse) so they can have a day together before he leaves. They drift around aimlessly a little, until they finally part with the rather corny lines: Madge: 'My dear, I love you. Come back safe'; to which Dennis replies: 'Rather! Good-bye darling!' We see Dennis's growing disillusion on his leave home in June 1917 (when he goes to Barford but is disappointed by Jimmy's ardency for war, and by his old masters' desire to interrogate him about it), and from the fact that he opts to pass a subsequent leave in Paris rather than going home. Madge is meanwhile working in the hospital kitchens temporarily, having come back from working in France because of a breakdown. Jimmy joins up and is eventually sent to France, where, having spoken to his Uncle Vincent (General Raleigh), he is sent to Stanhope's unit.

Thereafter, the course of the book is set by the course of the play, albeit with some cuts and additions, designed to illuminate the characters a little more. Trotter and Raleigh, for example, have an extended sequence in the trench together, where Raleigh realises how dissimilar they are, yet observes how well they get on together. Osborne, too, is given a few pages of exposition, seated, unobserved, behind the trench, contemplating the forthcoming raid. He thinks of his sons, and his wife, Joan: 'So many women found almost hysterical comfort in the thought that their sons or husbands had died while fighting for their country. But she was too clear-headed to be consoled by this manifestation of mob psychology.'[26] The two sentences nicely sum up Osborne's wife, while bathing the home front in a rather satirical light. There is a similarly satirical passage when Stanhope is in Barford, contemplating the war, 'this holy crusade of Right against Wrong, this campaign … to starve every German child.'[27] These passages are much more suggestive of Bartlett's influence than Sherriff's, but when Osborne stoops before going back in the dugout to pick a scarlet pimpernel to put in the letter he has written to his wife, it is pure Sherriff.

Some of the more interesting exposition relates to Hibbert, who is given the backstory of having come from a military family, but never having had the inclination to follow that career. He is described, at one point, as having a 'girlish' face, and Trotter dismisses him to Raleigh as 'a bit windy'. On the other hand, his outburst against Stanhope – his absolute determination to leave the dugout and go sick – is given some context, by occurring after he hears himself dismissed by Stanhope to the colonel as 'not the man' for the raid: while he is terrified at the thought of being chosen, he equally cannot stand the shame of being rejected in favour of Raleigh. All in all, Hibbert comes out of the book rather better than out of the play – but that may have been Sherriff's intention. In a timetable of the three and a half days 'C' Company are in the line,[28] he highlights a moment on the Tuesday morning (2.00

am) when Hibbert is on duty alone, having relieved Osborne. Sherriff asks: 'Would this make a chapter? Sympathetic description of H's fears might enlighten many who have misunderstood Hibbert in the play.'[29] The invention of a breakdown for Madge may also have been designed to solicit sympathy with the nerve-damaged.

One final scene warrants mention: the section just before the raid, where we see events unfolding from the German point of view. The chapter (XXII) begins with Ernst Scheffer in the German dugout, giving up the ribbons with which his daughter Gretel had tied up her birthday present to him – ribbons that would shortly be tied to the barbed wire to indicate the gaps down which the machine gunners should aim when the British came. No peacenik, Ernst hates the British because they are trying to kill him, because their conditions are better, because they are responsible for the shortages from which Gretel and his wife suffer at home, and because they are stopping him from joining them. He hopes that a couple might get through the gaps before dying in the trench, so he can steal their boots. In just a few pages he is deftly humanised.

The book was serialised in *Answers* magazine, beginning on 22 February ('The Year's Biggest Book'),[30] and was then published by Gollancz on 10 March. It received generally glowing reviews. 'So far as such a drama can be turned into a novel,' declared *Reynolds*, 'this book has been well done.'[31] *The Sketch* describes the first section as 'an excellent picture of youth and adolescence, and a lively narrative', before going on to commend the novel as 'having few blemishes'.[32] *The Irish Statesman*, in an article focusing on war books, felt that, in the novel, 'the character and outlook of the play are most adroitly retained'; the reviewer was relieved, as well, to be spared the 'harrowing details of the trenches and no-man's-land'.[33] Similar opinions were to be found in most of the major newspapers and magazines (it is 'gentler than many war books', noted *John O'London's*[34]; it is done with 'an admirable quietness and simplicity'[35] sighs *The Times*, in relief).

There was, however, one notable dissenter: Richard Aldington in *Referee* announced combatively that this was 'A War Book I Dislike',[36] and he proceeded to pound the book with all he had. Aldington was an imagist poet, four years older than Sherriff, who had joined the Army in 1916, and was wounded while in the Royal Sussex Regiment in 1917. He became a prolific writer and critic, eventually leaving poetry behind and moving on to novels (including a war novel, *Death of a Hero*) and biographies. In his review he began by admitting that he had been moved by the play – impressed by the accuracy of its setting and its obvious sympathy for 'the sufferings of the very young men'. But he had disliked its 'public school snobbery'; its 'gentlemanly officers in a gentlemanly war'; and its dismissal of the feelings of the 'vulgarians' (Mason and Trotter). Having said that, he then launched into the book:

> the novel – my hat, the novel! I should like to propose a public vote of censure
> on Mr Vernon Bartlett for writing such stuff ... there is nothing in this book

but unspeakable tripe, except for the dialogue taken from Mr Sherriff's play. ...
This novel is a panegyric of stupidity and ball-pursuing morons.

He hates the Stanhope-Madge goodbye sequence (for which it is hard to criticise him); he hates the public school sentiments; he hates what he sees as the implicit snobbery. On and on he goes, barely stopping for breath.

He also objected to what he had read in the pre-publicity: 'Thirty thousand copies before publication' – 'God pity England', he had written. But it was true. By Sherriff's reckoning, 28,000 sales in 1930, followed by another 6,000 in 1931 – and that was just in the UK. There were also the United States copies (published by Stokes). Not a patch on the money he earned from the play, of course, but worth another £800 in royalties.

Rosebriars

Over the preceding few months, while he was working on the novelisation of the play and the follow-up to *Journey's End*, Sherriff had been quietly focused on another event that would prove of great significance to him throughout the rest of his life: the purchase of a new house:

> Not far from where we lived the woodlands and open fields began. It was lovely country where people had built fine houses with enchanting gardens. We used to go that way for bicycle rides in days gone by, and look through wrought-iron gates at spacious lawns and rose gardens. On hot summer days we would catch the scent of heliotrope and honeysuckle, and I would go home to our old shabby house with the railway embankment at the end of the garden, and think enviously of those lucky people who lived in that fairyland. When *Journey's End* brought our dreams miraculously within reach, I set my heart on having one of those fine houses.[37]

Sherriff recalled that they had come across Rosebriars when driving home one evening, and that they took a chance on it, even though it had not been on the list of properties the agent had given them. They found out that the house was owned by an old couple who were thinking of moving to a smaller property, and were willing to sell to someone who would keep the house and garden together, and not sell it off piecemeal. Sherriff and his mother reassured them on that point, and so the sale went ahead – at a price of £6,500. The old couple of whom Sherriff wrote were the Nisbets – William and Ellen – in their seventies and sixties respectively, and married for nearly forty years. They had lived at the house for over ten years, having moved there after their children had left, but William died at the end of 1929, whether before or after the house was put up for sale is unknown.

Sherriff and his mother moved out of Rossendale, the family home, on 1 April 1930, prompting this reflection from Herbert in his diary:

> Bob and Connie finally left home for their new house at Esher – 'Rosebriars' – so family partly broken up after thirty-eight years here – not very nice to think of, but housekeeper Mrs Wright however seems a very capable person and cooks well so Bundy ought to be satisfied.[38]

Sherriff's brother Bundy had been back in England since October 1929. He had been out of the picture through much of the 1920s, moving to Calcutta in 1923 to take up a job in insurance. He had met his future wife, Hazel Leicester, in India, and she joined him in England in June 1930. They were married three months later, after which they moved into Rossendale with Herbert and the capable Mrs Wright. Bundy's return (and Hazel's anticipated arrival) may well have been the catalyst that sent Bob searching for somewhere bigger.

Sherriff is very coy about the decision he and his mother made to move out of the family home. Given the riches he had amassed from *Journey's End*, it is not surprising that he might want to move to a bigger house. The odd part is his decision to move with his mother and no one else. Connie had long had a stake in Bob – all the way back to those weekends when she travelled to Romford to visit him in the Artists Rifles. She had been a strong believer in his theatrical ambitions, and had been in attendance at all his premieres, including those in Europe. In an interview published in *The Times of India*[39] just a month before the move she said she had 'cherished a secret desire that my son should write' and she described how she had encouraged him in his efforts. If he was intending to move house, it was highly unlikely that she would let herself be left behind. In later years, it was observed by a friend of James Whale's that '[Sherriff] was very much under the thumb – fist – of his mother,'[40] and her domineering influence has also been noted by his godson, Chris Manning-Press: 'My father ... said Bob could not do anything without his mother's permission.'[41]

Accepting, then, that, if he was moving, she certainly was as well, the question remains as to why Herbert chose to stay at Rossendale. It is possible, of course, that he was not invited – possible but unlikely. Sherriff was unfailingly polite, and generally did everything he could to avoid conflict. It would have been out of character for him to invite only his mother and risk a fracture with his father, with whom he was on good terms. Rather, it is likelier that Herbert was invited, but that his pride led him to decline. Herbert had seen himself supplanted – massively – by his son. Bundy had noted Herbert's discomfort at Bob's wealth,[42] and it may have been more than he could bear to live in his son's house rather than stand on his own feet. He had been greatly excited when he finally bought Rossendale in 1906 (after having rented it for the previous fourteen years),[43] and perhaps, like Tom Spooner in Bob's 1934 play *Windfall*, he felt his pride grow as each year he paid down the mortgage and more and more of the house belonged to him.[44] He was very much a Victorian figure – fourteen years older than Connie – and his position and status as a middle-class office worker had been of great importance to him. That status had already been dented by his retirement, but he nevertheless had enough of a pension to maintain his house and wife: passing the burden of support to his son would have left him with even less of a purpose than he already had.

Bob's throwaway comment years later – about his father's advice about sticking with the firm and earning a pension for life (see page 106) – was a gentle tease but it revealed a fundamental difference between father and son. Herbert was happy to be a plodder, creeping inch by inch across the office floor over the years (see page 12), but Bob, although modest and unassuming, was willing to take a leap into the unknown: he had been doing so ever since he first formed The Adventurers. He could take a chance on the new house; Herbert could not.

There is no sign that the move caused any rift in the family. Herbert was obviously saddened by their departure, but he does not seem to have been upset beyond that. A couple of days before the move he went over to take a look and reacted very favourably: 'Sunday, 30 March: Bob took me over in his car to his new house, "Rosebriars" at Esher – magnificent gardens and grounds all beautifully kept and as interesting as Hampton Court Gardens. House also quite picturesque sort, and fine rooms.'[45] After the move there was a steady stream of Sherriff family visitors – Herbert recorded that Bundy, Beryl, Tudor (Beryl's husband) and he had all made the short trip to Esher in the weeks that followed.

Connie had long been more important to Bob than Herbert, and that would only increase in the years ahead. Once she moved in with him, he took her on almost every extended trip with him – certainly to Hollywood each time he went, and also to Oxford when he went to study there.[46] Herbert, by contrast, never went with him, although this may also have been due to the stroke that he suffered on 27 October 1931, not long after Connie and Bob departed for Oxford. A few years later, Rossendale was sold and Herbert, Bundy and Hazel moved into a new home quite nearby, which Bob had bought for them. Herbert lived there until he died in 1940, although he still did his best to provide for Connie's future, by leaving to her the proceeds of the sale of his beloved Rossendale.

Journey's End on Screen

About the time when Sherriff was closing on the purchase of Rosebriars, things were beginning to move with the new play. Sherriff told Peacock that he had been having discussions with Maurice Browne about it – where and when it might be produced, and whether it might be directed by James Whale, who was due back in England soon, to coincide with the premiere of the *Journey's End* movie.

The film had opened in New York on 8 April, at the Gaiety Theatre, and 'a seemingly stunned audience remained seated and inarticulate for a full minute after the picture had been completed and the lights had been turned up.'[47] Six days later – just enough time for Whale to cross the Atlantic and arrive in London – the film opened at the Tivoli cinema in the Strand. 'As good as, if not better than, it was as a play,' reckoned *The Star*, praising Whale for the fact that, where he opened out the play, he did it in a way that 'for the most part enhances the effect'[48] (notably in the raid scene). Sydney Carroll, in *The Sunday Times*, called it 'a triumph … technically first class, emotionally effective, dramatically powerful'.[49] Like many others, he celebrated the fact that the film, although made in Hollywood, was the product of a British studio, made almost entirely with British talent, including acting,[50] direction (Whale) and production (Pearson). Sherriff's contribution to the launch consisted of little more than supportive quotes and stories.

In its review, the cinema magazine *Bioscope* characterised the film as 'a triumph [that] cannot fail to break down any barriers which may operate reasonably against British films in the markets of the world'.[51] Unfortunately, that did not last long. The film was demolished at the box office just a couple of months later by *All Quiet on the Western Front*, which was seen as much more innovative, modern and dynamic than the rather stagey *Journey's End*. But the latter has actually held up remarkably well with time, and is well worth seeking out, for the performance of Colin Clive if nothing else. His Stanhope is a more tortured, snarling, self-pitying and bullying character than is typically seen in more modern versions of the play; yet despite the many faults that he shows us in Stanhope, we sympathise deeply with the young boy whom the war has so affected.

Settled in Rosebriars with his mother, with the movie launched and Whale back in town, it was time to focus on the new play. First the theatre had to be agreed with Maurice Browne, and then they had to think about the cast. Names were already being floated – Horace Hodges prominently among them. Hodges was a popular and highly experienced actor who would be perfect as the old and rather stuffy doctor – one of the key characters in the play – and having him on board was bound to generate valuable publicity, as would the fact that the Sherriff-Whale-Browne axis was back in business. The contract between Sherriff and Browne was settled relatively smoothly, although it is worth noting that Sherriff took some care in the assigning of the movie rights, reserving the sale of the rights to himself, with Maurice Browne to receive 40 per cent of the sale proceeds (it would be 'absurd', wrote Sherriff, to give him more than he had enjoyed with *Journey's End*).[52] Soon it was announced that *Journey's End* was coming off at the Prince of Wales Theatre on 7 June, and the new play would open there just five days later.

The final performance of *Journey's End* 'pulled the heartstrings':

Many of the audience in the stalls and dress circle had been at the first performance by the Stage Society and had come to say goodbye.... At the end the actors were called in front of the curtain and the audience stood up and cheered them. Colin Clive made a little speech of thanks, and it was over. There was a farewell party behind the curtain when the audience had gone. Maurice Browne made a speech, broke down and wiped the tears away. We were all close to tears, and I was glad when it was over.[53]

By the Monday morning the *Journey's End* signs had come down, the set had been packed away, and the 'dressing rooms were hung with cricket blazers and white flannels.' Outside, the men were putting up the signs for the new play: *Badger's Green*.

Badger's Green

The play is a reworked version of *Mr Birdie's Finger* – a comedy of village life, in which two important men in the village, originally arch-rivals, are brought together in their attempts to prevent the village being transformed by development. They succeed by enrolling the developer in the village cricket team, and by having him play in the match against their local opponents, delay his return to London to the meeting that will decide whether the development goes ahead. The two local rivals are again the doctor and the major – although their surnames are changed, as is the name of the developer (now Mr Butler) and the poor unfortunate whose finger is damaged by his fretwork (now Mr Twigg). The basic three-act structure is left intact, and the passage of time during the play is not altered.

The addition of a couple of female characters (the doctor's and major's wives) may suggest that Sherriff was keen to show he could inhabit his plays with women. Curiously, though, the changes from the earlier play actually diminish the importance of women in the play in general. In *Mr Birdie's Finger*, the developer's daughter (Joan) is shown as a very capable woman, and it is her sparring with Dickie (the doctor's son) that drives forward the plotting and counter-plotting. In *Badger's Green*, by contrast, the developer's secretary is not deemed worthy even of a name (she is 'The Girl' in the script), and the only exchanges she has are a little mild flirtation with first Mr Twigg and then Dickie.[54] The doctor's and major's wives have even less to do, other than annoy their husbands by being too solicitous of Twigg's welfare. Sherriff later acknowledged that he might not have put them to best use: 'There were women in the play, but, as a critic pointed out, they only came in to bring things to the men.'[55] By contrast, he expanded the role of the maidservant and gave her opinions and observations rather than being used more as a mobile prop; and she, at least, was given a name – Mary.

If the structure of the play is not too different, the tone is changed. The sparring between the doctor and the major becomes harder-edged in *Badger's Green*, and their dismissal of Mr Twigg and his efforts carries much more of the bully's swagger than in the earlier play. They are also rather brusquely dismissive of the pleas from the landlord of the local hotel (who argues that development will be of economic benefit to him and the other tradesmen in the village). As if to counter the more acerbic exchanges, Sherriff leavens the play with more slapstick, which is very effectively done. He also attempts to bring the cricket match on to the stage, by locating the whole of the last act in a village marquee that has an opening that allows us to see at least partly to the field beyond. The revision undoubtedly helps bring the action closer to the audience.

On the play's first night Sherriff was very hopeful. The cast was a good one and the rehearsals:

> were a joy. The play was built for comedy, and the cast squeezed every ounce of humour from it. They went out of their way to tell me how much they liked it: it was so different, they said, from anything at present on the West End stage. ... Blue skies and sunlight surrounded us.[56]

The first night was 'a glittering occasion', when, of course, literary London turned out to see whether Sherriff could hit the bull's-eye again. The applause from the audience at the end of the play suggested he had.

The press agreed. The next morning, the papers were almost unanimous in their opinion that Sherriff was not just a 'one-play man'. They all accepted, of course, that it was 'Not Another *Journey's End*' (in fact, Hannan Swaffer even underlined the 'Not')[57] – but this was seen to be something in its favour. They were almost unanimous, as well, in praising the play's characterisation and its observation, and celebrating its humour, although there were mutterings about its construction – even from those who, like Bill Darlington in *The Telegraph*, felt that the first act was 'brilliant'.[58] Nor were they happy with the female characters: 'Mr Sherriff is a very acute observer of men. He has either lacked the opportunity to observe women, or does not think them worth observing, for his women are just dummies.'[59] Nevertheless, the overwhelming impression was one of support for the play. In fact, so extensive was the praise that the reviewer for *Vogue*[60] felt compelled to remark upon it: noting that he himself had found it 'a sorry piece of work', he complained that 'among a score of criticisms I found only one to agree with me. The verdict of the press was emphatically favourable.' Sherriff told the *Daily Mail*[61] that:

> There was a time when I feared that the success of *Journey's End* might prove fatal to me in the future. Now I am contented because it has been acknowledged that I am not a one-play man. ... One or two critics have said that it is not another *Journey's End*; well, I never intended it to be.

All of which makes it difficult to understand why, in *No Leading Lady*, he gave the opposite account, describing the press as having been largely hostile. He begins with Hannan Swaffer's review, but misquotes it, and then, after conceding that a few reviewers had liked the play, he concludes that 'they were voices crying in the wilderness.'[62] He also mentions a review that began 'Poor Mr Sherriff!', as though it then went on to castigate the play as an unmitigated disaster; but that review[63] actually praises the play, and uses the phrase ironically, suggesting that the audience had come intending to see him fail, but, 'Sherriff thoroughly disappointed his loyal public by writing a very good play indeed. The next morning we read in a hundred papers, "Not another *Journey's End*". Well, who wants another anyway?'

Quite why Sherriff should have so completely misrepresented the press is not clear. It may just reflect his normal preference for a satisfying dramatic arc in his autobiography. Alternatively, it may be his way of trying to explain away the failure of the play – and it was a failure. Despite the glowing reviews the public just didn't turn out. The Prince of Wales Theatre was taking in almost £300 per performance when *Journey's End* was at its peak, but the very best it recorded for *Badger's Green* was the £192 on opening night, while it fell to less than £50 on average in each of the next ten performances.[64] Things got so bad that the cast took a 40 per cent pay cut, and Sherriff, summoned by telegram[65] from Henley to hear Maurice Browne address the company, agreed to hand back his £250 advance and forego his future royalties. But still the crowds stayed away and losses mounted to a total of over £4,000. Not even a broadcast of an extract on the BBC[66] could do anything to stop the slide. On 11 July, the papers carried the announcement that *Badger's Green* would close the following day.

The columnist for *Vogue* spent some time wondering why Sherriff's play should have failed when the press had given it such a fair wind, and concluded that the problem was that the public were not yet ready for the author of *Journey's End* to write a play that was not about the war.[67] For the same reason, people had been disinclined to attend an 'Ibsenesque' Barrie play, when what they expected from him was something more 'fantastical'; and they stayed away in droves from a 'musical play' by Edgar Wallace. *The Morning Post*, however, had a more prosaic explanation:

> Within three weeks, nearly twenty plays will have disappeared from the West End. Managers are inclined to the view that the slump is purely seasonal, and that London is rapidly returning to the pre-war custom when most of the theatres were closed in July.[68]

Maybe the 'blue skies and sunlight' were against it from the beginning.

Picture Work

After the play was taken off, Sherriff began to turn his mind to his other work again, writing to Walter Peacock that: 'I must settle down in earnest to new work which I am keen on doing. In the front of this is picture work.'[69] This had been on his mind ever since receiving a letter back in April from Universal Films, 'apparently suggesting I write a scenario for them.'[70] In fact, he had received several previous letters, from Universal,[71] and from others – including Samuel Goldwyn (who had offered him $1,000 a week for two months),[72] and the Fox Film Company.[73] He had declined in every case, but now he was beginning to think that he should be more receptive to their offers.

He told Peacock that he had been very impressed with *All Quiet*, which made him think that 'Universal seem to be good people to work with'.[74] But Whale had also written to him telling him that Tiffany were interested in a deal. He had begun mulling over ideas for scenarios, but was cautious of offering too much, preferring to develop the ideas as plays in the first instance. But within a few weeks, probably due to Peacock's assiduous representation, he was being approached by Percy Burton, a reader for Warner Brothers, who was keen to hear some scenario ideas, and was wondering whether Sherriff would be willing to come to Hollywood in December to develop them.[75] Sherriff promptly sent five different story ideas to Peacock, and let him know that he would be willing to go out to Hollywood if it was felt necessary – perhaps two months, including travel – but that December was much too early. January, on the other hand, would be fine.[76] The exact nature of the story ideas is unknown, but what is clear is that, just a week later, Sherriff had begun writing an extended scenario that he hoped would be of interest to the studios. That scenario was a sequel to *Journey's End*.

Journey's Other End

Sherriff never attached a title to his sequel, but he wrote a short story in 1932 about Trotter's return to no-man's-land, which he entitled *Journey's Other End*[77] – so that will suffice as a title for our purposes.

The story begins at the end of *Journey's End*, with the German attack. The Germans, as Stanhope feared, have pushed through the companies to their left and right, and open up their fire on the fifty men of the beleaguered 'C' Company from the rear. Their numbers dwindle rapidly, and next morning the Germans seek their surrender, but the wounded Stanhope refuses, leading his men in a madcap assault: 'It is soon over,' and only Stanhope and Trotter are left. The next scene, with Trotter and Stanhope as prisoners, is beautifully written – poignant and touching[78]: 'This is where we say goodbye to the Very Lights,' says Trotter, 'Goodbye to the war.' Stanhope is filled with self-loathing for having led his men to such bitter defeat and death, but Trotter tries to make him look on the bright side – they're still alive, and should be proud of the way their men fought to the end.

They are taken to a prisoner of war camp, where the next few scenes are described by Sherriff as 'fragmentary', spanning a passage of time. It starts with Stanhope being surly to his fellow prisoners; next we see Allied troops advancing, and Trotter being told that everywhere the British and Americans are winning; finally, the British soldiers are cheering their imminent release – all except Stanhope, who remains distant from it all.

Next, on the quay of an English port, on a fine winter's morning, the returning prisoners are being addressed by the local mayor who tells them that they are desperately needed by their country. Stanhope wears an expression of 'exultant joy'. He and Trotter part, promising to stay in touch – Trotter is quite convinced Stanhope will shortly be 'bossing round in a Rolls-Royce'. Back home, Stanhope has a long talk with Madge, telling her about his time in the trenches, how bleak things had been for him, and how he relied on alcohol to see him through. But he's come through it all, and feels much better; he's ready to work. He realised, 'I'd got a great job ahead: I was aching to get my teeth into it.' His father is less sure that he's ready to go to London to find employment, but Dennis is having none of it. He's going to see a major industrialist – Sir William Brand – with whom he was billeted before the war and who promised Stanhope help if ever he should need it.

But things don't go to plan. When he goes to see Sir William Brand, there are several men, ex-officers like Stanhope, waiting outside his office as well. When they eventually meet, Brand can offer him nothing. Not only that, he also learns that Brand is putting his son to work – a man younger than Stanhope, but someone who missed the war entirely. Thereafter we follow Stanhope to interview after interview, each situation meaner than the one before as his horizons gradually shrink. No one needs his ability to handle men; instead, what they need is experience of business, which he does not possess. Nor will they let him start at the bottom, because as a company commander with an MC it would be simply too demeaning to him. At an employment bureau for ex-officers he vents his frustrations, but for their part they are frustrated too – they keep sending him to employers, only for him to insult them and decline the lowly positions they are willing to offer. As a last gasp he is sent to Mr Ramsey, who offers him a job selling custard powder to grocery stores. He takes the job, but in the next scene we see him being rudely ignored by the grocer, who is too busy serving his customers to pay attention to Stanhope. As he trudges wearily down empty streets we see the contrast with his previous life, at the head of a body of men.

That was as far as Sherriff got with the individual scenes. Beyond that, Stanhope's tale darkens still further. He finds himself in a dreary industrial town and goes to the pub 'for the drink he longs for'. While there he meets a former sergeant, who tells him of the problems he and his colleagues are having at the steel works, which is now being managed by the son of the company chairman, Sir William Brand. The dispute is taking place in the shadow of a possible national strike, but the men have additional grievances and have left their union behind. Stanhope, intoxicated, agrees to be their spokesman, but the young man bests him in an argument when they meet. He promises violence unless their demands are met, but at the appointed time for the mass demonstration the men find him in his room, in a drunken stupor. When he awakes he realises what he has done and tries to commit suicide by turning on the gas taps. He is found in time, and Sir William Brand, who by now has calmed things down, visits him and hears his story. Stanhope has been broken by the war and realises that he must make way for those (both younger and older) who were untouched by it. In the end, Brand gives him the job of organising the men's sports and recreation, so he says goodbye to his dreams of leadership, and 'happy in the love of the girl who becomes his wife, he turns quietly down the bye-lanes.'

Ex-Officers of the Stanhope Type
Sherriff had been reluctant to write a sequel at all, feeling that there was nothing more he wished to add to *Journey's End*. But the movie companies – Warner Brothers especially[79] – had been very interested in the concept. Whale was keen on the idea too. Unfortunately, their visions were very different. Whale wanted an 'exciting and heroic kind of story', and to 'keep Stanhope in khaki',[80] possibly in the form of a prisoner of war movie (which would be of obvious interest to him, given his wartime experiences). For his part, Sherriff had no objection to writing a prisoner of war tale, but it would have to 'spring entirely from a fresh source'. If he were going to write another story about Stanhope it would be one that was true to the experiences of the 'ex-officer of the Stanhope type'.[81]

Sherriff was well aware of the struggles of ex-army officers to find employment after the war. He himself had returned to a job that he felt was less than he was capable of, and others of his colleagues had struggled similarly, or even to find a job at all. In 1921, just three years after the war had ended, unemployment had soared to over 2 million (over 12 per cent).[82] Officers were far from immune, especially those (like Stanhope) who had never had the chance to learn a profession, and those who had given up professional careers, or were nearing the end of their working lives.[83] And while ordinary soldiers who were unemployed could apply for an 'out of work donation' (an early form of unemployment benefit), officers, who were presumed to have means of their own, could not. That was what brought about 'the spectacle of destitute ex-officers selling matches on the streets or playing a barrel organ in the West End with an eye open for the police'.[84] The Officers Association, which was established in 1920, and then eventually folded into the new British Legion, worked hard to provide assistance to officers and their families, dealing with 24,000 cases in 1921 (twice that of the previous year).

The employment bureau that Stanhope visited may have been partly inspired by a similar bureau run by the Officers Department of the British Legion (which Sherriff must surely have heard about from comrades fallen on hard times). The bureau was staffed mainly by volunteers – ex-regular officers, who 'interviewed applicants, both able-bodied and disabled,'[85] as well as offering start-up loans or grants to help others into self-employment. Another section, which dealt with over 5,000 cases a year, provided 'relief' to ex-officers, but mainly in the form of loans or grants that would help them into employment.[86]

Quite where Sherriff got the idea for the industrial strife in the tale is not clear. The story is set, of course, just after the war, and in that regard he may have had upheavals such as the riot in George Square in Glasgow in 1919[87] on his mind. On the other hand, writing in 1930, he may have been influenced by the more recent unrest, such as the General Strike of 1926 (when Sherriff himself had joined up as a special constable). Whichever is the case, this is the only occasion in Sherriff's (original, non-adapted) writing, in which he tackles industrial working conditions and discontent.[88] His early plays and books in particular have much more of a pastoral feel, and his protagonists never veer very far away from the middle classes, about whom he was very well equipped to write.

Having fallen slowly from 1921, unemployment rose again in the late 1920s, and, as ever, old soldiers felt it worst. On Armistice Day 1929, General Sir Ian Hamilton, President of the British Legion, had written an open letter in the *Daily Express* to Erich Maria Remarque, and it was almost as if he was talking of Stanhope himself:

> In England we have over one million unemployed. More than half of these are old soldiers. When they went to the war they were the flower, not the dregs, of our people. Always I have tried to rouse them and stir them up by explaining to them the reason: namely, that education is most valuable from eighteen to twenty-two and that just during those very years, when the stay-at-homes were mastering their trades, they were standing in mud under a rain of shells. Therefore, when they came back, they were at a disadvantage. Therefore, when trade was slack, they were the first to be discharged.[89]

Sir Ian was not to know that the crash on Wall Street, which had taken place just a couple of weeks before, would usher in a major worldwide slump, during which UK unemployment would rise far above anything seen thus far – over 12 per cent in 1930, over 16 per cent in 1931, and rising to a peak of 17 per cent in 1932. The British Legion would find its finances stretched to the very limit, while the aid its Officers' Department could offer would be cut sharply as the flood of applicants threatened to overwhelm its meagre funds. It would take until the Second World War for ex-officers of the Stanhope type to see much improvement in their fortunes.

Regret Cannot Use

Journeys Other End is a depressing affair. It is also a surprisingly linear narrative; from the moment Stanhope returns home there is nothing but deepening gloom. It stands in contrast with Sherriff's later work, which has a pattern of light and shade, and a more typical story arc – often beginning optimistically, before the protagonists are faced with adversity, which is usually overcome in the happy ending. Such arcs are much more familiar in movies, and it may be that Sherriff learned the technique from his screenwriting work: his autobiography, in particular, is redolent with it.

But at this point, *Journey's Other End* was not at all what the studios had envisaged when they had asked for a sequel. He finished the manuscript in early November and sent it off to Warner Brothers in Hollywood. After a few weeks delay the reply came back in the form of a cable:

> Advise Peacock immediately Sherriff's story not suitable present form stop Liked original idea story but not last half therefore regret cannot use. Thank Peacock Sherriff their co-operation.[90]

Peacock noted that he was 'sorry and surprised', but the text of the cable would appear consistent with Warners having been sold the 'Stanhope in khaki' angle rather more aggressively than the tale of his subsequent struggle. Sherriff was not downhearted, and kept working on the sequel until he left for a Christmas holiday in Switzerland. But he came back to find another rejection letter on the doormat. This one was from John Maxwell, the founder of British International Pictures,[91] who thought there was certainly an idea in it, but turned it down because he doubted it would 'pass the Censor as he has laid a ban on anything that might incite to industrial strife'.[92] It is likely that Maxwell was just using the Censor angle as an excuse, and that he was simply not interested. Neither, as it happened, was Goldwyn.[93]

Sherriff, as always, was phlegmatic. He had wanted to pursue the story sincerely – 'to deal with the logical and natural results of such a man's war experience' – but he could understand the studios' caution. 'I imagine,' he wrote to Peacock, '[they] would … be quite keen on the picture if it rose to a far more spectacular climax than I have in mind.' Given, however, that the story had not been well received, he did not think he could muster the enthusiasm to see it finished, so at that point he put his pencil down on Stanhope's adventure. He later expanded on his concerns to Maurice Browne:

> I am far from being out of sympathy with the people who have turned it down. They are very likely right when they consider that while a past tragedy like *Journey's End* is eagerly accepted by the public, a tragedy that still surrounds them is very unlikely to meet the same response.[94]

A couple of weeks later, he heard from Whale that Tiffany were in financial difficulties, and would not be interested either. To Sherriff this was something of a relief; Whale was obviously still hankering to turn the story into something more heroic, and Sherriff felt that 'he and I would never see eye to eye over making the sequel.'[95] He was still willing to write a prisoner of war story (but not with Stanhope), and, more generally, would still be very happy to work for the studios. He encouraged Peacock to keep looking:

> The dialoguing of a novel or story for a Talking Film is something I would like to undertake from the point of view of experience, because it would give practice in the direction which does not often come a writer's way.[96]

There again is the evidence of Sherriff looking to expand his range, and take on new types of project – and, of course, the money would not be bad either.

At this point, the Savoy triumph was now two years behind him. He had been feted, and revelled in the acclaim. His bank balance, swollen by £41,000 in 1929, had added a further £31,500 or so in 1930 – almost entirely from *Journey's End*, but augmented a little by some touring performances of *Badger's Green* in the provinces, and the sale of the play by Gollancz. He was settled in Rosebriars, but his efforts in that big, new, panelled study, had been rewarded with little acclaim. *Badger's Green* had been, at best, a *succès d'estime* (if even that), and the three months he had spent practising his movie writing skills on *Journey's Other End* had received little more than a shake of the head from the studios. Sitting in his study in the evening, gazing at the bookshelves on which stood the many translations of *Journey's End*, bound in white vellum,[97] he must have wondered what on earth he was going to do next.

Up to Oxford

> I had got to get myself qualified for a profession before it was too late, and decided to go to Oxford, read for a degree in history and be a schoolmaster. Oxford wasn't a sudden inspiration. It was something I'd been hankering after for years. … To graduate at Oxford and become a schoolmaster would redeem my failure as a writer, give me back my self-respect, and provide me with a stimulating, worthwhile career.[98]

In *No Leading Lady* he describes his admission into Oxford as a rather tortuous process, beginning with an unnamed Fellow suggesting he study at Oxford, followed by an application to an unnamed college, where an unnamed rector turned him down because he had insufficient Latin.[99] This all took place, he tells us, in the autumn of 1930, followed by a miserable winter contemplating his writing failures, and his failure to secure a place at Oxford. But as with so many other tales in his autobiography, the story arc – from despair to triumph – is just too neat. There is no mention of such a trip in any of his letters; we have already seen that he expressed his willingness to travel to Hollywood in early 1931 if that was what the studios required.[100] We also have a letter to Thelma Cazalet in January 1931, thanking her for recommending him for her place on the London County Council, but declining, because he feared that his work would take him to Hollywood in the autumn.[101] So the initial part of his story is clearly unreliable.

Where the tale does begin to ring true, however, is when Mollie Cazalet enters, early in 1931. Sherriff said she encouraged him to put his writing aside for a while – 'Don't try to write until it comes back naturally' – and instead to go on up to Oxford and read history as he had long desired. She arranged for him to speak to H.A.L. (Herbert) Fisher at New College. He was the very antithesis of the stuffy old rector who had rejected him for his lack of Latin: Fisher was modern, a 'breath of fresh air', and he was happy to enrol Sherriff as a 'special student' from that autumn.

The timing of this story is consistent, at least, with the press cuttings in Sherriff's archive, for in April 1931 there is this: 'R.C. Sherriff ... will be unofficially in residence at Oxford during Term coaching eights and looking round to see if it is possible to fulfil an ambition of his to get an Oxford or Cambridge degree.'[102] On the face of it this seems rather an odd announcement to make, but in June the papers were reporting that special arrangements had been made to admit Sherriff to the university as a 'senior student': 'In view of the desire of Mr R.C. Sherriff, author of the famous war play *Journey's End*, to read for an honours degree at Oxford University, Congregation[103] yesterday decided to admit him as a senior student.'[104] The decision of Congregation in June suggests that the earlier press report may have been nothing more than a placeholder, designed to explain why Sherriff might be nosing around in Oxford.

It is more than likely that Mollie Cazalet had a hand in all this, as Sherriff says: she would certainly have been in a position to know Fisher and to speak with him on Sherriff's behalf, and her desire for him to go to Oxford can be seen from a letter she sent him in 1932, after it had been announced he was going to Hollywood to do some scriptwriting:

> I see from tonight's paper that Hollywood has claimed you at last. I don't know whether to be glad or sorry. I think the latter, first because I don't think you and it have much in common, and second because I want you to stay at Oxford and then come and join my family in helping to govern the country.[105]

Presumably she had earlier pressed upon him the idea of running the country – given Thelma's offer of the LCC seat to him, but also the fact that, by the time he actually went up to the university, he had rather changed his line about why he was going there. It was no longer solely with the view of becoming a schoolmaster, but:

> now my idea is politics. ... By reading history I hope to make better conclusions than by the superficial study of conditions such as modern life enables you to

make. The doings of the last few months have given me rather a feeling of humiliation at my own impotence to understand the conditions of the present day.[106]

Busy Summer

Having struck out with the play and the movie script, Sherriff's thoughts turned to the possibility of writing a novel. He had worked with Vernon Bartlett on the novelisation of *Journey's End*, and was probably eager to put his new skills to work. By July 1931, when he mentioned it to Maurice Browne, a book was well under way, with publication scheduled in the autumn.[107] During that summer he was also working on the adaptation of a play called *The Golden Watch*, for which Gilbert Miller had offered a fee of £250. The play had been written by Hungarian author Ernő Szép,[108] and had been a great success in Budapest, and was now 'sought after by almost every impresario in Europe'.[109]

Mid-August, he received an intriguing letter from James Whale in the United States: was he still interested in writing for the talkies?[110] There were two possible adaptations being mooted. One was *Dr Scerocold* by Helen Ashton (a tale about a day in the life of an English country doctor), which would appear to fit well with the kind of sensibility he had revealed in *Badger's Green*; the other was *The Road Back*, Erich Maria Remarque's sequel to *All Quiet on the Western Front*. Sherriff was tempted. He had hoped *Journey's Other End* might lead him down this road, but since its abandonment at the beginning of the year there had been no new offers, not even a response to the menu of projects he had offered up to Warner Brothers. He wrote back to Whale explaining that his work schedule was hectic – *The Golden Watch*, the new book, a possible adaptation of a French play[111] for Maurice Browne (a project that barely got off the launch pad) and a new play of his own that he was just planning. On top of that, of course, he was off to Oxford, which was bound to put a crimp in his available writing time. Nevertheless, the talkies were intriguing, so he indicated that he would be willing to take on an adaptation if he were given enough time to do it. He could, for example, take the book to work on while at Oxford during the winter, then he might think of a short contract in Hollywood beginning in March or in June (with his preference for the latter, so as not to disrupt his studies).

Before he could look that far ahead, however, he had to finish off his novel. Gollancz was intending to publish in October, so needed the manuscript urgently. On 16 September, he delivered the final typewritten manuscript of his first novel to the Gollancz offices in London's Covent Garden.[112]

The Fortnight in September

The new novel was published on 12 October 1932, coincidentally exactly the same date as he was pictured in the press arriving at New College, Oxford, with his mother. He was very embarrassed when he found the press out in force. He had not envisaged that any kind of fuss would be made, and yet there they were, waiting by the gate. He told them he had nothing to say – that he was just coming as a 'plain undergraduate' to read history. Nevertheless, the photographers:

> insisted on taking a picture of me walking up the garden path with a couple of suitcases, my mother beside me. It came out in several papers in the morning, the local paper heading it, 'Coming to Oxford with mother'. It was kindly meant, but there was something ridiculous about it, and I wished it hadn't happened.[113]

His embarrassment was short-lived, however, since the press focus switched rapidly to his new book. *The Fortnight in September* is a charming tale about a simple family holiday in Bognor, the idea having come to him when he was on a seaside holiday at Bognor himself, watching the crowds go by. The Stevens family take two weeks' holiday every September, always going to the same guest house (Seaview), run by the same landlady (Mrs Huggins), as they have for years. Mr Stevens has been a clerk for thirty years. Mrs Stevens is a housewife. Their three children are Mary (twenty), Dick (seventeen) and Ernie (just eight). In the course of their vacation we are given the opportunity to focus on each of them in turn, as they enjoy their individual moments of respite from the other family members:

> **Mr Stevens** contemplates his life during his long walk on the headland, and we learn that he is making the best of things, although he has been passed over for promotion, and made the mistake of resigning as secretary of the local football club, a job he had greatly enjoyed.
>
> **Mrs Stevens'** favourite moments are in the evening, alone, with a glass of port, while Ernie is sleeping, her husband is at the pub (something which he never would do at home, but enjoys as a holiday treat) and Dick and Mary are out walking. We learn that she has come to dread the holiday – that she is a nervous woman, frightened by the journey and by the sea when she gets there: she feels the children pull away from her on holiday, and prefers life at home, where she is mistress of her own domain.
>
> **Mary** and **Dick** each have their walks alone, during which they contemplate spreading their wings – they are getting to the age where they might think of holidaying with their friends, rather than their parents. Mary is keen to make friends, and meets a young woman who encourages her to stray beyond her usual boundaries, leading to her meeting a young actor, in a touring play, whom she befriends for the remainder of her stay. Dick, we discover, is unhappy in his job, and yearns for his schooldays, from which he feels he was plucked too early to be sent into the world of work; but he is trying to make the best of things, planning for something better in the future.

Ernie is just a child, free-spirited, the counterpart to the others' anxieties – he wants nothing more than to play with his yacht in the sea – but the joy he takes in the holiday is infectious.

Overlaying the holiday is a sense of change – Seaview is becoming more dilapidated as Mrs Hugget struggles to maintain it following her husband's death, and Mr Stevens is aware that there may not be many more years when the family will holiday together. The holiday itself revolves around straightforward pleasures – mainly walking and bathing – and one of their biggest decisions is whether to rent a beach hut, and for how long. The events that it portrays are mostly minor, but assume greater significance because of the Stevens' anxieties about their own status, and the way in which they are perceived by others. Aside from the beach hut decision, the most difficult challenge of the fortnight is the tea party to which they are invited by a wealthy client of Mr Stevens' firm (Mr Montgomery) – but they emerge with dignity intact, which, for the Stevens, is everything.

Although he writes of building up an 'imaginary story', Sherriff plundered liberally from his own experiences, and the comparison between the Stevens and the Sherriffs is an easy one to make. Both families live in old, shabby houses backing on to railway lines, and both have a minor clerk as father and housewife mother, with three children – an oldest girl, and two boys. Dick's experiences at school, his dissatisfaction with his first job (which even extends, like Jimmy Lawton, to the clothes he is forced to wear), and his feeling that he was wrenched from school too soon, all clearly mimic Sherriff's own. The Sherriffs also enjoyed their family holidays by the sea, in Selsey (near Bognor), albeit they stayed in their own holiday bungalow (Sleepy Hollow) rather than a guest house. In fact, they had been going to Selsey since August 1906, when Herbert noted in his diary: 'Spent till Saturday at Selsey – bathed twice a day – hired hut for a week – took short cycle rides and loafed about. All very much pleased with Selsey.'[114]

The description we have of Mr Stevens through his wife's eyes is similar to how Herbert appeared:

He had not altered much with passing years. His hair, of course, had thinned. ... He parted it almost behind his left ear, much further to the side than most men did, and brushed the long remaining wisps straight across his head. His moustache looked a little more ragged than it used to, but that was because waxing had gone out. It used to have beautifully glossy, sharp points.[115]

The relationship between the two also seems analogous to that between Connie and Herbert – one in which years of familiarity, rather than blossoming into closeness, have served if anything to separate them. When looking at her husband in the train carriage, for example, Flossie ponders how remote he seems from her:

It was hard, somehow, to think of him as the man she had lived so near for so many years. She felt that if he were suddenly to look up it would be quite natural for him to peer over his glasses and say: 'Let's see – you're my wife, aren't you?' – and for her to answer: 'Yes! – And – and – aren't you my husband?'

The only significant division between Sherriff's picture and that of real life is in his description of Flossie. Having once been vivacious (when acting on stage), she is now rather mousy, contenting herself with her home and family rather than seeking out her own friends. The contrast with Sherriff's mother is quite clear: after the birth of her third child she took to the theatre, skiffing and cycling with enthusiasm, forging a very distinctive path for herself. As a result, it is hard to believe that Flossie's other characteristics were shared with Connie – her nervousness at the sea, for example, or her general timidity. But maybe this is just symptomatic of his difficulty in drawing female characters: Mary, for example, has much less of an interior life in the book than Dick, and her ambitions as a result are much smaller and narrower. Mr Montgomery's wife, too, receives short shrift – 'her hand is soft and limp, her smile languid, and her conversation insipid.'[116]

The Montgomery character is interesting, carrying echoes of some of the nouveaux-riches businessmen in his earlier plays (the ones without the appropriate 'breeding' – such as Maraway in *Cornlow-in-the-Downs*, or the awful Squdge in *The Feudal System*), and pointing the way to some others in the future (such as the unpleasant and cowardly Mr Rose in *The Night My Number Came Up*). Quite why Sherriff had it in for such caricatures is a puzzle – he does not seem to have moved in the kind of circles where he might meet them: the rowing and skiffing worlds were gentlemanly, the suburban am-dram world genteel, Kingston Grammar School modest and serious. It is doubly surprising to see Mr Montgomery pop up shortly after Sherriff had enjoyed a sudden transformation in his fortunes, and enjoyed the material benefits of his success (in terms of better cars and house), in much the same way as Mr Montgomery.

Sherriff seems to have been aware of the autobiographical content of his work – perhaps at the time, but certainly later:

A writer has a special problem of his own when it comes to his life story. Every book he writes must draw a little from the well of his own experiences and from the people he has met. He draws more lavishly from these people and experiences in his early books – as he goes on the well begins to dry up. That's why with most novelists his early works are better than his later ones – but supposing he were suddenly to take it into his head to write an autobiography – he would put all his goods in the shop window and sell the lot in one go. That's why the wise novelist keeps quiet about himself and dishes himself out frugally in small bits in each book he writes.'[117]

When the reviews came in they were almost unanimously favourable – we know, because Sherriff tabulated them for us (maybe he had time between lectures): twenty were 'Good', three 'indifferent' and five 'bad'.[118] James Agate reckoned the book:

> a considerable advance on either of [his] plays. ... The book is as alive as 'Kipps', without any of Kipps's adventures, and I can only attribute this to a gift of narrative, a power to perceive and reproduce character, and a knack of actuality in dialogue, all raised to a power of felicity that suggests a born story-teller.[119]

Probably the best review was in *The Spectator*:

> Here is a subject which could have been treated satirically, cleverly, patronisingly, sentimentally, how you please. Mr Sherriff comes to it fresh, and makes it universal. There is more simple goodness and understanding in this book than in anything I have read for years.[120]

For others it was: 'within its limits, a perfect achievement'[121]; 'extraordinarily appealing'[122]; and 'a detailed, vivid and penetrating study'.[123]

Overseas, too, the book hit its mark. In Australia, 'his shy humour, his humanity and his gift for characterisation' were commended. When it was published in America, the *New York Times*[124] called it 'a book to read lingeringly, and presently to tuck safely away in that corner of your bookshelf where your most friendly volumes are stored', while the reviewer from the *Chicago Tribune*[125] saw it as a British version of Sinclair Lewis's *Main Street*. The *Kölnischer Zeitung* in Germany was equally captivated: 'in its finely observed and exceptionally charming and detailed portraiture, the book gives an excellent picture of the worth and solidity of the English lower middle class.'

Not all the critics were kind, however. *The New Statesman* (which had never been impressed with *Journey's End*) remarked that Sherriff handled his characters so affectionately that 'one gets the impression that not one of them is over 18 inches high.'[126] The reviewer in the *Glasgow Bulletin* found the story 'a little thin', and the *Birmingham Post*, while praising Sherriff's delicacy of touch, and touting him as a potential novelist of distinction, noted that 'Unsympathetic readers ... will find the book dull.'[127]

Thousands and thousands of book-buyers agreed with G.B. Stern (whose encomium appeared on the dust jacket),[128] and the critics; Gollancz had another Sherriff hit on his hands. The initial print run of 5,000 sold out in days, and before the end of the year, the book was in its sixth impression, with 15,000 copies sold. Sherriff was probably just as pleased with the comments of individual friends.

Mollie Cazalet, for example, busy campaigning for Thelma in East Islington in the General Election, wrote to thank him for the book: 'I have never enjoyed anything more and have lived with them for the last fortnight in Islington. Hundreds of Stevens live down here and you have helped me to understand them and to get them to vote for Thelma!' Thelma duly won for the Conservatives with a 23 per cent swing from Labour; since the national swing from Labour was only about 12 per cent, perhaps Sherriff's guide to the lower middle class was as helpful as Mollie suggested.

Hooray for Hollywood

Sherriff quickly settled into life at Oxford – attending lectures, joining the essay society in college, and, of paramount importance, joining the New College Boat Club. The president of the club was a young man of twenty-two, Gerald Ellison, a first-rate oarsman who would become a good friend of Sherriff's. They would remain good friends for the rest of their lives, communicating regularly while Ellison worked his way up the ranks of the clergy, becoming first Bishop of Chester in 1955, and then Bishop of London in 1973.

After about five weeks or so at university his peaceful routines were interrupted by a letter from James Whale in Hollywood. By this time Whale had moved to Universal Pictures, where he was working for the diminutive producer Carl Laemmle Junior, the son of the studio head (and founder) Carl Laemmle. Junior Laemmle (as he was known) had scored a great hit with *All Quiet on the Western Front*, and a further one with Bella Lugosi's *Dracula*, and on that basis had been given a certain amount of latitude in the organisation. In March 1931 he had hired Whale to direct *Waterloo Bridge*, a movie based on the play of the same name by Robert M. Sherwood, about a prostitute in wartime London. When the movie was released in August of that year, it was well enough received that Whale's one-year contract with Universal was extended to five years.[129] For his next project he was handed the reins to Universal's next big horror picture – *Frankenstein* – which was a huge box-office success upon its release on 21 November.

Shortly before the movie's release, Whale wrote to Sherriff asking if he were still interested in writing for the movies.[130] Sherriff replied very strongly in the affirmative. He had already received offers to undertake a lecture tour, but he knew how strenuous that could be. 'If I could get a moderately good offer for a couple of months or so in Hollywood I think it would be a pleasanter business.'[131] Now the hare was off and running.

Within two weeks, Sherriff received a letter from Peacock spelling out in detail what he should look for in a movie offer. Whale appeared to have settled on his choice of film project for Sherriff – *The Road Back* – and the suggestion was that he should go to Hollywood to do the writing. Junior Laemmle was interested in having Sherriff do the screenplay, adding, in a note to Whale, 'Please ascertain what we can get him for – naturally don't want to pay him too much money.'[132] Whale suggested Sherriff could go on the basis of a nominal fee, and having his expenses covered (with the promise of a larger fee if his adaptation were accepted), but Peacock cautioned strongly against that: 'There must be no talk of expenses and a nominal fee, because anything of this sort might make the trip hardly worth your while, and tend to damage your reputation.' If Universal were prepared to offer an appropriate fee it looked as though Sherriff might at last achieve his aim of writing for the movies.

Sitting in Rosebriars over Christmas 1931, Sherriff must have been hugely excited. From having had a gloomy start to the year, with the failure of *Journey's Other End*, he had gone on to achieve his dream of attending Oxford University and had seen his first novel become a success beyond anything he had imagined. Now he was on the threshold of a trip to Hollywood, and beyond that, possibly a career in scriptwriting. The delay in contract negotiations over the holiday period must have seemed unbearable, but by the time he was back up in his house at Belbroughton Road in Oxford, he was receiving word from Peacock that they 'very definitely want to close with you.'[133]

After further negotiation, Sherriff signed his first Hollywood contract on 9 February 1932.[134] It was agreed that he would leave during the third week of March, and no later than the eighteenth. While in California he would work 'in and about the production of motion picture films and in the preparation of stories, scripts, scenarios and or in any other way in which his literary and dramatic skills and talents shall be possible of employment by Universal'. His employment would begin on the day that he presented himself to Carl Laemmle Junior at Universal City, and would end sixteen weeks later. His payment terms were generous: $800 per week, with a safeguard against exchange rate changes, such that he was guaranteed at least £200 per week, unless that required Universal to pay him more than $1,000. *The Road Back* was not specifically included in the contract, but that was very much the understanding. Indeed, Junior Laemmle had already said as much to the press.[135]

The British press carried the story almost immediately, and Sherriff was left having to explain to Warden Fisher why he would not be in attendance for his third term at Oxford, despite having so recently insisted that Oxford was his true calling. In *No Leading Lady*, Sherriff recounts a very sympathetic meeting between the two, where Fisher tried to sum up the difference between a writer's career, and that of a schoolmaster:

A writer may influence a mass of people by remote control: he never meets them individually and never sees results at first hand. A schoolmaster has only a handful of boys, but he sees them every day and can watch the results of his work as it develops before his eyes.

Sherriff replied that he did not yet know which of the two careers he was better suited to, but going to Hollywood would help him decide. He and Fisher came to the compromise that he would take the summer term off, but that would mean, since he had to serve six terms before his exams, that he would need to come up for a third year.

Unfortunately, Sherriff's account of his meeting with Fisher must be taken with something more than a pinch of salt. In the first place, the discussion between the two takes place against a background in which Sherriff says he was heading to Hollywood to write *The Invisible Man* – but in fact it was *The Road Back* that was very firmly on the agenda. Next, there is some question as to whether there was ever any intention of Sherriff sitting for a degree. Certainly, Congregation had given him the status of a senior student, but according to New College records, he was admitted as a 'Special Status Student' (i.e. a mature student taking no examinations).[136] As a result, the college has no records of the supervision of his academic work, nor even if it was supervised in any formal way.

Finally, there is no real doubt as to Sherriff's career intention. He had worked since he came out of the Army to develop a career as a writer. He had set up The Adventurers to produce his plays; when it had folded he had taken them to Genesta. He had scrapped and chivvied to get *Journey's End* on to the ISS stage, and since the *Journey's End* days had begun to wane, he had diligently striven to produce work in a range of formats, albeit with variable success. Now he had the chance to become a screenwriter – in Hollywood, no less. No schoolmastering job could possibly compete with that.

Chapter 7

The Universal Years, 1932–35

*Do the things external which fall upon thee distract thee? Give thyself time to learn
something new and good, and cease to be whirled around. But then thou must also
avoid being carried about the other way.*

Marcus Aurelius, *The Meditations*, Book II.

Sherriff set sail for Hollywood, with his mother, on 18 March 1932 on the SS
Bremen. The ship arrived in New York some five days later, whence the pair
took the famous *Twentieth Century Limited* train to Chicago, and from there,
a day later, the similarly famous *The Chief*, to Los Angeles, a further two and a half
days away.

When they arrived in Hollywood, they found that Universal had booked them
rooms in the *Château Élysée*, on the fringes of the Hollywood Hills, and just a short
drive to Universal City, where the studio was based. Built as a replica of a French
castle, the chateau was run in hotel style, and housed many well-known Hollywood
movie stars. It came as a big surprise to Sherriff and his mother, but they were
instantly seduced by its grandeur and setting:

> It was very impressive and dignified in the twilight, with its majestic white walls
> and little corner turrets. ... Our apartment was at the top of the chateau, with
> an open balcony jutting out from the sitting room, and when we went outside
> the view was breathtaking. It was dark now, and the whole plain beneath us was
> lit with myriads of lights ... the enchantment of Hollywood enraptured us.[1]

At Universal City he was given an office and a desk, and set to work. He later wrote
to Gerald Ellison:

> The first month or two was immensely interesting because I spent most of that
> in the studios watching the mechanical side of the work, and trying to learn
> how films are made and sound recorded. I was in the studios mostly during the
> days and was working on my script during the evenings.'[2]

At the time, James Whale was directing *The Old Dark House*, a film based on the
J.B. Priestley story *Benighted*, about a group of misfits and grotesques in a house
in rural Wales. It was another horror story of sorts, and another starring vehicle

for Boris Karloff while also featuring several actors with whom Whale was familiar from the London stage.[3] The movie had been scripted by another English import, Benn Levy, but he had returned to England before shooting started, and it has been suggested that Sherriff was kept on hand to make last-minute script changes.

By the beginning of May, Sherriff had turned out a nine-page synopsis of *The Road Back*, and a two-page character guide. Remarque's book has a lengthy cast of characters, and proceeds, like its predecessor, in episodic fashion, although bound by a linear narrative. The young men return to a defeated Germany, fallen on hard times economically, with revolution in the air. Some of them adjust successfully to their new circumstances, but most find it hard, returning to fractured relationships, or to jobs and lives that seem trivial after all they have been through. One of their number, Albert, murders a war profiteer for seducing his girlfriend, another is gunned down during a riot, by soldiers now commanded by their former captain. Albert's trial is the climax of the book, with his sentence mitigated owing to the impassioned pleas of his friends, and the guilt of the court at having sent these young men into the cauldron of battle in the first place.

Sherriff enjoyed his time working on the film. He wrote to Ellison that 'Writing for the movies is a fascinating business – you seem to have such wonderful opportunities held out to you and yet you can seize so few.'[4] But he clearly remained true to his shy and private ways: 'I don't go out much to "wild Hollywood parties" because they are very dull and uninteresting – the most interesting people out here are working too hard to go to parties and a day's work in a studio is really exhausting.'

When he had returned to England, he told Maurice Browne that: 'Everyone connected with the firm of Universal Films was delightful to work with. They are excellent people, and gave me every chance of doing the best work I could by leaving me entirely alone to evolve the story upon my own ideas.'[5] His enthusiasm for the people at Universal was clearly a reflection of his more general enchantment with the American people:

> I like America for its people – the 'middle class' (if you can call them so) are charming – the most good-natured people in the world: they are abominably exploited and misused in every way by Big Business and politics and you feel terribly sorry for them sometimes. ... Yes Sir! I think on the whole the War of Independence was a Good Thing.[6]

Despite Sherriff's enthusiasm for America and the Americans, his sojourns in Hollywood during the 1930s were always rather brief, never more than a few months at a time, largely because of his (and his mother's) desire to return to his beloved Rosebriars. Even on this first occasion, he confessed to Gerald Ellison, 'I was feeling terribly homesick in America during Henley week: it was the first Henley I have missed since the war and I sincerely hope I will not miss another one.' His mind was clearly on his rowing friends earlier that summer as well. He had represented New College in the races in February that year, and was thinking of his friends at the start of the races in summer,[7] prompting him to cable them (and practise his newfound American dialect skills):

> Hope youse guys scram over de rival bozos in de stupendous boating blowoff dis week stop. Guess you're sure swell outfit and am pulling for you to push all de other lugs into de seakale stop. Good luck to all de buddies. Sherriff.[8]

His decision to stay in Hollywood only for short periods helped him avoid being sucked into the Hollywood system and lifestyle. Benn Levy believed it was important to stay no longer than three months at a time, so he could return to his proper work, which would prevent him being swallowed by the studios, but also increase his marketable value if he scored another hit as a playwright.[9] And P.G. Wodehouse approved of Sherriff's strategy as well: 'If I do make a hit with [Damsels in Distress] ... I shall do like Sherriff and come over here for visits of no longer than three months. I wouldn't take on a salaried job like the last one for anything.'[10] During the 1930s he never stayed in Hollywood for more than a couple of months at a time. Despite this, he was an active member of the Hollywood Cricket Club[11] (see Plate 22), and seems to have retained an unofficial membership of the English expatriate community (referred to by Sheridan Morley as the 'Hollywood Raj'),[12] which stood him in good stead when he was forced to stay for rather longer in the 1940s.

The Road Back

The Road Back script[13] was finished on 28 July 1932. It is a marvellously economical account of the book, trimming many of the side plots and secondary characters, but leaving intact the boys' sense of betrayal and confusion: Whale called it 'magnificent'.[14] Once it was completed it was submitted to the MPPDA (the Motion Picture Producers and Distributors of America), which encouraged filmmakers to subscribe to a voluntary 'Code' (known as the 'Hays Code', since the organisation was headed by Will Hays, a senior Republican politician and erstwhile Postmaster General). His main assistant was Colonel Jason Joy,[15] and it was to him that scripts and finished movies were submitted for censorial guidance. At this stage the Hays Office still only offered *guidance* on what local censor boards would or would not allow – it would take another two years before it would reserve to itself the right to *approve* movies for distribution, in the form of the Production Code Administration (PCA). As will be seen, several of Sherriff's movies of the 1930s and 1940s would undergo searching examination before receiving ultimate approval.

When Joy wrote his regular monthly round-up of movie productions to Will Hays at the beginning of August 1932, he commented that The Road Back 'should be an outstanding production.'[16] A more detailed note from Lamar Trotti on 5 August 1932 sets out the movie's story in detail, before offering a verdict:

> I think it is tremendously effective and a powerful argument against war. There is some small business to be watched, profanity etc. … I suppose the revolution scenes are the only things from a German standpoint to be worried about. To me it is a great thing for Germany, because the boys are sympathetic and nice and immediately we like them and realise how like our own problems their problems are.

Sherriff had also managed to excise several of the sexually related sub-plots that Trotti had identified as likely problematical when he had done his own synopsis of the story for the MPPDA[17] a year earlier.

Two weeks after finishing the script, Sherriff's contract came to an end and he left for home. A few weeks later he wrote approvingly to Maurice Browne about the story, noting that he had contemplated making a stage play of it. '*The Road Back*,' he wrote, 'gave me an opportunity of dealing with a problem which is very present in life today, and I sincerely hope the picture will turn out well.'[18] Unfortunately, his immediate hopes were to be dashed, on the rocks of financial exigency and Nazi intransigence.

Nazi Influence

The Nazis in Germany had first brought their influence to bear on the Hollywood studios even before they took power. *All Quiet on the Western Front* was released by Universal in August 1930. When it was shown in Germany in December of that year the Nazis were not in power, but they had gained some political success and their influence was growing. They organised demonstrations outside and inside the cinema where the film was being premiered (releasing white mice and stink bombs), and in creating a furore they succeeded in having the film banned in Germany.[19] The trouble attending the film led Frederick Herron (foreign manager at the MPPDA) to write to Jason Joy in January 1931, flagging up potential trouble with *The Road Back*:

> Following the trouble in Austria and Germany over the showing of *All Quiet on the Western Front* – which was finally banned in both countries – the second book by Remarque which I understand Universal is going to film, will have a little bit of trouble in all probability.

In the event, the German ban on *All Quiet* was only rescinded in August 1931, after Universal had not only acquiesced in a number of cuts to the print for distribution in Germany, but had also agreed to make those cuts to the version showing throughout the rest of the world.

At much the same time as Herron was writing to Joy, a German Foreign Office official named Martin Freudenthal was setting out on a year-long journey to the United States to 'study the American studio system'.[20] He spoke not only to the Hays office, but also to many of the most senior officials in the major studios, and seems to have met with some success in persuading producers to remove references that he felt were unsympathetic to the concerns of the German government. In relation to *The Road Back*, an August 1932 letter from Jason Joy to Carl Laemmle Junior at Universal shows that Freudenthal had voiced some concerns:

> [He] has told us that he has made the proper contacts with you and has asked for the privilege of contacting us if any misunderstanding arises. ... As I told you before, the important consideration is to make certain in your own minds that you are not giving offence to the German people as a people.[21]

Joy then went on to specify a list of changes that Freudenthal wanted to see made. In reply, Laemmle Junior said that 'it is my hope and belief that it is going to be handled in such fashion that the German people will find nothing in it to wound their sensibilities. We are taking advantage of your censorship suggestions.'[22]

But, with a terrible economic depression under way, times were hard in Hollywood. Universal Studios reported a $750,000 loss for the year, and against that background, it was hard to justify a picture with a $500,000 budget. In addition, the German government had just produced a new quota law (the latest in a line stretching back to 1925, designed to limit the number of imported films, and enhance the German film industry),[23] which included a clause (the so-called 'Article Fifteen') that threatened to refuse the allocation of import permits to studios whose output 'on the world market' was 'detrimental to German prestige'.[24] Universal had significant business interests in Germany, and with finances tight anyway, there was nothing to be gained from provoking the German government, and thus placing their interests in 'jeopardy',[25] so *The Road Back*, with Sherriff's 'magnificent' script, was put on the back burner. It would be revisited a few years later, upsetting the Nazis even more (see Chapter 8).

Oxford Fun

Sherriff left Hollywood with a generous offer in his pocket: 'When I was free to write again, Universal Studios were to have first option on my services to write three screenplays.'[26] For the moment, however, he was content to resume his studies at Oxford University.

Sherriff suggests in *No Leading Lady* that he returned to Oxford keen to make a case for his inclusion in the University Eight (to obtain his rowing 'Blue'), and that only illness prevented him doing so. But it is clear that he was no longer of that standard. In fact, he could not even compete to be in the best New College boats: he was thirty-six, and had not rowed at a consistently high level since the success of *Journey's End*. In Hollywood he had not even so much as stepped in a boat[27]; and he was still suffering from a back injury (from his Christmas holiday in Switzerland), which had given him trouble rowing in the spring races. In the end, rather than competing for a place in the best college boat, he settled, instead, for the role of 'general utility man' and coach: 'Much as I should like to row, I can find plenty of fun on the bank, taking the second or third boats.'[28] He still missed being in a boat though: after the summer races were over (and he had received a favourable mention in *The Times* as the coach of the Oriel crew)[29] he told Ellison how much he admired that 'very, very gallant race on that last evening', and how much he 'hated being on the bank after so nearly being in the crew and it was awful to hear that starting gun go and then do nothing but run importantly on the shore.'[30]

His letters to Gerald Ellison show a very different side than the rather shy and retiring Sherriff we are accustomed to. He seems to have assumed the role of the young student with ease, and his letters are filled with university slang[31] and a jollity that confirms his ability to mimic the speech patterns of those around him. And in the Ellison files in the Lambeth Palace Library is a menu card from the dinner following the Torpids races on 22 February 1933, which contains an uncharacteristically rude limerick from Sherriff about a young woman from Leicester ...

It is hard to understand quite why Sherriff went up to Oxford University. He obviously felt that he should have had the chance to go to university when he was younger, to prepare for a career in a profession: that much is clear from those of his stories (*Jimmy Lawton*, for example, or *The Fortnight in September*) that feature young men who feel they have been wrenched from school too soon. Perhaps, too, the idea of being a schoolmaster had stuck with him as a worthy profession, and it might have seemed more so when his post-*Journey's End* writings met with limited success. The desire to row in the Oxford–Cambridge Boat Race would also have loomed very large in his decision. So he perhaps went up to Oxford with a bundle of these thoughts in mind, only to find, on the day that he got there, that his book had been a major success, and within a few weeks, that a Hollywood writing career was beckoning.

Oxford must have looked good when his other choices were limited. But in early 1933, the factors that had taken him there had ceased to have much salience. He would never win a place in the Boat Race crew. As a special student, not sitting exams, and therefore unable to graduate in the conventional way, the route to becoming a schoolmaster was no clearer than it had been before. And he had left Hollywood with a lucrative writing contract just waiting to be exercised. By June 1933, therefore, it is not surprising to find Sherriff confessing that 'I don't seem to spend much time in Oxford these days ... such great activities are going on about my next film story that I had to spend a lot of time on it.'[32] In opting to activate his contract with Universal, he had clearly chosen the life of a writer, over that of a student (or schoolmaster). There would never be any doubt about his choice of profession again.

The Invisible Man

Sherriff's contract with Universal was for three screenplays a year, at a total price of £6,000.[33] The first three films he wrote would be *The Invisible Man*, *A Trip to Mars* and *One More River*.

By the time he was called in to write *The Invisible Man* the project had been bouncing around Universal for a year and a half. H.G. Wells had sold the film rights to the studio in September 1931 (while retaining the right to approve the final script), and although Whale was initially attached to the project, it was handed to Robert Florey when Whale opted to focus on *The Road Back*[34] instead. Despite employing a succession of writers, the studio seemed unable to settle on a satisfactory script. When *The Road Back* was shelved in November 1932, Whale produced a six-page treatment of his own, which was turned into a script by well-known silent screenwriter Gouverneur Morris. By January 1933, Junior Laemmle was happy enough to submit the script to the MPPDA, which had few problems with it. But Wells did – so it was back to the drawing board. Early in 1933, novelist John Weld was next to be given the task. By this time, he calculated that five treatments and six separate screenplays had been produced. He reported that, after reading them, he went looking for the original book, only to find that the studio did not have a copy, so he was forced to borrow one from the Hollywood Public Library.[35]

In *No Leading Lady*, Sherriff has a very different account, claiming that he was given the task of adapting *The Invisible Man* on his first trip to Hollywood, and that it was he who had to find a copy of the book in Hollywood (a tale he embellishes with a beautifully drawn account of stumbling across a copy in a tiny second-hand bookstore in LA's Chinatown).[36] This is one of the most obviously false accounts in his memoir, for he was undoubtedly in England when Whale cabled from Hollywood in early 1933 to ask him to develop Weld's initial screenplay.[37] The *Daily Herald* (among others) says so:

> Universal Pictures have had twelve scenario writers on the task of adaptation [of *The Invisible Man*] since last summer. But every one of the scripts has been rejected as not good enough. Lately, the company cabled Sherriff ... begging him to go to Hollywood at a handsome fee to put the story into screen shape. Mr Sherriff declined to leave England, but consented to write the script in London. ... It is expected that this, the thirteenth scenario, will be the lucky one.[38]

Wells's book[39] is fairly straightforward in its structure. A stranger – named later as Griffin – arrives in winter in the village of Iping, swaddled in clothing, and takes a room at the local inn. He is abrupt and rude, easy to anger, and the villagers are wary of him. Once his baggage arrives, full of books and equipment, he begins to experiment, causing much muttering among the locals. Eventually they provoke him beyond the point of endurance, and he removes his clothing: underneath he is completely invisible. This causes a furore in the village, which he flees, leaving a trail of incidents in his wake. Having left behind his diaries and notebooks, he recruits a tramp to help him recover them, and after some adventures it is the tramp who is the cause of his being shot and wounded, and seeking refuge in a nearby house, which happens to be owned by Dr Kemp, an old colleague. He explains to Kemp the principles behind his invisibility and how he has come to this point, but in due course Kemp reports him to the police, who eventually catch and kill him. Essentially the book is an extended chase, leavened with humour at the expense of the locals, and punctuated by Griffin's maniacal narcissism.

According to Sherriff, his problems with the previous versions of the script were mainly in the 'fabulous events' and 'unreal characters'[40] that they had invented. He saw a screenplay as 'halfway between a stage play and a novel'[41] – in that it could be opened up more than a play, but should not wander as far afield as a novel. The key was 'to prune away the side-shoots and keep to the main stem, and every line of dialogue was there to drive the story on.' He dramatised it, he tells us, 'chapter-by-chapter, and it was mainly a matter of turning narrative into dialogue.'

But here he does himself a disservice, for he took quite considerable liberties with the book, and the picture is likely the better for it. The beginning of the movie follows the book quite faithfully – the angry stranger, the curious locals, the removal of clothing, the run-in with the police – all are well handled. But, presumably to humanise him, the movie gives him a girlfriend (Flora) – the daughter of his kindly employer/mentor (Dr Cranley). Kemp is then changed from a decent fellow chemist to a coward and love-rival, and he meets a grisly end in a fiery car crash.

There is one other, even more significant, change in the script. Sherriff felt that 'an invisible lunatic would make people sit up in the cinema more quickly than a sane man.'[42] Whale agreed, and suggested that the fact of being invisible in itself should drive the man insane. But Sherriff rejected that tactic, feeling that it would 'take too long to show the gradual process of developing insanity' (especially in a man whose face was either wreathed in bandages, or invisible altogether). And so he came up with the idea of 'Monocane', a substance 'which draws colour from everything it touches' (according to Dr Cranley), but which might well make him 'raving mad'. This was the one aspect of the film with which Wells declared himself dissatisfied, telling the press that 'there was a difference in the sympathetic interest one could take in an invisible man and in an invisible madman.'[43] But in practice the madness was already there in the book – together with the rage and the monumental solipsism. Griffin's megalomania in the movie ('Don't you see what it means? Power! Power to rule! Power to make the world grovel at my feet!') is not so very far from the 'Reign of terror … to terrify and dominate'[44] that he proposes to Kemp in the book.

Sherriff delivered the screenplay of *The Invisible Man* in June 1933, and with the touching optimism of one clearly not fully versed in the ways of the film industry, wrote to Gerald Ellison in late July to say that, when they were both back from summer holiday, 'I'll give you a great treat and show you my new film, which ought to be finished in a month's time.'[45] Actually, following a slightly involved casting process, routine filming only began in July, finishing in August 1933. James Curtis notes that Whale (unusually) stuck closely to the script, albeit adding one or two ad-libs: when Griffin throws a rock through a grocery window, for example, he remarks (in echo of Roosevelt's National Recovery Act) that 'We do our part'. There is also a little in-joke when Kemp phones Dr Cranley, and asks the operator to connect him to 'Esher 1021', which was Sherriff's own phone number at Rosebriars.[46] After the routine filming wrapped there was to be much more work on producing the special effects in which Claude Rains became invisible, with the result that the film took another two months before it was ready to be shown.

It was first shown in trade previews in October 1933, but was not officially released until 13 November, when it opened at the Palace Theatre in Chicago.[47] It was a sensation. The *Hollywood Reporter* commented that '[It] is a legitimate offspring of the family that produced *Frankenstein* and *Dracula*, but a lusty, healthy, willing-to-laugh youngster who can stand on his own two feet.' *Variety* loved it as well: 'Considering the problems involved, both from a technical and entertainment standpoint, it is in many respects astounding.'[48] Mordaunt Hall, in the *New York Times*, thought it 'a remarkable achievement', and noted that 'Although various incidents may be spine chilling, it is a subject with a quota of well-turned comedy.'[49] The praise in the United States press quickly made its way back to the UK, where much emphasis was placed on the British connection: '*The Invisible Man* … has startled the most aloof of the critics and audiences and an Englishman, Mr Claude Rains, has been made famous in a night. … The cleverest brains of Britain had to be harnessed before the film could be completed … R.C. Sherriff made a perfect adaptation.'[50]

Audiences in Britain had to wait a few weeks before it made its way across the Atlantic, but it was finally previewed to the press at the Tivoli on 24 January 1934, with a celebratory lunch afterwards, hosted by Frank Ditcham, and featuring Sherriff, Whale and H.G. Wells himself, all of whom spoke. Wells's comments were the most widely covered, but that was all to the good, because he contrasted how well the film had captured his book with how badly some of his previous books had been treated. He was pleased that the love interest had been subordinated to the thrilling story, because 'conventional love relations … should be kept out of a fantastic picture.'[51] The reviews of the movie were almost entirely[52] in sympathy with praise it had garnered in the United States, and most of the praise directed towards the 'wizardry'[53] behind Rains's invisibility.

Sherriff's reputation emerged enhanced, and he was pleased enough with his efforts that, when approached by the writer Elizabeth Mackintosh[54] for an example of a script that might help her understand how to write for the movies, he sent her *The Invisible Man*, noting that it 'was shot almost word for word and scene by scene in the form in which I wrote it'.

Next Scripts

After Sherriff had turned in the screenplay for *The Invisible Man* at the end of June, he turned to the script of *A Trip to Mars* with some enthusiasm:

> *A Trip to Mars* is great fun and very *Boys' Own Paper*, but it's apparently the sort of thing the public want. I'm not putting any jokes in this letter – in fact I shall not be making any till at least November as I want them all for A *Trip to Mars*. You might, in fact, let me have any jokes you think of (simple jokes) as I haven't nearly enough yet.... I had lunch with Neville Chamberlain on Wednesday (such fun, chicks) but he didn't make any jokes about Mars.[55]

The only version of the script in Sherriff's files is one produced by Richard Schayer and Tom Reed in May 1932,[56] but it is not clear whether Sherriff was redrafting it, or whether he was working on an entirely new story. Whale was signed to direct the film in the autumn of 1933, at which time it was being touted as a vehicle for Boris Karloff. He arrived in England in December 1933 and stayed for a couple of months, part of the time with Sherriff, during which time they worked on scripts together, including *A Trip to Mars*. When he returned to the United States [57] he fully expected to begin work on the picture, but hard times at Universal meant that neither the budget nor the time could be found for what would likely be a complex picture, and it was put on a shelf, where it has languished ever since.

Sherriff next turned his attention to quite a different proposition: dramatising *Over the River*, John Galsworthy's last ever book, published shortly after he died in January 1933. The book was the final instalment in the *End of the Chapter* trilogy, which in turn was an extension to the well-known *Forsyte Saga*. It was a big hit in both the UK and the US (where it was published as *One More River*, Galsworthy fearing that the American vernacular would equate the title of his book with 'over the hill'). The story is seen largely through the eyes of Dinny Cherrell, who carries a torch for her departed lover Wilfrid, and who is being wooed by David Dornford, the local MP. The other, and primary, storyline concerns her younger sister Clare Corven, who leaves her sadistic husband and is eventually hauled through the divorce courts.

The subject matter was clearly likely to be difficult from the point of view of the Hays Code: on a list of 'Don'ts' the MPPDA had published in 1927, was 'Any inference of sex perversion', and on its list of 'Be Carefuls' was 'The institution of marriage'. To make matters even worse for Universal, they alighted on the project just as the censor's office in the United States was on the verge of undergoing a major change. The studios were facing economic collapse, as the Depression slashed ticket sales just as they were being forced to meet the costs of expensive new sound equipment; distributors found themselves with half-empty theatres: 'Informal enforcement of the 1930 Code was futile in such dire economic conditions, because the studios simply could not resist the temptation to produce ever more lurid films that might attract customers into empty theatres.'[58]

The industry eventually acquiesced in the face of continuing protests, and established the Production Code Administration (PCA), which went into effect on 11 July 1934. It was run by a Hays Commission employee – Joseph I. Breen, a tough, worldly, Irish Catholic with a wide knowledge of the film industry. Whereas the Hays Code had been *voluntary* in nature, the PCA had the power to *enforce* changes: movies would only receive an official PCA certificate after a final screening for the censors, and since no picture could secure funding nor distribution deals in the absence of that certificate, it meant that the studios were forced to do Breen's bidding. Since it was expensive for the studios to make changes after the final movie had been screened, in practice they evolved a means of working that involved showing scripts to the censors as the projects developed, after which there would be negotiations regarding the amendments that the PCA would require before the certificate would be granted. The PCA was always careful to stress in its negotiations that while it could recommend a course of action based on scripts it had seen, it could not guarantee the granting of a certificate until it had screened the final movie.

One More River

Galsworthy's book was full of adult themes and adult dialogue – fine for the publishing industry, not so much for the movie business. Sherriff had started work on the script as soon as he had completed *A Trip to Mars* and drew as much as he could from the book's source material. First, though, he trimmed the second plot line, about the romantic entanglements of Dinny, the older sister, making her simply a sounding board for her sister Clare. Clare is just twenty-four years old and married to a man seventeen years her senior – Sir Gerald Corven. He describes himself as 'an experimentalist … a sensualist',[59] and part of his pleasure comes from abusing her. The last straw is when he beats her with a riding crop, causing her to leave him in Ceylon (Sri Lanka), and return to England. On board the boat home she meets Tony Croom, a young man just a year or two older, and they form a friendship.

Corven pursues Clare to England, and insists she return as his wife. Her father at first appears to side with Corven, but when she mentions the riding crop incident he is horrified ('The Bounder … the swine!'). Despite Clare's distaste for him, Corven forces himself upon her in her apartment one evening. Her relationship with Croom is platonic, because she makes it clear that, after Corven, she has no interest in romantic love. But Corven has them followed by investigators, and when they are found to spend the night in a car (when their lights fail on the way back from Oxford), the worst possible spin is put on it, and Corven sues her for divorce and Croom for compensatory damages.

The climax of the tale is a dramatic court scene, in which Clare attempts to defend herself, pointing to the innocent nature of her relationship with Croom, and declining – perhaps because of her discretion, but perhaps because of her shame – to speak of the abuses she had suffered in her marriage. The most dramatic moment is when Corven is recalled to the stand to testify that 'the marital relationship [between him and his wife] had been re-established'. The revelation is crushing for Croom. Clare denies Corven's suggestion – believing that marital relations do not include rape – but Croom and everyone else appears to believe that she is perjuring herself. The trial goes against them, and costs are awarded against Tony (although damages are not). She attempts to make amends to Tony, but he struggles with the thought that Corven has had his way with her, and also with the idea that she would offer herself to him only because she feels indebted to him, rather than because she loves him.

Sherriff delivered the script on 6 March 1934,[60] and it makes compelling reading. Much of the dialogue comes straight from Galsworthy's pen, making it a vivid and authentic account of the upper middle classes in England in the 1930s. But when the script was offered to Breen at the PCA, there were fireworks.

The files of the PCA are housed in the Margaret Herrick Library in Beverly Hills, Los Angeles. Inspection of the PCA file for *One More River* shows that the studio first made contact on the subject on 10 April, in a meeting between Breen and Geoffrey Shurlock (a Hays Commission staffer) on the one hand, and Carl Laemmle, Harry Zehner (Laemmle's number two) and James Whale on the other. The text of the meeting was Sherriff's script; Breen's account of their conversations, and of their concerns with the script, ran to four and a half pages. He begins by stating baldly: 'As we told you this morning, the story of this play, based as it is upon sadism, is, in our considered judgment, a definite violation of the Code.'[61] He goes on to say that any story based on sadism, or suggestive of it, is 'in its very nature' forbidden by the Code. But he allows a way out:

> We can see no objection to your developing the character of Corven as that of a brutal man who has beaten his wife and thus compelled her to leave him, but we cannot allow any suggestion, directly or indirectly, referring to sadism.

There then followed a long list of specific changes that would be required to make the film compliant with the Code. There is the usual raft of tiny changes – deleting a 'God' here, or a 'Hell' there, but most of the criticisms focus on a few key aspects of the script:

Clare's description of her husband, on numerous occasions, as a 'beast' or a 'sadist'.

Corven's description of his own questionable morality, including his sexual adventurism.

The explicit references to the riding crop.

The awkwardness of Corven's testimony on the resumption of marital relations.

The suggestion that Clare is prepared to offer herself to Tony in the final scene.

There followed a sequence of back-and-forths on the script, with Whale writing to Breen on 5 May outlining the changes he had made.[62] He also indicated that he had cast three individuals in the main roles – Diana Wynyard as Clare, Colin Clive as Corven, and Frank Lawton as Croom – and that 'as they are all really gentle folks I think our problem is already solved.'[63] Breen, however, was not easily taken in. A further note in the PCA file indicates that their staffers had crawled over Whale's 'changes' to find that several that had been requested had not yet been taken on board. Breen had no power to insist at *that* point, since the PCA changes had not yet come into effect, so he wrote to Harry Zehner on 8 May to say that the dangerous elements in the script seemed to have been covered, but that 'particularly with regard to the element of sadism, we should like to say that our final judgment will depend pretty much on the manner in which the picture is shot.'[64]

Filming began on 11 May 1934, but Whale ran over on schedule and on budget. By the time that Breen viewed the film on 12 July, the new PCA arrangement had just been put in place, so he was no longer restricted to *suggesting* changes, but could now *compel* them. The film was due to be premiered on 2 August, so there was a very limited amount of time for any changes that might be required by Breen and his colleagues. An internal memo of 17 July points to thirty changes that still had to be made to satisfy the PCA – some of the changes having first been flagged up in April, but not yet implemented. By this time the changes required cuts, re-dubbing,[65] or even re-shooting of some aspects – and without it the film would not receive its certificate. On 27 July, Breen indicated in an internal memo that he was prepared to sign off on the film. The filmmakers were not quite so satisfied, however, since a preview in Santa Barbara on that evening indicated that the pacing of the film was a little slow for the audience's liking. By this time, Sherriff had arrived for his second time in Hollywood, so afterwards, according to *Variety*,[66] he, Whale and Junior Laemmle agreed a number of further cuts to speed the film up (and also to provide a happier ending).[67] But it took long enough for the cuts to be made that the movie missed its premiere date at the Hollywood Pantages Theatre on 2 August, premiering at Baltimore's Keith's Theatre on 6 August instead.

The changes to the movie seem to have done the trick, for the American papers were impressed:

> delightfully clear-cut screen drama … boasts … the deft writing of R.C. Sherriff'.[68]

> the picture compels attention by virtue of the surpassing skill of its production and direction and by the ultimate rightness of its casting. For its several virtues we have to thank James Whale for its direction, R.C. Sherriff for the adaptation and the cameramen and scenic designers for the beauty and atmosphere of the settings.[69]

> The Galsworthy story might easily have been made a cheap, daring and tawdry piece of sensationalism but the discreet Messrs R.C. Sherriff and James Whale … never ceased to be rationalists, intent upon rendering an intensely human narrative humanly, sympathetically and believably.[70]

When it opened in Britain on 19 January 1935 (as *Over the River*), it was not so well received. Its faux-Englishness was disliked, it was seen as overlong (*The Scotsman* remarked that it had been 'adapted carefully, if a little inconcisely'),[71] and according to Hannan Swaffer, it 'utterly fails to put Galsworthy on the screen, or to make you feel for the characters the slightest sympathy.'[72] The *Daily Telegraph* called it a 'story [that] does not grip'.

Once the movie was on general release, Breen wrote to Junior Laemmle noting the favourable nature of the reviews, but also the cuts that had been made by the censor board in Ohio (chiefly to the material relating to the courtroom scene), about which he had warned Laemmle in advance. More in sorrow than in anger he counselled that:

> we ought to make the corrections here in Hollywood, and not risk the mutilation of so fine a picture as this by censor boards. … I hope … you will readily appreciate that our purpose in this office is to save the picture from the rough treatment which this picture seems to have received at the hands of the Ohio censors.[73]

He also observed, regretfully, that: 'the Legion of Decency has condemned this picture as unsuitable for the Catholic patronage. … I suppose it is the divorce angle which brings down the condemnation of the Catholics … and I suppose we are helpless under the circumstances.' Perhaps, but Breen would learn from this mistake, so that it would be almost thirty years before the subject of divorce would be candidly dealt with in Hollywood again.[74]

The Play's the Thing

In the autumn of 1933, Jeanne de Casalis, actress wife of Colin Clive, had approached Sherriff and proposed a collaboration on a new play about Napoleon's years in exile, living in St Helena, surrounded by his closest confidantes. De Casalis had been educated in France, and spoke the language fluently, which had helped in her researches, where she had unearthed several volumes of memoirs and biographies that gave a comprehensive account of the French leader's final six years. According to Sherriff, however:

> Her problem was that she was an actress,[75] not a playwright. From her experience of the theatre she could recognise episodes that would go well on the stage, but it wasn't in her line to knit them together into the tight, dramatic structure of a play.[76]

For that she felt she needed a playwright collaborator, and Sherriff might do the trick.

At the beginning of the collaboration, Sherriff was clearly enthusiastic: 'It is hard in writing to you to prevent myself from appearing extravagantly gushing about the "Napoleon" play, because the more I read and the more I think about it the more superb the opportunity appears.'[77] De Casalis had clearly given him his homework to do, and over the next few weeks she set out more of the books he ought to read, while promising card indexes of the most salient scenes from a dozen volumes.[78] She also suggested Sherriff meet Norman Edwards, a historian who had been helpful in offering her access to his library of Napoleon and St Helena books.

By December of 1933, it was Sherriff's turn to begin card-indexing scenes, as he explained his approach:

> I don't want the play to turn into a kind of mechanical toy or jigsaw puzzle, but it seems to me quite vital to have a proper tabulated card index, so that we can 'play patience' with the cards, and get them to come out in their most dramatic order, consistent with chronology etc.[79]

Then he began writing the individual scenes. By 1 January 1934, he had written the first two scenes in draft, and 'skeletons' of the fourteen scenes they had planned at their previous meeting. When he sent the scenes to her on 4 January he cautioned that:

> I am awfully afraid you may be disappointed, but I know you won't judge them too hardly. If this were a film scenario I should be quite satisfied, but

we are both aiming at such a high standard that I think we must face early disappointments if we both get near our aim to begin with.[80]

He may have been especially aware, at this point, of the difference between play and film scripts, since he was working very hard with James Whale on the scripts of *A Trip to Mars* and *One More River*. While working with Whale he apologised regularly to De Casalis for not making enough progress with the play – notably when he was forced to rearrange a meeting because he and Whale were attending the Law Courts as research for the film. By 3 February, however, he could see light at the end of the tunnel, and he wrote to tell her that Whale would be leaving a week later. He recognised that with Whale's departure, 'as much as I shall miss him,' he could reorganise his work arrangements, and devote more time to 'the Napoleon play',[81] except that his plans were confounded by the studio, to his evident irritation:

I am *so* tired of *Over the River* [*sic*] … I keep having cables, practically making me feel that the whole studio is hung up, and after driving me nearly silly they usually get the script and put it on the shelf for six months before beginning.[82]

Whale and the movie were not the only distractions. There was, for example, the press screening of *The Invisible Man* on 24 January, and although he never mentioned this to De Casalis, the attendant publicity must have taken up a good deal of his time. There was also the opening night of his latest play, *Windfall*, his first since *Badger's Green*, which premiered at the Embassy Theatre on 26 February.

Windfall[83]
Sherriff had first hinted at the play in a letter to Maurice Browne in the middle of 1931, but likely made little progress before he again mentioned it a year later. By the end of 1932, he was writing optimistically to Walter Peacock that 'The new play is going ahead quite quickly.'[84] He and Peacock had discussed various production options,[85] but little progress was made during 1933, despite some interest from Gilbert Miller. However, just when the play appeared to be marooned, his agents suggested he take it to Ronald Adam, whose Embassy Theatre in Hampstead had become well known as a proving ground for new plays. He felt comfortable with the choice:

with *Badger's Green* still in mind … it was better not to go straight with it to a West End manager … we should have a fortnight to test it before a nightly audience, to polish off its rough edges and take advantage of any suggestions the critics might have made.[86]

Windfall is the story of Tom Spooner, who in losing in the final of the Bowling Cup in his local club, is awarded a derby sweepstake ticket as a consolation prize. It duly wins, netting him £80,000. Tom is anxious to carry on as usual, despite the win, but he is quickly confronted by the fact that others will behave differently as a result. His brother-in-law Syd, for example, quickly gives up his job and plans lavish holidays, whereas Tom, a great believer in the work ethic, is shocked, emphasising how proud he is to own the home in which he lives, having paid for it piece by piece.

Others seek to capitalise on Tom's good fortune: his employer, Mr Piggott, offers him a partnership but is really looking for a £3,000 capital injection; the glazier who comes to fix a window is disgruntled because Tom refuses to stump up for fancier glass; and when Jack Seymour, the Bowls Club secretary, tells Tom he should move to a big new house, he is conveniently in a position to sell him one. At the end of Act Two, the stage directions have Tom sitting with a look on his face 'as if he can hear the world crumbling about him.'

The third act opens with Tom dictating to a secretary, replying – usually positively – to requests for financial help. Syd arrives, drunk, and they have an exchange of words, which ends with Syd storming out, and drowning himself in the local canal. The next scene is quite unlike anything Sherriff had attempted before – a series of short sketches, played around the stage, lit as each one comes to the fore, showing brief proceedings in the coroner's court, and different groups of people commenting on the whole affair – from Tom's initial win to Syd's untimely death – but generally taking a dim view of Tom's behaviour. It has a very cinematic feel. The play ends with a very brief scene as the Spooners take a sad leave of their old house, before having their chauffeur take them to their new home.

The play was very clearly based on Sherriff's own experiences of sudden wealth (the £80,000 Tom Spooner receives almost exactly mimics Sherriff's 'windfall' from *Journey's End*), so it was a little unfortunate that the play's first outing was delayed until 1934, since the plot bore a resemblance to *Sheppey*, a play by W. Somerset Maugham, which had first been performed just five months earlier. But Sherriff was quick to dismiss the comparison:

> Maugham's play was mainly concerned with a man's experiment to live like Christ, and the play would have been just as effective if Sheppey had used money for this purpose which he had saved up in an ordinary way. My play deals with the direct effect of a large money prize, not only upon the recipient, but upon his circle of friends.[87]

Windfall had remarkably mixed reviews. *The Times*[88] felt that 'Mr Sherriff is searching all the while for a more significant story than the story he is telling,' while the *Evening News*[89] called it 'shrewd and funny', but noted that 'the audience expected something more.' The *News Chronicle*[90] speculated that the 'new play [was] like a film' and that it was 'superficial'. The *Daily Sketch*,[91] by contrast, found it 'most entertaining', and *The Morning Post*[92] liked it too, finding it 'a far, far better thing than *Badger's Green'*. In *The Observer*,[93] Ivor Brown enjoyed the first half of the play, but was unimpressed by what he saw as the 'muddle of realism and expressionism' in the second half. He chided that expressionist tricks 'will not blend at all with the naturalistic picture of an English suburb which Sherriff had earlier and most effectively presented.' The message to Sherriff seemed to be that he should stick to what people expected of him, and avoid trying anything new. But that would not suit Sherriff. He was eager to try his hand at different styles and subjects, partly to challenge himself as a writer, and perhaps also to disprove Bernard Shaw's dismissal of his 'journalistic' hand. In that context he would have been comforted by the glowing tribute that Geoffrey Dearmer sent in a letter to him: 'The unadorned way you continued to convey in the last scene Spooner's concession to the grasping unappreciativeness of his neighbours without ever conceding his self-respect is one of the tersest pieces of theatre I've seen.'[94]

Decent and generous as ever, he was very apologetic to Ronald Adam about the bad press, and was clear that there would be no West End transfer – not, at any rate, unless the last act were rewritten. Concerned that Adam might lose money on the play, he remitted his royalties (just over £17) back to him,[95] and also offered to share any royalties that might arise from repertory companies or from a published version of the play.[96] But even as he was making the offer, he was aware that other work would have to take priority, and as a result, *Windfall* was neither revised nor ever published. He did, however, sell the film rights to Embassy Productions the following year, for £225, and a quota quickie popped out before the end of that year.[97] The broad themes remained the same, but a number of changes were made to the details of the story, although probably not by Sherriff: while the story and dialogue are credited to him, there is no evidence he had anything to do with the movie whatsoever.[98]

Meanwhile, in St Helena

Distracted by the production of *Windfall*, Sherriff's inactivity on *St Helena* had clearly begun to chafe with De Casalis, who wrote at the end of February to ask if she should write a scene of the play. She was in disgruntled mood – unhappy with the demands placed on her by the opening of her new play *Success Story*: 'I am having a hectic time and *hating* it. … I wouldn't give two hoots if the whole thing fell through and I could concentrate with you on Napoleon. Unfortunately I am broke.'[99] But by 3 March, with *Windfall* out of the way and the script for *One More River* safely delivered, Sherriff was able to focus on the play once more. Over the next few weeks, a steady trickle of new scenes followed, so that by mid-April, Sherriff was confident enough to tell De Casalis that 'We are now drawing towards its close.'[100] Eight weeks later, after further meetings and redrafting they were nearing completion, which was just as well, for Sherriff was scheduled to make his next trip to Hollywood on 18 July. This was the trip on which he would collaborate on the reworking of *One*

More River (after the Santa Barbara preview), but he was also expected to take with him the screenplay for his next project (*Within This Present*).

Before he left, however, he wanted to discuss possible production arrangements for the play with Spencer Curtis Brown. Although Norman Edwards' agent wanted a say in the placing of the play, Sherriff was having none of it: he had an excellent relationship with Curtis Brown, and trusted him completely in matters relating to his literary contracts, so saw no reason to involve any other agent. He was very clear on this to De Casalis as well – typically being rather more assertive in tone when discussing financial matters with her, than when discussing details of the play, where he seemed genuinely willing to incorporate her suggestions. He probably felt that, given the range of contacts and experience he and Curtis Brown had acquired since *Journey's End*, they likely knew the literary terrain (and Sherriff's place in it) better than anyone else around.

It was important to finish off *St Helena* before he left, preferably with progress made on plans for production. There was a lengthy list of managements to whom they might pass the play,[101] and while Sherriff was engaged on other duties (including coaching rowing at Henley and reporting on the Third Ashes Test Match from Manchester!) it fell to De Casalis to hawk the play round likely producers. None took the bait, however, so that the only firm contract they did manage to sign was with Victor Gollancz. But that was pleasing enough: 'I know he will be glad that we agree to publication immediately,' wrote Sherriff the day before he sailed. 'It will be very exciting to get this out just as quickly as we can.'[102] That they did: by the time of his return from the United States in September, the book of the play would be ready for publication.

The Second Contract

Within This Present is a dynastic novel by Margaret Ayer Barnes, published in 1933, relating the story of a Chicago banking family, from just before the Chicago Fire in 1871, through the First World War to the roaring twenties and the Wall Street Crash and its aftermath. Junior Laemmle had bought the book hoping to use it as a vehicle for Margaret Sullavan, who had already appeared to good reviews in a couple of Universal pictures, and was about to appear in *Little Man, What Now?*[103] Sherriff was handed the book as the first assignment in his next three-screenplay contract, and had begun work on it after he had despatched *One More River*.

Ayer Barnes's 600-page novel follows the stories of the family members in some detail, making the job of adaptation a tricky one. There are too many incidents and characters to be crammed into one movie, so Sherriff took the route of concentrating primarily on one relationship as it evolves from just before the First World War, up to the point where the family's fortune is wiped out fifteen years later. Sherriff completed the script[104] as he returned to Hollywood, as the studio's promotional magazine *Universal Weekly* breathlessly reported:

With the unfinished manuscript of his screen version of *Within This Present* in his briefcase, R.C. Sherriff, noted stage and screen dramatist, left New York for Universal City Wednesday, 25 July, on the *Twentieth Century*. He will work on the script all the way across the continent in his train compartment. By the time he reaches Hollywood he will have his picture adaptation of this current popular novel by Margaret Ayer Barnes all in readiness to submit to Carl Laemmle Jr.[105]

The script was submitted to the PCA on 30 July, which gave it an easy run, registering only its objection to the usual profanities. But Whale, apparently, was not so happy, so Sherriff was taken off the movie *Edwin Drood* and set to work on redrafting the script he had just completed.[106] A subsequent script, dated 21 August, raised a few additional PCA objections but further amendments eventually secured a clean bill of health by 14 September. Although Sherriff's script was further rewritten later in the year, under the guidance of Leonard Spiegelgass (Universal's story editor), tight finances and the shift of James Whale's attention towards *Bride of Frankenstein* meant that *Within This Present* was eventually set aside.

St Helena

At the end of this second Hollywood visit, Sherriff left for England on 6 September on the *Empress of Britain*, his mother at his side, and a brand new Rolls-Royce 20/25 Thrupp & Maberley drop-head coupe awaiting his return.[107] In his autobiography he suggested that he was returning because the studio had asked him to work on *Bride of Frankenstein*, but he felt he would be writing 'pulp, and been ashamed of every page I wrote'.[108] But that can hardly have been the reason. He would be back over in Hollywood within a year, discussing his work on other projects (which would be less feted than *Bride*). It was far more likely that the trip had always been intended to be short; he preferred them that way anyway. This one had given him enough time to conference on, and finish, *Within This Present*, while also allowing him to adjust *One More River*, and then attend its premiere. That was more than enough, especially since he had two good reasons to be back in Britain by mid-September: one was the impending publication of *St Helena*, and the other was the release of the new movie version of *Badger's Green*.

Gollancz published *St Helena* on 17 September, and it proved to be unlike any other play that Sherriff wrote. It consists of twelve scenes, roughly similar in length, plotting Napoleon's time on the island, from his arrival in December of 1815, to just before his death, in May 1821. It features an extensive cast of principals, and takes place in six separate locations. Sherriff's motivation to write it clearly stems from his love of history, but his fidelity to his research (or to De Casalis's research) results in the play having a very episodic feel. It is symptomatic of Sherriff that he continued to try new techniques, adapting the cinematic writing skills he was acquiring to his work on the stage. In some respects the play seems to have more in common with a screenplay than with one of his more conventional theatre pieces – a series of incidents, linked primarily through Napoleon, each designed to shine a light on some aspects of his character. In fact, in one scene we even have two conversations occurring at the same time – almost as though inviting us to act as director, cutting from one to the other in our own minds.

Writing some fourteen years later (during which time he had produced no other plays), Sherriff recognised the problems in conveying history on the stage: 'The passage of time is an admirable vehicle for the screen, denied the theatre by the need for continual curtain drops.'[109]. But that is exactly what *St Helena* does. The first half of the play covers the first year of his stay, and the liveliness of much of the conversation remains undimmed, even while the constraints of the island are imposing themselves on a reluctant, and occasionally peevish, Napoleon. The second half covers four more years, which witness the steady deterioration in the Emperor's condition, the diminution of his energy, and the gradual departure – or premature death – of some of his closest confidantes. There is still some liveliness, but the overall tone is wistful, even melancholic, and the attempts of the Emperor and his staff to avoid dealing with the British authorities come across as wilful and childish. The Napoleon who inhabits the first half of the play is quite different from the character we see decline before our eyes in the second half.

In advance of publication, Sherriff had received encouraging letters from some of those to whom he had sent advance copies, including J.C. Masterman, a friend and Oxford Don,[110] and Rudolf Besier (author of the highly regarded and very successful *Barretts of Wimpole Street*). Many of the reviewers in the papers were equally intrigued (although it helped that some of them were good friends of Sherriff). G.B. Stern, for example, was very positive ('though undoubtedly written for acting … it is equally valuable … as a very perfect, concentrated biography'),[111] as was George Bishop ('The authors have shown fine selective artistry in building up the play. All the scenes are quick and vivid.').[112] *The Times* and the *New York Times* rated it highly as well, but Ivor Brown in *The Guardian* was less convinced: 'If ever there was a tiresome central figure of a play here is one, and it says much for the authors that they have managed to make something of their subject.'[113] Sherriff counselled De Casalis not to be too upset by Brown's review. 'It is perfectly clear that any reader of the play who has a prejudiced view of Napoleon will be influenced accordingly,'[114] he wrote.

Although the reviews were very satisfying, there was one slight cloud on the horizon, in the form of Norman Edwards. Shortly after the play was published Sherriff wrote to De Casalis that he had received a 'most extraordinary letter' from Edwards, listing a number of grievances, including 'that he, and he alone, suggested and inspired the play, and that we ought to say so in our book'. He also, noted Sherriff, 'defends you against my villainy in connection with Gollancz's first advertisement.' The advertisement to which he referred appeared in *The Observer* on 16 September, and highlighted Sherriff's name, with De Casalis's in much smaller type. Sherriff had had nothing to do with the advert, and Gollancz were presumably just highlighting the author who was most likely to influence book sales. But De Casalis would continue to feel that her role in the play had been downgraded below that of Sherriff (something that, she accepted, he did nothing to encourage), and later apparent slights would do nothing to improve her mood (see Chapter 8).

Sherriff has always been seen as a very modest and unassuming man – and so he was. But where his writing was concerned he could be robust and implacable. So he replied to Edwards' letter in kind, and was adamant that the inscription to him in the book would be nothing more than an acknowledgement of Edwards' assistance, by way of lending them his books. He made it clear to De Casalis that it was she alone who had inspired him with Napoleon as a subject, and he was unwilling to say anything other than that in the inscription. Further, he asked, 'Why on earth should we talk about our gratitude and about his invaluable help when, as far as I am concerned, he has been such a continual nuisance?'[115] Although he offered De Casalis the chance to change the inscription if she really wanted to, it was quite clear from the force of his objections that he would not settle for anything other than the briefest version possible, so subsequent versions of the play were published with only this short inscription included:

The authors wish to acknowledge the valuable help given by Mr Norman Edwards F.R.Hist.S. in placing his library and technical knowledge at their disposal.[116]

Badger's Green – The Movie

As with *Windfall*, Sherriff had no role in the movie of *Badger's Green*, other than selling the rights, but that had taken long enough: despite several expressions of interest from 1931 onwards, it took until 1934 before British and Dominions (B & D) Film Corporation produced it at Elstree as a quota-quickie for Paramount. This was a regular arrangement, with B & D producing roughly one film a month for them for 'several years'.[117] Production was in the hands of Anthony Havelock-Allan,[118] while the direction was placed with Adrian Brunel. Sherriff enjoyed a private showing in the Paramount projection room (arranged by Violet Powell, who had written the screenplay for the film), and also went to the trade show on 18 September, afterwards being quoted in support: 'Mr Sherriff said that he considered that the transition had been perfectly done, the casting was admirable and the atmosphere had been perfectly preserved. He had not one criticism to make.'[119] The reviews were positively glowing, with, for example, both *Kinematograph* and *Cinema* magazines labelling it 'delightful'.[120]

The public seems to have agreed, and the movie became a sizeable money earner – costing just £6,000 to make, but drawing over £60,000 at the box office.[121] Sherriff noted as much in a letter to Brown a few months later:

> There has been an extraordinary revival of interest in [*Badger's Green*] during the past few months, mainly, I think, attributable to the success of the picture. Although the picture cost so little money it has had the most extraordinarily good release.... I have had a request from the BBC to permit a broadcast version and there has been a steady and apparently increasing demand for the play in repertory and Amateur circles. ... All this brings back my long desire to repair the weaknesses of the stage play and give it another chance.[122]

Sherriff would, eventually, try to repair the play's weakness – although he would wait twenty-five years to do so (see Chapter 13).

Her Excellency the Governor[123]

Sherriff's next Universal commission was a script based on a short story by Nina Wilcox Putnam. The story had been published in *Liberty* magazine on 23 December 1933, and Universal seem to have acquired the rights early in 1934: several of Wilcox Putnam's stories had already made their way on to the screen with some success.[124] There were some complications around the awarding of the rights but by the end of the year Sherriff was hard at work.

The script relates the story of Judith Stonewall, whose mother had been a famous suffragette leader who died in a fire at a showground, despite the efforts of Tim Marshall, a circus juggler, to save her. Judith gradually falls for Tim – although they are from very different backgrounds – and eventually they get married, to the disapproval of many in her circle. Judith turns out to be a talented politician and rises to increasingly higher office, but Tim has a weakness for drink, and as she ascends the political ladder his occasional lapses are publicised by her opponents, so that, eventually, he feels that he must leave her or drag her down. In due course she becomes Governor and remarries (believing Tim to be dead), but Tim has fallen in with undesirable acquaintances, one of whom, discovering that he was the Governor's husband, threatens to blackmail Judith. Tim kills him to prevent him doing so, and is sentenced to death, the warrant signed by the new Governor – Judith. When she finds out who he is, she grants him a full pardon and resigns her governorship, so that they can escape to a life of anonymity together with their daughter.

This assignment was something of a departure for Sherriff, for nearly all his scripts so far had been adapted from books. In this case, however, the short story provided no more than a template, leaving him to flesh out the detail. James Curtis remarked,[125] vis-a-vis *Within This Present*, that Sherriff had struggled with the

American milieu; in practice, however, the upper-middle-class family of Ayer Barnes' novel was not a million miles away from the equivalent settings in England. *Her Excellency*, by contrast, focuses heavily on American politics. Politics and ideas were never Sherriff's strong suit: he specialised in observation, sketching his characters by the accumulation of small details. American politics, in particular, was a closed book. The political programme that he bestows on Judith is a cumbersome one, and the speeches that pop up in the script are unconvincing. His unfamiliarity with the political system in the United States is also apparent – in his confusion, for example, of the position of State Senator with that of United States Senator. Writing the script in England he was particularly at sea, as he recognised in a note in the script: 'I have not the necessary references at hand in England but I assume there is some colourful scene in connection with a governor's election in the United States.'[126]

Sherriff's script was first presented to Joseph Breen at the PCA at the end of January 1935, where an internal memo notes:

> The one difficulty in granting this story deals with the action of Judith, as Governor, granting a full pardon to Tim, her husband, who has been convicted of first-degree murder. This action is unethical and unsocial, to say the least. We suggested [to Spiegelgass and Russell at Universal] that the killing of Bill by Tim be made manslaughter in self-defence, leaving Tim really innocent. … Spiegelgass promised to change the script accordingly.[127]

Alternative endings, such as Tim committing suicide, proved no more acceptable. The wrangling with the PCA would continue for several more months, and through further script iterations (not all of them by Sherriff), before, in August, Universal finally pulled the plug on the project.[128]

Dracula's Daughter

Sherriff was nearing the end of his time with Universal. His first movie, *The Road Back*, had been praised by everyone who had seen the script. Two of the films in his first three-movie contract – *The Invisible Man* and *One More River* – had been very successful, and very well reviewed, but both had been set in firmly English locations (largely rural towns and villages). On the other hand, he had struck out with the first two films in his next contract, both of which had been set equally firmly in the towns and cities of the United States. With his second contract coming to an end, he probably felt that he needed another win – preferably something set outside the United States – and there was a chance that *Dracula's Daughter* might fit the bill.

Junior Laemmle had always wanted to make sequels of his main horror pictures[129] – *Frankenstein*, *Dracula*, *The Invisible Man* and the *Wolfman* – and he wanted James Whale to direct the first two. He acquired the rights to a Bram Stoker short story

(*Dracula's Guest*) from David O. Selznick, at MGM,[130] and planned to have Whale direct it straight after completing *Bride*, with Sherriff as scriptwriter (because of the good job he had done on *The Invisible Man*). But after *Bride*, Whale wanted a break from horror, hoping instead to direct a remake of *Show Boat*, which had been a massive stage success and – as a big-budget movie – had been featured on the Universal schedule at various points in the previous few years.

After completing his final script for *Her Excellency*, he began work on the screenplay in May 1935.[131] The first section of the script[132] sets up Dracula's backstory. It opens stirringly, with the Count's men rampaging through the countryside abducting young women from their villages and transporting them to the castle for the pleasure of the Count's guests, who play dice for the privilege of first choice among the captives. Dracula seduces one of the young women, and calls her his daughter. The villagers enlist the help of the ancient magician Talifer,[133] who turns the Count into a vampire, and his guests into various other creatures. The castle is then condemned to age a thousand years in an instant.

Still at the castle, in the present day, four young people (two brother-sister engaged couples) hear the vampire legend, and the boys decide to explore the castle at night: one (John) falls under the spell of Dracula's daughter, and is kept in the castle, while the other (David) escapes but is driven almost to madness. The vampire hunter Van Helsing comes to help, and when they find that Dracula's daughter has been shipped to London in her coffin (with John at her side), they follow closely behind. They eventually track her down (she is now the Countess Szelenski), and when she realises they are closing in she quickly arranges to be shipped back to Transylvania in her coffin, again with John as an escort. On board ship, they try but fail to get through to her coffin, and when they finally persuade the captain to inspect it, she summons up a mighty storm, causing the ship to founder, but not before Van Helsing drives a stake through her heart, lifting the spell on John.

With its very obvious satanic, sexual and sadistic themes it is a wonder that anyone at Universal felt they would be given the opportunity to make the film. According to the PCA records, the film was submitted 'off the record' by Harry Zehner to Breen on 5 September 1935. He was horrified, writing in an internal memorandum on 13 September:

> This story ... contains countless offensive stuff which makes the picture utterly impossible for approval under the production code. Messrs Shurlock and Breen talked with Junior Laemmle about the matter yesterday afternoon, and told him definitely, we could not approve the picture.[134]

He went on to note that he had spoken to Junior, who had assured him, that 'Mr Sherriff, the playwright' was rewriting the story entirely, 'cutting out much of the dangerous material which it now contains.'

The film had also been submitted to the British Board of Film Censors, whose chief censor, Colonel John Hanna, was equally abrupt:

> Dracula was ghoulish-weird-eerie and every other adjective in the language that expresses Horror, but *Dracula's Daughter* would require the resources of half a dozen more languages to adequately express its beastliness. I consider this absolutely unfit for exhibition as a film.[135]

It seems likely that not everyone at Universal was surprised, or even disappointed, at the results of the PCA's deliberations. There seems little doubt that Whale was not keen to begin work on *Dracula's Daughter*, preferring to continue his preparations for *Show Boat*, which he would eventually begin shooting in December 1935. It has been suggested that Whale may have egged Sherriff on to write a script that was much more outrageous than he would normally have ever written, while also adding some embellishments of his own.[136]

Sherriff left from Southampton on the *Empress of Britain* on 21 September, arriving in Hollywood on 1 October, rushing round to Universal with an updated screenplay. Over the next couple of weeks, Zehner, Sherriff and Breen met up, and further redrafting took place, with a new script sent to the PCA on 21 October. Breen replied to Zehner two days later urging further changes, in particular, 'we suggest, respectfully, that you take out of the script those elements in scene, dialogue or action, which tend to flavour the story with sex.'[137] He then sets out an extensive list of suggestions, most amusingly that, in the early part of the script:

> where Dracula's soldiers sweep the countryside and bring to his castle a group of young women, with the sprinkling of men, that you affirmatively indicate that the purpose for which the young girls have been abducted is to provide dancing partners for the Count's assembled guests at the banquet.

He reinforced the point by suggesting that Dracula's speech to his guests could be amended to include the line 'You shall choose your partners for the dance in order of your rank'. The rest of the detailed points were made along similar lines, but with additional proscriptions on religious or sadistic imagery, or excessive drunkenness. It was clear, though, from the generally conciliatory tone of Breen's letter that the PCA felt that things were moving in the right direction.

But the whole business had dragged on long enough that no progress was possible with James Whale, for he was now very firmly engaged in *Show Boat*. Sherriff, too, had moved on. Once he had delivered his third screenplay, Universal gave him permission to sign with Irving Thalberg at MGM to write the screenplay for *Goodbye, Mr Chips*.[138] Universal carried on with *Dracula's Daughter*, with the need to begin production before February 1936, or the rights would lapse to Selznick: a new script was completed by Garret Fort and the film was handed over to director Lambert Hillyer. It bears little resemblance to the project as conceived by Sherriff and Whale, although it was well reviewed when it was eventually released on 11 May 1936 – just six days before Whale's triumphant *Show Boat*.

Plate 1. Bob and Beryl, c. 1898. (*C KGS: SHC 3813/14/1/5/6*)

Plate 2. Family group, c. 1906. From left: Beryl, Bundy, Connie, Bob, Herbert. (*C KGS: SHC 3813/14/1/5/10*)

Plate 3. Rowing team, c. 1912; Bob is seated on the far left. (*C KGS: SHC 2332/6/6/1/4*)

Plate 4. Akron the Magician! c. 1914.
(*C Kingston Rowing Club: KX142/5,
KRC Bx 5*)

Plate 5. Proud Artist, March 1916. (*C KGS: SHC 2332/6/4/1/19*)

Plate 6. Percy High, seated back left, with pipe. (*C KGS: From* Memories of Active Service, *facing p.20. SHC 2332/3/9/3/2*)

Plate 7. Officers of the 9th East Surreys, March 1917. Including: seated, Lt Warre-Dymond (extreme left), Capt Tetley (extreme right), Lt Clark (second right). First row: standing, 2nd Lt Sherriff (centre), 2nd Lt Lindsay (extreme right). Second row: standing, 2nd Lt Douglass (extreme left). (*C SHC: Ref: ESR/25/Clark/7*)

Plate 8. Officers of 'C' Company, 9th East Surreys, Bully Grenay, April 1917. Front row, left to right: 2nd Lt Douglass, Capt Warre-Dymond, 2nd Lt Trenchard. Back row, left to right: 2nd Lt Kiver, 2nd Lt Sherriff, 2nd Lt Toplis. Seated: 2nd Lt Homewood. (*C KGS:SHC 2332/6/4/2/3*)

3rd EAST SURREY CRICKET ELEVEN, DOVER, 1918.

Sgt. C. Stratford,   Pte. F. Lazenby,   C.Q.M.S. I. Stevenson,   C.Q.M.S. J. Rowe,   Cpl. Penfold,   Sgt. J. Elsmore.
Lt. J. L. Crompton,   Lt. V. F. S. Crawford,   Col. R. F. Sulivan,   Lt. W. G. Kent,   Lt. R. B. Bettson.
Captain.
Lt. R. C. Sherrif,   Lt. R. C. Gold.

Plate 9. 3rd East Surrey Cricket XI, Dover 1918. Sherriff is seated left, front row (name misspelled on the caption). (*C SHC: Ref: ESR/4/2/3/16*)

Plate 10. Cast of the *Woods of Meadowside*, 1922. Sherriff seated on the floor, far right, with Beryl behind him. (*C KGS: SHC 2332/6/10/1(2)*)

Plate 11. Portrait of James Whale, signed 'To Bob with best wishes, Jimmy. Hollywood 1930'. (*SHC: 2332/6/13/4*)

DESIGN FOR "JOURNEY'S END".   James Whale - 1929 -

Plate 12. Set design for *Journey's End*, by James Whale, 1929. By permission of the David Lewis Estate. (*SHC 2332/6/13/4*)

Plate 13. Colin Clive as Stanhope, and Robert Speaight as Hibbert, from the Savoy production of *Journey's End*, 1929. (*Photo by Stage Photo Company, Ref: ESR/19/2/6(5)*)

Plate 14. Maurice Browne and Sherriff, c. 1929. (*Portrait by Cigarini, courtesy of University of Michigan Library (Special Collections Library) Ellen Van Volkenburg and Maurice Browne Papers*)

Plate 15. Sherriff on the boat for the US, probably 1929. (*C KGS: SHC 2332/6/6/2/1*)

Plate 16. Victoria Cross recipients at *Journey's End*, Prince of Wales Theatre, 1929. (*Courtesy of University of Michigan Library* (*Special Collections Library*) *Ellen Van Volkenburg and Maurice Browne Papers*)

Plate 17. King George V and Queen Mary with the Duke and Duchess of York at the Prince of Wales theatre for *Journey's End*, 14 November 1929. (*Courtesy of University of Michigan Library* (*Special Collections Library*) *Ellen Van Volkenburg and Maurice Browne Papers*)

Plate 18. Sherriff, in Kingston Rowing Club blazer, c. 1929. (*C KGS: SHC 2332/6/6/11/6*)

BACK TO THE DUG-OUT. 1930

A hundred and thirty officers and men of the 9th East Surreys, with whom Mr. R. C. Sherriff served in France, saw his war play, "Journey's End" at the Prince of Wales Theatre last Saturday, previous to the Battalion's reunion dinner. After the play Mr. Sherriff conducted some of his guests behind the scenes, and the dug-out on the stage was also inspected, when the photograph reproduced above was taken. (Left to right): Mr. R. C. Sherriff, Mr. L. H. Webb, M.C., Capt. L. C. Thomas, M.C., Capt. G. Warre-Dymond, M.C., Capt. C. A. Clark, D.S.O., M.C., Capt. L. A. Knight, Capt. H. Ellis, Mr. G. Harris, Mr F. J. Hardy.

Plate 19. On stage, after the special matinee performance of *Journey's End* for the East Surreys, 25 January 1930. (*SHC ESR/25/CLARK/15(20)*)

BADGERS GREEN — ACTS I , II.   James Whale -1930-

Plate 20. Set design for acts 1 and 2 of *Badger's Green*, by James Whale, 1930. By permission of the David Lewis Estate. (*SHC 2332/6/14/2/3*)

Plate 21. The New College Torpids VIII, February 1932 (Sherriff seated far left). (*C. Gillman & Soame; reproduced with permission of New College, University of Oxford*)

Plate 22. The Hollywood Cricket Club, mid-1930s. Sherriff seated front row, second left. First row: Boris Karloff (second left), C. Aubrey Smith (striped blazer), Ronald Coleman (3rd right), H.B. Warner (second right). (*SHC 2332/6/6/12/6*)

Plate 23. Bundy, Hazel, Beryl and Tudor, c. 1930s. (*C KGS: SHC 3813/14/1/4/4*)

Plate 24. Jeanne De Casalis (a qualified pilot) with Sherriff (her passenger), c. 1936. (*SHC 2332/5/2/71*)

Plate 25. Sherriff at the door of Rosebriars, late 1930s. (*C KGS: SHC 3813/14/2/5*)

Plate 26. Sherriff selling books, probably 1939. (*Photo by Frank W. Crouch, SHC 2332/6/9/19*)

Page 27. The 1st East Surreys repel the Sudanese natives, in filming for *The Four Feathers* (1938). (*Photo by Major P.G.S. Hill, reproduced by permission of the Surrey History Centre, ref: ESR/25/3/15(1)*)

Plate 28. Sherriff with director Gabriel Pascal, 1939. (*C.* Western Morning News *Co Ltd, SHC 2332/6/9/18*)

Plate 29. Connie in nurse's uniform in America in the Second World War, helping organise 'Bundles for Britain'. (*C KGS: SHC 3813/14/1/2/4*)

PEOPLE BEHIND THE PICTURE

*ROBERT CLARK, Director in charge of production,
Elstree Studios; President of the British Film Producers
Association and a Governor of The British Film Institute*

*MICHAEL ANDERSON, director of "The Dam
Busters."*

W. A. WHITTAKER (Production Supervisor)

*R. C. SHERRIFF, famous author who wrote the
screenplay.*

*PAUL BRICKHILL, on whose book "The Dam
Busters" the film is based.*

Plate 30. The men behind *The Dam Busters*: page from a commemorative brochure, 1955. (*C Studio Canal Films Ltd. Ref: SHC 2332/8/13/5*)

Plate 31. Production of *The Long Sunset*, at the Mermaid Theatre, 1961. Left to right: Gawain (David Pinner), Portius (Jerry Verno), Julian (Joseph O'Conor), Lucian (Kenneth Edwards), seated, Arthur (Peter Prowse). (*Photo by John Miles. Ref: SHC 2332/6/10/3/2/4*)

Plate 32. Sherriff in his later years, probably 1960s. (*C KGS: SHC 2332/6/9/25/1*)

Chapter 8

Pastures New, 1935–37

Observe constantly that all things take place by change, and accustom thyself to consider that the nature of the Universe loves nothing so much as to change the things which are and to make new things like them.

Marcus Aurelius, *The Meditations*, Book IV.

Having travelled out to the United States on the *Empress of Britain* in September, Sherriff and his mother returned on the same ship, battling through a gale[1] to arrive back in a cold and wet Southampton on 12 November 1935. Their spirits were probably lifted, however, by the arrival of yet another new Rolls-Royce – a drop-head coupé again, although perhaps winter wasn't the best time to make use of it.

Arriving back, he wrote to his old friend Bill Darlington about the problems facing his employers: 'The Universal Film Company, with whom I have been under contract for several years, are now in a tremendous upheaval, and it is rumoured that old Carl Laemmle is selling his interests.' The rumours were correct; by the beginning of 1936 an east coast syndicate had taken over, and the Laemmles were out, with Charles Rogers (an experienced film man, but with no particularly notable pictures to his credit) taking over as head of production. Sherriff told Darlington that the new people would take over the remains of his contract, but that in the meantime he had been:

> given freedom to do a film script for Metro-Goldwyn [MGM], which is to be *Goodbye, Mr Chips*, and I believe that Charles Laughton is to play the part. I wonder if you have read the book. It is a charming little book, though rather sentimental.[2]

Sherriff had been communicating with James Hilton, the book's author, since the beginning of the year, to see whether they might collaborate on an adaptation for the stage.[3] He had also mentioned the book to Alexander Korda[4] when they had met in March[5]: Korda had offered Sherriff a three-picture deal, which he reluctantly had to decline, because he was still bound exclusively to Universal. Some time after meeting Korda, with Universal in a state of flux, and no screenwriting assignments on the horizon after *Dracula's Daughter*, Sherriff had sent his agent to see Irving Thalberg[6] at MGM (which had acquired the rights to the book shortly after its publication in

1934), to see if Thalberg would be willing to try to get Universal's permission for Sherriff to be released to write the script. He must have been delighted when he was offered the contract: after a succession of difficult screenplays, this one looked right up his street.

Goodbye, Mr Chips

Hilton's story is a short and simple one. A Latin master at an unremarkable public school[7] looks back over his life. While many of the memories are about aspects of life at the school, he also remembers with great fondness the young woman whom he met and married, and who had a profound effect on his personality, even though she was with him for a relatively short time before dying in childbirth. Thalberg 'wanted the story developed as that of a man who "started his career as a failure and was bound to mediocrity. He never really improved, but he met a woman who … turned his mediocrity into success."'[8] Sherriff gave his own view of the adaptation in an article a dozen years later:

> This was the most perfect story I ever handled for the screen, but in many ways the most difficult. It was a very short novel, barely 100 pages. There was very little dialogue and its charm lay in its beautifully suggested retrospect. The focussing point, for the screen, was the character of Mr Chips himself. In the novel, the old man of eighty is dreaming by his fireside. His memories float back to him, inconsequently and frequently out of their true time sequence. I had to disentangle these memories and build them up into a series of living scenes.[9]

Sherriff's first script was dated 3 March 1936,[10] and it does an excellent job in some respects of capturing the character of Mr Chipping (known to his boys as Chips), although his tendency to strictness before he meets his wife makes the character more isolated from his peers than he is in the book. Sherriff adds a number of scenes rather than simply dramatising the book, largely to amplify Chips's character, and he also invents three generations of one family (the Colleys), to establish a thread of continuity during Chips's time at the school. But the framework of the film is Hilton's, as are many of the jokes (the *Lex Canuleia* scene, for example; Chips's protestations at the new Latin pronunciation ('We kiss 'em'); or the wonderful scene when the school is gathered in the hall at the height of a Zeppelin raid and Chips has them read from Julius Caesar's *The Conquest of Gaul* ('in this way did the Germans fight'). Even the final montage of boys remembered by Chips, with the admonition that he's had thousands of children – 'and all boys', is courtesy of Hilton. He also follows the book in having Chips's chance meeting with Katherine (his future wife) in the Lake District, rather than in Austria (that particular alteration would come later, and by a different hand).

It is no surprise that Hilton thoroughly approved of the script, drawn as it was so faithfully from his book. He wrote to Sherriff:

> Quite frankly it is one of the most beautiful things of its kind I have ever seen and if you think this sounds exaggerated I can add that David Lewis[11] thinks the same.[12] I don't know Thalberg's opinion yet, but I should imagine that nobody could fail to approve such a fine piece of work. I had known, of course, that it would be good, but the way you have entered into the spirit as well as the letter of my work exceeds my highest expectations.

Thalberg's opinion came shortly thereafter, following a story conference with Lewis and Hilton. A lot of changes were suggested, but Hilton wrote to Sherriff to reassure him that the changes shouldn't affect 'more than 10 per cent of the story'.[13] Furthermore, Thalberg had described it as 'the best first script he had ever received', and Hilton was glad that the rewrite would be in Sherriff's hands.

St Helena, Again

Even as he had been working hard on *Chips*, Sherriff had been shepherding *St Helena* towards its long delayed stage premiere.

Ever since its publication in September 1934, he and De Casalis had tried to find a sympathetic theatre management to produce it, but they had come up empty-handed. This was not altogether surprising. There had been a number of Napoleon-themed plays and films in the preceding months, and none had fared well.[14] Against such an unpromising background, *St Helena* had additional problems:

> From a box-office point of view everything was against it. There was no love story; no romance or glamour; no element of suspense, when from the rise of the first curtain the audience would know that Napoleon was doomed to die in exile. It was a play of a fight against boredom and fading hopes. ... On top of all was a big cast of more than thirty actors, and the difficult technical problems of numerous scene changes.[15]

As 1934 came to an end, Sherriff worked diligently to reduce the play's running time (by forty minutes from its original three hours), in the hope that the play might find a home. Over the following months there were discussions with various potential financial 'backers' but when it came down to specifics – producers, actors and theatre managements – the plans fell through, and the play languished in production limbo throughout the spring and summer of 1935. During that time Sherriff and De Casalis were able to enjoy another collaboration; this time on an adaptation of a French play, *Espoir*, by Henri Bernstein. Their partnership was again successful, and they were offered a generous deal by Howard & Wyndham (Britain's largest theatre management group), with Sherriff characteristically insisting that De Casalis receive the lion's share of the proceeds, since she had done the bulk of the work. But, at the very last minute, the play was mysteriously pulled from the theatre production schedule, leaving Sherriff aghast: 'I, too, am astonished at this news about *Espoir*. Nothing of the kind has ever happened to me personally before.'[16]

Good Old Vic

With the foot-dragging on *St Helena*, and the cancellation of *Espoir*, Sherriff gave vent to his frustration, writing to De Casalis that: 'I am absolutely sick to death of the word "backers" and the vague talk which tired us so much some months ago. It is not good for either of us to have the play lying unproduced.'[17] But just when the theatrical gods seemed against him, there came an unexpected approach from Henry Cass, a senior producer at The Old Vic, who wanted the play for their spring season.

Sherriff was a huge admirer of The Old Vic (and its 'coterie of genuine theatre lovers'),[18] and of its indomitable manager, Lilian Baylis. He wrote glowingly of her in his autobiography:

> When I first met her about *St Helena* she had been sole manager for more than twenty years. She had made it the home of Shakespeare, the only theatre in London that had produced all his plays. It had become a national institution.[19]

But just because Cass had come knocking did not mean that the deal was yet secure: Baylis had first to hear what her Committee of Management thought of the idea. Sherriff was keeping his fingers crossed:

> it will be a great thing for us if The Old Vic does it. It will be such a relief to stand aside and let them go ahead without all the worries we have been through. Thank goodness there will be no question of 'backers'!'[20]

Just a couple of weeks later, in early September 1935, he was able to tell De Casalis that The Old Vic had finally made a definite offer to produce the play.

That offer came in just before he disappeared to Hollywood (the trip that would see him grappling with Joe Breen over *Dracula's Daughter*). After such a gruelling experience he must have hoped he'd come back to some good news, but it was not to be, for production plans for *St Helena* were up in the air once more. Ronald Adam now seemed to be in the mix, clearly unfazed by the poor reception *Windfall* had received at his Embassy Theatre. But Sherriff was still keen on an Old Vic production, and meeting Cass again, was delighted to find that they were now definitely going ahead.

The production was scheduled for February 1936, and before the end of December the wheels were in motion. Cass proposed Kenneth Kent (an actor of considerable experience) as their Napoleon, and although he was far from their first choice, they bowed to his wishes. Sherriff saw significant advantages to an Old Vic production: 'The very fact of The Old Vic performance is inclined to place the play in the same category as the Tchekov/Ibsen type, which is not only a great compliment but assures it of future attention and revival.'[21] Somewhat surprisingly, he also wrote that 'I am not a great believer in meteoric West End productions,' and that he would far sooner see the play 'firmly established with a good repertory company', but he was probably making the best of a bad job. As he himself pointed out, it had been almost two years since the play had first been announced, and most managers were no longer interested: The Old Vic was their only option, and without it, 'the play may go upon the shelf for good.'[22]

Sherriff seemed fated to have plays rehearsed under difficult circumstances. With the ISS they had almost no access to the Apollo Theatre until the final rehearsals, and now they had to rehearse in the theatre in the morning with the scenery from the current production on the stage round about them, for there was no room in The Old Vic's finances for the stage to be empty for a week. Many of the actors[23] rehearsing the play would go on stage in the other production in the evenings, making it a long and difficult day for them. But somehow they made it through, and by opening night, on 4 February 1936, everything was ready.

In his autobiography, Sherriff writes that the 'critics hadn't got a good word to say for St Helena'[24] – but in fact the critics were much more in favour of the play than against it. Admittedly, The Times' critic was at best lukewarm, and The Standard's critic called it 'inexpressibly tedious', but the others were more positive. the New Statesman called it 'a brilliantly contrived mosaic of recorded remarks', noting that 'the authors show an extraordinary sense of the theatre.' The Observer described it as 'interesting', and the production 'a credit to The Old Vic'. The Post noted: 'It is very seldom that The Old Vic puts on a completely new play, and I am glad that the one that has been chosen ... is such a satisfactory production.' The Morning Post called it 'a haunting stage portrait ... an event to be remembered', The Guardian an 'admirable documentary'.[25]

Despite the press, the play got off to a very rocky start. In part this was because its opening night had been scheduled for the same night as the opening of Follow The Sun, C.B. Cochran's latest revue, and Sherriff knew in advance that this would suck all the publicity (and most of the critics) away from them. But even after the notices came out, the box office failed to pick up – and Sherriff was reminded of Journey's End's first faltering steps. He tells of looking in at the theatre one evening and doubting that 'there were more than fifty people there'.[26]

Out of the blue, however, some help arrived from an unlikely quarter. Winston Churchill had happened to go along to the play (without, rather surprisingly, the knowledge of The Old Vic or its patrons), and afterwards felt compelled to write a letter to *The Times*. In the letter he noted that he had very nearly been dissuaded from coming to the theatre by the weight of poor reviews in the press, but, having nevertheless gone along, he had been thoroughly impressed by the play. Being very knowledgeable about both Napoleon and the era in which he lived, he was very complimentary regarding the play's portrayal of the great general, and this he attributed to the efforts of Sherriff as the playwright, and to Kenneth Kent's performance in the leading role.

In No Leading Lady, Sherriff recounts how, having read the letter:

> I got the car out and drove up to the theatre. I wanted to be around to see what happened, but I never expected things to happen as they did. When I got there at about ten o'clock, there was already a trickle of people coming in to the box office. This in itself was an event, because until that morning there hadn't been anybody at all. By lunchtime it had turned into a stream. There was a queue as people came across the bridge to book their seats in the lunch hour. The box office telephone was ringing all the time and Lilian Bayliss put in an extra girl to attend to it. The West End ticket agencies ... had people coming in to their offices all over London and they had to ring up the theatre for seats, taking ten or twenty at a time.

The result was that, whereas on the evening before Churchill's letter there had been perhaps sixty people in the theatre (which could seat a thousand), the following night there were more than 500, and on the next evening the theatre was packed: 'Every seat sold with people standing at the back of the pit and the gallery. It must have been the most complete turnaround that had ever happened to a play before: all in a couple of nights.'[28]

So Lilian Baylis now had an unfamiliar problem on her hands. In The Old Vic season, each production was pencilled in for a number of weeks: it was a repertory company, and their regulars expected the productions to change. But, with *St Helena* doing great business, there was the temptation to keep it on for a longer run, which would bring in more desperately needed cash, but at the expense of upsetting her regular clientele. The run was extended, for a week at first, and then for a further week (with *The Winter's Tale*, which was to follow, being postponed indefinitely as a result), before a transfer was arranged to a West End theatre. The transfer came not a moment too soon: *The Manchester Guardian* reported:

> the regular Old Vic audience were not too keen on the play, and have been complaining to Miss Baylis about the alteration of the Shakespeare timetable. The cheaper parts of The Old Vic, always the most crowded, have not been well patronised, but the stalls and boxes have been full of strangers.[29]

Although a godsend, the Churchill letter did have one unfortunate repercussion – one that clearly troubled Sherriff for the rest of his life. The partnership between Sherriff and De Casalis had been one of equals: De Casalis provided the original idea, the fluent French, and the Napoleonic research; Sherriff had his skills as a dramatist – and vitally, of course, his name. But therein lay the problem: almost everyone regarded the play as Sherriff's. He had already been forced to apologise to De Casalis for the Gollancz advert, and then along came Churchill's intervention – saving the play, but at the expense of omitting De Casalis's name. It clearly upset Sherriff enough that he remembered it some thirty years later when he wrote this draft paragraph for his autobiography (although it was not incorporated in the published version):

> The only fly in the ointment was that in his letter he hadn't mentioned Jeanne De Casalis, bringing me in alone as if I'd been sole author of the play. I was sorry about this, because Jeanne deserved as much credit as I did, if not more. She was too happy about what had happened to let it worry her, but some of her friends were very indignant and rang me up saying I ought to do something about it. ... I pointed out that Jeanne's name was in the programme and in all the advertisements as part-author, so no harm was done, but it threw a cloud across a happy collaboration that I was sorry for.[30]

Go West

And so, a couple of weeks after Sherriff had mailed his script of *Goodbye, Mr Chips* to Thalberg at MGM, his attention was focused very firmly on the transfer of *St Helena* to the West End – his first on a West End stage since *Badger's Green*. The theatre chosen was Daly's, just off Leicester Square. It had a seating capacity of about 600, so no one was expecting crowds of the order of *Journey's End*, but nor was it exactly boutique. Sherriff and De Casalis held a grand party at the Savoy hotel on its opening night on 19 March, to which were invited a wide range of notables, including Sir Edwin Lutyens, Mrs Neville Chamberlain (wife of the Chancellor of the Exchequer) and the Cazalets (to whom Sherriff owed his initial introduction to the Chamberlains). De Casalis, for her part, invited a collection of 'big theatre people'.[31]

This time Sherriff felt the reviews were very positive ('the united criticisms published next morning were as good as any we had for *Journey's End*'), but he overstates his case. They were, again, broadly favourable, but no more, with the occasional encomium (*John O'London's Weekly*: 'It is an exquisite study in dying falls, autumn leaves, and sunsets as they really happen to great men'),[32] but some other irreconcilables (*The Saturday Review*: 'I am still unrepentant in thinking that it is not a very good play').[33] But as much fun was had with the melodrama of Churchill's intervention as with the play itself. Hannen Swaffer, for example, joked in *The People* that 'Winston … happened to go down [to The Old Vic] after a week or so … feeling, no doubt, rather like Napoleon on St Helena himself these days.'[34]

In *No Leading Lady*, Sherriff reckoned the transfer to Daly's didn't work: 'In its new and glamorous West End surroundings,' he wrote, 'the play was a flop. A complete, unadulterated flop.' This he ascribed to the play's failure to cross the bridge from The Old Vic to the West End: 'It was part of the attraction to cross the river and see the play in the shabby, romantic surroundings in which it had been born.'[35] While it is true that some of the critics (like Swaffer) drew attention to the extent to which society had enjoyed 'slumming', the play was not the flop that Sherriff describes. Using his own cash books we can see that royalties from The Old Vic (after Churchill's intervention) and Daly's were much the same (about £36 a week, of which he received half). Admittedly, that was a far cry from the £200 a week he had enjoyed with *Journey's End*, but the play still ran until 23 May, for a total of seventy-six performances – more than twice as many as *Badger's Green* had managed.

If *St Helena* was not the flop he made it out to be, neither was it a roaring success. Also, unlike *Journey's End* and *Badger's Green*, there was no hope that it would play in repertory to any great extent, nor was it likely that it would ever be picked up by amateur dramatic societies. Perhaps that was the trouble. Sherriff had spent a great deal of time on the play, and two years' worth of emotional energy in trying to have it produced. As another *succès d'estime*, it had done his reputation as a playwright no harm, but equally, it had not cemented his reputation in the way he would have liked. It was no surprise that he should have begun to sour on the business of play writing:

> While *St Helena* was on the crest of the wave, nothing would have tempted me back to screenwriting again. I had recaptured the excitement and fascination of the theatre: the exhilaration of working with a group of people who shared everything with you. The theatre could be cruel and merciless, but when it smiled it gave you something beyond price. Then *St Helena* collapsed, and I began to get second thoughts. My agent was waiting with alluring offers from Hollywood, and it was no good pretending I didn't enjoy the easy money from the studios. So all the good resolutions to stick to the theatre went west.[36]

Other Avenues

That left two other avenues open to Sherriff, and as luck would have it, his efforts in both were coming to a head.

On the scriptwriting side, he had been forging ahead with the *Mr Chips* redraft throughout the whole of April, and by the end of the month, was able to send copies out to Hilton telling him he was much happier with it, and that he hoped Hilton would:

fight hard to keep it in its present form. I know from experience what a danger there is when there are so many people in a studio all anxious to show their originality. Once somebody is allowed to get their teeth into a script all the rest fall upon it like a lot of vultures and rend it into fragments.[37]

Hilton reassured him that he liked the second draft as much as the first, and that David Lewis agreed. They did not yet know Thalberg's mind, but were sure things would be all right. Thalberg must have liked it, because he was happy to offer Sherriff another contract, as the trade press announced in August 1936:

> Irving Thalberg has signed R.C. Sherriff, author of *Journey's End*, to a term writing deal through the Myron Selznick office. Writer will do series of complete screenplays for producer's unit. Under terms of contract Sherriff will do most of his writing in London, confining studio work to a couple of visits yearly.[38]

The other avenue open to Sherriff was novel writing, and in that context he had another significant event looming on the horizon. He had been working on a new novel 'in fits and starts'[39] around the beginning of 1935, and by April (when he was discussing *Espoir* with De Casalis) was optimistically aiming to complete it by mid-August.[40] By the time he left for Hollywood in September, he had finished enough of it to allow it to begin to be serialised in *Good Housekeeping*,[41] and he finished it upon his return, delivering the completed manuscript to Gollancz by mid January.

Greengates

Sherriff's novel tells the story of Tom Baldwin, a clerk in the City (in insurance, inevitably), who retires at the relatively young age of fifty-eight, and plans a fulfilling life for himself – decorating the house, rejuvenating the garden, and writing historical studies. But things don't go according to plan – the house remains fusty; the soil in the garden is too tired and sour to bear the weight of his hopes; and his histories are rejected by publishers. Tom begins to despair, slow down and lose interest. His wife Edie, meanwhile, finds the pattern of her day changed by his expectations, to the extent that she can no longer even enjoy a nap in her comfortable armchair because Tom lays claim to it. Whereas once they would have things to discuss in the evenings, they now find themselves with little news to share, having been together most of the day. A long and unhappy retirement seems to stretch out before them both, when they are inadvertently saved by taking a walk in the countryside. The walk had been a favourite walk of theirs before the war, but when they take it now they find their precious Welden Valley forested with new houses. At first horrified, they are tempted into one of the show homes by a young salesman, and instantly fall in love with it, envisaging the bright new life they could have in it, and contrasting it with Grasmere, their old and shabby home.

The second half of the book relates their efforts to raise the capital to buy Greengates, with their emotions swung this way and that as they yearn for their new home, yet face a barrage of small obstacles. Eventually, they make the move, and quickly make friends through their involvement in a scheme to establish a sports and social club in the new development. In a final coda, written in the first person (from the perspective of an erstwhile colleague of Tom's, come to visit him in his retirement), we see both Tom and Edie busily and happily engaged – he in running the club, she in her garden and working with the Ladies' Committee. As he drives away, the visitor is struck by the City 'men and girls' returning home from the station, passing the many new shops that have recently been built. Welden was well on the way to becoming an established community.

Greengates was not the first time that Sherriff had tackled the story of suburban development. In *Mr Birdie's Finger* the key men of the village mobilised to resist the developer's plans. Rewritten as *Badger's Green*, the outcome was the same, although by then some of those in favour of development had also been given a voice. By the time we come to *Greengates*, Sherriff appears to have come round to the idea of development in previously rural areas. In fact, the feelings of well-being that Tom and Edie experience are very like those that the developers in the earlier plays suggest will affect transplanted city dwellers. There is nothing to tell us why Sherriff changed his mind on the subject, although it may simply be that, as a man of a 'small-c' conservative inclination, he was minded to support the status quo – and at that time the status quo was very firmly in favour of suburban development. The extension of the Tube lines to new tracts of countryside, and the offering of grants to private house builders to encourage development, resulted in an explosion of housebuilding around the fringes of London – Betjeman's 'Metroland'[42] – and his local area of Kingston-Surbiton-Esher was very much part of the boom. As someone who had cycled around the country lanes near his home in his younger days (and now was very contentedly driving around those same lanes), he would first have seen ribbons of housing form along the roads in the 1920s, followed by further infill behind them, until previously separated villages had become one conglomeration.

It may have been the development in his local area that prompted the idea of the book, but it may also have been a desire to reflect on the difficulties of retirement, as witnessed in the case of his father. Herbert had reluctantly retired in 1923, and his diaries betray the same determination to get to grips with other aspects of his life as soon as he was freed from the shackles of employment (barely a day passes, for example, when he was not busy in the garden). As ever, Sherriff probably mined his family seam rather heavily: his discussion of the building of the new house, and the subsequent removal from the old house, probably drew from the experiences of Herbert, Bundy and Hazel, when they moved from Rossendale in 1935 to the newly built home that Bob bought for them in Couchmore Avenue, Esher.[43] Other incidents in the book, the Baldwins' dealings with their maid,[44] for example, also appear to have been drawn from real life.

Gollancz again gave the book the G.B. Stern treatment on the dust jacket: 'It couldn't be better … you tear from page to page with the same breathless intensity as though you were plunged into a first-class thriller. Power – magic – he's got both of these.' But now they could also add a word (literally – 'Enchanting') from James Hilton, to whom Sherriff had sent what must have been a proof copy. The reviews were very positive, so much so that Gollancz took adverts in *The Observer* to trumpet them. It was: 'Brilliantly composed and splendidly persuasive' (*Daily Herald*); 'A magnificent work' (*Daily Dispatch*); 'A most engaging novel' (*Daily Telegraph*); and many others, best summed up, perhaps, in the *News Chronicle*'s 'How good it is!'

There were, inevitably, some who didn't like it: James Agate, usually a strong Sherriff supporter, found the book 'on the whole … a disappointment' (while conceding that Sherriff 'cannot write badly'). L.P. Hartley, however (another who could not write badly), implicitly disagreed with Agate, finding *Greengates* 'a simple story, simply but subtly told'. His review had one or two nice lines itself. Summing up Tom's difficulties with house and garden he remarks: 'Like the house itself, [the garden] had seen better days, but could not recall them.'[45] He continues later, highlighting Sherriff's perennial problem with female characters:

> For [Sherriff] and for his reader too, Mr Baldwin is the centre of the universe. Mrs Baldwin does not occupy quite such an important position: she is less firmly individualised. Like a thermometer, she does not affect the temperature of the story; she only registers when it goes up or down.

His friends loved it too – Hilton, as we have already seen, but many others as well. The most direct was his old friend Gerald Ellison, now in a curate's post at Sherborne: 'RCS does it again! Heartiest congratulations on your brilliant notices re *Greengates*. And what with *St Helena* going hot & strong – heaven knows where you will be next.'[46]

A Chancy Business

Sherriff would write three more novels before entering on to the stage again. Shortly after the book was published he told a friend that 'I am afraid I shall never write many plays: all my ideas fall into novel form, and rarely have sufficient dramatic highlights for the stage.'[47] Maybe he was right – maybe the stories that came to him were more suited to novels than plays. But he had spent the 1920s eschewing the novel in favour of drama, and seemed to have no difficulties coming up with ideas. He had, after all, managed to produce not far short of a play a year while with The

Adventurers. Perhaps the more plausible explanation was that *St Helena* was the final straw: no play he had written in the 1930s had survived more than a few weeks on stage, and every failure was viewed through the prism of *Journey's End*. His novels, by contrast, had been well reviewed by the critics, and by the public. If he stuck with novels he would not have to worry about producers or theatre managers or even, God forbid, the dreaded 'backers': the only approval he would need would be that of Victor Gollancz.

He was aware, however, that publishing novels might not be enough. As he told a young novelist friend of his who was seeking to make the break into movies:

> Writing is … a very chancy business … you might spend six months on a play or a novel and get practically nothing in return. With screenplays you do at least get payment on a definite basis, and if eventually you come to some plan upon the same lines as mine, under which you write, say, three screenplays a year for several years, you can feel the assurance of a regular income, and have plenty of time to do other and more chancy work in the bargain.[48]

The problem with his existing approach, however, was that he was tiring of his frequent trips across the Atlantic, and that there was considerable upheaval at Universal. But maybe there was another approach:

> Screenwriting suited me if I could do it under good conditions. If I could work with an English company I should get the best of both worlds. Their studios were all near London, within a short journey from my home. I could write the scripts in my own library, yet be in daily touch with the directors while the pictures were being made.[49]

That had been the reason for the initial meeting with Alexander Korda, where *Chips* had been discussed, after which he regretfully wrote to Korda that, because Universal had taken up their option, he could not work for anyone else:

> I am very disappointed indeed if this means I shall be prevented from working for you. Not only would I like to be associated with one of your productions, but it would also be very stimulating and interesting for me to work in close touch with the studio. I have asked Mr Ham to approach Universal with the suggestion that I do one of my next three screenplays for you. … I very much hope this can be arranged.[50]

Unfortunately, however, it could not – although Ham, his agent, probably had a part to play in securing his contract with Thalberg.

At the same time as he was meeting with Korda, he may well have been in discussions with another of the big names in the British movie world – Michael (or Mick, as he called him) Balcon. Now at Gaumont-British, Balcon had first met Sherriff when he won the film rights to *Journey's End*. In 1935, whether with Universal's agreement or not, he persuaded Sherriff to do some work on the film *Rhodes*,[51] beginning even before he finished writing *Dracula's Daughter*. The job does not appear to have amounted to much – probably just script polishing – since he received only three small payments (of £225) in June and July 1935 for his efforts.

It seems likely that the upheavals at Universal loosened the strings on Sherriff's contract there, but it took a little while to do so. His final fee for *Dracula's Daughter* was paid in September 1935, but there were no additional payments beyond that, other than a series of 'Universal settlement' payments – amounting to about £1,000 in total – during March–April 1936.[52] By June 1936 he was also receiving his third and final payment for *Mr Chips* – the combined total payment amounting to some £3,000. By contrast, his royalties for *Greengates* came to £1,700, and for *St Helena*, less than £800,[53] so it appears he was right about the cash benefits of writing for the screen.

Bicycle for Two

At the beginning of June, Sherriff started work for Korda. The contract was to run for twelve weeks (at £250 a week), but was extended by a further three weeks at the end, taking him into early autumn. His first big project was a screenplay, to be produced by Erich Pommer, and directed by René Clair,[54] based on the old song *A Bicycle Made for Two* – an Edwardian comedy of the early days of bicycling.[55]

He had sent a very early, partial, draft to Korda on 9 June, and thereafter drove regularly to Denham, where Korda had built Britain's largest studio complex in 1935, to have discussions with Pommer and Clair. This was something of a departure in working style for him, as he had pointed out to Pommer early on in the process:

> In all my previous engagements I have written my screenplay straight off from beginning to end in rough shooting form, and, following conferences with the director and executives, have re-written straight through to embody all suggestions offered ... this is the first time I am working in close touch throughout with those concerned in the production.[56]

He was pleased, at last, to be working in England, avoiding the Hollywood back and forth, and learning more about the detailed process of filmmaking at the same time.

The August 1936[57] script that he sent to Clair and Pommer sets out the story, which is a simple one: boy (Peter, a bike shop assistant) meets girl (Margot, a chorus girl); boy pretends to be something he's not (in his case, Lord Sloane), as does girl (who pretends she's from money); girl falls for boy, but is pursued by the real Lord

Sloane; her father approves the match with the lord, but she prefers Peter; Peter and Margot are brought together in the end, once Lord Sloane and his father reject the marriage, realising that Margot and her father are 'show folk'.[58]

Sherriff was happy with how things were going with *Bicycle for Two* when he delivered it, and had been hoping to see it through to completion before his contract ended in mid-September, but it was not to be. Korda does not seem to have liked the script, and whether for that reason, or some other, Clair and Korda abruptly parted ways.[59] Sherriff wrote to both Clair and Pommer telling them he had very much working with them, and thought they had the basis of a good script, one they could perhaps take up again in a few months. For the moment, however, he would have to leave Korda behind, and turn his attention to Hollywood once more.

SOS

On 14 October 1936, Sherriff and his mother set out from Southampton on the *Queen Mary*, bound for Hollywood. As he later told De Casalis, 'I got a most violent SOS to go out to Hollywood at once, as they were just upon the brink of starting one of the pictures I had written, and they wanted urgent alterations made.'[60] While he was there, he would also take the opportunity of entering discussions with MGM, which was in a period of flux, following the death of Irving Thalberg on 13 September. As executive vice president at MGM, he had been involved in all aspects of the company, and his death meant changes in personnel assignments and contracts. Sherriff was probably worried about the status of the three-picture deal he had just signed in August (which, at his going rate of £3,000 a picture, was very lucrative), but to his relief he was kept on.[61]

The trip gave Sherriff a chance to check up on the progress of *St Helena*, which by now had transferred to Broadway. The American producer Max Gordon had acquired the US rights, despite the play's relatively lacklustre performance in London. This was in part because he was working as a play spotter for MGM who were willing to help fund a Broadway production to decide if it was worth their while bidding for the movie rights. Gordon had hoped to make the play more popular by bringing in a movie star (having Paul Muni[62] in mind), but in July, it became clear that he would not be available. So he turned instead to an old friend of both authors, Maurice Evans, about whose casting neither Sherriff nor De Casalis were ever completely convinced.

Gordon began rehearsals in August, and was willing to pay travel and expenses for Sherriff and De Casalis to go to New York to help with the production. Sherriff cried off ('Personally I would love to go, but unfortunately I am bound up, because a contract I have with Alexander Korda runs alongside one with MGM'),[63] so De Casalis went out on her own. It was not a happy experience for her, and she wrote often to Sherriff, citing a long list of complaints.[64] One wonders how Sherriff felt about her unhappiness: her correspondence was always very frank (and entertaining), and it may be that he just viewed it as business as usual. Possibly he felt a little guilty at not being there to support her; most likely, he gave thanks for Korda and MGM.

The play opened at the Lyceum Theatre on 6 October to generally poor reviews – mainly critisising the structure of the play, and a general lack of sympathy for its leading character. Reviews of Evans's performance were very favourable, however, and led to him receiving a very generous offer to stage his own play on Broadway, which set him on the path to US stardom. Sherriff popped in to see it on his way through New York a couple of weeks later, and was told by Gordon that the play was on the verge of coming off: 'I was so upset that I really could not trust my judgment; the house was obviously full of paper;[65] the company had all taken cuts and there was an atmosphere of disappointment about everything.'[66] Gordon told him that, to keep the play going, De Casalis had agreed to forego her royalties, as had Daniel Mayer (the production company), so Sherriff agreed to pitch in as well. But it was not enough: the play limped on for a little while, but finally closed in late November, after a total of sixty-five performances.

When he returned to London in mid-December it was to an irate De Casalis, who said she had never agreed to give up her royalties. Indeed, she was determined to receive her full share, if only to offset the loss she had made by being out of London during the autumn booking season (important for her Mrs Feather act). This led to an angry back and forth with producers and agents (although not with Sherriff, whom she felt had been misled by Max Gordon), before she finally received her due. When Sherriff later tried to discuss with her the sale of various foreign rights to the play she replied, flamboyantly as ever:

> I have already told Curtis Brown that as far as I am concerned I don't care who has the rights to *St Helena*. The American adventure was such a financial disaster, as far as I am concerned, that the very name *St Helena* stinks in my nostrils![67]

Back to *The Road Back*

Probably rather relieved to be leaving *St Helena* behind him in New York, Sherriff took the train to Hollywood wondering what was in store for him. He knew that the ownership of Universal had changed, and that the Laemmles were out, but he had never met Charles Rogers, the new head of production, nor was it likely he had any idea of the minefield into which he was stepping.

In the few years since Sherriff's script had been shelved, the Nazis had become considerably more active in their monitoring and pressuring of the Hollywood Studios. In 1933, they had appointed Georg Gyssling – a career diplomat and long-standing Nazi Party member – as vice consul in Los Angeles. Gyssling was much less charming and accommodating then Freudenthal had been, and from the moment he arrived, began to take a very active interest in the activities of the Hollywood studios. Whenever he heard of scenes he disliked he would put pressure on the producers directly, or through the MPPDA, to have the scenes changed. The ultimate threat was not only that the film would not be shown, but also that – following the guidelines in Article 15 – the studio's entire slate would be at risk.

Gyssling was always alert to new projects that might prove undesirable to the Germans. Accordingly, he wrote to Breen on 30 September 1936 saying that he had heard that Universal were considering making *The Road Back* again, and asking him to 'use your influence on behalf of correct relations between the American Film industry and Germany'.[68] Breen brushed him off with a holding reply, but two weeks later, after receiving a copy of the latest script, he was suggesting to Zehner that 'you consult your Foreign Department as to the acceptability of this picture abroad, in view of its powerful anti-militaristic flavour.'[69] He reminded him of the treatment meted out to *All Quiet on the Western Front*, and suggested that this film might run into even worse trouble.

The shooting script for the film is dated 11 December 1936,[70] and is credited to Sherriff, with 'Additional Scenes by Charles Kenyon'. Sherriff acknowledged, in sending a script to Remarque's London representative some six months later, that he had worked on the revised script, adding a few extra comedy scenes at the studio's request.[71] As Sherriff noted, the script is not so very different from his 1932 original,[72] although the tone is altered somewhat due to the inclusion of the comedy scenes, especially those between Tjaden and Willy. The other notable change is the introduction of Elsa, Ernst's girlfriend, who appears in a couple of scenes to show how much the two have drifted apart. She does not feature in the book at all, so her inclusion at this point is probably an attempt to increase the number of female characters. One additional scene is that of the tattered remains of the company parading before its demobilisation, to be joined by the spectral images of their dead comrades. This scene effectively shows just how large and proud it had stood, before the war had shattered it so completely. There is also one very obvious Sherriff trademark: in the final scene, when Ernst and Ludwig encounter the group of schoolboys being led in military manoeuvres by an adult officer, Ernst remarks, 'It all seems rather silly, doesn't it?', and Ludwig replies, 'Yes – and the silliest thing is that everybody knows it's silly.'

The script was submitted to the PCA four days later, and Breen replied with a number of changes, ranging, as ever, from the banal (the filmmakers were not to refer to geese flying overhead as 'on their way to make a mess of the pyramids') to the significant ('Albert should not fire repeatedly when killing the war profiteer, and great care should be taken in the riot episode to avoid inflaming tensions'). In early January, Breen and two of his staff met with Rogers, Granger and Whale at Universal, and again repeated their warnings about Gyssling's objections. Rogers replied that 'the company was not very much concerned about German protests, because it was almost impossible for the company to operate in Germany at the present time.'[73] Breen and his people were concerned about the riot scene, but Whale tried to reassure them that it would be shot carefully. He also remarked that he 'had so changed the story from the book that the finished picture was not likely to give serious offence to anybody and more especially to the Germans.' But even while he was shooting the film, Whale was to be disappointed, as Gyssling continued to protest to Breen, who summarised the Germans' problem:

> The script does not, in our judgment, seriously reflect on the Germans, except that it pictures the Germans, after the Great World War, as a defeated people, highly hysterical, and groping blindly to re-establish themselves both as a nation and as a people. It may be that the German government will vigorously protest such a suggestion, at this time. They may not want to have their people shown as dejected and demoralised.[74]

Gyssling and Whale met in mid-February, three weeks after shooting had begun on the movie, but there was to be no compromise. By this time, Whale had been shooting the film for several weeks, having started at the end of January. The shoot went badly; bad weather delayed the schedule, and the death, on set, of one of the explosives experts, cast a gloom on the enterprise. Whale was also at loggerheads with the studio, which wanted the work completed more quickly. Then, on 25 March, almost a month before the movie was finally completed, Gyssling sent a letter to Breen informing him that he had sent to Universal – and in particular to James Whale and nine of his actors[75] – a warning concerning their participation in the film.[76] A warning that suggested, because of their involvement in this film, potentially every other film in which they might be involved could also be adversely affected. There was an immediate outcry, with the State Department being dragged in, and an eventual rebuke to Gyssling from the German authorities. But the strength of the Germans' objections had been set out for all to see.

The film was eventually signed off by the PCA on 26 May, and it premiered in New York on 17 June, but not before *Variety*[77] reported that Universal had made seventeen cuts to the movie to please the German ambassador (who still would not assure the studio that the movie would get a showing in Germany). The reviews were not kind. Frank Nugent, of the *New York Times*, felt that while Sherriff and Whale had done workmanlike jobs, the casting of Slim Summerville and Andy Devine in the (partially) comic roles of Tjaden and Willy had unbalanced the film. He ends:

> If you leave your recollection of the novel out of it, then I suppose *The Road Back* must be considered one of the year's better pictures. But that is an untenable hypothesis, for Remarque's *The Road Back* must be held in mind and, holding it, then we cannot avoid realising how maladroit a version the film

is. There seems to be no explanation of its weakness other than the ineptness of its producers.

Other reviewers were also unimpressed, but interestingly, – perhaps because of the *Variety* article – Whale and Sherriff generally got off scot-free.

The studio was still not happy at the film's reception, and felt that it would not be well received on general release. So they called back Ernst and Elsa (John King and Jean Rouverol), together with a different director (Edward Sloman) to shoot additional scenes before its general release in July. The studio's intention was to offer something of a happy ending with Ernst and Elsa getting back together again after the court scene, so other scenes showing their disaffection had to be dropped. As a result, the film now ended, after the court scene, with a syrupy, and utterly unmoving reconciliation between Ernst and Elsa, replacing the ominous scene of the boys practising their manoeuvres in the forest. The film then dissolves on Elsa's repeated hope that there would now be 'peace', phasing to a montage of scenes of rearmament – from all nations – bolstered with newspaper headlines. Quite how the studios felt this would be more acceptable to the general public is not clear, but they were sadly disappointed when the film was released to general disdain, and a very poor box office. To make matters worse, James Whale paid for a full-page advert in the *Hollywood Reporter* the day after its general release, praising Sherriff's script, and effectively washing his hands of the whole movie.[78] This is what it said:

Render to Caesar
The things that are Caesar's

This page is a tribute to
R.C. SHERRIFF
For his
SCREENPLAY
and
DIALOGUE
based on
ERICH MARIA REMARQUE'S
THE ROAD BACK

JAMES WHALE

Quite what Sherriff made of the whole affair is unclear. He had enjoyed successes during his time at Universal – his scripts for *The Invisible Man* and *One More River* were made into successful and highly regarded movies – but he had also experienced disappointments. His partnership with James Whale had not been the guarantee of success that he might reasonably have expected, given the triumph of *Journey's End*, and Whale's status as one of Universal's most critically acclaimed directors. In *No Leading Lady* he has very little to say about *The Road Back*, beyond the suggestion that he felt the studio had been disappointed in it. This is really quite a curious omission: it was his first big job in Hollywood and his script had been widely acclaimed; it had created a ferment of publicity due to Gyssling's activities and the studio's cuts prior to release; and James Whale's advert had placed a very definite exclamation point at the end of the process. Whale had become rather used to throwing his weight around at Universal, but Sherriff was not that kind of man. Given his modesty and his tendency to shun the limelight, the whole episode may just have been very uncomfortable for him. Besides, by the time the film was screened, he had already moved on to other projects, in particular, a screenplay for yet another Remarque movie, this time for his new employers, MGM.

Chapter 9

Korda and MGM, 1937–40

Be not either a man of many words, or busy about too many things.
Marcus Aurelius, *The Meditations*, Book III.

T hree Comrades was Remarque's latest novel, and while he had allowed the first two (*All Quiet* and *The Road Back*) to go to Universal he felt they had mishandled them, so took this one to MGM instead.[1] A first draft script was prepared by Harvey Gates by October 1936, but the studio then summoned Sherriff for a redraft. He produced a synopsis when he was on his trip to Hollywood[2], yet the full script took a little longer (perhaps delayed by his script doctoring on *The Road Back*), and was only completed in February 1937.

Three Comrades

Three Comrades is a tale of three old army friends – Robert (Bobby) Lohkamp (the main character), Otto Köster, and Gottfried Lenz, who run a struggling car repair garage in an unidentified German city, sometime in the late 1920s, when economic conditions are harsh. Bobby falls in love with Patricia Hollman, a beautiful woman from what was once a wealthy family, although she too has fallen on hard times. In due course, Patricia falls ill from a recurrent lung disease (probably TB), but the young couple try to make the most of their time together, sharing their hours with Bobby's two friends, and a cast of characters from the bars and clubs of the local demi-monde. Eventually, Pat's condition weakens and she makes her way to a sanatorium in the mountains. However, after she has left, Gottfried is shot and killed following a political demonstration, although he is quickly avenged by his comrades. When Pat takes a turn for the worse, Bobby joins her at the sanatorium, and stays with her until she dies. The final pages of the book are a melancholy portrayal of the people in the sanatorium, doing their best to live their lives in the shadow of imminent death.

This short summary leaves out many of the details and side stories that are so typical of Remarque, and make the novel so atmospheric. Confronted with the book's range, Sherriff opted to simplify the story considerably, judging that the romance between Bobby and Pat was its key feature. He therefore had to omit one major event: the death of Lenz. He explained his reasoning to the producer in a note he attached to the script,[3] arguing that, because the main concern of the story is the illness and death of Pat, all interest should be concentrated upon the efforts of the three men to lighten her burden. To include Lenz's death would be to include the politics that preceded it, which the movie could not accommodate while doing justice to Pat's story.

After he delivered the screenplay, little seems to have happened for several months, but by May the script had been sent to Breen at the PCA. He wrote back to Louis B. Mayer at MGM that, while the basic story met the requirements of the Production Code, the script in its present form was not acceptable 'by reason of the great number of scenes and lines of dialogue having to do with liquor and drinking.'[4] He then itemised forty-eight separate cuts, thirty-three of them having to do with omitting references to drinking (most of the rest relating to mild oaths). In June 1937, Sherriff wrote to Remarque's Agent in London, Otto Klement, sending him the screenplay that had been submitted to Breen, and noting that 'I have not yet had conferences with them upon it. These will doubtless take place when I am in Hollywood in August.'[5]

Somewhere along the line, however, the producer, Joseph L. Mankiewicz, seems to have had second thoughts about Sherriff's script, and turned to F. Scott Fitzgerald to rewrite it[6] ('who better to capture the disenchantment of the post-war "lost generation" and capture the ethereal character of Patricia?')[7] There is no explicit reason for Mankiewicz's dissatisfaction, although there was clearly disagreement about whether the death of Lenz should be incorporated. The inclusion in the final script of Lenz's death, and the political upheaval surrounding it, suggests that clearly, Sherriff and his and producer were not of one mind.

Whatever the reason, Sherriff was paid the final instalment of his fee (for a grand total of £4,000) in July. If he was following the trade press, he probably reckoned he was well out of it, for at the end of June, *Variety* was reporting that '*The Three Comrades* has political production problems believed by the studio to be fully as critical, from the showman's angle, as had *The Road Back*.'[8] That was prescient indeed, for Gyssling was all over the studio and the PCA trying to find out what was going on. When the film was finally released in June 1938, the main elements of Remarque's plot – the comrades, and the consumptive heroine – remained, but much of the flavour of the book had been toned down to meet the censor's demands. The changes forced by anticipation of the Nazis' reaction – in particular the shifting of the time frame to the immediate post-war period – helped further to diminish the overall thrust of Remarque's tale. Ironically, if Mankiewicz had stuck with Sherriff's original script – which largely eschewed any political content – the film might have retained much more of Remarque's original, and passed more easily through the censor's hands.

Frustration with Korda

Shortly after he despatched his *Three Comrades* script in February, Sherriff picked up another contract with Korda, for twelve weeks' work (again at £250 a week), running from 5 March to 18 May.

During the three months he was employed on a number of projects, none of which ever seem to have made it very far off the drawing board. This was not entirely surprising as Korda's company was struggling, deep in debt to its primary financial backer, the Prudential Assurance Company, and he had begun to fight shy of some of the grandiose schemes that had marked his previous films, concentrating on limited budget fare. Even Denham Studios was struggling, owing to a downturn in movie making more generally, so that fewer production companies were renting studio space. The upshot was that it would take a lot to get a project on to the screen in London Films' financial climate at that time.

Sherriff's first project was again *Bicycle For Two*, which had been passed to Victor Saville.[9] Sherriff delivered another script before reluctantly moving on to his next project, wishing he could see the film through to its completion. But even had he stayed with it, it would have made no difference, for Saville quickly turned to another project himself – an adaptation of Winifred Holtby's *South Riding* – and *Bicycle for Two* was put up on the shelf, never to be taken back down again. Sherriff was never quite reconciled to its fate, recalling it wistfully in his autobiography: 'Where the script is today I don't know, but if it is ever unearthed it will be the discovery of buried treasure.'[10]

Next he was set to working up a new story with Harry D'Arrast (an Argentinian director with whom Korda had worked occasionally in the past), but that went nowhere fast, although Sherriff seems to have escaped any blame for the lack of progress.[11] After a few weeks he moved on to another collaboration, with Hans Rehfisch (an émigré German Jewish playwright) on a screenplay about Disraeli – but not Disraeli in his pomp; rather the retired Disraeli, seeking to flex his diplomatic muscles again, in the aid of resolving a romantic problem for two young people, and in so doing, causing chaos in the halls of power. From his explanation of it, the story seems to have had some potential,[12] but Sherriff left the draft in Rehfisch's hands when his contract expired. When the draft came back to him he was not impressed, and rather washed his hands of the whole thing.

Summertime …

The employment in question was digging – of the archaeological variety. Sherriff's archaeological passion began when, as a schoolboy on a bicycling tour with his father, he had come across, in an old farmhouse, a 'cracked bowl containing an assortment of what looked like little green buttons'[13]: in fact, they turned out to be old Roman coins that the farmer regularly dug up while ploughing. His interest had been further piqued by Professor Collingwood's lectures at Oxford on Roman Britain. Soon Sherriff was keen to do some digging of his own and Collingwood referred him to Mortimer Wheeler, recently director of the London Museum, and a well-known authority on British archaeology. The site Wheeler suggested was a field near Angmering in Sussex, which was thought to contain the foundations of a Roman villa. Angmering was not far from Sherriff's beloved Selsey, nor from Bognor, where he was having a new holiday home (Sandmartin) built,[14] so he leased the field, secretly hoping that it might be the location of 'the legendary "Palace of Vespasian"'.[15]

For three summers in succession, Sherriff brought groups of young rowers down from Oxford University to take part in the digs with him. As to their trained supervisor, Wheeler recommended a star pupil of his – Leslie Scott – and one day Sherriff and Nigel Nicolson (a Balliol rower, and son of Harold Nicolson and Vita Sackville-West) went to the Ritz to 'meet this paragon', as Nicolson put it in his memoir:

> We watched the entrance of the hotel for a likely looking lad. None came. After half an hour I said to Sherriff, 'It couldn't be the girl over there, could it?' 'Oh no,' he replied, 'he would never have sent a girl.' But he had. She had been sitting in a corner of the foyer for the same half-hour. She might have been someone's niece or fiancée. She was neither. She was Leslie Scott. ... The next time that I saw her was at Angmering, in shorts and an Aertex shirt, grubbing up the remains of a hypocaust. She was not only supremely confident, but devastatingly attractive.'[16]

Sherriff used to take great care in organising his digs, which could last for several weeks at a time in the summer, but would also carry on, during weekends, through the winter. For digs at Angmering they would usually meet up at his Bognor house, and stay there, or move on to local hotels. On occasions they would venture elsewhere – to Mont Caburn on the South Downs, or the fort of Procolitia on Hadrian's Wall in Northumberland – when again, the trip would be organised by Sherriff with military precision:

> It was splendid working out there in the fields on those long summer days. It cost a good deal in labour and equipment, and I had ambitious plans for roofing over the parts of the villa worth preserving. But I reckoned the Hollywood studios would pay for all that. For the first time I felt that screenwriting was worthwhile. I didn't care whether they used my film scripts or not, so long as they provided the cash to excavate our Roman villa.[17]

Sherriff protests too much in this particular extract; the very fact that he mentions that his screenplays were not used suggests that it was, at the very least, something of a thorn in his side. He had already seen his *Three Comrades* script cast aside, and his months with Korda had produced nothing of significance. His next two projects for MGM would fare no better.

Development Limbo

Sherriff left for Hollywood, with his mother, on 7 August, taking the *Empress of Britain* to Quebec, and then on to Chicago and Los Angeles, as usual. But this was something of a flying visit – he would return again just six weeks later, rather less than the length of stay he was used to. With him he took the initial draft of his next assignment for MGM: an adaptation of a P.C. Wren story, *The Man of a Ghost*[18] (published in America as *Spur of Pride*,[19] as the film was so titled). He kept working on the script while in Hollywood, eventually completing it when he returned in October.

The story is a real *Boy's Own* yarn, about the court-martialling, cashiering (and apparent subsequent death) of a British officer, Captain Richard Wendover, who becomes a private spy for the British among the gun runners and bandits of the Afghan mountains, and after many adventures is finally exonerated, partly with the help of his friend Hazelrigg. It combines elements of many other adventure yarns, bringing to mind books such as *Kim*, *The Four Feathers* and Wren's other fort-bound books like the various *Beaus*, but its primary interest lies in the racist vitriol it heaps on the main villain – an Anglo-Indian doctor in the Indian Medical Service. Sherriff deleted the racist asides, and simplified the story considerably, while incorporating a wonderfully cinematic plot device of his own – gunrunning by pleasure steamer, which would have been intriguing to see. Yet his most interesting amendment was to the relationship between Wendover and the friend who helps him. In the book, Hazelrigg is slightly older (a major to his captain), while in the film he becomes a much younger lieutenant, prompted to action by his hero-worship for Wendover, with obvious echoes of the Stanhope-Raleigh relationship (although on this occasion, the young 'Raleigh' survived his adventures). But none of that was enough to see the script shepherded through the development process: beyond the copy of the script in Sherriff's files, no record of it appears to exist.

While in Hollywood he had contract discussions with some of the MGM executives, and when he returned he told Sydney Carroll, happily, that 'I am changing my present contract with MGM so that I can work for them in London instead of Hollywood.'[20] In fact, he was now working for MGM-British, which had been set up by MGM to operate out of the Denham Studios, making high-budget British films, using American actors and technicians, but also the British talent available at Denham. As to exactly why MGM chose to set up a high-end British operation, it may have been in part to weaken British competitors by co-opting their talent[21]; but it may also have been, as scriptwriter Sidney Gilliat suggested, 'window dressing'. Negotiations on a new quota act were underway, and MGM 'may have considered it good policy to make several high-budget pictures in Britain, to make the outcome more favourable for American interests.'[22]

The first head of MGM-British was Michael Balcon, who arrived in December 1936, taking with him a number of the projects from Gaumont-British, including

Shadow of the Wing, the film that Sherriff would be working on, which was intended as an 'aerial adventure' promoting the RAF, starring Clark Gable. By the time Sherriff was assigned to the project it had been through a couple of draft scripts, and Balcon had already sent experienced aerial cameraman Elmer Dyer[23] to England to capture a range of flying shots.[24]

Sherriff's script, dated January 1938, begins with the twentieth reunion of a wartime unit of the Royal Flying Corps, and amidst all the laughter and speeches it is notable that the participants give voice to the 'theme song' of the 7th Squadron, which just happens to be the same theme song as Sherriff's old 'C' Company of the 9th East Surreys – *Call Round Any Old Time*. Thereafter the story concerns Tim Burke, the veteran pilot who is put in charge of the testing of a grand new flying boat that the Air Ministry is building (essentially as a weapon of deterrence, the logic of which is interesting given the growing military pressures at the time the movie was being scripted). The flying sequences are leavened by Tim's ongoing clashes with his technologically minded second-in-command, and the development of a 'hate-at-first-sight' love interest. The film went nowhere, however, after the RAF withdrew its co-operation (probably shortly after Sherriff's version was completed), supposedly after they learned that an American would be taking the lead role. Some of Dyer's shots were put to good use, however, in Alexander Korda's 1939 propaganda movie *The Lion Has Wings*,[25] promoting the power of the Royal Air Force, and Sherriff recycled some of the themes in subsequent wartime scripts, notably *Flight Command* (1940) and *Stand By for Action* (1942).[26]

There is no evidence that Sherriff ever questioned why nothing became of his script (or, indeed, of *Spur of Pride*) – it was just one of the routine perils of being in the movie business. MGM were especially notorious for it, having a 'factory-like approach to screenwriting'.[27] Most of the MGM-British projects did not become movies, but 'this was not a remarkable fallout rate for a studio that employed hundreds of writers.' That was never more evident than in *A Yank at Oxford*: it was the first film that MGM-British actually brought to the screen (in fact, the only one that Balcon ushered on to the screen before quitting, frustrated by the interference from Louis B. Mayer), and is recorded as having utilised the talents of fully thirty-five scriptwriters.[28] Balcon also invited Sherriff to comment on the script, but he is not named among the thirty-five.[29]

The Hopkins Manuscript

After writing a string of unproduced screenplays, Sherriff was itching to get back to his own work, free of the quarrelsome demands of directors, producers, actors and even other scriptwriters, keen to steal a march. Still gun-shy, as far as plays were concerned, he alighted on an ingenious plot for a new novel – something unlike anything he had done before, rather familiar in its main character.

The Hopkins Manuscript is a story about a catastrophe that occurs when the moon falls out of its orbit and collides with the earth. The resulting tornado, earthquake and flood wipe out large parts of the civilisation of the northern hemisphere, but some pockets survive – one of them a small village in England called Beadle. The story is told in the first person by Edgar Hopkins, a 47-year-old man with a distinct resemblance to Charles Pooter, familiar to Sherriff from *Diary of a Nobody*, and to some extent, from the diaries of his own father. Hopkins, as a member of the British Lunar Society, receives advance knowledge of the impending disaster, something that makes him even more insufferably self-important and snobbish than usual. But eventually, as the moon is seen to come gradually closer to the earth, the authorities inform the people and preparations begin to be made, fostering a new sense of community among the village residents.

Afterwards, most of the villagers, trapped in a flooded shelter, are killed, but Edgar survives along with two young people from the local manor house: Pat and Robin. Forced back only on their own resources, they forge a self-sufficient lifestyle, supported by Robin's hunting and Edgar's gardening and chicken farming. The pride Edgar takes in his chickens (winners of multiple prizes at local poultry shows) is a theme throughout the book – and one that Sherriff could discourse on with ease, given his own expertise on the subject.[30] Eventually, the three plucky survivors, joined by an old retainer, are brought into contact with other survivors in the nearby town of Mulcaster, and they hear about the tremendous efforts that have been made to rebuild society. They even take a trip to see the moon, which collapsed into the Atlantic, forming a land bridge from the west coast of Europe to the east coast of America. There are plans across the governments of Europe to divide the moon up into separate sections for each country, but problems arise when the plans are confronted with the reality that some parts of the moon contain more valuable minerals and natural resources than others. The desire to claim the most valuable parts feed the most nationalistic impulses across the countries of Europe, and previous plans of co-operation are discarded in favour of an approach in which the spoils go to the strongest. That, rather than the fall of the moon itself, is the real catastrophe in the book.

Sherriff structures the tale very well indeed – almost like a 'whodunnit'. We begin with a foreword, from which we know that something cataclysmic has happened, and that the book is the only record of it: we know that the Western world has been wiped out, but that life goes on in Africa. So from the beginning we are hooked, eager to find out what and how. In the next scene we see Edgar Hopkins in the remains of Notting Hill, writing his account of the cataclysm[31] by the light of a piece of string soaked in bacon fat. Now, we see there were survivors but that they are dying out, and again our curiosity is piqued. That is when Hopkins returns to the beginning of his tale.

There is not much to be said for Sherriff's science-fiction device, of the moon spinning out of its orbit. In an introduction to the Persephone version of the book,

Michael Moorcock writes that 'the unscientific qualities of the story can be safely ignored'[32] – and he is absolutely right. The book is not about the falling of the moon, but about what happens to people and societies when that happens. One of the book's strongest features is that we are allowed to witness the events through the eyes of a very well-defined, but hardly likeable, character – operating in a milieu both strange and yet familiar from Sherriff's earlier novels. In fact, his three novels brilliantly illuminate the preoccupations of the 1930s Home Counties lower middle class – almost like Betjeman, but without the poetry.

Why he alighted on this particular device, or why he chose to examine a civilisation during catastrophe and war is not clear – although he cannot have been immune to the growing threat of war in Europe in the second half of the decade. His description of the petty tyrants who seek to exploit the passions of their people is clearly based on the rhetoric he has observed, especially from Germany and Italy. The final section of the book – the descent into war and ultimate destruction – accounts for a little under a fifth of the book, and even although Sherriff may have been stirred to write it by the events that unfolded during the year, it was never likely to be the strongest section. His skill lay in characterisation and observation, not in politics. But it did add a relevance that was not lost on the reviewers when it was published the following year.

By July 1938, he had finished enough of the book to begin having it serialised in *Good Housekeeping*, beginning in August. It would run there until the following March,[33] and as the story developed one wonders whether Sherriff began to worry about just how prophetic it might be. Earlier that year, the Germans had marched into Austria, and the Sudeten crisis began shortly afterwards, with German occupation finally ratified when Chamberlain went to Germany in September. Sherriff had met Chamberlain several times (as Chancellor and as Prime Minister),[34] usually in the company of Mollie Cazalet, who could not contain herself, writing:

You must feel very proud to know our splendid PM – it was a wonderful gesture to go and see that Demon and how he must have hated doing it. Now he has to go again and as far as I can see we are giving in to nearly all his demands, which is a terrible thing to have to do, but what's the alternative? A war which would exterminate most of the world. Can't you think, Bob dear, of some way to get rid of him?'[35]

A couple of weeks after Chamberlain returned from Munich, Sherriff wrote an article in the *Sunday Dispatch* entitled 'Tell us Now What to Do'. It was illustrated with pictures of preparation for war, and focused on a grand plan for 'Schools of National Service', to which, he believed, all school leavers should be sent – not solely for the purposes of army preparation, but as an apprenticeship for all aspects of industry and the services. He breathed a sigh of relief that war had been averted, but he feared that the country was unprepared for emergencies, and that it should begin by teaching its children what their role in such an emergency should be. Leaving aside the viability of his case the article goes some way to illuminating the anxieties that were felt at the time.

The Four Feathers

Early in March 1938, Sherriff had received his final payment for the *Spur of Pride* script. At that point he had received over £13,000 in fees from MGM since his first fee for *Chips* in November 1935, and yet only one of the four scripts he had worked on would ever make it into theatres with his name on it. His experience with Alex Korda had been no more productive – over £6,500 in fees since June 1936, and nothing anywhere close to a movie screen. But he enjoyed working with Korda at Denham, and was very happy when, as of 1 April 1938 and after the end of his assignments with MGM, he was able to finally start on his next contract with London Films. It would be another twelve weeks at £250, but this time with something to show for it besides a bigger bank balance. What followed was one of his happiest times working on a movie:

> It was the perfect way for a screenwriter to work: in the midst of things from the day the picture began. The studio was only a few miles from my home. I could spend the day there, and at night I could sit down and re-write or rearrange scenes in my library.[36]

The film was *The Four Feathers*, an adaptation of a novel by A.E.W. Mason, which had already been filmed three times before. He began writing the script as soon as he was employed by London Films and by mid-June had produced a first draft of the entire film.[37] Thereafter, he worked very closely with the director (Zoltan Korda, or 'Zolly', as he was generally known) on the scenes as they were shot.

The basic premise of both novel and film is similar: a young army officer, resigning upon hearing that his regiment is shipping out to the Sudan is presented with four white feathers for his 'cowardice' – three from fellow officers, and one from his fiancée (called Ethne in the book, and in the film, but – curiously – renamed Daphne in Sherriff's script).[38] He then travels out to the Sudan to perform various feats of bravery in assisting his brother officers, thus redeeming him in their eyes, and allowing him to return their feathers, the same to be said of Ethne. Within this overarching premise, however, Sherriff takes considerable liberties with Mason's story.

The most obvious (if trivial) is changing the hero's name from Feversham to Faversham (perhaps for ease of pronunciation), but there are more significant alterations, in particular when he brings forward the action by fifteen years, so that it focuses on Kitchener's expedition to the Sudan, ending with the thrilling British victory at Omdurman in 1898. The other main changes are with the stripping away of subplots, with two in particular: one relating to Ethne's family background; and a love triangle between Ethne, Durrance and a third character, Mrs Adair.

The character of Ethne is significantly changed in the film: as the reviewer in *The Manchester Guardian* put it: 'I had wondered what the film would do about Ethne, who, in her small way, is about the nastiest of all minor fiction's heroines. In Mr Sherriff's hands she became positively pleasant – and with no apparent difficulty at all.'[39] But changing Ethne's character gave Sherriff a problem, because while Harry's motivation for leaving the regiment is the same in both cases (fear that he may prove to be a coward), this impulse is strengthened in the book by the shame that Ethne would feel being married to a coward: were he not betrothed to her he would take his chances. The force of that particular impulse is much muted in the movie, meaning that Ethne's acceptance of her white feather has to be delivered in a different way.

In the event, it is done with humour, which was quite a feature of the film in general, and was quite risky in a film celebrating imperial victory, in so far as it subverts the very soldiers who had once been fighting for queen and country themselves. The particular focus of the humour is General Burroughs, who is Ethne's father in the movie (and completely invented by Sherriff)[40] and perfectly played by C. Aubrey Smith, the go-to actor for pompous military men (whom Sherriff knew from the Hollywood Cricket Club and *One More River*). Much of the satire came not from Sherriff's pen, but from that of Arthur Wimperis[41] (credited, along with Biro, for 'additional dialogue' in the movie), although in part at Sherriff's direction.[42]

The English scenes of the film were largely filmed during the summer months, and then it was time to sit down with Zolly and work through a rough cut of the film. This was so that he could revise the script and do everything necessary to it before director and crew left for the Sudan to film the big desert and battle sequences (a letter on 5 October recapped everything that had been done on the script thus far).

In the Sudan the filmmakers were assisted by the First Battalion of Sherriff's old regiment – the East Surreys – who went to a great deal of trouble establishing a separate camp in the desert, at Sabaluka Gorge, some 50 miles from Khartoum, whence came the supplies needed for a filming party of forty-five, over 200 soldiers, and perhaps 2,000 Sudanese natives. Water could come from the Nile, just 3 miles away. To help the filmmakers (and prevent soldiers having to spend a long time in make-up each morning), the soldiers were encouraged by their regiment to take part in a moustache-growing competition ('not of the "Charlie Chaplin" type, but long and flowing ones as favoured by our Grandfathers'),[43] with prizes awarded to the top three competitors (£1 for the winner). A number of soldiers had close-ups in the film, with one or two even having speaking roles. The camp lasted for the best part of a month, before most of the filmmakers (and their 160 packing cases) returned home in time for Christmas.[44]

In later years, Sherriff would tell a story he had picked up second-hand from the filmmakers[45] – namely that, when the Sudanese natives (cast as the Mahdi's army) were charging the 'thin red line', they tended to the over-zealous, and so the British soldiers were forced to shoot them in the legs. Whether Sherriff got hold of the wrong end of the stick, or was exaggerating the story for effect, the actual story was less dramatic. Osmond Borradaille, who was in charge of photography in the Sudan, reported that in fact the natives were hit by wadding from the blank cartridges – painful enough, but not fatal. Once they complained, Zolly 'walked nearer and nearer to the British guns until he too was hit. He then ordered that the attacking forces should stop just before that point. But he himself bore a nasty welt on his side, where a wad had hit him hard.'[46]

1939

Spring of 1939 was an exciting time. Sherriff had handed *The Hopkins Manuscript* to Gollancz at the beginning of the year, and it was due to be published, in a very respectable print run of 15,000, on 27 March. In addition, after three years working for MGM and Korda he was going to see two of his creations on screen at last: *The Four Feathers* was due to be premiered on 17 April, and *Goodbye, Mr Chips* on 15 May. He had enjoyed busy launch periods before, but never anything on this scale.

Before any of that, however, there was still a lot of work to do. When *The Four Feathers* footage had returned from the Sudan after Christmas, and the editors had begun their work, Sherriff was encouraged to continue his involvement in the film – viewing a cut of the whole movie and offering his thoughts to Zolly's assistant, Eileen Corbett. This was a considerable departure for him: he had never before enjoyed so much access to a film in the production stages, nor had his views been sought by directors and producers to anything like the same extent, which may be another reason why he would later recall his time working on the film with such fondness.

Besides the extra involvement with Korda, he also had plenty of work on hand for MGM – two screenplays in particular: the first an adaptation of a Nevil Shute novel, *Ruined City*[47]; and following that, a screen version of his very own *Journey's End*.

Ruined City was published in 1938, and after snapping up the rights, MGM had handed the project to Sherriff in the autumn.[48] The novel tells the story of a banker, Henry Warren, who arrives in Sharples, a northern shipbuilding town fallen on hard times. At the urging of a young local woman (Miss McMahon), Warren decides to try to help restore the town's fortunes. This he does, but only by means of engaging in a shady deal in the Balkan country of Laevatia, and by issuing a misleading prospectus for his newly formed shipbuilding company. As a result, just as the town is beginning to recover – orders are being placed for ships, and men returning to work – Warren is sentenced to five years for fraud. He accepts his punishment, arguing that it was well deserved, but that his fraud had achieved its objective. When he emerges from prison he returns to Sharples to find a plaque in his honour on the shipyard wall, and the girl, inevitably, waiting for him.

The book was ripe for translation to the screen, with several key scenes that would work well on film, all of which feature in Sherriff's script.[49] He also adds an additional one from his own memory banks – namely when Warren and Miss McMahon spend the day at Henley Royal Regatta together. Sherriff also simplifies the story somewhat, bringing together different characters into composites, just for ease of narrative drive. The biggest change he brings to the film is in the two main characters. Henry Warren in the book is far from likeable – a humourless workaholic with a keen sense of entitlement; and Alice McMahon in the book is very much younger than Warren. In Sherriff's script, Warren is humanised, and Miss McMahon is now Daphne (a name that seems to have stuck with him following his *Four Feathers* script) spars with him on several occasions, so much so that it is not difficult to imagine the two parts being taken by the usual duelling Hollywood couples that were such a feature of the late 1930s and 40s.

After submitting this version of the script, Sherriff continued on the project, through successive drafts, for another few months, before handing it back to Victor Saville. Before he received his final payment in March, he had already started work on the *Journey's End* adaptation.

Journey's End

MGM had acquired the film rights of *Journey's End* in 1937 from Maurice Browne, although not without 'many disputes and the usual time-taking skirmishes',[50] according to Browne himself. By the time he sold the rights he had long since frittered away his profits from *Journey's End* and was reduced to asking the Elmhirsts to guarantee an overdraft at the bank, in anticipation of the new film rights cheque dropping through the letterbox. Once Sherriff received the commission[51] actor friends started asking if he could arrange for them to get choice parts (Frank Lawton, for example, who had played Tony Croom in *One More River*, had his eye on the part of Raleigh, despite being thirty-five years old): Sherriff, as he always did, pleaded that he took no part in casting.

There is one script in Sherriff's files that may have been his proposed film script: it is labelled 'Screen Adaptation',[52] and begins with a 'Prefatory Note', which describes an opening, wordless scene, in which men are moving up to the front line, and we see the silhouettes of war, glimpsed against the halo thrown by the flares and star shells. After the scene setting, we see the soldiers as they walk through the communication trench – they are being shelled now and again, and talking with each other, followed by them establishing their defences in the trench. The scene is reminiscent of Sherriff's description in his memoir of bringing one company of men up to relieve another – of the difficult decisions the company (or in his case, platoon) commander has to make to decide when and how quickly to move to avoid the shelling.[53]

The dialogue is as it is in the play, but Sherriff does open things out – a number of scenes are shown in the trench, or in no-man's-land (during the raid). The draft screenplay is reminiscent of the novelisation rather more than the play, especially in Raleigh's first scene in the trench alongside Trotter (when they relieve Hibbert). But there are also clear differences: Hibbert is no longer given the justification for his outburst that he is in the novel (Sherriff may be less troubled by the possible misinterpretation of Hibbert's character); and there is no attempt to replay the view from the Germans' perspective.

A great deal of Sherriff's reworking of the script goes to consideration of how the camera can be put to best use, with close-ups, medium close-ups, long shots; varying camera angles; and in one case (the fight between Stanhope and Hibbert), a suggested series of swift shots, in close-up, in which the action is fully choreographed. From Sherriff's consideration of the action sequences he clearly seems intent on making the picture more visceral: there are occasions when the camera is enjoined to get down to ground level, almost to feel the bullets pass by. The screenplay is undoubtedly an exciting one, and less studio bound than what may have been expected.

He was hoping to finish the script by May, so that Victor Saville[54] could take it with him to Culver City to plan out the MGM-British slate for the months ahead. *Ruined City* would also have been tucked under his arm. There was speculation later in the summer that the latter was to be made in England, and would feature Robert Donat as Warren and Margaret Sullavan (fresh from a very engaging performance in *Three Comrades*) as Miss McMahon, to be directed by King Vidor (who had had great success with Robert Donat in *The Citadel* in 1938, also for MGM-British). The script continued to progress after Sherriff had handed his version over to Saville,[55] but the outbreak of the war in September 1939 brought the project to a halt. The worsening in the international political situation also likely did for *Journey's End* – no one was in the mood for a war movie with the real thing apparently inevitable. Unlike some of the other MGM-British properties, neither would be revived in California during the war.

On the Launchpad

With the *Ruined City* script complete, and *Journey's End* well in hand, the first of Sherriff's big spring launches was suddenly upon him, and he waited, no doubt rather anxiously, to find out what the critics thought of his new book. He must have been very gratified, because *The Hopkins Manuscript* was a great success, applauded widely – though not universally – by the critics.

Although there had been something of a spate of end-of-the-earth books in the recent period, Sherriff's was felt to stand out because of the characterisation of Hopkins himself, and the descriptions of village life both before and after the disaster. Frank Swinnerton in *The Observer* felt that 'in its imagining and in its minor perceptions of character and behaviour it has a quality transcending all but the finest of the prophetic novels of the last forty years.'[56] Forrest Reid in *The Spectator* believed that Sherriff had made the science 'quite plausible', but argued that its 'strangeness and excitement are not its only qualities; the humour and the character-drawing are alike excellent.'[57] *Punch* said it was 'thrillingly told – from Mr Sherriff one would expect nothing less,'[58] while *Country Life* thought it was 'uncommonly well done, and especially in the important matter of keeping us guessing, from stage to stage, all the time.'[59] L.P. Hartley – a big fan, it may be remembered, of *Greengates* – wrote that the author 'cannot describe any kind of life – however solitary, poor, nasty, brutish and short – without making it seem worth living. ... In all its final implications [the book] is extremely gloomy; but the path by which the author arrives at them ... passes through many a pleasant scene.'[60] Novelists Frank Swinnerton and Sylvia Townsend Warner also came down on Sherriff's side – although Hugh Walpole did not: 'I don't believe that once the moon had struck the earth anything happened as he said it did. That's probably my fault.'[61] The man from *The Times* was unconvinced as well, dismissing it as 'vague and unterrifying'.

Another Triumph

On balance, Sherriff would have been very happy with the reviews, especially for a book that was a departure from his previous novels, and it certainly got his launch season off to a good start. Next up was the premiere of *The Four Feathers*, which had its preview on 17 April at the Odeon in Leicester Square – Sherriff attending with a party of friends.

The film would be the first on the slate of a new company – Alex Korda Film Productions, which had emerged from a reorganisation of London Films, following an extended period of financial crisis. Essentially, London Films merged with the Pinewood Group (which included the Rank organisation and Pinewood Studios), and would no longer produce its own films, instead running Denham Studios. Korda, however, received a settlement that allowed him to set up his new company, which would stay in the business of movie making.[62] The reorganisation was announced to the press on 20 March 1939. A week earlier, Sherriff had received a letter from Basil Bleck, Korda's contracts manager, offering him a deal worth £6,000 for six months' work with the new company.[63] There were various contingencies attached, and nothing could be finalised until the new company had been formally established, but Bleck was at pains to point out:

Alex has often told me that you are one of the few people with whom he feels absolutely confident when working on scenarios, and I am sure, too, that the more general duties, which he suggested at our meeting you should also assist in, will greatly increase the success of the effects of your collaboration.[64]

The new company could hardly have wished for better press. 'Another triumph for the Korda studio', trumpeted the *News Chronicle*,[65] and the other papers almost unanimously agreed (though, again, not *The Times's* critic, who dismissed it rather sniffily).[66] The credit was spread around widely: the Kordas were praised for their production, design and direction; the acting was first rate (especially Ralph Richardson as Durrance, John Clements as Faversham and the newcomer June Duprez as Ethne); the cinematography outstanding (especially in the Sudan): '*The Four Feathers* lives because it gives you the feel of a cracked, parched, blistering-hot Sudan in wartime.'[67] Unusually, however, there was also praise for the screenplay (which is generally overlooked): 'It cannot fail to be one of the best pictures of the year,' wrote *The Spectator*, and 'it is impossible to divide the credit between Mr Zoltan Korda, the director, who has wiped out the disgrace of *Sanders of the River*, and Mr R.C. Sherriff, author of the film play. They seem to have perfectly fulfilled each other's intentions.'[68] There was even more in *The Guardian*, which, in one section of the review, highlighted Sherriff's contribution:

What calls for most praise in this film is not the acting or the directing but the contribution of that often overlooked individual, the scenario writer. R.C. Sherriff had taken great liberties with A.E.W. Mason's well-known, schoolboyish, but rather mistily elusive novel. One of the effects, of course, was to admit the Battle of Omdurman in a big way, but altogether the story had been so stiffened as to give far more drama to the vindication of Harry Faversham's honour and so rationalised that all these sons and daughters of regiments seemed a lot less like Mason's Jingoist prigs.[69]

The film was also well reviewed in the United States when it was eventually shown there, a few months later, although its story was occasionally viewed with bemusement: 'These movie Britishers are always off on quixotic errands. Their reasoning may not make much sense, but it often makes for a good movie,' and this one was, 'English spectacle at its best, banners flying, unabashed sentimentality, and stunning action shots'.[70]

And *Chips* Makes Three

Long before *The Four Feathers* reached the United States, Sherriff had one more launch ordeal to withstand, when *Goodbye, Mr Chips* was finally shown on the screen, more than three years after he had written its first draft.

He had been keeping an eye on the script during the development process, and had not been happy at how it had changed (by additional writers Claudine West and Eric Maschwitz), writing furiously to Victor Saville in July 1938[71]:

If the director said that the second half of my script was the best he had ever read, why in the name of reason has he mutilated it beyond recognition? The whole thing is inexplicable to me and an insult to me as a writer. ... If the script remains as it is, I know you will support my wish to have my name removed from it. ... If you feel I should take this up personally with Louis B. Mayer or [MGM Vice President] Eddie Mannix I will do so, and I will wait to hear your view.[72]

At some point in the following few months, at Saville's urging, he took the time to document the differences between the two scripts, and sent them on to Saville and Sam Wood (who had taken over as director from Sidney Franklin), whereupon Saville had tried to mollify him: 'I think you will find after certain revisions we have made when preparing for production, that the similarity of feeling is now identical.'[73]

But Saville was wrong: the feeling in Sherriff's script is quite different than in the later versions (and the movie), which are much more sentimental. Sherriff's original school scenes were much watered down, both in terms of time and authenticity, so that the school is no longer the one envisaged by Hilton (which mostly 'turned out merchants, manufacturers and professional men, with a good sprinkling of country squires and parsons'),[74] but is now the home of barons and knights.[75] Chips's relatively brief time with Katharine is expanded significantly, and they now no longer meet in the Lake District, but in Austria, where Chips is accompanied by his friend Staefel. Chips's own character is also altered – his disciplinarian tendencies exaggerated at the beginning to highlight more vividly the transformation wrought on him by Katharine's personality.

Despite Sherriff's fears, the changes in the script enhanced its box-office success, on both sides of the Atlantic, but especially in the United States. Alexander Woollcott, who was quoted in the ads for the film, cabled Hilton telling him, 'No film has ever moved me so deeply as *Goodbye, Mr Chips,*'[76] while Frank Nugent (the *New York Times* critic who would go on to become a pretty decent screenwriter himself, writing John Ford's cavalry trilogy and *The Searchers*, among many others) described it as 'one of the nicest pictures we have seen this year'. The British critics were occasionally a little sniffy about the portrayal of England, but the spirit of the movie won the public over and it did very well at the box office.

After the movie came out, Hilton wrote to congratulate Sherriff, who poured his heart out in reply: 'I have not seen the film yet, but I am very glad to hear you like the result. I went through the most awful time over it, and was completely heartbroken with what happened.'[77] He had calculated that 92 per cent of his script had been removed,[78] and felt, in particular, that the school scenes were badly done in the re-write, and that they were 'not only out of spirit, but rank bad screenwriting'. He told Hilton that he had thought of cabling him, but was already working for Korda, so had thought better of it. On the whole, though, he felt that 'my protest had some degree of effect, because a good many scenes which had been cut from the script were returned, and I think some of the worst of the additions removed.'

In his article on screenwriting in 1948, he commented on the difficulties of adapting the film:

> I remember the studio was very concerned because the only important female character would appear for such a brief time – from her marriage to Mr Chips and her early death. The studio was afraid that no leading star would accept a part that put her on the screen for so little time. I argued that she would remain indirectly and most potently on the screen all through the sequences following her death because it is her memory that shapes the character of Mr Chips's later years. I think this actually happened. Greer Garson accepted the part and it was the greatest success of her early career.[79]

Of course, he is absolutely correct that the memories of Katharine guide Chips long after her death – but in the film version, in the end, it was not Sherriff's hand that elevated Greer Garson's role, but rather those of Maschwitz and West (and likely Sidney Franklin as well). Their work was sufficient to earn Garson an Academy Award nomination for Best Actress, at the same time as the three screenwriters received a nomination for best script – ironically, given Sherriff's dislike of it. But they were not to be successful; other than Robert Donat for Best Actor, the film lost out in six other categories to *Gone With the Wind*.

Given his outrage at the liberties taken with his script, it is surprising that Sherriff made very little of it in his own memoir – not much more than a page, much of which is taken up with a remembrance of Donat on the studio lot in character. When *No Leading Lady* was published in 1968, Nigel Nicolson had written to him telling him how much he enjoyed it, but adding that he would have liked to have seen more on the difficulties of scriptwriting in Hollywood and Denham. But Sherriff's autobiography is refreshingly free of score settling – he was, after all, a very decent and gentlemanly type – and maybe, looking back, he was also a bit embarrassed at his own outbursts, especially since the script that so frustrated him was the only one he ever wrote that received an Oscar nomination.

What Is to Be the End of All This?

Sherriff wrote in *No Leading Lady* that he did not view the Second World War in the same romantic way as he had the First: 'I was over forty. ... I wasn't a junior clerk on a high stool this time. ... I wasn't straining to get back into uniform, but didn't want to appear a shirker.'[80] The key word in that final sentence is 'appear', since it was an essential part of his psychology that he must be seen to do the right thing, and it is to his credit that, even in circumstances where it would be inconvenient or dangerous or uncomfortable, he was always willing to do what was expected of him. It was probably what drove him into uniform in 1915, when he joined the Artists Rifles, and he listened to the voice of convention in his head again now, and sought out the colonel commanding the depot of his old regiment – which was in Kingston, just a stone's throw from Rosebriars. But there was nothing doing.

The same was not true of other ex-comrades. Warre-Dymond had contacted him several months before the outbreak of the war, explaining the efforts he had made to be placed in a regiment. At the suggestion of some friends, he wrote, he had tried the Royal Sussex, but received nothing more than an acknowledgement of his application: could Sherriff possibly pull some strings?[81] Sherriff tried his best, writing in praise of his former company commander, in such glowing terms that Warre-Dymond noted that 'it was all I could wish, in fact, I don't quite see how I can live up to it,'[82] but nothing came of it. In the end, however, Warre-Dymond did make it into the Army again, serving as a major in the Royal Army Ordnance Corps – perhaps not as much action as he might have wanted, but at least he was back in uniform.[83] Lechmere Thomas (Tommy the Bomber) was also in uniform (indeed, had never left), and he went on to fight at Dunkirk, and subsequently commanded brigades in Burma. Nobby Clark, too old for the Army, became Chief Air Raid warden for Folkestone. Another who was back in service was Dacre Stoker (who had played the colonel in the original *Journey's End*, and had remained a good friend ever since). He had also, according to his wife,[84] Peg, been promoted to captain, and was now Chief of Staff, Northern Ireland, doing an 'interesting', but 'hush-hush' job. Meanwhile, Mollie Cazalet had written to him, reporting that her 'two soldiers' (her sons Victor and Peter) were 'in charge of anti-aircraft guns', that her house, Fairlawne, 'has ninety cripples and sixteen attendants' and that her cottage, too, was crammed. 'Bob,' she asked, 'what is to be the end of all this?'[85]

But Bob had no answer for Mollie – in fact, he was frustrated trying to work out what his own part might be. After being turned down by his old regiment he took himself round to the Ministry of Information, who told him that he was on their list of authors whose services might be useful to them. He advised them that he could best help in film production, no doubt with an eye to breaking into the propaganda market. He then wrote to Korda, saying, 'If it is a matter of supplying the Ministry with the names of authors you want, then I hope you will add my name to the list, because I would far sooner work with you than with any other producer.'[86] Everything was being upended, everyone turning to new jobs, and yet there seemed to be no war work for Sherriff.

Unwanted, but not Unoccupied

But there was still a lot of other work for him to do. Since May he had been working for Korda on an adaptation of *Manon Lescaut*, the classic story of a nobleman (Des Grieux) who falls for a woman (Manon Lescaut herself) of whom his father disapproves. He worked jointly on it with Lajos Biro, completing the script in early August,[87] after which there was a flurry of press reports, confirming plans to make it with Merle Oberon (now Korda's wife) in the lead, and possibly having it renamed *Sinner* (on the grounds that the title *Manon Lescaut* would hardly be a box-office draw).[88] But like his MGM screenplays, it was shelved on the outbreak of the war, never to be revived.

In July Sherriff had signed a contract with Macmillan of Canada, to prepare an autobiography, for completion sometime before the autumn of 1940; there was a plan for a novel that he hoped to serialise in *Good Housekeeping*.[89] During September he also kept in close touch with Korda, and 'lent a hand'[90] in Britain's first 'propaganda' movie of the war – *The Lion Has Wings*. According to Korda's biographer, the film was something of a 'freelance effort', which caused all manner of problems between Korda, the Foreign Office and the Ministry of Information.[91] It was generally viewed as quite crude propaganda, but it was still impressive, especially given the short timespan in which it had been produced – about eight weeks from conception to distribution.[92]

There was one other interesting job on the books as well: the screenplay of George Bernard Shaw's *Major Barbara*, on which he would work alongside producer Gabriel Pascal. Pascal had enjoyed great success the previous year with the film version of *Pygmalion* (starring Leslie Howard and Wendy Hiller), to the point of receiving an Academy Award nomination for Production, and was becoming known for his collaborations with Bernard Shaw, who thought very highly of him indeed. The contract with Pascal was due to begin at the end of September, but Sherriff wrote to him asking to delay it for a week; with petrol rationing, he could no longer simply motor up and down to Denham in his Rolls-Royce, and he would need time to rent a house closer to the studios. There were further delays thereafter, mainly to do with Pascal seeking authorisation to begin production, and with construction of a complete scenario. Sherriff was reluctant to get dragged into the process too early and told Pascal that he would move closer to him once the picture had received production approval, and a final draft script was in hand. He kept trying to reassure Pascal that he had not lost interest in the work,[93] although he also flagged up a meeting with General Beith[94] at the War Office, and cautioned that, if he were required for 'official work I may be obliged to go right into the job.'[95]

He probably had not lost interest, but was just feeling a little at sea: he must have been excited at Korda's mobilisation of resources to get his propaganda film made so quickly, and the fact that he told Pascall about Beith's overture suggests that he was hopeful of something arising from it. Still, however, no one seemed to have much wartime use for him. His frustration can be glimpsed in a letter he sent to Peg Stoker in November, once he had actually started with Pascal:

It seems a queer business working on a film script in these distracting days, but apparently Pascal has some kind of government encouragement, because he hopes to get his company together and begin the picture sometime early in the New Year. I hope to goodness it happens. There are so many good people without jobs at present.[96]

He finally started work on the script at the beginning of November, staying at Stoke Court, near Denham, and cycling to Pascal's house each day. After a couple of weeks, however, Pascal decided to finish the job down at his house in Devon, and asked Sherriff to come along, which he did, albeit a little reluctantly. They finished work on the script[97] in time for Sherriff to return to Rosebriars for Christmas. He was happy with the finished script, and also, no doubt, with the extra £2,200 in his bank account, which would help to pay for some of the improvements he had in mind for Down House Farm, the farm that he had purchased at Eype in Dorset earlier that year.

1940

The year got off to a bad start. On 22 January, after a long period of infirmity, Sherriff's father died. Herbert had done well to struggle on since his stroke in 1931, and surviving till the age of eighty-two was no mean feat. But eventually he succumbed to pneumonia (and 'senility' – probably just meaning simple old age) and was cremated in Woking Crematorium on 25 January. Sherriff had not been especially close to his father for some considerable time, and it would not have been unexpected, but it would nevertheless have come as a blow, especially to Connie.

After *Major Barbara* he kept working at his novel, but seems to have made little or no progress on his autobiography – about which he had anyway appeared a little conflicted, as Pamela Frankau had observed some months earlier: 'How,' he had asked her, spreading out his hands in despair, 'does one do self revelation?'[98]

The film contracts all but dried up – he still hadn't been picked up for war-related work, and there were few other avenues in the film industry – but there were two small jobs that came his way. The first was with British National Films (part of the Rank organisation, and a company with which he had not previously been associated), where he was commissioned to work on an outline story on the sinking of the *Graf Spee*. The German battleship had been chased into the River Plate by a group of British warships in December 1939, and her captain had chosen to scuttle her, rather than have her captured. There are a couple of small payments in his cash book (two, of just over £100 each) suggesting the work had been no more than introductory. A later letter from Baron Strabolgi[99] (author of *The Battle of the River Plate* in 1940) indicates that he had tried to sell the story to Darryl Zanuck, at Twentieth Century Fox, but it had been turned down. Strabolgi hoped that it might get picked up if Sherriff could press the case upon his return to Hollywood, but nothing came of it.[100]

The other job, which came in April, was some script doctoring on the film *Freedom Radio*[101] (which was also released as *A Voice in the Night*). This one was a wartime propaganda movie, in which Hitler's doctor, finally becoming aware of the brutality of the Nazi regime, as some of his friends are sent to the camps, engages some engineer friends to set up a radio station to broadcast against the Nazi government. The payments in Sherriff's cash books (a total of £450) suggest that his involvement was relatively minor, and he certainly received no script credit. It did, however, introduce him to the production company Two Cities Films, which would be useful after the war.

A Call to Arms

Sherriff recalls busying himself in his garden at Rosebriars – 'Digging for Victory', as it were:

> I decided that we must make ourselves completely self-supporting, and talked things over with my gardener. We extended the vegetable garden and bought some additional pullets and young cockerels that were moved into the meadow, where they ran loose and picked up plenty of natural food. On the old chicken run we grew potatoes.... By March, the vegetable garden was something to be proud of.... Our plans for being self-supporting were working fine.[102]

He had already rented out Sandmartin[103]: petrol rationing meant that motoring to the coast was not something he could do on a regular basis, and with contracts hard to come by, it was important to have his various properties at least earning their own keep. The land of Down House Farm was also rented out to a local farmer.

But then, out of the blue, came a call from Alex Korda. Could Sherriff come to see him at Claridge's to discuss a film he was planning, on Nelson and Lady Hamilton? It would have to be made in Hollywood, and he wanted Sherriff to come along to write the script. Sherriff recalled that he was, at first, unwilling to take up the offer, but as Korda described it to him, the proposal 'began to sound attractive'. The government, he explained, wanted good British pictures made, the sort that 'would relate valiant episodes in Britain's not too distant past.' But the pictures should not 'wave the British flag too obviously', and they should be well made – which would be impossible in a Britain struggling with shortages. They had turned to Korda to help, and he, with his links to United Artists, had managed to secure the Hollywood facilities, and the necessary financial backing. He had even managed to secure the services of Laurence Olivier and Vivien Leigh as the two stars.[104] Sherriff felt that the offer was 'a great compliment: a great opportunity that any screenwriter, in

England or America, would have jumped at with open arms, and it was difficult to say I couldn't do it because of my potatoes and my chickens.'

Sherriff has a long and touching tale in his autobiography about his reluctance to leave Rosebriars, and his hope that the whole thing would be called off, especially once the Germans invaded the Low Countries and France, beginning on 10 May 1940. He also has a tale about how, at the last minute, there was a change in the sailing time of the boat. But letters from his files confirm that he was actively making preparations despite the latest turn of events in the war,[105] and that he had received notification of the ship's sailing date and time almost a week before it sailed.[106] He had made up his mind to go, and he was taking his mother with him.

It must have been a difficult decision, leaving his home and country in wartime, and taking a chance on a perilous Atlantic voyage when the U–boats were prowling the sea lanes. Yet Korda had asked him to Hollywood personally, and this was not a relationship he would wish to prejudice. The most crucial factor was probably the money. His earnings had all but dried up, and he had huge expenses at Rosebriars and Down House Farm. As he wrote himself: 'I'd got my own home in Esher, a house by the sea and a farm in Dorset. I wanted to look after them and go on with the screenwriting that made it possible to keep them.'[107] In which case, Hollywood was the only option available.

Chapter 10

Semi-Official Business, 1940–44

If men do rightly what they do, we ought not to be displeased; but if they do not right, it is plain that they do so involuntarily and in ignorance.
Marcus Aurelius, *The Meditations*, Book XI.

The *Duchess of Richmond* set sail from Gladstone Dock in Liverpool in the early evening of Thursday, 30 May 1940. 'The ship looked tired and shabby. We had the feeling it didn't want us,'[1] wrote Sherriff. 'Our cabins were small and low-down in the ship, stuffy from months of sailing with blacked-out portholes.' Small and stuffy, perhaps, but at least one of them came with a bath, since he had taken the precaution of upgrading both cabins.[2] Sherriff was a man who enjoyed his bath – indeed, he fell out with his old friend Joe Cowley on one occasion, because, having said he would call after his morning bath, he forgot to do so, leaving Cowley to fume that 'You spend more time in your bath than is prudent for one who appears to be as busy as you are.'[3]

The crossing must have been a very anxious one. The usual time taken was about five days, but this journey took ten, to avoid the areas where the U-boats were most likely to hunt. And this was no idle threat; just a few months later, Arthur Wimperis, Sherriff's writing partner from *The Four Feathers*, would travel across on the *City of Benares*, which was torpedoed on 18 September with the loss of 260 lives (including about eighty child evacuees),[4] although 'Wimp' survived.

According to Sherriff, the 'misery of our U-boat-haunted voyage was mild compared with the ordeal that faced us when we docked at Montreal.' He goes on to recount a traumatic tale of arriving in Canada with little money,[5] and finding his way to America barred because of a sudden edict against writers entering the country. Sherriff paints a harrowing tale of the two of them stranded in cheap lodgings with only a $100 advance to keep body and soul together. In the end, Myron Selznick, Sherriff's Hollywood agent, saves the day, organises the entrance visa and arranges for Sherriff to be given all the cash he needs to get him to Hollywood. Hurrah!

Once again, however, Sherriff's tale is just too movie-neat for credence. In fact, we know, from a letter to him from Basil Bleck (who had moved to the Hollywood offices of Alex Korda Films),[6] and a cable from Sig Marcus[7] (at Myron Selznick), that some $300 was made available to him, although a few days may have elapsed after his arrival on 9 June before he could draw on the money. But he also had the resources of Curtis Brown to fall back on, and their New York offices also advanced him $500 to tide him over.[8] Money, then, was unlikely to have been the problem. There is, though, another puzzle, which is to do with his onward journey to Los Angeles, which did not begin until 20 June[9]: why did he wait around in Montreal for eleven days? Sig Marcus's cable sheds a little light on this, since it notes that Bleck 'will request your postponing starting date with Korda until Korda returns.' It then goes on to say that Bleck has authorised that Myron Selznick may offer Sherriff to 'all studios immediately for one assignment before your Korda job commences'.[10]

This, then, may be the real source of the anxiety Sherriff was able to recall in his autobiography years later. A delay of a day or two in receipt of expenses was nothing much, and would not likely have left much of an impression on him. But to be in Montreal and to be told that his contract would not now begin immediately would surely have left a cavernous doubt. He had come to work, to earn the money he needed to finance his houses and his farm. If he could not begin work he would be even worse off than he had been in England, where at least his expenses would be less. The big question he had to face was: would another studio offer him work? Until that question was answered, he would be forced to wait, anxiously, in Montreal – because he was unlikely to be admitted to the United States unless he had a very clear job of work to go to. Happily, it took less than a couple of weeks for Sig Marcus to arrange a contract with MGM, beginning on 27 June. Armed with the promise of work, he was probably then able to secure his entry visa to the United States, and to arrange his onward itinerary.

Sherriff and his mother finally left Montreal on 20 June, heading first to Toronto, then to Chicago, where he arrived early in the morning of 21 June, breathing a sigh of relief that, after being in transit for three weeks, he had finally crossed the border into the United States. From Chicago it was the usual two-day run to Los Angeles, where they arrived around noon on 23 June. He was due to begin work for Metro just four days later, at a rate of $1,000 per week, with the proviso in his contract that, as soon as the call came in from Korda, he could answer it. He and his mother took an apartment initially at the Garden of Allah Hotel,[11] on Sunset Boulevard (ten minutes from MGM studios), and Sherriff got to work, initially script doctoring on the screenplay of *Flight Command*,[12] which was based on a story by ex-navy commander, Harvey Haislip, about a young navy pilot joining an elite group in training. He was only there a few weeks, however, before he received from Korda the summons for which he had been waiting.

That Hamilton Woman

Sherriff began work for Korda on 12 August, and was teamed with Austrian-born writer Walter Reisch, who had enjoyed a peripatetic screenwriting career,[13] but had lately landed at MGM with a reputation as 'a writer of strong roles for female stars'.[14] They were given the challenge of distilling the life of Emma, Lady Hamilton, and especially her relationship with Lord Nelson, into a patriotic blockbuster. The historical subject matter would have appealed to Sherriff, and having not so long ago written about Napoleon he would at least have been familiar with the history of the period, if not the real-life stories of the two main protagonists in the film.

The tale is told by old Emma, after she has been thrown into debtors' prison in Calais, and her narrative follows a chronological progression, touching the highlights of her life: her meetings with, and subsequent marriage to, Britain's ambassador to Naples, Sir William Hamilton; her encounters with Nelson, his battles and woundings; their very public affair and ultimate decision to live together, in spite of their marriages to other spouses. Nelson, of course, is killed at Trafalgar, and afterwards Emma falls on hard times, which takes her to the debtors' prison, where the story began.

The broadly sequential narrative would have appealed to Sherriff – it is reminiscent of the way in which he and De Casalis structured *St Helena*, while the narration of the tale by Emma herself has echoes of *The Hopkins Manuscript*. No doubt the writers reached for easy and familiar structures, because time was of the essence. Money was tight, and the plan was to produce the film as quickly as possible – so that Sherriff and Reisch only had about six weeks to produce the script before shooting began on 18 September.[15] Sherriff describes the pressure:

> We scrambled through an outline of the screenplay to give them what they wanted to design the sets and get on with the casting, but only the first sequences were down in dialogue when they began to shoot the picture. From then on it was a desperate race to keep up with them. It was like writing a serial story with only a week between your pen and the next instalment to be published.[16]

With such a tight schedule, it was important that the PCA be kept informed, and a week before production started a letter went off to Joe Breen containing what they had of the script so far (about eighty-seven pages). In his reply[17] Breen set out a number of detailed suggestions for changes that would be required, but he prefaced the list by warning Korda to be careful, because this was basically a story about adultery, and as such 'to be acceptable under the Production Code, it will be necessary to inject into it what we call "necessary compensating values".' He then set out what that might mean:

> Under the Code it has been found necessary, in dealing with stories of adultery, that:
>
> (A)   You definitely establish the adultery to be 'wrong';
> (B)   the adulterous situation be not condoned, nor justified, nor made to appear 'right and acceptable';
> (C)   the adulterous parties must be punished.

The warning from Breen could not have been any clearer.

On 19 September, George Bagnall replied to Geoffrey Shurlock at the PCA enclosing a longer script (now 105 pages); Breen was still not happy, noting that they still had not seen the 'necessary compensating moral values'.[18] The filmmakers tried again on 12 October, by which time Sherriff and Reisch had pushed the page count up to 160, with only another ten or so to come; but on 15 October they received a frosty reply[19]: 'We regret to have to report that the material so far submitted does not seem to contain the full necessary compensating values for the treatment of adultery on screen.'

He then went on to specify in detail a number of scenes that appeared to support Nelson's adultery, and seems to have been particularly annoyed that Nelson's father – a minister – does nothing to condemn Nelson's adultery. There followed a further three pages of suggested deletions and amendments, presumably to show he meant business.

In *No Leading Lady*, Sherriff recounts some of this tale, putting himself at the centre of events, but his timing is a little awry. He suggests that the movie was all but completed before Korda sent him to see Breen, whereas Korda had been smart enough to involve the PCA from the very beginning. But he does get right the fact that the scene with Nelson's father was turned around so that the father no longer implicitly condoned the son's adultery, instead rejecting it out of hand. Towards the end of October, Korda himself replied to Breen enclosing additional scenes (including one between Nelson and his father) that were designed to show that the filmmakers had been paying attention. Breen was beginning to come around, but still wanted more, even going so far as to suggest the type of dialogue that Korda might want to put in the mouth of Nelson's father[20]:

It would help if the father would come out frankly and say, in words of one syllable, something like this:

'This alliance of yours cannot help but end in disaster and I beg of you to break it up. Don't be fooled by any seeming happiness that you may think you are now enjoying … you can't defy the laws of God without being made to pay the price. Unless you catch yourself now, both of you will surely end up in the gutter.'

Amusingly enough, he then said that he didn't want to suggest how the dialogue should be written, but rather just 'give you our thoughts. … We think it would help us all very much if you have this very positive condemnation and prediction of disaster, which will follow as a result of their sin. This, we feel, is very, very important.'

By the time that Korda was receiving Breen's final missive, Sherriff had already moved back to MGM, his work with Korda ending on 12 October, so whether he was on hand to 'punch up' the final dialogue on the scenes is not clear. It is entirely possible he was doing both jobs at once – and he did have a track record of assisting with rewrites on projects long after his formal involvement had ceased. The final scene with the father is not quite as Breen had suggested, although the old parson makes clear his distaste for Nelson's adultery, and, when Nelson declines to deviate from his course, tells him that he then chooses to go with his son's wife, Lady Nelson. Even if the parson's words were not quite the PCA's, at least they could be satisfied that Emma's misery and decline after Nelson's death conveyed the kind of disapproval of adultery that they expected.

Filming finished at the beginning of November,[21] and the movie finally received its PCA certificate on 1 March 1941, with the world premiere of *That Hamilton Woman* (with the less implicitly judgmental title of *Lady Hamilton* in the UK release) taking place at the Four Star Theater in Hollywood on 19 March 1941. Given the timescale to which they had been working, the film is something of a marvel: it is sumptuously produced, with superb sets and costumes ('The production must have cost a fortune,' wrote Louella Parsons).[22] Vivien Leigh is perfectly cast as the courtesan who cannot help following the great love of her life, and Olivier makes a marvellously heroic Nelson. Several scenes stay in the mind long afterwards. On a domestic level, her interactions with the King and Queen of Naples (and their large brood of children) are very funny, displaying flightiness on her part, which is gradually modulated as the film progresses and her love affair with Nelson deepens. Then there is a wonderfully lit scene on board Nelson's boat, which is moored in the Bay of Naples: when Emma arrives and is taken to Nelson's cabin she is shocked by his appearance because he has been wounded in his campaigns, losing an eye and an arm[23] – her simple gasp and his fumbling for a bandage to cover his eye are brief but very moving gestures. When Nelson comes to see her on another occasion, and she is told in her bedroom that he is waiting on the balcony, such is the magnificence of Vincent Korda's sets that it takes her almost thirty seconds to run to him – through rooms and hallways and along apparently endless miles of balustraded balconies.

The film was not intended solely as a love story, but as a paean to Britain's historical past and her virtues as a nation with a long record in opposing tyrants. So there are action scenes[24] playing up Nelson's heroism, scenes of grandeur and pageantry in palaces and at Westminster, and there is a famous speech by Nelson in which he warns the men of the Admiralty that they should not try to make peace with a dictator:

> Gentlemen … you will never make peace with Napoleon. He doesn't mean peace today. He just wants to gain a little time to re-arm himself at sea and to make new alliances with Italy and Spain – all to one purpose. To destroy our Empire! … Napoleon can never be master of the world until he has smashed us up – and believe me, gentlemen, he means to be master of the world. You cannot make peace with dictators. You have to destroy them. Wipe them out![25]

In New York showings, 'the last lines never failed to draw a round of applause.'[26] The *New York Times* critic Bosley Crowther, while not impressed with the love story ('Perhaps if it had all been condensed and contrived with less manifest awe, the effect would have been more exciting and the love story would have had more poignancy')[27] clearly grasped the film's purpose, noting Nelson's 'timely opinions about dictators who would desire to invade England', and that 'coming at a moment such as this, it should stir anyone's interest.'

It is often suggested that Nelson's speech came neither from the pen of Sherriff, nor of Reisch, but instead was offered to Korda by Churchill himself. It is certainly true that it has something of a Churchillian tone – but such mimicry would have come easily to two experienced screenwriters (and especially Sherriff, who had a wonderful ear for such things). Michael Korda suggests that his uncle would not have included such an 'unsubtle' scene if he had 'not felt obliged to do so because of its authorship'.[28] With such inference aside, there is not one shred of evidence to suggest that Churchill had a hand in it. Churchill appears twice in *No Leading Lady* – once after his letter to Sherriff regarding *Journey's End* (see page 105) and once in his letter to *The Times* praising *St Helena* (see page 186). Nowhere in any of Sherriff's papers, however, is the subject of Churchill's authorship of the Nelson speech ever broached – yet he would have been beyond proud to have been associated with such an intervention. Multiple sources agree that the movie was one of Churchill's favourites, and that he saw it many times, also showing it to Roosevelt (at their Atlantic Conference) and later to Stalin as well.[29] For his part, Sherriff simply noted in *No Leading Lady* that 'Churchill had a copy sent to him, and he saw it many times in his private projection room. If it gave him a few evenings of relaxation in those arduous days it well repaid its making.'[30]

Mrs Miniver

Wrapping up his work on one big British propaganda movie, Sherriff was quickly shunted on to another one when he returned to MGM. Kenneth McKenna, story editor at MGM, had written to him a week before he was due to finish with Korda, enclosing a copy of *Mrs Miniver*, by Jan Struther,[31] and asking whether he thought that Metro should take an option on it.[32]

The Mrs Miniver character had first appeared in the court pages of *The Times* in October 1937, and ran until December 1939. She was a very well-to-do upper-middle-class housewife (from the 'top drawer but one', according to E.M. Forster),[33] living in Chelsea (with a second house in Kent) with her architect husband Clem and her three children. Struther's columns had mostly been written before the war, although the last few, written in the autumn of 1939, began to mention it. The columns were collected into a book that was published in the United States in July 1940. What McKenna saw in it was 'somewhat of a tribute to the stirringly courageous way that the British people continue their simple daily life under the present conditions', and he felt that Sherriff might be interested in tackling it.

Before Sherriff had returned to MGM, producer Sidney Franklin had taken out the option, and decided that Sherriff and James Hilton would be ideal for the project, putting them to work on it together. By 6 November, Sherriff had produced some initial thoughts on what the film might look like, and set them down in an outline.[34] This consisted of a 'prologue', followed by a dozen suggested scenes illuminating past episodes in their lives, and then an epilogue; the scenes would show such things as the people of the village, the children's schools, how they fell in love with the house and so on. The next day he provided a script for the prologue,[35] which begins with Mrs Miniver reading from *Alice in Wonderland* (that old Sherriff standby), then pans across the gas masks hung in the dugout (which, amusingly, showed everyone's gas masks with their name, except for the one showing 'Mrs' Miniver), before leading on to the conversation between the two adults, which is peppered with typical Sherriff-style jokes. As they converse, the sounds of the air raid grow ever nearer and the strain begins to tell in their conversation, although they do their best to mask their fears.

Despite setting down the first thoughts, Sherriff was moved on from the project by mid-December, although quite why is not clear, especially since additional writers George Froeschel, Claudine West and Arthur Wimperis were brought on board, to work alongside Hilton. Much of the one scene he had scripted did remain in the movie, although it no longer formed the prologue, instead taking place towards the end of the movie (and with the dog which he had scripted – he was something of a dog-lover, after all – becoming a cat), but it remains one of the scenes which sticks most in the memory.[36] Sherriff has also occasionally been mooted as the author of the first scene in the final movie – where Mrs Miniver is shopping in London for a hat – but there is no evidence that he had a hand in anything other than the dugout scene.[37]

The film was eventually released in June 1942, and shortly before then Sherriff bumped into Sidney Franklin in the street, prompting Franklin to write to him afterwards telling him much he had appreciated his efforts on the film:

> I'm sorry it didn't work out that you received screen credit, but this much I can do – and that is to let you know that I appreciated your work and the suggestions and thoughts of yours that did go into the final script. I hope that some day I will have the opportunity of working with you again, and that it will result in a credit.[38]

Shirkers

Shortly after arriving in the United States Sherriff was present at the formation of a brand new committee, designed to 'assist the various organisations conducting patriotic work in Southern California', and also to support the members of the British community in Los Angeles (and especially Hollywood). At the inaugural meeting on 21 August were Ronald Colman and Cedric Hardwicke (both of whom Sherriff knew well), and in subsequent meetings they would be joined by actor Herbert Marshall. Eric Cleugh, the British Consul in Los Angeles, popped along to lend his support, and to endorse their chosen title: 'British Consulate War Charities Advisory Board'.[39]

The British community in Hollywood had been accused of 'shirking' by staying in or going to Hollywood when their country was at war. The criticisms had been coming from England since early 1940 (at first in a rather lame attempt at humour in *Picturegoer* magazine),[40] and were particularly pointed in an interview given by Michael Balcon to the same magazine in May 1940, when he said that he was 'disgusted'[41] by British filmmakers heading to Hollywood. Here he had in his sights his long-time rival Korda,[42] but Sherriff was probably aware of the general criticism of 'cowards' and 'tax evaders' and would likely have been sensitive about it. He might also have seen the letter from Sir Seymour Hicks[43] (a well-known actor-manager), which poked fun at the Hollywood Brits 'gallantly facing the footlights', and suggesting that Charles Laughton, Alfred Hitchcock and Marshall might consider making a new movie, *Gone With the Wind Up*. However, as the British Ambassador to the US, Lord Lothian, had made clear to a delegation from Hollywood in July (including Cedric Hardwicke, Cary Grant and Laurence Olivier), only those between the ages of eighteen and thirty were required for military service. Britain did not want its middle-aged Hollywood stars to return, for they would add nothing to the war effort, and would be a drain on its resources: far better for them to remain in Hollywood and make pro-British pictures.

A few days after the inaugural meeting of the Advisory Board, Balcon again took aim at the expats, in the *Sunday Despatch*, criticising 'people who prefer to remain in Hollywood instead of returning home to aid their country's war efforts'. He singled out 'a plump young junior technician ... whom I promoted from department to department. Today he is one of our most famous directors and he is in Hollywood, while we who are left behind shorthanded are trying to harness the films to our great national effort.'[44] The man in his sights this time was Alfred Hitchcock, who, as chance would have it, screened his new film *Foreign Correspondent* (featuring Herbert Marshall, and starring Joel McCrea) for three members of the new board just three days later (with the minutes recording that they found the film 'of undoubted value to British prestige'). After the screening they were joined by the other board members, and adjourned to Hitchcock's house, where 'they were favoured with the gentleman's views regarding the "Background" of the *Sunday Despatch* article.'[45]

In response to Balcon's article, the board thought it would be a good idea for the British ambassador to issue a statement to the local press, clarifying the issue with regard to English actors. It started with a list of fourteen actors who had 'fought for or otherwise served their country in the last war', noting that many had been wounded or decorated[46]; then came six young actors (including Richard Greene and David Niven) who had been working in the US at the beginning of the war, but who had since enlisted in England or Canada; and then it noted that those of 'intermediate age' had 'reported and registered their names at the British Consulate, placing themselves unreservedly at the call of their native country.' The hope was that a cablegram to that effect could go to the *Sunday Despatch* to 'correct the misstatements'[47] it had made, and Sherriff even offered to write a piece for the same newspaper. It was decided, however, on the suggestion of a PR man with whom they consulted, that the best thing for them to do was ignore the *Despatch* article altogether.

The situation worsened that same day, with a broadcast given by J.B. Priestley to the United States in which he called the British actors in Hollywood 'deserters'. This prompted a cable from Lord Lothian back to the Foreign Secretary, Lord Halifax, saying that the actors were only following his guidance on military service, and that Priestley's accusations were undesirable:

> The maintenance of a powerful British nucleus of older actors in Hollywood is of great importance to our own interests, partly because they are continually championing the British cause in a very volatile community which would otherwise be left to the mercies of German propaganda, and because the production of films with a strong British tone is one of the best and subtlest forms of British propaganda.[48]

This appears to have been the high point of the cross-Atlantic megaphone diplomacy, and tempers seem to have cooled thereafter – with the suggestion that government officials may have had a quiet word with Balcon to let him know that Hitchcock was working in America 'at the express request of the British government'.[49] Ironically, after being attacked from the British side, the Hollywood film-makers would, in the following year, be attacked by the 'America First' lobby (which was a combination of those who sought American neutrality in the war, and those more sympathetic to the German cause, including some well-known anti-Semites). Both Victor Saville and Alex Korda were identified as potential British spies (and, indeed, there is a suggestion that they may have passed information to British authorities, and in Korda's case, may have directly facilitated Britain's spy networks through his offices in New York and Hollywood). The America First lobby became sufficiently exercised by what they saw as a barrage of pro-British films that Senate hearings were engineered beginning in September of 1941, with Korda being summoned to testify on 12 December 1941. But the bombing of Pearl Harbour on 7 December brought the hearings to an end, and Korda was spared an appearance.

Sherriff seems to have remained sensitive ever after to the charges of desertion or disloyalty: his absence even caused a rift with his old friend Manning-Press.[50] Consequently, in his public comments he would tend to downplay his time in the United States: in *No Leading Lady*, for example, he wrote that he and his mother were keen to go home and implicitly suggested that, shortly after the attack on Pearl Harbour, they did so.[51] But in fact they would not leave until mid-1944. In the same vein, after he returned, he would tend to play up the nature of the work that took him out to Hollywood in the first place, suggesting it was 'semi-official'[52] business. Of course, he had nothing to upbraid himself for – he had been offered no useful wartime work at home, and was keen simply to earn his living. Had he been offered the chance to do so in the UK, he would probably have stayed. But given that he left for Hollywood, it was at the very least important that he be seen to have done so for the right reasons.

Cargo of Innocence

By the end of November 1940, having just left work on *Mrs Miniver*, Sherriff was shunted on to a quite different project. *Cargo of Innocence* started as a short story of the same name in *Ken* magazine in May 1938. By Laurence Kirk,[53] the story was an account of an incident during the Spanish Civil War, when a group of refugee children, accompanied by some pregnant young women, were picked up in the Bay of Biscay by the British ship HMS *Tremendous*. Metro had commissioned a treatment in 1939, and had even submitted the story outline to the PCA, but then seem to have put it on the shelf.

Sherriff got to work quickly. His first notes on the subject are dated 18 December, and set out the main strands of the story, most of which remained even after he had moved on. The story should focus on the life of a British destroyer under war conditions, to familiarise people with a routine Atlantic patrol. He suggested a young captain being given, as his first command, an old boat that had fought at Jutland, but had been renovated and brought back into service. Many of the men assigned to the boat would be disappointed with their posting, but the new captain would strive to instil a fierce pride in the crew, and he would be assisted by an old sailor who had fought in her all those years before and maintained a watching eye over her ever since. Only once the rhythms of the voyage had been established should the surprise of the babies confront the crew. A story outline a couple of days later expanded on the theme, adding an extra character – a young lieutenant from an upper-class family who serves as the admiral's aide-de-camp, but whom the admiral feels would benefit from a tougher job.[54]

Next came a sixty-page script treatment by Sherriff, in conjunction with Harvey Haislip (with whom he had worked briefly on *Flight Command*). The script hews to Sherriff's outline fairly closely, but now the ship is engaged in a search and rescue mission, as well as joining a convoy. It is while steaming to join a convoy that they encounter a small tramp steamer, holed by a mine and limping home. The steamer has a party of women and babies on board – refugees from the Spanish Civil War. The final quarter or so of the script shows how the sailors look after the babies, and focuses on the successful births by the three pregnant women, all carried out under the watchful eye of the commodore, who is charged with leading the convoy.

There were subsequent changes to the script – an extra plot about the old seaman dying, and the rookie lieutenant disobeying the captain's orders in order to help him – but by 14 March 1941, Sherriff and Haislip handed in their final script. MGM seems to have been thinking about perhaps shooting some of the scenes in the UK, with Robert Donat and Edmund Gwenn, but wartime production difficulties convinced them to shoot in Hollywood. When the US entered the war after Pearl Harbour in December, the focus of the film changed from the Royal Navy to the US Navy, and the ocean from Atlantic to Pacific. By that time the assistance of the US Navy had been sought by the producers, and some action scenes added. Production took place during 1942, with the final release date set for the very end of the year.

The film was eventually released, as *Stand By For Action*, in the United States on 31 December 1942 (although it remained *Cargo of Innocence*[55] in the UK); it starred Brian Donlevy as the ship's new captain, and Robert Taylor as the Harvard-educated lieutenant whom the admiral wishes to teach a lesson: the admiral, in this case, was a hopelessly miscast Charles Laughton. Walter Brennan played the old sailor who had been with the ship, man and boy. The reviews were not good. This from the *New York Times*[56] sums up the flavour:

> It sandwiches within a serious war plot some of the most incredible farce you ever saw. … Charles Laughton plays … the admiral like a character out of HMS *Pinafore* and Walter Brennan seems on the verge of tears perpetually as an ancient mariner who is devoted to the ship.

Sherriff – well away from MGM by the time the film was distributed – would likely have been disappointed, but not surprised, given what he later wrote to Haislip:

> The happiest months of my stay in America were those when I was working with you on *Cargo of Innocence*, I enjoyed every moment of that collaboration and do hope one day that we shall work together again. It was a pity the picture was so horribly mutilated, but that is the luck of the game.[57]

After finishing his work on *Cargo of Innocence*, Sherriff carried on with MGM until the end of June 1941, during which time he seems to have been called on for some general script doctoring work, including on the Clark Gable/Rosalind Russell vehicle, *They Met in Bombay*. But he was unhappy in the US, anxious to return home, and wrote to Victor Cazalet asking if he might be able to find him a job back in England: 'I would prefer it to be an active job, instead of a journalistic one, but I would do anything or go anywhere.'[58] The studios were willing to release him to do any work requested by the British authorities, he wrote, and if Victor could find a definite job to do he would come straight back.

His keenness to return may have been due to frustration with his projects at MGM, and perhaps also a desire to rebut the 'shirker' charge, but he probably also felt the urge to get back to his houses, farm and gardens. His cash books show that the upkeep of Rosebriars was not cheap, and he had several projects progressing (very expensively) at Down House Farm, such as new farm buildings and infrastructure, and the little cottage he wanted as a weekend retreat. He would have relished the opportunity of being on hand to supervise things. But there was nothing Cazalet could do for him, although he did promise to keep a lookout in the future, so an early return seemed out of the question.

This Above All

Two days after his contract with MGM ended, Sherriff's agent approached him with an unexpected offer from Twentieth Century Fox: would he be interested in adapting Eric Knight's novel, *This Above All*, at a fee of $1,250 a week ($250 more than MGM was paying him), with the promise of a bonus when the screenplay was completed? He would indeed, and he started work almost immediately.[59]

This Above All was published in 1941 and is the story of embittered British soldier, Clive Briggs. Clive is working class, and has lived a hard life. One night he meets Prue, a rather sheltered WAAF[60] from an upper-middle-class family, and they quickly become romantically and sexually involved (the novel, while not exactly blatant about the sex, does not shy away from it). Soon they take a trip to a south coast town, where much of the novel takes place, and their (long) conversations shed light on his hardscrabble upbringing and his experiences at Dunkirk, all of which have made him despise the ruling class. Why, he asks, should he fight for a country that has treated him and others like him so badly, and would likely do so again once the war is over?

They are joined by his army pal Monty, from whom we hear a great deal about Clive's heroics at Dunkirk and Douai, and learn more about his character. Prue argues in favour of the prosecution of the war, believing that Britain will emerge changed afterwards; during one long night of bombing they thrash out their respective views of their country and the war, with Clive offering remarkably positive views of the effect that Hitler has had on Germany and Prue offering the vision of England for which they should be fighting. When the holiday is over, she returns to her barracks, and Clive goes on the run, encountering various characters along the way; but he soon tires of it and decides to return to the Army. He contacts Prue and they agree to marry, but on his way to meet her, he is injured in an air raid and the doctors find he has a brain disease arising from the pneumonia he contracted at Dunkirk. Prue's father operates on him, but there is nothing much he can do, and Clive dies, leaving a pregnant Prue, determined that her child will grow up in a better England.

The book was published in 1941, while the memory of Dunkirk was fresh, and the war still delicately balanced. It was very provocative, airing arguments against Britain at the very point when morale had to be maintained, and critics on both sides of the Atlantic regarded it as a powerful and important work. Provocation aside, it is an incredibly 'conversational' book – the two of them talk endlessly, often at cross-purposes, and usually with overtones of snappy defensiveness. It is frequently harsh and cynical, so it is surprising that it would be optioned for a wartime movie – when 'actioners' or films shot through a romantic lens (like *Mrs Miniver*) might have been thought to be more of a box-office draw. But Darryl Zanuck, who picked up the rights, knew what he was doing. He had been a writer and *wunderkind* producer at Warners before leaving to co-found Twentieth Century Fox. He had a string of British themed movies behind him (most recently, *A Yank in the RAF* (1941), with Tyrone Power, who would be chosen to play Clive), and he saw that the key to making the film successful at the box office was to play up the romance, and downplay the politics. Zanuck engaged as his director the highly respected Anatole Litvak, a Russian émigré, by way of films in Germany and France, who had been working in Hollywood for Warners for several years. While Sherriff would not necessarily be the first choice screenwriter for anyone making a romance, his credentials had been burnished by the fine job he and Reisch had done on *Lady Hamilton*, and his work on *Chips* and *The Four Feathers* showed an ability to bring novels to the screen.[61] He would also be able to navigate his way through the British class system and was familiar with the milieu, so he had a number of points in his favour.

The movie is out of the run of the usual pro-British Hollywood war movie. In the first place there are very few action scenes: like the book, it is mostly talking, first as Clive and Prue (played by Joan Fontaine) get to know each other, but as their relationship deepens, and she begins to probe his secrecy, they arrive at the point where they can share their competing views of the country. The adaptation does not open the book out much – in fact, it could almost be handled on a stage, with everything stripped away except Clive, Prue and Monty. Yet Clive's life story could easily have been rendered in flashback, and it is surprising that at least the battle scenes at Dunkirk – which, after all, are a large part of why he is so embittered – are not brought to life, especially in a wartime movie. But of course, that would have drawn the attention away from the love story. The movie opts, sensibly, to focus more on Prue's perspective than Clive's. It maintains the air of mystery around Clive, and it also highlights the more likeable of the two characters – Prue is seen to be open and friendly, while Clive is always restrained by his bitterness and his past (although the movie Clive remains consistently more likeable than his novel counterpart).

According to studio memos,[62] Sherriff's initial treatment, finished during July, was felt by Zanuck and Litvak to be too 'preachy':

Mr Zanuck emphasised that this story is first and foremost a LOVE STORY, in which the story of wartime England is combined but is not our focal point. Or, as Mr Litvak put it, it is a story about two people in England, and not England with two people in it.

Throughout the period of script development, both Zanuck and Litvak took a very active hand in the redrafting. Zanuck urged him to find 'ways and means of getting the sex attraction of the novel into our story without offending the Hays Office', and 'stressed the importance of injecting as much of the sex element of the book into the script as we can get away with … as much as decency will allow.' Sherriff was continually urged to get to the sex scenes more quickly – although ironically it was Zanuck and Litvak who delayed things by drafting an opening scene showing Prue upsetting her upper-class relatives[63] by telling them she's become a WAAF.

Trying to avoid offending the Hays office was – as always – quite a tall order. On 5 November, the producers received this discouraging reply:

In our opinion, this is a story of illicit sex without the compensating moral values required by the Production Code. In addition to the basic theme of illicit sex, the script also contains a very questionable element in the showing of two unmarried people going away for a week, for immoral purposes.[64]

Zanuck had tussled with the PCA many times.[65] On this occasion he jumped to the film's defence,[66] arguing that the PCA reviewers were bringing their sense of the novel to the film, not viewing the film independently. He went through a detailed analysis of the potentially contentious areas of the film, underscoring that at no time are Clive and Prue seen to be having an affair:

I will bet my best walking-stick that if the so-called haystack scene were laid in another locale, no one would bat an eye from the censorship standpoint because the fact remains – Prue and Clive do not have an affair in this scene, nor in any other scene in the entire film.

The film was eventually approved after further negotiation, and Zanuck had done well to skirt the edge of what was allowable – even having Fontaine disrobing, discreetly, perhaps, but suggestively, during a couple of conversations with Clive. While Zanuck was correct that there is no clear example of their consummation of the relationship, the cutaways at certain scenes (especially the haystack scene) were clearly designed to make cinemagoers use their imaginations.

As in the book, an important part of the film is the clash, within the romance, between Clive and Prue's competing views of England. In the book, Clive's bitterness and resentment are partly explained away by his brain disease, but in the movie he is not provided with that excuse. As a result, his arguments are softened (there's certainly nothing in praise of Hitler), and Prue's are emphasised. Knight himself (born in England, but raised in the US from the age of fifteen), was convinced that England had to change, but was in no doubt that the first job was to defeat Hitler,[67] so even in the book, Prue wins and Clive is willing to return to the Army. In the film the scales are weighted even more heavily in Prue's favour by a long speech (billed at the time as the longest continuous speech ever made by a woman in a movie), beautifully delivered by Joan Fontaine, in which she tells him what England means to her, and what Clive and his friends should fight for.[68] In the book, Prue is given about three pages to make her point, but Sherriff does a masterful job of whittling the word count down to a much more cogent 361.

The studio had planned to begin shooting in England in late September, and in August 1941, *Hollywood Reporter* announced that Zanuck would shortly be heading to England with Sherriff and producer Robert Kane. That was certainly Sherriff's impression, as he wrote to Victor Cazalet: 'I feel practically certain I shall be on my way home soon, because this studio is working out plans to produce pictures in England.'[69] But before long the studio changed its mind, sending Kane to England on his own to shoot background footage, and building a special set on a sound stage (at considerable expense) to match Kane's footage.

At the end of November, shortly before production was due to begin in the US, Zanuck sent Sherriff a note saying, 'You did an excellent job on *This Above All*. The changes that we discussed worked out perfectly.'[70] Zanuck was a man of such immense significance at Fox (indeed, in Hollywood more generally), that it cannot have done Sherriff's employment prospects any harm that he was so pleased. Of course, the $5,000 bonus he received for the completed script was a very tangible expression of the studio's satisfaction.

When the film premiered in New York in mid–May 1942, the critics were generally kind, seeing in it no faults that were not already in the book (in particular the lack of any serious rationale for Clive's sudden volte-face when he returns to the Army), and generally applauding its sincerity. 'Its strength and disarming distinction is that it tells a very moving love story with a sensitive regard for tensile passions against a background of England at war,'[71] wrote Bosley Crowther in the *New York Times*, although he cautioned that 'There is a prudence about this romance which is not in keeping with nature, and which belies the frank disposition of the two participants.' He also criticised the film for its failures to justify Clive's animosities, by explaining his poverty-stricken background, although he acknowledged that Sherriff and the producers might well have wanted to avoid revealing 'the degradation out of which the character rose, for fear of giving offense'. Knight himself was not a fan of the movie[72] (although he felt it easily surpassed *Mrs Miniver*), but the public did not agree with him, for the film did well at the box office, drawing $2.4 million – not far outside the top ten (although well short of *Mrs Miniver's* table-topping $6 million).[73]

Knight died in January 1943, in a plane crash in Dutch Guiana (now Surinam), along with a number of other military personnel. James Hilton was shocked, writing to Sherriff that 'It is only a short time since I was lunching with him at the Brown Derby and we were discussing taking some trip together similar to the one on which he met his death. I am sure, as the scenarist of *This Above All*, you must feel something of a personal loss.'[74] Shortly after Knight's death another of his books would be made into a film that would win worldwide box-office acclaim, starting up something of a franchise: *Lassie Come Home*.

Blind Man's House/House of Chedworth

Sherriff's first contract with Fox had been for the time of his work on *This Above All*, but before his work was complete, on 25 November 1941,[75] Fox had already exercised their option to engage him on another six-month contract, with a bump up to $1,400 a week.

The next project they had lined up for him was an adaptation of Hugh Walpole's *Blind Man's House*. The book was published in 1941, just before Walpole died, and was the story of Sir Julius Cromwell, a blinded ex-serviceman, who brings a young wife home to a country estate in the village where he grew up. Sherriff had a treatment[76] ready by 10 December, and added a brief foreword discussing whether changes might be needed now that the United States had just entered the war. He then went on to specify his new story, which was actually only loosely related to Walpole's novel, being based instead on a story he had himself been preparing at the beginning of the war[77]:

> That of a distinguished British airman who was disabled in an early raid over Germany and who returned to his old English manor house in the country with a young wife. The whole story dealt with this man's struggle to keep his home against the inrush of time.[78]

He would work steadily on the project during the next few months, but was still interested in finding a way home. To that end he contacted Eric Cleugh at the Los Angeles Consulate in March, asking for his help, although Cleugh was pessimistic about his chances of finding a berth on a 'clipper' (flying boat) service. When, in April, that request became moot (with Fox picking up its option on his services for yet another six months)[79] he put his name down for a sea passage, in the knowledge that it would take some time before he and his mother made it to the top of the list. He was clear that they would be going back together (he wrote to Gerald Ellison that 'She is so earnest about wanting to come home at the same time I do, I could not leave her here'),[80] and to make themselves more flexible, should the call come, they even gave up their house on Ocean Way, and moved into one of the garden bungalows at the Beverly Hills Hotel.

By September 1942, Sherriff had managed to produce a temporary script[81] for *Blind Man's House* that was largely complete, although the final section was still in synopsis. Almost everything had changed from the initial treatment, but it would change still further in the months ahead. In the meantime, he also worked on other projects, most unusually when he was 'loaned' to Disney for a period, working on a script for Seversky's *Victory Through Air Power*. This was an interesting project, essentially harnessing the might of the Walt Disney studio (through Disney himself) to a largely animated movie devoted to proselytising for air power, according to the theories advanced by Russian émigré Alexander Seversky in his book of the same name. In the end it proved a commercial failure – audiences could not quite work out what kind of movie they were watching, education or propaganda[82] – but it did pave the way for Disney's attempts at educational movies in the future. Sherriff received no writing credit, although he had been there for six weeks by the time he wrote to James Hilton telling him what a 'fascinating' job it was.[83]

Forever and a Day

Another film that utilised Sherriff's talents was *Forever and a Day*. This was a unique film, in that it represented the Hollywood British community's attempt at a pro-British movie that would raise funds for good causes (like a 1940s version of Geldof's Band Aid). The film, with the original working title of *This Changing World*, had been conceived in March 1940[84] (just as the criticism of the Hollywood Brits was beginning to gather pace) at a meeting between Cedric Hardwicke, Alfred Hitchcock, Victor Saville and Herbert Wilcox, and the idea was that it would harness all the talents of the community – writers, directors and stars – to produce a charity film that would also bang the drum for Britain. It was conceived as an episodic film, which would be easier to make as people became available during their existing movie work. Sherriff was very much part of the British community, involved in the Advisory Board, and through it, in entertaining British officers who happened to be in California (including, at the end of 1941, Gerald Ellison, at that point attached to the Cruiser HMS *Orion*).[85] So, even although the film had been conceived before he arrived, he was likely to have become involved quite quickly.

The approach adopted was taken from Noel Coward's hugely successful play (and later film), *Cavalcade*, and featured a house in Britain during a passage of time. It would begin in 1804, with the house being built by an admiral returning from war with Napoleon, but the end date was not agreed at the beginning of development. The script took some time to finish (the story and treatment being credited to W.P. Lipscomb and Robert Stevenson), and shooting eventually began at the RKO Studio in May 1941. The first five sequences, featuring a galaxy of British movie stars, and showing the house's development through the Victorian era, up to the end of the First World War, were completed by 14 December 1941. But that still left one final scene to be shot. Various suggestions were made: one was that it should end in 1939, although that was seen as 'evasive'; another was to show the house being bombed in the war, but there were box-office concerns over that; a third was to end at some point in the future, but no one seemed struck on that idea. The discussion was crystallised, however, by the US entry into the war, as was noted by a report on the progress of the movie:

> Due to the new situation created by America's entry into the war, this part has had to be revised and a first treatment on the part, based on suggestions by various authors, including Sinclair Lewis, Thornton Wilder, R.C. Sherriff, Charles Bennett and Gene Lockhart, is now in Sir Cedric's hands and under discussion. Although there is, as yet, no agreement on details, the general line of part VI has been decided upon. The sequence in the main will take place in the cellar of the house, now changed to an air raid shelter.[86]

Sure enough, that was the final sequence: an American (a distant relation of one of the earlier owners), arrives at the house during the Second World War, to be told its history by the woman who is its existing owner. While he is there the house is bombed, and all that remains is the cellar archway, welcoming 'All who shelter here', which had been installed when the house was first built by the admiral (played, inevitably, by C. Aubrey Smith). The final section featured no significant UK stars, since a number of those who had said they would take part had pulled out, and RKO, concerned about cost overruns, forced the filmmakers to begin filming with two of their relatively unknown leads lent to the production (Kent Smith and Ruth Warrick).

The film was released in March 1943, and much was made in the publicity of the vast collaborative effort undertaken. Seven directors were named in the trailer (with Cedric Hardwicke given a director's credit, since he had conceived and led the project. The film itself opens with the names of eighty actors involved (and a comment to the effect that there were others who would like to have participated but were 'unavailable'), and twenty-one writers (including Sherriff). With such a lengthy list it is not easy to detect Sherriff's hand, although he was clearly involved in discussions on the final section, and may have commented on the first section given his expertise in the area (C. Aubrey Smith has a line, for example, about the possibility of Napoleon invading if 'Parliament doesn't stir itself', which clearly has echoes of Nelson in *Lady Hamilton*).

The reviews from the quality press were as condescending as might be expected – but this was never intended to be high art. Others were prepared to see it for the entertainment it was: Bosley Crowther in the *New York Times*, for example, commented on the 'amusing and affecting passages', while the *Evening Standard* commended the film's 'charm and comedy and emotion'. It is a film that is well worth viewing, for a number of fine performances, but also for a game of 'spot-the-actor' in the cameos (Victor McLaglen as a doorman, for example, or June Duprez and Elsa Lanchester popping up briefly). By the time it was released, of course, the US was firmly engaged in the war and the sentiment against the Hollywood Brits had long vanished, so its propaganda elements were less required. But after RKO's costs were settled it still succeeded in raising more than $800,000 for charitable causes, with donations made in each of the countries in which it played, many to the Red Cross.[87]

Leave to Remain

Towards the end of 1942, Sherriff was trying even harder to make his way home, and he contacted the embassy in Washington, asking their opinion. He was probably rather disappointed to be told that 'Taking everything into consideration, it would be more advisable for you to remain in this country where your knowledge of Britain would … continue to be of considerable service to us.'[88] But they also suggested he might want to consult with the studio, to see if they'd be prepared to offer a leave of absence for him to explore conditions back home. Sherriff thought this an excellent idea ('I am certain the best and most significant stories of wartime England are hidden away in the towns and countryside and the only way to find them is to go there and hunt them out for one's self')[89] and immediately sent a memo about it to Jason Joy[90] at Fox. He hoped they might contract him to make the tour, but if not, he would be happy to be given a leave of absence, and make the trip 'as a freelance'. Within a month, however, the studio showed it was not yet ready to part with him, for his option was picked up again, this time for a full year, with a guaranteed minimum of forty weeks' work at $1,500 a week. On the letter from Sig Marcus telling him the new terms, it is possible to see his handwritten calculation where he converts the weekly total into the rather grand annual sum of $60,000.[91] At the prevailing exchange rate of $4 to the pound, that would net him more than enough to meet all the costs he was incurring in renovating Down House Farm.

On 5 February, he completed the second draft of a shooting script on the project that had been *Blind Man's House*, but was now renamed as *House of Chedworth*.[92] The story is about a young chorus girl (Peggy Fortescue) who falls for a blinded ex-airman (Sir Derek Chedworth), owner of a large estate in Cornwall. The day after they meet (when he admires her fortitude in continuing to sing on stage during a bombing raid), he sweeps her off to Cornwall, where they get married, and she becomes Lady Chedworth. She realises that the estate, and Sir Derek, are in dire financial straits: they cannot even afford to maintain the barn, which is washed away in floods. She tries to encourage him to ease up on some of the charity he doles out around the village, and to spend the money on the fabric of the estate, but he tells her not to interfere. The US Air Force comes to use the estate as an airfield, with Derek's enthusiastic agreement, but Peggy, in helping the men organise a concert, becomes attracted to a young lieutenant (Roger Lindsay). When he begins to fly raids over Germany she worries about him, and rushes into his arms when he returns. She realises the situation is untenable, and pleads with Derek to leave with her, but he refuses, saying he must stay at Chedworth, no matter the burden that falls on him. At that moment there is an air raid, during the course of which Derek helps guide the American bombers away from the estate, and back to a safe airfield. In doing so he is killed, but not before leaving a written note to Roger, asking him to take care of Peggy. The film ends with Peggy and some workmen rebuilding the barn, Roger leaving, and Peggy committing herself to staying, as the last of the Chedworths.

Sherriff passed the completed script over to the studio, where it appears to have undergone some further changes – although nothing too significant – before it was finally submitted to the PCA in July. They had the usual minor objections – suggestions of impropriety, or potentially vulgar language – but also two major issues: one was a concern that, in one of Derek's speeches, he 'practically hands his wife over to her lover'; the other was that Derek's death at the end could almost be construed as a suicide. The issues never seem to have been resolved, however, because the film, like so many others, ended in development limbo, never to reappear.[93]

Having completed the screenplay and handed it over, Sherriff contacted Alan Collins at Curtis Brown's New York office. He had written to Collins the previous November, telling him he was hoping to make a novel out of his work on the *Chedworth* screenplay, and fretting a little that people might suspect some plagiarism on his part, given that Walpole's book was also a 'country house' story. Collins had replied that, if nothing of Walpole's story remained, there was no need to worry. Sherriff was grateful for the advice, feeling that the issue would be straightforward as long as the studio did not produce the finished film under the *Blind Man's House* title (which he did not think they would).[94] A few months later, he was able to write to Collins telling him that the studio's legal department 'raises no objection to my using in novel form the story and material which I have embodied in this screenplay,'[95] and that he was now about to embark on the novel.

Signed with their Honour

In mid-February, Spencer Curtis Brown cabled Sherriff from London[96] to let him know about an intriguing offer that had come his way. Paul Soskin (who had a production company bearing his own name, and had recently completed the wartime movie *The Avengers*) wanted Sherriff to script a new movie, *Signed with their Honour*, which would be based on a novel of the same name by a young Australian war correspondent named James Aldridge. The book, which had come out in 1942, told the story of the RAF's defence of Greece and Crete against the Luftwaffe, and was a big success, critically and commercially.

Soskin was offering generous terms and was willing to have Sherriff write the treatment in the US, before coming back to London to prepare the script.

Immediately on receiving Curtis Brown's cable, Sherriff had cabled in reply, saying he was interested.[97] Actually he was very interested, because he was keen to get back home, and this might be the way to do it. He would need to get the agreement of Fox – which, of course, had him on contract for the next year – and he would need verification of the assignment to allow him to move up the sailing lists (which, at that point, he had been on for nearly nine months). Curtis Brown then cabled him with Soskin's offer (£2,500 for the preparation of a shooting script, or £150 a week on a twelve-month contract, possibly with a profit-sharing arrangement and co-producing status),[98] but Sherriff did not reply. After a couple of weeks' silence, Curtis Brown implored him: 'Please reply concerning *Signed Their Honour*. Is Soskin proposition unacceptable?[99]

It was. Fox had put him to work on a new screenplay and he felt unable to ask them for a release. But he hoped he would finish by the end of April, and then he would press to be freed from his current contract. He still seemed to be hoping that he could work out a scheme along the lines of the one he proposed to Jason Joy – even if it involved a leave of absence – but otherwise he seemed to be stuck. If he were to come back, however, and start working on UK films, he was clear about one thing:

> Primarily I would like to have a writer-producer agreement – not because I am
> interested in the business side of film-making, but to retain some control over
> the scripts I write when the time for production comes. Although in most cases
> I have been pleased with the pictures that have come from my screenplays, I
> have had one or two unfortunate experiences where the script was garbled and
> distorted beyond reason.[100]

Perhaps it was just having moved on to the new screenplay that held him back from the Soskin deal, but there is something odd in the delay in reply, especially given the alacrity with which he had seized on the first cable he received. It may just have been that he would find it difficult to opt out of his one-year deal at Fox. But that had clearly not been a factor in his thinking when he had jumped at that first telegram. And although he reckoned he would be working on the new project until the end of April, there was no reason he could not have made a counter-offer to Soskin, delaying the start date. There was, however, one other factor involved: Soskin was not actually offering a great deal of money. Sherriff's deal at Fox was paying him nearly £400 per week – and to drop from that to Soskin's £150 would be painful. He had long maintained that he was not too worried about the payment he might receive in England, if only he could just get home. But perhaps, faced with the prospect of such a large cut, he decide he could do better staying at Fox. Letters that he sent to Alan Collins in New York[101] and to the New College bursar in Oxford[102] hinted that he hoped to be sent to England by Fox in the near future, and to negotiate a writer-producer contract with them. Staying with Fox (at his present salary) and working on their stories in England looked a far better proposition than moving back to work with Soskin.[103]

Flare Path

Sherriff's optimism about a possible return to England seems to have coincided with the next project handed to him by the studio: an adaptation of Terence Rattigan's recent play, *Flare Path*.

Rattigan was an RAF tail gunner posted to Coastal Command, and he used his experiences there to write the play, which was completed in 1941.[104] The play is set in a boarding house adjoining an airfield, from which bombers set out nightly on their raids over Germany. Some of the men are planning to spend the weekend there with their wives: Teddy Graham, a pilot; Dusty Miller, Teddy's tail gunner; and Count Skriczevinsky, a Polish pilot. Teddy's wife Pat, an actress, is surprised at the arrival of her lover (Peter Kyle, an ageing movie star), who hopes to take her away with him. The Count's wife is a down-to-earth former barmaid called Doris, who speaks no Polish; the Count speaks no English, and communication is difficult, although they seem to be in love, but there is scepticism about how suited they are for each other, given the difference in their social status.

The men are called back to the aerodrome for a late scheduled mission, leaving the women at the hotel to agonise about their return. There is always concern when the flare path is lit up to allow the planes to take off, for that is the precise moment when the Germans can attack, and one of the planes crashes on take-off. They are all relieved when they find their husbands are not on board. Early the next morning, Teddy and Dusty return, but the Count has not come back. Teddy confesses to his wife about his fears while flying; this wins her over, so she tells Peter to leave without her. Before he goes he translates a letter from the Count to Doris, left behind in case anything should happen to him, in which he tells her he loves her, and would have wished to go back to Poland with her after the war. But the Count eventually arrives safe and sound, his delayed return explained by having ditched in the sea, and the play ends happily.

The play was first produced in London (by Binkie Beaumont) at the Apollo Theatre in August 1942 and was a huge hit, running for eighteen months. The Broadway transfer was not so successful, beginning on 23 December 1942, and ending just ten days later. Despite that lack of success, Fox had bought the rights to the play (for £20,000) and Sherriff was already at work on the adaptation on 1 March, when he told Alan Collins about it.

Sherriff's script[105] takes quite considerable liberties with the play, opening it up with a ludicrous backstory between Ted and Pat (albeit with a nod to *One More River*, when they stay the night in a car together), yet downgrading the poignant relationship between Doris and the Count. He changes the character of Peter for the worse, stripping him of his vulnerability and turning him into little more than a Hollywood egotist, whose relationship with Pat becomes that much more difficult to fathom. Even the few action sequences carry less tension than the off-screen action in the play (when the characters watch, through the hotel windows, the 'flare path' being lit up and then wait anxiously to see if the planes will take off successfully). All in all, it must count as one of Sherriff's least successful adaptations.

In his article for Nigel Nicolson's *Contact* magazine in 1948, Sherriff commented on the difficulty in adapting a play for the screen:

> I think the average stage play completely unsuited to the screen. The tighter its construction the more unsuited it is. ... I have seen reasonable films made from plays but I have never seen the play improved upon by the film version. And yet producers have always been attracted by stage successes and have bid high prices for them, mainly because they contain the valuable commodity of 'dialogue', never realising that the success of a play depends so much upon the construction of it which they cheerfully destroy for the screen.[106]

It is unlikely that he had *Flare Path* in mind when writing these words, since he prefaces the section by noting (incorrectly) that 'I have never accepted an assignment to turn a stage play into a screenplay.' Perhaps he preferred to forget about it.

Like *Chedworth*, *Flare Path* never made it to the screen with Fox. The script as Sherriff finished it was handed to the PCA straightaway, and they had a number of objections, raising that old chestnut 'compensating moral values'. Changes were made and it was sent back to the PCA, which responded with a long list of further changes. There is no sign that the script was ever redrafted thereafter, and the project, like so many others, disappeared without trace.[107]

Leave of Absence

On 26 June, after completing his initial *Flare Path* script, Sherriff at last got a six-month[108] leave of absence, and armed with a letter vouching for the helpful services he had rendered the British Consulate in LA, he and his mother made their way to New York to try to secure passage to England. He hadn't quite burned his bridges, however, and continued to work for Fox out of New York – mainly on redrafting *Flare Path* in light of comments from the PCA and others – until the very end of July.

The plan was to stay in and around New York until a passage became available, but as he later explained,[109] his difficulty came in trying to secure passage for his mother, and he would not travel without her. (Indeed, in May 1944, when she was offered passage but he was unavailable to go, she declined to take up the offer because she was unwilling to travel alone.)[110] Nor did things ease as the summer months wore on, because restrictions had been placed on all but essential passenger travel. They made the best of it, however, enjoying their time in New York and in Chatham (on Cape Cod), where they spent about six weeks, perhaps reminiscing about their seaside homes in England. Sherriff's cash books[111] show items including massages, sightseeing, theatre and pictures, as well as a trip to Atlantic City (which may well have been made at his mother's request, since she enjoyed a flutter on the horses back in England). In all, they spent almost $6,000 on their trip – a bit more than he had received from Fox for his work in July.

By the end of September, they were getting restless; they seemed no nearer to securing a berth home, and Sherriff had no film income coming in, although he was at least working on the novel of *Chedworth*. At the end of September he got in touch with the Thomas Cook office in New York and told them that he and his mother were 'ready and willing to travel on the first available British ship to England'. If no British ship were available, in the next six months or so, they would be willing to travel on a Portuguese ship, via Lisbon.[112] In the meantime, as long as he could be guaranteed enough notice in the event of a ship becoming available, he would travel back to Hollywood, where at least he could find work. Accordingly, by the end of November, they had left the Waldorf-Astoria in New York and were back again at the Beverly Hills Hotel in Los Angeles.

He kept working on *Chedworth*, reporting happily to Alan Collins at the beginning of 1944 that he'd completed about two-thirds of it.[113] While working on the manuscript he and Collins discussed potential publishers, and he eventually signed a contract with Macmillan, who had published him before.[114] Trying to concentrate on completing the book was difficult, especially with his mind firmly fixed on going home,[115] but he was still able to send Collins the last chunk of the book at the beginning of May – which was just as well, because by then he had also taken on a new screenwriting contract.

Heading Home

The contract, with Warner Brothers, was for the adaptation of Dodie Smith's play *Autumn Crocus*,[116] which they intended as a vehicle for Bette Davis. Written in 1931, the play is a wistful romance, about a 35-year-old English schoolmistress and a cheerful, but married, Tyrolean innkeeper, which had already been made into a not especially successful film in Britain. Sherriff knew Dodie Smith,[117] so he would likely have been happy to adapt her work for the screen; he would have been even happier that Warners were guaranteeing him ten weeks at $1,500 a week.[118] The contract began on 20 March, and it was due to finish at the end of May, so that Sherriff could leave Hollywood immediately thereafter and make his way back to New York to await a ship. There had been no further updates from Thomas Cook, but he was busy making sure his papers were in order so that he could go as soon as the need arose.

In April he received an offer from Alex Korda that suddenly made the possibility of a quick passage home seem much more likely. Korda had made a deal with MGM at the beginning of 1943, whereby they would provide 100 per cent of the finance he needed to make pictures in England, and he would receive 25 per cent of the profits.[119] Nothing much had come of it, owing to the exigencies of wartime production in the UK, but it looked as if it would be a powerful partnership. So Sherriff was delighted with Korda's offer: 'They tell me all arranged for me to join you in England and am very glad. Ready to leave immediately complete Bette Davis script at Warners beginning June. ... Looking forward to good work with you.'[120] He was also delighted that Korda's offer would bump him up the priority list for the passage home. As he later wrote in *No Leading Lady*:[121]

> Alex Korda came to the rescue. He gave me a contract, all signed and sealed and bound in silk tape. It looked very important and stated that I was engaged to write and produce three pictures for him in England and that I was due to begin preparation for them in London with as little delay as possible. Whether we should ever be able to fulfil the contract didn't matter. Korda knew that as well as I did. He wrote it to help me to get home, and it did the trick.

The contract wasn't quite as duplicitous as Sherriff suggested – Korda really did want him to work in England; the question was just how best to get him there. Reeves Espy, Sherriff's new agent at Myron Selznick, suggested that he go on the MGM payroll in the US as of 1 July, allowing him to go to England with them when transport became available. But Sherriff was not happy at that idea: he wanted to work for MGM in England, and not take the risk that he might be engaged on something with them in the US that might prevent him taking a ship home if one presented itself. Henry Blanke (the producer of *Autumn Crocus*) had already asked him to put in an extra two weeks, which would take him into early June, whereupon he intended to travel immediately to New York and await passage, which he was fairly confident would come quite soon:

> They tell me it is almost definite that we shall have a passage on a Portuguese ship if the British line cannot take Mrs Sherriff. So you see it seems better not to get tied up with any other complication and just go right along with the Metro deal to work in England.[122]

So he completed his work for Warners in early June as anticipated, and set out for New York, leaving the script in the hands of Henry Blanke. The following year, enquiring about the film's fate, Sherriff was told that, if Blanke re-signed with Warners, it would probably be 'one of his earliest productions'.[123] It was not.

Back at the Waldorf-Astoria, Sherriff and his mother were probably confident that their long wait was over; they had been assigned to a Portuguese ship that was expected to sail around 29 June. But with just three days to go, their hopes were dashed and they were told there would be a delay of 'about three or four weeks'.[124] Upset, they opted to get out of New York until closer to the sailing date, and they headed back to the coast at Chatham. A few weeks later they were unexpectedly offered a passage on a British ship, likely sailing on 25 July, and Sherriff immediately cabled his acceptance from the Chatham Bars Inn, where he was staying: 'Returning New York twentieth to have four clear days preparation British ship which you advise me as possibly sailing about twenty-fifth.'[125]

This time there would be no last-minute alterations, and at 3.00 pm on Tuesday, 25 July, he and his mother left a rain-soaked New York behind them and finally headed home.

Chapter 11

Back to Blighty, 1944–50

Often think of the rapidity with which things pass by and disappear, both the things which are and the things which are produced. For substance is like a river in a continual flow, and the activities of things are in constant change.

Marcus Aurelius, *The Meditations*, Book V.

Sherriff and his mother arrived back in Liverpool on 7 August 1944: it took the Cunard-White Star ship MV *Rangitata* thirteen days to make the journey, rather than the five that was more common in peacetime. The weather was 'wonderful', and the voyage 'interesting and happy … in spite of about nine people in each of our cabins'.[1] When they arrived home it was 'just in time for a dose of flying bombs which were at their height. … Luckily our own house escaped with a few broken tiles and cracked windows.'[2] He made light of it, but the flying bombs were terrifying, as Alice Head (editor of *Homes and Gardens*) told him a few months later:

> We had a rocket bomb in the early morning only a few yards from where I live. I saw a ball of fire coming down, then there was an explosion, then the glass from my windows [flew] all over the room, all in about five seconds.[3]

His good friend G.B. Stern had also been bombed out,[4] while Beryl's house had been damaged in one of the first raids of the war.[5]

He had a lot to catch up on: four years of maintenance on his houses and farm, and in particular, the reorganisation of his finances. He calculated that, between 1 June 1940 and 1 October 1944, he had spent more than £21,000 in England: £2,450 for the upkeep of Rosebriars and Sandmartin (his house in Bognor); £2,800 for the wages of the staff at Rosebriars, and his secretary; £3,700 for new building work on his farm, including a new house (Greystones); and a £6,600 tax bill. His income in Britain, totalling only £6,700, was not nearly enough to cover the expenses, but he had also sold property and investments to the tune of £9,500 and happily he was bringing back £10,650 with him from the United States.

He did not stay long in London, but spent most of the rest of the war at Down House Farm. This may have reflected his desire to return to the coast: his trips to Chatham on Cape Cod show how much he missed the sea, and he could not go to his homes in Selsey or Bognor as they had been rented out. But there was also the added bonus that the Dorset coastline was a long way from those flying bombs.

Chedworth

Two months after he arrived back in Britain his novelised version of *Chedworth* was launched in the United States. The book followed the contours of the screenplay in most particulars, albeit with some digressions on the historical significance of the great house, and on the difficulties of trying to maintain an estate in modern England. The biggest difference between film and book, however, is in the ending: in the film Derek is killed in the burning watchtower, as he heroically redirects the returning American bombers, while in the novel he survives the destruction of the house.

The book also delves more deeply into Peggy's backstory than was possible in the screenplay, presenting her as strong and resourceful, and well respected by the others in her London circle. As well as being successful in her own career, she is the level-headed one in the marriage, attempting to insist that Derek changes his ways if his estate is to survive, and not afraid to lock horns with the locals. In fact, she is the only example, in all of Sherriff's own output (as opposed to his adaptation of works by others) of a female leading character. Unfortunately, she turns disappointingly limp when confronted with Derek's intransigence, and it is also fair to say that Sherriff never successfully generates any real electricity between the two principals: indeed, it is amusing that the novel appears to adopt the old PCA trick of leading the couple to the bedroom door, only to have them close it behind them, leaving us on the outside.

The book was released in October 1944, to broadly favourable reviews. The most flattering was in *The Saturday Review*,[6] where respected critic Richard Cordell described it as 'a quiet, literate and unadorned novel … reminiscent in character and setting of *Rebecca* … which achieves finally a significance missing in … [that] feverish work'. He was impressed with Sherriff's handling of the American characters and of their language, unlike the reviewer in the *Chicago Daily News*,[7] who, however, did appreciate the 'natural, often humorous, heroism of the English under fire'. The *New York Herald Tribune*[8] was also complimentary, calling it a story told 'with simple sincerity'. *The Chicago Tribune*[9] also commended the tale as 'an easy-going and charming story', with characters that 'are likeable and clear-cut', and bestowed the ultimate compliment on Peggy: 'The heroine … might have been an American, she is that resourceful.' But there were naysayers as well – most notably *The Commonweal*[10]: 'There isn't a line which has the tang of *Journey's End* – or the humour.' Sherriff would not have been impressed that the *Journey's End* stick was being brought out to beat him with again – after fifteen years of literary labours and success.

Suppress It

Sherriff pressed Curtis Brown and Gollancz on the subject of publishing the book in the UK, but met with a disappointing response. Jean Curtis Brown told him that she and Spencer (her husband) felt the book to be a bit dated,[11] although when Sherriff appeared to take umbrage at the remark she hastened to reassure him that it was the 'wartime setting' that she had in mind.[12] Gollancz was rather blunter:

> I think in view of your letters that you will want me to write absolutely frankly about *Chedworth*. Well, with my life in my hands, here goes. The book would sell big, and perhaps very big: but in my view it would seriously harm your reputation: and if I were you I should suppress it.[13]

On the other hand, Alice Head liked it well enough that she offered to serialise it in *Homes & Gardens*, which left Sherriff rather scratching his head on the question of publication. He asked Gollancz for a more detailed view of the book and pressed Curtis Brown to send it out to one of his readers, but the report that came back was not good: 'This is a puzzling business. I know that Sherriff is a good writer, but judged by any but the lowest standard, this is almost worthless – light romance in the cheapest Hollywood manner.' It went on to criticise Sherriff's attempts to give a picture of life in wartime England ('the result is ridiculous'), and condemned the plot ('banal and crude') before concluding, 'I assume that Macmillans are not going to do it over here – and who can blame them?'[14]

Nevertheless, it had done quite well in America – 8,000 copies in three months – and he was convinced it could be rewritten for the English market. He told Curtis Brown that he had never really liked the melodramatic ending either – it had been 'more of a sop to the film producer at Twentieth Century Fox' – and if the story were taken out of its wartime setting, he envisaged a 'quieter' ending. He also promised: 'Besides the end of the book, I will work over the whole story revising certain parts which were deliberately "overwritten" for an American reader.'[15] But he never did find the time for the rewrite, thus permitting his English fans to see it only in the pages of *Homes and Gardens*, where, according to Alice Head, it gave 'a great deal of pleasure'.[16]

Bricks upon Dust

Sherriff had sailed across the Atlantic with a contract from Korda in his back pocket, but there were further negotiations upon his return, with the upshot that, around the end of October, he signed an agreement committing him to delivery of two screenplays, each within a sixteen-week period (which in subsequent discussions would be extended to two six-month periods): for each screenplay he would receive a fee of £8,000.

His first project was the adaptation of a recently published novel by Paul Tabori, *Bricks upon Dust*. Tabori was a Hungarian journalist and writer who had moved to England, whom Korda had employed as a writer at MGM. Tabori, by his own account, had little to do, and so spent some of his time writing a novel about the first year of 'a completely ruined city in Eastern Europe after the war'.[17] When it was finished he sent the typescript to Korda, and was promptly summoned to meet him, and Ben Goetz (MGM's top man in London), both of whom were very enthusiastic about the book.

Bricks upon Dust is an engrossing tale about a 37-year-old soldier, and former schoolmaster, Luke, returning to his hometown, in an unidentified, but presumably Balkan, country after he has been invalided out of the Army. The combatant countries are never identified, and the protagonist's names are generic enough that the piece has the feeling of a parable. The challenge facing Luke is to begin the rebuilding of the town, which means finding food and shelter, and putting people to work in the areas in which they are most suited. As the months roll by they are joined by a growing number of refugees and ex-soldiers, which presents them with opportunities to harness their skills, but also with the challenge of having to cater to their needs, and to find means of making decisions as a collective. Ultimately they make contact with their nation's government, but the demands that their country makes upon them leads to conflict in the town, which is only resolved in another battle. Luke's side wins, but he moves on after his father is killed, and he loses Joanna, the girl he admires, to his friend.

The script in Tabori's papers was probably completed in late 1944,[18] and appears to have been drafted by Sherriff and then sent on to Tabori for comment. It is a very unsatisfactory adaptation, because he takes great liberties with plot and, especially, character. In the first place, Luke is stripped of all depth, most of which is revealed in the book through his interactions with his father and his sister, neither of whom appears in the film. Instead of having Luke's father as an *éminence grise*, Sherriff invents two characters: an engineering colonel and a medical major, who try to wrest control of the town from Luke to implement their own ambitious schemes. In the book the engineer and the doctor are just two among several soldiers who come back from the war, and unlike Sherriff's versions, have no grandiose designs of their own. There are scenes in the film, in which the doctor and engineer scheme and squabble, which are reminiscent of nothing so much as *Badger's Green*, but without the humour. It is also quite clear from the script – and from Tabori's exasperated (and frequently very funny) marginalia – that Sherriff had no idea of just how devastated such war-torn cities could be.[19] Some of the script, in which Luke interacts with the children (mainly boys) who have remained in the town, resembles a rather jolly the Scout-themed romp; and the film ends with an utterly improbable romantic resolution in which Luke agrees to marry Joanna, despite having hardly spoken to her except in the early scenes of the film.

Sherriff seems to have largely finished the script in May, and handed sections, as they were completed, to producer Ian Dalrymple,[20] probably finishing up towards the end of July. When asked what he thought about it, Dalrymple was guardedly neutral, replying that he liked 'much of it', but he cautioned that 'further work on it would be extremely difficult until production is actually, even if remotely, scheduled. 1947 would be the earliest production date over here, and therefore any work before mid-1946 is wasted.'[21]

But the film would never make it into theatres. In October 1945 Korda resigned as head of MGM-British (on account of 'ill health', but more likely because he chafed at the interference of Louis B. Mayer, who in turn was sorely aggrieved at Korda's tendency to regard the company almost as his own), and although he departed, *Bricks upon Dust* stayed the property of MGM. Korda later sent Tabori back to Ben Goetz to try to buy back the rights to the book, and Tabori recalls that 'I dutifully went along ... but Korda's plan did not work. MGM wanted exactly seven times as much for the property as they had paid originally and this was a bit too steep even for Alex.'[22] This was a pity: the book would have made a good film, even if not in the version that Sherriff had scripted.

Immense Relief

In April 1945, Sherriff had written to Alice Head from Down House Farm, complaining a little about his work on *Bricks upon Dust*, but saying he hoped he would shortly be able to come to London to work on the shooting script.[23] In replying, she noted, almost with a sigh, that 'the relief of being free from bombs is very great.'[24] He sympathised with her: 'What an immense relief it is that at last you [are] having some peace and quiet. One almost dreads saying this in case it is a false alarm, but I really think it is the real thing this time.'[25]

A few weeks later, on 7 May, the Germans unconditionally surrendered, and on 8 May, VE Day was celebrated throughout the UK. Alice Head may well have been among the crowds in London who thronged Whitehall and Piccadilly Circus and revelled in the streets. Sherriff may also have been there, having planned to return from Dorset in early May.

Bundy and Hazel arrived back from India at the end of June 1945, but found they had nowhere to live, since Couchmore Avenue (where they had lived with Herbert) had been requisitioned by the council at the end of 1944.[26] Bundy was not keen to come back to Couchmore Avenue – he would have preferred a house where he could do some small-scale market gardening, expanding it as he retired[27] – but he was not wealthy, and Bob was still happy to provide Couchmore Avenue on a rent-free basis (although Bundy paid everything else, including the property taxes). Although Bob had been back in Rosebriars for about six weeks when Bundy returned, he obviously did not want to share his house with his brother and sister-in-law, and so had tried to obtain a hotel room for them. He was unsuccessful, so they opted to stay with Beryl and Tudor, until Couchmore Avenue was released on 18 July.

That meant that the whole family was again based in London when the war finally came to an end with the surrender of Japan on 15 August. In fact, Sherriff actually bumped into his old pal David Hatten on VJ Day, while they were walking on the

Portsmouth Road in Kingston.[28] Sherriff may just have been enjoying a stroll beside the Thames, but it is also possible he had been paying a visit to the East Surrey HQ, for he had recently agreed to write the regiment's Second World War History at the urgings of Major Sutton, the officer in command. Although there was some communication between the two from 1945–46, the project seems, at some point, to have been quietly dropped.

As soon as the war was over, Twentieth Century Fox pressed him to return to the US, to fulfil the contract that they had terminated in 1944 (to allow him to go back to England): by their view they had the right to ask for at least another ten weeks of his services in Hollywood. But Sherriff disagreed, believing that all he had to do by the terms of the previous contract was to offer them first refusal on his services *if* he returned to Hollywood. For the next two years, Fox would continue to pursue their claim, only for him to bat them away with a variety of excuses. He was very clear about one thing, however: he would not be pressurised into going to Hollywood, even at the expense of giving up scriptwriting opportunities.

Although his resistance to Fox's pressure to go to Hollywood was clear and persistent, he also expressed the desire, to others, to maintain links there, and to work there on a regular basis to maintain his contacts.[29] Why he should have been so conflicted is not clear, unless, perhaps, it had something to do with his mother. He knew that continued links with Hollywood would be beneficial to his career, but he would have been unwilling to leave his mother behind, and Connie (now over seventy, and happy to be back in England) may well have been reluctant to disturb her routine once more. Whatever the reason, he never did return to the United States, instead working off his obligations to Fox at home. Whether that had an adverse impact on his career is rather doubtful. He would find plenty of lucrative screenwriting work to occupy him in England – largely with British companies – although the fondness with which he describes California in *Another Year* suggests that maybe he was at least ambivalent about his decision.

Another Year

Just as the war was coming to an end, and he was finishing his work on *Bricks upon Dust*, Sherriff pitched a story to Korda for his next MGM screenplay. As he wrote to David Henley (the latest in a long line of contacts at Myron Selznick):

> I have got an original story which I want to do. I have told it to Alex. He likes it very much and I am now writing a short outline of it. If the outline is accepted I shall go right ahead with the screenplay as my second assignment, but as it happens to be a story which I had planned as a novel, I shall probably write the screenplay and the novel side by side.[30]

Another Year is the story of Roger Matthews, a late-50s clergyman who leaves his cushy country parish for the challenge of an East End slum. When he arrives there he finds the locals unwelcoming and church attendance poor. His desire to establish a sports and social club in the community is thwarted by the Church Council, led by the deeply unpleasant Mrs Bannister Paget. Mr Matthews nevertheless attempts to befriend the local lads, in part because he sees them being led astray by the landlord of the local pub, the Fighting Cocks, who encourages the boys to fight each other while drunk. Eventually he is able to reach out to young Peter, inviting him to a boathouse that he has found on some undeveloped land nearby. Peter and his friends are drawn to the idea of a boat club, and begin to practise and train in earnest. When they hold a show to raise funds one evening, the vicar's daughter, Rosemary, is talent spotted by a Hollywood agent, and the vicar, his wife and daughter are soon whisked away to Hollywood, where the daughter proves unsuccessful, the vicar becomes an unlikely hit, and is offered a juicy contract. He takes the job, but only to earn enough money to buy the land on which the boat club stands, so that he and the boys can build the boat club together.

A ten-page outline was enough to persuade Korda to commission the screenplay, and by the end of summer Sherriff was asking MGM for secretarial support, since his erstwhile secretary, Ellie Bentley, was still in the forces.[31] After a brief hiatus, the support was forthcoming and Sherriff made enough progress that, by the end of January, he was assuring Ben Goetz that the whole thing would be with him within a few days,[32] but also warning that, since he had accelerated the completion of the screenplay, the novel would not be completed until the autumn. That would turn out to be a very optimistic prediction, as additional commitments and a serialisation deal would combine to delay the novel's completion (and publication) until 1948. But at least it would eventually see the light of day, unlike the movie, which, without Korda's backing at MGM, simply disappeared from view.

Odd Man Out

At the beginning of 1946 Sherriff received an unexpected phone call from Carol Reed, asking him if he could take on some script doctoring work. Reed was a highly respected British film director, still only forty, but with an impressive track record, including classics such as *Kipps*, *The Stars Look Down*, and the successful wartime propaganda picture *The Way Ahead*.[33] Reed had come across *Odd Man Out*, a novel by F.L. Green about the troubles in Northern Ireland, and optioned it for Two Cities Films. Green came to Reed's flat for a week, and the two knocked a screenplay into shape, but once the draft was complete, he gave Sherriff a call, and asked him to 'give it a criticism and a polish up'.[34]

The film is the story of Johnny McQueen, an important man in 'The Organisation' (an unnamed terrorist group), who is wounded while stealing the payroll from a local mill. He and his companions make their getaway, but he falls from the car, and spends the next eight hours on the run from the police, growing steadily weaker. Part of the film examines the fate of his co-conspirators, but mostly it focuses on Johnny, and the people who help him along the way. In the end he is tracked down by his girlfriend Agnes, who engineers their death at the hands of the police.

There are various script fragments in Sherriff's papers relating to the film, and one complete script with his manuscript amendments. The latter appears to come from fairly early in the process[35] and may well be the one prepared by Reed and Green and then passed to Sherriff for comment. In some of the fragments, and in his letters, Sherriff made a number of suggestions regarding the ordering of scenes, and the best way to approach specific aspects of the drama, but most of the suggestions that can be identified do not seem to have made it into the final film. He was, however, being consulted by Reed, and was clearly discussing the film with him: indeed, even as late as June, when Reed was shooting at Denham, Sherriff was responding to his request for assistance and promising to come to the studios so they could talk over ideas for the opening of the movie in between shots.[36] Sherriff's influence must have been felt to some extent, since he was paid £3,000 in April for his work on the script[37] (more than would be expected for simple script doctoring) and earned a screen credit into the bargain.

London (Films) Calling

Working with Carol Reed was a pleasant diversion, but by the early spring it was time to make progress on the novelised version of *Another Year*. He had shown the outline to Alice Head in January 1946, and she had proven very enthusiastic: 'I am thrilled with the story … and should love to have it.'[38] The only snag was that she could not start running it until December: was he willing to wait? Actually, the delay suited him better, giving him more time to finish the draft, and dovetailing better with the movie, which, if it did make it into production, would probably not be until spring of 1947 at the earliest.[39]

In the end he would be disappointed by the studio's failure to proceed with the film, but the extra space to write the book gave him the chance to develop some new ideas and projects. On the home front he had begun exploring the possibility of establishing a permanent Scout camp at Down House, while also talking to the National Trust about whether it would accept the farm as a bequest.[40] As far as work was concerned, he was in discussion with BBC producers about possible adaptations of his earlier works (in particular *The Fortnight in September* and *The Hopkins Manuscript*), but he was also pitching a possible children's serial to his old friend Geoffrey Dearmer, now working in the Children's Hour department. Having completed his two scripts for MGM, he was once more in the market for movie work.

First in line was Alex Korda, now running London Films as his own company once again, who had approached Sherriff in January 1946, with further discussions in May. Sherriff kept him at bay while finishing *Another Year*, but by the beginning of September he had joined Korda again, on a salary of £1,000 a month.[41]

His first few months seem to have been taken up by a project he dubbed '*African Story*'. No outline or script survives, but from his correspondence with his collaborator, D.L. Murray,[42] it appears that the story concerned an adventurer who moves to Africa and engages in various escapades, during which he is imprisoned and escapes, changes his name and ultimately rises to a position of some status; but then, after seeing his family die off, or desert him, he eventually takes his own life. Sherriff was convinced that 'there is enough in the body of this outline to let [Korda] see that he has got a good, eventful story.' But he had worked with him many times before, and so told Murray:

> I have thought it wise to soft-pedal a little bit over the final sequence. I have a feeling that it would be policy to be deliberately vague about the final ending of the story, in order that Korda will give full reign to his ideas ... if we crystallise our own ending too firmly we are only inviting an equally crystallised 'yes' or 'no' from Korda.[43]

There is no evidence to suggest they ever managed to show him the story, and before long Sherriff had moved on to script doctoring on *Bonnie Prince Charlie*. His efforts were highlighted by the studio publicists, who reported in March 1947 that 'immense care has been lavished on the script, revised over and over till the final version, by R.C. Sherriff, is pronounced tip-top.'[44] This was part of a typical movie studio puff piece – in this case surrounding the search for an unknown to play the key part of Flora McDonald. But the movie was still some way from production, and would not be in cinemas for another eighteen months, by which time Sherriff's involvement in the script had disappeared from the record (as had the name of James Curtis, the original scriptwriter, leaving the 'laurels' in the hands of Clemence Dane).[45] By that time, however, Sherriff was long gone from London Films, and was lucky to be no longer associated with the film, which went down in flames when it was released in 1948.

Sherriff's time with Korda in the post-war period was frustrating. The screenplays he had written were almost certainly never to be produced, because Korda had moved on from MGM, and the bulk of the work he had done for London Films (the '*African Story*') had gone nowhere. Sherriff was sufficiently exercised to write to Korda to tell him, 'I'm not at all happy about the way our affairs are going,'[46] and in particular, the fact that he and Murray had received very little guidance on the kind of story he wanted. But the frustrations he felt could not have been very surprising, for Sherriff was familiar with his style, finding his interference both exasperating and inspiring, while recognising that it came about 'because of his immense responsibility to other persons who have invested their money in the picture'. In that regard, he was far from unique:

> Every famous producer I have worked for, such as Darryl Zanuck, Irving Thalberg, Sam Goldwyn and others have all 'interfered' just as much, or even more so than Korda, and it is quite beyond me to say whether the films they made were better or worse for this. ... Against Korda's failures must be placed his successes. Among these I wrote for him the scripts of *Lady Hamilton* and *The Four Feathers* – both outstanding successes, and both undoubtedly successful because of Korda's continual supervision.[47]

Looking Ahead

Sherriff's irritation with Korda may have been symptomatic of more general frustrations. While in the United States he had tried for the best part of eighteen months to secure a passage back to England, and he had clearly yearned to return to his old life. But the England he had come back to was very far from the one he remembered. Still in the middle of a war, with rationing and blackouts, England must have seemed a very cheerless place, particularly when set against the sunshine and plenty in California. He must also have been acutely aware how people, including his friends, had suffered in the intervening years, while he had chosen to go to the US. Some would have been loath to forgive him, and even if they did, he would probably have felt guilty for a while, perhaps until the more obvious scars of war had begun to heal.

Even in the post-war period things were very far from normal, with rationing only slowly disappearing. Petrol – a substance of great importance to a man who enjoyed motoring in his Rolls-Royce – was variously restricted and rationed until 1950, meaning that short trips to the coast, or down to the farm in Dorset, were treats that had to be severely curtailed: in fact, by the beginning of 1947, Sherriff was already trying to rent out Greystones (having only lately eulogised it in *Homes & Gardens*).[48] His frustrations would have been compounded by his irritation with Gollancz, the poor reaction to *Chedworth* in the UK, and Fox's apparent insistence that he should return to the US. All in all, the two and a half years since his return must have been a disappointment, certainly compared with how he probably imagined it from 5,000 miles away.

By spring 1947, however, things were beginning to look up. The war was two years past, and any guilt he may have felt about having spent so much time in the US was probably beginning to dissipate. He was well settled in Rosebriars once more, and was slowly knocking it back into shape. Business in the film industry was picking up again, and he had established his old contacts, so when his contract with Korda ran out in April, he declined the offered extension, preferring, for a while at least, to keep himself free of screenwriting assignments (even turning down offers from Paul Soskin and Sam Goldwyn).[49] He intended to enjoy his farming for a while, and he had a number of ideas for his own work that were slowly beginning to percolate.

Despite his best intentions, his screenwriter's interest was piqued in early summer by an offer from Sidney Box,[50] who asked if he might be interested in preparing a screenplay for a prisoner of war movie. What he had in mind was an examination of the mindset of the 'unrepentants',[51] those who had been most committed to Germany's pursuit of the war, and who could not reconcile themselves to their loss. It made for an intriguing prospect. The plan had been for Sherriff to begin on 1 July,[52] and he had already begun to do some research into the camps in Britain where the Germans had been stationed, when Box told him that the film had been shelved, because of the arrival of a new film on a broadly similar theme – *Frieda*, from Michael Balcon's Ealing Studios.[53] Box reassured him that an alternative project would be forthcoming, and after some delay, he came forward with a rather unusual sort of job: the adaptation of several Somerset Maugham short stories for inclusion in a portmanteau picture. Sherriff agreed, although he was not entirely happy with the brief, feeling that Box was expecting him to adapt six stories for the price of one: 'Of course, each of these six will be in the nature of a short picture but the amount of work involved is far greater than in a normal assignment because each story needs separate construction and characterisation.'[54]

While Box was selecting his Maugham stories, Sherriff agreed to undertake some polishing work for Twentieth Century Fox, offering them four weeks' work (at £500 a week), and thus finally absolving himself of his long-standing contractual obligation. The film in question was an adaptation of John Galsworthy's 1926 play *Escape*, in which a British army captain accidentally kills a police detective while assisting a prostitute who is being arrested. Sentenced to jail for manslaughter, he escapes and is hunted as he embarks on a journey through the English landscape, providing 'a study of the various reactions of various strata of British Society to the problem of an escaped convict'.[55] The film starred Rex Harrison (as a squadron leader, rather than a captain), and was directed by Joe Mankiewicz (whom Sherriff knew from *Three Comrades*), who came to England to work on the film at Denham (and then complained, constantly and bitterly, to Fox executives back home).[56] Before the start date of his contract Sherriff had been handed a copy of the script,[57] which he had annotated with all of his suggested dialogue alterations and improvements, and returned to Mankiewicz to await his instructions. He was certainly involved in redrafting at least a couple of scenes,[58] but in the absence of the scripts it is impossible to know quite what effect he had on the final movie – certainly not enough to earn himself a screen credit, which went entirely to Philip Dunne. When the film was released, about a year later, it was generally well received, despite the wordiness that betrayed its stage origins. No mention was made of Sherriff's involvement.

Quartet

Immediately after finishing the polishing on *Escape*, Sherriff moved on to the Somerset Maugham project. Rather than six short stories, it was Box's wish that Sherriff adapt just five – with the intention of putting them all in together in one film, tentatively entitled *Quintet*.[59]

The five stories were as follows:

The Facts of Life[60] (directed by Ralph Smart): A young man (Nicky), bound for a tennis tournament in Monte Carlo, is warned by his father to avoid gambling, lending money, and women. But in visiting the casino he manages to break all of his father's injunctions, and ends up sleeping with a woman he meets there. When she thinks he is sleeping she takes his winnings and puts them in a vase, not knowing he has seen what she is doing. Before he leaves, he empties the money from the vase, only to find, when he counts it later, that he now has much more than he had before.

The Alien Corn[61] (directed by Harold French): An English upper-class family is of Jewish extraction, but has concealed it over the years. Their oldest son (George) just sent down from Oxford, is dissatisfied at the prospect of the life of an English country gentleman, and discovering his German-Jewish roots, goes to Munich to become a pianist. His family despair, but acquiesce, as long as he agrees that, if he does not display sufficient talent after two years' study, he will take up the respectable life his father has chosen for him. In due course, he returns home and plays for a famous pianist, who judges him no more than a gifted amateur. Asking to be alone, he wanders off to clean his gun, which discharges, killing him with a shot through the heart.

The Kite[62] (directed by Arthur Crabtree): A young man (Herbert), who is a keen flyer of kites, falls in love with, and marries, a girl (Betty) who has no interest in the sport. Eventually he and his wife separate over his unwillingness to give up his kite flying but he continues to give her a weekly allowance, until the day when she destroys his kite. In defiance of a court order he refuses to give her any more money, and is hauled off to jail for contempt of court, where he vows to stay, rather than pay up.

The Colonel's Lady[63] (directed by Ken Annakin): Colonel George Peregrine, a staid, old-fashioned country gentleman, is surprised to find his wife has published a successful book of poems, which, he is told, is 'hot stuff'. Discovering that it tells the tale of an older woman who has a passionate affair with a young man, who later dies, he contemplates hiring an investigator to find the name of the young man. He is dissuaded, however, and reconciles himself to the idea of doing nothing about her past infidelity, realising he would be lost without his wife. But still, he says, he'll never understand: 'What in the name of heaven did the fellow ever see in her?'

The Sanatorium[64] (directed by Harold French): A writer with TB goes to a sanatorium, where he observes the lives of the other patients in the strange setting: two older men, long-term residents, who delight in making each other's lives miserable; a patient (Mr Chester) who resents his wife's good health; and a woman who is pursued by a middle-aged major with an eye for the ladies. In due course, one of the old men dies, leaving the other bereft; the young woman and the major fall in love and leave the sanatorium to get married, despite knowing that their health will be adversely affected; and Chester, chastened by their willingness to sacrifice for their love, apologises to his wife for his unpleasantness to her.

Five turned out to be too many for one picture, and so only the first four were used in the film – now named Quartet – while The Sanatorium was used, along with two additional short stories, in a sequel, entitled Trio.[65] The films were bookended by Maugham speaking from what appeared to be his house in the South of France, but was actually a very carefully constructed simulacrum at Gainsborough's studios in London.

Sherriff faced quite a challenge in adapting the stories, which had very different viewpoints, and tones. The Facts of Life remained substantially unchanged, except for the fact that it was the story to which the censor took the greatest exception, because Nicky slept with the woman from the casino who tried to rob him: 'This story ... is nothing more than a story of illicit sex without any compensating moral values. Moreover ... the illicit sex affair described here is glamourised, justified, and made to appear the right and acceptable thing to do.'[66] As a result, poor Nicky was not permitted to sleep with the woman from the casino who attempted to rob him, but instead was forced to bed down rather chastely on her sofa. Despite complaints from some critics,[67] this did not change Maugham's story in any material way.

Two of the other stories were altered to provide rather happier endings than Maugham himself had offered. In The Kite, his story ended with young Herbert in jail for the foreseeable future; in the film, however, Betty is made to see sense, and withdraw her claim for support. In the final scene she is flying a kite on the common, with Herbert moving to be by her side – a 'syrupy ending'[68] perhaps, but one more satisfying from the moviegoers' perspective than Maugham's rather bleaker version. The other story that was changed in the end is The Colonel's Lady, but this time by means of a rather inspired addition (which apparently came via Sydney Box)[69] in which the colonel's wife, when confronted as to the identity of her paramour, replies that it was actually the colonel himself, in his younger days; but that young man, increasingly absorbed by other interests, had died from her perspective, leaving her only with memories. The colonel's response to this confession is to appreciate his wife all the more, leaving the way open for a redemptive reconciliation between the two. Sidney Box's biographer describes the adaptation as 'deft', writing that it 'arguably augments the original'. It is certainly much less bleak.

The story that came in for the most criticism was *The Alien Corn:* 'Sherriff's adaptation ... rips out the heart of Maugham's story by excluding its focus on race ... [making] the rebellion of George solely a clash of art against convention.'[70] There is no doubt that George's Jewishness (and that of his family) plays absolutely no role in the story, but one is tempted to wonder how it ever could. Maugham's story is not short, by any means,[71] and is told through a first-person narrator who interacts with the family over a long period, illuminating their attempts to mask their Jewishness to fit in with British landed society. How such years of secrecy could ever be conveyed in a movie is difficult to imagine, while Maugham's depiction of George going to seed, while revelling with his student friends in Munich, might at the very least have been seen as distasteful, if not worse. It is not clear whether the decision to exclude race came from Sherriff, or whether it was one that was agreed by all parties early on. But even without the racial dimension, the story is powerfully told, and very well acted.

The expectations for the film were high, mainly because of the involvement of both Maugham and Sherriff.[72] When it was released in November 1948 the film was a success with the public, doing well in the UK, and exceptionally well in the US; indeed, it ran for two years in one theatre in New York.[73] The reviews, however, were more mixed; everyone seemed to have an opinion about this or that story that was corrupted by Sherriff's adaptation. The most critical review was in the *Glasgow Herald*: 'From at least two of the stories R.C. Sherriff has succeeded in utterly eradicating the point, a third has been bowdlerised.'[74] On the other hand, Sherriff must have been delighted to see that Bosley Crowther in the *New York Times* was still a fan:

> Of course, there is no continuity among the quartet of tales, and the four have been separately directed for the production of Sidney Box. But the scripts of all four were written by R.C. Sherriff, who has maintained a general uniformity in the spirit and tempo of the overall work, so that you're likely to leave the theatre feeling that you've seen not only a large-sized entertainment, but a rounded, stimulating view of life.[75]

Sherriff also heard from G.B. Stern that '[Maugham] spoke highly indeed of you and your job on *Quartet* when I saw him last night. That's unusual for [him]!'[76] He probably also enjoyed the fact that the film did well enough at the box office to generate not just one sequel, but two: *Trio* in 1950, and a further Maugham compendium in *Encore*[77] in 1951.

Publishing Woes

After returning from America, Sherriff was annoyed that his earlier books were out of print, complaining to Ian Dalrymple that '[Gollancz] got so political that he had no spare paper for keeping my novels in print. The supplies have therefore dried up entirely.'[78] Spencer Curtis Brown suggested that he might think about changing publishers, and pointed him towards Hutchinson's, so that by mid-1945 he had signed a deal whereby they would publish *Chedworth* and his next two novels as well. Within a year, however, he started having second thoughts about the move, partly because of Geoffrey Dearmer, who had put him in touch with one of Heinemann's directors, Dwye Evans. 'I wish we had met earlier,' Sherriff wrote to Evans. 'I have always felt that if I changed my publisher I would like to be with Heinemann's. But for some reason Curtis Brown Ltd suggested that I should go to Hutchinson's.'[79]

Despite having already fixed a deal with Hutchinson's, he soon cut a deal with Evans for Heinemann to publish *Another Year* when its serialisation was eventually completed. He fobbed off Hutchinson's with the suggestion that they had signed up for *Chedworth* and the subsequent two novels, but since *Another Year* was coming out first, he was perfectly entitled to sell it to Heinemann's. But he never did get around to completing an English version of *Chedworth*, and the contract with Hutchinson's was never enacted.

Why he was so quick to jump ship from Hutchinson's is not clear, although he did suggest to Curtis Brown that his soft spot for Heinemann's dated back to the days of Evans's father.[80] Probably more important in the decision, however, was Evans's expressed support for reprinting his previous novels, which Sherriff was very keen on. At one point, in drawing up the contract with Heinemann's, it looked as though Evans might resile on his commitment to reprinting: quick as a flash, Sherriff emphasised that he could still return to Gollancz: 'As you know, I never at any time had any personal differences with Victor Gollancz. In one sense we have not even parted company, because he has never refused publication of anything yet.'[81] That was enough to clear the way for a very explicit contract for the reprint, and for Heinemann's to become the publishers for his novels, at least for the foreseeable future.[82]

Another Year

Another Year was finally published at the beginning of 1948. It is similar to the screenplay in most aspects, but it darkens the end of the story quite considerably. After Mr Matthews's unexpected success in the film, the movie company offer him a generous contract, and they pay for him to return to Woodford to talk things over with the bishop. But when he arrives he finds that Mrs Bannister Paget, with the connivance of the substitute minister, has managed to scare the boys away from the boat club with threats to bring in the police. Peter has returned to the Fighting Cocks, where, according to his mother, he has been soundly beaten and incurred serious injury. 'You're not going away again, are you?' she pleads to Roger, who replies, 'No, I'm not going away any more.'

The reviews must have been a disappointment. There were a handful that liked it. According to *The Sunday Times*,[83] 'You can enjoy the story, no matter how much, or how little, of it you really believe … a most attractive affair'; George Bishop in the *Daily Telegraph* viewed it as 'a disarmingly simple story'[84]; and John Betjeman felt that Sherriff had 'written a gripping novel with one live and beautiful character – young Pete, the reformed drunk, with his touching faith in the slum parson.'[85]

The other reviewers were less convinced. *The Times*[86] referred to the book's 'various nuances of unreality', and the *Guardian*[87] felt it was 'not a very distinguished novel'. Many who were taken with the first half of the book felt that it lost its way as soon as it departed for Hollywood, most notably the well-known novelist Pamela Hansford Johnson, writing in the *Sunday Chronicle*[88]: 'Grand disappointment of the year, so far, is Mr R.C. Sherriff, who has contrived to crack his novel in two pieces, like a walnut, and one of them is bad.' *The Observer*[89] lauded the 'quiet persuasion' in his East End scenes, but felt that his characters lost 'their local and lifelike quality under the arc lamps' in Hollywood. *John O'London's Weekly*[90] rather simply, but acerbically, observed that 'it can be described in a quotation from it: "It was all so unexpected and astonishing that he hardly dared to believe it was true."'

The criticisms of Sherriff's descriptive powers are unwarranted. The sequences in which he describes the Matthews' journey to Hollywood – their awe at the *Queen Mary* as she is loaded at the dock; the journey across the Atlantic; their brief tour of New York and subsequent trip across America – are lively, informative and precise. Life as the Matthews family see it in Hollywood is painted in brilliant colours – suggesting, perhaps, that Sherriff, marooned in post-war austerity Britain, rather longed for the sunshine and citrus life in California. The Los Angeles scenes stand out all the more vividly because of the contrast he makes with the gloomy industrialisation of the wharves and riverside of Woodford.

Some of his characters, too, are exceptionally well drawn. We see in Mr Matthews, for example, a constant struggle between his urgent desire to do good – to reach out to Peter, for example, or to confront the thuggish pub landlord – and his shy and rather nervous disposition. Peter, too, is a complex character, balancing boyish eagerness with a bully's bluster. But there are blemishes, too: Mrs Bannister Paget might as well be wearing a black hat and twirling a moustache since she has no redeeming qualities; and the American movie people are brashly one-dimensional.

But it is the plot that really lets the book down: the arrival of a Hollywood agent at a small show in a broken-down boathouse by the river clearly stretches credulity (as does Mr Matthews's instantaneous elevation to the ranks of movie stardom). But the biggest plot problem comes right at the end, when Matthews promises to pay for the boathouse land (which means having to go to Hollywood again), and then promises Peter's mother that he will stay. The two promises are completely irreconcilable, a plot hole that was identified by Madge Duncan, a sub-editor at *Homes and Gardens*, before the final instalment of the serial was released. She wrote to Sherriff pointing out that Mr Matthews had signed a post-dated cheque in the sum of £2,500, but could no longer earn the money, since he was no longer going to Hollywood.[91] Sherriff replied that, in the original draft, Matthews had sent a letter back to his wife in America to tell her that he 'had been obliged to run round and see the estate agent and cancel his cheques, when he realised that he would not earn the money after deciding not to go back to Hollywood.' He further commented (rather impatiently), 'I took it for granted that the reader would realise that Mr Matthews would have a great many things to readjust when he made his decision not to go back to America.' He promised to try to rectify it, 'because the whole point at the end is that he sacrifices all this for the work in his Parish,'[92] but failed to do so.

About ten months later, after the book was serialised by the BBC, Sherriff gave a talk on *Woman's Hour*, in which he explained that the story had come to his mind when he watched a clergyman coaching a four-oared boat on the river, and he had 'wondered who the boys were, and what they thought about the clergyman, and what he thought about them, and one day I thought I would try and find out by writing a story round them.' He then explained that, when it came to the last chapter, 'I didn't know until the last page whether Mr Matthews would go back to Hollywood ... or whether he would give everything up and stay in Woodbank to work for those boys.' A handwritten addendum to his talk showed that even at that point he was still not entirely sure of Matthews's decision:

> You all know how the book ends. Matthews tells Pete's mother that he's not going to leave Woodbank again ... but do remember he only said that ... on the spur of the moment. It's quite possible, isn't it, that he may have changed his mind by the following morning? After all, it wasn't only Peter and his friends to be considered, but all those thousands of boys he would be able to help with the money he could make in films. Well, I don't know the answer to that.[93]

Nor, frustratingly, did anyone else.

Miss Mabel

While he had been working on *Quartet* an intriguing new idea for a play had come to him, and during the autumn of 1947 he began work. By March 1948, he was able to circulate a draft to Curtis Brown and to some friends, including David Hatten, to whom he suggested that, if Genesta were interested, he would let them take a run at it. Hatten did not like it, and told Sherriff so,[94] but everyone at Curtis Brown was very positive – Spencer himself, but also Archie Batty, who was in charge of their Dramatic Department, and whose advice Sherriff clearly valued very much. Very soon, Batty was reporting that theatrical managers Alec Rea and E.P. (Paul) Clift (of the company Reandco) were keen to put the play on in the autumn, featuring the very well-known actress Lilian Braithwaite as the box-office draw. Their plan was to start with a short tour in the provinces, to bed the play down properly, and then move to a London theatre after a few weeks. It looked as though Sherriff would finally have the opportunity to savour the agonies of a West End premiere once more, for the first time in twelve years.

Miss Mabel is a charming and funny play about an old lady who forges her twin sister's will and then kills her, to ensure that her twin's riches go to good causes.

The play begins with the beneficiaries of the will gathering in Miss Mabel's sitting room, to hear it read by Mr Smurthwaite, the lawyer. A number of generous bequests are made, and all the recipients are astonished because Mrs Fletcher (Miss Mabel's twin) had been such an unpleasant woman with nothing good to say about anyone – the very opposite, in fact, of Miss Mabel. Once the recipients disperse, however, the lawyer and doctor chat, and it quickly becomes clear that it was not Mrs Fletcher who had instructed the lawyer, but Miss Mabel herself. On that bombshell the first act curtain drops.

The first scene of the second act features most of the beneficiaries discussing the surprising turn of events, and the legal ramifications of the forgery of the will. There is general agreement that, because Miss Mabel forged the will for a good reason (to ensure her sister's money went to good causes, rather than risk it going to the Treasury), they should take no action (a course with which the lawyer naturally disagrees). But things take an unexpected turn just before the curtain drops when Miss Mabel infers that her sister was poisoned. The next scene features yet more discussion of what should be done, albeit no one is yet entirely sure of all the details.

The first scene of the third act ultimately confirms the suspicion that Miss Mabel did, indeed, kill her sister by toadstool poisoning. Her logic was simple. Her unpleasant sister was being wooed by an Australian man, and was likely to leave, taking her wealth with her. Miss Mabel felt the money could be put to much better use. In the second scene of the act the consequences are seen through to their conclusion, with Miss Mabel gamely confessing to the crime, but not to the forgery: nor will she offer any mitigation, for to do so would be to admit the forgery, and thus to invalidate the will. She will take her punishment, and the money will remain in the hands of the beneficiaries, where it can do most good.

The play is deftly written, with a fresh shock guaranteed before each curtain. There is plenty of Sherriff's trademark humour, but also a deeper examination of the responsibilities of professionals to follow the demands of their vocations, as opposed to their personal feelings. In the end there remains the question of whether the end justifies the means, and whether the morality of good works can ever trump the immorality that leads to it. As Sherriff put it himself: 'Could I make the old lady commit a murder for such an admirable purpose that all manner of honest, law-abiding people would set aside their scruples and become accessories to the murder?'[95]

The Production

By the end of August, plans for the tour were well in hand, but Lilian Braithwaite unexpectedly took ill, and had to be replaced at short notice. Her replacement, Mary Jerrold, was the natural choice, since she had acted alongside Braithwaite in the West End production of Joseph Kesselring's play, *Arsenic and Old Lace* (playing the two spinsters who murder old men by poisoning them with arsenic-laced elderberry wine). Sherriff was very pleased with her performance, but was concerned that they had lost their big box-office draw. The omens must have seemed even worse when Braithwaite died just ten days before the play opened at the Theatre Royal in Brighton on 27 September.

Although he was very skittish, Sherriff needn't have worried; from its very first outing in Brighton, the play was a hit. The *Brighton Gazette* made the inevitable comparisons to *Arsenic and Old Lace*, but found Sherriff's characters 'more finely delineated and its humour and pathos more subtle'.[96] The *Brighton Herald* commended the play's 'unexpected twists in the plot and excellent curtain lines',[97] and, like the *Gazette*, commended much of the acting, including Jerrold. The only London paper that seems to have made the journey to Brighton was *Stage*, which was even more strongly supportive than the Sussex papers, commending the 'remarkable series of comic and dramatic situations', the 'bright and snappy' dialogue, and the 'convincing' characterisation. Sherriff reported to Charlie Hamilton (Maurice Browne's old business manager) that, after its first performance in Brighton, the play enjoyed capacity audiences, taking over £1,500 during the week.[98]

The play went down equally well in its next three stops, in Reading, Birmingham[99] and Bolton. During the course of the tour one or two of the cast members were changed, although the principals remained the same throughout. And Sherriff apparently experimented a little as well, never quite able to decide how the play should end[100] (which sounds familiar after *Another Year*, and would be a problem in his next play as well). During the tour the producers were trying to fix up a London theatre, but with Christmas approaching availability was rather scarce. Nevertheless, after a few stumbles, an agreement was reached for the play to open at the Duchess Theatre on 22 November.

The London critics were even more enthusiastic than those in the provinces. *Punch* found the play 'endearing' and noted that 'Sherriff amuses himself by putting the amateur among the professionals, and showing lawyer, vicar and doctor, casuists all, trying to square their affection for Miss Mabel with their professional responsibilities,'[101] or, as the *Daily Herald* put it, 'Ethical issues afford well-argued dilemmas ... soundly but never ponderously put over.'[102] 'Casuistry' would pop up in a number of reviews, most pithily in *The Times*, which described the play as 'a comedy of red herrings and professional casuistry',[103] which is a very neat encapsulation. J.C. Trewin, long a fan of Sherriff's, called the play a 'fine specimen', and a 'most benevolent and diverting piece'.[104] There were, of course, some who were less taken with the play, the most notable being the reviewer for the *Liverpool Post*, who tut-tutted that 'There was a minority – perhaps only of one – who felt that murder and forgery are unsuitable subjects for laughter, and that Mr Sherriff could have exercised his talents to better purpose.'[105]

The play stayed at the Duchess until 22 January 1949, when it transferred to the Strand (receiving another favourable batch of notices), playing there until 30 April, for a total of 180 performances, better than any Sherriff play since *Journey's End*. Nor was it yet finished. In August, Rea and Clift took it on a three-month tour, taking in Cardiff, Cambridge, Bath and a number of seaside towns, including Margate in September, where Sherriff went to see it. On 2 October it premiered in Paris, where, featuring the acclaimed French actress Ludmilla Pitoeff as *Miss Mabel*, it was a great success.[106] Once the tour was finished the play was released to the repertory companies. By the end of 1950, it had already earned more in royalties for Sherriff than all of his previous plays combined (excepting *Journey's End*, of course). It would continue to earn money through amateur performances (it was very popular with amateurs, since the cast was fairly small), as well as radio and television. All in all, *Miss Mabel* had proved a very satisfactory return to the theatre, whetting Sherriff's appetite for further plays.

No Highway

While *Miss Mabel* was embarking on her successful journey towards a West End home, Sherriff had picked up another screenwriting contract, again from Darryl Zanuck at Twentieth Century Fox, and had begun work on an adaptation of Nevil Shute's book *No Highway*.

The book tells the story of eccentric but dedicated scientist Theodore Honey, as narrated by his boss at the Royal Aircraft Establishment, Dr Scott. Honey believes that there may be a problem with metal fatigue in the tail section of a newly designed aircraft, the Reindeer, and that it may fail after 1,440 hours of flying. Sent to Canada to investigate a crashed plane, he realises that he is flying in a Reindeer, and when the pilot ignores his pleas to turn back, he confides his fears to two women: Marjorie Corder, the stewardess, and Monica Teasdale, an ageing movie star. Once they land at an intermediate destination Honey retracts the undercarriage, damaging the plane quite badly, but at least preventing it from flying further. With Honey stranded in Canada for a while, the two women come back and take turns in helping his daughter Elspeth (his own wife having died in the war). Although the movie actress reluctantly returns to her own life, Marjorie remains in Honey's home, cleaning, organising, and looking after Elspeth.

The final section of the book has Scott trying to persuade the powers that be to ground the Reindeers, but he is hampered by the reputation Honey has acquired through his oddball beliefs. Scott is sent to Canada to retrieve the evidence from the downed plane, but the Russians beat him to it. His only hope is to find the missing tail section of the plane, which could be miles away, but Honey puts Elspeth in a trance, and by means of 'automatic writing',[107] has her produce a message that helps Scott find the tail, confirming the metal fatigue diagnosis. The planes are grounded and Marjorie and Honey walk off, engaged, into the sunset.

Sherriff delivered his script to Fox on 30 April 1949.[108] It followed Shute's story reasonably closely, except that it (very wisely) removed any reference to Russians, trances and 'automatic writing', instead sending Honey to Canada to help Scott with the search. Up to the point where Scott goes to Canada, Sherriff's script is compelling, with one or two outstanding scenes, in particular Honey's flight on the Reindeer, where he meets Monica and Marjorie; but he never satisfactorily replaces Shute's ending.

After delivering the script, Sherriff moved on to a number of other projects, including a boys' adventure story that he had been discussing with Dwye Evans; a BBC adaptation of *The Hopkins Manuscript*, due to be broadcast at the end of September; and an idea for a new play on which he was very keen to make progress. In the midst of this burst of creative activity, the last thing he wanted was to be called back to for script revisions, but in August, not long after *Miss Mabel* began her seaside tour, he received a letter from Zanuck.

Zanuck liked the script – up to a point: 'This is a good first draft script, and I put emphasis on first draft. ... You might say the first half of the story is better than good, and the second half much less than good.'[109] The script was too long: 'There is, of course, entirely too much stuff with the kid,' and there was insufficient drama: 'I doubt very much if we ever want him to go on the long drawn-out hunt for the missing tail piece – they look for it, they find it; it is as flat as a pancake.' Instead he wanted to raise the stakes for poor Mr Honey – have him much more invested in his theory, rail at the powers that be, only to have his theories questioned when another Reindeer is found that has been flying longer than his estimated maximum, but with no ill effects. At stake should be his entire scientific reputation and sense of himself. In the script as it stood, the very worst that might happen to him is that he would lose his job, and have to work in a private laboratory funded by Monica Teasdale: 'To most of the people in the audience this would sound like a pretty good thing.'

Sherriff's original contract for the movie gave the studio an option to call on his services for revisions, but he told Louis Lighton (who had taken over as producer from Bob Bassler) that he could not begin work in the near future – he had too much going on, and needed to clear out an undisturbed period for the movie. He suggested he might start by 10 October 1949, and would be able to block out six weeks for the work. But, he cautioned:

Having put a great deal of time into the original, I couldn't undertake the revisions with a proper detachment until we have gone right over the script together, scene by scene, and you have given me your full reactions to what is good and what is bad – what must stay and what must go.[110]

Hopkins on the Radio

Before he began work on the revisions there was just time to enjoy the BBC's dramatisation of *The Hopkins Manuscript*, which was transmitted in two episodes, the first on 5 October, and the second the following day. The billing was as follows: '*The Hopkins Manuscript*, by R.C. Sherriff. Dramatised version by E.J. King Bull and R.C. Sherriff',[111] and thereby hangs something of a tale.

The BBC had first sought to adapt the book in spring of 1947, and the task was handed to Mr King Bull. But, with four discrete sections, it is a difficult book to adapt. Sherriff was unhappy with King Bull's version because, by starting the story two-thirds in (i.e. at the beginning of the final section, when the nations of Europe are beginning to squabble over their shares of the moon) he was 'letting the cat out of the bag',[112] whereas Sherriff's story had been carefully written to avoid giving away any surprises. He suggested a couple of ways in which King Bull could structure the story to preserve the mystery, but also to get things moving along more quickly. But King Bull was having none of it, feeling that, once the moon was down, the drama was over: if they got to that point at the end of the first episode there would be no interest in the 'political parable' in the second part.[113] Just in case Sherriff was not minded to compromise, King Bull assured him that he wasn't just speaking for himself. Rather, he had consulted with the producers and with the Director of Drama, all of whom agreed with him, meaning that there would be no big changes to the script they already had.

Sherriff's final reply was a masterpiece of the passive-aggressive. After explaining how he constructed his novels and plays, he noted that the BBC had 'made several quite successful broadcasts of my plays, without having to start them with a few scenes out of Act 2.' But he understood that 'the producers, Director of Drama etc., know better what I was trying to do than I did myself.... I am sure, in the circumstances, it would be far better to call the whole thing off, and cancel the contract.'[114]

And that's where it had remained until the BBC had taken the dramatisation out of mothballs and enlisted Sherriff's help in the preparation of the new script. This time, in deference to Sherriff's wishes, the drama was structured much more in line with the novel, beginning as Hopkins starts to write his manuscript, giving us the knowledge that something has happened, but allowing the exact contours of the cataclysm to unfold as the drama progresses. It is an excellent adaptation, more satisfying, in some respects, than the book, possibly because Edgar's character is more congenial. Sherriff was very excited because the BBC seemed to be throwing its weight behind it in a big way, having special music composed, and an all-star cast headed by Eric Portman. After it was over Ayton Whitaker wrote to him to thank him for the telegram he had sent, and to say the programme had been well received. Sherriff was pleased, for 'a good broadcast is such a good advertisement for one's work in general that the fees are a secondary matter.'[115]

Cold Haddock

Just four days after the excitement of the broadcast, it was back to work on *No Highway*. Sherriff was not enthused, as he later told G.B. Stern: 'It is a dreary business rewriting something you have already given months to – what they call in Hollywood, "warming up cold haddock". But there it is.'[116]

Fox wanted him for the revisions, and that would be his primary work for the next eight weeks, despite the siren call of his new play, which he would shortly begin to circulate for comment and advice. This probably explains some of his frustration with the revision, but it went deeper as well. He had revised scripts before, and what mattered most was that it was not done in a vacuum, but in collaboration with the producer and the director. That was clearly not happening on this occasion, as he explained to his agent:

> I am not very happy about things. You may remember I had to refuse the previous suggestion that I sat down and rewrote the script without any indication of what additional material they wanted. Louis Lighton has now taken over ... but his own suggestions are not very clear or definite, and I am not sure whether I am not wasting my time.[117]

He kept going without detailed direction, and eventually finished his assignment on 3 December.[118] That was as far as his revisions went, but he offered to hold himself available in a consultative capacity (which enabled him to defer the payment from Fox to the following financial year, which he hoped would prove advantageous in tax terms). But Lighton then seems to have gone his own way, commissioning a whole new script from Oscar Millard. Thirty years later, Millard wrote an article[119] in which he claims to have been surprised by Sherriff's writing credit, voicing that neither he nor Lighton were aware of Sherriff's earlier draft: as far as Lighton was concerned, he was obviously mistaken. In fact, Sherriff had toiled at the script, on and off, for almost a year and a half, and much that remains in the movie came from his pencil, as the arbitrators clearly acknowledged in awarding him the credit.[120]

The movie was released in the UK in June 1951, about eighteen months after Sherriff finished his part of the job.[121] It starred James Stewart as Honey (a much more sympathetic version than in the book); Marlene Dietrich, perfectly cast as the ageing movie star Monica; Glynis Johns as Marjorie; and Jack Hawkins (last seen in these pages as Hibbert in *Journey's End* on Broadway in 1929) as Dr Scott.

It is an engaging movie, in large part because of the charm of the principal actors, but also because it is directed with pace by Henry Koster. The story follows the book in much the same way as Sherriff's script, until Honey's return from Canada, but thereafter the story bears more resemblance to Zanuck's prescription than to Sherriff's original, and is the better for it.

Despite his frustrations at having to undertake the revisions when he was longing to work on other things, Sherriff did very nicely out of the job, having received £9,000 for the original script, and another £4,000 for eight weeks' worth of revisions (as well, of course, as a screen credit). This was by some considerable margin the most he ever received for a script, so it was probably worth a few bumps along the road.

Home at Seven

The play on which Sherriff had been working during the summer was called *Dark Evening* when he circulated it to friends and colleagues in mid-October. It was quickly taken up by Rea and Clift, who had enjoyed their West End success with *Miss Mabel* (although not, unfortunately, with her small-town tour, which had proved unprofitable) and they envisaged a similar roll-out on this occasion: a short provincial tour to iron out the kinks, and then on to London.

The box-office draw they were hoping for this time was Ralph Richardson, with whom Sherriff had worked before (when he played Durrance in *The Four Feathers*) and by mid-November 1949, Sherriff was trying to arrange a meeting to discuss some of Richardson's criticisms of the play.[122] The meeting seems to have gone well, and plans were put in place for a production early in the New Year. Somewhere along the way, however, Richardson began to get anxious, becoming 'desperately depressed about his part during rehearsal and several times [he] wanted to give the part up.'[123] Nevertheless, he was persuaded to go on, and the play, now titled *Home at Seven*, finally began its provincial tour, at the Theatre Royal in Brighton, on 6 February 1950.

The play is a three-act mystery about senior bank clerk David Preston, who comes home one evening to find his wife very upset. She explains that he has been missing for a day, but he struggles to believe her – he is convinced he has come home on a Monday evening at the normal time, but she demonstrates to him that it is actually Tuesday. At first it seems that the missing day is of no consequence, but during the next few scenes David's absence becomes harder to explain in the light of a robbery and a murder at the social club of which he is treasurer. As the circumstantial evidence against him mounts up he begins to wonder himself whether he committed the crimes. With each passing scene the pressure builds, leaving him bewildered and confused. But the mystery is resolved in the very last scene when we learn that he had been in the habit of calling into a pub for a private drink after work each evening, and on this particular occasion, he had taken a nasty turn and had remained there for the day before returning home. At the same time, the police confirm the identities of the criminals involved at the social club, and all suspicions against Preston are lifted.

That final scene presented particular problems throughout the run in the provinces. The thorniest problem was that the original ending showed Preston, overwhelmed by the evidence piling up against him, committing suicide before being exonerated. But that did not go down well with the audience:

> During the first weeks of the try-out in the provinces, Sir Ralph Richardson played the 'suicide ending' and the 'happy ending' on alternative nights with the intention of judging audience reaction. We finally decided that the suicide ending was too abrupt and harsh. Although dramatically very impressive, it sent the audience away unhappy because they had grown to like Preston and his wife and didn't like the idea of tragedy overcoming them. We accordingly opened the play in London with the happy ending and had no cause to regret our choice.[124]

Sherriff's willingness to redraft his play in the light of his audience's reaction shows a flexibility borne of many years of revising movie scripts (maybe all that 'cold haddock' had a way of working out after all). Certainly on this occasion, it meant that, after touring to Glasgow and Hull (and doing very good business all along the way), the play arrived in London, at Wyndham's Theatre on 7 March, in a much more audience-pleasing format than it had entered Brighton just four weeks earlier.

The play is much more than a whodunit, although that part of it is skilfully executed, with regular shocks deployed just before curtain falls. What makes the play much more interesting is its focus on an ordinary middle-class man, buffeted by events. Sherriff himself described his play as one that depended on 'mystery and suspense', but actually what deepens the play is Preston's overwhelming sense of helplessness and his reaction to the destruction of his well-ordered world. Sherriff had proved in his earlier works that he understood the lower middle class as well as anyone, and *Home at Seven* demonstrated that he could take that understanding and stretch it to examine their reaction to utterly unexpected events. In that respect, the play has something in common with *Miss Mabel*: on the surface, it appears like a whodunit of sorts, a mystery play where each curtain shocks us with a new turn of events, but in practice the interest lies in the characters' responses to those unforeseen events.

It was, in the words of *Theatre World*, 'another splendid example of Sherriff's skill in presenting the English middle-class background'.[125] Richardson himself was seen as key to the success of the play, since 'it is essential that the audience should believe in this man and no actor is more skilled in conveying absolute sincerity and integrity.' *The Guardian* was unconvinced by the play, but agreed that Richardson was important, as he lent 'a sorely needed touch of distinction' to the 'humdrum and repetitive idiom the author imposes'.[126] J.C. Trewin, by contrast, lauded both: 'Dramatist and actor bring off their play perfectly, because they keep us anxious about its central figure.' He also noted that the doctor, lawyer and policeman were credits to their real-life counterparts, and that 'if there is an Incorporated Association of Barmaids, then Meriel Forbes[127] should take its diploma.'[128]

Out with the Old

At the beginning of 1950, Sherriff could afford to be pleased.

He had come back from the US while the war was still on, and had endured a rocky year or two – not financially, perhaps, but in terms of adjusting to the way of life in England. Working with Korda had proved more difficult than expected, especially when Korda quit MGM, and it was frustrating to have spent three years on screenplays that went nowhere. But he had enjoyed his time with Carol Reed on *Odd Man Out*, *Quartet* had been well received, and he had earned £48,000 from his movie work in just six years. Furthermore, he was still in demand in the film business, with regular offers of work. As for his novels, *Chedworth* had done reasonably well in the US (although it had not travelled across the Atlantic) and *Another Year* had been modestly successful in both the US and the UK, and had paved the way to a new publisher. Most pleasing of all were his two new plays: *Miss Mabel* had done well in the West End and was thriving in Paris, while *Home at Seven* was just about to begin its provincial tour before heading for London. He was once more enjoying the thrill of casting and rehearsals, and with a couple of new ideas in mind, had high hopes of re-establishing his dramatic credentials.

The 1940s had been a difficult decade, but Sherriff had come through it successfully, and was looking forward to the years ahead, in the hope that they would be productive, successful and rewarding. He could not have imagined just how rewarding they would prove to be.

Chapter 12

Pinnacle, 1950–56

He who loves fame considers another man's activity to be his own good; and he who loves pleasure, his own sensations; but he who has understanding, considers his own acts to be his own good.

Marcus Aurelius, *The Meditations*, Book VI.

At the beginning of 1950, petrol was still rationed. But the Conservatives campaigned in the February general election to have all rationing restrictions removed, and although they were defeated by the Labour Government, their gains reduced the government's majority to only five.[1] The days of rationing were clearly numbered, which may have been why, just six days after the election (and a week before *Home at Seven* was due to premiere at Wyndham's) Sherriff placed a deposit on a new Rolls-Royce. Four months later, with petrol rationing finally ended, he proudly took possession of the new car, and could enjoy his motoring once more.

He had also resumed his rowing coaching, offering his services to his old school. The Kingston Grammar boys were very impressed that such a famous man had come to help them. Derek Finlay would later recall how it started:

> We were being watched by a gentleman in an open-top Rolls-Royce wearing a soft grey fedora style hat with the brim turned down. He got out of the car, strode over and asked in a soft voice, 'Would you like some coaching help? I used to row here myself years ago.' From then on the Old Kingstonian, well-known author of *Journey's End* and playwright R.C. Sherriff, was increasingly generous of his time and support. He provided us with a new shell eight and was in fact a good coach.[2]

When the new boat was purchased, in the early summer of 1950, it was christened *Home at Seven*, and he took the entire First VIII up to Scott's in the West End for dinner before taking them on to the Wyndham's, having held the curtain to accommodate their late arrival, so that they could see the play for which their boat had been named. This would be the first of many boats he would buy for the school, and the first of many occasions on which he would treat members of the KGS First VIII to a 'slap-up feed' and a show.

Although he chose not to, he could have taken the boys to see another of his screenplays brought to fruition, when Sydney Box's *Trio* (containing his adaptation of Maugham's *Sanatorium*, as well as *The Verger* and *Mr Know-It-All*) came to the screen in August 1950. *The Guardian* gave it a very positive write-up ('almost as lucky a dip as *Quartet*') and when the movie opened in the United States two months later, Bosley Crowther also gave it an enthusiastic endorsement ('Another delightful screen potpourri'), noting that Sherriff's adaptation was 'considerably broader in its sweep' than the other two stories. 'As a matter of fact,' he continued, '[it] was considered at one time ... as the stuff for a full-length picture, and well it might have been. But told as it is in this instance, it is brilliantly concise and emotionally full.' Of course, a lot of credit had to go to the actors, who were uniformly excellent (but especially Jean Simmons as the young woman who chooses love, whatever the cost to her health), and to Harold French's 'smooth, unobtrusive and precise direction, in which not a frame is wasted'.[3] All true: *Sanatorium* is an excellent short film.

All Good Things

Home at Seven carried on at Wyndham's until New Year's Eve 1950, for a total of 342 performances, easily outstripping any previous Sherriff play except *Journey's End*. Six months after it was taken off, the whole cast was reunited in a BBC radio production on 9 June 1951, playing in the prestigious *Saturday Night Theatre* slot, to an audience of about 8 million.[4] The play had averaged the best part of £150 a week in royalties at Wyndham's, and over the course of the next couple of years it would yield more than £10,000 in revenues for its author, partly from the sale of the screen rights to Maurice Cowan, whose first producer's credit this would be. Sherriff felt that Cowan was unlikely to secure stars such as Richardson on his own, and that a better plan would be for him to operate within Korda's operation[5] (by which he meant British Lion Films, which was part-funded by government loans, and in which Korda had taken a major shareholding in 1946),[6] which was exactly what happened.

In the meantime, Sherriff continued working on a new play, initially titled *The Shade in Laburnum Terrace*, or *Be Gone and Live*, which had been occupying him for the past year. As early as June 1950, he had been discussing a draft with theatre manager Binkie Beaumont, producer Peter Brook,[7] and also with Ralph Richardson, who had maintained a keen involvement throughout ('Every thought I give to your play is an excitement to me,' he told Sherriff)[8]; indeed, the part of the main character – Sir John Greenwood – was effectively written for him, and he was keen enough on the part that he acquired the English speaking rights for himself[9] (although the downside to that was that any production would have to fit in with his busy schedule, which would inevitably delay things). By September 1951, just before Sherriff went off on another archaeological digging holiday on the south coast, it looked as though a production might be possible in the New Year, but that fell through. Nevertheless, Richardson, writing to Sherriff from Shepperton Studios, where he was making the film of *Home at Seven*, held out hope for a production in the autumn of 1952, once he was free of his obligations. He told Sherriff that Korda liked the play, and had no objection to him appearing in it in that time frame. Korda had also, it seems, suggested a title: *The White Carnation* (because of the flower the principal character wears in his buttonhole at the beginning of the play). Sherriff, who had long complained of his inability to think up catchy titles, felt this one was 'an inspiration'.[10]

With pressure building on Korda to keep costs contained at British Lion, *Home at Seven* was something of an experiment – a play that would be rehearsed for three weeks on the set at Shepperton, and then shot within a fortnight – compared with the eight weeks that would normally be taken. Rather than directing it himself, he handed the reins to Richardson, who worked to a script prepared by the very experienced Anatole de Grunwald.[11] Alongside Richardson in the cast were two of Korda's contract players – Margaret Leighton (as Preston's wife) and Jack Hawkins as Doctor Sparling.[12] The film was released in the UK in 1952, and in the US (as *Murder on Monday*) in 1953, to rather lacklustre reviews ('static, wordy – in short, "stagy"').[13]

Although he had handed the film over to Cowan and Korda, Sherriff had remained on hand for advice (Shepperton could be reached from Rosebriars in just twenty-five minutes in his shiny new Rolls-Royce), so he would likely have felt the dismissive reviews rather personally, not least since much of the complaint was about the structure of the play and its denouement. His mood would not have been helped by the death of one of his greatest supporters, Mollie Cazalet, in January 1952. He had sent her copies of all of his books, and taken her to see his plays and films, and she had reacted almost like a second mother, or at the very least, an indulgent aunt. He wrote a touching tribute in a letter to *The Times*, acknowledging her 'genius for helping the shy newcomer to the world of art and literature and music', and observing that 'the most cherished memories will not lie in the meeting with great people in her house, but in the sweetness and humanity of Mollie Cazalet herself, and the days one spent with her alone.'[14]

The Dam Busters

Towards the end of 1951, with the prospect of a production of *The White Carnation* pushed at least a year into the future, Sherriff seems to have thought it was time to pick up his screenwriting pencil again. He had not written for the movies since *No Highway*, partly because he had been busy with his plays, but also because no especially attractive film offer had come his way. As luck would have it, however, a British movie company had just acquired a property that, they felt, with the right script, could be turned into one of the best British war movies of the time.

Robert Clark[15] was the director of productions at Associated British Picture Corporation (ABPC), which was one of the biggest players in the British movie industry at that time. Clark was a believer in making movies from existing properties that had already shown themselves to be popular, and at the suggestion of Frederick (Fritz) Gotfurt[16] (ABPC's scenario editor) he bought up the rights to Paul Brickhill's *The Dam Busters*,[17] a history of the RAF's 617 Squadron.

The squadron had been formed especially to take part in the 1943 raid on three German dams (the Möhne, the Eder and the Sorpe), and this occupies the first eight chapters (out of thirty-one) of Brickhill's book. It begins with Barnes Wallis's work designing new, larger sized 'earthquake bombs' designed to attack Germany's sources of power, including mines and dams, and then goes on to describe the problems he faced in trying to shepherd his ideas through Whitehall's network of committees. Wallis, who was an important source for Brickhill, felt that he had been obstructed in his efforts to put his theories into practice, but subsequent accounts, based on fuller sources, suggest that Whitehall was not as obstructive as he described.[18] But even taking that part of his account with a pinch of salt, it did still take Wallis some time to give his idea practical form, and there were numerous tests to be run regarding the shape, size, launch trajectory and speed of the final bomb. Eventually, he had enough in place to be able to persuade Sir Arthur Harris ('Bomber' Harris, Chief of the Air Staff) to give him the go-ahead.

At that point the book turns to the formation, training and development of 617 Squadron, under its young, but experienced new commander, Guy Gibson. This section is based in part on Guy Gibson's own memoir, *Enemy Coast Ahead*[19] (especially in some of Gibson's direct quotes), and recounts the difficulties of bringing together an entire squadron from scratch. In due course, Gibson meets Wallis at his office in Weybridge, where the theory behind the bomb is explained to him (although Wallis does not tell him the targets). On Gibson's return to his base at RAF Scampton, he is shown models of the dams that he and his men will be attacking. Thereafter, with the deadline for the raid just a few weeks away, each man has his own problems to deal with: Wallis to perfect his bomb, and Gibson to ensure that his men could deliver it in exactly the way that was needed for the dams to be breached. That required, in particular, the ability to fly at very low altitudes over water, and a means of aiming the bombs accurately every time. The problems are eventually overcome, with backroom assistance, and the final three chapters of the first part of Brickhill's book describe the preparations for the raid, the raid itself and the aftermath, including the successful breaching of the Möhne and the Eder dams. It also reveals the high casualty rate, with eight of the nineteen planes being shot down, fifty-three men killed and three taken prisoner.

Clark began thinking of making the film in October 1951, buying up the rights to Brickhill's book, with the intention of using it as a vehicle for Richard Todd, at that time on contract to Associated British.[20] That same month he met 'high officials of the Air Ministry for general discussion of projected film', according to the diary of A.W. (Bill) Whittaker, a production supervisor at ABPC's Elstree Studios in North

London.[21] Whittaker and script editor Walter Mycroft then produced a suggested treatment of the story, which could be used to brief the screenwriter, once one had been chosen. That particular decision took a couple of production meetings, with various names being bandied about, including Terence Rattigan, Emlyn Williams and C.S. Forester, but in January of 1952, Clark settled on Sherriff.

The 'Briefing Treatment'

Brickhill and Mycroft's treatment[22] notes at the beginning that it is 'an attempt to explore one possible line of adaptation, i.e. with the flyers as the main thread', and it 'takes the story as far as the successful test of the full-sized bomb, which was the immediate prelude to the raid itself.' But, it cautions: 'As the Wallis bomb is still secret it evidently cannot be shown, any more than it is described in the book,' and also that 'the frustrations of Barnes Wallis have been condensed in this version because it might be against public policy ... to suggest that a brilliant war shortening invention could be held back by lack of imagination on the part of Authority.'

The surprise in their approach is that it turns Brickhill's previous narrative approach on its head: in both his book and a radio dramatisation he wrote for the BBC[23] (broadcast on 8 May 1951), the narrative had begun with Wallis, and only when he had taken the bomb far enough to persuade Harris did it switch to the formation of the squadron. But the new treatment focuses on Gibson until he meets Wallis, whereupon Wallis's own struggles are depicted in a sort of montage flashback. It is in this treatment that the (mistaken) suggestion is first made that the idea came from watching spotlights in a show, rather than (as Brickhill wrote) from the Ministry of Aircraft production.[24] Thereafter it follows the book quite closely, until the successful test at Reculver a couple of weeks later, whereupon the treatment ends, with the words 'There follows the sequences dealing with the hurry and tension of the last days of final preparation and then the great drama of the raid itself.'

Some three months after completing the briefing treatment, Whittaker offered a further elaboration in the form of a script,[25] but by that time, Sherriff had begun to read his way into the job.

Sherriff Arrives

According to Whittaker's diary,[26] Sherriff attended an initial script meeting on 7 March, with Clark 'presiding', in which he outlined his ideas for the treatment of the story. 'He feels that it should be told simply and naturally, with no recourse to tricks of any sort.... It was also agreed that there should be no effort to introduce a feminine influence.' This was an interesting decision, because it cut away two romantic sub-plots that had featured in the book. It may be that Sherriff felt that the martial atmosphere might be enhanced in the absence of women (as in *Journey's*

End), but, of course, the airmen were not at the front, and women were part of their daily lives, so excluding women seems a less obvious choice to make than in a Western Front setting. Since the flyers involved in those sub-plots (Shannon and Maltby) came home, there would not have been the deeper sadness that might have come from seeing a wife or girlfriend mourn their loved one. On the other hand, it may simply have been that Sherriff felt that there was more than enough to shoehorn into the script without adding a love interest.

After the meeting, Sherriff visited Wallis at his home in Effingham,[27] once on his own, and once in the company of Brickhill, Mycroft and Whittaker, the latter of whom recorded:

> Mr Wallis has set up the catapult, water tub etc. with which he did his original experiments. Mr Wallis proudly conducted us to them and said, 'It's just as it was at the time. Now I'll show you how it works.' It didn't.[28]

With the information from Wallis, and his experiments, in hand, Sherriff set about preparing his own treatment.[29] It is twenty-three pages long, and departs radically from the briefing treatment, returning instead to the book's original structure. It begins by showing Wallis's back-garden experiments, which had only been alluded to by Brickhill. The fact that Sherriff could begin with the experiment suggests that there had been a noticeable easing in security restrictions, as does the presence in his files of a 'TOP SECRET' memo written by Wallis on the 'Spherical Bomb'[30] (or 'Surface torpedo'). The diminished secrecy clearly meant that Wallis's part of the story could be played up, and that was what Sherriff's treatment set about doing, for the first eleven of its twenty-three pages. The next three pages begin Gibson's story, and thereafter we are in familiar territory as the stories are intercut as each tries to solve his own specific problems. The treatment ends with a short description of the way in which the raid will be treated, although at that point a detailed scene sequence could not be compiled because 'much of this is technical and dependent upon facilities as yet unidentified.'

Several points are worth noting about Sherriff's treatment:

> First, it does, indeed, completely exclude the 'feminine influence'. It omits Gibson's humiliating dressing-down of those who breached security regulations, presumably because it might look like bullying;

> It includes several short scenes (almost in montage fashion) that show the manufacture of the bomb, and the modification of the Lancasters to take the bomb;

It includes Wallis's Chesil Beach test, but only as seen through the reaction of onlookers: there would be 'no authentic shots of the falling bomb ... nor anything else that might infringe security';

It continues to suggest that the spotlight idea came from an airman watching a show – only this time it's Gibson himself, in a West End theatre.

As David Cottis points out,[31] Sherriff's treatment is highly innovative – essentially shifting the focus of the movie one-third of the way in, when we leave the story of one hero and begin following that of another; eventually the two storylines are woven together. The problem Sherriff faced was how to dramatise a story that elapsed over several years (which involved a good deal of scientific experimentation, and is hardly filmic at the best of times), and in which a second major protagonist does not appear until towards the very end. Brickhill's book actually begins Wallis's story in 1939, just before the outbreak of the war; Gibson, by contrast, does not feature until Harris orders the formation of what would become 617 Squadron on 15 March 1943. That is a lot of elapsed time to show in flashback, as the earlier treatment did, and it would seriously impede any forward narrative impulse. At least Sherriff's construction has the benefit of narrative progression, even if it takes a big risk in making us suddenly transfer our interest from one hero to an entirely different one. But the producers at Associated British seemed happy with Sherriff's new approach.

From Treatment to Script

Whittaker records that the 'Final complete script' was delivered on 15 July, and that, at meetings held from 12–14 August, a cast of characters from ABPC (including Clark, Gotfurt, Whittaker, Mycroft and Brickhill) read it through and discussed it: 'The script met with universal approval, but suggestions and discussion took place on a large number of points of detail.'[32] Although the original script is no longer to be found, a subsequent version, dated 24 October, can be examined in Sherriff's papers.[33] There are a number of changes from his own initial treatment:

A suggested shot of the bomb being placed in position under the Wellington bomber before the test run is deleted in the later script;

In Brickhill's book, Wallis was given a dressing-down by the managing director at Vickers (who reported that Whitehall felt he had been making a nuisance of himself), prompting him to resign. This scene was no longer included;

An important change was the omission of scenes showing the bomb being manufactured, and the Lancasters retrofitted to take the missile. Whether this was due to security concerns or just time constraints is not clear;

Gibson and Hay's crash, in a light aircraft, when returning from Reculver, described in Brickhill's book, is omitted entirely.

Several other scenes are trimmed and cut here or there, presumably to speed the action along, but the overall impression, especially given Sherriff's experiences in most of his other films, is that his original vision for the movie was broadly maintained throughout the script development process.

The script contains a few sightings of Sherriff's trademark humour. One of the better ones is when Wallis is asking for a Wellington bomber for his trials, and the civil servant asks him what argument he can advance to secure the use of one, and Wallis replies, 'If you tell them I invented it … don't you think that might help?' Another joke that survived the script process is the one where Wallis (after the final successful test at Reculver) credits the idea of the bouncing bomb to Nelson, who, at the Battle of the Nile, 'dismissed the French flagship with a yorker'.[34] The irate chicken farmer writing to complain about low flying is another obvious Sherriff touch (only he would have thought to make it chickens, rather than any other farm animal).

But there is not much use for humour in the script as a whole, since the overall tone is serious and restrained (in fact, Laurence Thompson, in the *News Chronicle*, described it as 'a little reverent, an Albert memorial rather than a transcription of life').[35] It was almost bound to be so, given how recently the raid had taken place, and the presence of so many survivors. But probably no one did restraint better than Sherriff. He had shown as much in *Journey's End*: in the scene where Trotter hears about the raid, for example, he remarks, 'What a damn nuisance!', to which Osborne replies, phlegmatically, 'It is, rather.'[36] The echo can be clearly heard some twenty-five years later, in Wallis and Gibson's exchange after the second unsuccessful test at Reculver: Gibson: 'It's the devil, isn't it?'; Wallis: 'Yes. It is rather.'

There is also a resonant echo from Sherriff's past in the final scene between Gibson and Wallis. Wallis is upset at the loss of fifty-six men and tells Gibson, 'If I'd known it would be like this, I would never have started it,' to which Gibson replies:

You mustn't think that way. If all these fellows had known from the beginning that they wouldn't be coming back, they'd have gone for it just the same. There isn't a single one would have dropped out. I know them all and I know that's the truth.

Gibson's sentiment is very similar to what Sherriff had written to Pips all those years before:

> It is no good dwelling on the awfulness of it all, for you know it only too well – the men who go up for a tour of duty in the trenches go up absolutely resigned ... they go because they must – and although they are always cheerful, they go with that thought that, although there is every possibility of them coming back safely, someone isn't.[37]

The final scenes in the script are delicate and sombre, and deeply touching. We watch the pilots as they prepare in their rooms before the raid. Afterwards we see the same rooms, now largely empty, as the announcement of the raid comes over the wireless. The heroism of the men is reinforced by the exchange between Wallis and Gibson, and is brilliantly underscored in Gibson's last line, when Wallis asks: 'Aren't you going to turn in?', and he replies, 'I've got to write some letters first.' That line, and the salute that he shortly thereafter returns to a young airman, perfectly symbolises Gibson's code of duty and takes us straight back to the 'uncomplaining' duty that Sherriff first described in the trenches in France.

The bulk of Sherriff's work on *The Dam Busters* probably ended with the production of the October 1952 script, although given his commitment to the project he was probably happy to remain available for script conferences and advice. His third (and final) payment (of £1,250) came through in August 1952, after which there would be no further payments until after the film was released (suggesting that his contract had been structured such that he was paid a slightly smaller amount than normal for the preparation of the script, but with a further final payment when the film was eventually released).[38]

The White Carnation

In August 1952, just as Sherriff was working through *The Dam Busters* script redrafts, word came through that Peter Brook was unlikely to be able to take the reins on *The White Carnation*, but within a month they had found a replacement in Noel Willman, an experienced actor who had been directing for about ten years, and who clearly impressed Sherriff:

> I think he would make a very good stage director for *Carnation*. He has a clear understanding of the play and his criticisms are sensible and constructive. I was in fact stimulated by his enthusiasm and shall feel quite happy if you decide to engage him.[39]

Sherriff immediately set to work on further revisions to the play, promising to have a final version delivered by the time Richardson had finished a very difficult season in Stratford.[40] By the end of November, rehearsals were underway, in preparation for an opening in Brighton on 5 January.

The White Carnation is a ghost story. During the war, at the end of his Christmas party, Sir John Greenwood, a wealthy stockbroker, gets locked out of his house. He knocks on the door but there is no answer, so he climbs in through a window, only to find that there is no one there and the house is dilapidated. His entrance has been noted by a policeman who comes to investigate: Greenwood protests that the house is his, but the policeman, doubting his claims, fetches his sergeant, whom Greenwood claims to know. When the sergeant arrives he is horrified to see Greenwood, whom he knows to have died in a flying bomb strike seven years before. The policeman calls the local coroner and a doctor to examine Greenwood and they come to the conclusion that he is a ghost – though Greenwood does not support their diagnosis. The problem then becomes how to remove him from the house, which is due to be demolished by the council to make way for a block of flats. There will have to be discussions with the town clerk and other officials, but in the meantime Greenwood is given some of his furniture (which has been in storage), and a policeman on guard provides conversation, as does Lydia, the niece of the town clerk who has an interest in ghosts, and talks Greenwood through the delicacy of his position.

As the second act begins, Greenwood has resolved to make the most of the eternity available to him. During his life he was a businessman, obsessed with finance, and had no time for higher culture; now is his chance to put that right, and he asks Lydia if she will help him. He is peeved when he finds that the classic books brought from his library are not in the pristine condition he imagined, but had already been read by his wife, a woman he had thought very far from his intellectual equal (although socially she ranked above him). Conversations with the vicar and an elderly neighbour make him realise that perhaps he had been unfair to his wife while alive. Greenwood struggles with this idea, just as he struggles with his self-improvement scheme, soon preferring the financial pages to the great books. All the while the functionaries are trying to remove him from the house, even seeking the assistance of a senior official at the Home Office. In the end the council plans to demolish the house at midnight on Christmas Eve, but just before the appointed hour Greenwood's loneliness, and his desire to make amends to his wife, take his spirit back to the Christmas party from which it had left, leaving him and his wife together as the flying bomb falls.

The rollout format, which had worked so well for *Miss Mabel* and *Home at Seven*, was used again for *The White Carnation*. It opened at the Theatre Royal, Brighton, on 5 January 1953, and played there for two weeks, to very good houses. Thereafter it made its way around the country, calling in to eight other locations,[41] on each occasion grossing over £2,000 a week. Sherriff (and Richardson, who was invested in the production) probably had high hopes for its reception in London, where it arrived, at The Globe Theatre, on 20 March. Unfortunately, the reviews were rather mixed. *The Tatler* felt that 'Mr Sherriff is himself puzzled with what to do with the ghost. He never really makes up his mind whether to be frivolous, fantastic or philosophical,'[42] while Harold Hobson, influential critic at *The Sunday Times*, felt that the dialectical battle between ghost and humanity was never effectively argued, although he did note that the play did well in showing the growth of Greenwood, 'not spiritually or intellectually, but humanly. ... The ending of the play is, in fact, quite extraordinarily moving and beautiful.'[43] Even his old friend Bill Darlington was unsure what to make of the play: 'Mr Sherriff hardly seems to have made up his mind what kind of play he has set out to write. At one moment he is verging on farce; at the next he is writing quite serious scenes.'[44] All the same, he observed, 'the play holds one's attention throughout.'

While the play may have been regarded with some misgivings, the acting was generally very highly commended, especially Richardson's Greenwood, as Hobson proclaimed: 'Sir Ralph is on the stage almost the whole evening and his performance is magnificent. There is no other player who can touch the ordinary qualities of ordinary people with such a radiance, nor so marry the commonplace with the sublime.' He also singled out Meriel Forbes, who was 'altogether delightful as a breath of fresh air from the public libraries'. Even Kenneth Tynan, the *enfant terrible* of theatre criticism, was impressed by Richardson, praising him (although not the play) as a '4D character in a 3D world' and noting how he 'guides the play through its shallows with a touch of a master helmsman'.[45]

The reviews were sufficiently lukewarm that the play struggled from the beginning. In its best week it just scraped over the £2,000 mark – below every single week in the provinces – and by the end of April it was down to receipts of just over £1,600. At that point Sherriff agreed to forego his royalties, but the play gradually wound down, and ended its run (after ninety performances) on 6 June – a very unwelcome 57th birthday present.[46]

It is difficult to explain quite why the play failed to catch the public's imagination. It is very funny, in particular in the way in which it takes an extraordinary occurrence and examines it from the most banal of perspectives. Nevertheless, the reviewers were correct in asserting that the play seemed caught between several stools. Was it simply a comedy of frustrated officialdom? Was it a meditation on spirituality and humanity? Or was it an examination of a man's capacity for emotional improvement? Certainly Sherriff achieves the latter, because while we view Greenwood with distaste initially (brusque, self-satisfied and narrow-minded), we warm to him as he grapples with the functionaries, and then we applaud how he reacts to the difficult lessons he learns from those who help him examine his life. By the end he wins us over, and we thrill to his reconnection with his wife.

In Lydia Truscott we have one of the strongest female roles that Sherriff ever wrote. She is brave and smart, and is willing to stand up to Greenwood even when he attempts to bully her. She is the voice of reason in the play, negotiating between the two sides, intermediating between the individual and the public spheres. As a librarian she is also representative of culture, the element that was most missing from Greenwood's life, and as a woman she makes him aware of how he had (albeit inadvertently) mistreated his wife. He gets a glimpse from the vicar and the neighbour as well, but it is Lydia who suggests why he is here, and what he needs to do to be gone. She is easily the strongest female character in any of his plays since he first invented Joan Winter, the developer's daughter in *Mr Birdie's Finger*.

Perhaps the lack of success was simply a variant on the old issue that once a playwright has established a style, the audience will come to expect the same in the future. Sherriff's two recent successes had been whodunits of a sort, and it may have been that a 'mystery play' was what the audience now expected of him.

But he no longer needed to worry about what the audience wanted. Because of his screenwriting work he could focus on just the types of stories that gave him pleasure to write. One such story was occupying him in the summer of 1953 – the boys' adventure story that he had been promising to Dwye Evans these past two years. Before *The White Carnation* had finished its run he had sent Evans a completed draft of the book, now entitled *King John's Treasure*, and in an exchange of correspondence, secured Evans's promise to see that the book was well illustrated, in exchange for taking a 'pretty modest' royalty.[47] As he observed: 'I am sure a well-illustrated boys' book has a much better chance of re-printing than a cheap affair, so that in the long run I think we shall gain by accepting a lower royalty.'[48]

At that point he could afford to be generous where his royalties on the book were concerned, for children's books were seldom huge sellers, and any slight reduction in the agreed rate of royalties would be unlikely to have much effect on his income. In fact, his boys' book would net him less than £200 over the following five years, whereas at precisely that moment he was receiving the second of three payments of £1,500 for a script that he had agreed to write for Warwick Films[49]: an adaptation of *Prize of Gold*, a thriller, written by Max Catto, about a heist that goes badly wrong. He completed the script in August, and as late as December (when it was submitted to the PCA), his was still the only name on the script. At some point thereafter, however, the producers took the story in a different direction, and when the film was released in 1955,[50] to generally poor reviews, there was no word of Sherriff's involvement.

Having despatched the draft of *Prize of Gold*, and while waiting for the proofs of *King John's Treasure*, Sherriff began to turn his attention to a new play – one that had been in his mind for some time. It was unlike anything he had attempted before: a story about a Romano-British family at exactly the point in history where the last Romans left the British Isles (about AD 410). He sent early drafts of the first act to Mortimer Wheeler, who liked it very much, and to Ralph Richardson, who replied:

I think you have made a wonderful start, and I send to you all congratulations and my prayers that you may be guided by your genius, to the terribly difficult stage that lies ahead – to gain the summit of the conclusion. Everest is not to be compared with the feat![51]

King John's Treasure

On 15 March 1954, in the midst of his exertions on the new play, Sherriff's boys' book was published – an exciting tale of two young schoolboys who go in search of the treasure that King John was reputed to have lost in the marshes at the mouth of the Wash. The boys hear the tale from their history master, and Peter, the book's narrator, is so enthralled that he persuades his friend Simon to accompany him to the marshes to begin their search. But the area is now very built up, and just as they despair they come across an old lady who tells them a tale that suggests that the treasure was never lost, but instead was stolen by one of King John's courtiers. Following one clue after another, they eventually come to the home of the family descended from the courtier. Sneaking secretly into the grounds, they observe the trappings of a court, and a young boy (Michael), about their age, who is treated as the rightful king, crown jewels and all. When they tell the boy that his family's wealth is built on treason, he agrees to abdicate and return to London with them, and in the end the story is resolved happily: the treasure is returned to its owners, the crown jewels to the nation, and Michael lives with Simon's family and discovers the joys of being a normal boy.

The story brings together Sherriff's love of history and archaeology, and is absorbing throughout, if not as action packed as some adventure stories. There is no great character development, but the locations they visit – especially the Fens and the Peak District – are evocatively drawn, and the individuals they encounter on their quest are very well sketched. The critics liked it too: 'The blend of fact and fantasy is convincing and the characterisation excellent,'[52] wrote The Birmingham Post; 'a most readable book', noted the Surrey Comet, 'for Mr Sherriff writes for young readers without writing down to them,'[53] while Housewife magazine felt he wrote 'with … gusto and confidence'.[54] The Times Literary Supplement accredited it the best of the history fiction books it was reviewing, and clearly felt it was appropriate for adults (apart from the 'Ruritanian' ending).[55]

Sherriff had sent copies of the book out to a number of people, including various colleagues from archaeological digs, as well as old friends such as Gerald Ellison, Geoffrey Dearmer and G.B. Stern. Mortimer Wheeler wrote to him that he envied him 'the easy swing which carries your reader on with irresistible momentum'[56]; he also told him that he would be reading it to his step-daughter, whom he was sure would enjoy it as well (thus rather backing up the reviewer for BBC Children's Hour who felt that although the book was described on its dust jacket as a book for boys, most girls would enjoy it too!)[57]

Dakota Story

About a month after the publication of *King John's Treasure*, location shooting finally began on *The Dam Busters*, almost eighteen months after Sherriff had completed his script. Part of the delay was due to the need to secure the full co-operation of the Air Ministry, which offered access to RAF facilities and crews, as well as help in 'overcoming vested interests within the government that wanted to stop or to limit the project on security grounds.'[58] But the extra time also allowed for the preparation of special effects, and for the script to be sent far and wide for comment and approval, including to survivors and next of kin. The script was also sent to 'Bomber' Harris, who complained that it made him look like an 'irascible, unapproachable moron',[59] which prompted Walter Mycroft to rewrite the sequence in which Wallis first visits Harris. But Mycroft's cuts may have been less about Harris's complaint than about the need to reduce running time: in fact, between the December 1953 script (an updated version of Sherriff's October 1952 version) and the film itself, a total of twenty-five scenes would be excised.[60]

Sherriff meanwhile was busily working on the draft of the 'Romano-British' play as well as a new commission from Michael Balcon, at Ealing Studios. His cash books refer to the film as the 'Dakota Story',[61] but it would eventually become *The Night My Number Came Up*. Three payments, in May and June, suggest when the script was written, but it is impossible to be sure since, aside from a passing reference in a letter to Ayton Whitaker,[62] there is nothing about the movie in his correspondence files whatsoever. The cash book suggests he received his first two payments for the work on an outline story, with the further (larger) payment for a subsequent screenplay.

The film was based on a short story in the *Saturday Evening Post* in 1951,[63] which in turn was based on an event in the life of Air Vice Marshal Sir Victor Goddard. Just after the war, at a cocktail party in Shanghai, he encountered a Royal Navy officer who'd had a vivid dream about Goddard's death, along with three British civilians (a woman and two men), in the crash of a Dakota airplane along a rocky shoreline. Later that night, Goddard learned that his military flight the next day would (unusually) take three civilian passengers (one woman, two men) and would be made in a Dakota. The flight unfolded exactly as the officer had foreseen in his dream, except that it ended only in a crash landing, not in the air vice-marshal's death. The film was to be directed by Leslie Norman, his first film as director, after fifteen years as an editor and producer. In an interview in October 1992, he noted that he had come across the story and thought it would make a good film, but Balcon would not let him write the screenplay.[64]

No version of the original script exists in Sherriff's files, so we have to examine the film itself for evidence of how Sherriff may have developed the basic story. The broad outline is much the same – a man is trapped in an airplane apparently living out someone else's dream, which will end in his death. The film begins with the dinner party at which the dream is retold, amidst much discussion of oriental-style superstition, leaving the air marshal with a lingering unease. Thereafter, a series of random events gradually presents us with the same set of circumstances as those in the dream. For example, towards the beginning of the movie it looks as though the air marshal will be travelling on a Liberator airplane; but at the last moment, problems with the plane mean that a Dakota must be substituted instead. Then it appears that the number of people on the plane does not match the number in the dream, but at the last minute, some additional passengers are taken on board. Just as it appears that the plane will take a route avoiding a rocky shore, a storm conspires to throw it off course. Bit by bit, the circumstances of the dream are gradually put in place, until it seems inevitable that it must come true. The tension is ratcheted up steadily as the film proceeds, so that the initial idea is developed in a very original way.

The story is fleshed out by a much wider cast of characters than in the original short story, and from a diverse set of backgrounds. To what extent they were drawn from Sherriff's pen is difficult to know, but it is hard to look at the awful businessman, Mr Rose, and not see echoes of earlier variants in Sherriff's books and plays (think of Mr Montgomery in *The Fortnight in September*, for example, or Maraway in *Cornlow-in-the-Downs*). Just as the tension rises as each piece of the dream falls into place, so the characters gradually become aware of the dream and its implications, and much of the complexity of the movie is derived from their respective attitudes to the dream itself, and whether it can be forestalled by action on their parts. Movies in which individuals react differently to some imminent peril are not at all unusual, but what makes this one different, and much more interesting, is that it deals with the characters' attitudes to a potential peril, one that they may or may not be convinced of, depending on their backgrounds and attitudes. It is a cleverly constructed piece of work.

Drawing the Threads Together

Sherriff most likely finished his work on the 'Dakota' film during the summer of 1954, and thereafter his priority was the new play. After returning from a trip to Hadrian's Wall he sent a copy of the latest version to Kitty Black, in the play department of Curtis Brown. She read it immediately and replied enthusiastically:

> I love the new version – you really are as clever as paint to have done it so beautifully, and it hangs together and moves along in the most promising manner. I love all the new bits, and suddenly saw that you had written in the loveliest possible title. What do you think of '*The Long Sunset*'? It sounds absolutely perfect and I do hope you will like it.[65]

He did, so that was what it became.

The play was sent to Binkie Beaumont, at H.M. Tennent, with the suggestion that he might want to try it at the Lyric, Hammersmith (traditionally a more adventurous venue than the normal West End theatres), but he did not. Black wrote to him that 'It is so different from your usual style that I think they are rather afraid of departing radically from the usual.'[66] But all was not lost: 'I wonder whether it wouldn't be more sensible to let the script go to Ayton Whitaker immediately,' she mused. 'Doing a play on the air can never prejudice its chances in the theatre, and in the case of several scripts I know, the stage production has resulted directly from the interest caused by the radio transmission.' Sherriff immediately wrote to Whitaker, to see if he might be interested.

Early in January 1955, while awaiting Whitaker's reply, he received an invitation to lunch with Frederick Gotfurt, at Associated British. The company was obviously pleased with the job that Sherriff had done on *The Dam Busters* (which would be coming to the screen in just a few months), and wondered if he might be interested in writing a script on Mary, Queen of Scots. He was indeed, and after some initial discussions hoped he might be able to begin in February, but things were delayed by three weeks' additional script doctoring work (at the tidy sum of £500 a week) for Dino De Laurentiis on the movie *War and Peace*.[67] He eventually signed the contract on 22 March, with the promised end date set for 28 July, a little later than originally envisaged, but for good reason: he had finally heard back from Ayton Whitaker, who, having taken Sherriff's proposal to his department heads (one of whom was Sherriff's old friend Val Gielgud), reported that they would be keen to see the play broadcast in the *Saturday Night Theatre* slot on the Home Service on St George's Day, 23 April 1955.[68] Sherriff was very excited: he had enjoyed several radio broadcasts of his plays in the past, but this would be the first occasion on which a new play of his was given its *first ever* performance on the radio. He was particularly pleased, as he told Kitty Black, that the BBC 'will do it in a really top class way.'[69] Admittedly, the need to reshape the play for radio transmission would take up a little of the initial time he had envisaged spending on Mary, but that was a small price to pay for something as exciting as a genuine broadcasting first for him.

Sherriff was now set for almost an exact repeat of the glorious experience he had enjoyed in 1939. Back then, a launch of a piece of his own work (*The Hopkins Manuscript*) had been sandwiched between the launches of two films, *The Four Feathers* and *Goodbye, Mr Chips*; this time it would be *The Long Sunset* between two aircraft movies – one featuring a Dakota, and the other an entire squadron of Lancasters.

On the Launch Pad (Again)

First on the launch pad on this occasion was *The Night My Number Came Up*, which featured Michael Redgrave as the air marshal, with Alexander Knox as the consul, Denholm Elliott as the air marshal's aide, Michael Hordern as the officer who has the unfortunate dream, and a cast of other British regulars (including Nigel Stock, Sheila Sim and Alfie Bass) alongside them.

The film was never intended as a prestige project in the way that *The Dam Busters* had become for Associated British, but Balcon would have been happy with the reception of the film nonetheless. It was seen as enjoyable and well crafted, although Sherriff's script was generally seen only as 'functional'[70] (which seems harsh, given the ingenuity in the film's construction). Nevertheless, while 'it lacks the supreme excitement of complete uncertainty … there is enough shock and ticklish detail in it to set the average attendant's nerves on edge.'[71] Redgrave himself was rather dismissive of the film in his memoir, but the general reception would have done Sherriff no harm whatsoever: indeed, Gotfurt congratulated him on his success. Ealing were happy enough with his work that they were already looking to commission him for another film. They would be successful in the end, but for now he had all the work he could handle, preparing for the launch of the new play.

The Long Sunset
Shortly before the St George's Day broadcast, Sherriff explained the play, rather evocatively, to readers of *Radio Times:*

> What did these Romans do to meet their own disaster, and how did they face the end? Nothing is known. When the last of the legions sailed out of the British harbours, the history of the island went with them. When light returned two centuries later, the homes of the Roman settlers were in ruins and a new people occupied their land. In *The Long Sunset* I have tried to follow one of these Roman families into the darkness.

Sherriff's Roman family, wealthy landowners in the Kent downs, comprises Julian and his wife Serena, and their two late-teen children, Otho and Paula. At the beginning of the play they watch as their friend Marcus leads the last of the Roman legions to the coast, leaving the inhabitants at the mercy of foreign invaders. Julian tries to organise the defence of his part of the island with the help of a mercenary Brittonic soldier, named Arthur, and his men. Arthur helps to organise defences and train Julian's men, but eventually moves on to his headquarters at Winchester, accompanied by Julian's children: Otho wants to fight by Arthur's side, and Paula is sweet on Arthur's nephew, Gawaine. Julian continues to try to organise the defences, with the help of his friends, local landowners Lucian and Portius, but the former is murdered by his slaves, and the latter opts to leave. Just after Portius announces he's leaving, Julian's chief slave, Lugar, tells him that he and the rest of the Caledonian servants have been called north by their new king. As the sun falls, Julian and his wife leave their house as they await the arrival of the Saxons, but before doing so, Julian becomes a Christian, like his wife, so they can be together forever.

The play is undoubtedly one of Sherriff's best, a labour of love that combined his deep historical knowledge of the period, and his playwriting 'genius', as Richardson put it. It was also his own personal favourite.[72] The *structure* is reminiscent of *Journey's End*, with Julian and his neighbours preparing for the onslaught (by, coincidentally, Germans), which they know is coming (it may be recalled that Sherriff had contemplated calling the earlier play *Waiting*); the play's *tone*, by contrast, harks back rather more to *St Helena*, owing to the sense of elegiac decline that suffuses the play – the memory of happier days contrasted with the sunset of the empire.

An important character in the play is Arthur, who is portrayed as a red-haired, West Country native who, with his 'band of adventurers'[73] (a couple of hundred strong), had already helped Romans in the Severn Valley organise themselves, and was now being looked to more widely to keep invaders at bay. In advance of the play being broadcast, in discussion about casting options, Sherriff explained the character of Arthur, and the relationship between him and Julian:

> He is a fascinating character because he is so elusive, but I think we have come as close to the truth as anybody about what Arthur really was ... [he] should be rather slow and deliberate in his delivery. We want to convey a sincere, honest man with no background or education to help him. If you can play him in this way, it will be a good contrast with Julian, who has the vigorous assurance of a man of good position and education. ... In his scenes with Arthur one should feel that Arthur is rather on the defensive from the intellectual point of view. He has a sort of feeling that Julian is laughing at him because he is little more than a barbarian. But in their hearts there is mutual respect.[74]

Bill Darlington felt the theme was 'fine ... extraordinarily modern in some of its implications and echoes', and he regarded the linking of Roman history with ancient British myth (the legend of Arthur) as a 'bold and happy stroke'.[75] But it was more than that. The entire play is a very patriotic one, in which Sherriff very clearly identifies with both the Romano-Britons, and those Britons relatively untouched by Roman influence, against the threat of the invader. Julian is given several speeches in which to plead the glory and nobility of his way of life, and the words cannot help but recall the speeches in Sherriff's wartime movies. In fact, there is one passage, in which Julian attempts to persuade Arthur to make use of Romano-British boys, where his words echo Joan Fontaine's speech in *This Above All*:

> If I did [say why Arthur needs Romans] then you'd laugh at me and say I'm using fine words again. They are fine words, but you don't hear very much of

them today. Ideals: loyalty: devotion to great purposes that make a man stand by his leader in defeat as well as victory.[76]

The arguments he puts at Julian's disposal may have been influenced in part by his digs at Angmering and by his instinctive empathy (as Vernon Bartlett remarked)[77] with ordinary people, but the anxieties of 1939–40 may not have been far from his mind either.

While the play is very good, it is not flawless. One major criticism (which was made by Richardson after he had read the early draft)[78] is that it lacks theatrical power and character development. There is a momentum to the play, an inevitability of progression from Marcus's initial departure, but the action – such as it is – is always subdued: it is difficult to believe that the Romano-Britons would have been quite as calm about their fate. In fact, the only moment of high drama takes place offstage, when Arthur and his men (including Otho and Julian) confront a small group of invading Saxons. It is almost as though Sherriff conceived of his main characters as too civilised to have turbulent emotions (even the 'barbarian' Arthur). There is no emotional upheaval (not even when the two children depart with Arthur), no voices raised, no sense of panic: the lights never go out completely, they just slowly dim. Perhaps, as a result, Sherriff was wise (or lucky) to have had the play performed first on radio, rather than on the stage, where more challenge and emotion might have been demanded.

The other major criticism of the play, and it was made by the reviewer in *The Times* after the initial broadcast, was the language that he deployed – not in the speeches, but in the ordinary conversations. Particularly grating is the brief exchange after the Britons return from repelling the initial Saxon invasion:

'Well, Gawaine, are you all right?'
'Yes, great show, wasn't it?'

'How may one suggest so mysterious a past,' asks the reviewer, 'in language so barely modern?' Sherriff, as ever, was happy to respond to criticism, and when the play was performed on stage later that summer he counselled the producer that 'There are not many of these [lines] but wherever they occur, then by all means cut them.'[79] There is no doubt that some of them do sound unhappily modern (or, to our ears now, rather dated), but it is difficult to know how else the dramatist should tackle the problem. The rather pompous circumlocution that tends to be used in more modern films is neither more nor less authentic than Sherriff's dialogue, but at the very least the ability to differentiate between characters from different social strata would be a good start. Some years before, Sidney Gilliat[80] had criticised Sherriff for having characters who all spoke in the same way, and that is probably the more pertinent criticism in this case.

The language problems notwithstanding, *The Times*' reviewer thought well of the play ('it contains one or two happier moments one would not have missed'),[81] and his views were shared by listeners. Sherriff wrote excitedly to Curtis Brown:

> All my other plays have been done after their London run and didn't produce more than a dozen letters between them. But *The Long Sunset* has produced stacks of them from all kinds and conditions of people from every corner of Britain and Ireland. It seems to have appealed more than I really thought and I hope that it will become a valuable play in repertory and amateur circles.[82]

Within a month, Barry Jackson (who had been one of the only two theatre managers to attend the first performance of *Journey's End* at the Apollo Theatre) had contracted to present the play at the Birmingham Rep for four weeks from 30 August, under the directorship of Bernard Hepton.[83]

Before the play enjoyed its stage premiere in Birmingham, the BBC gave it another outing, on 8 August (as he wrote to Gladys Day at Curtis Brown, 'a second performance of the play so soon after the original one suggests that it met with popular approval').[84] And that approval was endorsed by the critics who made the trip to Birmingham. '*The Long Sunset* is more theatrical but less theatrically effective than *Journey's End*,' wrote the *Daily Mail*, 'but it comes nearer to that play than anything Mr Sherriff has written in the interim.' *The Illustrated London News* was a fan too: 'Here is a play entirely without fuss and parade. … It is a valiant, lucid play. Sherriff has never over-written.'[85] J.C. Trewin wrote of how the play 'lights the mind', and that it 'strongly challenges the imagination'. *Stage* magazine, meanwhile, reckoned that 'It is not so much the matter [but] … the manner of its telling that gives an impressive air to [Sherriff's] speculations on the last of Roman Britain.'[86] Not everyone was so happy, however. The reviewer in *The Guardian* wrote:

> It looks an excellent idea taking a blank of history and filling it with plausible invention, though the result is disappointing. It gathers no real tension, though it achieves a number of affecting moments and some theatrical power right at the end.[87]

Moreover, Kenneth Tynan, while commending Sherriff's conception as the most original for many years, regretted that Sherriff's 'verbal gift cannot take the strain. … One laments a chance missed, and wishes that this great outline had been filled in by another pen.'[88] The same largely linguistic criticisms were directed at the play when it was revived by Bernard Miles at The Mermaid theatre in 1961 ('The dialogue is relentlessly drawing-room'),[89] although Bernard Levin, who was also free in his criticism of that aspect of the play, felt it was more than outweighed by Sherriff's 'astonishing creative leap of the imagination', and by the play's construction, which was 'an object lesson in playwriting'.[90]

The Dam Busters

The Long Sunset's opening night in Birmingham was still a good three months away when Sherriff savoured the splendours of his third launch of the year, and this one was on a different scale to anything he had enjoyed since *The Four Feathers* (if even then). It premiered at The Empire in Leicester Square, in the presence of Princess Margaret, and massed ranks of luminaries from the movie world and the RAF, as well as the survivors of the original Dam Busters raid, and next of kin of those who had been shot down. A thick commemorative programme remembered the fallen, celebrated the skill and courage of the men who had been involved in the operation, and set out in detail the process by which they had been immortalised on screen.[91]

The film was directed by Michael Anderson, who was relatively inexperienced, having only half a dozen films to his credit, but for whom this film would establish his reputation. Richard Todd was, of course, a compelling Gibson, prompting a congratulatory letter from Gibson's father,which was included in the commemorative programme.[92] Michael Redgrave, having delivered one Sherriff script so recently, now delivered another even more proficiently, while both Ursula Jeans (as Wallis's wife) and Nigel Stock (as Gibson's bomb aimer) made the jump from the earlier film as well. The rest of the cast were the sort of reliable senior officer types familiar from so many other recent British war movies, but with a sprinkling of new faces among the young aircrew, including Robert Shaw (as Gibson's engineer) and George Baker as Maltby. (Patrick McGoohan also popped up in a brief, uncredited role.)

The press could not have been more positive, both about the film and its script. 'Princess Margaret saw a great film last night,' announced the *Evening News*,[93] adding that 'the human, exciting and admirably explanatory screenplay of R.C. Sherriff matches in excellence the firm direction of Michael Anderson.' *The Guardian* argued that the film exhibited the virtues of typical British war films, noting that 'the difference this time is that they are to be found, so unalloyed, in such a long film.' It continued: 'R.C. Sherriff wrote the script, thus (incidentally) achieving the distinction of having found the right dramatic dialogue for the men of 1939–45 as well as those of 1914–18. The script was, surely, the foundation of the film's fineness.'[94] *The Star* also put the 'magnificent script'[95] as number one in its reasons for the film's success (with, for those who are keeping score, Redgrave and Todd at joint second, and Anderson next), and *The Times* called it 'faultless'.[96] *The Daily Telegraph* credited the film's success ('despite its length and tempo') in part to the epic subject, but also to 'skilful treatment', and commended Sherriff's script for avoiding 'outmoded slang' and for its dry English humour (singling out

Wallis's comment on Nelson's yorker).[97] The *Financial Times* was less enthusiastic about the overall impact of the film than some papers ('it hardly seems that this is the deeply memorable war film we may have expected'), but was nevertheless very positive about the script, which had a 'veracity which makes the stiff-upper-lippery of some recent war films seem very artificial indeed'.[98] Dilys Powell, the doyenne of British film critics then, and for many years after, was the only critic to comment on the genius of Sherriff's ending, the 'hush', as she called it, of an 'ending which leaves mourning to the imagination. ... The very last sentence leaves grief hanging in mid-air, and there is no neat securing of the emotions with tears or triumph.'[99] It is, indeed, a very powerful ending, one that Sherriff had crafted from the beginning, and she was right to highlight it.

The Canine Actor

After Britain, the film would show in the United States, but not in the same cut as had just been seen. Associated British was part owned by the American studio Warner Brothers, with British films being distributed through Warners' US cinemas (and vice versa). The Distribution Agreement for *The Dam Busters* gave Warners the right to distribute in the US and Canada, but it also gave them the right to make cuts and changes to the movie.[100] Consequently, in April 1955, ABPC had sent copies of the film and soundtrack to Warners for them to amend as they saw fit.[101] A number of changes were made to the print, notably the inclusion of a foreword setting the raid in context (which Jack Warner himself had requested), and a number of other cuts to speed the movie along. There was also one other major difference between the two versions: the name of Gibson's dog.

Gibson's dog was called Nigger. There was no pejorative implication; it was simply the fact that he was a black Labrador retriever, and at that time (and for many years afterwards in Britain) the word was in common use as an adjective to qualify a colour such as brown or black. The dog's name presented no issues to any of the people involved in writing or producing the film in the UK – in fact, it is used very freely in the final version of the film – nor did it crop up as an issue in any of the reviews. But the sensitivities to the word were obviously much greater in the US, so the film was overdubbed to change the dog's name, to Trigger. Indeed, the sensitivities were such that they even extended to the publicity material prepared for the film. In a section of the PR hand-out that discussed how the welfare of the dog had been handled on set, a draft section was amended to exclude the dog's name and replace it with the formulation 'the canine actor'.[102]

The film was released in the US in July, inevitably to relatively muted applause. In the UK, by contrast, the film remained a great success, topping the box-office charts for 1955, and over the years, establishing itself as one of the great British war films of all time. As for Sherriff, it took him 'to the top of the world with the film studios'. From then on, he wrote, 'in those golden years, I could write anything

I wanted to.'[103] Unfortunately, none of those subsequent scripts would ever be produced, meaning that, at the very height of his powers, he had just attended the premiere of one of his own new films for the very last time.[104]

Mary Stuart

Sherriff had started preparations on the Mary, Queen of Scots film (or *Mary Stuart*,[105] as it was subsequently titled) in a very similar way to his work on *St Helena* – simply reading through biographies and plays about the subject,[106] and setting down a 'series of events in chronological order which will form the basis of a structure'.[107] Within a few weeks he and Gotfurt had embarked on a series of meetings that would continue from June all the way through until the beginning of November,[108] during which time Sherriff produced, in late July, a 'Scenario' (although it looks much more like a screenplay), and then a final completed script on 17 November.[109]

The early sections of the script are excellent, presenting a wonderfully vivid account of Mary – pretty, smart, talented and strong-minded. She is shown as loving her young French husband, and reinforcing him in his kingly duties, and she herself is seen as embracing the duties and status of her role with some relish. The early scenes are by far the most engaging, because by the mid-point of the script (which, at 240 pages, is on the long side) it begins to get lost in the weeds of Scottish politics. Nevertheless, there are some excellent character portraits: Bothwell, in particular, is a magnetic presence on the page. Mary's half-brother James, and Darnley, are much less sympathetic, but still very well-written characters whom it is easy to picture on screen.[110]

Sadly, however, their characters would never make it off the page, and Sherriff grew increasingly puzzled about the lack of action on the studio's part. In September 1957, he asked his agent, Bob Fenn, to make discreet enquiries. The studio had been enthusiastic about the final screenplay, he noted, but there had been dead silence ever since. 'It is very depressing to do such work under these conditions,' he grumbled. No satisfactory answer seems to have been forthcoming. He would probably have grumbled even more if he had known that Robert Clark, a strong supporter of the project, would, in January 1958, be replaced as executive in charge of production at Elstree (although moving to a different role in the company), having upset Jack Warner with what were perceived to be his anti-American sympathies.[111] In due course, the studio sold off the rights to Sherriff's screenplay[112] for just £2,000, considerably less than the £5,000 they had paid him for writing it.[113]

Deluge

Before finishing on *Mary Stuart*, Sherriff had picked up another commission from Michael Balcon. His Ealing Studios had found some success in the late 1940s and early 1950s (especially for the comedies to which its name is now indelibly attached), but had been rather adrift ever since. Now Balcon announced a major tie-up with MGM in which MGM would provide worldwide distribution, and the major portion of the finance, and also the studios in London where the films would be shot. One of the films that was front and centre when the new tie-up was announced was *Dunkirk*, to be written by Sherriff. He was a very obvious choice for the job. He had the success of *The Dam Busters* behind him, he was on very good terms with Michael Balcon, and the director of the film would be Leslie Norman, the man with whom had worked on *The Night My Number Came Up*. The contract was signed in early October, and the screenplay was to be completed by the beginning of March.

Just as he was beginning work on the new script, however, he received a surprising message from Val Gielgud at the BBC, asking what he thought of the BBC hosting a Sherriff festival on the radio, in the same way as they had previously hosted festivals for two other prominent writers – Somerset Maugham and J.B. Priestley. This would be quite an honour, marking, as Sherriff later noted, the 'high tide' of his playwriting.

The Priestley festival had included six radio dramas, as well as an eight-part serial based on one of his books (*Angel Pavement*). For Sherriff's festival they envisaged new (radio) productions of five of his existing plays: *Journey's End*, *Badger's Green*, *Miss Mabel*, *The White Carnation*, and *Home at Seven*.[114] In addition, Gielgud expressed the BBC's hope that he would be willing to write a brand new radio play, which would be prominently featured as the highlight of the whole affair.[115]

Sherriff was delighted, but also a little overwhelmed, as he tried to sketch out for Gielgud what his next few months would look like:

> What I plan to do is this. I am under contract to write the story of Dunkirk for Ealing Studios, and this will take me to the beginning of March. I shall then accept no further assignments so that I can give all my time to the new play, and anything else which you want me to do for the festival, such as adaptations etc.[116]

They must have been difficult words to write, because he had also been sounded out by Betty Box[117] and Ralph Thomas, working for Rank at Pinewood Studios, about preparing the screenplay for another Nevil Shute novel, *Requiem for a Wren*. He told Nevil Shute at lunch that he would love to do it, but only if they could wait. As luck would have it, they could.

Just when it appeared that his cup was already running over, it was topped up by the BBC yet again – this time on the television side. Shortly before Christmas they approached him with the suggestion that they broadcast *The Hopkins Manuscript* on television the following year, in six episodes of thirty minutes each. They were prepared to pay a fee of £250 for the permission to broadcast, and for Sherriff's help in adapting the book. This was nothing compared to the money he could obtain from a screenplay, but he was keen to see the book adapted: 'Ever since you made the radio version with Eric Portman I have thought what a good television play it ought to make,' he told Ayton Whitaker.[118]

Dunkirk

Over Christmas 1955, and into the early part of 1956, Sherriff's main focus was *Dunkirk*. This was not a simple adaptation, for he was challenged with devising a storyline from the various accounts that were already available.[119] The difficulty he faced was how to dramatise an event that was relatively short (lasting a couple of weeks at its peak), but featured a variety of different military forces, and resulted from a number of complex political and military factors. Early on in the process he sketched out a possible treatment, focusing on four men: Viscount Gort (the commander-in-chief at the time); a colonel of an infantry regiment; a lance corporal separated, with four of his men, from his own regiment; and the owner of a small cabin cruiser who sails to France to help pick the men up. His aim was to 'hold an even balance between the strategic side of the campaign and the human side.'[120]

By mid-February he was writing to H.E. Alexander (literary editor at Ealing), explaining that he was anticipating delivery around early March, as the contract had envisaged.[121] He was uneasy, because, in contrast with the close way in which he had worked with Gotfurt on the *Mary Stuart* story, he was operating in something of a vacuum, since Michael Balcon was in America for part of the time, and Leslie Norman in Australia.[122] Nevertheless, he finished the first draft of the *Dunkirk* script at the beginning of March, as he had promised.[123] It was broadly in line with his earlier treatment, except that Gort was no longer featured, the story now focusing on the three other men; it did an impressive job of conveying the events that led up to the evacuation at Dunkirk, as well as the organisation behind taking the men off the beaches.

After receiving the script, Balcon wrote a memo to Norman with a number of criticisms, most of which can be boiled down to the view that the script took too long to get going (much of the early part explored the strategic build-up to the conflict); that characterisation was too limited, and left too late (for example, much time is spent at the beginning with the colonel, who then does not feature until towards the very end); and that there was an absence of any significant Belgian or French perspective. He also felt that the owner of the cabin cruiser (Thompson) was initially shown as too smug and complacent, when 'at the time of Dunkirk there was a realisation of the position and one felt the first real stirring of the soul of the nation.'[124] The script contained only two female characters, neither of whom had much to do, but Balcon was not troubled by that: 'There are no women characters of any importance,' he noted, 'and in my view the women of the period should be symbolised.'

Sherriff responded to the criticisms that had been made of the script by writing some notes explaining his approach, choosing (intriguingly, given Laurence Thompson's critique of *The Dam Busters* script) to assert that the last thing he wanted was 'an Albert Memorial with the characters placed around it as symbolic statues'.[125] He took on the criticisms one by one and made a stout defence of his script, while remaining open to ways in which it could be improved. Overall he set out not just a cogent case for the screenplay he had written, but almost a manual of his approach to screenwriting, and it is well worth reading in that context.

At that point the discussion between Sherriff and the producers came to a halt, at least for a couple of months, since everything went quiet at the Ealing end. At the end of July, Sherriff seems to have written to Ealing summarising his position regarding the script. Having heard nothing from them since he sent them his notes in May, he would now see his job as largely complete, except that he would be happy to do further work on the script if required, provided it could be fitted around his existing work. He received a reply from H.E. Alexander, reminding him that his contract committed him to be available for revisions and further work, and then informing him that the studio were now hiring David Divine (who had already written a book on Dunkirk) to help write another draft, and that 'when this is ready we would like to send it to you for your comments and any additional scenes and dialogue that may be required.'[126] Sherriff's agent, Bob Fenn, was not impressed, finding it 'most unreasonable' that they should expect him to work on someone else's draft script, which might bear no resemblance to his original:

> We should point out that as the circumstances which prevented you from completing the screenplay at the time were not of your making, you can only be called upon to 'make such minor alterations and additions as they may reasonably require' as per your contract.[127]

Two weeks later, Fenn told Sherriff that Ealing were 'disturbed by your reaction not to do further work', but he felt that they were now prepared to be more reasonable, and it might be worth his while agreeing to do some work on the new script, if only to maintain his relationship with Michael Balcon.[128]

At that point, Sherriff was on holiday, staying at the Royal Crescent Hotel in Brighton, which had become a favoured destination for him since he had sold his Bognor home, Sandmartin, at the beginning of 1955.[129] The advantage of staying in Brighton was that the journey back to Esher was easy and short, and when he closeted himself there (usually to concentrate on his writing), he could make occasional trips home to deal with his correspondence. On this occasion he returned to find Fenn's letter waiting for him. He was extremely unhappy with Ealing, feeling that he had delivered the script as promised, and that it was not his fault if it had taken them months to decide it was not what they wanted, by which time he had moved on to other work. He felt they were being extremely unreasonable in expecting him to drop everything at their command.

> I can't write [the letter] for you to show the Ealing Studio at the moment because it needs some thought, and certainly some restraint because I am very angry at the way this thing has been handled by Ealing and some of the things are quite unforgivable.[130]

A month later, he was no nearer the emollient letter Fenn was after:

> I will write you a letter to give to Ealing when I have time, but I am terribly busy just now. I ought to warn you that it won't be a pleasant letter because I will have to say exactly what I think. The whole thing was the most disappointing and unpleasant experience I have had in all these years of screen writing.[131]

Dunkirk eventually went ahead without any further involvement from Sherriff. The film was released in 1958, to good box-office and favourable reviews. It starred John Mills as Binns (Sherriff's lance corporal character, although designated a corporal in the film), and Richard Attenborough as one of the small boat skippers (although not the same character as Sherriff had delineated, and curiously, one who was even less committed to the war effort than the Thompson character that Balcon had criticised). Interestingly, the film was much more negative about the failures that lay behind the disaster than Sherriff had been, and omitted most of the positive examples that Sherriff had included to demonstrate the Navy's organisation behind the small flotillas. Despite having criticised Sherriff for not including the Belgian and French perspectives, the film largely skipped over them as well.

Hard at Work

After sending Ealing his notes in May, Sherriff was able to concentrate rather more on the new play (although his work on the TV adaptation of *Hopkins* was proceeding alongside). The story was one that he seems to have had in mind since 1949, when he had contacted the minister of an East End parish, the Reverend D.H. (Peter) Booth, to ask his help in exploring the juvenile court system. What he seems to have had in mind was a story about a clergyman who intercedes on behalf of a young offender, and thereafter tries to help him see the error of his ways. It had elements of *Another Year* contained within it, but focusing more on the boy's path this time. During the months since hearing about the festival he had been researching the story in more detail, with visits to the London Police Court Mission, and to the Approved School it ran, known as the Cotswold School. He also made visits to the juvenile courts near his home to make sure his play was accurate in all its details. This quest for accuracy was very much a part of all of Sherriff's writing.

Early in July, despite all the distractions of *Hopkins* and *Dunkirk*, the first act of the play was ready to send to Val Gielgud. He cautioned that he was writing it as a stage play, because that was the form that came most naturally to him, but that meant it would probably be about two hours in length, which might be longer than Gielgud wanted. He was also having trouble with the title (he never was good with titles), having rejected *The Needle's Eye* as too suggestive of a parable, which was something he was very eager to avoid.[132] He also sent a copy to Canon Booth (with whom he had kept in contact, owing to Booth's interest in the theatre), asking if he would read it over: 'I needn't ask you not to pull your punches and would like you to go for it like the sourest dramatic critic.'[133]

By the time he came back from his holiday in Brighton, the play was nearing completion, although it was not yet finished because *Hopkins* continued to get in the way. To complicate matters, another previously postponed project was hurtling towards him. Earlier in the year he had agreed to script an adaptation of Alistair MacLean's first novel, *HMS Ulysses*, for Associated British. This was set to be a prestige project for the studio, and, when agreeing to the work, the tentative start date had been fixed as 1 July. As work had begun to pile up he had pushed the start date back to 1 September – but he knew that it could be postponed no further: it was likely to be a complex project, and he had to make a start. So now he was juggling three jobs, but the most time critical was the new play, and he was greatly relieved when it was finally done, although it had been a 'heart-aching job' to cut it down for broadcast: 'the BBC are adamant that ninety minutes is the proper length for a play unless it be a Third Programme classic.'[134]

The Telescope[135]

This play is set, in all three of its acts, in the study of St Mark's Vicarage, Canbury,[136] in London's Dockland. It is the story of a young clergyman (John Mayfield) who comes to the neglected parish of Canbury in the East End of London, motivated by the desire to atone for the sins of his family, whose activities in trade and commerce had built the area, while exploiting the local inhabitants. Like Roger Matthews, he finds the parish struggling, controlled by a church board run by an objectionable elderly lady (in this case, Miss Fortescue), and he spends some of his time trudging the streets to encourage people to come to the church.

Mayfield is visited by the mother of Joe Palmer, a young hooligan, who asks him to attend the Juvenile Court to speak on behalf of her son, who is accused of stealing a bike. Mayfield is reluctant (he does not know the boy) but is curious, and goes along. The chairman of the magistrates agrees that the boy can avoid being sent to Approved School if Mayfield stands surety for him, which means he has to visit Mayfield on a regular basis. As the weeks go by, Mayfield cannot connect to the boy and begins to feel he has failed, but when Mayfield's wife lets the boy use a telescope to view the ships on the river, he is transformed. The promise of a berth on a training ship excites him even more, and the vicar and his wife feel they are finally getting through to him.

Everything seems to be going well and Joe is about to leave for the training ship, when a policeman makes an appearance asking Joe's whereabouts the previous night, when a telescope was stolen from a local junk shop. Joe, who took the telescope, asks the vicar to cover for him, otherwise he will not go to the training ship. But the vicar refuses, insisting that Joe tell the truth, for if he lied his way to the ship, he would just be a phoney. The play ends with Joe taken into custody and railing at the vicar.

The BBC Festival

The Telescope was first broadcast on 31 October 1956, and the BBC trumpeted it as a 'world premiere' (which Sherriff found 'rather pretentious … could we not just leave it by saying "the first performance of a new play"?').[137] Before that had come five of his previous plays, in chronological order, on successive Wednesdays, beginning with *Journey's End* on 26 September.[138] Each play (except the latest) was prefaced by a short talk by Sherriff, explaining its background and history, and he also contributed an introductory article to the *Radio Times* about the need to maintain the theatre, given its role as a testing ground for new playwrights and actors.[139] Nor was his fiction neglected, for *The Fortnight in September* was adapted to be read, aptly enough, in September.

At the end of the festival, Val Gielgud passed him some listener feedback that the BBC had commissioned, and he was very gratified to see that *The Telescope* had held its own.[140] He had been worried that such a difficult subject, with such a downbeat ending (which Peter Booth had described as 'rather strong meat'),[141] would not attract the average listener, and yet the BBC figures showed that the actual audience for the play, at 11 per cent of the adult population of the UK, was higher than for any other in the festival.[142]

The most popular play of the festival, entirely unsurprisingly, was *Journey's End*, but *The Telescope* was, along with *Home at Seven*, the second most popular, followed, in sequence, by *Miss Mabel*, *Long Sunset* and then *Badger's Green* in last place.[143] The feedback contained summaries of listener responses that highlighted a wide range of viewpoints. There were some who had found it a damp squib, and were unsure of the author's intentions, but they were in the minority. Far more had found it absorbing, and also felt that it had tackled a difficult topic very well. But even among those who enjoyed the play there was some dissension, especially about the way in which Sherriff had brought the play to its conclusion.

The dissension was not so much about the quality of the ending, but about whether John Mayfield had done the right thing in handing young Joe over to the police. Sherriff would not have been upset that people took issue with the resolution he had offered, since that is exactly the type of disagreement he would have invited. And besides, the people whose opinions he respected, whose advice he had taken in its construction (like Canon Booth, or Morley Jacob, at the London Police Court Mission) told him that they liked the ending, and that it rang true. He was especially pleased to receive a complimentary letter from C.A. Joyce, the head of the Cotswold School, 'because of all people, you are the one to judge,' replied Sherriff. He went on: 'What you have said encourages me to go right ahead with the plan to extend the story to cover the boy's experience at an Approved School. I shall be talking to the television people in a few days.'[144]

If *The Long Sunset* was Sherriff's favourite play, *The Telescope* is his most committed. He clearly sympathised deeply with boys like Joe, who turn to the bad due to parental neglect. His desire to steer boys on the right path can be seen from the moment he came back to Down House Farm and set up a camp for boys (used, in the first instance, by a reverend at Southwark Cathedral, as it happens),[145] which he then wanted to turn into a fully fledged Scout camp. He had first become interested in the subject when writing *Another Year*, and since then had been thinking about how he might be able to help, even reaching out to the Cotswold School to offer to set up a rowing programme (a scheme that foundered on the rocks of impracticality). The research he had done in the youth courts and at the Cotswold School had obviously struck a chord, and his willingness to write a television series about young Joe at the school was much less about his desire for another commission, than it was to tell the stories of boys like Joe, and the institutions to which they are sent. Nothing came of the plans, unfortunately, for it would have been an interesting programme to watch, but Sherriff was very clear from the moment *The Telescope* was broadcast that he was going to refashion it as a play, and see it performed on stage. This, at least, was something practical he could do for boys like Joe.

A Long Way Down

The year 1956 had been glorious for Sherriff. He had seen his two most recent films nominated for BAFTA awards, and although they had lost out to *The Ladykillers*, *The Dam Busters* had cemented its reputation as one of the best British war movies of the time. He had written a well received new play and the BBC's festival of his work represented the absolute pinnacle of his reputation as a dramatist.

The year had not been blemish free, however, and the sting of his disagreement with Balcon at Ealing would linger long enough that he would never work with him again. He had also been working steadily on the script for *The Hopkins Manuscript*, passing the finished product back to the BBC, only to find they were still dragging their feet about a production date. But he was confident it would come, and in the meantime he had more than enough movie work to be going on with. He was very much in demand, and work on *HMS Ulysses* was well in hand, while Rank were waiting in the wings with a contract for *Requiem for a Wren*, whenever he was ready to start.

But there was a worm in the apple of his success, for in May 1956 the staid 1950s theatre world had been rocked by a new play, written by John Osborne, called *Look Back in Anger*. This would be the first of many plays by a number of new playwrights – the 'angry young men' – that would explore themes and individuals very different from those that Sherriff and his contemporaries had portrayed on stage. Sitting in his library at Rosebriars at the end of 1956, revelling in the acclaim that his work had received, and with a schedule full of current and prospective projects, he had no idea of just how much things might change for him in the years ahead.

Chapter 13

Curtain, 1956–75

Thou hast embarked, thou hast made the voyage, thou art come to shore; get out.
Marcus Aurelius, *The Meditations*, Book III.

There was no holiday for Sherriff during Christmas and New Year 1956: he was much too busy for that.

The most important job was the adaptation of HMS *Ulysses*. Alistair MacLean's first novel was published, to enormous acclaim, in the autumn of 1955, and Robert Clark quickly snapped up the rights to his fellow Scot's book for £30,000.[1] The story is that of a light cruiser, escort of an arctic convoy headed to Murmansk. En route they encounter the many perils of the crossing, including a fierce storm and enemy ships, U-boats and aircraft. Almost all of the convoy ships are sunk, and HMS *Ulysses* sacrifices itself attempting to ram a German cruiser. The action in the book is raw and brutal but its authenticity was never in doubt, given MacLean's wartime service in the Navy.

The project was an important one for Associated British, as can be seen from a report in the *Scottish Daily Mail* (obviously a puff piece from the studio) on 5 January, which raised it as a potential successor to *The Dam Busters*. Two weeks later came a publicity still in *Today's Cinema*, showing Sherriff and Clark at Elstree, alongside Gotfurt, Bill Whittaker, W. Collins (from the book's publishers) and Admiral Sir Robert Burnett, who was acting as the film's naval advisor.

The naval aspects of the film made the going difficult for Sherriff: he could not simply adapt the novel as it stood, but had regularly to conference on the technical details with the film's advisors and producers. As early as October 1956, he was telling Ayton Whitaker that 'At present I am being chased about by Associated British Pictures. I have kept them waiting many months while I wrote the television play and I have got to give them everything now and this includes numerous talks with technical advisers on naval affairs.'[2] Four months later, he was still complaining: 'At the moment I am up to my eyes in the screenplay for *HMS Ulysses*, with all manner of experts and naval specialists sending in advice.'[3]

One of the problems was that he was still working on *The Telescope*, trying to recover it from its radio shape, and make it look like a stage play once more. Gladys Day at Curtis Brown had already circulated it to the repertory companies, many of whom were interested, although she complained that, as ever, she did not have enough copies to send out. She encouraged Sherriff to have some photocopies made, but he initially baulked at the cost, suggesting instead that they wait for the script to be published by Elek Books (who had also published *The Long Sunset*). But that would take months,[4] so Sherriff hurried along with his redraft. The main changes were twofold: first, about twenty minutes of acting time had been pruned (although the structure remained the same); second, the final two scenes were now to be played as one, avoiding what would have been a curtain drop followed by a very short last scene. Sherriff explained the cuts to Peter Booth when he sent him a copy of the play, 'all nicely washed and brushed up for the theatre'.[5] He promised him that, while Bryan Bailey at Guildford would have the honour of the first repertory performance, Booth could enjoy the accolade of staging the first amateur production in Brighton, on 26 April.

All the while, *Hopkins* rumbled on in the background. Although the original thought had been that it might form a six-part series, Sherriff and the BBC (in the form of Ayton Whitaker, script editor Donald Wilson and BBC Head of Drama, Michael Barry) had come to an understanding that it might fit better into two ninety-minute episodes, presented a week apart. That was certainly the understanding as late as November 1956, but just a month later, the plan had changed, and it was now to be produced as a 'whole play in one evening'.[6] Despite the pressures of *Ulysses*, and his own misgivings about the impact the cuts might have on the continuity and build-up of the piece itself, Sherriff spent several long evenings in December trying to hack the piece into shape. Back it went to the BBC, and by the end of January, Whitaker was able to return it to him as a single, two-hour play, while still suggesting it might be twenty minutes too long.[7] Sherriff was not happy and wrote bluntly to Whitaker (which must have been difficult, since he considered him a friend):

> I spent weeks of time writing and revising this work, giving it the greatest care, and it will be most disappointing and depressing if the whole of this work now gets thrown down the drain and the play just becomes a slick piece of science fiction in which the characters play second fiddle to the events.[8]

Gielgud Calls

Curiously, not long after he had fired this broadside off to the BBC's television department, he received a welcome letter from Val Gielgud, who was in the market for new plays, specifically written for radio. He was very much hoping that Sherriff might be able to offer an idea or two.[9]

The basic premise was that the play should be completely new (and not an adaptation), between sixty to ninety minutes long, and be of a theme and style that would be appropriate to a BBC Monday night Home Service audience: in return, the BBC would pay a fee of £500 for the rights to three radio broadcasts. All other rights would remain with the author. This all sounded perfect to Sherriff, who was toying with a new idea for a play anyway. His only caveat was that he was unlikely to be able to deliver the play by 30 September, which is what Gielgud had requested. He was very close to finishing his work on *Ulysses*, but thereafter would start immediately on *Requiem for a Wren*, which would take him through until August.[10] Gielgud was obviously keen to have his old friend involved, airily swatting away concerns about the timing, and offering him a two-month extension, to the end of November. Sherriff's recent radio ventures had been very successful, and it would likely add some lustre to the new series if he were to be involved.[11]

Sherriff's resilience has to be admired. Having wrestled with the BBC for months over *The Hopkins Manuscript* – a book that he was very proud of, and was keen to see adapted, and thus a project to which he was absolutely committed and had given many hours of his time without any financial recompense (beyond the initial fee) – it would have been only natural if he had sent Gielgud away with a flea in his ear. But he was never one to hold a grudge. He did his work, and he did it as well as he could. If people asked for changes (in moving from one medium to another, for example), he would do his best to accommodate them. If writers at other organisations wanted to amend his work, he was not precious or over-protective, although he did like to be given approval, to prevent damage being done to his original concept. But he was generally willing to listen to criticisms, and respond where necessary, and always behave in a professional way. If he had difficulties with one part of the BBC on one project, there was no reason why that should have an impact on his work elsewhere. It was in part his resilience that resulted in a steady flow of work coming his way: if he had been perturbed every time someone requested an alteration with which he disagreed, the number of movie companies with which he might have worked would have dwindled rapidly.

On 1 April he sent off the final scenes of *Ulysses* to Associated British, but quite what he sent off is unknown: no copy of the script appears to exist. A few months later, having heard nothing from them, he asked his agent what was happening (he had thought it was going to be a 'big and very expensive picture',[12] after all), but no answer seems to have been forthcoming. Nor was there to be any further public acknowledgement by ABPC until 1959, by which time Robert Clark had been replaced as head of production at Elstree by Bill Whittaker, and the project was listed as one of a number of movies that the company had committed to making that year (indeed, was seen as the most significant of them):

> Britain's film studios are booming back into big business. And last night a new proof came that cinemas are beating the slump. It was from the powerful Associated-British company at Elstree. … Epics include *HMS Ulysses* scripted by R.C. Sherriff.[13]

Later that year it would be described in the trade press as 'one of the largest to be undertaken by the company'.[14] Again, though, the publicity proved premature: the film never made it into production, and about a decade later, Associated British sold the rights on. The film has still never been made.[15]

Barely pausing for breath, Sherriff moved on to *Requiem for a Wren*, although he had already had a number of conferences with Box and Thomas, and with Joyce Briggs, the story editor. The novel was first published by Heinemann in 1955 and is the story of Alan Duncan, a lawyer returning to his native Australia, to find his parents' housekeeper has committed suicide. On delving deeper he finds that the woman had been the former girlfriend of his (deceased) brother Bill, a girl for whom Alan had searched after the war. She, tormented by guilt from killings during the war, had come to her dead boyfriend's parents' home as some kind of atonement, but hearing that Alan would be returning, and might reveal her secret, she commits suicide. It is far from a happy tale, but vivid, and with plenty of potential cinematic incidents. After beginning work on the script Sherriff had taken advantage of some holiday time to tour locations on the south coast that might be of use in the film. He seemed happy in the work – it was clearly less technical than the *Ulysses* story, and Shute was an author with whom he obviously had a connection (he had already adapted two of his novels for the screen),[16] and it seems that they may have been friendly enough that Shute even invited him to Australia for a six-month tour, although Sherriff declined.[17]

Sherriff carried on working on *Requiem* until mid-August, when he delivered the script to Joyce Briggs, along with an accompanying note, which, reading between the lines of a letter to his agent, intimated that he would be willing to undertake revisions, but only for a certain period after delivery of the script (he was keen to avoid, he wrote, 'a repetition of that awful *Dunkirk* affair'). *Requiem* is, however, another of those scripts that no longer appears to exist, and was never made into a movie. But the studio must have liked his work, for he was quickly signed to another contract by Joyce Briggs at Rank – this time for *Gold in the Sky*, another Max Catto thriller, which he would begin in the New Year.

On Stage Again

A month before he had finished work on *Ulysses*, and picked up his pencil on *Requiem*, Sherriff had written to Peter Booth in Brighton, telling him that the plans of Guildford Rep to stage *The Telescope* in April had become 'somewhat ambitious', and that, knowing it would by now be too late for him to change his plans, would he mind not advertising it too widely: 'If, for instance, you were to give a story to a London paper it would take the edge off the repertory production, and as they have to earn a living under precarious conditions, I would like to let them have this little extra fillip in calling it the "premiere".'[18] Booth was happy to oblige, and nothing seems to have made its way to the London press, despite the fact that, according to Sherriff, the St Peter's Players 'made a fine job of the play, and I was very glad to see you get an immediate response with a full house on Saturday night [the second and final night of performances].'[19]

The main event, of course, was still to come, for the play opened in Guildford on 13 May as part of an interesting experiment, part funded by the Arts Council. Four repertory companies were involved, each performing one play for a week at the home of each repertory company. Guildford Rep would thus play *The Telescope* first in their home theatre for a week, and then for a week at three venues in Canterbury, Hornchurch and Salisbury.[20] Shortly afterwards, the BBC co-operated with the festival by giving the radio play another outing on the Home Service on 8 June.

The reviews for the play, in Guildford and beyond, were generally very positive, balancing criticism of the obvious radio origins of the first two acts, with strong praise for the power of the final act:

The climax … is fine theatre, and not the less so when Mr Sherriff in the end leaves the vicar in the air, without an answer to his accuser, without even the curtain line to himself. Sheer sincerity here turns what is provisional to good effect. The play comes alive because the author at last speaks up frankly.[21]

The *Birmingham Post*[22] called the last act 'truthful and fine, and "uncompromising" theatre into the bargain'. J.C. Trewin[23] noted that Sherriff's 'sincerity, vigour, shrewdness and theatrical command are all present here', while *The Daily Telegraph*[24] reviewer found the play 'a deeply absorbing discussion of Christian values in a commercial society … [arising] neatly out of a strong and moving little story'. The most deeply gratifying review came in *The Manchester Guardian*:

Having given us two acts of mild domestic drama … [Sherriff] suddenly changes pace. The third act has the savagery and brute force of *A View from the Bridge*. And when the curtain rings down on its tragic, yet inevitable ending, Mr Sherriff has achieved the catharsis we have come to expect from Mr Arthur Miller.[25]

Sherriff was not the only one singled out for praise, however. There was unanimity about the quality of Bryan Bailey's production: 'Excellent', wrote *The Telegraph*, while Tynan (who, unusually, preferred the first two acts to the third, which he called 'vinegar-sour') felt it had a 'polished oaken gleam' throughout.[26] The acting was generally held to be first-rate as well, especially Edward Woodward as Mayfield, the vicar, and Melvyn Hayes as Joe. *The Guardian*, in passing, pointed out one additional benefit that accrued to the Guildford production, which was that, because the theatre operated as a club theatre, it 'remained outside the strictures of the Lord Chamberlain' – which meant that the language in the last act (Joe: 'They always said you'd let me down, you bastard. You dirty bastard.') did not need to be censored for the performance.

After the play had completed its run at Guildford, Bryan Bailey wrote to let Sherriff know that it had produced the best box office they'd ever had in May, and also the best box office of any new play,[27] so very quickly he tried to capitalise on the play's success by alerting his film industry contacts.[28] He also wrote to Michael Barry at the BBC, noting that 'If you were thinking about a television performance with this company, then it would have my full support,' although 'the only provision I would make is that it would be a normal ninety-minute broadcast.'[29]

Hopkins on His Mind

As the summer wore on, Sherriff kept trying to develop opportunities for *The Telescope*, and worked steadily on *Requiem*, which he finished by mid-August. But throughout the period, *The Hopkins Manuscript* was never far away from his thoughts.

For a year he had been in discussions with George Kamm at Pan Books about a reprint of the book. Originally, the idea had been a straightforward reprint, but Sherriff had become convinced that, with the upsurge in interest in space, it might be better to rework the book, 'shortening and streamlining'[30] it, and bringing it into a size more suitable for a Pan publication. Even before he was fully engaged in his revisions, however, he received word from Donald Wilson at the BBC that they had yet to finalise the script for the two-hour version of *Hopkins*, promising something as soon as possible, but alerting him to the fact that the production date might well be pushed back further.[31] There was then silence for a few weeks until, on 16 August, Wilson wrote apologetically to Sherriff's agent, Bob Fenn, saying that, despite his best efforts, and those of his staff, he had been reluctantly forced to cancel the project.[32]

Fenn passed Wilson's letter on to Sherriff with a note saying that he felt they had no redress under the contract, which clearly stated that 'after the initial payment to you there would be no further financial obligation.'[33] Shortly afterwards, Michael Barry sent his own letter to Sherriff, apologising for the cancellation of the adaptation, and trying to explain what had gone wrong. Sherriff replied to Barry that it may simply have been that everyone had been 'thinking in too ambitious a way', and hoped it might be done in a simpler way, but it was not to be.

Sherriff had always known that he was taking a risk with the work he put into the BBC version, but he did it because of his commitment to the story – one of his favourites that he always felt could be well dramatised, on TV or on film – and because he felt that a successful dramatisation would open the way up to more book sales, and possibly the sale of the film rights. He could not understand why they had changed their minds: 'It still puzzles me, because in all our talks, extending over a year, I was continually assured that they definitely meant to do it, and that was why I went on working at it, giving so much of my time.'[35]

Swallowing his disappointment, he turned to the redrafting of the original book and quickly made progress, reporting to George Kamm by the end of September that he had removed about thirty pages from the first seventy. By early in October, he had finished his editing on the book, now entitled *The Cataclysm*, trimming, by his count, some sixty pages. Most of the cuts were just in detail – side events, for example, which illuminated the rather petty and pompous nature of Edgar's character, or much of the early scene-setting material. One noteworthy exclusion is the Foreword from the Addis Ababa research institution, which makes the extent of the 'Cataclysm' a little less instantly obvious: it was a nice touch in the original book. Generally, the cut-down version, although it fitted more neatly within the covers of a Pan book, has the feel of being slightly chopped up, a little less smoothly flowing than the original, which is undoubtedly the better book. It would be published a year later, on 8 November 1958, to critical indifference, but at least, from Sherriff's perspective, it would finally be back in print.

Having finished his editing work, Sherriff's resilience made him return to the fray with Michael Barry, whom he informed about the new book, prefacing his remarks with a wonderfully passive-aggressive (and funny) question:

> Apropos the *Hopkins* script that you sent me the other day, who is the ardent young critic who has sprinkled my carefully composed intentions with rude epithets? ... In this particular case he has missed the purpose of the lines so entirely that I'm sure his appeal to Jesus would fall upon deaf ears.[36]

Clearly Sherriff was still aggrieved at the treatment of his work by the BBC, but he was nevertheless willing to try again:

> The news of the past week [the launch of Sputnik] has given so much topical interest to it that it seems well worth going on with. ... I am sure that the ideas we recently discussed are not beyond reach of a competent writer, and if you can let one of your people do it, I will gladly give all the help I can.

Seventy-Five and No More

It seems, however, that Sherriff was not destined to see eye to eye with Mr Barry, for at the same time as he was again trying to promote *Hopkins* to him, he was tussling on another front: the television adaptation of *The Telescope*, which was due to be broadcast on 5 November. Sherriff had made his opinion on the broadcast very clear, when writing to Bryan Bailey in June:

> I hope the television production will be done, with all the company who have played through the festival. There should not be much problem in preparing

a television version because it could follow very closely upon the one used in sound radio, which was a ninety-minute production.[37]

Ayton Whitaker was in touch with both Sherriff and Bailey in cutting the script during the summer, but by the end of September, having cut the play to seventy-nine minutes, Sherriff was questioning the wisdom of cutting the play further, having already cut it 'to the bone'.[38]

> If my cutting was so massive as to bring it down to seventy-nine minutes, then I achieved more than I expected, but if an attempt is made to cut four more minutes, then I think the thing will draw perilously near the point of disintegrating into a series of mutilated scenes.

When a letter from Barry made it clear he wouldn't budge[39], Sherriff reluctantly acquiesced:

> Concerning *The Telescope*, I have agreed, with considerable foreboding, to granting a licence for a seventy-five minute production, when, strictly speaking, it ought to receive the normal ninety minutes to give it a proper chance. But had I withheld the licence, it would have been a great disappointment to the Guildford Theatre Company, and after all, as they gave such a good stage performance, I think they deserve the opportunity to appear in it on television.[40]

The reviews were again generally favourable, but the cuts were noticed ('That the play had been ruthlessly slashed was glaringly obvious'),[41] as was the fact that it had originally been devised for radio, 'so there was little for the actors to do in the way of action.'[42] Nevertheless, it was seen as 'eminently viewable',[43] and generating a 'true tension'.[44] After being briefed by the BBC, Sherriff seemed very happy with the whole affair, as he told Peter Booth:

> *The Telescope* seems to have had a very big audience and the results were most interesting. Some people thought it was a bore and a waste of time, saying they have had enough of Teddy Boys in the documentaries (this was regardless of the fact that every attempt was made to show that Joe was not a Teddy Boy!). There were some letters from clergymen who were indignant at the suggestion that the Church was not all that it should be in the East End, but I think we had a good majority in our favour. Joyce wrote a most enthusiastic letter about it. He had a large audience of his delinquent boys looking in with him at the Cotswold School, and Joyce tells me that their unanimous verdict was that Joe deserved all he got![45]

The TV production neatly dovetailed with the publication of the play in the Elek Books *Plays of the Year* volume; Samuel French were rushing through a version that the amateurs and the reps could use; and Sherriff was still trying to hawk the play round the film companies. But the most curious development of all came when he was approached by Peter Powell, who had produced the play in Birmingham, and was interested in producing a musical version: he had already succeeded in interesting The Players Theatre in the idea, and also the composer Antony Hopkins in writing the music. Sherriff wrote to Gladys Day, slightly bemused at the idea:

> It all sounds very odd, but the last thing I ever want to do is to discourage anybody from doing something they are enthusiastic about, and I have told him to go ahead with the best of luck and see what happens.[46]

Over the following months there would be various contractual details to iron out, but to all intents and purposes, Powell had been given the green light, and a musical version of *The Telescope* would soon be in the works.

Cards with Uncle Tom

Even while he was editing *The Telescope* and *The Cataclysm*,[47] Sherriff had been working hard on the radio play, now called *Cards With Uncle Tom*,[48] which he had promised Val Gielgud back in the spring. He had sent a first draft to the BBC at the end of September, but as it was a legal drama, they would have to take advice from their lawyers. Almost inevitably, given the pattern of the rest of his dealings with the BBC during the year, he was also advised that it was too long, which alarmed him, because 'I was patting myself on the back about the close cutting and pruning I had done for the final version.'[49]

A five-page report came back from the corporation's solicitor, and Gielgud sent it on with word that they had timed the play, and it needed to be cut by at least ten minutes, and probably a little more, to allow a margin of safety.[50] On the suggestion of the solicitor, Sherriff went along to see Mr J.P. Eddy, a barrister who was accustomed to giving advice on plays and films, and was relieved to find that there were no overwhelming problems, and to receive some very helpful suggestions on the language that might be used by the judges and barristers in the play. On 12 December, not long after his meeting with Eddy, he was told that the production date had been set for 2 February. Setting to work quickly on his final revisions,[51] he was able to put the final script into Gielgud's hands by 4 January.

Sherriff set out the first part of the plot very cogently, in an earlier letter to Eddy:

> A young man named Edward Bradley is suspected of a murder and is questioned by the police. He did not, in fact, commit the murder and is in no real danger of arrest because he has a cast-iron alibi. He was actually playing cards with

his uncle, and two of his uncle's friends, when the murder happened. Two servants in his uncle's house also saw him there at the time in question. There are therefore five people who can speak on his behalf. He only has to inform the police of this to clear himself.

But he happens to be a freelance journalist by trade and it occurs to him that he can provide himself with an excellent (and financially valuable) story if he allows himself to be arrested, tried and convicted of the crime. He can do this by refusing to give any account of his whereabouts at the time of the murder, and by arranging with his uncle, and the other witnesses, not to come forward with proof of his innocence until after he has been convicted.[52]

Bradley arranges that the others will make depositions testifying to the fact that they were with him at the time of the murder, and then, when he is nearing the date of his execution, the statements can be brought forth, exonerating him, and providing him with the material for a best-selling book. Unfortunately for him, things take an entirely different turn from what he has planned. A week before his scheduled execution, he tells the police he did not do the crime, and that his uncle, and his friends and servants, can verify his account, and have already done so in legally binding documents. But when the police approach his uncle, he maintains that Edward was not with him on the night; his friends also say they were not there; and his servants have left the country and cannot be contacted. Edward pleads with his uncle, who replies that Edward must be delusional to think such things. In the absence of any corroboration, Edward is executed, leaving Uncle Tom to receive a sizeable inheritance that had been held in trust for Edward, some of which he shares with his two card-playing friends.

Sherriff was pleased by the reaction of the public: '[The play] appears to have been well received over sound radio the other night, judging from the number of letters which have come in,'[53] although there were also quite a number who had written 'rather indignant that the old uncle got away with it'.[54] He was straightaway in contact with Curtis Brown to see whether there might be interest in foreign broadcasts, or in the film rights. But he did not simply wish to part with the play for a fee: 'I have got a lot of ideas about the story, and would not want to sell it unless I can hold some rights in it myself, including the screenplay.'[55] Fenn advised him that, given the state of the British movie industry, none of the big players were likely to be interested, so the best he might hope for was a small budget producer, or perhaps television.[56] A few weeks later, the BBC duly expressed interest in a TV adaptation, which Sherriff was content to authorise, but 'I would ask that it is a ninety-minute version because I don't think the story could be cut down so drastically to seventy-five minutes without damage.'[57] Alas, he would be disappointed once again.

Back to the Big Screen

On 1 January, Sherriff had started his adaptation of *Gold in the Sky* for Pinewood Studios, a story about the attempt by a professor, his daughter and a mining engineer to salvage the eponymous airliner from a swamp in the Congo, and float it downriver to Tanganyika.

On 17 January, he wrote to Teddy Baird, the film's producer, commenting:

> The story is original and exciting, and full of opportunity. The whole enterprise of salvaging the aircraft from the swamp, and the sequence of events upon the river, right through to the final achievement, makes an odyssey that could scarcely be bettered for the screen.[58]

But the characters (and there were only three significant ones) were unbelievable, and no decent reason was given why they were in the jungle in the first place, nor why they would embark on such a massive enterprise. To compound matters, their constant bickering (especially between the daughter and the mining engineer) was tedious. But Sherriff had a solution, which was to keep the basic story of the aircraft being floated downriver, but to widen the cast of characters by making several passengers in the stricken aircraft part of an archaeological expedition to find a lost city in the jungle. By this means he could populate the film with a number of quite different individuals, each with a particular talent that would be important in the enterprise. 'The interplay of the various characters would provide the light and shade to the story. Divided counsels may bring them near disaster and add to the natural difficulties of the enterprise.'

After about six weeks, Sherriff reported to Joyce Briggs that things were going well with the script, but the initial deadline (21 April) was looking tight: 'As you know, I am having to construct an almost entirely new story around the central idea, with new characters and a new development, which means … that the screenplay is taking rather longer than usual.' Could he have a three-week extension? Briggs agreed; the delivery date was pushed back to 21 May.

That presented another problem, however, which was that it now overlapped with the start date on another screenplay that he was taking on for producer David Henley, on behalf of British Lion, namely, the story of William the Conqueror. He had already spent six weeks at the end of 1957 on a treatment for the play, and after some discussion the basic structure had been agreed, allowing him to begin work on the full screenplay on 1 May. That same day he reassured Bob Fenn that the overlap looked worse than it was: in fact, he was only correcting the final draft of *Gold in the Sky*, 'and work on *The Conqueror* can go right ahead.'[59] In practice, the delivery time slipped a few weeks further still, so that it was eventually dated 13 June.

The final script of *Gold in the Sky*[60] would have made a first-rate adventure movie, although thanks to all of Sherriff's invention, it had moved some considerable distance from the book. But it was another that disappeared into the film company's files, never to make it into production. When, at the end of 1957, the film was announced as part of the Pinewood slate for 1958, it was noted that 'there is a large schedule out of which twenty films will finally be set for … production.'[61] Since it would probably have been one of the most expensive, it might have been felt prudent to direct resources elsewhere, but it is impossible to know.

William the Conqueror

The producer of the film at British Lion was to be Steven Pallos, a Budapest-born émigré with an undistinguished track record, and Henley told Sherriff that Pallos and British Lion were happy with the treatment, although they hoped that 'the historical aspect will be the background and the people will dominate the scenes'.[62] This, of course, was a concern familiar to Sherriff from some of his previous movies (he may have recalled Zanuck and Litvak's concerns about This Above All being a movie about two people in England, not England with two people in it), but he reassured Henley that he would write the 'whole story in terms of human endeavour', although he was worried that 'some people may exert pressure upon you, and upon me, to cut down everything of the historical background to make room for flirtations of unimportant characters.'[63]

After some further discussion, Sherriff eventually started work on the screenplay on 1 May, and during the following months produced a script[64] that is lively and engaging, with a number of highly cinematic scenes hung around a fairly straightforward account of William's life. It begins when his father has to secure the services of a tanner's daughter to provide him with a bastard heir, moving through the many revolts he faced initially (in part because of his lack of royal blood), his subsequent mastery of Normandy, and finally his invasion of England. It is altogether too respectful of its principal characters (who are generally portrayed as thoughtful and considerate, although William does show the odd display of temper), and the narrative is linear and largely unabsorbing (we know from the outset that it will end with William's victory at Hastings). Nevertheless, there are some very well-executed scenes: his brutality at Alençon, for example, when he cut off, and then catapulted into the town, the hands and feet of those who had tried to resist him; his destruction of the army of the French king's brother by the use of massed archers; his whipping of Matilda of Flanders, the woman he had intended for his wife; and the preparations for the invasion of England and its subsequent successful resolution. The script provides quite detailed accounts of the mundane details attached to preparations for battle or invasion, and he exhibits a relish in his knowledge of the detail of mediaeval warfare and provisioning. Historical detail clearly always fascinated him, and would be put to good use some years later, in a boys' book about a mediaeval siege.[65]

One rather personal element jumps out from the script, where he considers William's apparent disinterest in girls. There is no suggestion that he is gay, just that, to a certain point, he had been interested in other pursuits (soldiering, or hunting, for example), and could not share the interest for women that he observed among his young friends. He has a short speech with Lanfranc, a famously devout and celibate cleric, where he laments their lack of passion:

> What's wrong with us, Lanfranc? – with all of us who have been dukes of Normandy? – Most of us have had the vigour of a dozen men – and passion, too: passion for war and hunting and drink and gambling ... but for women? ... it seems as if some curse has been put upon us that drains away our passions to these other things: that leaves us cold and dead to the one desire that most men call the supreme happiness of all.

For William, the passion surges shortly afterwards when he meets Matilda of Flanders, who will become his wife. But for Sherriff, the passionless condition, which he described with such understanding, would never change.

As ever, the writing process took him longer than he had originally envisaged, and he had to ask the studio for an extension from the original end of August deadline. Towards the end of September, he was reassuring Henley that it would be with him in a couple of weeks, but Henley was urging him to move quicker, since a competing project had sprung up in Hollywood. He finally delivered the script on 23 October, and Henley wrote back quickly saying he liked it, and that the challenge now was to find the appropriate director. Thereafter, Sherriff could only wait to hear how Henley's efforts were going, and he would have been pleased to see some press interest early in 1959, when Pallos announced that they were seeking American partners:

> We had to get an American company interested because of the high cost. If it were only £500,000, we could do it easily on our own, but it will cost one and a half million. R.C. Sherriff has written a wonderful script.[66]

A few months later, Henley said that he and Sydney Box had been to New York to sign a contract to have the film made for an American company, so it looked as though progress was being made.[67] But six months later, Henley was reporting that the American company had merged with MGM, so no longer had their own slate, and he was in the process of trying to buy back the rights to the film.[68] At that point, the mists envelop the movie and it slowly disappears without trace.

The Play's Still the Thing

Sherriff had been glad to polish off *The Conqueror* script, for he was keen to get to work on a new stage play, and he only had a small window of opportunity, for another screenplay was beckoning in the new year – an adaptation of Mika Waltari's *The*

Dark Angel, which had been offered to him by Italian producer Dino De Laurentiis (with whom he had briefly worked on *War and Peace*). He also had a rather loose commitment to write a play for Bernard Miles, who was on the verge of launching The Mermaid theatre in the City of London.

Miles and Sherriff had been in contact since the beginning of the year, when Sherriff had first visited the building site that would become The Mermaid (which still stands in Puddle Dock in the City today). Miles was searching for a play that might get the theatre off to a flying start, and they discussed constructing an episodic structure around the basic story of a school in the City that develops through the ages. This appealed greatly to Sherriff, but as he was swamped with other work, he put it on the back burner, promising to read around the subject before putting pencil to paper. He progressed far enough that he was able to offer a scene to Miles by the end of 1958 (which he liked very much), but thereafter counselled that, with his forthcoming work for De Laurentiis, progress would be slow for a while. He wouldn't be putting the play 'up on the shelf'; it wasn't the kind of play he could 'sit down and work on night by night like an ordinary play, because every scene needs an awful lot of thinking out and reading up before it is written.'[69] Of course, if he didn't sit down and write it night by night, it might never be fully written, which seems to have happened, since it exists in Sherriff's papers only as an incomplete version of a play, and as a novel, entitled *The School*.[70]

He made more progress with the other play, which was of a much more conventional type, and by the end of the year he had finished the first two acts, although it remained untitled. At that point he reported to John Barber, in the drama department at Curtis Brown, that he would have to put the play aside for a little, for his 'holiday from screenwriting'[71] had ended, and he was about to embark on the treatment of *Dark Angel* for De Laurentiis. The last act would not take him long, he felt, for it was already fairly clear in his mind,[72] but in the meantime he would take the chance to obtain some advice about the behaviour of the solicitor in the first two acts: 'I have trained up my own lawyer, Kenneth Ewart, to advise me on these things.'[73] As well as roping in Barber as a critic, he also sent a copy to Archie Batty, who had been so helpful with advice on his late 1940s–early '50s plays, and he was delighted (and relieved, he told Batty)[74] when both he and Barber told him how much they liked it.

Dark Angel

On 1 January 1959, Sherriff began work on *The Dark Angel*, a historical novel by Mika Waltari, set during the siege of Constantinople in 1453. The novel is in the form of a diary, written by the hero, John Angelos (in Waltari's original Finnish, the title is *Johannes Angelos*), and it combines a detailed and dramatic account of the city's fall, and a love story between the mysterious Angelos and Anna Notaras, daughter of Lukas Notaras, the Lord High Admiral of the city. The novel is very complex, especially because the character of Angelos himself is so slippery – his background is very mysterious, and it is never clear which side he is really on – but the love story is at the very heart of the characters' motivations and beliefs, and thus of the book itself.

Bearing that in mind, it is not entirely surprising that the project would become one of the most difficult that Sherriff had ever undertaken: it was absolutely ripe for a conflict between a highly cultured producer who wanted to use the love story to explore important philosophical and religious issues, and a writer who was much more fascinated by the historical and mechanical details of a mediaeval siege.

It all started off well enough. Just after Christmas, De Laurentiis sent Sherriff a long memo outlining his ideas about the picture, and above all letting him know that he would like to be sympathetic to the Turkish besiegers, and not just because he was hoping to have the co-operation of the Turkish army and navy.[75] Sherriff replied, agreeing that this was not a struggle between Christian and 'infidel', or right against wrong: 'I would, in fact, prefer to leave religion entirely out of it so far as it concerns a conflict between different faiths. This story is a conflict between men rather than between rival theologies.'[76] He also suggested that, while the love story was absolutely integral to the book, it could not occupy as much space on the screen, because he also wanted to 'capture the mystery and romance surrounding a great city besieged'.

He finished his initial treatment at the end of February, and a couple of weeks later received a four-page memo in return: he cannot have been optimistic when, from the very first paragraph, De Laurentiis made it clear that he had found the screenplay lacking in drama from the very beginning. His particular complaint was that the string of events portrayed in the screenplay completely missed out on converting the dark and tragic atmosphere that had influenced him to make a picture of the book in the first place.[77] A further letter a few days later asked him to think hard about the three-cornered relationship between John, Anna and Anna's father, and although he apologised for upending Sherriff's carefully constructed treatment, he suggested that it might give him the chance to improve it.[78]

At this point, Sherriff was not quite sure how to proceed. The contract had three stages: treatment, first draft screenplay, and final screenplay, and Sherriff suggested that, if they could not hash out their ideas in face-to-face conferences, perhaps it would be better if the initial draft were written in Italy (where De Laurentiis was based), with an Italian writer he trusted. Sherriff could then come in at a later stage, when the framework was in place. De Laurentiis declined the offer, instead sending Ivo Perilli to London to act as his representative in discussions with Sherriff. The conferences seemed to go well and soon enough Sherriff was able to begin on the screenplay, finishing the first half by mid-June, and the whole thing by the end of August.[79] He sent it off quite confidently, feeling that it embodied all the earlier criticisms, and fully reflected everything that had come up in discussion with Perilli (in fact, perhaps too fully, because, at 206 pages, it was really much too long).

He would have been unpleasantly surprised when, a month later, De Laurentiis wrote to him telling him just how much he disliked the screenplay. He saw no way in which it could possibly be livened up, the main problem being that he had spent too much time on the setting, the history, and the clash of civilisations, and not nearly enough time on the love story between Anna and Angelos. He seemed to think that Sherriff had put in the foreground the conditions of the time, relegating the love story to the background, although that was what most people would be interested in. His first draft was a very long way from what was wanted.[80]

There was no way back from this, and Sherriff tried politely to bow out. There was clearly no point in him preparing a final screenplay, when the draft was so unloved, so he suggested that they now view the contract as complete, and De Laurentiis pay him solely for the treatment and first draft screenplay. In a spirit of co-operation, however, he also offered to look over any subsequent drafts that De Laurentiis might commission from other writers, and even 'bring the dialogue into shape for the English or American actors who will play the parts.'[81] De Laurentiis was not inclined to be co-operative, however, telling Sherriff that he did not see any way in which the screenplay might be amended or used as the basis for another screenplay, and hinting that Sherriff had not lived up to the terms of the contract.[82] But Sherriff was not having it. He had produced the treatment and screenplay, after extensive discussion, and if it turned out that it was not what was wanted, that was unfortunate, but not his fault. He had lived up to his part of the deal, and De Laurentiis should do likewise, and he was willing to take legal action if that was necessary.[83] Whether he did or not is unclear, but he received a final settlement payment of £1,000 in March 1960, bringing the whole saga – which he had found very unpleasant – to a welcome end.[84]

New Plays

Back in March, when he had just sent *Dark Angel* over to Italy, he had taken the chance to start work on the final act of the untitled play that he had sent to Barber and Batty for comment. By the end of the month, he despatched the last act and Archie Batty responded immediately:

> I think the third act is STUPENDOUS! I may say I took a dose of digitalis before reading it [he had a heart condition] and very nearly had to take another when I came to the curtain. ... I could hardly breathe when I came to the end, but then I am probably not a very good example, because I find difficulty in breathing in any case.[85]

Even as he began working on the *Dark Angel* screenplay again, he kept working on the play, and was happily able to send a fully revised version to Curtis Brown on 1 May. By now it finally had a title: *The Strip of Steel* (although by the time it was first performed, that had been changed to *A Shred of Evidence*). As soon as Curtis Brown got hold of the script they sent it to Paul Clift, who instantly expressed an interest in producing it, but although he had been fairly confident that he could put the production in place quite quickly, it took him longer to find the right people than he had expected, and so for a while things went quiet on that front.

That was just as well, because as well as grappling with De Laurentiis, Sherriff was engaged in another no–holds–barred bout with the BBC, over the fate of the televised version of *Cards with Uncle Tom*. After leaving the play in the corporation's hands in April 1958, he had kept well away, until approached for his comments, later in the summer, by Donald Bull, the scriptwriter attached to the project. Sherriff was not happy with the changes Bull had made, and proposed various alternatives, resulting in a series of discussions lasting all the way through to November, when Sherriff, feeling that his views had been incorporated, left it to Bull to wrap things up. They renewed their exchange in March 1959, and when Sherriff saw the latest version of the script he was again unhappy, and decided to pull the plug entirely. He told Bull that he had been thinking of preparing a short series of television plays,[86] and that he now intended to include *Uncle Tom* as one of them, but 'I will tell my agents that, as the BBC were first to ask for the story, they shall have first refusal of my script.'[87]

He had probably been hard at work on the adaptation already (notwithstanding the demands of *Dark Angel*), because just two weeks later he was writing to his agent enclosing a copy, and asking him to let the BBC have first refusal.[88] He quickly received word from Donald Wilson that he and Michael Barry very much liked it and wanted to buy it. Sherriff was happy to sell it to them as long as the contract specifically stated that the script was subject to his approval. This they were happy to do. The biggest difference relative to the radio version was at the end, where, to prevent Uncle Tom getting away with it, there is a denouement in which the governor of the prison tricks him into giving himself away, shortly after he has visited Edward in his cell. That would at least prevent the kind of letters they had received in protest on the previous occasion.

Uncle Tom was broadcast on 8 September, with an impressive cast, including Eric Porter as Bradley, and Ronald Leigh-Hunt as the detective superintendent. It earned some very good reviews: the *Liverpool Post* called Sherriff a 'thriller writer of considerable ingenuity',[89] while *The Listener* called it 'an expertly carpentered thriller'.[90] *The Yorkshire Post*, although disappointed in the twist at the end, felt it 'provided a first-class model for a production designed to hold an audience to the very end',[91] much the same sentiment as *The Sheffield Star* ('[it] immediately captured enough interest to banish any thought of switching over.')[92] Like several of his plays before, however, the reception in the provinces was much more favourable than in London, where some of the papers were not impressed, calling it 'unconvincing and old-fashioned',[93] and, even worse, a thriller that didn't thrill.[94]

1960

Sherriff's last few years had largely been disappointing. Not a single movie script – of which there had been several, some of high status, and many of good quality – had made it into production since *The Dam Busters*. It was not his fault, of course, that the British film industry was in some disarray, with revenues down and fierce competition from the two national TV networks. But even though Sherriff would have been aware of the economic woes of the industry, it must still have been galling to spend so much time and effort, just to see the results disappear high upon a shelf. At least, since the troubles with Ealing, the people with whom he had been dealing in the British film industry – especially those at Rank and Associated British – had been congenial colleagues, with whom he had been able to work productively and well. The same could not be said, of course, of De Laurentiis, and whether because of that experience, or just because he was becoming a little bit old fashioned and out of touch (many of his contacts moving on or retiring), it would be three years before he would script another movie.

His experiences with the BBC had also been mixed, with enjoyment on the radio side, which had now broadcast three premieres of his plays, balanced by some difficult experiences on the TV side, especially the whole unrewarding saga of *The Hopkins Manuscript*.

But the plays had done well. The festival in 1956 had been a great success, and the transfer of *The Telescope* to the stage had been better than he might have hoped. There were no film offers in the wings for any of his new plays, nor were there likely to be given the problems in the industry, but he could count himself satisfied that the past few years had reaffirmed his credentials as a dramatist. Hopefully, 1960 would do the same, because in the early months of the year there were to be three high-profile Sherriff productions.

The first was a TV revival of *Journey's End*, on 6 March. Next would come the premiere of the musical version of *The Telescope* (now named *Johnny the Priest*), which would premiere at the Wimbledon Theatre on 25 March, before moving on to The Princes Theatre on 19 April. Finally, and probably the most important from Sherriff's point of view, would come the rollout of the new play, starting in Brighton on 28 March, and taking in Bournemouth, Oxford and Blackpool before its West End debut at the Duchess Theatre on 27 April. This was another of those periods when everything seemed to be coming up Sherriff.

On 6 March 1960, the BBC Sunday Night play was *Journey's End*, featuring Richard Johnson as Stanhope, Joseph O'Conor as Osborne, Derrick Sherwin as Raleigh, and Peter Sallis as Hardy. The play went down well, as always, with George Bishop noting that the presentation 'showed how little his 30-year-old play ... has dated.'[95] *Johnny the Priest*, however, was conspicuously *not* a success. There was little coverage of its try-out fortnight in Wimbledon, but the critics were out in force at the Princes Theatre, and tore into it like a pack of hungry wolves. Its biggest flaw, it would appear, was that it was not *West Side Story*, for which the blame was laid at composer Antony Hopkins' feet, Sherriff's basic story being seen as strong enough to sustain a musical adaptation. Reynolds castigated Hopkins for not including a 'single hummable tune', but it is much too unfair: the soundtrack still exists, and is markedly better than the critics suggested, even if it is not quite in the same league as Bernstein's classic. There was praise from one or two quarters – *The Sunday Times* in particular, which called the play 'remarkable'[96] and the ending 'very fine', while also commending Jeremy Brett as the clergyman and Stephanie Voss as his wife. But the consensus of the critics was so damning that the show shut down on 30 April, after a run of just eleven days, costing its backers some £25,000.[97]

A Shred of Evidence

Three days after *Johnny* opened in Wimbledon, Sherriff's new play arrived in Brighton for its opening night. It is the story of Richard Medway, a successful middle-aged businessman who fears that, driving home drunk from a rugby club dinner, he may have knocked a man off his bicycle and killed him.

The play is of the mystery-thriller type,[98] as Sherriff would call it. Medway is shown in the first act as happy and successful, with a younger son (whom we never see) at prep school, and a daughter who is keen to go to Oxford to study to be an archaeologist. A prospective promotion permits him to pay for her course, and sign his son up for Winchester. All is looking good, until he hears a news report that a man had been killed by a car early that morning – coincidentally, on a stretch of road that he may have used, and at a time when he may have been using it.

Medway knows he drove home drunk, but remembers little of the drive home. As circumstantial evidence mounts, appearing to implicate him, he takes action to dispose of what might be incriminating evidence, and to seek the assurance of the two people he had driven home that they will say nothing of his inebriation, which he fears would be taken as an indicator of guilt by the police, since he already had two drink-driving convictions on his record. One of the passengers, Captain Foster, was a good friend, and assures him he will say nothing incriminating; but he barely knows the other man, Bennett, and when it appears possible that Medway might have been involved in the crash, Bennett and his domineering wife seek to blackmail him to ensure their silence. On the advice of a solicitor friend he refuses to pay, so they take their suspicions to the police. In doing so, however, they make the mistake of taking with them a strip of steel that had fallen from Medway's car when he collided with a lamp post outside their house – the very strip that Medway had noticed was missing, and which he feared he might have left at the scene of the collision with the bicycle, if he had been involved – thus effectively allaying his fears. When the police inspector passes the strip of steel to him he also confirms that the crash had involved another car, and he is exonerated. He decides to take his wife and daughter to the local restaurant to celebrate, but in opting to take his car, he suggests he might not yet fully have absorbed the lesson about drink-driving.

The tour reviews were generally positive but those in the West End were more mixed, with a clear division emerging between those who appreciated the older-fashioned dramas, and those in the more modern camp. J.C. Trewin was clearly one of the former, comparing the play with two other newcomers (Ionesco's *Rhinoceros* (with Laurence Olivier) and Pinter's *The Caretaker*) and finding firmly in favour of *Shred* ('exciting and touching').[99] Irving Wardle in *The Observer*[100] acknowledged that the characters were cardboard, and had his complaints about the daughter especially, but 'once under way the plot exerts a fair grip.' *The Star*[101] found Sherriff's second West End first night in eight days 'exciting', while Paul Rogers is 'brilliant, as the man tormented by fear. ... Round the shred of evidence has been woven an exciting play.' To the *News Chronicle* it was 'neat, quiet and absorbing'[102]; *The Manchester Guardian*[103] found it 'entertainment of quite good value, well-constructed, well-timed, holding its punches nicely'; and Bill Darlington, while unhappy with 'a certain dryness in the working out of the earlier parts of the play', found that 'the all-important last act comes fully to life.'[104]

Against these generally favourable reviews can be set a few stinkers, mainly reflecting a change in the view of what made good drama. *Drama* magazine felt it old-fashioned:

Very likely, back in 1930, this harmless little play might have been thought an excellent discussion of an urgent moral problem. In 1960, however, its cosy evasiveness, the absolute certainty of a happy ending, its twists of plot which take the place of exploration of character, leave us cold.[105]

Unlike Trewin, *The Sunday Times* felt that the comparison with more modern plays did Sherriff few favours: 'After the fantasies of Ionesco and Pinter, R.C. Sherriff's doggedly realistic little play impresses, if at all, only by its total lack of connection with reality.'[106] The *Daily Mail* took much the same view, although was a bit more entertaining in getting there:

Ideas? Characters? Not for one moment. ... Cardboard! ... There is so much interminable waffle about the roads to and from Guildford, Effingham, Bookham, Ripley and Godalming that anyone still not discouraged from seeing this play is well advised to bring a set of road maps. ... PS While this dodo was being offered for inspection, another new play, Harold Pinter's *The Caretaker*, was being presented for the first time at the Arts Theatre.[107]

The play stayed at the Duchess for four weeks, before transferring to the Fortune Theatre, where the *Daily Express* reported that 'business was good. Except possibly in the bar. ... During the play's one-month run at the Duchess it was noted that the bar business during the intervals declined'[108] (all that drink-drive discussion, they surmised). Maybe it was the shortage of bar takings, but the play only lasted two more weeks before it slipped from the West End altogether. But that was far from the end of it. Just as had happened with some of Sherriff's previous plays (especially *The White Carnation*), it went on to great success throughout the rest of the country. From July 1960 to October 1961 (with a short gap over Christmas and New Year), the play was performed in sixty separate venues, usually for a week at a time, but sometimes for longer, raking in over £2,000 in royalties for Sherriff – including £190 royalties from several weeks worth of performances in Butlin's camps. It might not have been the play of tomorrow (or even, for some critics, of today), but it was certainly the type of play that was popular with the public and would remain popular with the reps and amateurs for some time to come.

Old Friends

While *Shred of Evidence* was touring the country, Sherriff was busy with other work – so busy, in fact, that he even turned down a request from the BBC for a specially commissioned radio piece: 'I would like to write another original play for sound broadcast ... but I am rather tied up at the moment, finishing off a novel, and I've got to get on with a play for the theatre which I am behind with.'[109] The novel would eventually become *The Wells of St Mary's*, and would be published in 1962. The play was most probably *The Siege of Ogburn Manor*, which he started thinking about before the year was out, but which would be in development for some time, and would never make it to stage or screen.

As his new work was proceeding, he was also tied up with prospective productions of his previous plays, and two in particular: a newly revised *Badger's Green* at the Wimbledon Theatre and *The Long Sunset* at The Mermaid. The latter would involve less of his time, since Miles would make most of the changes himself, but the production of *Badger's Green* gave him the chance to take another go at the play, which was something he had been wanting to do for some time.

Peter Haddon was the man in charge of Wimbledon Theatre, and Sherriff had been talking to him since April the previous year, telling him how keen he was to make a new edition of the play. Within a couple of months he had revised most of the play, summarising the changes for Haddon. The doctor was now a man torn by doubt, whereas before he had the same certitude as the major (who was unchanged); the boy and the girl were now given their own points of view, to prevent them being quite so colourless as before; Twigg was now 'not such a complete simpleton'; and – probably most interestingly – the girl was now Butler's daughter instead of his secretary, and had a much more active part to play (in fact, in large part, the development becomes her idea). The interesting aspect to the changes is that, in some respects, it moves the play closer to the dynamics of *Mr Birdie's Finger*, particularly in what he does with Joan.

By December, Sherriff was again writing to Haddon to let him know his thoughts about the third act. In *Mr Birdie* the act was played in the doctor's study; in *Badger's Green* it was moved to a marquee; but now he envisaged splitting the stage between the doctor's study and part of the village green, so that the scoreboard, and scorer's table and some spectators could now be seen. This seemed an ingenious way of bringing the action onstage to some extent, while minimising the work (and cost) involved in a major scene change.

The first performance of the newly 'washed and brushed-up'[110] *Badger's Green* was given on 5 June 1961, and Sherriff was sufficiently enthusiastic about his revision of the play to offer Peter Haddon a share of any royalties (in the end, an equal share) that accrued from the production being picked up by other repertory companies (which it was). He was also enthusiastic about the production, sending a telegram to Haddon (who was then at Weston Super Mare) that 'Your company at Wimbledon did a beautiful job last night.'[111] In subsequent correspondence he lamented that the play, which had gone down very well with the audience, would be unlikely to get an outing in the West End, so 'I put my faith in the provinces.'[112] He also put his faith in the amateurs, and encouraged Samuel French (partly through foregoing some of his royalties) to scrap their copies of the existing version, and replace them with the brand new version (which, because it now involved no change of scenery, he was confident would be much more popular).

Over at The Mermaid, Bernard Miles was making a number of small changes to *The Long Sunset*, but his primary concern, as he put it to Sherriff, was to 'detrivialise a couple of hundred expressions in the play, retaining the speeches completely except for paring away these manifestations of the trivial.'[113] But there was also one other interesting, and rather significant, change that he wished to make: at the end, when Sherriff has Julian and Serena take their picnic to the woods, to await their inevitable deaths, Miles preferred instead to suggest they might try to make for Winchester so 'we can … be left at the end with grave doubts, but some hopes.'[114] Sherriff's reaction was very positive, feeling that it was all of a part with Julian's character to remain strong to the end. He even compared the 'hope with grave doubts' idea to the closing scene of *Journey's End*:

> The men in the dugout strapped on their equipment and went out into the darkness to meet an overwhelming attack. I don't know what happened to them and never shall, and this is rather how I feel about Julian and Serena.[115]

As the production approached, Sherriff made additional changes to the play, mostly of a minor nature, but it is indicative of his willingness to absorb criticism and suggestion, and to revise constantly, that he was willing to put in the time, unpaid of course, to make the changes. Unfortunately, no revised version of the play exists, because it was never a strong enough favourite with the amateurs to make a new version worthwhile. The reviews of the performance were rather more mixed than they had been at Birmingham (the acting was generally not well regarded), and there were still criticisms of some of the dialogue, but on the other hand, some of the speeches (especially Julian's in praise of Rome) were singled out, deservedly, for special praise, and he would have been content with Bernard Levin's encapsulation: '*The Long Sunset* is a remarkable piece of work.'[116]

The Wells of St Mary's

Sherriff was completing *The Wells of St Mary's* around the time that he was revising *Badger's Green*, with which it has a few similarities, although it also has echoes of *Miss Mabel* in its examination of people's willingness to compromise their principles in the service of an apparently greater good.

The story is told, in a first person narrative, in a manner reminiscent of Edgar Hopkins, although the character of the hero, in this case Peter Joyce, is much more congenial. Peter's family have long been important in the area, but their landholdings have gradually been trimmed due to economic hardship, but they still retain an old well, which, even in Roman times, had a reputation for healing waters. Peter invites an old friend to stay with him (Colin, now Lord Colindale), a formerly vigorous man, a newspaper magnate who had been a national figure during the war (the parallels with Beaverbrook are obvious), but who was now crippled with rheumatism. While staying with Peter, Colin drinks the water from the well and is miraculously cured.

In due course, his cure becomes known, and there is a surge of interest in the well and the town, which the local mayor (and pub owner) is keen to harness. He organises the town to get together to form a public company, with Peter as chairman, and everyone in the town invests, with the money being used to build up all the facilities, and construct a casino. While everything seems to be progressing, the old man whom Peter had employed to look after the well tells the board that the water had actually dried up long ago, but that he had arranged for a local plumber to pipe water in from the neighbouring duck pond. He tells them that, for a price, he is willing to remain silent.

Shockingly, the old man is murdered, probably by someone on the board, the members of which now face the dilemma of whether to report what they know of the motive for the murder, and whether to declare that the water is from a duck pond, thus potentially ruining everyone in the town who has contributed to the company's share capital. Each of the members gradually finds a way to come to terms with their connivance in the deception, and the murderer is never officially discovered, although the mayor privately confesses to Peter. The casino is launched and the well is a huge success but Peter ends his narration waiting for some disease to arise from the duck pond water, thus bringing the whole edifice crashing down around him.

Sherriff once again hits a bullseye with his examination of a group of small-town citizens, examining each member of the board individually to highlight foibles and weaknesses. The plot is straightforward, but much of the last third of the book is taken up less by the hunt for the murderer than by an examination of the motivations of the members of the board, and their interactions with each other. It has its moments of humour, but it is also an examination of conscience, individual and collective, albeit with a light touch.

The reviews were not hugely complimentary. The best *The Sunday Telegraph*[117] could say was that it had a good, strong plot, but it cautioned that 'the characters are mere puppets'. *The Sunday Times* described its 'plain-spoken account of the nasty vapours that rise in a small town when a press baron puts it on the map. He entertains, but too casually.'[118] The *Birmingham Mail*,[119] while noting that 'Sherriff, of course, cannot handle any theme dully, and this story has its moments of high tension', found itself wondering if the theme was really the right one for 'the author of those fine plays *Journey's End*, *The Long Sunset* and *Badger's Green?*' *The Northern Echo*[120] countered by noting that 'Mr Sherriff, who drew so attractively the Englishmen of *Badger's Green*, takes his opportunity here and gives us a very entertaining story.' Perhaps the closest to the mark was *John O'London's Weekly*,[121] which recognised a satirical mind at work:

> The style of the narrative is restrained, unfussy and urbane. Mr Sherriff is an expert in understatement by implication. (The whole thing could just happen. Well, couldn't it?) In its own quiet, deceptively casual way, *The Wells of St Mary's* is sharp satire, packing a potent punch indeed.

Still Writing

When the book was published, Sherriff was sixty-seven, and was still writing, if not quite as much as before. But more and more of the projects on which he was engaged seem to have flown from his pen, but never on to the printed page. *The School* was one, on which he corresponded with Bernard Miles from time to time. In fact, Miles expressed a renewed interest in it in 1971,[122] and Sherriff immediately promised to send him a copy of the narrative on which he had been working: but it remains in his files, intriguing, but unpublished.

Then there was the *Ogburn Story* – which started life in 1960 as a potential stage play, before becoming a possible TV play – a tale of a landowner driven to declare his estate an independent nation by the constant demands from government. This was another on which he spent a lot of time, and where the BBC all but promised a production, only to pull the plug after some considerable delay. It exists in his files as both a TV play and as an unpublished novel, some nineteen chapters long.

There were film scripts, too. In December 1961, he had begun discussions with Leonard Key, of the American company Entertainment Industries Ltd, about the possibility of him writing a treatment, and then a screenplay, of *Peter Pan*, with the intention that it would star Audrey Hepburn. But several months later, after he had completed a seventy-page treatment, the project foundered on the withdrawal of the rights by the lawyers of the children's hospital that held them. Sherriff was very frustrated, partly because he longed to take on the subject, but also because he had turned down an alternative screenplay offer when he thought he would be tied up with *Peter Pan*.

There was one other film script, commissioned by his old friend Bill Whittaker at Associated British. The movie was called *Eddie's Acre*, and was intended as a vehicle for comedian Charlie Drake. Discussions seem to have begun early in 1963, and the drafting process carried on through that year and into the next, with the contract structured in the way he preferred: treatment followed by draft screenplay and final version. The story has Charlie Drake as Eddy, the ordinary man, but extraordinary grower of roses, who is the only person in the village who refuses to sell up when a developer comes calling. Like so many others, it never made it into production.

By the time he had finished *Eddie's Acre* in 1964, his screenwriting income had dwindled to almost nothing (which may be one of the reasons he opted to sell his coin collection). But he continued to enjoy significant royalties from his past works, in the form of payments from amateurs and rep companies, and also from TV companies buying the rights to produce his plays on the small screen. As time wore on he appears to have started thinking about writing the autobiography that he had dismissed on so many previous occasions. Correspondence in 1964 and 1965 with Geoffrey Dearmer and Nobby Clark pointed to the fact that he was beginning to try to marshal his thoughts. He was probably also looking back because, by 1964, his 94-year-old mother was beginning to show signs of infirmity, and had to be provided with nursing care at home. It seems safe to assume that his mother's illness both distracted him from his writing, but also encouraged him to think back on the time they had spent together. She died on 31 May 1965, and it may be as well to think that she did so in the manner described in *No Leading Lady*:

For my mother, it was always the garden that counted most, and she grew the more devoted to it as the years went by. One summer evening when she was very old she came for her last walk with me. 'I'm feeling rather tired,' she said. 'I think we will have a rest. We sat by the summerhouse talking of some new planting we would do. I asked her something and she didn't answer. Her eyes were closed, and I thought at first she was dozing. It had happened very peacefully. Had such things been ours to choose, it was the end she would have asked for, sitting out there in the garden in the sunset.'[123]

His mother's death, while a blow, would not have been surprising, especially given her infirmity. But the following year he would likely have been hit hard by the death of his sister Beryl, who died on 18 October, aged seventy-three. We know that they stayed in touch at least throughout the 1950s, when Beryl would sweep into the drive at Rosebriars to visit her mother,[124] and, from Bob's inscription to Tudor, Beryl's husband, in a copy of *No Leading Lady*, we can deduce that the relationship had most likely been maintained.

When his autobiography was published in July 1968, it was very well received, and when he was interviewed on the BBC he was asked, 'Have you still got ideas rattling around in your mind for other plays?' He replied:

> Oh yes – certainly. I think one goes on all the time. I'm writing a book now. I don't want to tell you what it's like, or you'll say it sounds terrible. It's been my habit all my life. You see, when I was in an insurance office there was no time to write until the evening and it used to become such a looked-forward to thing after your supper to go upstairs and shut the door, turn on the light and begin this little journey into the fantasy. And I've never given that up – and to this day I always do that. I don't think I've ever written a word in the daylight.[125]

The book he said he was writing could have been any of the unpublished stories that can still be found in his files, or it may have been an early draft of the final book he ever published, which, rather fittingly, was a children's story about a medieval siege. It was published in 1973.

The Siege of Swayne Castle[126]
The story is set in the time of King John, when Earl Valmont accuses Lord Swayne of treachery so he can seize his lands on the coast, and obtain the harbour his family has coveted for so long. The book is the tale of how the Earl and his mercenaries mount their attacks, and the ingenious ways in which Swayne defends his home, including, among other things, using boiling oil to repel an attack, bolsters to protect his tower from missiles, and foraging expeditions in the quiet of night to defray impending starvation. The Earl is a nasty piece of work: when his teenage son Godfrey is captured by Swayne's men, he would be happy to see him killed. Instead, Godfrey is befriended by Swayne's teenage son Roger, and their conversations tell us much about the Earl, and also about Lord Swayne, who is honest and decent, and loved by his men. Swayne's ingenuity keeps the Earl's men at bay for a while, but he is gradually pushed back into his last remaining refuge, with the prospect of imminent starvation, when suddenly the good news arrives that the Earl has died, and the siege with him.

The book exhibits considerable knowledge on Sherriff's part of the nature of siege warfare, and is a lively page-turner. There is not much plot: an initial set-up, and then the siege itself. The interest lies in the different ways in which the attackers mount their assaults on the castle, and the ways in which Swayne and his forces repel them. The side plot of the relationship between the two boys is uninvolving, because neither boy is convincing as a character. The same is true of the Earl and Swayne himself – there is so much to describe in the siege that Sherriff is forced to draw with a very broad brush, to the detriment of the story. There are only really three other characters of significance: a friar on Swayne's side, and two mercenaries on the Earl's, but they are little more than outlines. Nevertheless, the book has pace and sweeps the reader along with the desire to discover just how Swayne will escape from each of the perils that he faces.

Gollancz managed to place a small piece on the book in *The Sunday Times*, which noted that Sherriff had 'been turning his hand to the theme of war again'. Noting (incorrectly) that it was 'not only his first children's book, but his first work of fiction since the 1930s', it then set out his reasons for writing the book:

> I wanted to write it for myself; it's the sort of book I like. I was fascinated by the idea of the day-to-day life of people under sieges and as far as I know, it's never been treated in the form of a book. ... It's a good adventure story with real people in it. Just the type of book I like to do.[127]

The reviewers expressed their approval of the book. *The Sunday Times* itself was the most positive (so much so, in fact, that the extract went on the paperback version of the book published a couple of years later by William Collins): 'The techniques and tragedies of mediaeval siege can seldom have been described in such a clear-cut, practical way; this exciting one-thing-after-another tale should be spread widely among history-lovers.'[128] *The Tablet* agreed: 'Good on the boiling oil and the battering ram, characterisation a little wooden, exciting plot.'[129]

But there were criticisms too, notably of the Godfrey/Roger relationship: 'There is lots of movement, fighting and intrigue ... but the language is trite and ungainly ... there is no sense of time and place, and therefore no flavour ... the friendship between ... Roger, and Gregory ... carries no conviction,'[130] wrote the *Times Educational Supplement*, and the *Times Literary Supplement* was similarly sceptical: 'Sherriff tells a carefully worked-out story of mediaeval siege warfare with much convincing technical detail. ... But his boys are the schoolboy contemporaries of the young officers of *Journey's End*, with public school inability to show emotion.'[131]

Writing for children suited Sherriff's simple style. His strengths had always lain in description and in dialogue, and his world view was very straightforward. From his very first writings – *Jimmy Lawton* and his memoir, through to his autobiography, he excelled when reporting and recording, but floundered in deeper philosophical waters. He could have been a very successful latter-day G.A. Henty, writing historical stories involving brave young lads. He had, of course, raised with Dwye Evans the possibility of writing more children's stories, and it is to be regretted that he did not receive more encouragement.

The Final Curtain

After his mother died Sherriff was alone in Rosebriars, and seems to have become something of a 'recluse', according to his doctor.[132] Even when he opened his garden to the public, he would remain upstairs in the house until the guests had gone. 'Latterly, almost the only strangers he would accept were the youngsters who came and helped him with his garden, and they would return again and again.'

But although he was alone, by his own account he was never lonely. When John Ellison asked him if being a writer was a lonely life, he replied:

> Oh no – it's crowded with people that you're working with – I mean the characters are all with you, and they're all alive – and most of them are much more interesting than the people would be if I asked them in to supper.[133]

Bob died on 13 November 1975, and was cremated at Randalls Crematorium in Oxshott on 20 November. His ashes were interred in a special chamber set in the wall of St Wilfrid Church in his beloved Selsey, next to those of his mother, which seems entirely fitting.

Conclusion

It is hard to locate the real R.C. Sherriff, for throughout his life he took great pains to hide his true nature. The story he told in *No Leading Lady* was much the same as the story he had told throughout his entire life: a young writer who chanced upon a play that made him a household name, and who ever after was expected to live up to that success, but was often thought to have failed. He ends his autobiography with this exchange:

> The other day I went to give the prizes away at a nearby school. Afterwards there was a little reception, with coffee and cakes. An old lady who brought me a cup of coffee said: 'I did enjoy *Journey's End*, Mr Sherriff. Why don't you write something else?'

If that old lady existed, and it is highly doubtful that she did, she must have led a very sheltered life. From *Journey's End* in 1929 to *The Dam Busters* in 1955, no one could fail to hear when Sherriff had written something new: it was not so much that his writing was always compared with *Journey's End* (although that did happen), it was simply that the fame from *Journey's End* never left, burnished as it was by further successes: well-regarded plays; highly praised novels that shone a revealing light on the lives and attitudes of his social class in the 1920s and 30s; and a clutch of classic movies. Not bad for someone who felt that his headmaster had 'written me off as a flop'.[1]

Of course, he had many setbacks as well, as the blurb for *No Leading Lady* acknowledged:

> His autobiography makes an engrossing tale all the more human because it is not a story of unalloyed triumph … his career as playwright, novelist and screenwriter, like that of most writers, has been a series of ups and downs, of agonising waits for first night notices, and for box-office queues which might, or might not, materialise.

But in the end, his persistence pulled him through. This is not something he dwelt upon in his own account of his life, because it rather contradicts the picture he portrays of the lucky writer stumbling across success in a series of happy accidents. But the real Sherriff was someone who decided when he left the Army (or, possibly, before) that he was going to become a writer; who then worked for several years to perfect his craft; who thereafter worked to master different mediums; and who, whenever he failed at something he had written, would either attempt to improve it, or discard it, move on and try again.

The most obvious example of his persistence is in the saga of the West End production of *Journey's End*. From the play's dismissal by the first two people who read it, through its travails with the Incorporated Stage Society Committee, his willingness to take a chance and send it to George Bernard Shaw, his pursuit of Basil Dean the morning after its success at the Apollo, and his willingness to grasp at the straw provided by Maurice Browne: these were the actions of a man who was willing to do whatever it took to have his work performed. Similarly, at the other end of his career, when he was lucky enough to have the resources to write what pleased him, rather than what he thought audiences might want, he was willing to make the compromises necessary (foregoing royalties, for example, or cutting deeply into his text) to have his work shown on stage, or screen (whether television or cinema). When his work could not find a home in the West End theatre because it was dismissed as old-fashioned, he took it around the provinces, or on to television, or into books. He never stopped writing, and never stopped trying to find ways of bringing that writing to the public's attention.

The source of his resilience is not easy to find, because he was not confident as a child, or a young adult. His letters home, from army training camp, and then from France, are riddled with his insecurities – especially intellectual, but also social, and even sporting (despite his obvious prowess in that regard). Those same insecurities – the fear of not being good enough, of letting people down – may also have been the main source of his nervousness in the trenches: 'Like everyone else I can admit that there were times when I was afraid – but more afraid of being afraid than of the actual danger.'[2] But somewhere over the next few years – perhaps in the context of his growing success with his theatre groups (at first The Adventurers, and then Cymba) – he seems to have acquired an inner confidence that would allow him to continue his work whatever the reaction. As he put it himself, in a newspaper article in 1930:

> The modest, sensitive child has the hardest battle to fight: the fear of others' laughter eats into his simplicity and, unless as time goes by, he develops sufficient courage and sense of humour to face the issue – to say: 'This is the real me and be hanged to you!' – he will lose his simplicity beyond recovery in later years. It is possible to go on presenting an artificial character to the world until we begin to believe it is actually our own.[3]

The other source of his confidence may have been his mother, who obviously had great belief in her son's abilities: she expected much from him, felt that he could make a great success as a writer, and went out of her way to support him at every step in his career. Probably the only first night she ever missed was on Broadway, and she never made that mistake again. Nor did she make the mistake of allowing him to be distracted, accompanying him on every extended trip he ever made. Their exceptionally close relationship is probably also the best explanation for why he remained free from romantic encounters throughout his life: he was perfectly able to forge good working relationships with women, but that was as close as his mother ever allowed.

One thing that hardly changed was his writing style. It is possible to go back to his earliest work of fiction, the *Jimmy Lawton Story*, and find passages that would fit into his final adult novel, *The Wells of St Mary's*. He was admired for never 'over-writing', but at the same time it was that simplicity that gave some critics the chance to dismiss his work as cold, or lacking in drama. Stanhope's outbursts in *Journey's End* are unusual in his own work (rather than his adaptations), which is generally free from melodrama and histrionics. It is true that he tended not to favour deeper philosophical or political issues, but his work serves as a window into the lives and attitudes of the people that he knew best – the middle-class people of his time, the 'little people', as Vernon Bartlett put it, with whom he was able to empathise better than anyone. *Journey's End* was praised for its authenticity at the time, but all of his works – right up to *The Dam Busters* and beyond – share that same characteristic.

Charles Morgan, *The Times* critic who felt that Sherriff's great play would exhibit no 'endurance', would be surprised, no doubt, to see how it has become the most common drama-based interpretation of the First World War: it has been regularly revived in the commercial theatre (most recently in David Grindley's production, which began in the West End in 2004, before touring widely); it immediately became a staple of schools and village halls, making the low-roofed Western Front dugout symbolic of the First World War experience; and it now influences new generations of British schoolchildren through its inclusion in the GCSE syllabus (and, though to a much lesser extent, through its parodic version in *Blackadder Goes Forth*).

And yet, Sherriff's name remains relatively unknown today, a victim, to some extent, of the public's tendency to be relatively unacquainted with the names of the screenwriters of their favourite movies. While writing this book I have often been asked about whom I am writing, and the stares remain blank until I mention the movies: *The Dam Busters* usually produces the first nod of recognition, but other favourites from long ago – *Goodbye, Mr Chips, The Four Feathers, Odd Man Out, Quartet* – transform the nod into a smile. Through his generosity he is remembered at Kingston Grammar School, and in his home Borough of Elmbridge, where the R.C. Sherriff Trust, funded by another of his bequests, has long supported the arts and continues to do so. If this biography succeeds in widening the recognition of his name and his achievements, it will have done its job.

Notes

Introduction
1. Sherriff, R.C., *No Leading Lady*, Gollancz, 1968. Hereafter: *No Leading Lady*.
2. Lucas, M., *The Journey's End Battalion*, Pen & Sword, 2012.
3. Gore-Langton, R., *Journey's End: The Classic War Play Explored*, Oberon Books, 2013.

Chapter 1: Into Uniform
1. The *Jimmy Lawton Story* (JL), p.1. Surrey History Centre (SHC) 2332/3/8/2/3. There are four *Jimmy Lawton* fragments in Sherriff's papers, all with the initial reference 2332/3/8/2. The fragments are, respectively:
    (1) A Brief Chapter, one of the earliest sections written, in August 1917.
    (2) A version written, in good hand, in ink, on foolscap paper. This is the latest version written, incorporating (and extending) much of the other versions, but ending much sooner (chronologically) in Jimmy's adventures.
    (3) This is much the longest version, and the one that is primarily used in the discussion in this chapter. It is written, largely in pencil, in a notebook, and is clearly a first draft of the story. It ends with Jimmy being posted to France.
    (4) Like (3), this is a first draft, and written in pencil in a notebook. It follows on from (3), beginning when Jimmy boards the train to France, and recounts his initial experiences overseas.
2. Letter to Mother, 16 November 1916. SHC 2332/1/1/2/112.
3. *JL*, p.20.
4. *No Leading Lady*, *op. cit.*, p.317.
5. *JL*, p.25.
6. *Ibid*, p.27.
7. *Ibid*, p.27.
8. *No Leading Lady*, *op. cit.*, p.317.
9. *The English Public Schools in the Great War*, contained in *Promise of Greatness: The 1914–18 War*, Panichas, GA., (Ed), Cassell, London, 1968.
10. National Archive Ref: WO339/169081 [C641557].
11. According to Kingston Grammar School staff records, Walter Parker Etches had come to the school in 1907, after ten years of teaching. As well as his duties as second master, he also taught French and German.
12. The opening scene of the later-written fragment of the *Jimmy Lawton Story*. SHC 2332/3/8/2/2.
13. SHC 2332/3/9/2.
14. Letters from G. Leonard Clayton, 13 February 1914 (SHC 2332/1/1/1/2) and 24 April 1914 (SHC 2332/1/1/1/3). This exchange is captured in the *Jimmy Lawton Story*: 'He sought out an old schoolmaster friend of his – he introduced himself to him – the old man smiled and asked him whether he would be a schoolmaster and immediately a new light and a new hope came over his life. Oxford or Cambridge were out of the question – but a degree at London wasn't, and for months he worked quietly in the evenings at his old school books again.' (*JL*, *op. cit.*, p.15.)
15. Despite Sherriff's obvious misgivings about the length of his school career, in fact his record of admission at Kingston Grammar School shows that he was there for eight years, a perfectly average amount of time, and, like his contemporaries, he had sat the Cambridge Prelim, Junior

and Senior exams in successive years prior to his departure. To have stayed on any longer would have been the unusual course.

16. To be found in the Kingston Borough Archive, KX142/5, KRC, Bx 5.

17. Letter from George Mead to Causton Freeth, 21 January 1915, SHC 2332/1/1/1/6. Sherriff probably wrote to the manager of the Oxford Street branch of Sun Fire Insurance (Freeth) in the first instance, since the reply from Mead is addressed to Freeth.

18. For example, a postcard from his old Sun Insurance colleague Laurence Woodley in November 1914. He was training with the County of London Battalion, of the 4th London Infantry Brigade, and wrote: 'We are roughing it here quite a lot, although we have just had straw mattresses for the first time and feel quite luxurious at night. We have now all three passed well in the Shooting Tests – I finished mine today in a snowstorm. If I don't get pneumonia I must be jolly fit. Standing about in a field all day, this weather is a bit damp and cold.' He also enquired about the progress of Sherriff's application for a commission. SHC 2332/1/1/1/5.

19. See letters from Mead to Freeth (30 June 1915) and from Mead to Sherriff (22 July 1915). SHC 2332/1/1/1/7 & 8.

20. A similar type of sentiment is expressed in a letter to Sherriff from Laurence Woodley, now serving in the London Brigade, who replies, on 29 July, to Sherriff's recent letter: 'I can quite realise what a rotten time the recruiting sergeants give those they consider eligible', and hoped the manager would find his way to 'reconsider the situation'. (SHC 2332/1/1/6/65.) Taking this and Mead's letter together suggests that part of Sherriff's concern was that people would think that he had not been prepared to do his duty and enlist.

21. Letter from Mead to Sherriff, 27 October 1915. SHC 2332/1/1/1/9.

22. SHC 2332/3/8/2/2.

23. In the earlier version of the story (SHC 2332/3/8/2/3) the dead colleague is named Wilson, and Jimmy's departure is not dated precisely to his death: rather, it serves instead to make him 'even more restless'. In fact, the catalyst in this version is when they 'brought in girls to help – the shame of it cut into his very soul.' The arrival of girls is confirmed by letters to Sherriff from his former colleagues in early 1916, which contain gossip about the girls newly arrived in the office. (SHC 2332/1/1/8, passim).

24. An excellent selection of photographs of Romford, the Hare Hall camp, Gidea Hall and other locations of relevance to the Artists is provided online by the Havering museum: http://www.haveringmuseum.org.uk/docs/ArtistsRiflesVisualResource.pdf.

25. Higham, S.S., *Artists Rifles Regimental Roll of Honour and War Record 1914–1919*, Naval & Military Press, 2001 (reprint of 1922 edition).

26. Gregory, B., *A History of the Artists Rifles*, 1859–1947, Pen & Sword, 2006, pp.122–3.

27. Higham, *op. cit.*

28. Higham, *op. cit.*

29. No. 429 of 1915.

30. SHC 2332/1/1/2/1.

31. SHC 2332/1/1/2/2.

32. C. (Charles) A. Trimm had the service number 5225, while Sherriff's was 5217 (the numbers were given out sequentially). He was gazetted to the Royal Artillery in January 1917 as a second lieutenant, and won an MC on 17 August 1917. (See Higham (1922).) He ended the war as a lieutenant and soon went to work at Kingston Corporation, where he remained for thirty-four years, retiring in 1954 as the Chief Assistant Architect of the Borough. (*The Kingstonian*, January 1954.)

33. SHC 2332/1/1/2/3.

34. See SHC 9314/7 and SHC 9314/4/7.

35. Including, for example, socialite Mollie Cazalet; playwriting collaborator (and successful writer and performer) Jeanne de Casalis; and noted novelist G.B. Stern, among several others.

36. Letter to Father, 13 January. SHC 2332/1/1/3/1.

37. He wrote about it in a letter to his father on 15 January (SHC 2332/1/1/3/2), but the Field Day was the previous day.

38. The commanding officer was Major Sir Richard Nelson Rycroft ('unofficially known as "Piecrust"', according to Sherriff) who had been appointed temporary major on transfer from The Rifle Brigade in February 1915.

39. *JL*, p.54.

40. Letter to Mother, 9 February 1916, SHC 2332/1/1/2/14.

41. Letter to Father, 24 February 1916, SHC2332/1/1/3/18.

42. Letter to Father, 22 February 1916, SHC 2332/1/1/3/16.

43. Letter to Father, 2 February 1916, SHC 2332/1/1/3/10.

44. Letters from Manning-Press, 9 January 1916 and 19 January 1916, SHC 2332/1/1/6/27 and 2332/1/1/6/28.

45. Letter from Doland, 23 January 1916, SHC 2332/1/1/8/19.

46. Letter from Watson, 28 January 1916, SHC 2332/1/1/8/16.

47. Letter to Father, 25 January 1916, SHC 2332/1/1/3/6.

48. Letter to Father, 16 February 1916, SHC 2332/1/1/3/15.

49. Letter to Mother, 23 February 1916, SHC 2332/1/1/2/16.

50. Letter to Father, 29 February 1916, SHC 2332/1/1/3/19.

51. Beryl Constance was born on 30 January 1893. Bundy was born Cecil Herbert Methuen Sherriff on 10 November 1899.

52. 7 December 1857.

53. 2 May 1892.

54. 14 October 1871.

55. Diary of H.H. Sherriff, 1892, SHC 3813/16/6/12.

56. Draft of Sherriff's Autobiography, probably written about 1966–67. This section never made it into the finished book, nor did very much related to his early childhood. SHC 2332/3/9/7/1.

57. *Ibid.*

58. SHC 3813/16/6/7.

59. SHC 3813/16/6/13.

60. The average earnings figure comes from ONS: 'A Century of Labour Market Change' (2003). The KGS teacher's salary is from the staff record of W.P. Etches, who began at the school in 1907. Indexing Herbert's salary by the Retail Prices Index would give a figure of about £45,000 in the present day; indexing by wages would yield a value of £163,000 (http://www.measuringworth.com/ukcompare/relativevalue.php).

61. Herbert retired on Friday, 16 March 1923.

62. SHC 2332/3/9/7/1.

63. SHC 3813/16/6/14.

64. Ladies cycling appears to have really taken off during the 1890s – Herbert records in his diaries the swarms of cyclists – men and women – in the streets and towpath around Kingston and beyond. And the ladies cycling races seem to have been very popular – see, for example: http://www.sheilahanlon.com/?p=1556.

65. SHC 3813/16/6/13, January 1906.

66. 21 August 1909, SHC 2332/9/11 p.26.

67. Week beginning 8 September 1896, SHC 3813/16/6/12.

68. SHC 2332/9/12 p.11.

69. SHC 2332/3/9/7/1.

70. SHC 9314/7.

71. https: www.autismspeaks.org

72. Letter to Father, 2 March 1916, SHC 2332/1/1/3/20.

73. Letter to Mother, 3 March 1916, 2332/1/1/2/17.

74. Nor, it should be briefly pointed out, was he with two other famous literary artists – Wilfred Owen and Edward Thomas, although both were in camp at the time. Owen was in Hut 6A, while Thomas was in Hut 15. Owen had arrived there in November 1915, and left in late May. Thomas arrived in late 1915, and left in the summer of 1916.

75. Letter to Mother, 6 March 1916, SHC 2332/1/1/2/18.

76. SHC 2332/3/8/2/3, p.47.

77. Letter to Mother, 15 April 1916, SHC 2332/1/1/2/33.

78. Letter to Mother, 7 April 1916, SHC 2332/1/1/2/31.
79. Letter to Mother, 17 April 1916, SHC 2332/1/1/2/34.
80. Letter to Father, 14 April 1916, SHC 2332/1/1/3/35.
81. Letter to Mother, 5 April 1916, SHC 2332/1/1/2/30.
82. His father noted in his diary for 10 June 1906 that 'The Grammar School sports on Wednesday caused much interest in our family, Bob competing and winning two prizes – a bat and an egg cup – band and everything done tiptop – quite a large crowd and the racing good and well managed.' SHC 3813/6/6/14.
83. *The Kingstonian*, April 1914.
84. There is a little bit of *Chariots of Fire* to the report in the magazine: 'Stoneham was leading for some considerable time, but Sherriff drew up and passed him in fine fashion in the last lap, winning by about 14 yards.'
85. It seems only fair to mention, in passing, that Bundy had quite a successful day too – coming second in the under-14 100 yards and in the under-15 220 yards, third in the under-14 mile race, and (with Driskell) winning the 220-yard three-legged race.
86. Letter to Mother, 19 April 1916.
87. *No Leading Lady*, *op. cit.* p.217.
88. SHC 2332/8/1/1/1.
89. *JL*, p.39.
90. Mr Keetch features in a number of letters, usually appearing glum or unhappy – which is perhaps understandable for a middle-aged schoolmaster suddenly having to accommodate himself to the ways of the Army. There were two Keetches who taught at the school, and he could have been either one. Happily, both survived not only this war but also the next.
91. Letter to Mother, 19 May 1916, SHC 2332/1/1/2/45.
92. From an earlier letter (15 April) there appeared to have been a possibility he came across Edward Thomas, since he refers to a day spent map reading with a corporal – an 'interesting man' (and Thomas was a corporal and map reading instructor). However, he also says the man was a schoolmaster, and Thomas was never that.
93. Letter to Mother, 25 May 1916, SHC 2332/1/1/2/46.
94. Letter to Father, 20 May 1916, SHC 2332/1/1/3/45.
95. Letter to Father, 6 June 1916, SHC 2332/1/1/3/51.
96. Letter to Father, 8 June 1916, SHC 2332/1/1/3/52.
97. Letter to Mother, 19 June 1916, SHC 2332/1/1/2/53.
98. Letter to Father, 1 July 1916, SHC 2332/1/1/3/60.
99. *JL*, p.79.
100. Letter to Mother, 6 July 1916, SHC 2332/1/1/2/58.
101. Letter to Father, 18 July 1916, SHC 2332/1/1/3/64.
102. D.A. White, who was at Kingston Grammar from 1912–1914, a good hockey player and cricketer. He left a year after Sherriff and was posted to the 7th East Surreys when Sherriff went to the 9th. White was listed as missing during the great German offensive on 23 March 1918.
103. Letters to Father, 24 July 1916 to 31 July 1916, SHC 2332/1/1/3/66-69.
104. Letter to Mother, 9 August 1916, SHC 2332/1/1/2/71.
105. Letter to Father, 30 August 1916, SHC 2332/1/1/3/76.
106. Letter to Mother, 16 September 1916, SHC 2332/1/1/2/79.
107. Letter to Father, 16 September 1916, SHC 2332/1/1/3/79.
108. Letter to Mother, 17 September 1916, SHC 2332/1/1/2/80.
109. *JL*, final page.

Chapter 2: In the Trenches

1. Quoted by Sherriff in *Memories of Active Service in France and Belgium, 1916–1917*, SHC 2332/3/9/3/2. Sherriff wrote his memoir from about 1918 to 1921, and it covers the first three months of his time in France. Hereafter, MAS.
2. Letter to Pips, 29 September 1916, SHC 2332/1/1/3/86.
3. Letter to Mother, 28 September 1916, SHC 2332/1/1/2/84.

4. MAS, *op. cit.*, p.13.
5. Letter to Pips, 29 September 1916, *op. cit.*
6. Sherriff's 'Movement Order' is posted in MAS, opposite p.18.
7. MAS, *op. cit.*, p.22.
8. *Ibid*, facing p.29.
9. *Ibid*, pp.30–1.
10. See Lucas, M., *op. cit.*, 2012, pp.3–9 for a comprehensive account of the battalion's beginnings and composition, and pp.10–24 for an account of its role in the Battle of Loos. The book is an invaluable resource for information on the battalion (and its officers and men) throughout the war.
11. MAS, *op. cit.*, p.37.
12. MAS, *op. cit.*, p.39. Sherriff's comment, about the respect given to Nobby *despite* his dropped H's is an intriguing one. Sherriff was never an intellectual snob – in fact, he was intellectually rather insecure – and it is not the kind of comment he would have made much later in life. Perhaps it was youthful arrogance, or perhaps a veneer to conceal his self-doubts.
13. MAS, *op. cit.*, p.40.
14. The 26-year-old Hilton had joined the Territorial Civil Service Rifles in 1912, and come to France with them as a sergeant in March 1915. He was commissioned into the East Surreys in December 1915. The nickname came from his youthful looks.
15. MAS, *op. cit.*, p.41.
16. The open sheath attached to the belt in which a sword would be placed.
17. MAS, *op. cit.*, p.43.
18. *Ibid*, p.47.
19. *Ibid*, p.48.
20. Letter to Mother, 2 October 1916, SHC 2332/1/1/2/85
21. *Ibid*.
22. Letter to Mother, 4 October 1916. SHC 2332/1/1/2/86.
23. See Lucas, M., 2012, *op. cit.*, p.184.
24. Those familiar with *Journey's End* will recognise this as the very first scene, when Osborne encounters Captain Hardy.
25. MAS, *op. cit.*, p.81.
26. Letter to Pips, 14 October 1916, SHC 2332/1/1/3/92.
27. Letter to Mother, 9 October 1916, SHC 2332/1/1/2/89.
28. Sherriff wrote a vivid description of a stand-to in MAS, pp.177–80.
29. In Act 1 of *Journey's End*, just before Trotter takes Raleigh up into the trench, he remarks: 'You don't want a walking stick. It gets in your way if you have to run fast.' *Journey's End*, Penguin Classics Edition, 2000, p.27.
30. MAS, *op. cit.*, p.114.
31. *Ibid*, p.119.
32. Six months, was the answer: Penrose would be killed by a shell at Bully Grenay in April 1917.
33. MAS, *op. cit.*, facing p.156.
34. *Ibid*, p.160.
35. *Ibid*, p.170.
36. Letter to Mother, 12 October 1916, SHC 2332/1/1/2/92.
37. MAS, *op. cit.*, p.211.
38. *Ibid*, p.217.
39. *Ibid*, p.244.
40. *Memories of Active Service*, p.255, SHC 2332/3/9/3/3.
41. Letter to Pips, 21 October 1916, SHC 2332//1/3/94. He was one of four officers with the group, one from each company; the officer from 'B' Company was Abrams, the man who had come out to France with him.
42. *Memories of Active Service*, p.277, SHC 2332/3/3/4 (henceforth MAS 3).
43. *Ibid*, p.291.
44. Marcus Aurelius, *Meditations*, Book V.
45. MAS 3, *op. cit.*, pp.286–7.

46. The most famous being the Lochnagar mine at La Boisselle on the first day of the Battle of the Somme on 1 July 1916; and the series of mines exploded at the Battle of Messines in June 1917.
47. Lucas, M., *op. cit.*, 2012, p.79.
48. Lucas, M., (2012), p.51, notes that Tew's predecessor as commanding officer, lieutenant Colonel H.V.M. De La Fontaine, was conscious of the need to give men a break if they had been under heavy stress, and this would have been a perfect time to do it for one of the longer serving officers.
49. MAS 3, *op. cit.*, p.308.
50. *Ibid*, p.312.
51. *Ibid*, p.378.
52. SHC 2332/1/1/3/100. In the same letter, Sherriff commented on the *Alice Through the Looking Glass* quality of the opposed forces, each doing exactly the same as the other, as if they were simply reflections.
53. Letter to Pips, 21 November 1916, SHC 2332/1/1/3/111.
54. Letter to Mother, 27 November 1916, SHC 2332/1/1/2/116.
55. Letter to Pips, 29 November 1916, SHC 2332/1/1/3/116.
56. Letter to Mother, 10 December 1916, SHC 2332/1/1/2/122.
57. Letter to Mother, 14 November 1916, SHC 2332/1/1/2/111.
58. MAS 3, *op. cit.*, p.364.
59. Letter from W. Howard Webb to Sherriff, 23 December 1916, SHC 2332/1/1/8/17.
    Webb was with the Royal Field Artillery, and had been shot through the hips while acting as an observation officer on 19 September. There are two cuttings about him in Sherriff's scrapbook, SHC 2332/9/11, p.100.
    A detailed account of the Kingston Grammar School casualties can be found in Davies, J., *Kingston Grammar School War Dead*, KGS History Department, 2014.
60. Letter to Pips, 12 December 1916, SHC 2332/1/1/3/122.
61. MAS 3, *op, cit,,* p.450.
62. *Ibid*, p.459.
63. *Ibid*, pp.480–90.
64. *Ibid*, final page.
65. Letter to Pips, 28 December 1916, SHC 2332/1/1/3/130.
66. Tetley would commemorate the day by sending letter cases to the officers of the company, with a card saying 'In memory of New Year's Day'. Sherriff sent the card on to his mother, remarking, 'New Year's Day will always be memorable as I was with him all day from three in the morning till two in the afternoon, during which time we were shelled almost incessantly.' SHC 2332/1/1/2/50.
67. Battalion diary, to be found online at www.queensroyalsurries.org.uk, January 1917.
68. A mobile medical unit.
69. Letter to Mother, 25 January 1917, SHC 2332/1/1/2/140.
70. Letter to Pips, 25 January 1917, SHC 2332/1/1/3/138.
71. As described by Nobby Clark, some years later. See Lucas, M., *op. cit.*, 2012, p.84.
72. *Ibid*.
73. The account in the battalion diary suggests around twenty.
74. After the war, Summers would go on to an illustrious career in films, as director and screenwriter. See his potted biography on BFI Screenonline: http://www.screenonline.org.uk/people/id/543945/. Michael Lucas has also written an article on Summers' time in the East Surreys in *Stand-To!*, Issue 104, September 2015.
75. Letter to Pips, 27 January 1917, SHC 2332/1/1/3/139.
76. Letter to Mother, 1 February 1917, SHC 2332/1/1/143.
77. Letter to Pips, 27 January 1917, SHC 2332/1/1/3/139.
78. Letter to Pips, 10 February 1917, SHC 2332/1/1/3/141.
79. Letter to Pips, 19 February 1917. SHC 2332/1/1/3/143.
80. MAS, *op. cit.*, p.48.
81. Letter to Mother, 8 March 1917, SHC 2332/1/1/2/152.
82. See Sherriff's short story, *The Cellars of Cite Calonne*, SHC 2332/3/8/1.

83. The description of their dugout matches that in his letter to his mother, and his description of 'Petles' (whose name was clearly written first as Tetley, until the 'T' and the 'y' were obviously overwritten) exactly matches that of Tetley. The company commander is called Childs (a reference that may have come from Hilton's nickname as 'Baby'), and there is also a Dougall (clearly Douglass) and a Homedale (Homewood).

84. The tune would even pop up in a film script he wrote some twenty years later – *Shadow of the Wing*, SHC 2332/3/6/13. See discussion in Chapter 9. It would also appear in a letter to him from Godfrey Warre-Dymond (undated), inviting him to a 'Gallants' reunion dinner, SHC 2332/7/9/14.

85. He wrote three short stories about his time in the Army, and they were probably his first attempts to harvest his military experiences. But this story is the only one that does not appear in typescript (which was expensive, and thus indicative of an intention to publish), suggesting it may have been the earliest.

86. Letter to Mother, 18 March 1917, SHC 2332/1/1/2/153.

87. Letter to Pips, 18 March 1917, SHC 2332/1/1//3/151.

88. Letter to Mother, 18 April 1917, SHC 2332/1/1/2/165.

89. Letter to Mother, 7 April, 1917, SHC 2332/1/1/2/159.

90. Letter to Pips, 14 April 1917, SHC 2332/1/1/3/163.

91. Letter to Pips, 17 April 1917, SHC 2332/1/1/3/164.

92. Letter to Mother, 22 April 1917, SHC 2332/1/1/2/166.

93. Letter to Pips, 20 April 1917, SHC 2332/1/1/3/165.

94. Letter to Mother, 23 April 1917, SHC 2332/1/1/2/167.

95. Letter to Mother, 30 April 1917, SHC 2332/1/1/2/168.

96. Lucas, M., *op. cit.*, 2012, p.99.

97. Letter to Pips, 8 May 1917, SHC 2332/1/1/3/173.

98. Letter to Pips, 17 May 1917, SHC 2332/1/1/3/175.

99. Letter to Mother, 9 April 1917, SHC 2332/1/1/2/160.

100. Letter to Mother, 15 May 1917, SHC 2332/1/1/2/172.

101. The casualty figures are taken from the battalion diary for June, and from Lucas, M., *op. cit.*, 2012, who has a very useful chart of the battalion's fatalities during the war (Appendix 2).

102. Letter to Pips, 7 June 1917, SHC 2332/1/1/3/183.

103. Letter to Pips, 7 June 1917, SHC 2332/1/1/3/183.

104. Letter to Mother, 6 July 1917, SHC 2332/1/1/2/186.

105. Battalion diary, *op. cit.*, July 1917.

106. MAS, *op. cit.*, p.48.

107. Letter to Mother, 21 July 1917, SHC 2332/1/1/2/187.

108. Their graves are pictured in Herbert's account of the trip he and Bob took to the battlefields in 1921, SHC 2332/9/7.

109. See Lucas, M., *op. cit.*, 2012, for full account.

110. Panichas, G. (Ed), *op. cit.*, 1968, p.145.

111. Battalion diary, *op. cit.*, August 1917.

112. See Panichas , G. (Ed), *op. cit.*, 1968.

113. Shells from 5.9-inch howitzers.

114. Panichas, G. (Ed), *op. cit.*, 1968, p.150.

115. Letter to Mother, 2/8/17, SHC 2332/1/1/2/192. Although the letter is dated 2 August, the relief did not begin until 5.00 pm, and was not completely finished until 1.30 am. So by the time he was at the hospital and able to have someone write for him, it was probably 3 August, which was also the date on the letter he wrote to Pips.

116. Letter to Pips, 5 August 1917, SHC 2332/1/1/3/203.

117. Letter to Pips, 14 August 1917.

118. Letter to Pips, 18 August, 1917, SHC 2332/1/1/3/206.

119. Letter from Warre-Dymond to Sherriff, 15 August 1917, SHC 2332/1/1/6/58.

120. Killed by a sniper while inspecting a position in the front line, he was described in the battalion diary as 'a personal friend of, and beloved by, every man in the battalion, he died a soldier, carrying out his duty and anxious for the safety of his men.'

121. Letter from High to Sherriff, undated, but probably August 1917, SHC 2332/1/1//6/10.
122. Letter from Tetley to Sherriff, 17 September, SHC 2332/1/1/6/54.
123. Letter from Tetley to Sherriff, 17 September, SHC 2332/1/1/6/54.
124. Letter from Tetley to Sherriff, 2 February 1917, SHC 2332/1/1/6/52.
125. David, H., *On Queer Street*, Harper Collins, 1997, p.56.
126. Letter from Lindsay to Sherriff, 11 September 1917, SHC 2332/1/1/6/24.
127. Letter from Lindsay to Sherriff, 23 September 1917, SHC 2332/1/1/6/25.
128. Houlbrook, M., *Queer London*, University of Chicago Press, 2006, p.19.
129. The ban on gays in the military was lifted in January 2000 as a result of a ruling from the European Court of Human Rights.
130. Hall, E., *We Can't Even March Straight*, Vintage, 1995, p.3.
131. Porter, K. & Weeks, J., *Between The Acts: Lives of Homosexual Men*, 1885–1967, Routledge, 1991, p.6.
132. I am grateful to Michael Lucas for this point.
133. Ackerley, J.R., *My Father and Myself*, New York Review of Books, 2012, p.153.
134. *Ibid*, p.151.
135. Quoted in Fussell, P., *The Great War and Modern Memory*, OUP, 2000, p.275.
136. While Tetley was some nine years older, Lindsay was only two years' Sherriff's senior, but it seems highly likely that Sherriff's modest and quiet demeanour would have made him seem very much the junior partner.
137. Houlbrook, *op. cit.*, p.45.
138. *Ibid*.
139. Letter from Sherriff to Webb, 13 October 1917, SHC 2332/1/1/6/61.
140. According to a letter from his colleague, 2nd Lt Beard, SHC 2332/1/1/6/1.
141. See two letters from Cyril Manning-Press in June 1918, SHC 2332/1/1/6/31 & 32.
142. See Lucas, M., *op. cit.*, 2012, pp.120–41.
143. *Ibid*, p.139.
144. *Ibid*, p.149.
145. Letter to Pips, 3 February 1919, SHC 2332/1/1/3/210.

Chapter 3: A Writer in the Making

1. SHC 2332/1/1/6/35, letter from John Staddon, 6 March 1919.
2. SHC 2332/1/1/6/36, letter from John Staddon, 19 March 1919.
3. SHC 9314/11, copy of Sherriff's Army Service Papers held at the National Archives.
4. A third short story – *A Ghost on Vimy Ridge* (SHC 2332/3/8/3/4) – is in manuscript and typescript form, suggesting it was completed later than the other two, most likely with a view to publication.
5. The *On Active Service* series was published by John Lane at the Bodley Head Press. They consisted of first-hand accounts of wartime experiences. The most complete listing is to be found at: http://www.greatwardustjackets.co.uk/page48.html.
6. One thing he had almost certainly not been writing was a movie called *The Toilers* (1919). This is mistakenly attributed to Sherriff in the IMDB Movie Listing website, and first seems to have been suggested by Max Will in his 2004 book *Schmucks with Underwoods*. But there are several reasons why this is highly unlikely: (i) The screen credit is given to Elliott Stannard, who was already a prolific screenwriter, requiring no additional help; (ii) neither of the two available contemporaneous reviews mentions Sherriff ; (iii) He is not mentioned in this context in Rachel Low's definitive *The History of the British Film Industry 1918–1929*; (iv) The film was released on 27 March 1919 – which means he would have needed to write it while still in the Army; (v) Sherriff himself never mentioned any scriptwriting experience prior to his engagement by Universal Studios in 1932 – not even in letters to his agent preceding that appointment; (vi) When International Productions Ltd (a British studio) was seeking film rights to *Badger's Green* he evidently had no idea who Elliott Stannard was, before he met him for discussions (letter to Walter Peacock, 4 March 1931). Of course, it is impossible to prove a negative, but the probability that Sherriff was engaged in any way at all with *The Toilers* is vanishingly small.
7. Letter to Pips, 18 August 1917, SHC 2332/1/1/3/206.

8. *Westminster Gazette*, 21 April 1930.
9. Journal of the East Surrey Regiment, November 1936 – May 1939. SHC J/553/65-70. The text was lightly edited to remove personal comments about some officers.
10. *The Kingstonian*, July 1919, Vol.II, No.2, Kingston Grammar School. The Memorial Tablet was unveiled at the school on 19 September 1920, and it continues to have pride of place in the school's main hall today.
11. *No Leading Lady*, *op. cit*. p.317. In fact, he applied for his wounds gratuity on 12 February 1918, so it may not have been quite as closely linked to the sculling boat purchase as he remembered (not least since he also remarked in *No Leading Lady* (p.32) that he had bought a 'fine eight-volume History of England' with the same gratuity – in all probability, Charles Knights' *Popular History of England* (1856)). But his desire to get back on the water – even to the extent of organising a whole new Boat Club – cannot be doubted.
12. Fundraising memo, Kingston Rowing Club. Kingston Borough Archive, KX142/5. The memo is undated but must be after 1958, since it refers to the club as being founded 'more than a century ago'. Sherriff remarks that 'The first breakthrough [in club membership] came when the grammar school and Tiffins [another grammar school in Kingston] took up rowing. It was a long time before the committee of the club would accept them because they weren't public schoolboys. In 1919, I was one of the first grammar schoolboys to be accepted. I was told by my sponsor that I squeezed in by one vote: five committeemen in favour and four black balls.'
13. In 1932, when his work at Universal Studios took him away from England for three months, he told a friend how much he regretted missing his first Henley Regatta 'since the war'. Letter to Geoffrey Ellison, 19 August 1932, Lambeth Palace Archive.
14. SHC 2332/8/18.
15. Which we can tell because the Editorial is in his handwriting.
16. See page 5 above.
17. Sherriff, Herbert Hankin: *A Tour to the Battlefields of France and Belgium*, 1921, SHC 2332/9/7.
18. Lt Picton, 2nd Lt Bogue, and Captain Pirie. See page 47 above.
19. We do not have a copy of the final letter, but there is a draft in a notebook containing sketches of Roman coins, SHC 2332/8/4/4.
20. *Journey's Other End, John Bull*, 12 March 1932.
21. SHC 2332/3/2/1.
22. *No Leading Lady*, *op. cit.*, pp.17–25.
23. With brickwork eroding because of its location on a busy stretch of road, it inevitably still requires funding for further repairs.
24. Programmes relating to *A Hitch in the Proceedings*, SHC 2332/8/12/10.
25. Warner came to the school in 1919. He had been in the Queen's Own Oxford Hussars in September 1914, but after a serious accident received a commission in the London Divisional Cyclist Company. He went to France in 1916 and was at Ypres, Arras and Cambrai, before coming home temporarily disabled in January 1918.
26. From a conversation with Lt-Col Christopher Manning-Press, Cyril's son and Sherriff's godson, SHC 9314/7.
27. *No Leading Lady*, *op. cit.*, p.31.
28. *Surrey Comet*, 7 March 1925.
29. *No Leading Lady*, *op cit.*, p.17.
30. Herbert Boret, who had rowed for Cambridge in 1921 in the Boat Race, and for Leander at Henley, rowed in the KRC Wyfold Four at Henley in 1922. His younger brother, David Boret, was the spare for that crew.
31. See the description on the London gardens online website: www.londongardensonline.org.uk.
32. A nice picture can be found of its use as a hospital at the Oakhill Community Heritage Project: ochre.org.uk/timeline.
33. According to a press clipping in Sherriff's files from *The Star* on 22 July 1937, part of the grounds, including the theatre, was sold off in 1937 to make way for a block of flats. SHC 2332/5/2/62.
34. *No Leading Lady*, *op. cit.*, p.19.

35. *Surrey Comet*, 23 November 1921.
36. Born in 1888, Mr E(dward) W(illiam) H(arold) (Jimmy) James arrived at the school early in 1921 as second master, fresh from active service as a lieutenant in the Royal Garrison Artillery. He remained in that position until he took over as (Acting) Headmaster from C.A. Howse in 1941. His leaving of the school in 1949 has a *Chips*-like quality about it – and the boys even performed a scene from *Goodbye, Mr Chips* in his honour at his final speech day.
37. Born in 1889, he was a new master who arrived in July 1921, and was, among other duties, helping with the cadet corps. He had been an acting captain in the Manchester Regiment, winning the Belgian Croix de Guerre, before transferring to the Balloon Company, and then the Royal Flying Corps. Known as 'Giff', he became a stalwart of the group, and a good friend of Sherriff's.
38. Sanders arrived at the school in 1919, after serving in Egypt and in France. He was commissioned into the 2nd London Regiment in August 1915, and after some months in Egypt, returned to France in time to take part in the Battle of the Somme. He was twice sent home wounded, the second time from Passchendaele.
39. He would go on to cox the KRC Thames Cup Eight at Henley Royal Regatta in 1924.
40. *No Leading Lady*, op. cit., p.29.
41. SHC 2332/3/2/2/3.
42. *A Privy Council*, by W.P. Drury and Richard Pryce.
43. The producer on this occasion was another KGS old boy – David Hatten, his colleague from the East Surreys. He was about nineteen years older than Sherriff, and as well as school and the East Surreys, they had the insurance business in common. Sherriff must have written a flattering letter to him afterwards, because he replied in kind, noting that the success was down to the rest of the company. SHC 2332/1/1/9.
44. One of the friends is called Mrs Trayler-Gush, and was played by Beryl. The name of the character was in all likelihood a tease by Sherriff, for Beryl was married in the spring of 1926 to Edward Tudor-Mash, for whom her fondness may already have been apparent when the play was written.
45. See Plate 10.
46. *No Leading Lady*, op. cit., p.37.
47. Letter from Curtis Brown to Sherriff, 22 June 1922, SHC 2332/1/1/9.
48. There are four copies of the play in the Surrey History Centre. The most nearly final version is 2332/3/2/3/4, which is identical in typescript form to 2332/3/2/3, but with later handwritten amendments. There is no published edition.
49. *No Leading Lady*, op. cit., p.27.
50. Letter from Frank Randell to Sherriff, 14 December 1922, SHC 2332/1/1/9.
51. Played by Cyril Manning-Press, who made rather a speciality of crusty old buffers.
52. Played by Sherriff himself.
53. *Surrey Comet*, 13 January 1923, SHC 2332/5/2/62.
54. In the very first act, when Dick arrives home, and his mother tells him something wonderful has happened, he says: 'You don't mean Aunt Jessica's dead?' 'No Dick,' she replies, 'something better than that.' Shortly afterwards, when everyone is planning how to use the extra money Mr Jottings will receive, he cautions them that 'Rome wasn't burnt in a day.' Music Hall and malaprop – the staples of his first two plays.
55. Some years later, in *Windfall*, a rather similar character – Tom Spooner – decides to hew to his old life when he receives a large lottery win; although even this has unwelcome consequences.
56. Letter from Curtis Brown, 7 March 1923, SHC 2332/1/1/9.
57. Letter from Reginald Higgins, 7 March 1923, SHC 2332/1/1/9.
58. *No Leading Lady*, op. cit., p.230.
59. SHC 2332/3/2/4/4.
60. *Surrey Comet*, 7 March 1925.
61. In the 1930s, Sherriff would develop a friendship with Hilton, following his screen adaptation of Hilton's novel *Goodbye, Mr Chips*, and especially when they both lived in the US during the Second World War.

62. Including *Mr Birdie's Finger* (1926), *Badger's Green* (1930), *The Hopkins Manuscript* (1939), and *The Long Sunset* (1955). He also considers the issue of housing development in *Greengates* (1936), but on that occasion from a fairly favourable perspective.

63. *Surrey Comet*, 12 December 1923.

64. SHC 2332/3/2/4/5.

65. Rossendale had enough bedrooms for them to have one apiece, and in *The Fortnight in September* (1931), which can be seen as a depiction of Sherriff's own family, we can see the parents sleeping in separate rooms.

66. Even when, eventually, Connie moved out of the family home to join her son in his new home following the success of *Journey's End*, she continued to remain married to Herbert.

67. Almost, but not quite. The protagonist in *The Hopkins Manuscript* is a lonely, and rather irritating, bachelor. In the movies, he would address the issue of divorce in *One More River* (1934), and of adultery in *That Hamilton Woman* (1941). It is impossible to imagine him writing a play or novel of his own with similar themes, although *Chedworth* (1944) does feature a marriage in difficulties. Sex of any sort is absent from all of his own (non-adapted) work.

68. Letter from G. Patching to Sherriff, 30 July 1924, SHC 2332/1/1/9.

69. Letter from G. Patching to Sherriff, 17 October 1924, SHC 2332/1/1/9.

70. Royal Academy of Dramatic Arts.

71. SHC 2332/3/2/5/3.

72. Letter from G. Patching, 14 November 1924, SHC 2332/1/1/9.

73. SHC 2332/8/12/14. The source of the quote is, unfortunately, unknown, but likely one of Sherriff's history books. The quote also appears on the front of the script.

74. *Surrey Comet*, 4 March 1925.

75. There is a very entertaining letter, dated 21 August 1925, from Giff to Sherriff in the files of the Kingston Rowing Club, in which he discusses – among many other things – Sherriff's (self-confessed) inebriation at Henley Regatta that summer. Kingston Rowing Club Papers, KX 142/5.

76. Howse had written to Sherriff to tell him about the review, in a letter dated 19 March 1925. Kingston Rowing Club Papers, KX 142/5.

77. Letter from Oldham to Sherriff, 10 September 1925. Kingston Rowing Club Papers, KX 142/5.

78. See, for example, the editions of *The Kingstonian* in March 1926, March 1927 and March 1928.

79. SHC 2332/3/2/6.

80. See her (undated) letter of 1925. SHC 2332/1/1/9.

81. *Surrey Comet*, 27 February 1926.

82. Undated, unsourced review in Sherriff's files. SHC 2332/5/2/53.

83. *No Leading Lady, op. cit.*, p.30.

84. *Surrey Comet*, 7 July 1926.

85. The Leander Club has long been one of the powerhouse rowing clubs in the country.

86. *Surrey Comet*, 22 September 1926.

Chapter 4: The Writing of *Journey's End*

1. Being a little picky, he wasn't actually in Selsey at the time of the Bank Holiday – which was in early August at that time – but he was there by late August, which is when he presumably began his work. (Draft Script for *The Birthday Party*. Letter from Gale Pedrick, 17 June 1939, SHC 3813/1/53.)

2. He tended to write his first drafts in pencil, then either rewriting in ink in good hand, or, later, having them typed.

3. *No Leading Lady, op. cit.*, p.35. Unfortunately, no fragment of the novel appears to exist.

4. *Westminster Gazette*, 21 April, 1930.

5. Published in German in 1928, with the English translation available in 1929.

6. In its English translation. It was first published in German in 1920.

7. Quoted in Cunningham, V: *British Writers of the 1930s*, Oxford University Press, 1988.

8. Hynes, S., *A War Imagined: The First World War and English Culture*, Pimlico, 1992.

9. Quoted in Fussell, P., *The Great War and Modern Memory*, Oxford University Press, 1977.

10. Brittain, V., *Testament of Youth*; Gollancz, 1933. Interestingly, she later wrote that it was watching a performance of *Journey's End* alongside Winifred Holtby that prompted her to write her memoir, convinced that the 'young men' should not 'have the war to themselves'. (*War Service in Perspective*, in Panichas, G., *op. cit.*, 1968.)

11. *No Leading Lady, op. cit.*, p.40.

12. The date comes from George Bishop's book of recollections: Bishop, G., *My Betters*, Heinemann Ltd, 1957.

13. *No Leading Lady, op. cit.*, p.42.

14. Founder of the Agency, and father of Spencer Curtis-Brown, who took over from him, and was Sherriff's main point of contact with the company.

15. Curtis Brown, A., *Contacts*, Cassell & Co Ltd, 1935.

16. Woodfield, J., *English Theatre in Transition 1881–1914*; Routledge, 2015

17. One actor to express his appreciation of the society was its secretary in 1903, C. Aubrey Smith, who noted that actors could find satisfaction in 'interpreting a play that has real acting value although commercially worthless' (Woodfield (2015)). He would go on to great success in Hollywood in the 1930s and 1940s, and major roles in a number of Sherriff-scripted movies.

18. Parker, P., *A Life of J.R. Ackerley*; Constable & Co Ltd, 1989.

19. *No Leading Lady, op. cit.*, p.43.

20. See, for example, his obituary in *The Independent* on 23 October 2011.

21. While on the surface it might seem a trifle odd to encourage an unknown playwright to send his manuscript, unbidden, to the leading light in the English stage, Bernard Shaw's longstanding commitment to the society, and his place on the committee would likely guarantee at least a perusal of the manuscript.

22. William S. Kennedy (1878–1957) – a writer and critic, was a long-standing member of the Stage Society Committee, having been its treasurer before being elevated to the chairman's role, which he relinquished in 1929.

23. Ervine was a very well-known playwright and journalist, who had been wounded in the First World War (losing a leg).

24. Letter from W.S. Kennedy to St John Ervine, 30 January 1933. From the Archives of the Incorporated Stage Society at the V&A Theatre and Performance Archive, V&A THM/136/5/7.

25. *Good Housekeeping*, 1929. In the press cuttings of the ISS, V&A, THM /136/1/10.

26. Letter from Kennedy to St John Ervine, *op. cit.*

27. The quote was used in pre-publicity for the play, and is to be found in the ISS press cuttings at the V&A (THM 136/1/10). Mottram had written the *Spanish Farm* trilogy (1924–26) about the Western Front. In the late 1930s, Mottram was chairing an event in Norwich, at which Sherriff was giving a talk on Hollywood and the movies, and he told the audience of the 'admiring opinion' he had given of *Journey's End* not quite ten years earlier. (Cutting in SHC 2332/5/9/2.)

28. Letter from Geoffrey Dearmer to W.S. Kennedy, 30 January 1933, V&A, THM/136/5/7.

29. *No Leading Lady, op. cit.*, p.45.

30. 'Editors do not sufficiently realise that Mr Sherriff has in him the makings of a really great commentator on public spectacles, and for their failure to realise this we may be devoutly thankful.' *The Observer*, 11 November 1934.

31. Quoted in Gore-Langton, R., *Journey's End: The Classic War Play Explored*, Oberon Books, 2013.

32. *The Daily Telegraph*, 8 November 1928.

33. *No Leading Lady, op. cit.*, p.39.

34. *Ibid.*

35. *New York American*, 7 April 1929.

36. Letter to E.P. Jones, 31 May 1939, SHC 3813/1/50.

37. Matthew Norgate suggested that they had first approached Miles Malleson for the job, but, although he liked the play 'enormously', he had turned them down in favour of something that would bring him a 'more commercial remuneration'. *Variety News*, 12 March, 1936.

38. *No Leading Lady*, op. cit., pp.46-7.

39. The biographical material on Whale is taken from Curtis, J., *James Whale: A New World of Gods and Monsters*, University of Minnesota Press, 1998.

40. Thomaier, W. and Fink, R.F., *James Whale; Films in Review*, October 1962, quoted in Curtis, J. *op. cit.*, 1968, pp.19–20.
41. *Filmland*, May 1930, quoted in Curtis, J., *op. cit.*, 1998.
42. One of the productions on which he worked was Ackerley's *The Prisoners of War*, where he was set designer.
43. Curtis, J., *op. cit.*, 1998, p.46.
44. The play was written by ex-MP Noel Pemberton-Billings, a notorious conspiracy theorist and homophobe, who was involved in a sensational libel case in 1918.
45. Note that Curtis (p.51) has Whale's fee at £15, while Norgate himself (*Variety News*) recalls offering the play to Malleson at 15 guineas. He is unlikely to have offered Whale any less.
46. *No Leading Lady, op. cit.*, p.47.
47. *Ibid*, pp.47–8.
48. *Ibid*, p.49.
49. See Dean, B., *Mind's Eye: An Autobiography 1927–1972*, Hutchinson of London, 1973.
50. See Darlington, W., *I Do What I Like*, McDonald & Co, 1947, p.331.
51. See Wearing, J.P., *The London Stage 1920–1929: A Calendar of Productions, Performers, and Personnel*, Rowman & Littlefield, 2014.
52. Melville Cooper's most memorable role in Hollywood movies was probably as the Sherriff of Nottingham in the Errol Flynn version of *Robin Hood* in 1938. Maurice Evans achieved great success on Broadway, but is best known for his roles on *Planet of the Apes* and the long-running TV series *Bewitched* (as Samantha's father).
53. Olivier, L., *Confessions of An Actor*, Penguin, 1984, p.69.
54. This was especially evident in the guidance he would give to Jeanne De Casalis when she went to Broadway to assist with the production of *St Helena* in 1936.
55. *No Leading Lady, op. cit.*, p.53.
56. Evans, M., *All This and Evans Too*, University of South Carolina Press, 1989, p.39.
57. Speaight, R., *The Property Basket: Recollections of a Divided Life*, Collins & Harvill Press, 1970, p.103.
58. Evans, M., *op. cit.*, 1989, p.39.
59. At this point it is appropriate to note that, despite many internet references to the contrary, there is no evidence that Sherriff was ever awarded the MC. Michael Lucas has done sterling work to demonstrate that it was, however, presented to F.G. Sherriff (Yorks & Lancs Regiment) and G. Sherriff (Army Ordnance Corps). The tunic appears to be long gone, but the Sam Browne belt can still be found at the Victoria and Albert Museum.
60. *No Leading Lady, op. cit.*, p.54.
61. SHC 3813/16/6/20.
62. *No Leading Lady, op. cit.*, pp.54–5.
63. Curtis Brown, A., *op. cit.*, 1935, p.132.
64. Hodges, S., *Gollancz: The Story of a Publishing House, 1928–1978*, Gollancz, 1978, pp.46–7. Gollancz made a lot of money from the play, and its subsequent novelisation, and it made such an impression on Victor himself that 'in later years he often referred to it as his "first publication", though in fact it was more like his seventy-first.'
65. See Browne, M., *Too Late to Lament*, Gollancz, 1955, p.306.
66. Monro, a friend of Browne's from Cambridge (and formerly married to his sister), was a well-known London literary figure, proprietor of the Poetry Bookstore, and promoter of Wilfred Owen, among others.
67. Dean and Barry Jackson were the only significant stage figures in the audience, since critics preferred the Monday matinee. Madeleine Carroll would go on to a very successful Hollywood career, starring in Hitchcock's *The Thirty-Nine Steps*, among many other movies.
68. Dean, B., *Mind's Eye: An Autobiography, 1927–1972*, Hutchinson, 1973, p.51.
69. SHC 3813/16/6/20.
70. *No Leading Lady, op. cit.*, p.56.
71. Bishop, G., *op. cit.*, 1957, p.41.
72. Agate, J., *My Theatre Talks*, Arthur Baker Ltd, 1933, p.133.
73. SHC 3813/16/6/20.

74. *Evening Standard*, 11 December 1928. *Havoc* had run at the Haymarket for several months back in 1924.

75. *The Daily Telegraph*, 11 December 1928. Years later, in his autobiography, Darlington took issue with American critics ('who never saw service') who dismissed the play as sentimental, and recounted an exchange with his wife after the first performance: '"Was it like that?" Marjorie asked. ... "Exactly like that," I answered, hardly able to say the words.' Darlington, W.A., *op. cit.*, 1947, p.329.

76. *The Manchester Guardian*, 11 December 1928.

77. *Daily Mail*, 11 December 1928.

78. *The Times*, 11 December 1928.

79. Dean, B., *op. cit.*, 1973, p.51.

80. *Ibid.*

81. Letter from Sherriff to Basil Dean, 11 December 1928, University of Manchester, John Rylands Library, Special Collections, DEA/1/2/2144.

82. Letter from Basil Dean to R.C. Sherriff, 12 December 1928, University of Manchester, John Rylands Library, Special Collections, DEA/1/2/1502.

83. *No Leading Lady, op. cit.*, p.84. He also tells an amusing story about having thought of raising the issue with the King when he met him at a *Journey's End* production in November 1929 (but having chosen not to).

84. Evans, M., *op. cit.*, 1989, p.40.

85. *Ibid.*

86. Agate, J., *op. cit.*, 1933, p.133.

87. Bishop, G.W. *op. cit.*, 1957, p.41.

88. Leonard Elmhirst was a progressive agronomist who had met heiress Dorothy Payne Whitney while studying agriculture at Cornell University in the early 1920s, and together they came back to England, where they acquired the Dartington Hall Estate in Devon, where they sought to implement progressive ideas on rural reconstruction, development and education, while promoting literature, music and the arts.

89. Devon Heritage Centre (DHC), Dartington Hall Trust Archive (DHTA), LKE General, Transcripts 2. Interview with Leonard Elmhirst re Maurice Browne.

90. *No Leading Lady, op. cit.*, pp.65–9.

91. Browne, M., *op. cit.*, 1955, p.306.

92. Bishop, G.W., *op. cit.*, 1957, p.40.

93. Dean, B., *op. cit.*, 1973, p.53.

94. Interview with Leonard Elmhirst, *op. cit.*

95. 'Maurice was an enigmatic character,' wrote Basil Dean. 'His autobiography is a confused tale of enthusiasm, conceit, arrogance and utter unreliability in financial matters ... he seems to have been the victim of muddled ideals, coupled with a ruthless determination to put them into effect at other people's expense.' Dean, B., *op. cit.*, 1973, p.53.)

    We must exercise a little caution in taking Basil Dean entirely at his word here, since he clearly harboured some resentment at Browne for nabbing both *Journey's End* and the Savoy from under his nose (letter from Browne to the Elmhirsts, 24 December 1928); and for a deal regarding Colin Clive, which fell through towards the end of the *Journey's End* run. Dean, B., *op. cit.*, 1973, p.112.

96. Browne, M., *op. cit.*, 1955, p.307.

97. *Ibid*, p.307.

98. *Ibid*, p.307.

99. De Casalis would later collaborate with Sherriff in the writing of *St Helena* (1934).

100. Evans, M., *op. cit.*, 1989, p.41.

101. *Woman's Pictorial*, 15 November 1930.

102. *No Leading Lady, op. cit.*, p.75.

103. *Bristol Times*, 22 October 1930. (To be found in SHC 2332/5/9/2.) He stuck to that line in his autobiography, some twenty years later.

104. *No Leading Lady, op. cit.*, p.75.

105. University of Michigan, Collection Code: AMSHW, Call Number VV-B General Correspondence. Memorandum of Agreement between R.C. Sherriff and Maurice Browne.

106. Browne was true to his word, and the play did stay at the Savoy until the theatre was refurbished. It closed at the Savoy on Saturday, 1 June, and began its run at the Prince of Wales theatre on Monday, 3 June. Note that some sources mistakenly have the Savoy run at three weeks, or a slightly more plausible three months (the latter figure, curiously enough, comes from Browne's own autobiography).

107. See *The Star*, 5 January 1929.

108. *No Leading Lady, op. cit.*, p.73

109. *Ibid*, p.78.

110. Clive died just eight years later, from an illness aggravated by his chronic alcoholism. While it has been suggested that Sherriff may have set him on the slippery slope, that seems far-fetched.

111. They were accompanied by a disclaimer written to Dame Adelaide Livingstone, of the League of Nations Union on 4 November 1929:

> I understand that you want to have some formal letter from me concerning the authenticity and completeness of the MS. For its authenticity I can, of course, give you a complete guarantee. As to its completeness, I can only tell you that so far as I know every word written in the preparation of the play is contained in the batch of papers that I have handed to the League of Nations Union. It is impossible for me to guarantee this further, because the play was written some time ago, and as sheets were finished with they were placed together for further reference. I cannot, of course, guarantee that every sheet is here, but so far as I can possibly say, it is complete.

> ([1] Imperial War Museum Documents.4999. Manuscript of *Journey's End* by R.C. Sherriff, 1927 [*sic*].)

112. SHC 2332/3/1/1/3.

113. GB, 71 THM/136/3/2.

114. The SHC manuscript is stamped with a mark indicating that it was used as evidence in the plagiarism case that was heard before the New York South District Court in October 1931 (see page 124), thus supporting the idea that Sherriff himself viewed it as his earliest manuscript copy.

115. *Bristol Times*, 22 October 1930. To be found in SHC 2332/5/9/2.

116. The main changes are set out in Wales, R.L., *You're Playing for England Now: Revisions to Journey's End*, 2016, www.rolandwales.com.

117. In the otherwise very positive review in the *Evening Standard*, 11 December 1928.

118. From H.H. Sherriff's diary (SHC 3813/16/6/21), and *No Leading Lady, op. cit.*, p.82.

119. Browne, M., *op. cit.*, *1955*, p.309.

120. All of the reviews are dated 22 January 1929, unless otherwise specified.

121. *Daily Mirror*, 23 January 1929.

122. *The Sunday Times*, 27 January 1929.

123. SHC 3813/16/6/21.

Chapter 5: The Aftermath

1. See his cash book, SHC 2332/4/1/1.

2. And that was after Curtis-Brown's 10 per cent fee had already been deducted.

3. Hamilton had been a theatrical manager, and had organised the tour of *The Unknown Warrior* around the country, costing himself some money in the process. But Browne would remember his generosity, and see it repaid in the future.

4. *No Leading Lady, op. cit.*, p.100.

5. SHC 3813/16/6/21.

6. *The Era*, 30 January 1929.

7. Browne, M., *op. cit.*, 1955, p.310.

8. *The Era*, 20 February 1929.

9. See Gollancz Black Production Book 2, Warwick University Modern Records Centre, MSS 318/2/1/2.

10. Winthrop Ames, a veteran producer, known for his interest in Shakespeare and his American revivals of Gilbert and Sullivan in the 1920s.

11. Browne, M., *op. cit.*, 1955, p.311.

12. See Bloom, K., *Broadway: An Encyclopaedia*, Routledge, 2013.

13. It had also been home to Gershwin's first complete Broadway score in 1919.

14. Browne, M., *op. cit.*, 1955, p.311.
15. *No Leading Lady, op. cit.*, p.171.
16. Letter from Churchill, SHC 2332/1/8.
17. Letter to Churchill, SHC 3813/1/1.
18. *See No Leading Lady, op. cit.*, pp.113–14
19. Fragment of a draft letter from Sherriff to Maurice Browne, undated (but probably early April 1929), SHC 3813/1/5.
20. Script for BBC *Books and Authors* programme, 1947. While all of this must have been very uncomfortable at the time, at least it gave him some source material for a play, *Windfall*, which he would write a few years later (see below).
21. Script for BBC *Books and Authors* programme, 1947, i*bid*.
22. See *No Leading Lady, op. cit.*, pp.120–23.
23. In *No Leading Lady*, Sherriff pegged the leave of absence at twelve months (p.122). George Bishop, in *The Era* on 20 February, wrote that Sherriff had asked for six months, and that was the figure Sherriff mentioned in a letter fragment written in about early April (SHC 3813/1/5). A press cutting in his scrapbook also has him comment that 'My leave expires in August,' SHC 2332/9/12, p.53.
24. *No Leading Lady, op. cit.*, p.123.
25. *New York Herald Tribune*, 3 March 1929.
26. According to Jack Hawkins, he auditioned in the final week of the run of *Beau Geste*. Hawkins, J., *Anything for a Quiet Life*, Coronet, 1975, p.45.
27. *Ibid,* p.46.
28. Cash book, SHC 2332/4/1/1.
29. In fact, Hawkins was happy that at least one of the critics felt he would have made a better Stanhope. Hawkins, J., *op cit.*, 1975, p.48.
30. *No Leading Lady, op. cit.*, p.131–2.
31. Hawkins, J., *op. cit.*, 1975, p.48.
32. *No Leading Lady, op. cit.*, p.135.
33. *Good Housekeeping*, April 1930, SHC 2332/5/4/1.
34. Hawkins, J., *op. cit., 1975*, p.49.
35. *The Era*, 27 March 1929.
36. Cable from Maurice Browne, undated, but probably 23 March 1929, [Punctuation added], DHC, DHTA, LKE/BR/1/B.
37. Cable from Gilbert Miller to the Elmhirsts, 25 March 1929, DHC, DHTA, LKE/BR/1/B.
38. SHC 2332/4/1/1.
39. Letter from Maurice Browne to the Elmhirsts, 27 March 1929, DHC, DHTA, LKE/BR/1/B.
40. See Curtis, J., *op. cit.*, 1998, p.76.
41. Letter from Mollie Cazalet to Sherriff, 23 March 1929, SHC 3813/1/4.
42. Letter from Geoffrey Dearmer to Sherriff, 12 April 1929, SHC 3813/1/2.
43. Letter from G.B. Stern to Sherriff, undated, but likely early April 1929, SHC 3813/1/5.
44. Letter from Leonard Lodge, 16 March 1929, SHC 3813/1/2.
45. Letter from C.D. Fair to Sherriff, 9 April 1929. SHC 3813/4/1.
46. Letter from Maurice Browne to Dorothy and Leonard Elmhirst, 7 February 1929, DHC, DHTA, LKE/BR/1/B.
47. For some unknown reason, each maintained in their respective autobiographies that the split was 50:50.
48. Cash book, SHC 2332/4/1/1.
49. See Memorandum by G.A. Hill, 12 June 1930, DHC, DHTA, LKE/BR/4/F.
50. Sherriff's account of the dispute is set out in *No Leading Lady, op. cit.*, pp.162–8.
51. SHC 3813/1/5.
52. Cable from Browne to Directors and Managerial Staff, Maurice Browne Ltd, 8 April 1929, DHC, DHTA, LKE/BR/1/B.
53. The account of the meeting comes from *No Leading Lady, op. cit.*, pp.166–7.
54. Fragment of letter from Sherriff to Browne, undated, but probably April 1929, SHC 3813/1/5.

55. Letter from Fred Gwatkin to Messrs Baldwin Hutchins and Todd [Maurice Browne Ltd's American lawyers], 9 April 1929, DHC, DHTA, LKE/BR/1/B.
56. Letter from Gwatkin to Leonard Elmhirst, 9 April 1929, DHC, DHTA, LKE/BR/1/B.
57. For example, with Jeanne De Casalis in the adaptation of *Espoir*, and with Sheila Bush in the editing of his autobiography.
58. Fragment of letter from Sherriff to Browne, undated, but probably April 1929, SHC 3813/1/5.
59. According to a letter from Gwatkin to Leonard Elmhirst, 25 April 1929, DHC, DHTA, LKE/BR/1/B.
    That number is supported in Browne, M., (1955), although Michael Balcon set the figure at £15,000 in his autobiography. Balcon, M., *Michael Balcon Presents ... A Lifetime of Films*, Hutchinson, 1969, pp.39–42.
60. Balcon, M., *op. cit.*, 1969.
61. Letter from Peacock to Sherriff, 24 April 1929, SHC 3813/1/8.
62. *Sunday Express*, 28 April 1929.
63. Quoted in *The Cape Times*, 30 May 1929.
64. Who was now, following her marriage in 1922, known as Kathleen Hilton Young.
65. Jones, M., T*he Last Great Quest: Captain Scott's Antarctic Sacrifice*, OUP, 2004, p.276.
66. Published by Nicholson & Watson in 1933, and a sequel to *The Great Victorians* (1932).
67. *The Post Victorians, op. cit.*, 1933, p.547.
68. See letter from Gwatkin to Leonard Elmhirst, 26 May 1930, DHC, DHTA, LKE/BR/2A.
69. *The Era*, 8 May 1929.
70. More than 160 performances in all.
71. *New York World*, 6 June 1929.
72. *New York Herald Tribune*, 16 June 1929.
73. *News of the World*, 9 June 1929; *Variety*, 19 June 1929.
74. Mills, J., *Up in the Clouds, Gentlemen Please*, Penguin,1980, pp.86–7.
75. Woollcott, A., *While Rome Burns*, Simon & Schuster, 1989, p.286.
76. Mills, J., *op. cit.*, 1980, pp.124–7.
77. On his way back to the UK from Singapore, Coward is thought to have written his own First World War play, *Post Mortem*. See Gore-Langton, R., *op. cit.*, 2013.
78. Drei Masken were grateful that he was prepared to see the play altered slightly, so that the young German prisoner no longer cried when captured.
79. Letter to Sherriff from Ann Bernstein, 28 February 1929. SHC 3813/1/2.
80. Translation of a letter from Thomas Mann to Hans Reisiger, 27 April 1929, SHC 3813/1/4.
81. Letter from Morley Peel to Sherriff, 15 July 1929, SHC 3813/1/8.
82. See *The Observer*, 1 September 1929. The same nationalist spirit was abroad in Italy, where Mussolini had banned war plays, and in Austria, where the army had forbidden its men to read *All Quiet on the Western Front*.
83. *Times Weekly Edition*, 5 September 1929.
84. *Times of India Weekly*, 29 September 1929.
85. *The Morning Post*, 31 August 1929.
86. *Sunday Dispatch*, 29 December 1929.
87. See cuttings in SHC 2332/5/1/3/25.
88. Quoted in *The Englishman*, Calcutta, 21 October 1929.
89. Quoted in the *Ceylon Observer*, 25 October 1929.
90. *The Era*, 20 November 1929.
91. *Sunday News*, December 1929.
92. *The Era*, 18 September 1929.
93. *Theatre Arts Monthly*, May 1929.
94. *Sunday Times*, 6 October 1929.
95. It had, however, already been made into a movie, and a variant of it – using the same characters – had been made into a talkie in 1929 called *The Cock-Eyed World*, produced by the Fox Film Company (as it then was), who commissioned Sherriff to write an appreciation of it. British Library YV 1985, a.256.
96. *The Baltimore Sun*, 31 March 1929, article by Robert Sisk.

97. Quoted in *The Toronto Star*, 8 August 1929.
98. Darlington, W.A., *op. cit.*, 1947, p.329.
99. O'Casey, Sean, *Autobiographies 2*, Pan Books, 1980, p.335,
100. Sisk, R., *op. cit.*
101. *New York World*, 24 March 1929.
102. *Theatre Arts Monthly*, May 1929.
103. *New York World*, 24 March 1929.
104. *Theatre Arts Monthly*, May 1929.
105. See the discussion in the *New York Post*, 6 December 1929.
106. *New York Evening Post*, 16 March 1929.
107. Balcon, M., *op. cit.*, 1969.
108. Letter from Walter Peacock to Sherriff, 21 September 1929, SHC 3813/1/8.
109. Pearson, G., *Flashback: an Autobiography of A British Film Maker*, George Allen & Unwin, 1957, p.162.
110. See the letter from Joe Cowley to Sherriff, 24 October 1929, SHC 3813/1/1.
111. Letter from Sherriff to John Bush (Gollancz), 28 May 1968, SHC 2332/1/5/6.
112. The manuscript of the novel is largely in Bartlett's handwriting, SHC 2332/3/1/2.
113. *St Louis Democrat*, 10 November 1929.
114. *South Wales Argus*, 8 November 1929.
115. *Glasgow Herald*, 9 November 1929.
116. The newspapers had a wonderful circumlocution to avoid spelling out the word in print: they referred to it as 'The word which was first used on the stage in G.B. Shaw's *Pygmalion*' (*The Glasgow Record*, 9 November 1929).
117. Act III, Scene 2: the scene in which Stanhope is upbraiding Raleigh for not having come down to dinner.
118. *Glasgow Record*, 4 November 1929.
119. *Glasgow Evening Citizen*, 12 November 1929.
120. See *Glasgow Evening News*, 13 November 1929.
121. The most senior among them was Colonel James Henry Reynolds, better known as Surgeon Reynolds of Rourke's Drift. He was eighty-two at the time, and would be in the company of another Rourke's Drift veteran – Private John Williams, late of the 2nd Battalion of the 24th Foot. *The Morning Post*, 9 November 1929.
122. See Sherriff's long and funny account of the evening in *No Leading Lady*, *op. cit.*, pp.181–9.
123. Browne, M., *op. cit.*, 1955, p.315.
124. Or 'switch-back railway', as Beryl called it in her charming letter to Bob of 12 August 1917, SHC 2332/1/1/5/10.
125. *New York World*, 30 November 1929.
126. *The Morning Post*, 30 November 1929.
127. SHC 2332/4/1/1.

Chapter 6: What Next?

1. Clive left London on 21 November 1929.
2. Maurice Evans has a comment on Clive's departure in his autobiography, which is amusing in its rather blatant self-regard: "Such offers did come for Colin Clive and me to play our parts in the motion-picture version, which James Whale was to direct, but we were still doing sell-out business at the Prince of Wales Theatre, to which the show had been transferred. The management baulked at giving leaves of absence to both of us simultaneously. They felt that, since my name was at the top of the billing, it would be less noticeable if Colin was the one allowed to go to Hollywood while I continued to hold the fort in London.' The reason Clive had to go and not Evans is because Stanhope is the fulcrum of the play, and Clive was the *ne plus ultra* of Stanhopes. Evans, M., *op. cit.*, 1989, p.44.
3. *No Leading Lady*, *op. cit.*, p.191.
4. From September to January, average weekly receipts fell by 38 per cent in New York, and 26 per cent in London. See Sherriff's cash book, SHC 2332/4/1/1.
5. At a weekly salary of £500 – a big improvement on the £30 he was getting from Maurice Browne.

6. For a detailed account of the travails behind the film, see Curtis, J., *op. cit.*, 1998, pp.91–105. Also, Pearson, G., *op. cit.*, 1957, pp.159–76.
7. Bartlett has a nice paragraph recalling some of their explorations: Bartlett, V., *This Is My Life*, Chatto & Windus, 1938, pp.243–4.
8. H.H. Sherriff Diary, 1930, SHC 3813/16/6/22.
9. Frankau was twelve years older than Sherriff, and had joined the East Surreys in 1914, before moving to the Royal Field Artillery in 1915. He had published several books of poetry and novels during the war, before publishing the novel based on his East Surrey experiences, *Peter Jackson, Cigar Merchant*, in 1919. Frankau also wrote (with a byline) for the *Wipers Times*, something that Sherriff never did: see his letter of 12 September 1972 to Patrick Beaver, SHC 2332/1/1/27.
10. *Surrey Comet*, 1 February 1930.
11. See Chapter 2.
12. *The Evening News*, 5 January 1929.
13. *Western Morning News and Mercury*, 23 January 1929.
14. *Westminster Gazette*, 21 April 1930, SHC 2332/5/4/7.
15. *Liverpool Express*, 27 February 1933, SHC 2332/5/3/13.
16. See Page 31.
17. Recall Sherriff's reference to his dropped H's on page 24 above.
18. Many of the details on the East Surrey officers are taken from Lucas, M., *op. cit.*, 2012.
19. On 16 April 1972, the *Sunday Times Magazine* carried a profile of Sherriff, illustrated with a number of pictures, including the Bully Grenay photo, and the caption included the comment that Warre-Dymond 'bore more than a passing resemblance to Stanhope.'
20. Clark and Warre-Dymond were really the only two officers with whom Sherriff kept in contact during the 1930s and beyond, which says much for the high regard in which he held them both. Tetley died of consumption on 29 May 1928, at the age of forty.
21. *East Surrey Regimental Journal*, May 1955, SHC J/553/88. Warre-Dymond died on 23 January 1955 of a heart attack. He was sixty-four.
22. Letter from Nobby Clark to Sherriff, 5 January 1936, SHC 3813/1/61.
23. I am grateful to Michael Lucas for his observations on Hilton.
24. See, for example, *Inverness Courier*, 7 January 1930. The *Daily Mail* also reported on the story, according to an exchange of letters between Walter Peacock and Sherriff. SHC 3813/1/15.
25. *The Era*, 5 February 1930. The same column noted that the play *Charles and Mary* had just opened at the Everyman. The play would later be produced (at a loss, almost inevitably) at the Globe by Maurice Browne. The author was Joan Temple, the person who had offered Sherriff advice on how to reshape his earlier play *Cornlow-in-the-Downs*, to have it more likely to be performed by the RADA players. She acknowledged as much in the article.
26. *Journey's End* novel, p.219.
27. *Journey's End* novel, p.66.
28. Probably prepared for Bartlett.
29. SHC 2332/3/1/1/1.
30. *Answers*, 22 February 1930.
31. *Reynolds*, 9 March 1930.
32. *The Sketch*, 26 March 1930.
33. *The Irish Statesman*, 29 March 1930.
34. *John O'London's Weekly*, 29 March 1930.
35. *Times Weekly Edition*, 20 March 1930.
36. *Referee*, 30 March 1930.
37. *No Leading Lady*, *op. cit.*, p.208.
38. SHC 3813/16/6/22.
39. *The Times of India Weekly*, 2 March 1930, SHC 2332/5/4/11. This is likely to have been a syndicated interview, although there are no other copies in the files of press cuttings at the Surrey History Centre.
40. Remark made by Jack Latham, quoted in Curtis, J., *op. cit.*, 1998, p.233.
41. Email to author, 26 October 2015.
42. Letter from Bundy to Bob, 24 April 1929, SHC 3813/2/3,

43. See the entry in his diary for 24 November 1906, SHC 3813/16/6/14.
44. He never quite paid down the entire mortgage, leaving a balance that Sherriff paid off in 1932 – see his letter to Bundy on 23 June 1954, courtesy of Ann Hutton.
45. SHC 3813/16/6/22.
46. When he was writing *No Leading Lady* in 1968 he was aware enough of how odd this might look to raise it with his editor: 'It is quite a trifling matter, but in the straight read-through I got an uneasy feeling that the business of taking my mother with me on so many journeys might open up a target for a critic that wants to find something to make fun of … I am sure you know what I mean by this, and no doubt feel as I do that we are on slightly dangerous ground. My mother obviously did not come on all these excursions by any means but it rather looks as if she did. … This can be quite easily remedied by making clear that there were obvious reasons for taking her along, and this naturally applies to the war.' (Letter to Sheila Bush, 6 February 1968, SHC 2332/1/5/6).
47. George Gorbard, of the *New York World*, quoted in Curtis, J., *op. cit.*, 1998, p.103.
48. *The Star*, 15 April 1930.
49. *The Sunday Times*, 20 April 1930.
50. It was pointed out, in more than one review, that the only non-English actor played the German soldier.
51. *Bioscope*, 16 April 1930.
52. Letter from Sherriff to Walter Peacock, 27 May 1930, SHC 3813/1/15.
53. *No Leading Lady, op. cit.*, p.197.
54. Sherriff revised *Badger's Green* for a revival at the Wimbledon Theatre in 1961. He made a number of changes (see Chapter 13), one of which was to restore Joan's name, and relationship to her father, but also make her a more significant player in the planned development.
55. 'Why I Am a Bachelor', by R.C. Sherriff, *Good Housekeeping*, December 1930.
56. *No Leading Lady, op. cit.*, p.198.
57. *Daily Express*, June 13 1930.
58. *The Daily Telegraph*, 13 June 1930.
59. Christopher St John, *Time and Tide*, 28 June 1930.
60. *Vogue*, early July 1930, SHC 2332/5/2/4.
61. *Daily Mail*, 14 June 1930.
62. *No Leading Lady, op. cit.*, p.201.
63. *Sunday Dispatch*, 15 June 1930.
64. The figures are taken from the Maurice Browne Ltd Statement of Account for *Badger's Green*, HC, Dartington Hall Trust Archive, LKE/BR/6/E1.
65. Telegram from Walter Peacock, 27 June 1930, SHC 3813/1/15.
66. The broadcast took place on 5 July, and featured all the main cast members.
67. *Vogue*, early July 1930, SHC 2332/5/2/4.
68. *The Morning Post*, 11 July 1930.
69. Letter from Sherriff to Peacock, 19 August 1930, SHC 3813/1/15.
70. Letter from Sherriff to Walter Peacock, 8 April 1930, SHC 3813/1/15.
71. In *No Leading Lady*, Sherriff wrote that Carl Laemmle had sent a telegram to him while he was in the US for the Broadway production of *Journey's End*, asking him to write the script of *All Quiet*. This seems unlikely, for he would probably have mentioned it in at least one of the letters he exchanged with Walter Peacock. *No Leading Lady, op. cit.*, p.156.
72. Letter from Sherriff to Peacock, 11 April 1930, SHC 3813/1/15.
73. For which he had written the review of *The Cock-Eyed World* (see above).
74. Letter from Sherriff to Peacock, 19 August 1930, SHC 3813/1/15.
75. Letter from Sherriff to Peacock, 20 September 1930, SHC 3813/1/15.
76. Letter from Sherriff to Peacock, 26 September 1930, SHC 3813/1/15.
77. SHC 2332/3/1/4.
78. The scene has been acted just once since it was written – in November 2009, at a Kingston Grammar School 'Sherriff Night' – when it was very well received. Stanhope was played by Mark Gillis; Trotter by Pavle Dimitrijevic.
79. Letters from Peacock to Sherriff, 1 October 1930 and 3 October 1930, SHC 3813/1/15.
80. Letter from Sherriff to Peacock, 29 January 1931, SHC 3813/1/27.

81. Letter from Sherriff to Peacock, 24 January 1931, SHC 3813/1/27.
82. Gazeley, I., *Poverty in Britain, 1900–1965*, Palgrave Macmillan, 2003. Table 4.2. The unemployment numbers in the interwar period are highly dependent on the definition chosen. Most figures quote insured workers as a proportion of total insured employees. This understates the number of unemployed (because many important occupations were not covered by National Insurance), but overstates the rate (because, paradoxically, the rate of unemployment among the insured was higher than in the population as a whole).
83. Of course, it was especially difficult for those who were disabled. In 1922, the number of disabled servicemen in receipt of pensions was over 934,000, and the British Legion estimated that about 100,000 disabled had found no employment. (See Reese, P., *Homecoming Heroes*, Pen & Sword, 1992, p.94.)
84. Harding, B., *Keeping Faith*, Pen & Sword, 1990, p.191.
85. *Ibid.*
86. *Ibid.*
87. See page 56 above.
88. The problem of high unemployment in an industrialised northern city does crop up in a screenplay he wrote in the late 1930s, *Ruined City*, based on a novel by Nevil Shute. See Chapter 9.
89. *Daily Express*, 11 November 1929.
90. The cable was quoted by Peacock in a letter to Sherriff on 11 December 1930, SHC 3813/1/28.
91. The company was created from the merger of British National Studios (based at Elstree) and Maxwell's ABC Cinema chain. It was renamed Associated British Picture Corporation (ABPC) in 1933, and it was as ABPC that Sherriff would work for it in the 1950s, producing *The Dam Busters* in particular.
92. Letter from John Maxwell to R. Golding Bright, 6 January 1931, SHC 3813/1/28.
93. Letter from Peacock to Sherriff, 21 January 1931, SHC 3813/1/27.
94. Letter from Sherriff to Maurice Browne, 31 March 1931, University of Michigan, Collection Code AMSHW, Call Number VV-B General Correspondence. Correspondence between Maurice Browne and R.C. Sherriff.
95. Letter from Sherriff to Peacock, 7 February 1931, SHC 3813/127.
96. Letter to Peacock, 6 February 1931, SHC 3813/1/27.
97. The vellum binding is referred to in a letter to Lighton-Straker Bookbinding Company, 3 June 1937, SHC 3813/1/47.
98. *No Leading Lady, op. cit.*, pp.213–14.
99. *Ibid*, pp.212–24.
100. See various letters to Peacock.
101. Letter from Sherriff to Thelma Cazalet, 22 January 1931, SHC 3813/1/28.
102. *South Wales Argus*, 27 April 1931.
103. 'Congregation' is the governing body of Oxford University, made up of its academic staff, senior representatives from colleges and other staff members.
104. *Daily News and Chronicle*, 3 June 1931.
105. Letter from Mollie Cazalet to Sherriff, 12 February 1932, SHC 3813/1/28.
106. *Evening Standard*, 10 October 1931.
107. Letter from Sherriff to Maurice Browne, 15 July 1931, University of Michigan, Collection Code AMSHW, Call Number VV-B General Correspondence. Correspondence between Maurice Browne and R.C. Sherriff.
108. Szep was a Hungarian Jew, born in the eastern part of Austria-Hungary (now Ukraine) in 1884, who had made a name for himself as a poet and journalist as well as a playwright. He was rounded up by the Nazis in the 1940s, and only escaped because he was given a Swedish passport by Raoul Wallenberg. He later wrote an account of his experiences in *The Smell of Humans: An Account of the Holocaust in Hungary* (reprinted in 1994).
109. *The Era*, 12 August 1931.
110. Outlined in a letter from Sherriff to Walter Peacock on 17 August 1931, SHC 3813/1/28.
111. *L'Orgue du Stade*, possibly based on André Obey's book of the same name about the Paris Olympics, published in 1924.
112. See Hodges, S., *op. cit.*, 1978, p.20.

113. *No Leading Lady, op. cit.*, p.234.
114. SHC 3813/6/6/14.
115. Sherriff, R.C., *The Fortnight in September*, Gollancz, 1931, p.76, (8th Impression).
116. *Ibid*, pp.266–75.
117. Sherriff's thoughts prepared for the Authors and Books programme with Arthur Calder Marshall in 1947, SHC 2332/1/2/12.
118. SHC 2332/5/2/28.
119. *Daily Express*, October 1931.
120. *The Spectator*, 17 October 1931. When the book was reissued by Persephone Press in November 2006, the *Spectator* review was almost as glowing: 'It remains a masterpiece – and one that surprises through its understated but irresistible power to move.'
121. *The Tatler*, 4 November 1931.
122. *John O'London's Weekly*, 31 October 1931.
123. *The Era*, 8 April 1932.
124. *New York Times*, 6 March 1932.
125. *Chicago Tribune*, 2 March 1932.
126. *New Statesman & Nation*, 31 October 1931.
127. *Birmingham Post*, 20 October 1931.
128. 'To read *The Fortnight in September* is comparable to listening to a violin played with unconscious mastery. In *Journey's End*, Mr R.C. Sherriff achieved universality by the simple means of not concerning himself with it; and in [this book] he repeats the same magic formula.'
129. Curtis, J., *op. cit.*, 1998.
130. In *No Leading Lady* (p.241), Sherriff is vague about exactly when Whale's letter appeared. Sherriff wrote to Peacock on 23 November saying he had received a letter from Whale, so it must have been before then. But Peacock also refers (in a letter on 8 December) to Sherriff's letter to Whale of 29 October, suggesting Whale had contacted him before that date. Sherriff does say that Whale complimented him on the success of *Fortnight*, so it must have been after 12 October.
131. Letter from Sherriff to Peacock, 23 November 1931, SHC 3813/1/28.
132. Quoted in Peacock's letter to Sherriff, 8 December 1931, SHC 3813/1/28.
133. Letter from Peacock to Sherriff, 20 January 1932, SHC 3813/1/31.
134. SHC 2332/1/1/10.
135. Letter from Peacock to Sherriff, 3 February 1932, SHC 3813/1/31.
136. Email to the author from Jennifer Thorp, Archivist at New College, Oxford, 23 October 2014.

Chapter 7: The Universal Years

1. *No Leading Lady, op. cit.*, pp.251–2. They later moved to the equally plush Miramar: 'One evening we drove down to the coast at Santa Monica and found an old timber-framed hotel on the palisades overlooking the Pacific. There was a bungalow in the garden that we rented for the rest of our stay.' *No Leading Lady, op. cit.*, p.264.
2. Letter to Gerald Ellison, 19 August 1932, Lambeth Palace Library, Bishop Ellison Papers, File P/10/4/7 – correspondence between Ellison and R.C. Sherriff.
3. Whale had an exaggeratedly English habit of halting production twice a day, for 'elevenses' and 'foursies', which rather annoyed the two main American actors – Melvyn Douglas and Gloria Stuart – who were not invited. Stuart played the ingénue in the film, and was back on set for Whale a year later for *The Invisible Man*. Although both her performances were well received, there was no whisper of an Oscar nomination for her efforts; that would have to wait more than sixty years, until she featured in James Cameron's *Titanic*. See Stuart, G., *I Just Kept Hoping*, Little, Brown & Co., 1999, p.44.
4. Letter from Sherriff to Ellison, 10 June 1932, Lambeth Palace Library, Bishop Ellison Papers, file P/10/4/7 – correspondence between Ellison and R.C. Sherriff.
5. University of Michigan, Collection Code: AMSHW, Call number VV-B General Correspondence. Correspondence between Maurice Browne and R.C. Sherriff. Letter dated 27 August 1932.
6. Letter from Sherriff to Ellison, 10 June 1932, Lambeth Palace Library, Bishop Ellison Papers, file P/10/4/7. Correspondence between Ellison and R.C. Sherriff.

7. The inter-college rowing races involve short-distance races in which crews try to 'bump' the crews in front and take their place in the start order the following day. Races take place twice a year: in February (when they are known as 'Torpids'), and in May ('Summer Eights').

8. Telegram from Sherriff, Santa Monica, CA to John Bayly, Oxford, 19 May 1932. Lambeth Palace Library, Bishop Ellison Papers, file P/1/1/5, Books of Cuttings.

9. See Wilk, M., *Schmucks with Underwoods*, Applause Theatre & Cinema Books, NY, 2004, p.115.

10. *P.G.Wodehouse: A Life in Letters,* Random House, London, 2012, p.268.

11. The club was formed in 1932 by C. Aubrey Smith, who had played for Cambridge and England in his day. He would work with Sherriff on a number of projects over the next dozen or so years.

12. Morley, S., *Tales from the Hollywood Raj: The British Film Colony On Screen and Off,* Weidenfeld & Nicolson, 1983, London.

13. SHC 2332/3/6/1: *The Road Back* script. The script is undated (the cover page is missing), but it seems likely to be an early version. When contrasted with a 1936 shooting script (SHC 9314/13 – Copy of *The Road Back*, a screenplay held at the University of Southern California) it can be seen to hew much more closely to the source book.

14. See Curtis, J., *op. cit.,*1998, p.188.

15. Joy would later turn up as Sherriff's boss at Twentieth Century Fox – see Chapter 10.

16. Letter from Jason Joy to Will H. Hays, 1 August 1932, AMPAS, Margaret Herrick Library, PCA Files, *The Road Back* (1937). Henceforth, PCA Files, *The Road Back*, (1937).

17. Memo by Lamar Trotti, 7 July 1931, PCA Records, *The Road Back* (1937).

18. University of Michigan. Collection Code: AMSHW, Call number VV-B General Correspondence. Correspondence between Maurice Browne and R.C. Sherriff, letter dated 27 August 1932.

19. Urwand, B., *The Collaboration*, Kindle Edition, 2013, Location 551.

20. *Ibid.*, Location 990.

21. Letter from Jason Joy to Carl Laemmle Jr, 16 August 1932, PCA Files, *The Road Back* (1937).

22. Letter from Carl Laemmle Jr to Jason Joy, 23 August 1932, PCA Files, *The Road Back* (1937).

23. Urwand, *op. cit*, 2013. The same motivation gave rise to the Cinematographic Films Act of 1927 in Great Britain, which would result in the phenomenon of the 'quota quickie' – cheaply made films designed to satisfy the quota on British production. These included two based on Sherriff plays, namely *Badger's Green* (1934) and *Windfall* (1935).

24. Urwand, *op. cit.*, 2013.

25. Letter from Harry Zehner (Universal) to Joseph Breen (at the PCA), 13 October 1936, enclosing a script of *The Road Back*, 'which is pretty much in the shape in which we intend to shoot it. ... When this story originally came in four or five years ago we were loathe to produce same then, solely due to the jeopardy in which its production would have placed our German business at that time. However, since then the situation with regard to the American film industry has completely changed and we are now ready and anxious to produce this story.' PCA Files, *The Road Back* (1937).

26. *No Leading Lady, op. cit.*, p.276.

27. He wrote to Ellison: 'It will be a joy to see the river again after living in a desert for six months.' Letter to Gerald Ellison, 23 August 1932, Lambeth Palace Library, Bishop Ellison papers, File P/10/4/7.

28. Letter to Gerald Ellison, 17 March 1933, Lambeth Palace Library, Bishop Ellison papers, File P/10/4/7.

29. 'The only crew they [Magdalen] need to fear are Oriel, who have been well coached by Mr R.C. Sherriff.' *The Times*, clipping in Books of Cuttings P1/1/6, Ellison Collection, Lambeth Palace Library.

30. Letter to Gerald Ellison, 26 May 1933, Lambeth Palace Library, Bishop Ellison papers, File P/10/4/7.

31. E.g. his reference to Torpids as 'Toggers'.

32. Letter to Gerald Ellison, 1 June 1933, Lambeth Palace Library, Bishop Ellison papers, File P/10/4/7.

33. Not, as he writes in *No Leading Lady* (p.276), for £6,000 each. We know the terms of his contract from a letter to Maurice Browne on 9 October 1934: 'I am under contract with Universal Films Corporation of Hollywood to prepare them three screenplays a year, and my services so long

as the contract is in force are exclusive to them. I finished my first three pictures this summer, and they have just recently taken up their option for three more.' (Letter to Maurice Browne, 9 October 1934, University of Michigan, Collection Code: AMSHW, Call number VV-B General Correspondence. Correspondence between Maurice Browne and R.C. Sherriff.

34. Curtis, *op. cit.*, 1998, pp.196–9.
35. *Ibid*, p.199.
36. *No Leading Lady, op. cit.*, pp.259–62.
37. Noted film academic Paul Jensen wrote, in an email to the author on 30 March 2015, about a conversation he had with Sherriff in 1971: 'When the subject came up, I referred to what he said in *No Leading Lady* about writing *The Invisible Man* in Hollywood. He immediately said, quite definitely and without hesitation (or evident embarrassment), that his autobiography was wrong!'
38. *Daily Herald*, 7 March 1933.
39. Wells, H.G., *The Invisible Man*, Gollancz SF Masterworks 2001.
40. *No Leading Lady, op. cit.*, p.263.
41. *Ibid*, p.267.
42. Quoted in Curtis, *op. cit.*, 1998.
43. *Today's Cinema*, 25 January 1934.
44. Wells, H.G., *op. cit.*, 2001, p.115.
45. Letter to Gerald Ellison, 22 July 1933, Lambeth Palace Library, Bishop Ellison Papers, File P/10/4/7. Correspondence between Ellison and R.C. Sherriff.
46. Thanks to David Cottis for noticing this.
47. Curtis, J., *op. cit.*, 1998, p.213.
48. Quoted in Curtis, J., *op. cit.*, 1998, p.212.
49. *The New York Times*, 18 November 1933.
50. *Sunday Chronicle*, 26 November 1933.
51. *Today's Cinema*, 25 January 1934.
52. Apart from the man from *The Times*, who did not like the film at all.
53. *The Morning Post*, 29 January 1934.
54. Who wrote under the pen name of Gordon Daviot.
55. Letter to Gerald Ellison, 22 July 1933, Lambeth Palace Library, Bishop Ellison Papers, File P/10/4/7. Correspondence between Ellison and R.C. Sherriff.
56. SHC 2332/3/6/2.
57. On 15 February 1934, the *Hollywood Reporter* noted that James Whale was set to arrive in New York on the *Europa*, back from a vacation in London, with R.C. Sherriff's script for *A Trip to Mars* – a new Karloff vehicle. Quoted in Mank, G.W., *Bela Lugosi and Boris Karloff: The Expanded Story of a Haunting Collaboration*, McFarland, 2009.
58. Amish, M., *Divorce in the Movies: From the Hays Code to Kramer vs Kramer*, Legal Studies Vol.24, p.228.
59. *Over the River*, Kindle edition, location 1561.
60. SHC 2332/3/6/4.
61. AMPAS, Margaret Herrick Library, Production Code Administration records, *One More River* (1934), Margaret Herrick Library, (henceforth, *One More River* (1934) PCA file.)
62. Since Sherriff was in London throughout this period, the changes were made with the assistance of playwright William Hurlbut. See Curtis, J., *op. cit.*, 1998, p.225.
63. Other significant cast members are C. Aubrey Smith as Clare's father (General Charwell), and Mrs Patrick Campbell as Lady Mont (Clare's aunt).
64. Letter from Joseph I. Breen to Harry Zehner, 8 May 1934, *One More River* (1934), PCA File.
65. Some of the redubbing can be clearly seen in the finished movie.
66. *Variety*, 30 July: 'Carl Laemmle Jr., James Whale and R.C. Sherriff, English playwright, remained in Santa Barbara over the weekend for story conferences, following preview of Universal's *One More River* there Friday night.'
67. In Sherriff's original script (SHC 2332/3/6/4), Tony is upset by Clare offering herself to him, as though she is in his debt. In the revised ending (the one in the final cut, and also SHC

2332/3/6/5), he visits her at breakfast the next morning and they apologise to each other, and are thereby reconciled.

68. *New York Mirror*, date unknown, but probably 10 August 1934. To be found in SHC 2332/5/2/60.
69. *The New York Post*, 10 August 1934.
70. *The Washington Post*, 12 August 1934.
71. *The Scotsman*, 2 April 1935.
72. *The People*, 20 January 1935.
73. Letter from Joseph I. Breen to Carl Laemmle Jr, 17 August 1934, *One More River* (1934) PCA File.
74. Amish, M., *Divorce in the Movies: From the Hays Code to Kramer vs Kramer*. Legal Studies Vol.24, p.240 ff.
75. Which was true, but not the whole story. As well as being an actress, she was also something of a music hall turn, performing comic monologues in the character of Mrs Feather, a rather dim-witted middle-class suburban lady. Some of the monologues can still be heard and seen on YouTube.
76. *No Leading Lady*, *op. cit.*, p.299.
77. Letter from Sherriff to de Casalis, 20 October 1933, SHC 3813/1/26.
78. Letter from De Casalis to Sherriff, around 14 November 1933, SHC 3813/1/26 (De Casalis's letters are generally undated, but the dating can be inferred from Sherriff's replies.)
79. Letter from Sherriff to De Casalis, 8 December 1933, SHC 383/1/26.
80. Letter from Sherriff to De Casalis, 4 January 1934, SHC 3813/1/21.
81. Letter from Sherriff to De Casalis, 13 February 1934, SHC 3813/1/21.
82. Letter from Sherriff to De Casalis, 22 February 1934, SHC 3813/1/21.
83. The play was never published, but there are a number of typescript versions to be found in the Surrey History Centre. The version that is likely to be closest to the script used in the performance is SHC 2332/3/3/2/4 (i). It is identical to another script, version (iii), which bears the stamp of Curtis Brown but is missing a few pages; in its complete form, the latter was probably the script that was shown to theatre managements.
84. Letter from Sherriff to Peacock, 12 December 1932, SHC 3813/1/32.
85. Letter from Peacock to Sherriff, 3 December 1932, SHC 3813/1/32.
86. *No Leading Lady*, *op. cit.*, p.226.
87. Letter from Sherriff to Peacock, 9 December 1933, SHC 3813/1/11.
88. *The Times*, 27 February 1934.
89. *Evening News*, 27 February 1934.
90. *The News Chronicle*, 27 February 1934.
91. *Daily Sketch*, 27 February 1934.
92. *The Morning Post*, 27 February 1934.
93. *The Observer*, 4 March 1934.
94. Letter to Sherriff from Geoffrey Dearmer, 11 March 1934, SHC 3813/1/21.
95. Letter from Sherriff to Ronald Adam, 3 April 1934, SHC 3813/1/11.
96. Letter from Sherriff to Ronald Adam, 28 February 1934, SHC 3813/1/11.
97. *Windfall* (1935), Embassy Film Company. Produced by George King; Directed by Frederick Hayward.
98. The movie can be seen at the British Film Institute, Ref 51679.
99. Letter from De Casalis to Sherriff, Feb/Mar 1934, SHC 3813/1/21.
100. Letter from Sherriff to De Casalis, 17 April 1934, SHC 3813/1/21.
101. Including Bronson Albery, Barry Jackson, C.B. (Charles) Cochran and Sydney Carroll. Letter from Sherriff to De Casalis, 20 June 1934, SHC 3813/1/21.
102. Letter from Sherriff to De Casalis, 17 July 1934, SHC 3813/1/21.
103. The film was directed by Frank Borzage, and Borzage's biographer wrote that Sherriff had assisted in the script, 'incognito'. See Dumont, Hervé, *The Life and Films of a Hollywood Romantic*, McFarland & Co, 2009.
104. SHC 2332/3/6/8.
105. *Universal Weekly*, 28 July 1934, SHC 2332/5/13/1.
106. Curtis, J., *op. cit.*, 1998, p.233.

107. A postcard exists showing it outside Sleepy Hollow in Selsey.
108. *No Leading Lady, op. cit.*, p.284. Curtis suggests that Sherriff spent 'several listless and unproductive weeks on the film when he returned to England but nothing came of it.' (Curtis, p.236). This tallies with the AFI Film Catalog, which reveals no input from Sherriff, and also from his own cash books, which bear no trace of Whale's classic whatsoever.
109. *Writing for the Films*, Uncommon Pleasures: Contact Book 17, A.G. Weidenfeld 1949.
110. Sherriff would later contribute a foreword to Masterman's own play *Marshal Ney*, a play, on which Masterman had hoped they might collaborate. Masterman later wrote a nice acknowledgement to Sherriff in his memoir, *Bits and Pieces* (Hodder & Stoughton, 1961). Interestingly, it makes no mention of Masterman's role in the XX counter-espionage committee in the Second World War, which is an extraordinary tale.
111. *The Daily Telegraph*, 21 September 1934.
112. *The Sunday Times*, 16 September 1934,
113. *Books of the Day, The Manchester Guardian*, 24 September 1934.
114. Letter from Sherriff to De Casalis, 28 September 1934, SHC 3813/1/21.
115. Letter from Sherriff to De Casalis, 29 September 1934, SHC 3813/1/21.
116. Here was the inscription that Edwards wanted: 'The authors wish to thank Mr Norman Edwards, the Editor of the English edition of *The St Helena Journal of General Baron Gourgaud*, for his suggestion that we should write a play about Napoleon's exile on the island of St Helena, and for his kindness in placing his valuable St Helena library at our disposal, and for much general advice and assistance.' Letter from Sherriff to De Casalis, 4 October 1934, SHC 3813/1/21.
117. Low, R., *Film Making in 1930s Britain*, George & Unwin, 1985.
118. This was Havelock-Allan's first production credit. He would go on to a stellar career as producer, writer and occasional director, with a host of famous movies to his name (*In Which We Serve* (1942), *Brief Encounter* (1945), *Great Expectations* (1946), *Ryan's Daughter* (1970) and many more).
119. *Kinematograph*, 20 September 1934.
120. *Cinema*, 19 September 1934.
121. Brunel, A., *Nice Work: Thirty years in British Films*, Forbes Robertson, 1949.
122. University of Michigan, Collection Code: AMSHW, Call number VV-B General Correspondence. Correspondence between Maurice Browne and R.C. Sherriff. Letter from Sherriff to Browne, 26 March 1935.
123. SHC 2332/3/6/6.
124. She had, for example, collaborated in an adaptation that became *The Mummy* – a hit for Universal and for Boris Karloff.
125. Curtis J., *op. cit.*, 1998, p.233.
126. SHC 2332/3/6/6 *Her Excellency the Governor* (Revised Script), April 1935.
127. Internal Memo written by KL, *Her Excellency the Governor*, AMPAS, Margaret Herrick Library, PCA Files. Henceforth, *Her Excellency the Governor*, PCA File.
128. Zehner to Breen, 17 August 1935: 'At the present time it has been decided to suspend further preparation of this production but you have our assurance that if, and when, this story goes into production, the objectionable elements will be removed so as to overcome the censorship difficulties presented in the script sent you.' *Her Excellency the Governor*, PCA Files.
129. Interview with Carl Laemmle Jr, 1971. Contained in Riley, Philip J., *James Whale's Dracula's Daughter*, Kindle edition, Bear Manor Media, 2009.
130. AFI Catalogue, *Dracula's Daughter*. The Catalogue entry questions whether the story was in fact the source of the film, since it was not published until 1937. But Junior Laemmle's interview appeared to suggest that the story was less important for its content than for the filmmakers' acquisition of additional movie rights.
131. *Variety*, 28 May 1935.
132. *Dracula's Daughter: A Screenplay*, July-August 1935, SHC 2332/3/6/9. Although the typed cover shows the date July 1935, the second half of the bound screenplay is dated August 1935. A subsequent script, dated September 1935, and showing relatively few revisions, is published in Riley, Philip J. *op. cit.*, 2009.

133. Riley notes that Sherriff said: 'We got the name Talifer from a book that James had just read – *Talifer*, by Edward Arlington Robinson, a lyric poem published by Macmillan in 1933. One of us referenced him to a wizard who lived around King Arthur's time but I'm not sure of the connection.' Riley, Philip J., *op. cit.*, 2009, Locations 719–723.

134. Memo by Joseph I. Breen, 13 September 1935, AMPAS, Margaret Herrick Library, PCA Files. *Dracula's Daughter*, PCA (1936). Henceforth, *Dracula's Daughter*, (1936), PCA Files. In his monthly resume of activities to Will Hays, Breen remarked: 'The script submitted seemed to us to be completely unacceptable, as it contained a very objectionable mixture of sex and horror. We had a conference with the studio; they have agreed to rewrite it entirely.'

135. Quoted in Robertson, James C., *The Hidden Cinema: British Film Censorship in Action, 1913–1975*, Routledge, 1989, p.66.

136. Riley suggests that, while the initial script was prepared by Sherriff in London, he then handed it to Whale, who, with some of his friends, 'took the basic script and added into it scenes with gay and lesbian overtones, sadomasochistic action in some of the scene backgrounds, whips and chains, mutilations and amputations and worded it to look as if the main characters would be two male lovers travelling with each other's sisters for a cover.' He then suggests that Whale handed the script to the PCA anonymously, but there is nothing in the PCA file to suggest they had seen anything before Zehner handed Sherriff's recently completed script to Breen on 5 September. Riley, Philip J., *op. cit.*, 2009, Locations 502–10.

137. Letter from Breen to Zehner, 23 October 1935, *Dracula's Daughter*, (1936), PCA File.

138. *Hollywood Reporter*, 25 October, 1935. See copy in the Surrey History Centre, 2332/5/13/3.

Chapter 8: Pastures New

1. http://www.metoffice.gov.uk/media/pdf/c/8/Nov1935.pdf.

2. Letter from Sherriff to Darlington, 19 November, 1935. SHC 3813/1/46. Laughton was, indeed, the original choice for the part of Mr Chipping, but at some point the studio changed its mind, possibly because of his success as Captain Bligh in *Mutiny on the Bounty*.

3. See exchange of letters between Sherriff and Hilton, 4 January 1935 to 11 January 1935, SHC 3813/1/39. The collaboration never came to fruition, because both were engaged on other projects.

4. Korda was a Hungarian filmmaker who had come to England via Austria and Hollywood. In 1932 he founded London Films (familiar from the trademark Big Ben title card in its movies) and with the assistance of his brothers Vincent (who specialised in film design) and Zoltan (who worked as a director), he went on to produce many of the most important British films of the 1930s. See, for example, Drazin, C., *Korda: Britain's Movie Mogul*, I B Tauris 2011.

5. Mentioned in a letter to Hilton, 11 March 1935, SHC 3813/1/39.

6. Thalberg was three years younger than Sherriff, but had been in the movie business since he was eighteen. Beginning with Carl Laemmle at Universal, he quickly became General Manager, before moving to work with Louis B. Mayer, becoming head of production at MGM when it was founded in 1924. He was nicknamed the 'Boy Wonder'.

7. 'Public' in the English sense of the word, i.e. fee-paying.

8. Quoted in Glancy, M., *When Hollywood Loved Britain*, Manchester University Press, 1999, pp.84–5.

9. SHC 2332/3/7/7/1.

10. AMPAS, Margaret Herrick Library. Turner/MGM Scripts. 1093-f.G-846.

11. Born in 1903, David Lewis was an associate producer at MGM, and James Whale's lover.

12. Lewis may just have been keeping Hilton happy. James Curtis reports that Whale and Lewis were very unhappy with the 'lack of feeling' in the first script. Curtis, J., *op. cit.*, 1998, p.283.

13. Letter from Hilton to Sherriff, 16 March, 1936, SHC 3813/1/39. All Hilton extracts reproduced with permission of Curtis Brown, London, on behalf of the Beneficiaries of the Literary Estate of James Hilton, © the Beneficiaries of the Literary Estate of James Hilton.

14. The most recent had been *Josephine* at His Majesty's Theatre on 25 September, which, according to Sherriff, 'had the worst notices of any play I have read about for years.' Letter from Sherriff to De Casalis, 28 September 1934, SHC 3813/1/21.

15. *No Leading Lady*, *op. cit.*, p.299.

16. Letter to De Casalis, 14 August 1935, SHC 3813/1/37. The best guess is that the producers were unhappy with the adaptation, because an alternative version, entitled *Promise*, by H.M. Harwood, finally appeared on stage in the spring of 1936.
17. Letter from Sherriff to De Casalis, 21 August 1938, SHC 3813/1/38.
18. Letter from Sherriff to De Casalis, 28 September 1934, SHC 3813/1/18.
19. *No Leading Lady*, op. cit., p.301.
20. Letter from Sherriff to De Casalis, 30 August 1935, SHC 3813/1/38.
21. Letter from Sherriff to De Casalis, 23 December 1935, SHC 3813/1/36.
22. Letter from Sherriff to De Casalis, 23 December 1935, SHC 3813/1/36.
23. The actors included, among their number, Leo Genn as Montholon and a 13-year-old Glynis Johns as one of Bertrand's children.
24. *No Leading Lady*, op. cit., p.302.
25. Here are the relevant dates: *The Times*, 6 February 1936; the *Evening Standard*, 5 February 1936; *New Statesman*, 8 February 1936; *The Observer*, 9 February 1936; *The Post*, 15 February 1936; *The Morning Post*, 5 February 1936; *The Manchester Guardian*, 7 February 1936.
26. *No Leading Lady*, op. cit., p.304.
27. *The Times*, 14 February 1936.
28. *No Leading Lady*, op. cit., p.305.
29. *The Manchester Guardian*, 14 March 1936.
30. SHC 2332/1/5/6.
31. *No Leading Lady*, op. cit., p.307.
32. *John O'London's Weekly*, 28 March 1936.
33. *The Saturday Review*, 28 March 1936.
34. *The People*, 22 March 1936.
35. *No Leading Lady*, op. cit., p.308.
36. *Ibid*, p.309.
37. Letter from Sherriff to Hilton, 30 April 1936, SHC 3813/1/39.
38. *Variety*, 7 August 1936.
39. Letter from Sherriff to Gerald Ellison, 16 February 1935, SHC 3813/1/37.
40. Letter from Sherriff to Jeanne De Casalis, 25 April 1935, SHC 3813/1/38.
41. The serialisation began in October 1935.
42. See Juliet Gardiner's preface in the Persephone edition of *Greengates*, 2015.
43. The house, which is still standing today, was located about midway between the old house and Rosebriars, and convenient for Beryl's house, 'Pitkerro', in Weston Green.
44. See Zoe Karens' Sherriff Project blog: http://www.exploringsurreyspast.org.uk/sherriff-blog-18/.
45. *The Sketch*, 10 June 1936.
46. Letter from Gerald Ellison to Sherriff, 11 May 1936, SHC 3813/1/49.
47. Letter to Ernest Denny, 16 June 1936, SHC 3813/1/46.
48. Letter to Anthony (Toni) Thorne, 29 March 1935, SHC 3813/1/45.
49. *No Leading Lady*, op. cit., p.285.
50. Letter to Alexander Korda, 13 April 1935, SHC 3813/1/37.
51. The movie was released in 1936, but Sherriff received no writing credit. One of the credited writers was Miles Malleson, the man who had turned down the chance to direct *Journey's End* at the Incorporated Stage Society some eight years earlier.
52. Cash books SHC 2332/4/1/2.
53. *Greengates* royalties from 1935 to 1940 (incl), and for *St Helena* from 1934 to 1939 (incl). Cash books SHC 2332/4/1/2 & SHC 2332/4/1/4.
54. Erich Pommer had been a very significant figure in the German film industry throughout the 1920s, leaving it behind only after the Nazis came to power. He worked for Korda in 1936 and 1937, producing *Fire Over England* (about Elizabeth I and the Spanish Armada, and featuring Vivien Leigh and Laurence Olivier together for the first time). René Clair was a luminary of French cinema who came to work with Korda in 1935, before their falling out in 1936.
55. Sherriff recalled this project as having come after *The Four Feathers*, but he was mistaken. *No Leading Lady*, op. cit., p.294.

56. Letter from Sherriff to Pommer, 17 June 1936, SHC 3813/1/46.
57. SHC 2332/3/6/11.
58. The tenor of the tale may have appealed to Sherriff because it reminded him of an earlier 'playlet' he had written, called *Two Hearts Doubled*, which also featured a young couple, each concealing their humble background from the other. The play was written in 1934 as a sketch for inclusion in a revue being planned by J.B. Priestley's wife, Jane. Although the revue was cancelled, Sherriff opted to let the magazine *Printer's Pie* publish it in summer 1934. It was also published by Samuel French, for amateur companies.
59. Even Clair's biographer is at a loss to explain 'the suddenness, the completeness, of their break'. McGerr, C., *René Clair*, Twayne Publishers, 1980.
60. Letter from Sherriff to Jean De Casalis, 17 December 1936. SHC 3813/1/12,.
61. As was David Lewis.
62. Muni's two most notable movies at that point were *Scarface* and *I am a Fugitive from a Chain Gang*, for which he had received an Oscar nomination.
63. Letter from Sherriff to De Casalis, 11 July 1936, SHC 3813/1/62.
64. See, for example, her letter to Sherriff, undated, but probably mid to late August 1936, SHC 3813/1/30.
65. 'Paper' referred to people who had been offered free tickets by the management to make the house look fuller, and in the hope that they would pass on recommendations by word of mouth.
66. Letter from Sherriff to De Casalis, 17 December 1936, SHC 3813/1/12.
67. Letter from De Casalis to Sherriff, undated, but probably around mid-January 1937, SHC 3813/1/12.
68. Letter from Gyssling to Breen, 30 September 1936. *The Road Back* (1937) PCA File. Demonstrating the Nazis' reflexive dislike of Remarque, he asks at the end of the letter: 'Do you know the nature of a manuscript by Erich Maria Remarque *Three Comrades*, which is said to have been bought by Metro-Goldwyn-Mayer?' In reply Breen wrote that he knew nothing of it – but Sherriff would go on to produce the first script for it just a couple of months later.
69. Letter from Breen to Zehner, 14 October 1936, *The Road Back*, PCA Files.
70. SHC 9314/13. This is a copy of a screenplay held at the University of Southern California.
71. Letter to Otto Klement, 9 June 1937, SHC 3813/1/12.
72. SHC 2332/3/6/1.
73. Outlined in a memo from Breen to Hays, 12 February 1937. *The Road Back* (1937) PCA File. The memo gave a comprehensive account of all of the PCA's recent dealings with Universal.
74. *Ibid.*
75. Noah Beery Jr (Wessling), Richard Cromwell (Ludwig), Andy Devine (Willy), Henry Hunter (Bethke), John King (Ernst), Maurice Murphy (Albert), Slim Summerville (Tjaden), Louise Fazenda (Angelina), and Barbara Read (Lucy).
76. This was the text of the warning:
   The allocation of permits may be refused for films, the producers of which, in spite of warnings issued by the competent German authorities, continue to distribute on the world market films, the tendency of which is detrimental to German prestige. The same applies to pictures with which persons are connected who have already participated in the production of pictures detrimental to German prestige in tendency or effect. (Letter from Gyssling to Breen, 25 March 1937. *The Road Back*, (1937) PCA File.
77. *Variety*, 8 June 1937.
78. Curtis, J., *op. cit.*, 1998, p.308.

Chapter 9: Korda and MGM

1. And the decision would likely have been even more emphatic if he could have predicted the fate of *The Road Back* over the coming months.
2. Sherriff, R.C., *Three Comrades: Summary of Chapters*, 30 October 1936, AMPAS, Margaret Herrick Library, Turner/MGM Scripts, *Three Comrades* (1938) – T 1212.
3. Sherriff, R.C., *Notes on the Script of Three Comrades*, February 1937, AMPAS, Margaret Herrick Library, Turner/MGM Scripts, *Three Comrades* (1938) – T 1213.

4. Letter from Joseph Breen to Louis B. Mayer, 11 May 1937, AMPAS, Margaret Herrick Library, *Three Comrades*, (1938), PCA File.

5. Letter to Otto Klement, 9 June 1937, SHC 3813/1/12.

6. In the event, even Fitzgerald's screenplay did not sit well with Mankiewicz, who rewrote sections of it himself, remarking in the process that 'I personally have been attacked [by the literary world] as if I had spat on the flag. ... If I go down at all in literary history, in a footnote, it will be as the swine who rewrote F. Scott Fitzgerald.' See Dumont, H., *Frank Borzage: The Life and Films of a Hollywood Romantic*; McFarland, 2006.

7. *Ibid.*

8. *Variety*, 26 June 1937.

9. Saville was a year older than Sherriff, and another First World War veteran. He had worked in the film industry since the war ended, including stints as a director at Gaumont-British, working for Balcon. He set up his own production company – Victor Saville Productions – along with scriptwriter Ian Dalrymple, and made several films at Denham for Korda.

10. *No Leading Lady, op. cit.*, p.294.

11. Lajos Biro, Korda's scenario chief (another Hungarian, with extensive film industry and scriptwriting experience) dropped him a line to reassure him: 'Only two lines to ask you not to worry about the waste of time over your work with D'Arrast. Everybody knows it was not your fault, Alex in the first place.' Letter from Lajos Biro to Sherriff, 14 May 1937, SHC 3813/1/62.

12. Letter from Sherriff to Lajos Biro, 4 June 1937, SHC 3813/1/62.

13. *No Leading Lady, op. cit.*, p.309.

14. Sherriff owned two houses in Bognor (Lapwing and Fieldfare), before having Sandmartin built from August 1936–July 1937.

15. Letter from Sherriff to Nigel Nicolson, 26 April 1969, SHC 2332/1/1/27. In fact, a rather grand palace was unearthed in 1960 in Fishbourne, just 10 miles away from Selsey.

16. Nicolson, N., *Long Life*, Weidenfeld & Nicolson, 1997, p.223.

17. *No Leading Lady, op. cit.*, p.313.

18. Wren, P.C., *The Man of a Ghost*, Remploy Reprint Edition, 1973 (orig 1937), p.23.

19. The title comes from a well-known poem by Kipling entitled *Gentleman-rankers*, about ex-officers who had fallen on hard times and re-enlisted as rankers – ordinary soldiers – to scratch out a living. The poem records their dissatisfactions and despair.

20. Letter from Sherriff to Sydney Carroll, 20 September 1937, SHC 3813/1/47.

21. Glancy, H. Mark, *op. cit.*, 1999, p.81.

22. Brown, G., *Launder and Gilliat*, British Film Institute, 1977, p.82.

23. His experience included working for Howard Hughes on *Hell's Angels* and *Dawn Patrol*.

24. He visited the Hendon air pageant, and the airfields at Kenley and Felixstowe. AMPAS, Margaret Herrick Library, Elmer Dyer papers, 2.f-56 and 2.f-57.

25. The film was released in November 1939, and starred Ralph Richardson and Merle Oberon. It was the product of many talented hands, including Alexander Korda, Michael Powell, Adrian Brunel and Ian Dalrymple.

26. Known as *Cargo of Innocence* in the UK.

27. Glancy, H. Mark, *Hollywood and Britain: MGM and the British Quota Legislation*, in Richards, J., *The Unknown 1930s: An Alternative History of the British Cinema, 1929–1939*, L.B. Tauris, 1998, p.68.

28. Glancy, H. Mark, *op. cit.*, 1999, p.83.

29. Sherriff liked the script, and the film was a great box office success. But critics were less kind about it.

30. The egg-laying charts in his papers speak eloquently to his knowledge of poultry.

31. In 1958, Sherriff would produce a shortened version of the story for Pan books, entitled *The Cataclysm*.

32. Moorcock, M., *Preface*; in Sherriff, R.C., *The Hopkins Manuscript*, Persephone Press, 2005.

33. Sourced from his reply to Mollie Cazalet, 4 January 1939, SHC 3813/1/44.

34. In fact, his library contained *A History of The Kings of England* by Geoffrey of Monmouth, given to him, and inscribed, by Mrs Chamberlain.

35. Letter from Mollie Cazalet to Sherriff, 21 September 1938, SHC 3813/1/44. The letter was written after Chamberlain's visit to Berchtesgaden, but before his trip to Munich later that month.
36. *No Leading Lady, op. cit.*, p.290.
37. *Variety* magazine announced, in January of 1937, that Oliver H.P. Garrett (a very experienced American scriptwriter) was leaving for England to write *The Four Feathers*. No trace of that original script (if there was one) can be found, however, and he received no writing or story credit for the film. Nothing in Sherriff's account (or those of Korda's biographers) suggests that Sherriff was reworking an existing script.
38. *The Four Feathers*, Revised Draft Script, June 1938, SHC 2332/3/6/14.
39. *The Manchester Guardian*, 19 April 1939.
40. In *No Leading Lady*, Sherriff recalls talking to A.E.W. Mason about the screenplay, and that Mason felt Sherriff had not adapted the character of Fanshawe from the novel especially well. Sherriff smiled at Mason's protestations, noting that there was no Fanshawe in the book at all. We, in turn, can smile at Sherriff, since there is no Fanshawe in the movie either.
41. Wimperis was some twenty years older than Sherriff, and had fought in the Boer War and the First World War. He had written for theatre and lyrics for songs and musicals (including the First World War recruiting song *I'll Make a Man of You*) before going on to write for movies. He worked closely with Biro for Korda in the 1930s, and then for MGM in the 1940s, and would win an Academy Award for *Mrs Miniver*.
42. See, for example, Sherriff's letter to Eileen Corbett, Zoltan Korda's assistant, p.6: 'Wimp[eris] to write line for General Burroughs to open the scene at the Crimea dinner party. Remind Wimp that Burroughs must be comic relief, and all the menacing lines directed to intimidate the boy must come from General Faversham or some other guest who is not funny.' Letter from Sherriff to Eileen Corbett (Assistant to Zoltan Korda), 20 July 1938, SHC 3813/1/30.
43. Memo from Major C.D. Armstrong, Officer Commanding Film Camp, 1st Battalion, East Surrey Regiment, SHC ESR/2/8/10.
44. There are excellent accounts of the camp, from both the Army and the filmmakers' perspectives, in the *Journal of the East Surrey Regiment*, May 1939, SHC J/553/70.
45. Told to the author, in turn, by Chris Manning-Press, Sherriff's godson.
46. Borradaille, O., and Hadley, A.B., *Life Through a Lens*, McGill-Queen's University Press 2001, p.108. Borradaille and the principal cinematographer, Georges Périnal, would both be nominated for an Academy Award in 1939 for their work on the film, although they would lose out (as almost everyone did that year) to *Gone with the Wind*.
47. Shute, N., *Ruined City*, Pan Books, London, 1973. Also known as *Kindling* in the American edition.
48. His first payment was logged in his cash book in September 1938.
49. *Ruined City*, January 1939, SHC 2332/3/6/16. The script is subtitled 'Revisions', and from some of the notes inside it is clear that it is at least a second draft, if not later. There are a number of inherent contradictions in the script, and several 'montage' sequences that are offered almost as menus from which Victor Saville is invited to choose.
50. Letter from Maurice Browne to Dorothy Elmhirst, 9 July 1937, DHC, DHTA, DWE/4/14C.
51. Probably in February, judging by the first payment in his cash book.
52. SHC 2332/3/1/1/4.
53. See page 28.
54. Or Ben Goetz, depending on reports.
55. See the Jules Furthman papers at the Margaret Herrick library (20.f-173), and the revised script at the University of South Carolina, James Furthman Screenplay Archive, Box 5, Furthman A.5.17.
56. *The Observer*, 26 March 1939.
57. *The Spectator*, 2 April 1939.
58. *Punch*, 12 April 1939.
59. *Country Life*, 15 April 1939.
60. *The Sketch*, 12 April 1939.
61. *Daily Sketch*, 1 April 1939.

62. For a detailed analysis of the financial issues behind the establishment of Korda's new company, see Drazin, C., *op. cit.*, 2011, pp.196–203.

63. Letter from Bleck to Sherriff, 13 March 1939, SHC 3813/1/38. It is probably this contract that Sherriff recalled when he wrote *No Leading Lady*, in which (p.289) he suggested that Korda was paying him £6,000 per screenplay. His cash books show, however, that the contracts with Korda were always specified as a weekly salary.

64. Letter from Bleck to Sherriff, 15 March 1939, SHC 3813/1/38.

65. *News Chronicle*, 18 April 1930.

66. *The Times*, 18 April 1939.

67. *The Observer*, 23 April 1939.

68. *The Spectator*, 28 April 1939.

69. *The Manchester Guardian*, 19 April 1939.

70. *New York Sun*, 4 August 1939.

71. Saville had taken over as head of MGM-British when Michael Balcon had quit, owing to his frustrations at interference from Louis B. Mayer and the parent studio.

72. Letter from Sherriff to Victor Saville, 19 July 1938, SHC 3813/1/30.

73. Letter from Saville to Sherriff, 24 November 1938, SHC 3813/1/30.

74. Hilton, J., *Goodbye, Mr Chips*, Coronet Books, 2001, p.10.

75. Amusingly, in the film, when Chips is showing one of the new boys the commemorative arch on which boys inscribe their names, we see the name of Sir William Howe: one has to admire the boy who knew, at such an early age, that he was going to be knighted!

76. Quoted by Hilton in a letter to Sherriff, 1 May 1939, SHC 3813/1/39.

77. Letter from Sherriff to Hilton, 15 May 1939, SHC 3813/1/39.

78. The author's examination suggests that the amount of his script remaining is closer to 25 per cent than 8 per cent.

79. SNC 2332 2332/3/7/7/1.

80. *No Leading Lady, op. cit.*, p.318.

81. Letter from Warre-Dymond to Sherriff, 25 March 1939, SHC 3813/1/56.

82. Letter from Warre-Dymond to Sherriff, 8 April 1939, SHC 3813/1/56.

83. Details of former comrades' activities in the war are taken from Lucas, M., *op. cit.*, 2012.

84. Letter from Peg Stoker to Sherriff, 29 October 1939, SHC 3813/1/51.

85. Letter from Mollie Cazalet to Sherriff, 8 September 1939, SHC 3813/1/17.

86. Letter from Sherriff to Korda, 14 September 1939, SHC 3813/1/38.

87. AMPAS, Margaret Herrick Library, Paul Kohner Agency records, *Manon Lescaut* script, 125-f.115.

88. *Glasgow Evening Times*, 24 August 1939.

89. Letter from Sherriff to Pascal, 18 October 1939, SHC 3813/1/53.

90. Letter from Sherriff to David Michael de Rueda Winser, 12 November 1939, SHC 3813/1/48. Winser was later killed in action as a member of the RAMC, attached to 48 Royal Marine Commando, on 1 November 1944.

91. See Drazin, C., *op. cit.*, 2011, pp.221–9.

92. See Aldgate, A., and Richards, J., *Britain Can Take It: The British Cinema in the Second World War*, I.B. Tauris, 2007, pp.22–3.

93. Letter from Sherriff to Pascal, 2 October 1939, SHC 3813/1/53.

94. General John Beith, a successful author and First World War veteran, was Director of Public Relations at the War Office.

95. Letter from Sherriff to Marjorie Deans, 18 October 1939, SHC 3813/1/53.

96. Letter from Sherriff to Peg Stoker, 13 November 1939, SHC 3813/1/50.

97. The film and the script would carry on in development without him, so that when it was finally distributed in May 1941, his name was not attached to the writing credits.

98. *Daily Sketch*, 24 April 1939.

99. Formerly Joseph Kenworthy, an ex-naval man and Labour MP, who became Labour Chief Whip in the House of Lords after assuming the hereditary title of Baron Strabolgi.

100. The story was, eventually, made into a movie in 1956, *The Battle of the River Plate*, by Powell & Pressburger.

101. SHC 2332/3/6/17.
102. *No Leading Lady, op. cit.*, pp.319–20.
103. Letter from Sherriff to A. Flavell, 28 March 1940, SHC 2332/1/1/11.
104. As Drazin, *op. cit.*, 2011, p.232, points out, Leigh and Olivier made 'for perfect casting as the two lovers, since they were both at the height of their Hollywood stardom and, like their characters in the film, had themselves been engaged in a highly public affair.'
105. For example, arranging new passports and visas as late as 22 May 1940. See the letter to Sherriff from Northern Transport Travel Bureau, 22 May 1940, SHC 2332/1/1/11.
106. Letter from Canadian Pacific Railway Company, 24 May 1940, SHC 2332/1/1/11.
107. *No Leading Lady, op. cit.*, p.318.

Chapter 10: Semi-Official Business

1. *No Leading Lady, op. cit.*, p.326.
2. SHC 2332/1/1/11.
3. Letter from Cowley to Sherriff, 13 June 1939, SHC 3813/1/50.
4. See Nagorski, T., *Miracles on the Water*, Hachette, 2015.
5. Émigrés from the United Kingdom were only allowed to take about £10 each owing to exchange restrictions, although it was possible to take more, with the appropriate permits, or to take additional travellers' cheques. (Letter from Canadian Pacific Railway Company, 24 May 1940, SHC 2332/1/1/11.)
6. Letter from Basil Bleck to Sherriff, 1 June 1940, SHC 2332/1/1/11.
7. Cable from Sig Marcus to Sherriff, 12 June 1940, SHC 2352/1/1/11.
8. See cash book, 2332/4/1/5, p.100.
9. Itinerary from Canadian Pacific Railway Company, undated, SHC 2332/1/1/11.
10. Cable from Sig Marcus, 12 June 1940, *op. cit.*
11. The hotel had no religious connotations. Its original owner was Alla Nazimova, and when she sold the hotel the new owners added an 'h' at the end.
12. The film was released in December 1940, and starred Robert Taylor and Walter Pidgeon. It has some good flight scenes, but otherwise is a fairly conventional action movie.
13. Reisch started in Austria, but then moved to Germany where he worked with Erich Pommer (coincidentally alongside Billy Wilder). He returned to Vienna but left as the Nazis grew in power, heading first for London – where he worked with Korda – and then on to the United States, where he settled with MGM.
14. See Drazin, C., *op. cit.*, 2011, p.233.
15. Capua, Michelangelo, *Vivien Leigh: A Biography*, McFarland, 2003, p.79.
16. *No Leading Lady, op. cit.*, p.335.
17. Letter from Breen to George Bagnall (of Alexander Korda Films Inc), 16 September 1940. AMPAS, Margaret Herrick Library, Production Code Administration records, *That Hamilton Woman* (1941), (henceforth *That Hamilton Woman* (1941) PCA File).
18. Letter from Breen to Korda, 19 September 1940, *That Hamilton Woman* (1941) PCA File.
19. Letter from Breen to Korda, 15 October 1940, *That Hamilton Woman* (1941) PCA File.
20. Letter from Breen to Korda, 30 October 1940, *That Hamilton Woman* (1941) PCA File.
21. Drazin, C., *op. cit.*, 2011, p.235.
22. SHC 2332/5/2/87.
23. There is a nice tale in Michael Korda's biography of the Korda brothers, to the effect that Alex Korda, desperate to know which arm Nelson lost before shooting began, consulted an actor in Los Angeles who had played Nelson on stage. He was no wiser after meeting him, however, for the actor said he had changed arms in different performances to make things more interesting for himself. See Korda, M., *Charmed Lives*, Allen Lane, 1980, p.151.
24. The scenes were filmed mainly in a large tank, with model boats, about the size of dinghies, being pushed by discreetly concealed prop men in fishing waders.
25. *That Hamilton Woman* (1941), about 92 minutes into the film.
26. Calder, R., *Beware the British Serpent: The Role of Writers in British Propaganda in the United States*, 1939–1945, McGill-Queen's University Press, 2004, p.251.
27. *New York Times*, 4 April 1941.

28. Korda, M., *op. cit.*, 1980, p.154.
29. See Calder, R., *op. cit.*, 2004, p.251.
30. *No Leading Lady, op. cit.*, p.338.
31. The penname of author Joyce Maxtone Graham.
32. Letter from Kenneth McKenna to Sherriff, 5 October 1940, SHC 2332/1/1/11.
33. Quoted in Glancy, H. Mark, *op. cit.*, 1999, p.142.
34. In what he described as a kind of 'notebook', to which they could add or subtract as they worked on the project. See Notes from R.C. Sherriff, 6 November 1940 (AMPAS, Margaret Herrick Library, Turner/MGM Scripts, *Mrs Miniver*, 1942). He also appears to have scripted two possible scenes in advance of producing the notebook, neither of which made it into the movie. SHC 2332/3/6/18/ 1 & 2.
35. *Mrs Miniver* Prologue Script, by R.C. Sherriff, 7 November 1940, AMPAS, Margaret Herrick Library, Turner/MGM Scripts, *Mrs Miniver* (1942).
36. In fact, James Hilton sent him a clipping in which the actress Laraine Day described it as her 'favourite movie scene'. Sherriff replied to Hilton noting that it brought back pleasant memories of their time working on the film with Sydney Franklin, 'who used to turn up at conferences some mornings completely dressed as an Old Etonian and next morning as an Old Marlburian.' SHC 2332/1/1/17.
37. Given that he first wrote a 'prologue' scene, and that in the final movie the 'hat scene' is the first one, the two may have become mistakenly conflated.
38. Letter from Sidney Franklin to Sherriff, 5 May 1942, SHC 2332/1/1/11.
39. Minutes of meeting, 21 August 1940, SHC 2332/1/1/11. The committee later became known, more simply, as the British War Services Advisory Board. It was eventually wound up in January 1945, when Cleugh was posted to Cuba. (See his letter to Sherriff, 16 January 1945, SHC 2332/1/1/15.)
40. *Picturegoer and Film Weekly,* 27 January 1940.
41. *Picturegoer and Film Weekly*, 11 May 1940.
42. Balcon confessed his sins in his biography: 'It may be that I was at times mildly jealous of [Korda's] popularity and his achievements, and certainly I misunderstood his departure to Hollywood, with other members of his family, early in the Second World War. I was wrong then about Korda, but perhaps not so wrong about some of the others who left with unseemly haste immediately before or after the war began. Korda was generous in his forgiveness of one or two unseemly cracks I made.' Balcon, M., *op. cit.*, 1969, pp.93–4.
43. *The Times*, 24 May 1940.
44. *The Sunday Despatch*, 25 August 1940. Quoted in Morley, S., *op. cit.*, 1983, p.166.
45. Minutes of meeting, 28 August 1940, SHC 2332/1/1/11.
46. Glancy (1999) writes that a *Variety* article in July 1940, which was supportive of the Hollywood Brits, gave a shortlist of well-known actors who had fought in the First World War, and had noted that C. Aubrey Smith was 'old enough to have drawn a longbow at Hastings'.
47. Minutes of meeting, 28 August 1940, SHC 2332/1/1/11.
48. Cable from Lord Lothian to Lord Halifax, 31 August 1940, SHC 2332/1/1/11.
49. Calder, R., *op. cit.*, 2004, p.247.
50. As told to the author by Christopher Manning-Press.
51. *No Leading Lady, op. cit.*, p.340–1.
52. See letter to Richard West, 24 March 1945, SHC 2332/1/1/14
53. The pen name of Eric Andrew Simson, British writer and one-time Navy officer.
54. AMPAS, Margaret Herrick Library, Turner/MGM Scripts, *Stand By For Action* (1943) – Story Outline by R.C. Sherriff, 12-20-40.
55. Actually, *Cargo of Innocents* in the print at the British Film Institute.
56. *New York Times*, 12 March, 1943.
57. Letter to Harvey Haislip, 9 January 1945, SHC 2332/1/1/14.
58. Letter from Sherriff to Victor Cazalet, 24 June 1941, SHC 2332/1/1/11.
59. On Monday, 7 July 1941.
60. Women's Auxiliary Air Force.

61. Some of the work he had done for MGM in the late 1930s showed the same ability, but it's unlikely that Zanuck would have known about those unproduced screenplays.

62. The studio memos are quoted in Glancy, H.M., *op. cit.*, 1999, pp.135–42.

63. One of whom, her uncle, was played by an old friend of Sherriff's – Melville Cooper, who had played Trotter in the original *Journey's End*.

64. AMPAS, Margaret Herrick Library, Production Code Administration Files, *This Above All* (1942). Henceforth, *This Above All*, (1942), PCA File.

65. In fact, he was known for putting in extra lines that he would then allow the PCA to force him to omit, distracting them from other sections that he would prefer to keep. See Wilk, M., *op. cit.*, 2004, p.119.

66. Letter from Zanuck to Shurlock, 10 November 1941, *This Above All*, (1942), PCA File.

67. Letter from Knight to Paul Rotha. Rotha, P., (Ed.), *Portrait of a Flying Yorkshireman: Letters from Eric Knight in the United States to Paul Rotha in England*, Chapman & Hall, 1952.

68. The speech takes place 65:03 minutes into the film.

69. Letter from Sherriff to Cazalet, 22 September 1941, SHC 2332/1/1/11. This is the last exchange of correspondence Sherriff seems to have had with Cazalet, who died in a plane crash in 1943.

70. Memo from Zanuck to Sherriff, 27 November 1941, SHC 2332/1/1/11.

71. *New York Times*, 13 May 1942.

72. See Glancy, H. Mark, *op. cit.*, 1999, p.141.

73. *Variety*, 6 January 1943.

74. Letter from James Hilton to Sherriff, 22 January 1943, SHC 2332/1/1/12.

75. SHC 2332/1/1/11.

76. SHC 2332/3/6/2/2.

77. This may have been the one he referred to in a letter to Harold Boxall at Korda Film Productions on 22 December 1939, SHC 3813/1/38.

78. Letter from Sherriff to Alan Collins, 14 November 1942, SHC 2332/1/1/12.

79. With a contract beginning towards the end of May, and still paying $1,400 a week. See the letter from George Stephenson to Sherriff, 10 April 1942, SHC 2332/1/1/11.

80. Letter from Sherriff to Gerald Ellison, 28 November 1941, SHC 2332/1/1/11.

81. SHC 2332/3/6/23.

82. Watts, S., *The Magic Kingdom: Walt Disney and the American Way of Life*, University of Missouri Press, 2013, p.236.

83. Letter to James Hilton from Sherriff, 28 September 1942, SHC 2332/1/1/11.

84. See Glancy, H. Mark, *op. cit.*, 1999, p.170.

85. See the exchange of letters between Ellison and Sherriff, SHC 2332/1/1/11.

86. Report on *This Changing World*, 31 December 1941, UCLA Files, *Forever and a Day*.

87. See Glancy, H., Mark *op. cit.*, 1999, p.179.

88. Letter from Harold Butler, to Sherriff, 2 November 1942, SHC 2332/1/1/11.

89. Letter from Sherriff to Harold Butler, 10 November 1942, SHC 2332/1/1/11.

90. Last seen, in this book, toiling for the PCA in 1932. (See Chapter 7.)

91. Letter from Sig Marcus, 12 January 1943, SHC 2332/1/1/12.

92. SHC 2332/3/5/3/2.

93. A couple of years later, having heard that Warners might be interested in buying the project from Fox, Sherriff asked his agent what was happening. The reply came back from Hugh King at Myron Selznick that it was still on Bob Bassler's schedule at Fox: he was keen to produce it, but had not yet been given the go-ahead (SHC 2332/1/1/15). Finding the money for new productions after the war was difficult, and *Chedworth* would simply have been one project among many competing for resources. It had the added disadvantage of a very obvious and specific wartime setting, and as soon as the war was over studios reached out for other subjects, convinced the public had had enough.

94. Letter from Sherriff to Collins, 2 December 1942, SHC 2332/1/1/12.

95. Letter to Alan Collins, 8 February 1943, SHC 2332/1/1/12.

96. Cable from Curtis Brown to Sherriff, 18 February 1943, SHC 2332/1/1/12.

97. Quoted in a letter from Sherriff to Curtis Brown, 19 February 1943, but marked not sent.

98. Cable from Curtis Brown to Sherriff, 23 February 1943, SHC 2332/1/1/12.

99. Cable from Curtis Brown to Sherriff, 10 March 1943, SHC 2332/1/1/12.
100. Letter from Sherriff to Spencer Curtis Brown, 12 March 1943, SHC 2332/1/1/12.
101. Letter to Alan Collins, 1 March 1943, SHC 2332/1/1/12.
102. Letter to G.R.G. Radcliffe from Sherriff, 20 April 1943, SHC 2332/1/1/12.
103. Soskin eventually found someone else to write the screenplay, and production began later in 1943, with Osmond Borradaille hired to film dramatic aerial sequences over the countryside near Shrewsbury. But, for no very obvious reason, the production was cancelled indefinitely soon after the air sequences had been shot. 'To my deep disappointment,' wrote Borradaille, 'the film was never completed and I do not know what happened to our negatives.' Borradaille, O., *op. cit.*, 2001, p.150.
104. It might have been finished much later, for when his plane was shot up in 1941, and the crew were ordered to discard unnecessary weight, he successfully managed to hold on to the manuscript of the play's first act.
105. SHC 2332/3/6/25.
106. SHC 2332/3/7/7/1.
107. Elements from *Flare Path* did, however, make their way into the impressive, Rattigan-scripted British movie, *The Way to the Stars*, in 1945.
108. Letter from LA Consulate to Consulate General in New York, 12 June 1943, SHC 2332/1/1/12.
109. Letter from Sherriff to Barclays Bank manager, Esher, 3 January 1944, SHC 2332/1/1/12.
110. Letter from Sherriff to Reeves Espy, 9 May 1944, SHC 2332/1/1/13.
111. SHC 2332/4/1/6.
112. Letter from Sherriff to C.L. Hill, 28 September 1943, SHC 2332/1/1/13.
113. Letter from Sherriff to Alan Collins, 3 January 1944, SHC 2332/1/1/13.
114. Contract with Macmillans, 29 February 1944, SHC 2332/4/6.
115. He later wrote to Harold Latham, vice president at Macmillan, that: 'I wrote [the book] under rather difficult conditions, the last part of it while waiting in New York for a ship to England, never knowing when I should have to pack up and rush away to the docks at a few hours' notice.' (Letter from Sherriff to Harold Latham, 15 March 1945, SHC 2332/1/1/14.) Of course, he was exaggerating for effect – the manuscript was completed in California, where he knew he would receive at least a week or two's notice – but Sherriff never let anything get in the way of a good story.
116. Her first, written under the pseudonym of C.L. Anthony.
117. She came, at his invitation, to the West End premiere of *St Helena*, and had afterwards written him a fulsome letter in praise of it. SHC 3813/1/60.
118. His salary was roughly twice what they were paying the (soon to become) famous Ayn Rand, who was on a screenwriting contract with them at the same time. (Contract details are contained in the Warner Brothers archive, Specific Assignment Reports.)
119. See Drazin, C., *op. cit.*, 2011, p.255.
120. Telegram from Sherriff to Korda, date unknown, but likely April/May 1944, SHC 2332/1/1/12.
121. *No Leading Lady, op. cit.*, p.340.
122. Letter from Sherriff to Reeves Espy, 9 May 1944, SHC 2332/1/1/13.
123. Letter from Hugh King to Sherriff, 4 April 1945, SHC 2332/1/1/13.
124. Letter from C.L. Hill to Sherriff, 26 June 1944, SHC 2332/1/1/11.
125. Draft cable, written on a letter to Sherriff from C.L. Hill, 28 June 1944, SHC 2332/1/1/11.

Chapter 11: Back to Blighty
1. Letters to Harvey Haislip, 9 January 1945, SHC 2332/1/1/14, and to Frank Hodsoll, 31 May 1945 (SHC 2332/1/1/15).
2. Letter from Sherriff to Reeves Espy, 10 February 1945, SHC 2332/1/1/14.
3. Letter from Alice Head to Sherriff, 2 February 1945, SHC 2332/1/1/14.
4. Stern, G.B., *Trumpet Voluntary*, Cassell & Co, 1944.
5. Letter from E.W. Greene to Sherriff, 28 October 1944, SHC 2332/1/1/13.
6. *The Saturday Review*, 4 November 1944.
7. *Chicago Daily News*, 11 October 1944.
8. *New York Herald Tribune*, 15 October 1944.

9. *Chicago Tribune*, 15 October 1944.
10. *The Commonweal*, 1 December 1944.
11. Letter from Jean Curtis-Brown to Sherriff, 20 November 1944, SHC 2332/1/1/14.
12. Letter from Jean Curtis-Brown to Sherriff, 23 November 1944, SHC 2332/1/1/14.
13. Letter from Victor Gollancz to Sherriff, 7 December 1944, SHC 2332/1/1/13.
14. Reader's Report on *Chedworth*, contained in letter from Spencer Curtis Brown to Sherriff, 29 June 1945, SHC 2332/1/1/15.
15. Letter from Sherriff to Spencer Curtis Brown, 19 July 1945, SHC 2332/1/1/16.
16. Letter from Alice Head to Sherriff, 9 April 1945, SHC 2332/1/1/15.
17. Tabori, P., *Alexander Korda*, Oldbourne, London, 1959, p.10.
18. University of London Senate House Library, Special Collections. Paul Tabori Film Scripts. MS 1006/5/5.
19. Tabori urges him in one comment to examine the photos of Cologne.
20. Dalrymple was seven years Sherriff's junior, but was a very experienced film-maker, having worked in the industry since the late 1920s, mainly with Gainsborough and Gaumont-British, and with Victor Saville. He had been a producer for the Crown Film unit during the war, and had been nominated for an Academy Award for his adaption of *The Citadel* in 1938.
21. Letter from Ian Dalrymple to Sherriff, 10 August 1945. SHC 2332/1/1/16,
22. Tabori, P., *op. cit.*, 1959, p.13.
23. Letter from Sherriff to Alice Head, 5 April 1945, SHC 2332/1/1/15.
24. Letter from Alice Head to Sherriff, 9 April 1945, SHC 2332/1/1/15.
25. Letter from Sherriff to Alice Head, 12 April 1945, SHC 2332/1/1/15.
26. Letter from Sherriff to Bundy, 9 January 1945, SHC 2332/1/1/14.
27. Letter from Bundy to Sherriff, 16 January 1945, SHC 2332/1/1/14.
28. See David Hatten's letter to Sherriff, 15 August 1945, SHC 2332/1/1/16.
29. See, for example, letters to Charles Feldman, 11 October 1945, SHC 2332/1/1/17, and to Colin Tennant on 15 November 1945, SHC 2332/1/1/18.
30. Letter from Sherriff to David Henley, 17 May 1945. SHC 2332/1/1/15.
31. She had enlisted in the Women's Royal Naval Service.
32. Letter from Sherriff to Ben Goetz, 30 January 1946, SHC 2332/1/1/18.
33. The film was written by Eric Ambler and Peter Ustinov, and is the story of a group of army recruits coming together during training, and shipping out to fight the Germans in North Africa. It is an excellent picture, although I am not entirely unbiased because my father had a role in one of the training scenes in the film, albeit enclosed in his Sherman tank.
34. Letter from Sherriff to Colin Tennant, 8 January 1946, SHC 2332/1/1/18.
35. It excludes, for example, an important scene that was in the film, in which Johnny is helped by two older women, Rosie and Maude.
36. Letter from Sherriff to Reed, 21 June 1946, SHC 2332/1/1/18.
37. SHC 2332/4/1/7.
38. Letter from Alice Head to Sherriff, 22 January 1946, SHC 2332/1/1/18.
39. Letter from Sherriff to Alice Head, 26 January 1946, SHC 2332/1/1/18.
40. Which it did. The Farm is still in the hands of the National Trust, although leased to a local farmer.
41. Cash book, SHC 2332/4/1/3.
42. David Leslie Murray had been editor of the *Times Literary Supplement* from 1938–45, and was also well known as a novelist.
43. Letter from Sherriff to D.L. Murray, 10 January 1947, SHC 2332/1/1/20.
44. *Glasgow Sunday Mail*, 23 March 1947, SHC 2332/5/2/16.
45. Whose real name was Winifred Ashton.
46. Draft letter from Sherriff to Korda, undated, but probably early 1947, SHC 2332/1/1/30.
47. Letter from Sherriff to Alan Wood, 4 May 1951, SHC 2332/1/1/26.
48. He would, in fact, sell it in 1948, having barely lived in it.
49. Letter from Sherriff to Colin Tennant (Myron Selznick, London), 25 April 1947, SHC 2332/1/1/20.

50. Box, aged forty, had originally been a writer who had moved into films during the 1930s, and set up a documentary production company during the war. He moved into more general film production as the war drew to a close, and had a big hit with *The Seventh Veil*. After the war he was hired by Rank to run, and expand, Gainsborough Studios.
51. Letter from Sherriff to Lt Col Drake-Brockman, 11 July 1947, SHC 3813/1/77.
52. Letter from Sherriff to MCA (his agents), 15 August 1947, SHC 3813/1/76.
53. The film starred Mai Zetterling in a tale about an RAF flyer who brings home to England the German woman who helped him escape, only for their lives to be upended when her unrepentantly Nazi brother arrives to join her.
54. Letter from Sherriff to Robin Fox, 22 August 1947, SHC 3813/1/76.
55. Memo from Joe Mankiewicz to Darryl Zanuck, 3 September 1946, AMPAS, Margaret Herrick Library, Joseph Mankiewicz Collection: *Escape*, Correspondence Folder No. 156.
56. See in particular, a very funny letter from Mankiewicz to Bill Perlberg (the producer), on 2 October 1947, which includes the rather emphatic line: 'J. Arthur and his cohorts are really slipping us the finger, Bill … what they have handed us are the crummiest barrel-scrapings of the entire rank Rank outfit.' *Escape*, Correspondence Folder No. 156, *op. cit.*
57. SHC 2332/3/6/27.
58. See letter from Sherriff to Mankiewicz, 12 September 1947, in *Escape* Correspondence Folder No. 156, *op. cit.*
59. *Daily Mail*, 1 December 1947, SHC 2332/5/2/63.
60. Maugham, W. Somerset, and Sherriff, R.C., *Quartet*, Heinemann's, 1948.
61. *Ibid.*
62. *Ibid.*
63. *Ibid.*
64. Maugham, W. Somerset, *The Collected Stories, Volume Two*, The Reprint Society, London 1954.
65. The other two short stories in *Trio* were *The Verger* and *Mr Knowall*.
66. AMPAS, Margaret Herrick Library, PCA Files, *Quartet*, 1948.
67. See, for example, *The Glasgow Herald*, 3 January 1949.
68. *Ibid.*
69. Spicer, A., *Sydney Box*, Manchester University Press, 2006, p.119.
70. *Ibid.*
71. Indeed, in the film, which uses the old device of an opened book to suggest that the story comes straight from its pages, the story begins with George's twenty-first birthday, about twenty-four pages into a forty-six-page story.
72. See *Variety*, 3 November 1948.
73. See Annakin, K.: *So You Wanna Be A Director?*, Tomahawk Press, 2001.
74. *The Glasgow Herald*, 3 January 1949.
75. *New York Times*, 29 March 1949.
76. Letter from G.B. Stern to Sherriff, 1 November 1948, SHC 2332/1/1/22.
77. *Encore* featured the stories *The Ant and the Grasshopper*, *Winter Cruise* and *Gigolo and Gigolette*.
78. Letter from Sherriff to Ian Dalrymple, 28 May 1946, SHC 2332/1/1/19.
79. Letter from Sherriff to Evans, 17 May 1946, SHC 2332/1/1/19.
80. Letter from Sherriff to Spencer Curtis Brown, 17 January 1947, SHC 2332/1/1/20.
81. Letter from Sherriff to Curtis Brown, 24 January 1947, SHC 2332/1/1/20.
82. Gollancz would still publish one or two of his new plays, and ultimately, his autobiography and his final novel, *The Siege of Swayne Castle*.
83. *The Sunday Times*, 8 February 1948.
84. *The Daily Telegraph*, 20 February 1948.
85. In a clipping from an unknown paper, SHC 2332/5/2/12.
86. *The Times*, 21 February 1948.
87. *The Manchester Guardian*, 20 February 1948.
88. *The Sunday Chronicle*, 15 February 1948.
89. *The Observer*, 22 February 1948.
90. *John O'London's Weekly*, 20 February 1948.
91. Letter from Madge Duncan to Sherriff, 21 August 1947, SHC 3813/1/76.

92. Letter from Sherriff to Madge Duncan, 22 August 1947, SHC 3813/1/76.
93. *What Happened After*. Script for Broadcast on BBC Women's Hour, 25 June 1948, SHC 2332/3/4/5.
94. Letter from David Hatten to Sherriff, 21 May 1948, SHC 2332/1/1/21.
95. *Radio Times*, 16 March 1961.
96. *Brighton Gazette*, 2 October 1948.
97. *Brighton Herald*, 2 October 1948.
98. Letter from Sherriff to Charlie Hamilton, 15 October 1948, SHC 2332/1/1/22.
99. At Birmingham it was playing to houses of over £200 a night. Letter from Sherriff to Charlie Hamilton, *op. cit.*
100. See Interview with Christopher Manning-Press, SHC 9314/4/7.
101. *Punch*, 1 December 1948.
102. *Daily Herald*, 24 November 1948.
103. *The Times*, 24 November 1948.
104. *John O'London's Weekly*, 10 December 1948.
105. *Liverpool Post*, 25 November 1948.
106. Ludmilla Pitoeff had a previous tenuous link with Sherriff, insofar as Maurice Browne used some of his proceeds from *Journey's End* to employ Pitoeff and her husband, Edouard, in an international season in London in 1930.
107. A spiritualist belief, in which an individual's hands may be guided without conscious thought – typically by supernatural forces. The efforts are sometimes aided by use of a Ouija board, or a 'planchette'.
108. SHC 2332/3/6/29.
109. Letter from Darryl Zanuck to Bob Bassler, 11 August 1949, SHC 2332/1/1/23.
110. Letter from Sherriff to Lighton, 16 September 1949, SHC 2332/1/1/23.
111. SHC 2332/1/2/1.
112. Letter from Sherriff to E.J. King-Bull, 4 July 1947, SHC 3813/1/76.
113. Letter from E.J. King-Bull to Sherriff, 9 July 1947, SHC 3813/1/76.
114. Letter from Sherriff to King-Bull, 11 July 1947, SHC 3813/1/76.
115. Letter from Sherriff to Gladys Day, 2 September 1949, SHC 2332/1/1/23.
116. Letter from Sherriff to G.B. Stern, 17 November 1949, SHC 2332/1/1/24.
117. Letter from Sherriff to James McHugh (agent), 25 October 1949, SHC 2332/1/1/24.
118. Letter from Sherriff to James McHugh, 14 December 1949, SHC 2332/1/1/24.
119. *Los Angeles Times*, 28 August 1983.
120. Millard also suggested in the article that Sherriff, himself, had been surprised by the credit. But that cannot be so. Sherriff actually asked for a copy of the shooting script in 1951, to reassure himself that enough of his work survived to justify him receiving it. Exchange of letters between Sherriff and Fred Fox, February 1951; SHC 2332/1/1/25.
121. It was released in the US in September 1951, with the title *No Highway in the Sky*.
122. Letter from Sherriff to Richardson, 10 November 1949.
123. Letter from Sherriff to Madeleine Clive, 12 November 1953, SHC 2332/1/3/3.
124. Letter from Sherriff to Madeleine Clive, 29 September 1953, SHC 2332/1/3/3. Clive had attempted to take *Home at Seven* to the US, but had problems from her very first engagement in Syracuse, with the play's star – Paul Muni – very unhappy with the director and with the play's last act. Clive had planned to take the production on to Broadway but was unable to do so.
125. *Theatre World*, May 1950.
126. *The Manchester Guardian*, 8 March 1950.
127. Also known as Mrs Ralph Richardson.
128. *The Observer*, 12 March 1950.

Chapter 12: Pinnacle

1. Labour would last just twenty more months before another election, which returned Churchill to Downing Street.
2. Finlay, R. Derek, *Ten to Take Her Home*, The Memoir Club, 2006, p.15. Derek Finlay would go on to study at Cambridge, and thence to management consultants McKinsey & Co, before serving in senior positions at H.J. Heinz at WHQ Pittsburgh.

3. Spicer, A., *op. cit.*, 2006, p.121.
4. Letter from Sherriff to Victor Gollancz, 25 May 1951, SHC 2332/1/1/26.
5. See Sherriff's letter to Hettie Hilton, 20 April 1951, SHC 2332/1/1/25.
6. There is a detailed account of the relationship between Korda's London Films and British Lion Films in Drazin, *op. cit.*, 2011.
7. Brook was still in his twenties at the time, but had worked as a producer at the Shakespeare Memorial Theatre for several years. He would go on to have a long and storied theatrical career.
8. Letter from Ralph Richardson to Sherriff, 5 April 1951, SHC 2332/1/7.
9. Letter from Sherriff to Richardson on 11 July 1951, SHC 2332/1/7.
10. Letter from Sherriff to Richardson, 14 November 1951, SHC 2332/1/7.
11. De Grunwald already had more than twenty screen credits to his name, including adapting Rattigan's *Winslow Boy*. He also wrote the wonderful Leslie Howard wartime propaganda movie *Pimpernel Smith*.
12. See Hawkins, J., *op. cit.*, 1975, pp.169–70. Hawkins mistakenly attributes the play to J.B. Priestley, rather than Sherriff.
13. *The Manchester Guardian*, 2 February 1952.
14. *The Times*, 21 January 1952.
15. Clark was a Scottish lawyer, in his mid-forties, who had been mentored by John Maxwell, who had created British International Pictures in 1927, which then became Associated British in 1933. Maxwell had encouraged Clark, a fellow Scot, to study law, and brought him down to Elstree in 1929, after he had qualified. Although Maxwell died in 1940, Clark remained with the company, becoming Executive in Charge of Production in 1948.
16. Gotfurt was a German Jewish writer who had moved to Britain to escape the Nazis. He worked in theatre and movies, achieving some success with *Temptation Harbour* in 1947, before moving on to become Clark's scenario editor.
17. Brickhill, P., *The Dam Busters*, Pan Books, 1954 (first published in 1951).
18. See Ramsden, J., *The Dam Busters*, I.B. Tauris, 2003, p.25.
19. Gibson, G., *Enemy Coast Ahead*, Pan Books, 1955. Gibson wrote the book in the early months of 1944, before he was killed in a bombing raid later that year. It was first published in 1946.
20. See Harper, S. and Porter, V., *British Cinema of the 1950s: The Decline of Deference,* Oxford University Press, 2007, p.82. He also, according to Harper & Porter, bought the rights to *Enemy Coast Ahead*, although that was not enough to prevent Gibson's widow protesting that some of the material was used without her permission. [*Variety*, 10 November 1954.]
21. See *The Age,* 26 June 1954.
22. Dated 10 November 1951, SHC 2332/3/6/31/7. The treatment bears no names on the cover, but, given its date, was most likely written by Mycroft and Whittaker, since it roughly corresponds with the comments in Whittaker's diary.
23. SHC 2332/3/6/31/3.
24. The idea was not entirely an invention: Brickhill noted that Spafford (one of Gibson's crew) afterwards claimed to have had the same idea at an ENSA show.
25. SHC 2332/3/6/31/12.
26. Reprinted in *The Age,* 26 June 1954.
27. Which was just a quick 8-mile hop from Esher.
28. Whittaker's diary, 22 March 1952, *The Age, op. cit.*
29. SHC 2332/3/6/31/9. The date of its completion is not known – but since it begins with a scene involving Wallis's garden experiments, it suggests that it was completed after the 22 March meeting. It would have been completed at least several weeks in advance of him completing his 'Final Complete Screenplay', which, according to Whittaker's diary, was in July 1952.
30. SHC 2332/3/6/31/1.
31. See his email to the author, 21 July 2016.
32. Whittaker's diary, July 15 1952, and August 12–14, 1952. *The Age, op. cit.*
33. *The Dam Busters*, screenplay by R.C. Sherriff, 24 October 1952, SHC 2332/3/6/31/13.
34. The concept is noted in Wallis's Top Secret memo on the bomb, which includes the following section: 'Ricochet gunfire was known as early as the sixteenth century and was used in naval gunnery in the seventeenth and eighteenth centuries to extend the effective range of muzzle-

loading guns, firing spherical cannon balls.' The Nelson touch was probably pure Sherriff. SHC 2332/3/6/31/1.

35. Quoted in Ramsden, J., *op cit.*, 2003, p.47.
36. *Journey's End, op. cit.*, p.61.
37. Letter from Sherriff to Pips, 25 January 1917, SHC 2332/1/1/3/138. See page 38.
38. The £3,750 he was paid initially was matched by an equivalent amount in 1956.
39. Letter from Sherriff to Richardson, 24 September 1952, SHC 2332/1/7.
40. Richardson's biographer described the season as 'the lowest trough in [his] career', with mixed reviews for his *Volpone* following hard on the heels of damning reviews in both *The Tempest* and *Macbeth*. Miller, J., *Ralph Richardson: The Authorized Biography*, Sidgwick & Jackson, 1995, p.158.
41. Stratford, Edinburgh, Blackpool, Southport, Hull, Bournemouth, Newcastle and Bristol. See cash book, SHC 2332/4/1/10, p.185.
42. *The Tatler*, 8 April 1953.
43. *The Sunday Times*, 22 March 1953.
44. W.A. Darlington review. SHC 2332/5/2/93.
45. Quoted in Miller, J., *op. cit.*, p.161.
46. As Sherriff noted in *No Leading Lady* (p.346), Richardson took the play on a tour of the North after it left London, and did well with it.
47. Letter from Curtis Brown to Sherriff, 21 September 1953, SHC 2332/1/5/3.
48. Letter from Sherriff to Curtis Brown, 29 September 1953, SHC 2332/1/5/3.
49. Warwick Films was founded in 1951 by two experienced American producers based in London: Irving Allen and Albert (Cubby) Broccoli (later to become famous as the producer of the James Bond franchise). They had opted to operate out of the UK because it was more financially advantageous than remaining in the US, and in 1953 they began producing films in collaboration with Columbia Pictures. The first fruits of this collaboration were three pictures featuring Alan Ladd (including *The Red Beret*, which created something of a media firestorm because an American was playing a British paratrooper).
50. The film was directed by Mark Robson, and starred Richard Widmark as Joe, Mai Zetterling as Maria, George Cole as Roger, and Nigel Patrick as Brian. The writing credits went to Robert Buckner and John Paxton.
51. Letter from Richardson to Sherriff, 24 January 1954, SHC 2332/1/2/2.
52. *The Birmingham Post*, 15 April 1954.
53. *Surrey Comet*, 27 February 1954.
54. *The Housewife*, May 1954.
55. *The Times Literary Supplement*, 28 May 1954.
56. Letter from Mortimer Wheeler to Sherriff, 16 March 1954, SCH 2332/1/2/2.
57. BBC Children's Hour review, SHC 2332/1/5/3.
58. Ramsden, J., *op. cit.*, 2003, p.48.
59. Quoted in Harper, S. and Porter, V., *op. cit.*, 2007, p.83.
60. Some of the excisions were no more than a passing shot, but others included exchanges of dialogue. The most notable cuts were those scenes in which Sherriff had tried to show Britain's war apparatus jumping into action when the bombs and planes were finally given the go-ahead.
61. 2332/4/1/3. The cash books show the payments totalling £3,150, implying a fee of £3,500 (before commission). But in a later page in the book (p.185) listing his earnings from movie work, he shows a fee of £5,000, which was the same as he received for *Prize of Gold*.
62. Letter from Sherriff to Whitaker, 21 May 1954, SHC 2332/1/2/2.
63. *Saturday Evening Post*, 26 May 1951.
64. McFarlane, B., *An Autobiography of British Cinema.*, Methuen, 1997, p.441. In the course of the interview he also remarked that he didn't feel Sherriff had added anything to it.
65. Letter from Kitty Black to Sherriff, 23 September 1954, SHC 2332/1/2/2.
66. Letter from Kitty Black to Sherriff, 26 November 1954, SHC 2332/1/2/2.
67. The film was directed by King Vidor, and starred Audrey Hepburn, Henry Fonda, Mel Ferrer and Anita Ekberg, among many others. Eight writers were credited with the screenplay (although Sherriff was not among them). It was not a success.

68. Letter from Whitaker to Sherriff, 22 February 1955, SHC 2332/1/2/2.
69. Letter from Sherriff to Black, 23 February 1955, SHC 2332/1/2/2.
70. *New York Times*, 20 December 1955.
71. *Ibid.*
72. Letter from Sherriff to Ayton Whitaker, 20 December 1956, SHC 2332/1/3/5.
73. Sherriff, R.C., *The Long Sunset,* Longmans, Green & Co, 1960, p.26.
74. Letter from Sherriff to Whitaker, 7 March 1955, SHC 2332/1/2/2.
75. *The Daily Telegraph*, 31 August 1955.
76. *The Long Sunset*, op. cit., p.85.
77. See page 127.
78. Letter from Richardson to Sherriff, 25 April 1954, SHC 2332/1/2/2.
79. Letter from Sherriff to Bernard Hepton, 11 August 1955.
80. See Brown, G., *op. cit.*, 1977, p.10.
81. *The Times*, 25 April 1955.
82. Letter from Sherriff to Curtis Brown, 2 May 1956, SHC 2332/1/2/2.
83. At that point, just thirty years old. He would go on to an extensive career in TV and film acting, being perhaps best known for his role as the Commandant in the TV version of *Colditz*; and as the French café owner in *Secret Army*.
84. Letter from Sherriff to Gladys Day, 5 August 1955, SHC 2332/1/3/4.
85. *The Illustrated London News*, 10 September 1955.
86. *The Stage*, 1 September 1955.
87. *The Manchester Guardian*, 31 August 1955.
88. *The Observer,* 4 September 1955.
89. *Plays and Players*, December 1961.
90. *Daily Express*, 10 November 1961.
91. SHC 2332/8/13/5.
92. *Ibid.*
93. *The Evening News*, 17 May 1955.
94. *The Manchester Guardian*, 18 May 1955.
95. *The Star,* 20 May 1955.
96. *The Times Weekly Review*, 26 May 1955.
97. *The Daily Telegraph*, 21 May 1955.
98. *Financial Times*, 23 May 1955.
99. *The Sunday Times,* 22 May 1955.
100. Warner Brothers Archive, University of Southern California, *The Dam Busters*, 1955, agreement dated 18 April 1955.
101. Memo from Robert Clark, 19 April 1955. Warner Brothers Archive, *op. cit.*
102. Pre-publicity material. Warner Brothers Archive, *op. cit.* The dog's name continues to present difficulties today when the film is broadcast on television. It has also been reported that a proposed remake of the movie, which has been in the works for some considerable time, is likely to feature a screenplay in which the dog's name is changed to 'Digger' instead. http://www.bbc.co.uk/news/uk-england-lincolnshire-13727908
103. *No Leading Lady, op. cit.*, p.349.
104. This excludes *Storm over the Nile*, which came out in December 1955, and was hardly 'new', since it was a remake of *The Four Feathers*, using the same script, and much of the same location footage, but different principal actors. It was directed by Terence Young, and produced by London Films.
105. SHC 2332/3/6/32/8.
106. In this case, biographies by Agnes Strickland (*The Life of Mary Stuart*) and Eric Linklater (*Mary, Queen of Scots*) among others; and plays by Schiller (*Mary Stuart*) and Gordon Daviot (*Queen of Scots*).
107. Letter from Sherriff to Fritz Gotfurt, 19 April 1955, SHC 2332/1/4/7.
108. The minutes of the script conferences make fascinating reading, and offer an insight into the process by which a script is finally drafted, SHC 2332/3/6/32/6.
109. SHC 2332/3/6/32/8.

110. He also gave a little nod to his old school. There is a brief scene in 1561 when, just before Darnley visits Elizabeth in her throne room, she is discussing royal business with her secretary, who passes her some papers asking her to sign the Charters for the new Grammar schools. Kingston Grammar School received its charter in that year by Elizabeth's hand.

111. See Harper, S. and Porter, V., *op. cit.*, 2007, pp.89–90.

112. And to the Gordon Daviot play on the same subject, which they had also acquired.

113. *Evening Standard*, 11 December 1965.

114. In the end, T*he White Carnation* was dropped from the plans, and replaced with *The Long Sunset*.

115. Letter from Gielgud to Sherriff, 28 October 1955, SHC 2332/1/2/4.

116. Letter from Sherriff to Gielgud, 22 November 1955, SHC 2332/1/2/4.

117. Betty Box was Sydney Box's sister, and a powerful, prolific and well-respected producer. She had been with Sydney at Gainsborough, which Rank closed down in 1949, in favour of moving production to Pinewood Studios.

118. Letter from Sherriff to Whitaker, 19 January 1956, SHC 2332/1/2/1.

119. Including an Official Report, and two recently published books, *The Big Pick-Up*, by Elleston Trevor, and *Dunkirk*, by Lt Col Ewan Butler and Major J.S. Bradford.

120. *Dunkirk* (treatment). Undated, but probably early 1956, SHC 2332/1/4/1.

121. Letter from Sherriff to H.E. Alexander, 16 February 1956, SHC 2332/1/4/1.

122. Where he was working on one of the other films in the MGM-Ealing slate, *The Shiralee*.

123. SHC 2332/3/6/38/3.

124. Memo by Michael Balcon, 19 March 1956, SHC 2332/1/4/1.

125. *Dunkirk: Notes on a Screenplay*. 17 May 1956, SHC 2332/1/4/1.

126. Letter from H.E. Alexander to Sherriff, 31 July 1956, SHC 2332/1/4/1.

127. Letter from Fenn to Sherriff, 1 August 1956, SHC 2332/1/4/1.

128. Letter from Fenn to Sherriff, 13 August 1956, SHC 2332/1/4/1.

129. His property portfolio was growing ever smaller, and was now restricted to Rosebriars and Down House Farm (to which he seldom seems to have travelled), and a new property, Leeward, which he had bought in Ferring (near Worthing, on the south coast), although mainly, it seems, for the purposes of renting out.

130. Letter from Sherriff to Fenn, 22 August 1956, SHC 2332/1/4/1.

131. Letter from Sherriff to Fenn, 12 September 1956, SHC 2332/1/1/28.

132. Letter from Sherriff to Gielgud, 11 July 1956, SHC 2332/1/2/4.

133. Letter from Sherriff to Booth, 1 July 1956, SHC 2332/1/2/4.

134. Letter from Sherriff to Booth, 13 October 1956. SHC 2332/1/2/4.

135. The synopsis is based on the stage play. The BBC version was a good half hour shorter, and according to Sherriff, cut out Miss Fortescue altogether, and trimmed the role of the housekeeper, and the domestic scenes between Mayfield and his wife. (See Sherriff's letter to Booth, 13 October 1956).

136. He may have taken the name of Canbury from the part of Kingston in which the Rowing Club's boathouse is situated.

137. Letter from Sherriff to Campbell Nairne, 15 October 1956, SHC 2332/1/2/4,

138. Followed by *Badger's Green* on 3 October, *Miss Mabel* on 10 October, *Home at Seven* on 17 October and *The Long Sunset* on 24 October.

139. 'Why The Living Theatre Must Not Die', *Radio Times*, 21 September 1956, SHC 2332/5/3/15.

140. SHC 2332/1/3/5.

141. Letter from Booth to Sherriff, 6 November 1956, SHC 2332/1/2/4.

142. Letter from Sherriff to C.J. Morley Jacob, 2 January 1957, SHC 2332/1/2/4.

143. The exact order was calculated by a specific measure, which averaged the graded responses offered by listeners, from A+ to C-.

144. Letter from Sherriff to C.A. Joyce, 8 November 1956, SHC 2332/1/2/4.

145. See, in 1945, letters to and from Sherriff and the Reverend Colin Cuttell, SHC 2332/1/1/6.

Chapter 13: Curtain

   1. Webster, J., *Alistair MacLean*, Chapmans, 1991, p.63. A report in the *Scottish Daily Mail* on 5 January 1957, flagging the film up as the likely top film of the year, quotes a figure of £10,000 for the screen rights.

2. Letter to Ayton Whitaker, 6 October 1956, SHC 2332/1/2/1.
3. SHC 2332/1/2/1.
4. In fact, the play would only be published, as part of a *Plays of the Year* volume, in November, with a separate volume coming later.
5. Letter from Sherriff to Booth, 15 February 1957, SHC 3813/1/78.
6. Letter from Sherriff to Ayton Whitaker, 17 December 1956, SHC 2332/1/2/1
7. Letter from Ayton Whitaker to Sherriff, 25 January 1957, SHC 2332/1/2/1.
8. Letter from Sherriff to Whitaker, 7 February 1957, SHC 2332/1/2/1.
9. Letter from Val Gielgud to Sherriff, 14 March 1957, SHC 2332/1/2/6.
10. Letter from Sherriff to Val Gielgud, 30 March 1957, SHC 2332/1/2/6.
11. Letter from Val Gielgud to Sherriff, 2 April 1957, SHC 2332/1/2/6.
12. Letter from Sherriff to Bob Fenn, 26 January 1957, SHC 2332/1/1/28.
13. See *Daily Mail*, 12 February 1959.
14. *Films and Filming*, April 1959.
15. See Webster, J., *op. cit.*, 1991.
16. *Ruined City* and *No Highway*.
17. See interview with Olive Pettit, SHC 9314/7.
18. Letter from Sherriff to Booth, 7 March 1957, SHC 2332/1/3/5.
19. Letter from Sherriff to Booth, 1 May 1957, SHC 2332/1/3/5.
20. The theatres were the Marlowe Theatre in Canterbury, the Queen's Theatre in Hornchurch and the Playhouse Theatre in Salisbury.
21. *The Times*, 14 May 1957.
22. *The Birmingham Post*, 17 May 1957.
23. *The Lady*, 30 May 1957.
24. *The Daily Telegraph*, 14 May 1957.
25. *The Manchester Guardian*, 15 May 1957.
26. *The Observer*, 19 May 1957.
27. Bailey also told him that, although the audiences were very good wherever they went, the Hornchurch audience 'took the first act rather coldly. This dismayed him until he was told that quite a lot of them were £2,000 a year dockers now living in opulence outside the East End who might not have taken too kindly to the first scene, which talked about the East End nouveau riche rather freely.' Letter from Sherriff to Lionel Hale, 29 May 1957, SHC 2332/1/3/5.
28. See, for example, his letter to Fritz Gotfurt of 29 May (SHC 2332/1/3/5); his letter to Joyce Briggs at Rank, 15 May 1957 (SHC 2332/1/1/28), and his subsequent letter to Bob Fenn outlining his planned meetings with Janni and Lee at Pinewood, 20 June 1957, SHC 2332/1/1/28.
29. Letter from Sherriff to Michael Barry, 23 May 1957, SHC 2332/1/3/5.
30. Letter from Sherriff to George Kamm, 30 August 1957, SHC 2332/1/5/4.
31. Letter from Donald Wilson to Bob Fenn, 26 July 1957, SHC 2332/1/1/28.
32. Letter from Donald Wilson to Bob Fenn, 16 August 1957, SHC 2332/1/2/1.
33. Letter from Bob Fenn to Sherriff, 19 August 1957, SHC 2332/1/2/1.
34. Letters to and from Barry and Sherriff, August 1957, SHC 2332/1/2/1.
35. Letter to Bob Fenn, 19 September 1957, SHC 2332/1/1/28.
36. Letter from Sherriff to Michael Barry, 10 October 1957, SHC 2332/1/5/4.
37. Letter from Sherriff to Bryan Bailey, 5 June 1957, SHC 2332/1/3/5.
38. Letter from Sherriff to Michael Barry, 26 September 1957, SHC 3813/1/78.
39. Letter from Michael Barry to Sherriff, 2 October 1957, SHC 2332/1/5/4.
40. Letter from Sherriff to Lawrence Hammond, 17 October 1957, SHC 2332/1/2/6.
41. *Liverpool Evening Express*, 6 November 1957.
42. *Aberdeen Evening Express*, 6 November 1957.
43. *Birmingham Mail*, 6 November 1957.
44. *The Sunday Times*, 10 November 1957.
45. Letter from Sherriff to Booth, 4 December 1957, SHC 3813/1/78.
46. Letter from Sherriff to Gladys Day, 12 December 1957, SHC 2332/1/1/28.
47. Eventually published on 7 November 1958.
48. SHC 2332/1/2/6.
49. Letter from Sherriff to Val Gielgud, 17 October 1957, SHC 2332/1/2/6.

50. Letter from Val Gielgud to Sherriff, 25 October 1957, SHC 2332/1/2/6.
51. Letter to Val Gielgud, 12 December 1957, SHC 2332/1/2/6.
52. Letter from Sherriff to J.P. Eddy QC, 21 November 1957, SHC 2332/1/2/7.
53. Letter from Sherriff to Margaret McLaren, 13 February 1958, SHC 2332/1/2/7.
54. Letter from Sherriff to Connie Driskell, 13 February 1958, SHC 2332/1/2/7.
55. Letter from Sherriff to Bob Fenn, 20 February 1958, SHC 2332/1/2/7.
56. Letter from Bob Fenn to Sherriff, 17 February 1958, SHC 2332/1/2/7.
57. Letter from Sherriff to R.G. Walford, 10 April 1958, SHC 2332/1/2/7.
58. Letter from Sherriff to Teddy Baird, 17 January 1958, SHC 2332/1/4/3.
59. Letter to Bob Fenn, 1 May 1958, SHC 2332/1/4/3.
60. SHC 2332/3/6/42.
61. Newspaper clipping in SHC 2332/5/2/30.
62. Letter from Henley to Sherriff, 14 January 1958 [misdated as 1957], SHC 2332/1/4/2.
63. Letter from Sherriff to Henley, 16 January 1958, SHC 2332/1/4/2.
64. SHC 2332/3/6/41.
65. Sherriff, R.C., *The Siege of Swayne Castle*, Gollancz, 1973.
66. *Aberdeen Evening Press*, 9 April 1959.
67. Letter from David Henley to Sherriff, 3 September 1959, SHC 2332/1/2/4. Henley also reported that Sydney Box had suffered a stroke as soon as they arrived back.
68. Letter from David Henley to Sherriff, 15 March 1960, SHC 2332/1/2/4.
69. Letter from Sherriff to Bernard Miles, 1 January 1959 [misdated as 1958], SHC 2332/1/1/29.
70. SHC 2332/3/7/2.
71. Letter from Sherriff to John Barber, 1 January 1959 [misdated as 1958], SHC 2332/1/3/6.
72. Letter from Sherriff to John Barber, 15 January 1959, SHC 2332/1/3/6.
73. Letter from Sherriff to John Barber, 1 January 1959 [misdated as 1958], SHC 2332/1/3/6.
74. Letter from Sherriff to Archie Batty, 12 February 1959, SHC 2332/1/3/6.
75. Letter from De Laurentiis to Sherriff, 26 December 1958, SHC 2332/1/4/8.
76. Letter from Sherriff to De Laurentiis, 6 January 1959, SHC 2332/1/4/8.
77. Letter from De Laurentiis to Sherriff, 17 March 1959, SHC 2332/1/4/8.
78. Letter from De Laurentiis to Sherriff, 24 March 1959, SHC 2332/1/4/8.
79. SHC 2332/3/6/40/1 & 2.
80. Letter from De Laurentiis to Sherriff, 25 September 1959, SHC 2332/1/4/8.
81. Letter from Sherriff to De Laurentiis, 8 October 1959, SHC 2332/1/4/8.
82. Letter from De Laurentiis to Sherriff, 22 October 1959, SHC 2332/1/4/8.
83. Letter from Sherriff to Bob Fenn, 22 October 1959, SHC 2332/1/4/8.
84. De Laurentiis would try again with the film, commissioning Dalton Trumbo to produce another screenplay in 1963. That version was never made either.
85. Letter from Archie Batty to Sherriff, 31 March 1959, SHC 2332/1/3/6.
86. One of the ideas that came to him, via Spencer Curtis Brown, was that of a series about an insurance investigator. He went to the bother of preparing a twelve-page outline only to find that the idea had been used in America, and that the BBC were already considering their own version, SHC 2332/1/2/9.
87. Letter to Donald Bull, 27 April 1959, SHC 2332/1/2/7.
88. Letter from Sherriff to Gareth Wigan, 11 May 1959, SHC 2332/1/2/7.
89. *Liverpool Daily Post*, 9 September 1959.
90. *The Listener*, 17 September 1959.
91. *The Yorkshire Post*, 9 September 1959.
92. *The Sheffield Star*, 9 September 1959.
93. *Daily Sketch*, 9 September 1959.
94. *The Star*, 9 September 1959.
95. *The Daily Telegraph*, 21 March 1960.
96. *The Sunday Times*, 24 April 1960.
97. *The Daily Telegraph*, 26 April 1960.
98. See letter from Sherriff to Gladys Day, 12 December 1957, SHC 2332/1/1/28.
99. *The Lady*, 12 May 1960.

100. *The Observer*, 1 May 1960.
101. *The Star*, 28 April 1960.
102. *News Chronicle*, 28 April 1960.
103. *The Manchester Guardian*, 29 April 1960.
104. *The Daily Telegraph*, 29 April 1960.
105. *Drama*, Summer 1960.
106. *The Sunday Times*, 1 May 1960.
107. *Daily Mail*, 28 April 1960.
108. *Daily Express*, 1 June 1960.
109. Letter from Sherriff to Michael Bakewell, 15 February 1961.
110. Letter from Sherriff to Peter Haddon, 28 February 1961, SHC 2332/1/3/8.
111. SHC 2332/1/3/8.
112. Letter from Sherriff to Peter Haddon, 3 July 1961, SHC 2332/1/3/8.
113. Letter from Bernard Miles to Sherriff, 11 July 1961, SHC 2332/1/3/10.
114. Letter from Bernard Miles to Sherriff, 22 August 1961, SHC 2332/1/3/10.
115. Letter from Sherriff to Miles, 25 August 1961. Of course, following the Sequel he did know what happened to them. But perhaps he had forgotten.
116. *Daily Express*, 10 November 1961.
117. *The Sunday Telegraph*, 28 January 1962.
118. *The Sunday Times*, 28 January 1962.
119. *Birmingham Mail*, 7 February 1962.
120. *The Northern Echo*. 2 February 1962.
121. *John O'London's Weekly*, 22 February 1962.
122. Letter from Bernard Miles to Sherriff, 25 May 1971, SHC 2332/1/3/10.
123. *No Leading Lady, op. cit.*, p.212.
124. See the interview with Olive Pettit, SHC 9314/7.
125. *Journey's End and All That*, BBC interview with John Ellison, 22 August 1968.
126. Published by Gollancz, 1973.
127. *The Sunday Times*, 8 April 1973.
128. *The Sunday Times*, 30 September 1973.
129. *The Tablet*, 15 December 1973.
130. *The Times Educational Supplement*, 2 November 1973.
131. *Times Literary Supplement*, 23 November 1973.
132. SHC 9314/2/5.
133. *Journey's End and All That*, BBC interview with John Ellison, 22 August 1968.

Conclusion
1. *No Leading Lady, op. cit.*, p.217.
2. *Royal Magazine*, probably March 1929. To be found in Sherriff's scrapbook. SHC 2332/9/11, p.58.
3. 'I Believe in Simplicity', *Pictorial Weekly*, 29 November 1930.

Bibliography

Ackerley, J.R., *My Father and Myself*, New York Review of Books, 2012.

Ackerley, J.R., *The Prisoners of War*, Chatto & Windus, 1925.

Agate, J., *My Theatre Talks*, Arthur Baker Ltd, 1933.

Aldgate, A. & Richards, J., *Britain Can Take It: The British Cinema in the Second World War*, I.B. Tauris, 2007.

Annakin, K., *So You Wanna Be A Director?* Tomahawk Press, 2001.

Aurelius, Marcus, *Meditations*, Penguin Classics, 2006.

Balcon, M., *Michael Balcon Presents … A Lifetime of Films*, Hutchinson, 1969.

Barnes, M.A., *Within This Present*, Johnathan Cape, 1934.

Bartlett, V., *This Is My Life*, Chatto & Windus, 1938.

Bishop, G., *My Betters*, William Heinemann Ltd, 1957.

Bloom, K., *Broadway: An Encyclopaedia*, Routledge, 2013.

Borradaille, O. & Hadley, A.B., *Life Through A Lens*, McGill-Queen's University Press, 2001.

Bracco, R.M., *Merchants of Hope: British Middlebrow Writers and the First World War, 1919–39*, Berg Publishers, Ltd, 1993.

Brickhill, P., *The Dam Busters*, Pan Books, 1954.

Brittain, V., *Testament of Youth*, Victor Gollancz Ltd, 1933.

Brown, G., *Launder and Gilliat*, British Film Institute, 1977.

Browne, M., *Too Late to Lament*, Victor Gollancz Ltd, 1955.

Brunel, A., *Nice Work: Thirty Years in British Films*, Forbes Robertson, 1949.

Calder, R., *Beware the British Serpent: The Role of Writers in British Propaganda in the United States, 1939–1945*, McGill-Queen's University Press, 2004.

Capua, M., *Vivien Leigh: A Biography*, McFarland & Co, 2003.

Catto, M., *A Prize of Gold*, Lanesborough Publications Ltd, 1959.

Catto, M., *Gold in the Sky*, Mayflower Books, 1974.

Clough, E., *Without Let or Hindrance: Reminiscences of a British Foreign Service Officer*, Cassell, 1960.

Crowther, B., *The Lion's Share*, E.P. Dutton & Company Inc, 1957.

Cunningham, V., *British Writers of the 1930s*, Oxford University Press, 1988.

Curtis, J., *James Whale: A New World of Gods and Monsters,* University of Minnesota Press, 1998.

Curtis Brown, A., *Contacts*, Cassel & Co. Ltd, 1935.

Darlington, W.A., *I Do What I Like*, McDonald & Co, 1947.

David, H., *On Queer Street*, Harper Collins Publishers, 1997.

Dean, B., *Mind's Eye: An Autobiography 1927–1972*, Hutchinson of London, 1973.

De Casalis, J., *Mrs Feather's Diary*, William Heinemann Ltd, 1936.

De Casalis, J., *Things I Don't Remember: Short Stories and Impressions*, William Heinemann Ltd, 1953.

Doherty, T., *Hollywood and Hitler, 1933–1939*, Columbia University Press, 2013.

Drazin, C., *Korda: Britain's Movie Mogul*, I.B. Taurus, 2011.

Dumont, H., *Frank Borzage: The Life and Films of a Hollywood Romantic*, McFarland & Co, 2009

Evans, M., *All This and Evans Too*, University of South Carolina Press, 1989.

Finlay, R.D., *Ten To Take Her Home*, The Memoir Club, 2006.

Frankau, G., *Self-Portrait: A Novel of His Own Life*, 1941.

Fussell, P., *The Great War and Modern Memory*, Oxford University Press, 2000.

Galsworthy, J., *Over The River*, Kindle Edition.

Gardiner, J., *The Thirties: An Intimate History*, Harper Press, 2010.

Gazeley, I., *Poverty in Britain, 1900–1965*, Palgrave Macmillan, 2003.

Gibson, G., *Enemy Coast Ahead*, Pan Books, 1955.

Glancy, H.M., *When Hollywood Loved Britain*, Manchester University Press, 1999.
Gore-Langton, R., *Journey's End: The Classic War Play Explored*, Oberon Books, 2013.
Green, F.L., *Odd Man Out*, Penguin Books, 1948.
Gregory, B., *A History of the Artists Rifles 1859–1947*, Pen & Sword Books Ltd, 2006.
Hall, E., *We Can't Even March Straight*, Vintage, 1995.
Harding, B., *Keeping Faith*, Pen & Sword Books, Ltd, 1990.
Harper, S. & Porter, V., *British Cinema of the 1950s: The Decline of Deference*, Oxford University Press, 2007.
Hawkins, J., *Anything for a Quiet Life*, Coronet Books, 1975.
Higham, S.S., *Artists Rifles Regimental Roll of Honour and War Record 1914–19*, Naval & Military Press, 2001.
Hilton, J., *Goodbye, Mr Chips*, Coronet Books, 2001.
Hodges, S., *Gollancz: The Story of a Publishing House 1928–1978*, Victor Gollancz Ltd, 1978.
Houlbrook, M., *Queer London*, University of Chicago Press, 2006.
Hynes, S., *A War Imagined: The First World War and English Culture*, Pimlico, 1992.
Jensen, P.M., *The Men Who Made the Monsters*, Twayne Publishers, 1996.
Jones, M., *The Last Great Quest: Captain Scott's Antarctic Sacrifice*, Oxford University Press, 2004.
Knight, E., *This Above All*, The Musson Book Company Ltd, 1941.
Korda, M., *Charmed Lives*, Allen Lane, 1980.
Low, R., *Film making in 1930s Britain*, George & Unwin, 1985.
Low, R., *The History of the British Film Industry 1918–1929*, Routledge, 2013.
Lucas, M., *The Journey's End Battalion*, Pen & Sword Books Ltd, 2012.
Lucas, M. (Ed), *Frontline Medic: The Diary of Captain George Pirie, RAMC 1914–1917*, Helion & Company Ltd, 2014.
MacLean, A., *HMS Ulysses*, Collins, 1955.
Mank, G.W., *Bela Lugosi and Boris Karloff: The Expanded Story of a Haunting Collaboration*, McFarland & Co, 2009.
Mason, A.E.W., *The Four Feathers*, Penguin Books, 2001.
Masterman, J.C., *Bits and Pieces*, Hodder & Stoughton, 1961.
Maugham, W.S., *The Collected Stories, Volume Two*, The Reprint Society, 1954.
McFarlane, B., *An Autobiography of British Cinema*, Methuen, 1997.
McGerr, C., *René Clair*, Twayne Publishers, 1980.
Miller, J., *Ralph Richardson: The Authorised Biography*, Sedgwick & Jackson, 1995.
Mills, J., *Up in the Clouds, Gentlemen Please*, Penguin, 1980.
Morley, S., *Tales from the Hollywood Raj: The British Film Colony On Screen and Off*, Weidenfeld & Nicholson, 1983.
Nicolson, N., *Long Life: Memoirs*, Weidenfeld & Nicolson, 1997.
O'Casey, S., *Autobiographies 2*, Pan Books Ltd, 1980.
Olivier, L., *Confessions of an Actor*, Penguin, 1984.
Panichas, G.A. (Ed) *Promise of Greatness: The 1914–18 War*, Cassell, 1968.
Parker, P., *A Life of J.R. Ackerley*, Constable & Co Ltd, 1989.
Pearson, G., *Flashback: An Autobiography of a British Film Maker*, George Allen & Unwin Ltd, 1957.
Porter, K. & Weeks, J., *Between the Acts: Lives of Homosexual Men 1885–1967*, Routledge, 1991.
The Post Victorians, Ivor Nicholson & Watson Ltd, 1933.
Ramsden, J., *The Dam Busters*, I.B. Tauris, 2003.
Ratcliffe, S. (Ed), *P.G. Wodehouse: A Life in Letters*, Random House, 2013.
Rattigan, T., *Flare Path*, Hamish Hamilton, 1942.
Reese, P., *Homecoming Heroes*, Pen & Sword Books Ltd, 1992.
Remarque, E.M., *The Road Back*, Mayflower Books, 1979.
Remarque, E.M., *Three Comrades*, Random House Trade Paperback Edition, 2013.
Richards, J., *The Unknown 1930s: An Alternative History of the British Cinema, 1929–1939*, I.B. Taurus, 1998.
Riley, P.J., *James Whale's Dracula's Daughter*, Kindle Edition, Bear Manor Media, 2009.
Robertson, J.C., *The Hidden Cinema: British Film Censorship in Action, 1913–1975*, Routledge, 1989.

Rotha, P. (Ed), *Portrait of a Flying Yorkshireman: Letters from Eric Knight in the United States to Paul Rotha in England*, Chapman & Hall, 1952.

Sherriff, R.C., *Another Year*, Heinemann Ltd, 1948.

Sherriff, R.C., *Badger's Green*, Victor Gollancz Ltd, 1930.

Sherriff, R.C., *Badger's Green*, Samuel French Ltd, 1962.

Sherriff, R.C., *The Cataclysm*, Pan Books Ltd, 1958.

Sherriff, R.C., *Chedworth*, The Macmillan Company, 1944.

Sherriff, R.C., *The Fortnight in September*, Victor Gollancz Ltd, 1932 (8th imp).

Sherriff, R.C., *Greengates*, Persephone Books Ltd, 2016.

Sherriff, R.C., *Home at Seven*, Victor Gollancz Ltd, 1950.

Sherriff, R.C., *The Hopkins Manuscript*, Persephone Books Ltd, 2005.

Sherriff, R.C., *Journey's End*, Penguin Classics Edition, 2000.

Sherriff, R.C., *King John's Treasure*, Heinemann Ltd, 1954.

Sherriff, R.C., *The Long Sunset*, Longmans, Green & Co Ltd, 1960.

Sherriff, R.C., *Miss Mabel*, Samuel French Ltd, 1949.

Sherriff, R.C., *No Leading Lady*, Victor Gollancz Ltd, 1968.

Sherriff, R.C., *A Shred of Evidence*, Samuel French Ltd, 1961.

Sherriff, R.C., *The Siege of Swayne Castle*, William Collins & Sons Ltd, 1975.

Sherriff, R.C., *The Telescope*, Samuel French Ltd, 1957.

Sherriff, R.C., *Two Hearts Doubled*, Samuel French Ltd, 1934.

Sherriff, R.C., *The Wells of St Mary's*, Arrow Books, 1974.

Sherriff, R.C., *The White Carnation*, Samuel French Ltd, 1953.

Sherriff, R.C. & Bartlett, V., *Journey's End: A Novel*, Victor Gollancz Ltd, 1930.

Sherriff, R.C. & De Casalis, J., *St Helena*, Victor Gollancz Ltd, 1936.

Sherriff, R.C. & Maugham, W.S., *Quartet*, William Heinemann Ltd, 1948.

Shute, N., *No Highway*, Pan Books, 1963.

Shute, N., *Requiem for A Wren*, Vintage, 2009.

Shute, N., *Ruined City*, Pan Books, 1973.

Speaight, R., *The Property Basket: Recollections of a Divided Life*, Collins & Harvill Press, 1970.

Spicer, A., *Sydney Box*, Manchester University Press, 2006.

Stern, G.B., *Trumpet Voluntary*, Cassel & Co, 1944.

Stuart, G., *I Just Kept Hoping*, Little, Brown & Co, 1999.

Tabori, P., *Alexander Korda*, Oldbourne, 1959.

Tabori, P., *Bricks Upon Dust*, Hodder & Stoughton, 1945.

Urwand, B., *The Collaboration*, Kindle Edition, 2013.

Vaughan, T., *Odd Man Out*, British Film Institute, 1995.

Walpole, H., *The Blind Man's House*, Macmillan & Co Ltd, 1941.

Watts, S., *The Magic Kingdom: Walt Disney and the American Way of Life*, University of Missouri Press, 2013.

Wearing, J.P., *The London Stage 1920–1929: A Calendar of Productions, Performers and Personnel*, Rowman & Littlefield, 2014.

Webster, J., *Alistair MacLean*, Chapmans, 1991.

Wells, H.G., *The Invisible Man*, Gollancz SF Masterworks, 2001.

Wilk, M., *Schmucks with Underwoods: Conversations with Hollywood's Classic Screenwriters*, Applause Theatre & Cinema Books, 2004.

Woodfield, J., *English Theatre in Transition 1881–1914*, Routledge, 2015.

Woollcott, A., *While Rome Burns*, Simon & Schuster Ltd, 1989.

Wren, P.C., *The Man of A Ghost*, Remploy Reprint Edition, 1973.

Index

n = endnote